38   (14   4 - 50

GW01452653

The history of the Panzerkorps Großdeutschland

Helmuth Spaeter
Vol. 2

Translated by David Johnston

THE HISTORY OF THE
PANZERKORPS GROSSDEUTSCHLAND
Volume 2

By Helmuth Spaeter
English translation by David Johnston

Copyright 1995 by
J.J. Fedorowicz Publishing

Originally Published in German as
DIE GESCHICHTE DER PANZERKORPS GROSSDEUTSCHLAND 2
In 1958, Bielefeld, Germany

English Edition published by
J.J. Fedorowicz Publishing Inc.
106 Browning Blvd.
Winnipeg, Manitoba
Canada R3K 0L7
(204) 837-6080
Fax: (204) 889-1960

The material in this book is copyright by
J.J. Fedorowicz Publishing Inc., no part of it
may be reproduced in any way without the
written permission of the publisher.

Printed in the USA
ISBN 0-921991-27-4

Typesetting by George R. Bradford

Printed and Bound by
Publishers Press

PUBLISHER'S ACKNOWLEDGEMENTS

We wish to thank the following individuals who have contributed to the publishing of this book.

David Johnston – Translation

Tom Wilson – Proof Reading

Brian Molloy – Cover & Signing Box

Matt Reinert – GD Cuffband

We also wish to thank you the reader for purchasing this book, and all those of you who have purchased our other books, and have written us with your kind words of praise and encouragement. It gives us impetus to continue to publish translations of the best German books and specially commissioned books, as you can see by the additional books which are in preparation for publication in the near future. Other titles are either being negotiated or seriously contemplated, many as a result of your helpful proposals. Such proposals have also motivated us to pursue the start of a serious military art print series, focusing on the Waffen-SS and German armor. More on these in the near future, further suggestions are always welcome.

John Fedorowicz & Michael Olive

Books published by J.J. Fedorowicz Publishing
THE LEIBSTANDARTE (1 SS Panzer Division) volumes I, II, III and IV/1
EUROPEAN VOLUNTEERS (5 SS Panzer Division)
DAS REICH I (2 SS Panzer Division)
THE HISTORY OF PANZERKORPS GROSSDEUTSCHLAND I & 2
OTTO WEIDINGER
OTTO KUMM
MANHAY, THE ARDENNES; CHRISTMAS 1944
ARMOR BATTLES OF THE WAFFEN-SS 1943-45
TIGER: THE HISTORY OF A LEGENDARY WEAPON 1942-45
HITLER MOVES EAST
TIGERS IN THE MUD
PANZER ACES
FOOTSTEPS OF THE HUNTER
HISTORY OF THE 12 SS PANZERDIVISION HITLERJUGEND
GRENADIERS (Kurt Meyer)
FIELD UNIFORMS OF THE GERMAN ARMY PANZER FORCES IN WW2
TIGERS IN COMBAT I
INFANTERIE ACES
FREINEUX AND LAMORMENIL – THE ARDENNES
THE CAUCASUS AND THE OIL
EAST FRONT DRAMA – 1944
HISTORY OF THE PANZERKORPS HERMAN GÖRING
DAS REICH II
PRINZ EUGEN, THE HISTORY OF THE 7SS MOUNTAIN DIVISION "PRINZ EUGEN"
THE WESTERN FRONT 1944 – MEMOIRS OF A PANZER LEHR OFFICER

Books in preparation:
MICHAEL WITTMANN AND THE TIGER COMMANDERS OF THE LEIBSTANDARTE
THE LEIBSTANDARTE IV/2
THE BRANDENBURGERS – GLOBAL MISSION
SS-POLIZEI, HISTORY OF THE 4SS PANZERGRENADIER DIVISION, VOLS. 1 & 2

J.J. Fedorowicz Publishing Inc.

CONTENTS

PART III — THE DNIEPER

PART IV — FROM THE KIROVOGRAD AREA TO JASSY

INTRODUCTION

The second volume of the history of the Panzer Corps *Großdeutschland* should be dedicated to the memory of the actions and sacrifices of the Panzer-Grenadier Division *Großdeutschland* in the difficult battles on the Eastern Front in 1943 and 1944.

Wherever the division saw action it provided a shining example of bold offensive spirit and unshakeable steadfastness.

When, after the fall of Stalingrad, the Soviets hoped to destroy the southern wing of the German armies by driving into its deep flank by way of Kharkov, the division – together with the SS Panzer Corps and other units – threw itself against the vastly- superior enemy and brought them to a halt.

The Panzer-Grenadier Division *Großdeutschland* played a decisive role in the success of the German counteroffensive on that front.

In the course of the last German offensive in the east – Operation "Zitadelle"– the division was once again able to display its offensive power, until developments on other fronts forced a cessation of the German offensive and robbed the brave field forces of a victory that was already in sight.

In the heavy defensive fighting that followed, first in the area of Army Group centre, then again with Army Group South, west of Kharkov, in the battle for the Dniepr Line, in the defensive battles in the Dniepr Bend and later in the fighting withdrawal to the Bug and the Dnestr, the *Großdeutschland* Division repeatedly faced far superior enemy forces, inflicted powerful blows on them and held its own against the enemy's superiority in the field.

The division's unparallelled military accomplishments in this almost uninterrupted battle and the sacrifices that our comrades made for Germany will never be forgotten!

Generalfeldmarschall von Manstein

Münster, Westphalia
23 September 1958

1

This history of the units of the Panzer Corps GD bears testimony to the rule according to which the members of the units of this corps, no matter what their rank or specialty, joined and by which they acted always and everywhere:

Our honour is fulfillment of duty!

The book also describes the spirit of community and comradeship in action which existed in this formation. Furthermore it shows clearly its selfless readiness to assume responsibility for our people and fatherland.

The GD carried out every mission given to it, because every member of the unit could depend on the others, conscious of their obligations – including to their fallen comrades.

We, comrades, will not forget this obligation and wish to dedicate ourselves with equal devotion to building a new world.

If this history also awakens, promotes and strengthens the idea of service of the individual in the common good in the younger generation, then the suffering, misery and death of these brave men will have some sense, their sacrifices will have value in the sense that they were made.

General der Panzertruppe (Ret.)
Hasso von Manteuffel
Holder of the Knight's Cross with Oak Leaves, Swords and Diamonds

Neuß, Rhine
2 May 1958

Part I

CHAPTER 1

KHARKOV 1943
In the Defensive Battle

19. 1. 43 – 4. 3. 43	Defensive battle in Kharkov area
5. 3. 43 – 31. 3. 43	Attack in Kharkov area
1. 4. 43 – 3. 7. 43	Army reserve within Armeeabteilung Kempf

In the initial phase of the German summer offensive of 1942, the left wing reached the city of Voronezh on the Don after a bold advance and initially halted there. The right wing of Army Group B and the left wing of Army Group A followed these movements and were likewise able to advance to the Don. The western outskirts of Stalingrad were reached on August 25, 1942. At the same time the focus of the German offensive was shifted south and the advance toward the Caucasus begun. However this plan necessitated a denuding of the rest of the southern sector of the Eastern Front of German troops, which were needed for the drive into the Caucasus. As well, the flanks along the Don were so extended that the units deployed there were assigned excessively-long defensive sectors. As everyone knows, this resulted in the deployment there of armies belonging to three of Germany's allies, the Rumanians, the Hungarians and the Italians. While the German Sixth Army was embroiled in heavy fighting for the city of Stalingrad, the Romanian Third Army moved into position on its left, to the west along the Don. Situated in this area was the sole remaining Soviet bridgehead, south of Kremenskaya. This not insignificant bridgehead represented a constant, considerable danger to the German and allied units deployed there. To the west, beginning roughly near Veshenskaya, was the sector of the Italian Eighth Army, which consisted of six infantry, one motorised and three *Alpini* Divisions. Northwest of Rossosh began the sector of the Hungarian Second Army, with about ten divisions, while subsequently the German Second Army defended the front on both sides of Voronezh.

For some months it had been clear to Army Group B, which was in command of these armies, that employment of the allied armies was only an acceptable stopgap measure as long as the more than 400- kilometre-long front remained quiet. For the allied divisions were inherently weaker than the German divisions and were inadequately equipped, especially in the area of anti-tank weapons. Their artillery lacked the modern, large-calibre weapons used by the Germans and Russians. The few German reserves, which in the previous months had been positioned behind the front, had largely been committed to the fighting in Stalingrad.

Meanwhile the Soviets waited to launch their major offensive until considerable German forces were tied down by the western powers, and probably also in the belief that winter would offer the Soviet soldiers the same advantages as it had the previous year.

When it became evident that the offensive by the British 8th Army in Egypt was going to succeed, they struck: on 19 November 1942. The thrust led by General Vasilevsky was intended to envelop the Sixth Army in Stalingrad from the west and south. Under the command of General Rokossovsky, the Soviets advanced out of the Kremenskaya bridgehead with three tank and two cavalry corps, behind which were assembled 21 rifle divisions, and broke through the Romanian positions in the initial assault on a front of more than 30 kilometres. In conjunction with the attack across the Don south of Stalingrad, two further Russian tank corps and nine rifle divisions under General Yeremenko smashed through the Romanian Fourth Army. Simultaneously 20 rifle divisions, six tank brigades and two motorised brigades attacked Stalingrad's northern front (Sixth Army).

The objective was to recapture the city and surround the Sixth Army, and this was achieved on 22 November 1942. The Soviets' long-range objective was to drive in the direction of Rostov, with the intention of cutting off the German forces in the Caucasus (Army Group Don).

While the spearheads of these attacking Soviet armies all pointed south, a further offensive group, which began its attack on 16 December 1942, struck the Italian Eighth Army, which consisted of seven Italian and one German divisions. Two days later the entire front between Veshenskaya and Kalitva, south of Voronezh, had been broken. In several places the Soviets had driven deep armoured wedges into the front, so that the units on the German side completely lost control of the situation. The local reserves were used up on the first day. Soon there was a yawning gap more than 100 kilometres wide in the front, which had to affect Army Group Don, especially Second Army in the north.

Finally, on 14 January 1943, the Soviets launched their third attack across the Don toward the Donets, the full weight of which mainly struck the Hungarian Second Army. The desired breakthrough was achieved quickly; the Soviets exploited the opportunity to gain ground toward the west and simultaneously roll up the Hungarian divisions along the Don north of the breakthrough point from the south. The Hungarian divisions subsequently broke and streamed back toward the west and north before the Soviet onslaught.

The Russians veered north and northwest on a broad front, placing the German Second Army in extreme danger. The Soviet offensive quickly gained ground toward the west and its objective was obviously Gorshetshnoye, a road junction 80 kilometres west of Voronezh. Too late, much too late, the German divisions left the Voronezh bridgehead and fought their way west through the attacking Soviet formations as a moving pocket.

The Russian offensive which had begun on 14 January 1943 had meanwhile torn open a gap more than 350 kilometres wide in the front held by the armies of Germany and its allies. The German Second Army was badly battered, and the Hungarian Second Army had been virtually destroyed. The German army corps deployed in its sector was in retreat, attempting to fight its way toward Oskol. The remnants of the *Alpini* corps and XXIV Panzer

Corps were no longer fit for operations and sought to escape to the west. Two German panzer divisions and an infantry division, their northern flank unprotected, fought their way out of the area on both sides of Starobyelsk back toward Kupyansk against a vastly superior enemy.

The situation in this area threatened to become chaos bearing the seeds of a destructive defeat. At the cost of ruthlessly stripping other fronts, all available reserves were moved in. Even the Führer Headquarters sent a battle group to the southern sector of the Eastern Front.

"Battle Group Pohlmann" of the *Führer-Begleit-Bataillon* was thus one of the first GD units to be transferred into the threatened area. Consisting of a rifle company, the 4th (Heavy) Company under Hauptmann Mattheis and the 5th (Panzer) Company under Oberleutnant Kegel, it was a relatively weak force, but it was equipped with the latest weapons and was particularly well-suited for the anti-tank role.

Battle Group Pohlmann:

Commander:	Hptm. Pohlmann
Adjutant:	Oblt. Wegmann

1st (Rifle) Company: Hptm. Kessel (†)
(three rifle platoons, one   Lt. Christiansen
equipped with half-tracked   Lt. Frhr. von Richthofen
armoured-personnel carriers)   Lt. Gossrau   Lt. Stumpf (†)

4th (Heavy) Company: Hptm. Mattheis
2-3 Pak platoons
2 Flak platoons

5th (Panzer) Company: Oblt. Kegel (†)
Panzer III and IV   Lt. von Geisberg
                      Lt. Wilkens (†)
                      Lt. Arnold

The men wore grey assault gun uniforms and were outfitted with winter equipment. In their pay books the word FHQu had been obliterated with ink and replaced by the entry 51. Kp./I.R. GD (51st Company, Infantry Regiment GD).

The former 3rd Company, which was comprised mainly of orderlies, remained at headquarters and continued its guard duties. Several trains carried Battle Group Pohlmann to the front. The force was unintentionally split apart while still en route: while the main body, namely 1st (Rifle) Company and headquarters, elements of 4th (Heavy) Company and the maintenance shop, detrained in Alexeyevka, southwest of Voronezh, on 19 December and was soon sucked into the maelstrom of retreating units; the 5th (Panzer) Company and the 20mm flak platoon under Leutnant Grotewohl landed in Chertkovo on the Kalitva following a journey through Minsk, Orel, Kursk, Valuiki and Millerovo. The battle group had thus been split in two and its

Plan of Tachertkowe.
ca. 1: 50,000

5.(Pz.)Kp./ FBB.

● *da würde ich namen......*

+ *Die Gräber*

▪ *Gefechtstand Obert. Jräser*
▪ *1 Unterkunft des Jäger*
▲ *2. Unterkunft des Jyges*

III *Eisenbahnlinie am
Janet minowka aber
nebet Baum schleifer-
bank a nach Uulemmo*
--- *Abschnitts grenzen.*

Einsatz und Verteilung der Kräfte:
Commitment/Employment and Distribution of the Strength

Bottle-section	Commander	Strength	in addition units/forces
I	Hptsturmf. Schwarting	SS-Polizei Div. 7/538 1 Zug I/538 (Reserve)	5. Pz. Kp. Führer Oblt. Kegel
II	Obersturmf. Tigge	SS-Polizei Div.	Zug Lt. Grothewohl (Stück 2 cm Flak)
III	Hptm. Peters	I/538	
IV	Lt. Peters	Tross III/538 (ohne 1. Zug)	Schw. Pz. Jäger-
V	Hptm. Erhardt	Schneeräumkp. u. Wachbatl. 4/122 1/18	Komp. 517 Führer Oblt. Planschiefer
VI	Major Ullmer	Ital. Kdo. Fest. Pi. Btl.30 (25 M.)	12 St. 7,5 cm lg. (eingesetzt 10
VII	Hptm. Lewandowski	II/538 (ohne 7/538	Reserve 2) Sb-Batterie Krausse 10,5 Haubitze

6

striking power decisively reduced. Each of the two parts fought as separate entities well into January 1943. However, both were caught up in the wake of the retreating Germans, and in particular allied units.

Straightaway, on 19 December, the reinforced 5th (Panzer) Company under Oblt. Kegel became involved in heavy tank-versus-tank fighting near Mankovo. That same day the tank of the courageous *Oberfeldwebel* Steinhardt was knocked out by enemy fire. He and his entire crew were killed, with the exception of Gefreiter Lehmann. The company fought as part of Battle Group Schulte, a regiment-size formation of the 298th Infantry Division, which was attempting to fight its way through to the west. The following days saw bitter defensive fighting against the hard-pursuing and far-superior enemy, who finally succeeded in encircling the German force in Chertkovo. Together with other battle groups, about 9,000 exhausted men of the 298th Infantry Division dug in in Chertkovo. About half were wounded. It was the first day of the Christmas season.

Heavy fighting for possession of the city raged in the days which followed, costing the lives of many brave men. Fought out there was the desperate battle of a surrounded formation with no hope of relief. The German soldiers in Chertkovo were like a rock in the sea and they held on grimly.

There exists an account of the fighting by a Russian battalion commander who was later captured:

Battle Group Oberst Dr. Göller
Command Post, 23. 12. 1942 — 22.00 hours.
To the Battalion Ic – 3rd Mountain Infantry Division
Statements by the commander of the 3rd Battalion, 12th Infantry Regiment, 41st Guards Division, Styashin, Nicolaus, born 22. 10. 1909 – Russian.

Captured at about 07.00 in the morning on 21 December 1943 on the Mankovo – Kalitvenskaya – Chertkovo road.

He came across the Don to Nizhne Mamon with his battalion, accompanied only by sledge vehicles, marched to Mankovo without contact with the enemy. The battalion's preliminary objective was Chertkovo. – Final objective of the offensive was said to be Rostov. – Overtaking tanks said to belong to the 4th Tank Corps.

He stated that about 80 tanks drove past him on the road from the Don to Mankovo. The majority were medium tanks. A company equipped with submachine-guns was detached to Kantamirovka (prisoners from this company were brought in from that direction!).

Supply: Most supplies were delivered by horse-drawn vehicle. Only a few trucks were available.

The 41st Guards Division consists of:
3 infantry regiments (about 850 men per regiment)
1 battery of 76mm guns – 4 guns are towed by tanks
1 battery of 45mm guns
1 battery of 150mm guns 2 submachine-gun companies
1 radio company, 2 radiophone and telephone

1 platoon of combat engineers – about 40-50 men strong

1 company with anti-tank rifles.

The 89th Division is in reserve behind the 41st Guards Division.

Employed in the offensive were:

The army Lieutenant General ...., who received his attack orders personally from Stalin.

The army consisted of:

84th Rifle Division

85th Rifle Division

41st Guards Division

4th Tank Corps with 4 tank brigades, with about 1,200 tanks. Approx. 50 Stalin Organs (claims to have seen them).

Stalin's order is said to have read:

The army is to break through in the direction of Rostov and cut off the southern German army.

Soviet radio announced that 8 Italian divisions had been destroyed and that the line between Kantamirovka and Millerovo was in Russian hands.

St. is an enthusiastic soldier. As battalion commander he has under his command 600 cossacks, who follow him blindly. – He claims to know nothing about the treatment of captured German soldiers. He has only seen captured Italian soldiers. The soldiers who raised their hands were taken to the rear, others were shot. – He saw Russian prisoners who worked on our side being shot.

signed Göller

During an attempt by the 5th (Panzer) Company, Führer-Begleit Battalion to break out of Chertkovo toward Welizkozkoje, from which direction a relief attack by the German 19th Panzer Division was expected, the company commander, Oblt. Kegel, was killed by enemy mortar fire. As well, platoon leader Lt. Wilkens was mortally wounded while outside his tank. The following radio messages were exchanged between the tanks of 5th Company:

1 January 1943:

To 22 & 23:	Drive ahead further!
S to A:	Don't drive so far forward!
An to An:	On the extreme left; can you see anything?
An to An:	Pull back very slowly!
An to 22& 23:	Drive behind the self-propelled carriage!
An to An:	Two brave lads go up and bring back the chief (Oblt. Kegel) and Lt. Wilkens.
An to C:	Employ all means to engage the guns!
C to An:	C has no more high-explosive ammunition!
An to C:	Fire on the Russians with machine-guns!
An to C:	Continue firing and changing positions!
	A report to assault gun when Oblt. Kegel and Lt.

	Wilkens have been recovered and S has returned.
An to 24:	Recovery must take place quickly, otherwise you're likely to be hit.
S to 24:	Lt. Wilkens is lying over there, or what is it? Take him with you!
S to S:	Withdraw slowly!
S to 24:	Are they both dead?
24 to S:	Both are dead!
S to S:	S pull back and drive to quarters. Sequence: C, Af, Wn and An.
An to 24:	Drive back with the two dead, I must stay here to pick up infantry.
An to 23 & 24:	You drive back too.
An to 22:	Remain here and secure in the direction of Welizkozkoje and the village.

On 15 January 1943 the battle group of the 298th Infantry Division prepared to break out of Chertkovo. The few available tanks of the 5th (Panzer) Company, FBB were to spearhead the attack.

The breakout began at about 22.00 and was successful. In an approximately 9,000-metre-long column, with the wounded riding in the remaining serviceable vehicles and tanks, the 298th Infantry Division fought its way through in the direction of Strikavka. There it was taken in by the Jüterbof Assault Gun Training Battalion, which, like "Battle Group Pohlmann," had been thrown into action on the threatened front.

On 19 January 1943 the surviving elements of "Battle Group Pohlmann" were reunited in Starobyelsk, where the unit briefly rested and reorganised.

The battle group subsequently saw action under the command of the Infantry Division *Großdeutschland*, which had meanwhile reached the front. It remained with the division from the beginning of February until into the month of March 1943.

It was now clear where the path of the Infantry Division *Großdeutschland* was leading: toward Stalingrad! The men of the division heard and read of the collapse of the German front between Rostov and Voronezh on the radio and in the armed forces newspapers. They drew their own conclusions and gave up on their dream of going home to rest and refit.

On 15 January 1943 the division's advance detachment left the city of Smolensk, arriving in Kupyansk, on the upper course of the Oskol River, at about lunchtime on 19 January.

Already all hell was loose there. Retreating units, supply trains and workshop installations, decamping supply and foodstuffs dumps, all heading west, driven by the fury of fear of the advancing Soviets.

For the bulk of the Infantry Division *Großdeutschland* there were still a few days of rest, which were used to bring the units back up to strength and carry out necessary repair work on weapons and equipment. New plans for reorganisation arrived. It was announced that the Grenadier Regiment's I Battalion under Hptm. Remer was to become an armoured personnel carrier battalion. The former Motorcycle Battalion GD was redesignated the "Reconnaissance Battalion GD," and it was authorised to wear the gold-yellow service colour of the cavalry. The change of colours was made more quickly than anticipated, for it had been the wish all along to have this association with the cavalry.

Formation of a IV Artillery Battalion GD went ahead in Guben. The battalion commander was Hptm. Roeckner, while commanding the 10th, 11th and 12th Batteries were Lt. Hübner, Lt. Sporleder and Lt. Reisemann, respectively. The battalion's formation was completed at the end of January 1943, after which it was ready to join the division; its heavy howitzers and cannon represented a significant strengthening of the Artillery Regiment GD.

While the Grenadier Regiment GD received orders to entrain on 16 January 1943 — it was later moved back to 19 January — the Fusilier Regiment's I Battalion began actual entraining on 17 January. This battalion became the first of the division's units to begin transport.

Meanwhile the division's advance detachment, which had been in Kupyansk since 19 January 1943, had established contact with the German general in Headquarters, Italian Eighth Army and was placed under the latter's command. The *Großdeutschland* Division's assigned detraining area was Volchansk and the surrounding area.

The Italian headquarters characterised the situation as totally uncertain. All that they knew for certain was that on the left (northwest) the enemy had broken through the front of the neighbouring Hungarians along its entire width and were pouring into the Valuiki–Volokonovka–Novy Oskol area. Their objective appeared to be Kharkov.

The city of Valuiki on the Oskol was allegedly already occupied by the enemy. The Soviets were said to be approaching Kupyansk. As to which friendly units were still holding out somewhere and their strengths, nothing was known.

The first of the division's units to arrive was I Battalion, Fusilier Regiment, which arrived in Volokonovka on 19 January 1943 and immediately began detraining in the bitter cold. That same night the battalion occupied positions at the edge of village.

Loud engine noises were repeatedly heard east of Volokonovka during the night of 20/21 January. Then in the early morning hours of 21 January, seven enemy tanks broke into the village, causing great confusion. They shot up parked and dispersed vehicles of I Battalion, Fusilier Regiment, set the houses on fire and drove up and down the streets. After the fusiliers recovered from their initial shock, they killed some of the escorting Soviet infantry and put the rest to flight. The tanks subsequently withdrew. Four, however, were unable to move; they had become stuck in the deep snow and were destroyed with hand grenades. Thus, in spite of the initial surprise, I Battalion, Fusilier Regiment was able to chalk up a success for itself.

In the evening hours a planned withdrawal from Volokonovka was carried out and a new strongpoint further north in and near Novy Oskol was occupied. Meanwhile, I Battalion, Grenadier Regiment GD arrived at Belyi Kolodes station, southwest of Volchansk, at about 15.00 on 21 January 1943.

Detraining was completed by about 18.00 hours. The battalion commander meanwhile established contact with Volchansk and was assigned quarters for his unit. Late in the evening I Battalion, Grenadier Regiment moved into the village of Sinelnikovo, due south of Volchansk, and waited.

Finally, on 22 January 1943, sufficient units of the Infantry Division *Großdeutschland* had arrived for the division to be given its first assignment:

Block the roads to Olkovatka and Volchansk toward the east and
scout for enemy forces advancing out of Valuiki and Volokonovka.

Oberst Kassnitz, commander of the Fusilier Regiment GD, moved along the road toward Volokonovka with the available elements of his regiment. His forces were too weak for an attack on the city, and he was forced to content himself with blocking the Volokonovka–Volchansk road.

The enemy felt their way forward with reconnaissance patrols, but so far showed no greater offensive intentions. "Battle Group Bringmann," which had withdrawn from Valuiki on the Oskol, was placed under the division's command and was moved to Olkovatka, where it was assigned defensive responsibilities. The Grenadier Regiment GD, all of which had now arrived, established contact with the battle group in Olkovatka.

Almost completely in the dark concerning the enemy situation, the division command operated from Volchansk as if in an empty room. The division's reconnaissance battalion was still en route; it therefore had to depend on information acquired by the regiments. These dispatched motorised patrols to all sides in search of the enemy spearheads as well as German units. Slowly at first, the division began to get a somewhat clearer picture of the enemy situation. It learned that the Soviets had reached the Oskol on a broad front, with elements across the river in places. Enemy patrols were sighted in the Kosinka Valley near Borki and near the village of Kosinka. The Fusilier Regiment had only limited contact with the enemy at the Volokonovka—Volchansk road (west of Volokonovka).

On the German side, elements of the Fusilier Regiment GD were positioned west of Volokonovka, while farther south – east of Kosinka – were deployed alert units composed of bakers, supply train personnel, etc., about 300 men strong, and III Battalion, Grenadier Regiment GD. In the bottom land of the Kosinka, several kilometres south of Kosinka, was "Battle Group Bringmann," which defended the Kosinka Valley and the approach to Olkovatka. Between the two German battle groups there were only individual strongpoints. While in the past few days the enemy opposite this line had still been relatively weak, on 24 January 1943 concentrations were observed east of Kosinka, opposite "Battle Group von Platen," which suggested that an attack was imminent. Finally, late in the afternoon, the enemy launched an assault with tanks and infantry. This was repulsed in a joint effort by "Battle Group von Platten" and the Grenadier Regiment's III Battalion with heavy losses to the enemy.

However this attack caused the leaders of the Grenadier Regiment to place the battalions still at rest near Volchansk on alert and move them into this area. Further and heavier attacks by the enemy had to be expected east of Kosinka. During the nighttime hours of 25 January both battalions of the

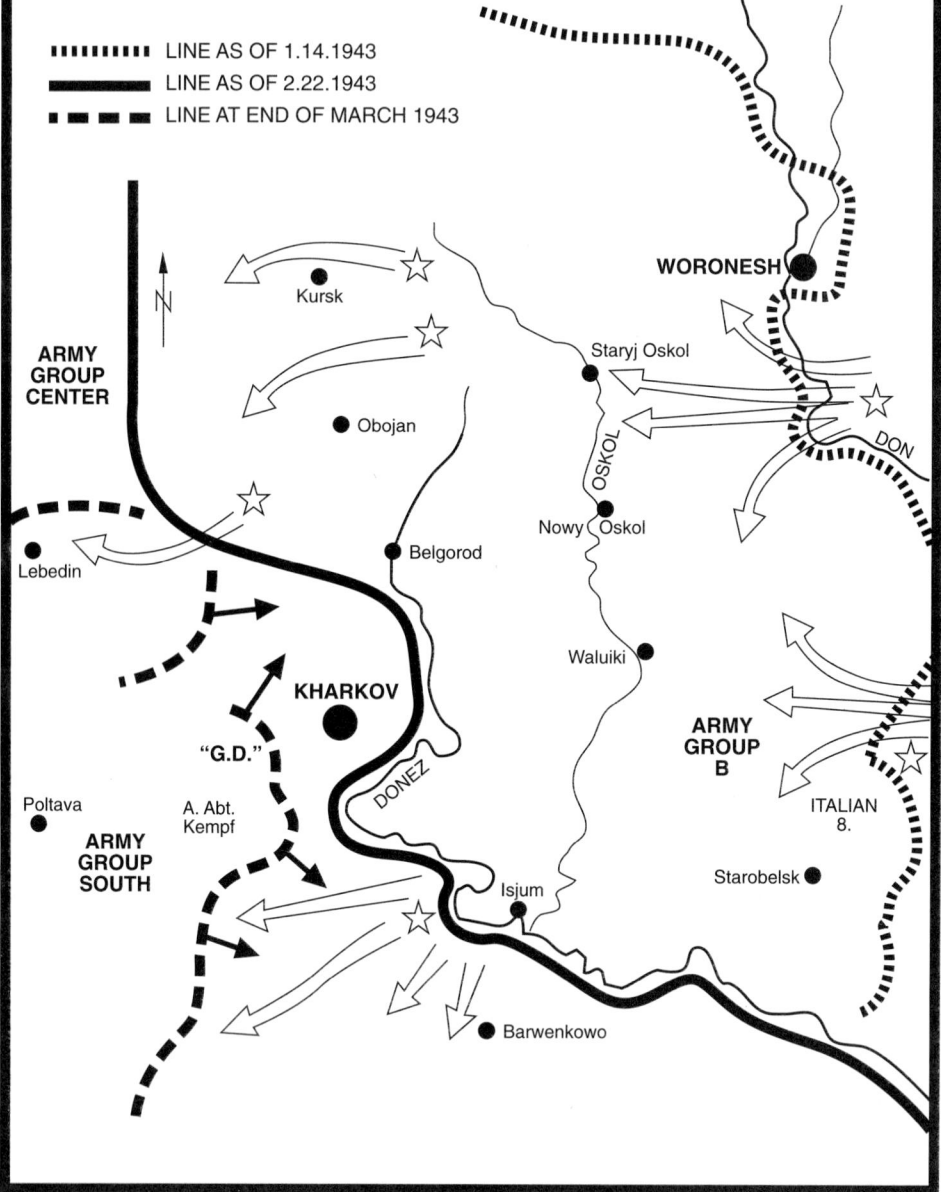

THE SOVIET OFFENSIVE
of Jan. 14, 1943
Between the Don and the Donez

ıııııııı LINE AS OF 1.14.1943

▬▬▬▬▬ LINE AS OF 2.22.1943

▬ ▬ ▬ ▬ LINE AT END OF MARCH 1943

N

WORONESH

Kursk

ARMY
GROUP
CENTER

Staryj Oskol

Obojan

OSKOL

Nowy Oskol

DON

Lebedin

Belgorod

Waluiki

KHARKOV

ARMY
GROUP
B

"G.D."

Poltava

A. Abt.
Kempf

ITALIAN
8.

ARMY
GROUP
SOUTH

DONEZ

Starobelsk

Isjum

Barwenkowo

Grenadier Regiment GD arrived in Chugonovka, near Olkovatka. "Battle Group von Platen" was placed under their command. Meanwhile the 1st First-aid Company had also arrived, immediately setting up a medical clearing station in Volchansk and a wounded forwarding post at the rail station. The number of wounded was still small.

The units of the division defended their sectors in the line Kosinka Valley near Borki, farther north in the village of Kosinka, and subsequently—by the Fusilier Regiment—the road west of Volokonovka. Both sides maintained lively patrol activity.

Unfortunately the infiltration of the German lines by the enemy had to be expected, for as a result of the shape of the sector and the limited combat strengths, the widely spaced strongpoint system could only be weakly manned. Typical combat strengths were:

2nd Company, Grenadier Rgt.:	1 officer and 27 NCOs and men.
6th Company, Grenadier Rgt.:	1 officer and 12 NCOs and men.
13th Company, Grenadier Rgt.:	2 officers and 25 NCOs and men.

Much use was made of patrols and diversionary manoeuvres. On the other hand, the countryside, with its numerous hollows and ravines, offered the enemy numerous opportunities to approach, so that it was impossible to prevent them from suddenly appearing from behind. Given the weakness of the German forces, combat was possible only in mixed battle groups, which included infantry, artillery, anti-tank forces, a few pioneers and anti-aircraft guns. These self-contained units had to be sent wherever the enemy appeared, and there were many such places. The enemy sought out the weak spots in the German strongpoints, and simply withdrew wherever strong opposition was met. Riding on the decks of their tanks, sometimes with several limbered anti-tank guns, the Soviet infantry drove into a village, fired wildly in all directions and usually caused a great deal of panic, especially among the Italians and Hungarians, who, completely exhausted, had taken shelter in the village.

At that time the German troops were perhaps unaware of the stresses to which these units of the allied armies had been exposed on the Don front. Inadequate anti-tank defences against a heavily-armoured opponent, overextended lines facing an enemy attacking in concentration and breaking through at one point, a brutal style of fighting, even against the sick and wounded, a Soviet force used to the cold and snow against southerners used to the warm southern sun.

It remained for the first German units, alone and unsupported, with open flanks, overextended routes and improvised supply, and without clear orders, to save what could be saved. It was vital that they, together with the German battle groups expected from the east, trying to fight their way to the west, and the divisions being hastily moved in, establish a new defensive line and thus bring the rampaging enemy to a halt. Only near and east of the village of Kosinka was there anything "up" in the *Großdeutschland* Infantry Division's strongpoint system – it was impossible to speak of a sector with neighbouring forces on the left and right. That meant that there was only the enemy showing any sign of his usual stubborn will to break through, in that they launched several heavy attacks each day. These were successfully repulsed by III Battalion, Grenadier Regiment, however, often with heavy losses to the attacker. In the Kosinka Valley itself, into which I Battalion, Grenadier Regiment had been moved in the meantime, there was only limited combat. In order to improve its defensive positions the Grenadier Regiment's I Battalion undertook an advance with the objective of blocking and defending the Kosinka Valley near Karabinovo and Babka. As well, on 28 January 1943 the advance detachment of I Battalion, Grenadier Regiment, under the command of Lt. Bernhagen, with three tanks, two 20mm flak, a rifle platoon, a heavy mortar squad of 4th Company and a 50mm anti-tank gun, set out on an advance through Budennovka in the direction of Rega Kosinka. The temperature was 32 degrees below zero. The village was reached without fighting and the advance continued toward the east with the following battalion. Karabinovo and Babka were subsequently occupied at about 14.00 hours and prepared for defence. Contact was established with Battle Group von Platen" to the north and III Battalion, Grenadier Regiment near the village of Kosinka. Thus a continuous defensive line had been established.

The *Großdeutschland* Reconnaissance Battalion, which was so eagerly awaited by the division command, meanwhile arrived in Belyi Kolodes and detrained. It initially took up quarters in Novaya Alexandrovka. The first reconnaissance missions were already on the table. These would soon be carried out by the armoured scout cars under such veteran patrol leaders as Lt. Gerhard, *Wachtmeister* Weichert and others. Farther north, at the road from Volokonovka to Volchansk, the fusiliers reported nothing out of the ordinary.

During the afternoon of 28 January a column of about 1,600 men approached the fusiliers' positions from the east. It was a group of Germans and Italian *Alpini*, who for the past ten days had been making their way westward through the Soviet lines. Almost all were suffering from frostbite or other injuries related to their trek or were wounded.

Measures had already been taken to supply these 1,600 men, as reconnaissance patrols had brought back reports of them the day before. A surgical group of the 1st First-aid Company, reinforced by the addition of three further division first-aid officers, was moved forward to Prikolotnoye. The first order of business was to house these completely exhausted men in warm farm cottages, feed them and provide preliminary medical care. After their arrival the five first-aid officers and the few available medical aides were kept busy treating the wounded, the sick and those suffering from frostbite. They were subsequently transported to Volchansk in empty vehicles, BVZ and ambulances, where the medical clearing station assumed responsibility for further care. In those days and nights great demands were made on all first-aid officers, NCOs and men.

The 29th of January brought new orders. The Infantry Division *Großdeutschland* was placed under a new command authority, the Cramer Corps Headquarters (Special Purpose), which from that point on assumed overall command in this sector. Among the units en route was the *Das Reich* SS Division, which was inserted into the sector east of Volchansk. *Das*

Reich, a volunteer division of the Waffen-SS, was part of the newly-formed II SS Panzer Corps, the bulk of which was still on its way from the West by rail. Following brief preparations the Infantry Division *Großdeutschland* was to launch an attack with these units against the Oskol sector in the north, in order to create a new defensive line. According to the map this section of the valley was particularly well-suited. It remained to be seen whether the Soviets had concentrated sufficient forces on the west bank of the Oskol to easily defeat this plan. It appeared that inadequate reconnaissance had led the commanding headquarters to make a false assessment of the situation— even to a premature launching of the counterattack.

To begin with, a fast unit had to be assembled quickly and sent north. The departure of "Battle Group Kassnitz" (the reinforced Fusilier Regiment GD) was planned for 30 January and the necessary orders issued. While these movements were being initiated the first relieving units of the *Das Reich* SS Division arrived. "Battle Group Lorenz" (the Grenadier Regiment GD) disengaged from the enemy one unit at a time and transferred to the rear for the time being.

The division command left its headquarters in Volchansk and occupied new quarters in Korotsha, where it immediately assumed command of the new sector. Early on 31 January, following a long, nocturnal march over snow-covered roads and paths, the reinforced "Battle Group Kassnitz" attacked Olkovatka from Mikhailovka (southwest of Novy Oskol). Well-built enemy positions and very noticeable flanking movements from north and south hindered the advance. The enemy soon counterattacked from Belomestnoye, which prevented the attack force from entering Olkovatka. Afterward the attack was broken off and instead "Battle Group Lorenz" made ready to advance out of the Goroshenoye area toward Sidorovka and Barsuk. Added to the several fatal casualties suffered by the fusilier regiment were the losses of the Assault Gun Battalion GD. The crew of Uffz. Günth, Gefr. August Hoffmann and gunner Alfred Harre were killed in action.

While the reinforced Fusilier Regiment dug in on the high ground southwest of Mikhailovka, on the evening of 31 January the Grenadier Regiment's II Battalion, which was temporarily under the command of the fusilier regiment, attacked Belomestnoye and entered the town in heavy fighting. Close-quarters fighting for every house in the village against a superior, determined enemy lasted through the entire night. Among those killed were the brave grenadiers Heften and Kannikowsky of 7th Company, Grenadier Regiment. The attack by II Battalion, Grenadier Regiment, which had begun so successfully, had to be called off, on account of the severity of the losses suffered by the companies and the troops withdrawn. The surgical group of the 1st First-aid Company reported treating 86 casualties, the bulk of which were attributable to the brave II Battalion, Grenadier Regiment GD.

Meanwhile the main body of "Battle Group Lorenz" was still en route through Volchansk into the Goroshenoye area. Blowing snow, as well as roads jammed with retreating Italians and Hungarians, limited the progress of the motorised columns. Leading elements of the reinforced Grenadier Regiment GD did not reach the assigned area until late in the evening of 1

February 1943.

"Battle Group Kassnitz" meanwhile held its defensive positions in a line Begorodskoye (the right wing had contact there with II Battalion, Grenadier Regiment)Point 212.1– Podwisloye. There was only limited enemy activity. The evacuation of wounded by ambulance also caused extraordinary difficulties. At the time the few ambulances of the 1st Ambulance Platoon were all that was available and these had to constantly shuttle to and from the medical clearing station in Korotsha over the poor, snow- and ice-covered roads.

In the meantime the rest of the 1st First-aid Company moved out of Volchansk to take over the medical clearing station in Korotsha. A forward dressing station with a surgical group was set up in Mikhailovka, near the reinforced Fusilier Regiment.

Dawn arrived on 2 February 1943 with temperatures of minus 35 degrees; this was the day when the last German resistance ceased in Stalingrad – *Generalfeldmarschall* Paulus had signed the surrender on 30 January. Plenty of movement was observed on the enemy side, suggesting further attacks, especially against the right wing of the Fusilier Regiment. The neighbouring II Battalion, Grenadier Regiment had dug in on the eastern outskirts of Begorodskoye, creating continuous contact to the left with the fusiliers. Farther south, however, there was no contact with the main body of the grenadiers, who had not been able to complete their preparations for the attack on Sidorovka, because III Battalion had not yet arrived. The observed movements by strong Soviet forces were directed at this gap—in the Novoselovka- Barsuk area. The enemy spearhead was able to enter Barsuk unopposed, as the Hungarian units had already decamped.

"Battle Group Kassnitz" subsequently received orders to take possession of Hill 231.4 and then attack to the southwest in order to drive the enemy out of Barsuk again. Meanwhile the Grenadier Regiment GD continued its preparations in the area southwest of Goroshenoye and Kalinovka, delayed by the slow approach of III Battalion. At 07.00 the Panzer Battalion GD tried a surprise advance on Sidorovka; however heavy anti-tank fire forced the panzers to turn back. The tank of Uffz. Herzer, with the crew of Gefr. Grohn, Stein and Ziegler (3rd Company, Panzer Battalion GD) was knocked out (it was hit six times in five seconds by anti-tank fire). Herzer and Grohn were fatally wounded.

A surprise attack was therefore impossible. However III Battalion, Grenadier Regiment finally arrived and the attack preparations were concluded. A combat report by I Battalion, Grenadier Regiment describes the attack:

"I Battalion had orders to attack the village of Sidirovka at 10.00 hours. It was to advance to the left of the road while III Battalion advanced to the right."

Attached to the battalion were: 6 tanks, which early in the morning followed from Kalinovka with mounted infantry, the 1st and 2nd Heavy Infantry Gun Platoons and a light infantry gun platoon from 17th (Heavy Infantry Gun) Company, as well as artillery support by the 4th and 5th

BATTLES AROUND WOLCHANSK AND THE 'OSKOL'
Jan. 28 - Feb. 3, 1943

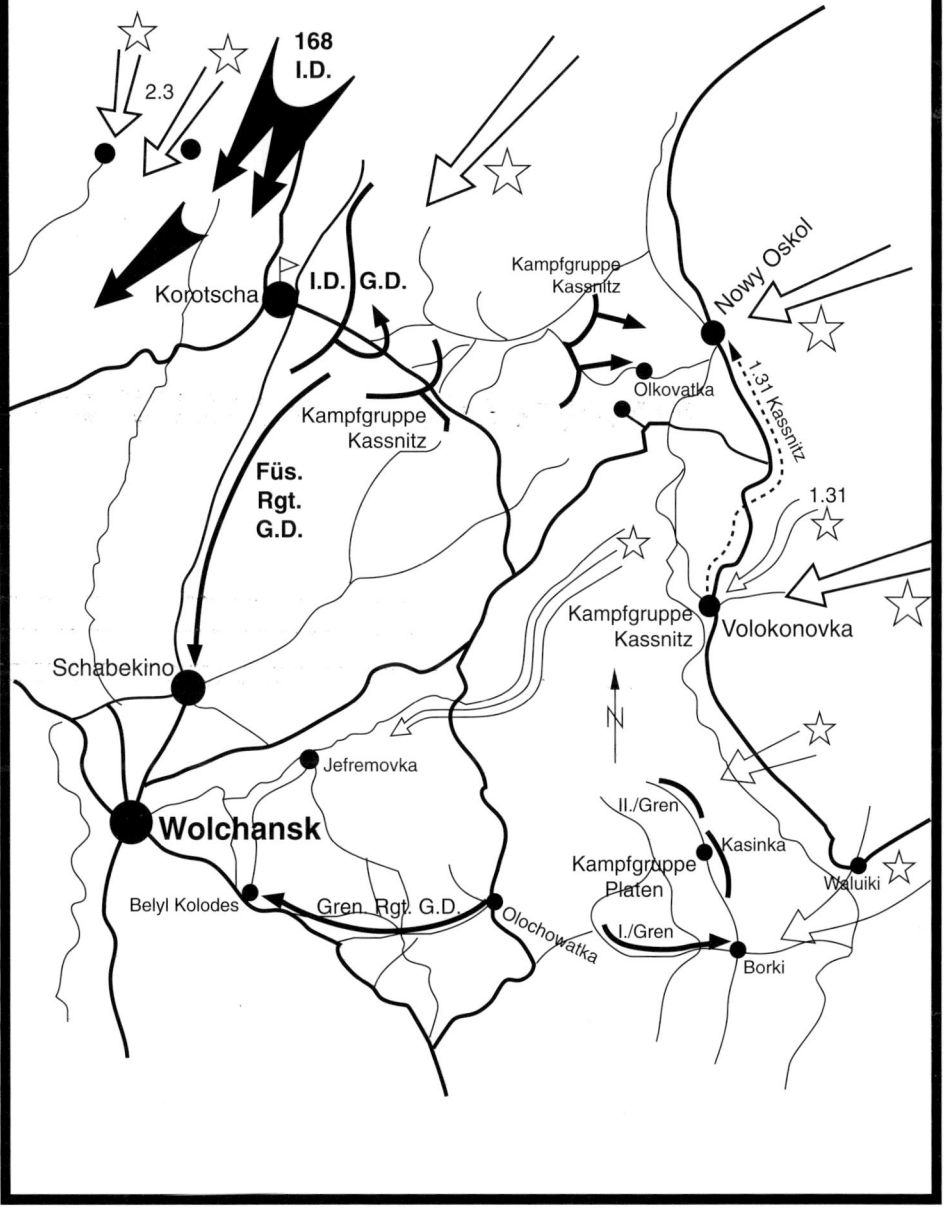

168
I.D.

2.3

Korotscha

I.D. G.D.

Kampfgruppe
Kassnitz

Nowy Oskol

Olkovatka

1.31 Kassnitz

Kampfgruppe
Kassnitz

Füs.
Rgt.
G.D.

1.31

Schabekino

Kampfgruppe
Kassnitz

Volokonovka

N

Jefremovka

II./Gren

Wolchansk

Kasinka

Kampfgruppe
Platen

I./Gren

Waluiki

Belyl Kolodes

Gren. Rgt. G.D.

Olochowatka

Borki

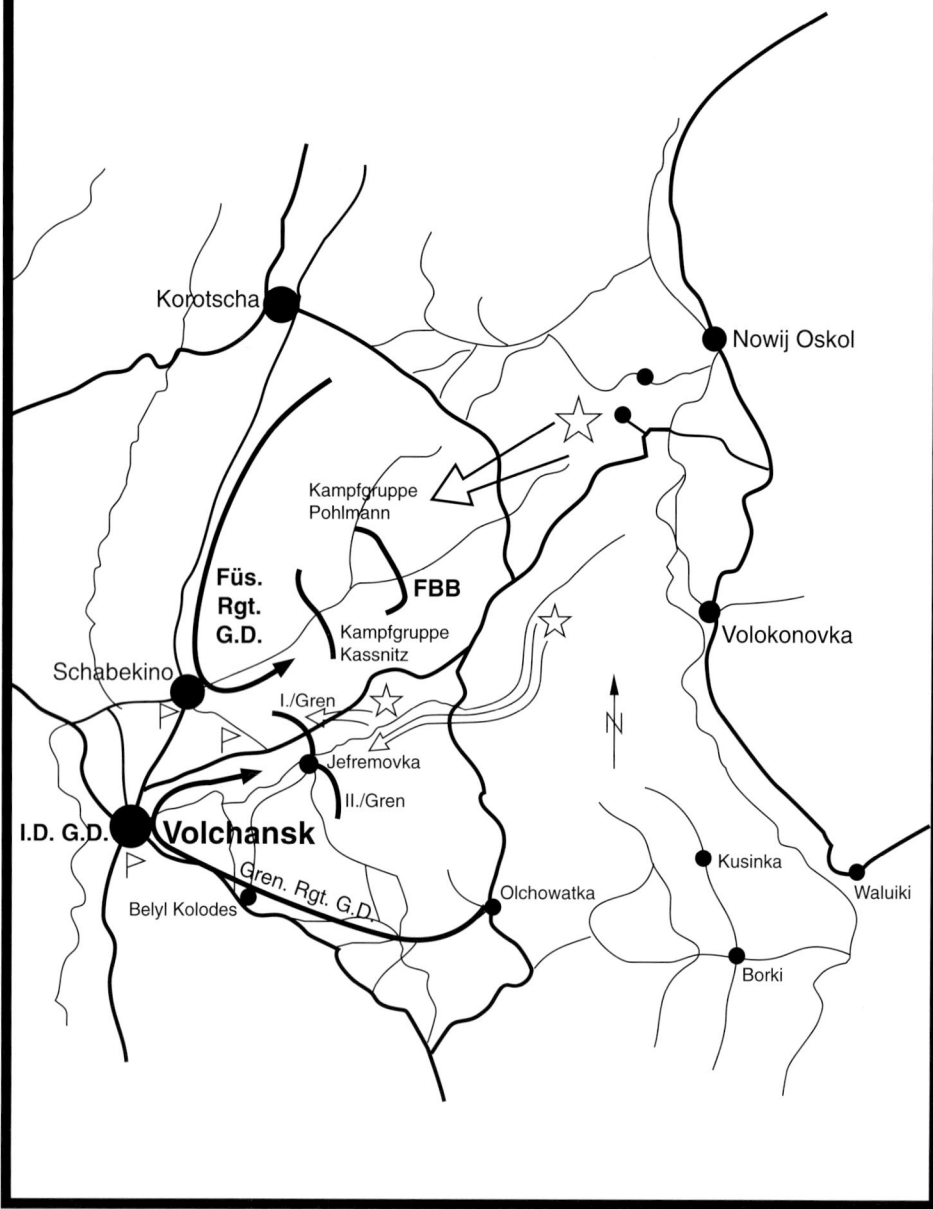

BATTLES AROUND NOWIJ OSKOL AND VOLCHANSK
From Feb.4 to Feb.8, 1943

Korotscha

Nowij Oskol

Kampfgruppe
Pohlmann

Füs.
Rgt.
G.D.

FBB

Kampfgruppe
Kassnitz

Volokonovka

Schabekino

I./Gren

N

Jefremovka

II./Gren

I.D. G.D. **Volchansk**

Kusinka

Waluiki

Gren. Rgt. G.D.

Belyl Kolodes

Olchowatka

Borki

18

Batteries of the Artillery Regiment GD. I Battalion waited in the open in freezing temperatures for III Battalion to complete its preparations. Already feeling the effects of the hardships of the past few days, the men stood around the exhaust pipes at the rear of the tanks seeking any opportunity to get warm. Attack at 13.00 hours, after III Battalion finally arrived.

Formation: I Battalion left, III Battalion right of the road. Organisation within I Battalion: 3rd Company mounted on tanks, attacked the village of Sidorovka after swinging wide left. — Following next on foot 1st Company, and far right 2nd Company. — 4th Company attacked right of the road with III Battalion, on its left wing. — Anti-tank guns and 5th Company's light infantry gun platoon went into position on the road and supported the attack by the infantry with their fire.

The attack was halted about 300 metres from the village, as the Soviets put up bitter resistance with dug-in anti-tank guns from behind a snow wall. The companies dug in at about 17.00. At about 19.00 4th Company sent an assault team into the village. It was able to enter as the Soviets had withdrawn. The rest of I Battalion was moved up at about 24.00. — I Battalion had 7 dead and 25 wounded in this attack, as well as 4 men lost through frostbite, which meant that the equivalent of an entire company had been "put out of action."

The day did not pass without crises developing elsewhere. Even though the Fusilier Regiment succeeded in taking possession of Hill 231.4, an attack by the Soviets from Barsuk was only stopped through the actions of two pioneer companies. On the left (northern) flank of the Fusilier Regiment GD, the Russians, after swinging north, succeeded in punching through the Hungarian units there and entered Mikhailovka with a small number of tanks. The surgical group of the 1st First-aid Company only just managed to load up the wounded in Mikhailovka and evacuate the village in time. That day the medical clearing station in Korotsha once again treated more than 85 wounded. The combat strengths of the infantry regiments at the front continued to decline.

Meanwhile the situation farther south had grown increasingly worse. The advancing Soviets, following the principle of not stopping to attack individual strongpoints, repeatedly changed course and sought other paths to the west. Their leading spearheads were already before Volchansk, had entered the Volchya Valley and were advancing along the Neshegol. This advance by the Soviets repeatedly forced the abandonment of favourable defensive positions—often without a shot being fired.

So, on 3 February, Army Group Lanz ordered the evacuation of the Mikhailovka-Sidorovka positions and the establishment of a new defensive line due east of Korotsha.

In the meantime the *Führer-Begleit-Bataillon* had been moved into the area. A small force from this unit, Battle Group Pohlmann, was moved hastily into the Neshegol Valley and deployed near Bolshe Troizkoje with orders to set up a blocking position. Several kilomctres farther east, near the village of Maximovka, sat Oblt. Spaeter, who several weeks earlier had still been the Division O1, with several armoured cars and volkswagens. His mission was to observe the enemy's movements and intercept individual advances at an early stage. As he watched, the enemy again veered north and simply drove past his position—there was nothing he could do about it. Meanwhile there were indications of a threatening situation farther north: aerial reconnaissance had spotted Soviet march and sledge columns, which included a large number of tanks, advancing toward Belgorod. Their leading elements were already on the upper course of the Severnyi Donets, roughly near Podilchi and Donetskoye; but to an increasing degree they were threatening the German defensive front east of Korotsha, into whose rear they were in the process of advancing. Aerial reconnaissance also reported a German column fleeing toward Belgorod before the Soviet forces moving in from the north.

Therefore, in a surprise move, the Reconnaissance Battalion GD under *Rittmeister* Wätjen was transferred to Belgorod with orders to block the valley of the Severnyi Donets as far to the north as possible. As a result of drifting snow and blocked roads the battalion did not arrive in the city until the evening of 4 February.

The situation became even more critical; Soviet spearheads had been sighted in numerous places, but the German forces were too weak to defend everywhere at once. Instead they were forced to fight delaying actions here and there and thus at least delay the Soviet advance. It was unclear to the headquarters, nor could it predict, how this was to continue or where it would end. The regiments were hastily withdrawn from their previous positions, which inevitably involved some fighting. Indeed in the area of Schtschetinowka II Battalion, Grenadier Regiment and III Battalion, Fusilier Regiment had to be committed to a counterattack to cover the withdrawal of all elements. The danger, which was especially evident in the Volchya Valley, in the defensive area of the *Das Reich* SS Division, was so great that the Grenadier Regiment's I Battalion, which was already on the march, had to be immediately diverted there. The vehicles carrying the grenadiers of I Battalion drove at high speed into the Volchya Valley in the midst of a snowstorm and in minus 30 degree temperatures. On arrival they immediately occupied new positions south of Pankov at the road. Under Hptm. Remer the rest of the battalion and the headquarters initially moved into Maryin. That evening the enemy attacked with several assault detachments, but these were repulsed with the help of elements of the *Das Reich* Motorcycle Battalion still there. Several Soviet rifle brigades and a tank brigade were also reported in the area.

The *Großdeutschland* Infantry Division moved its command post to Shebekino. The Reconnaissance Battalion GD was just about to reconnoitre to the north, when it was informed by radio by division that Belgorod was directly threatened from the north. The same day, 5 February 1943, measures were taken to defend the city. The diary of the Reconnaissance Battalion GD contains the following account:

"It is 15.00. We establish contact with the Belgorod city commandant. He is just in the process of arranging the distribution of several beds. Contact is also made with the commander of a security battalion in the city, at the very moment he is in the process of distributing a large shipment of goods. The quartermaster section of the Cramer Special Purpose Corps, which is located in the city, also knows nothing of the imminent dangers. When the commander informs them they all promise their help in defending against the enemy.

The battalion immediately dispatches two patrols into the Severnyi-Donets valley to the northeast; one on the large road to Kursk, the other in the direction of Korotsha, in order to get a clear picture of the enemy and to determine the location of the first branching-off of the road to Kiselevo, where the first line of resistance is to be established. A standing patrol will be sent to Gostishshevo in the evening.

The patrols return during the night; the one on the road to Kursk had no contact with the enemy and reports impassable roads to Kiselevo. The other patrol, likewise with no enemy contact, claims to have found a passable way into the Severnyi-Donets Valley. The commander therefore decides to start the battalion on the road to Korotsha."

In spite of eight advances by the enemy, some with tanks, the situation in the Volchya Valley had basically not changed for the units deployed there, I Battalion, Grenadier Regiment south of Pankov and III Battalion, Grenadier Regiment near the village of Yefremovka. Contact was made with elements of the *Das Reich* SS Division holding to the south and a continuous defensive line established. Meanwhile, elements of "Battle Group Kassnitz" moved into the Neshegol valley, relieving "Battle Group FBB-Pohlmann" and occupying a new defensive position near Ruskaya. There were increasing signs that the enemy was forming a new focal point in the Volchya Valley, while Soviet elements advancing into the Neshegol Valley were initially just advance forces. The situation in the Severnyi-Donets Valley north of Belgorod, where the Reconnaissance Battalion GD was occupying positions, was much more threatening. The 4th Squadron under Oblt. Schubert advanced toward Kiselevo, while the main body of the battalion initially remained in Dalnaya-Igumanka. On 6 February the leading elements of 4th Squadron even advanced as far as Sabyino, but were attacked by strong enemy forces before entering. That evening, when the enemy tried to go around the village, which was difficult to defend on account of its layout, the 4th Squadron was finally withdrawn toward Kiselevo. Two 88mm flak of the Heavy Flak Battery GD, which had meanwhile been sent by Division, were placed under its command, while 2nd Company, Assault Pioneer Battalion GD initially remained in Belgorod. The Reconnaissance Battalion GD was temporarily assigned to the 168th Infantry Division which was fighting its way through from Korotsha. All in all, it had to be assumed that the enemy were intent on breaking through toward Belgorod in the Donets Valley, in order to take possession of the city.

The enemy's movements provided an increasingly clear indication of their intentions: two powerful battle groups, one from the north toward Belgorod, the other in the Volchya Valley from the east toward Volchansk, had as their objective the city of Kharkov, which they intended to attack together. Given the situation their linking up was to take place in the area northeast of

Kharkov.

Armed with this knowledge, Army Group Lanz introduced its first measures. Where the Infantry Division *Großdeutschland* was concerned, this meant the deployment of a strong regimental group due east of Volchansk together with elements of the *Das Reich* SS Division. Together with other forces near Belgorod its mission was to fight a delaying action to hold off the enemy until...yes, until the remaining elements of II SS-Panzer Corps, which were on the way, and other German units had reached their areas.

Fighting a delaying action was difficult, especially with the appearance of strong enemy battle groups in a large area, which could not be kept under control given the low combat strengths of the defenders. With the appearance of enemy spearheads, small, mobile battle groups quickly established blocking positions at expected focal points and set up the defense. In such a case the vehicles were usually held at the far exit from the village or behind the nearest hill. Then followed first contact; all too often the enemy went around the blocking position and resumed their advance behind it. In that case all that could be done was to carry out a timely withdrawal, occupy new positions and break camp again. There was no rest, always outside in the snow and cold. As well, there was the depressing feeling of unwavering retreat—all of this ate away at the soldiers' will to resist.

An improbable level of flexibility had to be demanded of the German command, which in this period was forced to operate almost exclusively by radio. Only it, possessing as it did the overall picture of the enemy's movements, could see where the danger of being outflanked was greatest and where the encirclement of individual units was soon to take place. It had to coordinate each individual action and maintain the uniformity of its units. It became clear that the units deployed in the Donets Valley would have to be sent reinforcements continuously. The reinforced Grenadier Regiment GD, en route to Belgorod via Kharkov, its movements delayed by drifting snow, was not the only force heading for the city. Smaller battle groups were also hurrying toward Belgorod to at least hold the city as long as possible and cover the retreat of the 168th Infantry Division fighting its way through from the northeast. The first to arrive in Belgorod was the battle group of the *Führer-Begleit-Bataillon* under Hptm. Mattheis, which represented a welcome reinforcement to the Reconnaissance Battalion GD. Its five Panzer IV tanks, two assault guns, two 75mm anti-tank guns and the equivalent of two rifle companies helped bolster the garrison of Belgorod.

However the situation had become increasingly critical: on 7 February strong enemy forces were advancing along the Korotsha- Belgorod road, their leading elements already engaged in heavy fighting with elements of the reconnaissance battalion under Oblt. Heise in the northern part of Dalnaya-Igumenka.

The measures initiated by the division resulted in the withdrawal of the reinforced Grenadier Regiment GD on 8 February 1943. Its new orders were to pass through Kharkov, advance as far as possible toward Belgorod, establish a new north-facing blocking line at the road, and later take in elements of the reinforced Reconnaissance Battalion GD when they withdrew from

Belgorod.

The reinforced Fusilier Regiment GD was under orders to carry out a gradual withdrawal beyond the Severnyi-Donets and prepare a new defensive line at the riverbank. For the regiment a withdrawal over the Volchansk–Kharkov road was no longer possible; instead it would have to shovel a path through the snow to the west in order to reach the Belgorod–Kharkov road.

The 8th of February saw the fighting for the city of Belgorod reach its climax, and as well the abandoning of the city by the defenders. The best account of these events is once again contained in the diary entries of the Reconnaissance Battalion GD, which documented all the details of this tragic-comic battle:

"At about 06.00 the Russians attacked with tanks and infantry west of the Belgorod–Kursk road. The advance was initially repulsed by the FBB battle group, which was able to destroy three T 34s. 'Battle Group Schubert' (reinforced 4th Squadron) received orders to guard the rail and road bridge east of Belgorod while remaining close to the city.

The first regimental commander of the infantry division fighting in this sector arrived and assumed responsibility for the defence to the north with his regiment, which was approaching very slowly. A dreary, cold winter morning dawned. Everywhere one looked one saw soldiers coming from the already burning supply dump with boxes, sausages and large, round cheeses. In no time at all the stores, which until a short time ago had been guarded by an administrator as the apple of his eye, were distributed among our vehicles. The men sat around tubs in groups, smearing their bread with a thick layer of butter. There was everything in the supply dump, from toothbrushes to French red wine.

The battalion command post had been set up in the basement of the hospital, which had been left in a terrible condition. The first members of the previously mentioned infantry division arrived after us, tired and apathetic. Finding something to eat, sleeping or smoking, they had no thought of taking part in the defence of Belgorod.

Suddenly a T 34 raced out of a side street; it roared – with all guns firing – past the hospital. In no time the first men charged out of the hospital entrance, hollow charges swinging. But the anti-aircraft gun which had been installed on the crossing of the Kursk-Kharkov road on orders of the city commandant put the tank out of action with seven hits. Not content with this, an Unteroffizier placed a hollow charge, and the T 34 blew apart with an ear-shattering crash.

At that moment the staff of the infantry division arrived in the hospital. Scarcely had the excitement over the tank died down, when new, alarming news was received: the Russians had taken the Donets and rail bridges and 'Battle Group Schubert' was making a fighting withdrawal toward the city centre after requesting in vain that a battalion of this infantry division help hold the bridge. The battalion commander merely replied that he had no orders to take part in the defence. We were all furious at the infantry division; we had summoned all our forces to cover its retreat and then it was willing to do nothing. Two further enemy tanks had meanwhile roared up the streets of Belgorod and likewise become victims of the excellent shooting of the flak at the intersection.

The enemy now pressed from the north and east, and there was bitter street fighting. Then at about midday a radio message arrived from the Cramer Special Purpose Corps, stating that the mentioned infantry division should act according to its own judgement. It decided to withdraw to the northwest, through Tomarovka. The order to follow the division toward the northwest didn't sit well with the commander of the Reconnaissance Battalion GD; for his primary intention was to keep open the road to Kharkov in order to enable our division to fall back along this road.

All of the trains were immediately moved to Krasnoye (Grasnoye) on the road to Kharkov. Oblt. Spaeter and 3rd Squadron occupied a rear defensive position on this road.

Suddenly a breathless runner stormed in and reported that the enemy was advancing from the northwest toward Krasnoye in our rear. However, minutes later this unhappy news was contradicted by another report. An attempt by the enemy to outflank us to the south was frustrated by a counterattack by 'Battle Group Schubert.' It had meanwhile become dark. Houses burned everywhere. In places the streets were lit as bright as day.

An American-built M3 light tank appeared out of the darkness before 4th Squadron's sector; a Panzer IV coolly destroyed the tank from a range of 20 metres.

The departure of the 168th Infantry Division came to an abrupt standstill, for the enemy had meanwhile established themselves in the houses at the western exit from Belgorod. The pressure, especially from the north, increased. The rail bridge had just been recaptured, and the last infantry regiment of the 168th Infantry Division streamed into the city, where everything now bunched together. The situation was tense to the point of breaking. In the north the enemy broke into our lines against the 'Battle Group FBB,' but was stopped for the time being. Increasing losses to us and the FBB made the situation more difficult.

Finally the way to the west was free. Sleigh after sleigh stalled on the exit road. At first progress was slow, until the first shots whistled over our heads and the infantry tramped off toward Tomarovka in a disorderly throng. It was high time too, for our weak forces were no longer in a position to hold Belgorod.

The 1st Squadron and the flak had already left for Krasnoye. The last elements of 'Battle Group FBB' and 'Battle Group Schubert' now fought their way back toward the bridge at the southern exit from the city.

The withdrawal of the battalion from Belgorod succeeded at the last minute. It assembled in Krasnoye (Grasnoye). A hard day had ended; the retreat of the 168th Infantry Division had been covered. Eight knocked-out enemy tanks were left behind. All the elements of the Infantry Division GD deployed there, including a battery of the Artillery Regiment GD, had been withdrawn from Belgorod.

The grim nature of the battle for the city of Belgorod, in which, in addition to the squadrons of the Reconnaissance Battalion GD and the flak, the pioneers and to a great degree the "Battle Group FBB" took part, is revealed in an account written by *Oberfeldwebel* A. Müller. It also describes the death of the universally-loved Lt. Christiansen of the FBB on 8 February 1943:

"Our company had established defensive positions at the north end of Belgorod on the road to Kursk. Soon after moving into position, the men in our forward outposts were smoked out by 120mm mortars. At about midday Lt. Christiansen therefore decided to undertake an advance with the objective of capturing this enemy mortar position. The losses incurred by this advance, which was carried out to the right of the road without any tank or artillery support, were relatively low. Not until we reached the attack's objective, a large farm, did we request tanks by radio. Our GD Panzer Battalion then carried out a bold attack on and to the left of the road. But then, before dark, the Soviets launched a massive tank attack, so that we were forced to withdraw to the edge of the city again with considerable losses.

On reaching our starting point, we were pleased when Russian civilians gave us *chleba* (bread) and tea. In view of the likely capture of the city this type of behaviour was to be highly regarded. We were especially impressed by the behaviour of an elderly couple, who had certainly seen better times. The dignified old lady had been an interpreter in the city commander's office for almost two years. She spoke fluent German and had visited Germany often during the time of the czar. Her husband gave the impression of a pope, with his white, flowing beard. Both were completely resigned to their fate and waited for what was to come after our withdrawal. We were ready to help this couple, but they had been born in Russia and wanted to die in Russia.

Our FBB battle group manned its positions until it was completely dark; a GD anti-tank company had provided support, placing its guns at the hot spots. At about 19.00 the enemy suddenly attacked, firing everything they had. In barely an hour the city behind us was blazing fiercely. Most of our men now experienced heavy street fighting for the first time. The front as such had ceased to exist; for the front had now become the corner of a house. None of us knew whether the roaring of engines was caused by our own or by Russian tanks. There was firing in front, but then also from the right and then again on the left. At ten metres no one recognized friend or foe. The crews of the GD company's anti-tank guns gave their all in the close-quarters struggle with the enemy tanks. I can still see the crew of one gun, on a narrow street which led to the cemetery to the right of the road, which literally held out to the last man, until he too lost his life to a direct hit.

The clear winter night was brightly lit. Our winter clothing no longer gave any protection against the snow. Every movement could be seen from a distance. Our company's platoon leaders tried desperately to hold together and assemble their people. At the corner of a house in the centre of the city, I and four men of my platoon, which was now reduced to the strength of a rifle squad, ran into Lt. Christiansen and the *Feldwebel* of an infantry unit. The *Leutnant* was seeking a position from which he could best cover the passage of the infantry. He instructed me to move forward about 100 metres, to an intersection which was visible there, in order to keep the street to the north-east open for at least another hour. He positioned a two-man outpost halfway to my position, so that they could inform us if we were in danger of being cut off.

About ten minutes later Lt. Christiansen himself came crawling forward to fetch me, as Russian infantry had already dug in between us. We took a detour in an effort to reestablish contact with the other platoons. Lt. Christiansen took command of our party, while I and two men formed the rearguard. About 50 metres ahead of me, he reached an intersecting street, on which a T 34 had positioned itself. But Lt. Christiansen failed to see the tank, and when he tried to dash across the street he was caught by a burst of machine-gun fire from it. He cried out loudly and took a few steps back. I reached him in a matter of minutes, and when I picked him up all he said was, 'They got me!' Still in my arms, he fell silent. There was a large red spot on his winter clothing, level with his stomach.

Four of my men picked up the dead *Leutnant*, who we all thought a great deal of, for he really was an outstanding officer. We took his body in the middle and dragged him past the ruins of Belgorod to the spot where the enemy tank was still sitting on the corner.

We had no other choice, we had to get past the tank. The four men with the *Leutnant* hid in the ruins of some houses. An *Obergefreiter* and I decided on an act of desperation. We crawled to the corner of the house, pressed close to the wall, and readied ourselves for a mighty leap to the next house corner- - three metres in front of the nose of the T 34. Finally we worked up enough courage to make the dash, which had to cover 7-8 metres to the nearest cover. I made it across, but the *Obergefreiter* cried out and fell in front of the tank.

After about 100 metres I came upon the first German armoured vehicle; it was an assault gun, commanded by our *Leutnant* from Steiermark. I climbed up and quickly told him what the situation was. In the glow of the fires I could still see the *Obergefreiter* lying in front of the T 34, which sat there immobile. The assault gun made a brief, quick turn and fired a shell into the steel body of the unsuspecting T 34. That was its end.

I hurried to the scene and found the four men we had left behind. We placed the dead *Leutnant* and the dead *Obergefreiter* on the assault gun and drove with them to the aid station, which was housed in a school."

The battle for Belgorod was over. The vehicles of the reinforced Reconnaissance Battalion GD rolled down the easily-passable road south-west toward Kharkov, where another blocking position was to be established. These movements were covered by the few men of 3rd Squadron under Oblt. Spaeter, who held out in Krasnoye until the next evening.

In the focal point of the fighting on 9 February 1943 was "Battle Group Kassnitz" (reinforced Fusilier Regiment GD) on the lower course of the Korotsha. There the enemy pressured the battle group's withdrawal movements very strongly and during the morning hours surprised elements of IV Battalion, Fusilier Regiment in their quarters in Shebekino. Groups of enemy soldiers wearing German camouflage clothing entered the village and caused the battalion considerable losses in materiel, weapons and vehicles. Only by gathering all its forces did the battalion succeed in evacuating the village itself. Not until the afternoon, after heavy fighting, was the reinforced Fusilier Regiment GD able to break contact with the enemy and move back to new positions on the west side of the Severnyi Donets, due east of Arkhangelskoye, southwest of Shebekino. The enemy followed hesitantly at first, however stronger movements were observed on the Shebekino-Belgorod road.

It was still unclear how the main body of the Infantry Division GD was supposed to shovel a path to the Belgorod-Kharkov road in the short time available. It seemed almost impossible given the drifting snow, but work was nevertheless begun straightaway. For this was truly the last way out, the last chance of escaping this emergency situation unscathed.

This account by the commander of the Assault Gun Battalion GD, Hptm. Hans Frank, is typical for the situation that existed then:

"On account of the dispersed manner in which the division conducted the battle and in particular on account of the road conditions, which were especially difficult for the assault guns, during those days of fighting the individual batteries were placed under the command of the division's various battle groups. They repeatedly intervened successfully in the fighting, but there was little visible evidence of success, as the defence was directed mainly against enemy infantry and ski troops, which repeatedly disrupted the division's movements through attacks on the road. On reaching the bridge across the Severnyi-Donets east of Arkhangelskoye, the individual batteries were again placed under the battalion command. This was directed to cooperate with 'Battle Group Kassnitz,' which was supposed to occupy a new main line of resistance on the west bank of the Severnyi-Donets, which led through the middle of Arkhangelskoye.

The guns of 1st Battery under the command of Oberwachtmeister Wegener, who was known universally throughout the division, took up position in several cottages at the western edge of Arkhangelskoye. They received orders to scout approach routes within and on both sides of the village, so as to be able to intervene (even at night) if the need arose. Because, as noted, half of the village lay in front of the main line of resistance, accommodations conditions for the various headquarters and troops in the western part of Arkhangelskoye were very crowded. Since on the other side the Russians had ceased pressing hard late in the afternoon and as the river still lay between us and them, I felt able to justify moving with my battalion staff into a large house. It was in front of the main line of resistance which the division adjutant, my friend Theo Bethke, had occupied until the afternoon. Consequently, the quarters were clean and comfortably warm and thus extremely inviting to an overtired tactical operations staff. As a precaution, I established contact with the infantry commander behind us, letting him know we were there. This was to pay dividends later on. My tactical operations staff, which consisted of driver, dispatch rider, the adjutant Lt. Verch and the radio station (in total about ten people) soon settled down in its new quarters

RETREAT AND REGROUPING OF I.D.GD
from February 9-10, 1943 in the area of
BELGOROD – ARCHANGELSKOJE – LIPZY – KHARKOV

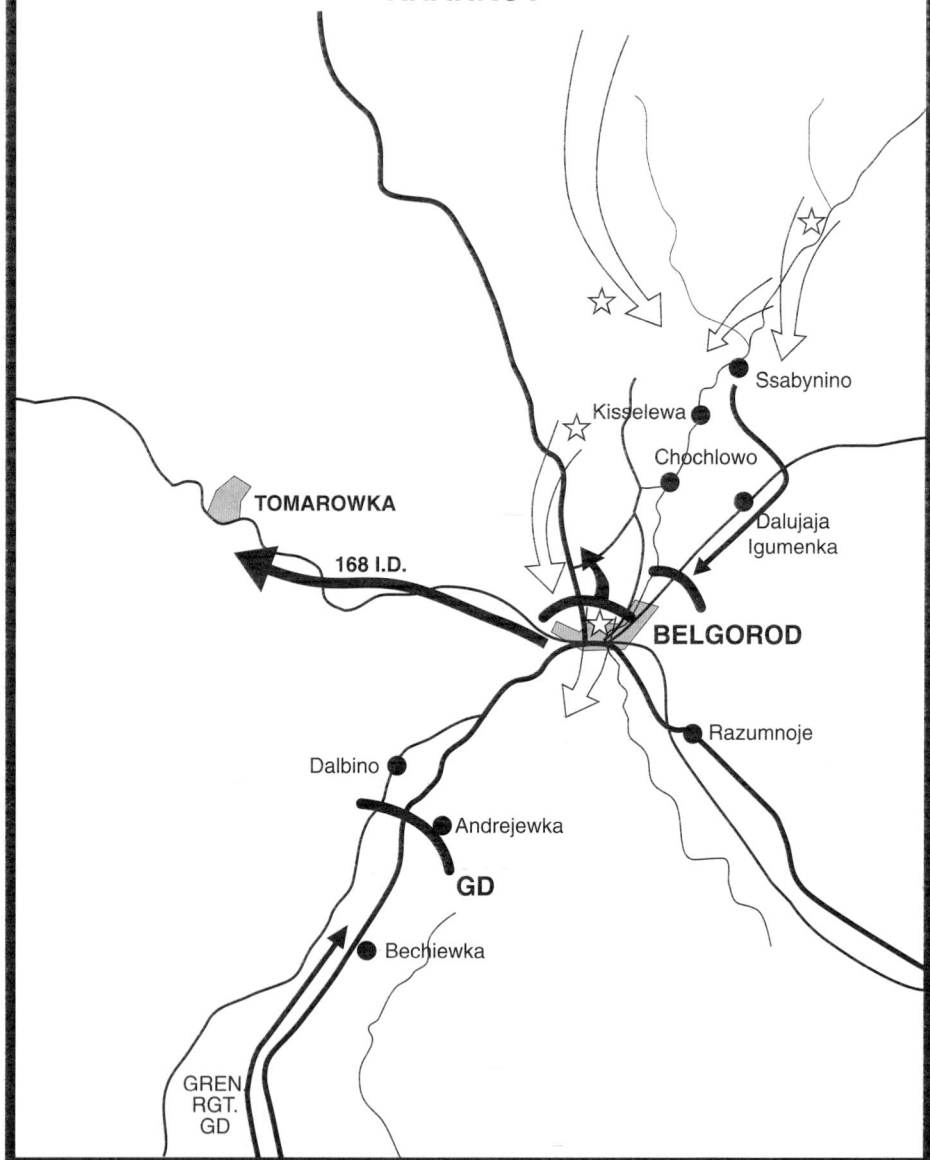

Ssabynino

Kisselewa

Chochlowo

TOMAROWKA

Dalujaja
Igumenka

168 I.D.

BELGOROD

Razumnoje

Dalbino

Andrejewka

GD

Bechiewka

GREN.
RGT.
GD

to rest. At about two o'clock in the morning the sentry woke me with the call: '*Herr Hauptmann, Herr Hauptmann*, the Russians are in the village! They're already on the main street. You can hear the shots clearly!'

I pulled on my fur-lined boots and coat, alerted everyone and ran out the back entrance and through the courtyard to the street. Just as I was about to turn onto the street from the entrance to the courtyard, a very tall Russian ran past right in front of me in the darkness. I squeezed the trigger of my 08 and – I had neglected to cock the weapon. The Russian, obviously just as terrified as I, jumped behind the courtyard wall. I ducked right, behind a shed. As the sound of battle was now directly in front of us, there was no possibility of our few people breaking through to our own troops in the vehicles. The only choice was to head back on foot to the right of the houses, parallel to the road, at double-time through the 50-centimetre-deep snow. The Russians matched our pace on the village street. Full marks to the infantry there, who opened fire at the right place, namely on the Russians, and let us through. In this way the battalion's tactical operations staff, on foot and without its four vehicles, reached 1st Battery's reserve guns. There was a brief conference, and an hour later Obwm. Wegener and two other guns, with the operation staff's drivers aboard, were rolling down the village street in a counterattack. The Russians, who had meanwhile taken up positions in the houses and who were obviously not in the clear as to the overall situation, fled or stood still. Wegener drove up to our house, was able to knock out an anti-tank gun at 400 metres and from there covered the drivers, who jumped in and onto their vehicles. In the end we got all of our vehicles out in one piece. Nothing had happened to them in the dark courtyard of our lost quarters in the intervening hour and a half.

It was once again proof of the energy of the Russian command that, in spite of the unclear nature of the situation, they had their infantry cross an only partially frozen river during the night and drove them forward until they regained the upper hand over the withdrawing German troops. Obviously losses on the Russian side were once again not limited. For the German command the resumption of Russian pressure during the night made more difficult the decisions for the next day."

"Battle Group Lorenz" had a much easier time disengaging from the enemy and by noon its elements were passing through Kharkov. For the first time the men were shown the mood of a city about to fall, something they were later to experience often. The populace fell on anything of value like vultures. With many houses already burning, one could see busy people stripping everything possible and plundering stores and storehouses. Marauding mobs prowled along the walls of houses. On the streets of the city, column after column, especially the supply units, pressed toward the southern and western exits. The vehicles of these rear-echelon services were loaded with beds, furniture, bottles and foodstuffs from the city's abandoned storehouses. Sitting atop the vehicles were women and children, auxiliaries released by the German posts. Once Kharkov had been the metropolis of the rear zone with cinemas, cafes, soldiers homes and other entertainment spots. Now it had become a front-line city, changed its face. Kharkov was to be the focal point of the coming resistance.

The battalions of the Grenadier Regiment GD arrived in Mikoyanovka, on the road to Belgorod, until late in the evening. It was there that they were supposed to establish their new northward-facing blocking line and take in the withdrawing Reconnaissance Battalion GD.

Finally, by the evening, the bulk of the division succeeded in shovelling a path as far as Lipzy, establishing a direct link from the former combat zone to the Kharkov-Belgorod road – without touching Kharkov. While at about 19.00 the division headquarters of the Infantry Division *Großdeutschland* began evacuating the village of Arkhangelskoye and further elements of the division left via the recently-cleared path to Lipzy, a Russian combat patrol entered Arkhangelskoye itself and dug in between the II and III Battalions, Fusilier Regiment GD. Heavy fighting went on through the night and it wasn't until the next morning that order was restored. The defenders continued to hold the positions on the Donets but realized that further attacks were likely in the coming days.

Evacuation of the wounded was also a cause for concern. Because of the way the situation had developed, it was no longer possible to transport them from Shebekino, which had accumulated large numbers of wounded, through Volchansk, because an immediate Soviet threat had made it necessary to hastily mine the road from Shebekino to Volchansk. While scouting a new evacuation route the division medical officer drove over a mine, suffering serious ankle injuries. As a result there was no choice but to take the wounded along over the makeshift road to Lipzy and house them there in hastily-improvised shelters. In the process it was impossible to prevent about sixty wounded from accumulating in Arkhangelskoye. Finally, that evening, they were evacuated in empty vehicles.

Meanwhile in Lipzy a battalion medical officer set up a new reception point for the wounded, where they could be given a warm bed, fed and provided initial surgical treatment. Reaching the main road, and with it access to the medical clearing station was still not possible. In spite of these difficult conditions all wounded were provided at least some care, while during the night the most serious cases received emergency surgery.

That day the wounded from the Belgorod area received treatment at the 2nd First-aid Company's medical clearing station in Mikoyanovka. The picture in the evening hours of 9 February 1943 showed the units of the Infantry Division GD fighting a delaying action on two different fronts against a superior, hard-pressing enemy. Two focal points were evident in this difficult winter battle: one against an enemy advancing east to west in and on both sides of Arkhangelskoye, and already on the west bank of the Severnyi-Donets; the river was frozen over and thus no obstacle. The opposition there was provided by "Battle Group Kassnitz" (reinforced Fusilier Regiment GD) and then the reinforced Reconnaissance Battalion GD under Rittmeister Wätjen at the Belgorod-Kharkov road, with trailing groups still near Novaya Derevnya ("Battle Group *Führer-Begleit-Bataillon*" together with 3rd Squadron, Reconnaissance Battalion). The first elements of the reinforced Grenadier Regiment GD, namely II Battalion, were just arriving, with orders to establish a new blocking position as far north on the road as possible, while taking in elements of the Reconnaissance Battalion GD, reinforced by "Battle Group *Führer-Begleit-Bataillon*."

Near Golovino the leading elements of II Battalion, Grenadier Regiment ran into the advancing enemy and took up position on both sides of the road.

The remaining elements of the division (especially heavy weapons, trains, vehicle columns, first-aid units) fought their way through the snow in the truest sense of the word, cross-country from east to west out of the Arkhangelskoye area in the direction of Lipzy, in order to link up with the main body of the division at the main road. The reinforced Fusilier Regiment GD covered this withdrawal, with orders to be the last to disengage from the enemy at the Donets and then follow.

The objective of the Soviet movements was obviously not just to cut off the avenue of retreat of the Infantry Division GD as it withdrew fighting. The goal was to link up north of Kharkov and together with the Soviet battle group approaching from the north take possession of the city. The Infantry Division GD's fighting withdrawal was supposed to delay this linking-up of the two Soviet battle groups for as long as possible, gaining time for the evacuation of the city of Kharkov.

Advancing along the road from Belgorod, the Soviet forces ran into the elements of the Grenadier Regiment GD which had been deployed there. At this point they turned to their standard tactic on encountering opposition: following a brief exchange of fire they simply headed into the terrain on both sides of the road and outflanked the German position, which due to inadequate forces and the lack of any contact with friendly elements usually had to be abandoned without any fighting whatsoever.

The 10th of February therefore saw the reinforced Grenadier Regiment GD occupying new positions on both sides of Shuravlovka, following the move south of the "Battle Group FBB"-reinforced Reconnaissance Battalion GD. The grenadiers lay in the deep snow in an icy east wind and tried to halt the enemy. Weapons were often little more than lumps of ice, which thawed out when fired but accrued a thick crust of ice during each pause. It was not just a battle against a superior enemy, it was equally a struggle against nature, which made every action so much more difficult.

The soldiers themselves had been without warm quarters for days, indeed weeks; frostbite, illness, weakness and wounds gnawed away at their strength as well as their numbers. The 1st and 3rd Companies of the Grenadier Regiment's I Battalion had to be amalgamated under the command of Lt. Bernhagen in order to produce even a relatively combat-capable formation. The 4th and 5th (Heavy) Companies were also merged under the command of Lt. Stangl and only 2nd Company was able to remain as it was.

The reinforced Fusilier Regiment GD had meanwhile been able to leave its positions at the Donets near Arkhangelskoye and was fighting a delaying action as it withdrew toward the Kharkov- Belgorod road. A serious situation arose for this battle group during the afternoon of 10 February, when, in a move which took the fusiliers by surprise, the SS units withdrawing farther to the south (the regiment's former neighbours) were moved to the outskirts of Kharkov. As a result the regiment's southern flank was ripped open. All the division's available forces had to be thrown against the vigorously-pursuing enemy. At the last minute the last reserves – 50 artillerymen, a handful of pioneers, two anti-tank guns and several light machine-guns – led by the commander of the Assault Pioneer Battalion GD, halted the enemy spearhead on the heights west of Veseloye until the alerted "Battle Group FBB" could come to their aid. The enemy saw themselves forced to veer farther south by this blocking position. The immediate threat to the division had been banished for the time being. As planned, the main body of the Fusilier Regiment GD occupied new positions on either side of Lipzy, in order to engage the advancing enemy. The movement of the division's units into one area and their unification there was just about complete. In the fighting at the road the grenadiers repeatedly destroyed advancing enemy elements to the last man. Conscious of the common danger and aware that they were lost if even one limb faltered, the men held out grimly and together.

They also took joint action when the enemy – as was so often the case in the fighting at the road during the retreat – broke through on the flanks and occupied the road farther to the rear. In such cases the visibly desperate situation was usually restored through the determined actions of individuals. In each case, however, there was heavy, often hand-to-hand, fighting associated with the skilful solution of such a situation.

A combat report by I Battalion, Grenadier Regiment GD, elements of which were encircled by advancing Soviet forces on the road to Kharkov, sounds very matter-of-fact. The events of 11 February 1943, which saw the battalion escape the enemy encirclement, are reflected in a factual, cold fashion:

"Regimental commander (Oberstleutnant Lorenz) informs the commander of I Battalion (Hptm. Remer) that the road to the rear in the direction of Kharkov is occupied by the enemy. Hptm. Remer receives orders to break through to the south with a battle group.

Composition of the battle group: available tanks of the Panzer Battalion GD, as well as several panzers of the SS; riding on these the Bernhagen Company. – 7th Company riding in trucks, then the 16th Company's 37mm flak, the 5th Company's 75mm Pak platoon and two rocket launchers. 4th Company assumes responsibility for guarding the flanks.

Attack begins late in the morning at about 10.40 hours against Hill 227.3. It proceeds as planned, two enemy anti-tank guns are destroyed by our tanks, a Soviet company is wiped out to the last man. the objective is reached at about 11.30 hours.

Advance renewed and breakthrough completed in the period between 12.00 and about 13.30 hours. Afterward the road is secured to both sides and the remaining vehicles of the battalion not belonging to the battle group and then those of the regiment, are sent through.

There are terrible scenes: plundered vehicles and murdered soldiers, surprised here the day before by the bolsheviks. I Battalion, Grenadier Regiment occupies quarters for the night in Lennoy, west of Lipzy. The companies themselves stand guard at a snow wall on Hill 200 in the following order: left attached 7th Company, II Battalion; a platoon of the Bernhagen Company left of the road, and a platoon of 3rd Company to the right (east) of the road. 2nd Company initially held in reserve. Three tanks and one 88mm flak remain under the command of the battalion."

East of Lipzy the reinforced Fusilier Regiment GD was engaged in heavy fighting with enemy forces advancing west and, in particular, south. The enemy broke into Lipzy itself but was thrown out again by counterattack.

In constant fighting, following a routine of heavy fighting by day in hastily-dug positions, a nightly evacuation of same and a move to the next hill, the Infantry Division GD drew ever nearer to the city limits of Kharkov. Trains, field kitchens and rear-echelon services had already set up quarters in the suburbs. The sound of gunfire, which went on day and night, drew perceptibly closer, heralding the abandonment of the city.

Both *Großdeutschland* regimental groups continued to fight a delaying action in an effort to check the enemy advance: the reinforced Grenadier Regiment at the road facing the northern enemy and near and southeast of Lipzy the reinforced Fusilier Regiment, trying to forestall a premature entry into Kharkov by the eastern group of Soviet forces. The reinforced Reconnaissance Battalion and its command post were in Dergachi. The battalion was under orders to scout to the northwest for the enemy forces expected from that direction. On 12 February elements of the reconnaissance battalion, namely the 2nd (APC) Squadron, were moved without delay to Peresetshnaya, north-northwest of Kharkov, to block the Udy valley there. The enemy had already been reported advancing past Kharkov to the west, in the direction of Olshany. It was accepted that there was a danger that the city might be encircled even before the Infantry Division GD, as well as the SS units still northeast of the city, reached Kharkov.

At dawn on 12 February 1943, the enemy achieved a penetration along the road north of Lennoy, but this was sealed off at once. Five enemy tanks were destroyed. The Soviets weren't stopped for long, however. Employing their familiar tactic, they went round the grenadiers' positions to the west and entered Prudyanka, meeting no resistance. An immediate counterattack was successful, returning the village to German hands and destroying four more Soviet tanks in the process. Afterward the enemy once again bypassed the defenders farther to the west and resumed their advance toward Dergachi.

It was realized that the GD units on the road and farther to the northeast were in immediate danger. They received orders to evacuate their positions during the night of 12/13 February and reorganise their resistance in the line Voskoya-Tishi–(Ruskyi Tishi)–Stulnevo.

The Reconnaissance Battalion GD, the bulk of which was still in Dergachi, was deployed against the enemy forces advancing in the Lopal Valley but in the face of increasing enemy pressure and forays into Dergachi by enemy tanks, was forced to withdraw toward Losovenka. The division command post occupied new quarters in Pomerki, next to the road just outside Kharkov.

The 13th of February saw the division, which formed a shallow semi-circle north of Kharkov, under extremely heavy pressure from the enemy. On the

Belgorod-Kharkov road the new positions on either side of Stulnevo were held by I and II Battalions of the Grenadier Regiment, and contact was maintained with the fusiliers on the right. During the course of the late morning the men enjoyed several quiet hours. In spite of this there existed a serious threat from the northwest near Dergachi. Superior enemy forces broke in; sleigh columns streamed into the village, individual tanks drove around on the surrounding hills. Elements of the Reconnaissance Battalion GD and the attached "Battle Group *Führer-Begleit-Bataillon*" were positioned in Losovenka and to the north, expecting the enemy advance at any minute.

The *Großdeutschland* Division command recognized the danger, especially of an advance by the enemy into Kharkov in the division's rear. Such a move would make an orderly withdrawal by the division questionable, if not impossible. The division command was therefore forced to send a battle group to attack the enemy forces in Dergachi, to either drive them out or deflect them toward the southwest.

The reinforced Reconnaissance Battalion GD received orders to carry out the attack on Dergachi with its own armoured vehicles as soon as possible. A report by the staff of the Reconnaissance Battalion GD on the course of this engagement, in which III Battalion, Grenadier Regiment participated in its later stages, contains interesting details:

"The first elements of the *Führer-Begleit-Bataillon* and the 75mm pak platoon of the Waffen-SS arrived at 05.30 hours. These were immediately sent on to 4th Squardon's command post in Losovenka. There orders were issued concerning details of the attack on Dergachi.

Then, suddenly, several loud reports from tank cannon at the northern edge of Losovenka. A small enemy tank, which appeared to be a T 60, approached our forward outposts slowly and was there set on fire by an anti-tank gun of the Waffen-SS.

The attack was to take place as follows: moving out at 09.00, the *Führer-Begleit-Bataillon*, with an assault gun and a tank, was to advance along the road, while 4th Squadron, which was still guarding the northern outskirts of Losovenka, was to drive west of the railway line and road into the western part of Dergachi, likewise supported by an assault gun and a tank. The 3rd squadron was initially to remain in reserve in Alexeyevka. A battery of the Artillery Regiment GD was to go into position at the southern end of Losovenka. The attack got under way as planned. In spite of being hindered by deep snow, the *Führer-Begleit-Bataillon* and 4th Squadron made good progress, meeting no opposition. The Division Ia went forward to the command vehicle to see for himself that the attack was making progress.

The men of the *Führer-Begleit-Bataillon*, who had been in action for some days without a night's sleep, advanced slowly through the deep snow to the right of the road. As soon as there was a halt the exhausted men dropped to the ground, but the advance was resumed immediately, the commander got even the most tired men on their feet with a few encouraging words.

We could see Dergachi before us, but then anti-tank shells began flying over our heads. One assault gun was hit twice straightaway and pulled back to find a good firing position. The artillery opened fire in support of the subsequent advance. An enemy tank, which interrupted our advance along the road from its position at the edge of the village, was hit and set on fire.

The outskirts of the village were reached. 4th Squadron also entered the western part of the village. The streets and houses were combed for enemy troops.

Suddenly several tanks appeared on the hills east of Dergachi; as well several rocket launchers graciously showered us with their rockets!

There were still heavy exchanges of fire in the northwest part of Dergachi as dusk fell. Dense clusters of fleeing Russians withdrew to the northwest with sleighs and cannon. Now and then the village street, where our vehicles sat parked close together, was struck by shells. The 3rd Squadron was summoned from Alexeyevka and deployed next to 4th Squadron to guard the village to the west. The battery of the Artillery Regiment GD made a change of position to the southern exit from Dergachi.

Meanwhile the first elements of III Battalion, Grenadier Regiment under Hptm. Peiler arrived and secured to the north. It was thus possible to pull the *Führer-Begleit-Bataillon* out of the line and give it a night's rest."

The arrival of III Battalion, Grenadier Regiment was due to a radioed order, which was passed on to the individual companies on message forms. The original order was worded as follows:

Originator:

III./ – GD   **Date:** 13. 2. 43

> To 11th, 12th, 13th Companies, anti-tank platoon
>
> Battalion to mount up immediately and reach Losovenka.
>
> 1 platoon of 12th Company
>
> 1 75mm anti-tank gun
>
> rest of 12th Company
>
> 1 75mm anti-tank gun
>
> Staff, combat elements
>
> 14th Company
>
> 11th Company
>
> 13th Company
>
> 15th Company
>
> Trains at rear. Later remain in Losovenka.
>
> Combat elements remain in vehicles in Losovenka.
>
> Earlier orders concerning whereabouts of supply vehicles no longer valid.

>   A.B.
>
>   Holzgrefe
>
>   Leutnant and adjutant

Once the main body of III Battalion, Grenadier Regiment had taken over responsibility for guarding Dergachi, the reinforced Reconnaissance Battalion GD received orders to immediately move through Kharkov and keep open the road west of the city near Lyubotin. As expected, following the attack on Dergachi and the capture of the village by German forces the enemy had veered to the west and especially the southwest, then resumed his southward advance west of the city of Kharkov. The 2nd (APC) Squadron under Oblt. Spaeter, which had several vehicles near Peresetshnaya, reported the first enemy advances north and northwest of the town. Increased reconnaissance activity in this area was urgently needed, which led to the transfer of the Reconnaissance Battalion GD into the Lyubotin area.

During the evening hours of this eventful day new positions were occupied at the road on either side of Cherkasskoye-Losovaya, as per orders. This was not accomplished without some fighting. It was characteristic of the enemy in these winter battles to shun the daylight for their advances, preferring to use the twilight of morning, or even better that of approaching nightfall. This was an unfortunate time for the units deployed before Kharkov, because in general their withdrawal movements were begun during the evening and had to be carried out during the night.

At dawn on 14 February the grenadiers assumed the following defensive arrangement near Cherkasskoye: III Battalion in Dergachi, contact on the right with II Battalion at Point 199.4. Directly on and on both sides of the road was I Battalion, with the pioneers of the Assault Pioneer Battalion GD on its right. From there the positions of the Fusilier Regiment GD extended southeastward as far as the collective farm due south of Zirkuny. There they linked up with units of the Waffen-SS (SS-Panzer- Grenadier Division *Das Reich*).

The imminent battle for the capital of the Ukraine, Kharkov, must be seen within a larger framework. In the area of Army Group South under *Generalfeldmarschall* von Manstein, the enemy, in the course of their winter offensive, were advancing rapidly toward Kiev-Poltava, as well as the Dniepr crossings. Together with the Soviet 6th Army, the 1st Guards Army had forced a deep penetration to the southwest. Its spearhead, the 267th Guards Division, was already approaching Krasnograd, while the 35th Guards Division had taken Pavlograd. These movements further increased the threat of encirclement of the German units on the Mius and the Donets. In the northwest the city of Kharkov was still holding, while the enemy undertook to continue their westward advance south, but especially northwest, of the city.

At this point the recently formed *Armee-Abteilung* Lanz, which belonged to Army Group B, had at its disposal only a few minor German and Italian units, as well as the Infantry Division GD and the SS-Panzer-Grenadier Division *Das Reich*. It was much too weak to offer major resistance to the sharply-pursuing enemy. This was roughly the situation when, on 15 February 1943, *Armee-Abteilung Lanz* and the sector as far as Belgorod were placed under the command of Army Group South. The result was the creation of rigid command structure at a decisive point in the crisis of those weeks.

The creation of *Armee-Abteilung Lanz* was a result of the situation on this front. It was an idea of Hitler's, who reserved to himself the right to interfere in the command affairs of Army Group South. Hitler gave the *Armee-*

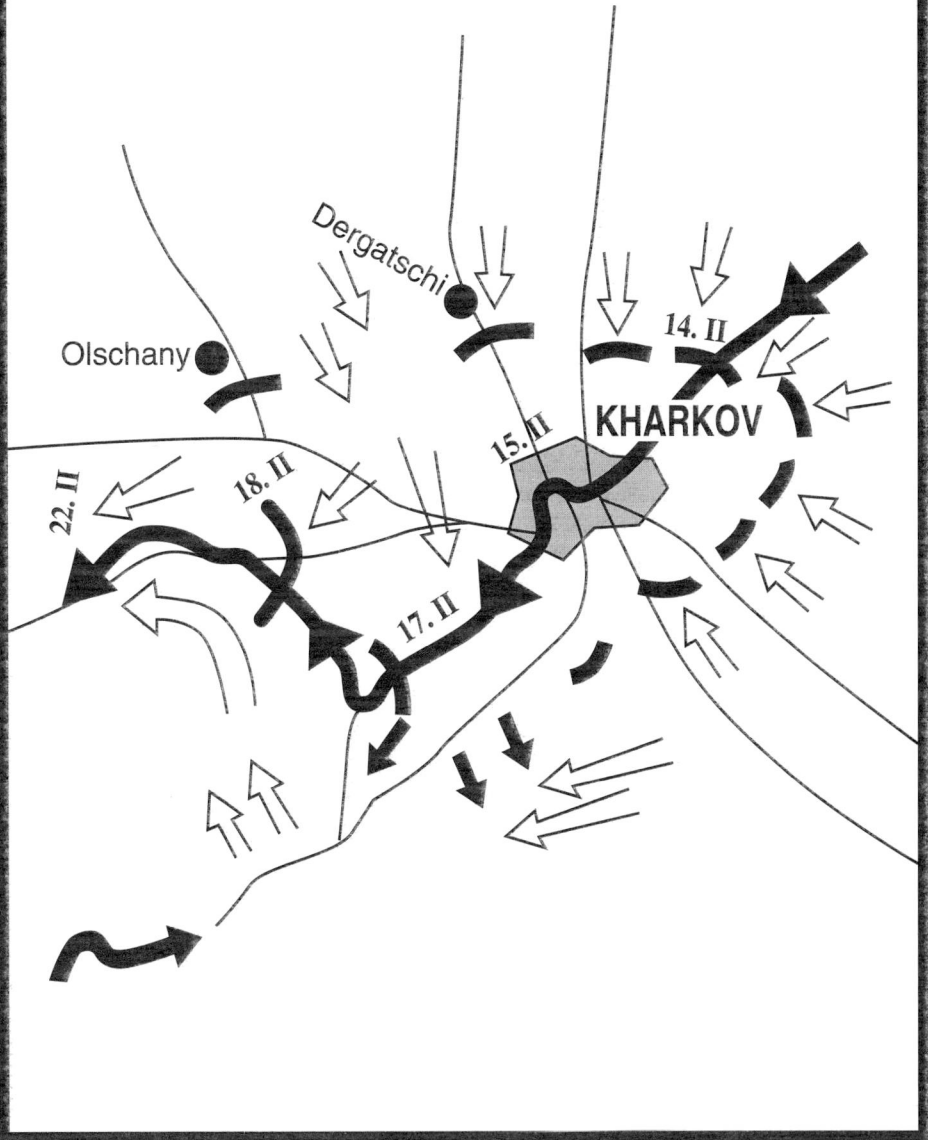

GERMAN LOSS OF KHARKOV
Feb. 14 to Feb. 22, 1943

Dergatschi

Olschany

KHARKOV

14. II

15. II

22. II

18. II

17. II

Abteilung strict orders to hold the city of Kharkov at all costs. Furthermore, it was supposed to advance in the direction of Losovaya to relieve the left flank of Army Group South. This advance was to be carried out by the SS-Panzer Corps, which formed the core of the *Armee-Abteilung*, but of which only two of three panzer divisions (*Das Reich* and *Leibstandarte-SS Adolf Hitler*) had so far arrived.

But *Armee-Abteilung Lanz* could not accomplish both tasks with the weak forces available. Hitler responded to a proposal by *Generalfeldmarschall* von Manstein, that the *Armee-Abteilung* initially ignore Kharkov and instead try to smash the enemy forces south of the city, by repeating his strict order that Kharkov be held at all costs. This was the situation on 14 February 1943, in which the Infantry Division GD and its units fought a desperate battle to maintain their positions on the outskirts of Kharkov.

The enemy pressure against the northwest part of the main line of resistance grew ever stronger as the day went on. The battalion's strongpoint-style positions were outflanked, resulting in some extremely serious situations in the often difficult terrain north of Kharkov.The enemy undoubtedly intended a large-scale encirclement of Kharkov; there were already strong Soviet forces in Olchany and others were driving toward the road to Valki. While, on the afternoon of 14 February 1943, preliminary steps were taken toward the evacuation of Kharkov in the coming night; that evening saw the release of the Führer Order to hold the city at all costs. A withdrawal from the present positions was probably only possible with heavy losses, since by evening the enemy had occupied, or at least was firing on, all the roads leading out of Kharkov. The city of Kharkov itself became ever emptier. There wasn't much to be seen of the inhabitants; lone, dark figures crept along the walls of houses or ducked behind windows and lowered blinds.

The German Army supply dumps located there had been plundered. Disassembled parts of tanks and motor vehicles still lay in the halls of the various army motor vehicle parks, replacement part dumps and motor vehicle workshops. These were sought out by the *Schirrmeister* (motor transport sergeants) of the units fighting nearby, who scavenged replacement parts for their damaged vehicles.

The division's situation grew increasingly critical during the night of 14/15 February. The enemy achieved a deep penetration north of Cherkaskaya-Losovaya, which extended into the area of Pyatichatka. Heavy fighting involving all the division's forces went on through the night until early morning in the difficult terrain of wooded areas and gardens. The Soviets kept up the pressure and in the late morning hours of 15 February advanced into the wooded area northwest of the city, pushing back the weak German defenders. The crisis reached its high point.

The enemy began infiltrating the northwest section of Kharkov at about 09.00. Quick action was required, but the supreme commander's order to hold the city loomed above all other considerations. The division closed ranks; it assembled in the northern part of the city in order to hold out as long as possible. The Reconnaissance Battalion GD, deployed near Lyubotin south of the city, received radioed orders to occupy new positions at the western edge of the city on the Grenadier Regiment's left, to prevent at all costs the enemy entering the city there. The commander of the reconnaissance battalion determined that surrendering Lyubotin would also mean abandoning the over-filled medical clearing station there, as well as the blocking of the road (the last one still open to the southwest) by the enemy. The first enemy spearheads had already been sighted near Shapkovka and Kommuna, advancing toward the main road, which traced an arc there. The first rockets and anti-tank shells were already falling on the road about four kilometres east of Lyubotin. The first direct contact with the enemy occurred in the late morning, northeast of Lyubotin. Hill 182.6, situated due north of the road, provided an excellent view of the terrain to the north and northwest. The hill fell away gently into the Udy Valley, along which ran the Kharkov-Olchany railway line; a goods train was still on the tracks. The villages of Peresetshnaya and Miranovka lay on the opposite, gently climbing, largely wooded, slope. Dense sleigh columns, heading south, could be seen clearly with binoculars. Even three artillery pieces, their muzzles pointed at Kharkov, could be seen standing in the open near a house. Southwest of Peresetshnaya "Battle Group *Führer-Begleit-Bataillon*" and the 2nd Squadron under Oblt. Spaeter were engaged in heavy defensive fighting against enemy forces advancing in the direction of the city and farther south. One T 34 was destroyed.

It became increasingly clear that the Infantry Division GD in the northern part of the city was in danger of being cut off from the south and southwest if a fundamental decision to evacuate the city was not made soon. The elements of the division south and southwest of the city were much too weak to stop the encircling movements of the enemy.

The command of the SS-Panzer Corps decided to evacuate the city during the midday hours against Hitler's orders. Without warning *Armee-Abteilung Lanz*, instructions were issued to the SS-Panzer-Grenadier Division *Das Reich* to began evacuation of the city without delay. The Ia of the Infantry Division GD overheard the order, which led him to initiate corresponding preparations for his own units, while simultaneously informing corps of what was happening. Not until about 16.00 did the commanding corps approve the proposal, at which time the necessary withdrawal and evacuation movements were carried out.

Assault guns and tanks barred the main and secondary roads into the city from the north and northwest, while the vehicle columns poured quickly, but in an orderly fashion, into the city and out of it to the southwest. In the city itself there was shooting everywhere, although the populace took no serious part in it. Fires still smouldered here and there. Pioneers had prepared important fixtures such as bridges, dumps and hangars for demolition. They waited beside houses in small groups for the order to detonate. It was nearing midnight; the bulk of the units were through, only lone vehicles and dispatch riders still drove through the streets toward the exits from the city. On the street corners the vehicles of the Assault Gun Battalion GD stood out as dark shadows against the night sky. They were to be the last to follow, transporting the pioneer demolition squads. It was just before midnight when a tremendous explosion shattered the night stillness. The big road bridge flew into the air, not without causing considerable damage to the nearby houses.

The following account describes those hours in Kharkov and the first actions after the evacuation of the city:

"We had disengaged from the enemy in a surprise move and were to abandon Kharkov today for a new defensive position. The trucks had been driven into position; it was just before departure and we stood together in small groups smoking cigarettes. A few lucky ones read their letters, which our kitchen had brought. I was one of these. I read of home and of theatres and concerts. Grimly I thought to myself: you're playing a winter sport here, and there's more concerts and theatre each day than we can stand! The sun seemed pale. It brought little warmth even though it was midday. The broad snow-covered fields glittered, a long row of black telephone poles led into the city, whose jumble of houses— in typical Russian fashion—lay strewn about randomly.

A large number of mighty structures, with storeys 4 and 5 metres high, towered in the centre of the city, the so-called show buildings: the party house, the GPU building and theatre, facades of Soviet culture and genius. Then there were long rows of tall apartment buildings. A piece outside the city sat the tractor works. A cold east wind blew over the road, blowing powdery snow horizontally across its surface. 'Mount up!' We climbed into the trucks and the battalion moved out. The flaps were folded back and everyone had his weapon ready to fire. The word was that partisan rabble were about, so be very careful! It seemed as if were driving through the streets of a dead city. Only a very few civilians scurried past, the large dumps and warehouses had been emptied or blown up, and there were fires in many places. We drove on silently, toward the western exit. Pioneers stood at crossroads and bridges; the last demolition squads.

When we rolled across the rail bridge we saw the station. It had been blown up, and the wreckage covered the tracks. We left the jumble of houses and drove into the open of the workers settlement at the western edge of the city. The road climbed somewhat near a brickworks and the column stopped. We were close to the front and about halfway up the grade. The squad in front of us had a bottle of schnapps and we were a little jealous, for in that cold a drink wouldn't have hurt. While we were shouting to them that they should leave us a little, someone noticed soldiers with white snow smocks and guns on a road about 300 metres to our left on the far side of a hollow. They also stopped and looked over at us, and as we watched they began moving an anti-tank gun into position to fire on us. 'Man, those are Russians!' Our column began moving, engines roared. Away from the road and into cover! The truck pulled away, drove slowly up the hill and stopped behind a house. We got down. The driver was supposed to follow the other vehicles but most of them had got stuck. Suddenly we came under small-arms fire and a Russian heavy machine-gun rattled from a brickworks. Behind us a 20mm flak on a self-propelled carriage opened fire; it was hit. Boom! Crash!! A scream, and there was nothing more to be seen of the anti-aircraft gun. Direct hit; a wounded man was dragged away by his comrades. They took him to the ambulance which was farther up the column.

The drivers who couldn't get their vehicles up the hill came running toward us. The trucks sat there. Shots whistled over the snow. The Russian anti-tank gun fired round after round at us, almost all of which exploded in a red brick building. The road continued on in front of us to the right, we were supposed to assemble there in the cover of the houses. Alone and in small groups the soldiers raced to cover. I suddenly realized I no longer had a rifle, only a stick hand grenade in my belt. I took this in my hand and ran. I was just squeezing past the ambulance, when I saw Jupp D. running in front of me. Boom! There was a crash and fragments whizzed past me. Jupp grabbed his head and shouted in terror, 'My back, my back!' Franz Schlößbauer rolled him over. Help me carry him! He was bleeding heavily. The three of us dashed over the snow in long strides. Bullets chirped and hissed after us. Damn this deep snow! An anti-tank gun had driven up beside the red house and returned fire. Our company assembled and moved into position.

We mortar people had been forced to leave our equipment in the truck and were employed as infantry, because mainly street and house fighting was expected in the city. What could I do with my one hand grenade? Goga had a rifle as well as his pistol. It was mine, but he only gave me the pistol. Now things went somewhat better. We had posted guards between the houses, but it was too closed-in in the gardens, sheds and houses. Lt. M. appeared and said to us that we should try and get to the road, the position there was more favourable. It was barely 500 metres to the road, we were a heavy machine-gun squad led by Obgefr. Sch. and a heavy mortar team under the command of Gefr. Schlößbauer. The machine-gun people moved toward the road on the left, we on the right. There was sporadic shooting. Cautiously we ran from house to house. We had almost all made it when a single shot rang out and one of us fell, shot through the head. We peeked cautiously around the corner of a house. There was a ping!!! and the bullet hissed past our heads, missing by a hair. Sch. called over to us from the left: 'Watch out, snipers!' Giving each other covering fire, we worked our way from a house to the haystack and from there to another house. We made good progress.

On the other side the machine-gun people had kept pace with us. We could already see the road before us. There was a long burst from an MG 42, then a loud scream: the sniper was finished! Firing as we went, we ran forward and reached then occupied the houses at the side of the road. Soon everyone had gathered there, including the machine-gun people. Pleased, we shook hands. That was excellent teamwork. A large number of dead Russians lay about. Then our sentry called: 'They're running, man! hordes of them!' and fired after them. We all raised our rifles, even pistols, and fired. There was a wild flurry of shots, but they stubbornly kept running and soon disappeared around the next corner.

We took up position in a house under construction, still without a roof. Later we were joined by a heavy machine-gun. In the fervour of battle we had failed to notice that it was already dark again. We also now realized that we had no contact to the left or right, but we didn't see this as too tragic. A despatch rider was sent out, after which we were relieved and had something to eat. There were still civilians in the houses everywhere, rather frightened. When I entered one house a young girl spoke to me in German, broken, but easily understandable. When I asked whether she had seen Russians here before, she answered: I saw many soldiers with sleighs and machine-guns at the railroad tracks about 3 km northwest of here. – Northwest? – Then the Russians, coming from the north, were already behind us and were trying to cut us off from the west. We put out extra sentries, not wanting to be taken by surprise. By now it was quite dark. We still had no news from battalion.

I visited the sentries in our small fortress. All peered strenuously into the darkness. After an hour our dispatch rider suddenly shouted, `Hello, 9th Company!' Soon afterward he was with us. His news was encouraging: we were not yet completely cut off and furthermore, an assault gun and a tank were supposed to be coming to get us. The entire city was on fire, there was shooting everywhere.

After half an hour we heard the sound of tanks in the distance behind us. We listened expectantly, but would they find us? The roar of engines drew ever nearer and then stopped, about 200 metres behind us. A messenger came to us: 'Leave here quietly at once and assemble at the tank.' We joined up quickly and set off. At the tank was Lt. M. 'Get on immediately, one after the other. Keep a sharp lookout to the left and right!' I was unable to get up on the tank, and I was forced to run behind it. The motor sprang to life with a roar. The tank gave a jerk and began to move. I held onto a hook with one hand, in the other I had my cocked pistol. In this way I stumbled along behind the loud, roaring steel colossus.

The tank threw up snow behind it and quite often a chunk flew into my face. But we were happy to have such protection, for the empty streets and the tall houses with their dark windows were eerie. Now and then someone fired a shot, a parachute flare lit our field of view for a few seconds. Our tank rolled on. Suddenly we heard German voices. There were trucks sitting there, soldiers walked about. The battalion was assembling. The tank stopped, everyone jumped off. We were to continue in a pioneer vehicle, to a new security position somewhere. The column began to move. Our three-axle vehicle tried to pass but was forced off to the side; it skidded and became stuck in the snow. The wheels spun futilely; it refused to move, get out and push! I and several of my comrades got behind the car and pushed, but we were unable to push the vehicle free. Suddenly the tires found traction. It moved slowly, then the whole car slid sideways. I fell to the ground and the rear wheels rolled over my left leg. The pain took my breath away. I wanted to scream but all I could do was moan.

The others had seen me fall and I was lifted onto the car. There seemed to be no feeling in my leg. The column rolled out of the city in a southwesterly direction. Flames leapt from the burning buildings. Entire houses collapsed with loud crashes and showers of sparks as we broke out of the encirclement to the southwest. Behind us the sky over burning Kharkov was red."

The units did not escape Kharkov totally unscathed. During the afternoon of 15 February columns of vehicles carrying elements of the Fusilier Regiment GD were fired on and even ambushed by enemy forces with anti-tank guns advancing from the north. More than fifty vehicles fell victim to the ambush, which took place on the road southeast of Kommuna. A number of men managed to make it to Lyobotin alone on foot. A battle group under *Major* Hacke, commander of the Anti-tank Battalion GD, was immediately dispatched from the east to reopen the road. All available forces were required to at least force the enemy back toward the hills north of the road and open the way for the division's vehicles leaving Kharkov. However bullets continued to whistle over the road and negotiating this dangerous stretch was only possible at top speed. The enemy also turned up close to Lyubotin itself, which was being guarded by the Reconnaissance Battalion GD, near Point 182.6 at a bend in the road. However the hussars of the reconnaissance battalion were able to put them to flight. The Reconnaissance Battalion GD remained responsible for the decisive task of ensuring that the division was able to move to the west and later southwest at all costs and consequently received a continuous flow of reinforcements. "Battle Group *Führer-Begleit-Bataillon*" was soon able to take over further defensive positions; assault and anti-tank guns also finally arrived. The initial threat to the road was alleviated.

Hptm. Frantz, commander of the Assault Gun Battalion GD, provided the following account of the fighting on 15 and 16 February:

"With the remaining combat-capable guns of my battalion, I had the mission of guarding against enemy tanks, infantry and so on, at the northern edge of Kharkov not far from the forward division command post. Since during those hours I was, out of necessity, often at the forward command post, I could observe the drama of the situation firsthand. Here the division was involved in the battle for a political objective (capital city of the Ukraine), which led Führer Headquarters to order that it be held at any price, regardless of the overall situation. The division commander thus faced a difficult decision for any leader: either withdraw from Kharkov contrary to the orders of the supreme command and take up the battle again west of the city, or allow the division to be encircled and destroyed in Kharkov together with the SS units fighting to the south. That the breakout order was finally given by the division, shows the high consciousness of responsibility of the division commander, *Generalmajor* Hoernlein, who listened to his conscience and carried out the right decision contrary to orders. In doing so he preserved the division's striking power for later successful defensive and offensive battles, which in the end led to the recapture of Kharkov. It is a typical example of how alone commanders are on the battlefield and how close to one another are glory and defeat.

Even while enemy situation reports, orders and decisions vied with one another at the northern exit from Kharkov, the division learned of the arrival of twenty new assault guns and crews from Germany. These guns, manned by inexperienced crews, had been unloaded in Valki that morning and were supposed to supplement the striking power of the assault gun battalion as quickly as possible. My doubts about employing these guns, whose combat value had to be rated very low on account of the inexperience of their crews, were naturally overruled by hopes of a significant strengthening of the exhausted division's firepower at that point. There was nothing left for me to do but fetch the twenty guns from Valki as quickly as possible. I did it myself, hoping to use the short drive to practice radio communication and assess the skill of the drivers. During the afternoon of the 15th my battalion's strength swelled to more than thirty guns. This was an enormous force at that time. What was more obvious, then to hand over to this force responsibility for covering the rear of the division as it withdrew from Kharkov? The last to fight on at the northern edge of Kharkov, while the remaining elements of the division marched off to the southwest, in some cases fighting, was Major Remer with the Grenadier Regiment's APC battalion. During this time the assault gun battalion remained in the centre of the city, at Red Square, securing to all sides. Its mission was to take in the APC battalion during the night and then follow to the southwest as the division rearguard. The order to blow up the large road bridge over the rail line in Kharkov was in the battalion commander's vehicle.

Night came. The only light in the huge square was from the burning ruins of houses; the sound of battle could be heard in the distance, especially in the southwest. In the north, from where we eagerly awaited the APC battalion, there was initially nothing to be heard. Radio contact with division could no longer clarify the situation in Kharkov as the other elements were already withdrawing. Hour after hour passed. The gun crews had strict orders to fire only from very close range and on clearly recognized enemy targets so as not to endanger the friendly unit we were waiting for. Every front-line soldier knew what a disaster nervous, premature firing could cause in such situations. Again we radioed division: 'Is it certain that I Battalion, Grenadier Regiment is still at the northern edge of Kharkov?' Answer: `Remer must still be there, as per orders! We are not in contact with him.' Time passed slowly. Shots were fired in the direction of the guns from the roofs of several surrounding houses. The sound of small arms fire from the east grew nearer. Here too the question facing the leader was: what is the right thing to do? Here was the division's last concentrated firepower in the form of 30 assault guns – there the infantry battalion, still holding at the northern limits. Several guns were moved somewhat farther to the east as a precautionary measure. The enemy infantry had to be prevented from getting in among the assault guns at all costs. An assault gun was sent to try and make contact with the Remer Battalion. For an assault gun, driving 7 to 10 kilometres at night, through an otherwise abandoned city which was already partly occupied by infiltrating enemy troops, was an undertaking which demanded daring and circumspection. Radio contact was maintained with the vehicle. Finally it was able to report that elements of I Battalion were on their way. The sound of the weight falling from my shoulders must have been heard for some distance! The bulk of the battalion came through at a quick pace.

Major Remer stopped to describe the last battles and the situation of the enemy. A platoon commanded by a Leutnant had been assigned as rearguard and we had to wait for it. Again minutes passed, then a quarter and a half hour. Finally this platoon came too; the infantrymen shrouded in their greatcoats, asleep in the vehicles from exhaustion. Only the drivers and co-drivers were still awake. The long-awaited order was now given to the assault guns. They formed up and likewise drove out of the city toward the west. At the end of the column was the commander's vehicle. This in turn was eagerly awaited by the division's pioneer commander, Hptm. Chrapowski, at the bridge, for the pioneers also felt that it was time to withdraw from the city. They too had been fired at from all sides while they waited. With a huge roar the large road bridge in the centre of Kharkov flew into the air. The crews of the assault guns fired rifles and submachine-guns at windows from which muzzle flashes were seen. We had no way of telling whether it was partisans or regular Russian troops doing the shooting. After a good two-hour drive the battalion drove into a small village just behind the new main line of resistance. The battalion was halted there and the battalion commander ordered to report to the Ia. General Staff Oberst von Natzmer wanted to issue the mission orders for the battalion himself. His orderly had some difficulty waking him. The division command, too, was at the limits of its strength after the weeks of fighting.

The briefing went as follows: 'The division's march column and all its vehicles are pinned down on the road to Lyubotin. Driving around Kharkov from the north, the enemy has already reached the road and is within small arms range of the vehicles. There have already been considerable losses of vehicles and men. A defensive perimeter has been established around the vehicles. Exploiting every possibility, the Assault Gun Battalion must ensure that by dawn the enemy pressure on the division is sufficiently relieved to allow the vehicle columns to flow as quickly as possible in the direction of Lyubotin-Valki.' What was there to do? The force in question, which included twenty guns with no combat experience, had been given a mission which could only be properly carried out by very experienced assault gun personnel. Therefore the decision to crush the enemy, who in the twilight could be clearly seen from the eastern edge of the village north of the road, with the bulk of the assault guns, especially the new arrivals, while those with the more experienced crews provided protection against anti-tank weapons.

The assault gun battalion moved out as twilight was falling—it may have been about six o'clock—at top speed and simply overran the enemy's infantry and anti-tank gun positions. The assault guns assigned to provide covering fire succeeded in destroying several anti-tank guns positioned farther back. Our own infantry in vehicles and part of the anti-tank battalion immediately set out toward the north in pursuit of the fleeing enemy. The road was clear. Within half an hour the division column was moving smoothly, leaving behind the vehicles which had been destroyed by the enemy during the night. Once again a critical situation had been mastered through the cooperation of all elements of the division. As the sun came up the assault gun crews stood proudly in their defensive positions, their guns facing north. They felt that in the past days they had made a considerable contribution to the division's defensive effort."

The 16th of February, following the breakout from Kharkov, saw little out of the ordinary, apart from the clearing and reopening of the Kharkov–Kommuna–Valki road. An advance against Kommuna, which had meanwhile been occupied by the enemy, by the Bernhagen Company of I Battalion, Grenadier Regiment GD, returned the village to German hands. New defensive positions were occupied; the northwards-facing front ran due north of the road, turned near Lyubotin and Korotich and then extended southeast in the direction of Budy, where it met the positions of the 320th Infantry Division.

It is all too understandable that the first day after the leaving of Kharkov brought no significant fighting: the capital city of the Ukraine acted as a magnet, which initially attracted all Soviet forces. And yet it had to be assumed that the next few days would see a resumption of enemy attacks, their objective being the city of Valki, halfway along the road to Poltava.

As expected, the focus of the fighting on 17 February 1943 was on the road, roughly between Korotich and Kommuna. At the eastern edge of Korotich was III Battalion, Grenadier Regiment, which absorbed the shock of the first thrust by Soviet forces advancing west out of Kharkov. This village also marked the left boundary of the Grenadier Regiment GD. In positions farther to the right were II and I Battalions, the latter in Budy. Elements of the Fusilier Regiment GD were in positions along the road and near Kommuna, with I Battalion near Kommuna. Meanwhile the weather had changed. Rain and a warm wind melted the snow; dark, black spots appeared through the snow. But the cases of freezing, caused by continually damp fur-lined boots and below-zero nighttime temperatures, increased and further reduced the fighting strength of the units.

A dangerous situation arose for III Battalion, Grenadier Regiment in the early morning hours of 18 February, when an enemy force consisting of infantry in roughly brigade strength and ten tanks broke into the battalion's weak positions. The Peiler Battalion fought desperately to avoid being overrun, and casualties were heavy. Reserves were brought in, including the Reconnaissance Battalion GD, and by evening the penetration had been sealed off.

Deployed at this focal point of the engagement near Korotich were two companies of III Battalion, the 12th and 13th (commanded by Lt. Hofstetter and Lt. Kollewe, respectively). *Leutnant* Kollewe provided this account of this bloody battle:

"I awoke at about four o'clock in the morning. Heavy fighting could be heard from 12th Company's positions; enemy tanks with mounted infantry were at work there. I reorganized my sentries and then walked to the forward command post. Then I saw what was going on and was scarcely able to believe my eyes: a long Russian column had driven up in front of my position, which was located along the road in the hollow about 1,000 metres away. The 12th Company was in position next to mine right at this road. An enemy patrol had just been wiped out there, but now enemy tanks with mounted infantry were attacking. Through my binoculars I watched their advance. Lt. Hofstetter had no anti-tank weapons. In this dangerous situation it seemed he was lost if they didn't succeed in pulling everyone back at the last minute. But his men stayed put; the enemy tanks made a wild drive through the positions, over the foxholes, and attacked the haystack. The poor company! It seemed to me as if all was lost there. The steel monsters fired in

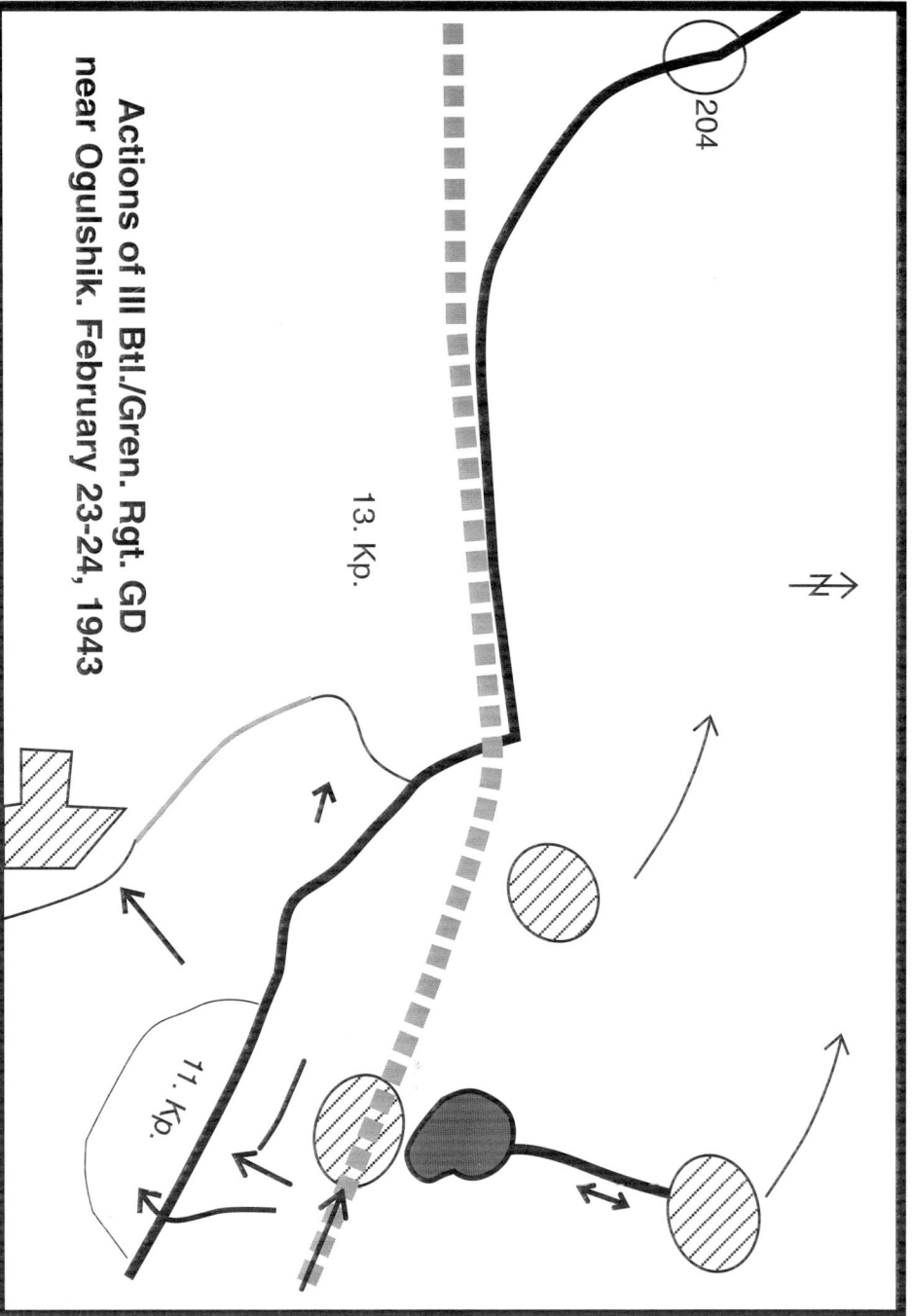

Actions of III Btl./Gren. Rgt. GD near Ogulshik. February 23-24, 1943

204

13. Kp.

11. Kp.

all directions; they turned, crushing everything beneath their tracks.

Eventually the bulk of the tanks moved away from their victims and, miraculously, a small group came running across the open field, pursued by machine-gun fire, pursued by a single enemy tank. It mowed down almost everyone on its death ride; only Lt. Hofstetter, dodging like a rabbit, finally managed to reach the safety of the village.

Meanwhile new tank assembly areas had been sighted. Six giants, loaded with riflemen, set out at high speed toward my positions. All I could do was order everyone to take cover. Then, to the left of my position, they broke into 1st Platoon's positions and then drove on, firing wildly. They ran over two of my machine-guns, and I believed that the affair was over and done with.

Heavy mortar fire smashed into our positions. The beastly shells fell to my left and right. I saw the flashes. Only a few metres separated me from the explosions. This is the end, so I thought; but no fragments tore my body. There were cries from the left, cries beside me. Lipke was wounded. Three men lay dead around me.

Then there was a cry from the bushes: "*Herr Leutnant, Herr Leutnant!*" It was *Feldwebel* Weber. I found him quickly. He was already yellow in the face. The sight was so painful I felt as if I'd been hit myself. They'd got Feldw. Weber, our "Franzl.' My best sergeant! I wanted to help him, hurried to get a blanket, but he had only one wish: '*Herr Leutnant*, shoot me! There's no point any more!' His leg was almost gone, his buttocks had been ripped up. Would he make it? He had to make it! There were tears in my eyes as he was carried off; all danger was forgotten at that moment. Our Weber, my old sergeant! I had little hope that he would pull through, his wounds were too severe.

And then, without warning, came the news that Lt. Braumüller had fallen. I had a bitter taste in my mouth. All these valuable men had been taken from us by the horror of war, men who would be impossible to replace.

I had meanwhile withdrawn my left, now open, flank toward the brush-covered terrain before the outskirts of the village. The Russians could have exploited the situation there to break in as they pleased. Instead they now came from the collective farm. I quickly moved a heavy machine-gun into position and raked the approaching column. Their losses weren't heavy, but at least I was able to force them to withdraw.

We still had no anti-tank defence. The enemy columns on the road were still unmolested. A large number of enemy tanks drove about; I counted at least twenty. Once again, the enemy infantry moved forward, veered left then right again, toward the collective farm. At least regiment strength, I estimated. How much longer would we be able to hold? Were they really going to allow us to be totally destroyed?

A runner brought me the news that Feldw. Weber had died at the aid station. He left us as a hero, just as he had lived. He left the battlefield with a 'Long live Germany!' His last words were, 'Carry on boys—to victory!!!'

How could I describe him, Weber the man? Words could not say what he had meant to us, what he was to his men. He was unique in his greatness. Even if talk of unforgettable comrades always has an empty ring to it, those who knew and lived with him will always remember Franzl Weber and keep him in their hearts. Many of my hardened soldiers had tears in their eyes at that moment. The fate which hung over us was inscrutable, unpredictable; for it passed sentence – over life and death!

In the meantime our command had finally taken steps. They had deployed a company there to cover an eventual retreat; as well we now had tanks on our side. Nevertheless a counterattack in the hollow toward the collective farm got nowhere; as well we were at first unable to close the gap at the road.

However the situation calmed down somewhat, even if the Russians were within 200 metres of my positions. Then a mass of bolsheviks appeared on my left flank. Again there were tanks with them. If they turn left now! Finally they disappeared somewhere into the terrain. It was getting toward evening.

We fell back to a new position on the outskirts of Lyubotin. Three of our tanks under Lt. Liebscher were on hand. I was thus able to assemble my small band in peace. Our losses were five dead, two wounded and one missing. – A black day for my 13th Company."

The 19th of February illustrated the threat to the Infantry Division GD, deployed near Lyubotin and Budy, posed by new withdrawal movements: the enemy forces sighted north of Lyubotin and near Olchany moved west across the white plains with large numbers of sleigh columns and tanks. Reconnaissance had already reported their leading elements before Novy Merchik and Bayrak. The danger thus existed of a further outflanking of the division's existing positions. Countermeasures had to be initiated immediately. Three companies hastily assembled in the area west of Bayrak were ordered to attack the enemy in the flank and halt their westward advance. Following the removal of these companies all that was available to man their former positions, whose evacuation was out of necessity only a matter of time, was weak security forces, which were forced to fall back in the early morning hours in the face of constant enemy pressure. These were subsequently attacked from the area near Merchik Station and withdrew farther to the south. The result was an even more precarious situation for the elements of the Infantry Division GD near Lyubotin and Budy.

The reinforced Reconnaissance Battalion GD received orders to secure the road, an important supply line, to the north at a point north of Ogulzy. However as the situation developed, it was instead moved to Kovyagy with orders to carry out an attack toward the north in the direction of Novy Merchik and further to Bayrak on 20 February, in order to halt the enemy there. Additional units were sent to take part in the attack: the Assault Pioneer Battalion GD, a battery of assault guns, an army flak battery, a battery each of light and heavy howitzers of the Artillery Regiment GD and elements of the SS Reconnaissance Battalion *Totenkopf*. The necessary preparations were made and reconnaissance patrols were sent into the area.

In the course of that day several assaults against the Infantry Division GD's eastern and northern fronts were repulsed with heavy losses to the enemy. A particularly serious situation arose on the division's right wing, as the neighbouring 320th Infantry Division had not moved close enough to eliminate a flanking threat there. Elements of the Anti-tank Battalion GD under *Major* Hacke were moved into the gap, but this was not enough to eliminate the threat. Hacke's command post was located in Budy.

As a result of the threat to Kovyagy Station a further evacuation by B.V.Z. (emergency wounded train) was not possible. The last wounded were transported out in freight cars in the early morning hours of 19 February 1943. Initially there was nothing left but to leave the rest in Valki until it was possible to transport them by road in the direction of Poltava. The 1st First-aid Company therefore set up a medical clearing station in Chutovo on the Kolomak to take in the wounded transported there from Valki. There too efforts were made to stay in communication with the nearest rail station, Skorochodovo, in order to ship the wounded on to Poltava by train.

Lyubotin, in which the Fusilier Regiment GD set up its command post on 21 February, was most unsuited for defence. It was a small city with many sections and properties covering several hills and small valleys over an area of several kilometres. The fusiliers' positions were at the northern outskirts of the city at the much-fought-over road. To the east by a small stream and valley lay the village of Kommuna and on the left on the hill the Kasarovka Farm, both in the hands of the fusilier battalions.

From these positions Lyubotin stretched southward roughly to the source of the small Merefa River. There were many properties on the slopes and waters, whose gardens created a most idyllic impression. At the moment, however, this idyll simply made it simpler for the enemy to infiltrate the city by night, with the help of local residents.

Farther to the northeast was III Battalion, Grenadier Regiment, then the regiment's II Battalion and at the eastern edge of Budy I Battalion. The Anti-tank Battalion GD constituted a welcome support to the grenadiers. Those of its guns not assigned to the infantry were positioned due east of Budy. It was responsible for the most uncomfortable mission at that time, namely covering the gap extending to the 320th Infantry Division against attempts by the enemy to break through.

Considerable enemy attacks continued to be reported against the northern – the fusiliers – and eastern – the grenadiers – fronts. On 20 February these totalled six against the Grenadier Regiment GD, some supported by as many as 15 enemy tanks. Using their unique instinct for weak points in the German defensive line, that day the enemy perceptibly shifted their focus onto the right wing of the Infantry Division GD and the gap between it and the 320th Infantry Division. Employing infantry and tanks, in the morning the Soviets attacked near Budy successfully and forced the German defenders to abandon their positions there. In this situation the arrival of the order for I Battalion, Grenadier Regiment to withdraw caused even more confusion. The Anti-tank Battalion GD defended somewhat longer and then likewise withdrew from its positions, not without losing a considerable part of its guns and suffering a large number of casualties. However the pressure from the enemy near Budy soon abated after they followed up through the gap between the Infantry Division GD and the 320th Infantry Division. Accurate German artillery fire inflicted heavy losses, but was unable to halt the onrushing enemy. Instead the sleigh columns deviated to the southwest, as a result of which there was no more contact with the enemy at that point.

The division command was now faced with a picture of the enemy passing by on both flanks, seeking less to engage in battle than gain further territory. Sooner or later the growing threat of being outflanked and subsequently encircled must compel the division command to abandon the existing main line of resistance and pull its forces back to a new, further shortened position. In any case, the division did a good job of tying down the outflanking enemy, allowing the regiments still in their positions to safely flow out of the open sack.

An attack early on 20 February by the reinforced Reconnaissance Battalion GD from the Grintsev Rog area in the direction of Novy Merchik and Dolina on the Mok Merchik served to screen the northern flank. Supported by a battery of heavy field howitzers, 2nd Company, Assault Pioneer Battalion GD and a reserve company moved on Krasnopolye, while 1st Company, Assault Pioneer Battalion GD and 3rd Squadron together with seven assault guns advanced directly toward Novy Merchik and Dolina as the focal point of the attack. An icy wind blew across the open plain as the men tramped through the deep snow on either side of the road, followed closely by the assault guns. By 10.30 they were able to enter the western part of Novy Merchik, where there was heavy fighting with the bolsheviks who were taken by surprise. An attack farther east by the reconnaissance battalion of the SS Panzer-Grenadier Division *Totenkopf* made itself felt in the afternoon, allowing Novy Merchik to be occupied completely. The village was a sorry sight. Dead horses and tipped-over sleighs lay everywhere, a gun crew had been wiped out by a direct hit, almost every second house was burning. The surprise of the Soviets was evident in the many abandoned weapons and pieces of equipment which lay scattered about the village streets; but once again the main body of the enemy had gone around the German positions and appeared to be on the march southwest, in the direction of Kovyagy. This assumption led to the Reconnaissance Battalion GD being ordered to give up the villages it had taken so as to reach the city of Kovyagy by evening.

The *Führer-Begleit-Bataillon* battle group was also sent there, while the 5th Battery of the Army Flak Battalion GD remained with the Reconnaissance Battalion GD. The elements of the Assault Pioneer Battalion GD under the latter's command were to be released for other duties. The light and heavy field howitzer battalions still under the command of the reconnaissance battalion remained in their positions near Grintsev Rog.

The growing belief that the northern group of enemy forces were advancing west toward Kolomak with the intention of outflanking the villages of Valki and Kovyagy, as well as the fact that ever more columns were streaming southwest through the gap near Budy, about which the division could do nothing on its southern flank because of a lack of forces, led the division command to issue orders for a withdrawal to a new line during the night of 21-22 February 1943. Patrols by the Reconnaissance Battalion GD had already spotted the advancing enemy in the Merla Valley – leading elements were already outside Kolontayev. Arriving elements of the SS-Panzer-

Grenadier Division *Totenkopf* were sent there as quickly as possible. It was thus certain that in the northwest the enemy had overtaken the retreating German forces and was advancing toward Poltava, threatening this important supply base.

On 22 February 1943 the division command post moved to Valki. Armoured Train 62 was assigned to the division by the army group to support its operations. The train was initially sent ahead as far as Skorochodovo Station on the Poltava–Kovyagy rail line.

With average temperatures still in the minus 20 degree range, the individual battalions reached their new positions in the early morning hours, occupying them by moonlight. Initially this proceeded without interference by the enemy. The new defensive line lay about 10 kilometres farther west, on both sides of the road, roughly in a line Malaya Lichovka (the right wing of the I.D. GD and border with the 320th Inf. Div.) northwest through Burivka collective farm–Pasetchnik collective farm–Point 204.3 and a generally westerly direction.

On the right wing of the division, I Battalion/Grenadier Regiment had scarcely occupied its positions when the enemy attacked at 05.00. The following combat report by I Battalion provides details of the engagement:

"I Battalion arrived in its new area of operations near Solochevski at about 03.00. A new main line of resistance at the road south of Malaya Lichovka was occupied immediately after arrival. Attached anti-tank company with rifle platoon of the Division Escort Company, then left the 1st and 2nd Companies with elements of 4th Company, battalion command post located at the southern end of the village near the mill.

Under the battalion's command were: light and heavy infantry gun platoons of IV Battalion, an anti-tank platoon of the 18th (anti- tank) Company, an 88mm flak combat team. No contact yet with the 320th Infantry Division on the right. On the battalion's left II Battalion.

At dawn at about 05.00 the enemy attacked the village of Malaya Lichovka from the direction of the Kovalenkovka collective farm with superior forces. The anti-tank company pulled back along the road and was taken in there by 1st Company and elements of 4th Company. The Russian attack finally came to a halt at the village's western exit. The anti-tank company, with attached rifle platoon, assembled and occupied new main line of resistance.

Nothing out of the ordinary throughout the day. With the onset of darkness the enemy again felt his way forward with infantry from the Kovalenkovka collective farm west along the road. When the moon rose, at about 20.00, they moved forward with 7 tanks and mounted infantry and tried to occupy Hill 205. Enemy attack was repulsed, however, the enemy infantry jumped off the tanks. Panzer Group Bernhard barred the road with blind fire. Inexplicably the Russians did not follow up and withdrew later during the night. Leutnant Stangl was killed in this counterattack."

While the two infantry regiments were essentially able to hold their own in their new positions, the main task of the reinforced Reconnaissance Battalion GD lay not in fighting but in the observation of the enemy and monitoring of his movements in the area Kolomak–Kolontayev–Kotelva. The division command, which based its decisions almost exclusively on the information provided by its reconnaissance battalion, awaited fresh details from it hourly. Aware of the great responsibility which had been placed on it, the battalion was very active, with numerous patrols under way.

The initial reconnaissance results revealed that in the north a powerful Soviet battle group was advancing from the Bogoduchov area in a south-westerly direction, probably with the objective of Poltava, while a further battle group was on the move through Akhtyrka toward the west. No further information was available concerning the whereabouts of the enemy battle group operating farther to the southeast; essentially the question no longer concerned the division's area of operations, rather that farther to the south-east, where other German units, including the 320th Infantry Division, were operating. Whereas the regiments remained in their positions—which must be seen as the last of this period of fighting—for reasons which will be examined in more detail, there was a series of movements and engagements by the reinforced Reconnaissance Battalion GD in the Kolotayev—Shelestevo area. It was from these that the grounds for the later deployment of the division in this same area developed.

The combat report by the reinforced Reconnaissance Battalion GD from 23 February is therefore reproduced here:

"Moving out at about 07.00 on 23 February 1943, the battalion, driving on good roads with thawing weather and a cloudy sky, with Headquarters, 1st and 4th Squadrons, the assault gun platoon of 'Battle Group FBB' and the flak battery, reached Skorochodovo Station; the other three squadrons were brought up immediately. The FBB tracked battle group did not move out toward Kolontayev until 03.00 this morning due to fuel reasons. –

Deployed from the battalion:

> 4th Squadron to secure Filenkov, with reconnaissance toward Otrada;
> 3rd (VW) Squadron in Ryabkovka, with reconnaissance toward Mikhailovka and Vyasovaya;
> 2nd and 5th Squadrons in Skorochodovo, with reconnaissance to Nagalnyi.
> HQ and 1st (Armoured Recon.) Squadron in Filenkov.

Following minor skirmishes with partisans the FBB tracked battle group occupied the village of Kolontayev. The reinforced reconnaissance battalion was thus watching over the approximately 25-kilometre-long stretch Kolontayev–Nagalnyi. Patrol under Lt. Gebhard, which had been under way to Kolontayev via Poltava and Rublevka since 05.00, reported good roads and had made contact with the 167th Infantry Division in Rublevka and the FBB tracked battle group in Kolontayev. An enemy mounted patrol was fired on about 1,000 metres north of Kotshubekevka.

At 15.15 the 2nd (APC) Squadron reported that the tracks in Izkrovka and Kolomak, with the exception of the main track, had been blown.

Armoured Train 62 observed strong enemy forces advancing toward the southwest from Pokrovka and Trudelyubovka as it steamed north through

Skorochodovo. Kolomak Station under enemy artillery fire. At about 16.50 the following radio message was received from division: 'Bravo reconnaissance battalion! The commanding general.'

While still twilight a 20mm flak on a self-propelled carriage was sighted on the Filenkov–Rublevka road and contact made there with II Battalion/315th Infantry Regiment.

At about 18.55 received radioed order from division to immediately take following positions on account of enemy situation: Shelestevo, exclusive of Petropavlovsk, Vyazovaya, Otrada. – Point of main effort on the right wing. – As well Hptm. Frantz and elements of his assault gun battalion en route to Skorochodovo."

There was undoubtedly an immediate threat near Kolomak; the 23rd of February saw the enemy assembling forces in the wooded area northwest of the city in preparation for further attacks. As well, the *Deutschland* Regiment of the SS-Panzer-Grenadier Division *Das Reich* was engaged in heavy fighting there and successfully defended its strongpoints against a somewhat superior enemy.

The regiments were positioned as follows: on the right the grenadiers, from Malaya Likovka–Lyunovka collective farm–Burivka collective farm—Pasetsnik collective farm, then the pioneers to Point 204.3, and the fusiliers from there to the Voytenkov collective farm–Mistchenkov collective farm. As before they had to fend off enemy advances, some with tanks, even though they weren't as strong as before. III Battalion/Fusilier Regiment characterised it as a day of close combat near the Voytenkov collective farm, where the enemy repeatedly, but futilely, tried to break through the battalion's positions.

With the battalions again installed in favourable positions, the artillery once more became the most loyal helper of the infantry. Concentrated barrages destroyed the enemy's assembly points and negated preparations for advances. Furthermore, there existed the as-yet-unconfirmed impression that the enemy there were growing weaker. The Soviet attacks had lost some of their impetus.

Among the engagements fought that day was one by the Grenadier Regiment's 11th Company in the wooded areas northeast of the Liovka collective farm. The commander of the company on the left, Lt. Kollewe, who had the best view of the engagement, wrote:

'Meanwhile the Russians had attacked 11th Company, but were beaten back in their first attempt. A subsequent attack by the Soviets achieved partial success. They succeeded in breaking into 11th Company's right wing. A furious battle now broke out in the forest, without my being able to assist.

Only my right machine-gun was able to provide flanking fire, but with the help of the artillery and its forward observer, Lt. Dulfer, the 11th Company was able to retake its positions during the night."

During the evening hours of 23 February 1943 the division was informed that it would be withdrawn from its positions in the next twenty-four hours and moved into the Poltava area to rest. This may have come as a surprise to the men up front in their holes in the snow and mud, but it was almost expected by the division command, which naturally had some idea of the overall situation.

Surveying the situation on the other fronts, it must be repeated that Army Group Kempf (Kempf had replaced General Lanz) had been part of Army Group South since 13 February.

However the fighting withdrawal of the past weeks had almost completely isolated the relatively weak army group, which was in no way equal to the onrushing enemy, from its superior command authority.

The objective of the Soviet advance had been to achieve a breakthrough southwest into the Pavlograd area with the 1st Guards and 6th Armies advancing from both sides of Izyum on the Donets, in preparation for a subsequent advance to the Dniepr near Zaphorozhye which would cut off all of Army Group South. They were only 100 kilometres short of their objective! A huge new Stalingrad seemed to be unavoidable.

Once the enemy had been halted on the Mius front after extremely heavy fighting, on 20 February, in a daring, brilliant operation, *Generalfeld-marschall* von Manstein committed the Fourth Panzer Army, which had been moved from the southern wing, in a flanking attack against this enemy near Pavlovgrad. Its objective was to drive the Soviets back toward the northeast and close the gap between the left wing of the First Panzer Army and the right wing of Army Group Kempf.

One of the consequences of this counterattack by the Fourth Panzer Army was the removal of Soviet units from the former attack areas in front of Army Group Kempf. Understandably, Soviet offensive strength in the Valki area diminished, which resulted in a weakening of the forces facing the units of the Infantry Division Großdeutschland.

The four-week winter battle between the Donets and the Dniepr had saved Army Group South from encirclement and brought considerable success. The bulk of the Soviet 1st Guards and 6th Armies had been destroyed.

But now, in spite of the thaw, following an all too brief pause the boil of Kharkov had to be burnt out, in order to advance the front to Belgorod and achieve a straightening of the lines. Without the recapture of Kharkov the success would not be complete, the great threat not averted.

The Infantry Division Großdeutschland was to play a decisive role in the victorious conclusion to the great winter battle.

CHAPTER 2

THE GREAT COUNTERATTACK

Beginning on 24 February the various units of the Infantry Division *Großdeutschland* transferred into the Reczetilovka area (about 30 km. southwest of Poltava), leaving behind a number of armoured battle groups. The division headquarters likewise moved to Reczetilovka. As soon as the units arrived they were placed in rest status. In the days that followed, the units were brought up to strength in personnel and equipment. It was expected that they would see action again in three or four days.

Meanwhile the reinforced Reconnaissance Battalion GD, with the assault guns, the FBB battle group, the Grenadier Regiment's II Battalion (which had been directed to work with the reconnaissance battalion) and the 4th and 5th Batteries of the Artillery Regiment GD, remained in the Skorochodovo–Filenkov–Kolotayev line of resistance under the direct command of the Raus Special Purpose Corps.

The reconnaissance battalion was responsible for screening the rest area northeast of Poltava, as well as guarding preparations under way by the new units which in recent days had arrived at Poltava Station to take part in the coming offensive. Among these units were II Battalion and the Regimental Headquarters of the Panzer Regiment GD under its new commander, Oberst of the Reserve Hyazinth Graf von Strachwitz, the 13th (Tiger) Company, Panzer Regiment GD, IV Battalion, Artillery Regiment GD and 6th Battery, Army Flak Battalion GD. At the same time field replacement battalions from Cottbus were standing by in Poltava to provide the regiments with replacement personnel. All in all, the few days available were used to reorganize and regenerate the units. The spirit of the forces was firming up as far as the coming offensive action was concerned, with a growing will to drive the enemy back to their starting positions with their new weapons and with the Waffen-SS at their side.

By 5 March 1943, the Fourth Panzer Army had reached its initial objective and smashed the enemy's southern wing, the 3rd Tank Army, at the Bestovaya southwest of Kharkov; on 7 March, after a quick regrouping, the SS Panzer Corps, under the command of *General der Waffen-SS* Hausser, attacked north from the Krasnograd area. Its objective was to take in the flank the enemy forces attacking west from the area of Belgorod and Kharkov, force them away from Kharkov and reestablish contact with Army Group Centre to the north.

At the same time as the Fourth Panzer Army resumed its attack, Army Group Kempf was supposed to set off from the area northeast of Poltava, engage the enemy frontally and then drive in the general direction of Belgorod. The Infantry Division *Großdeutschland* formed the army group's left wing, which was to advance to Belgorod via Bogodukhov. It was expected that the deep flanking thrust by the SS Panzer Corps on the left wing of the Fourth Panzer Army, with Kharkov as its objective, would very soon make itself felt on the enemy units in the Poltava–Akhtyrka area as well. The

Infantry Division GD's brief period of rest ended on 5 March 1943; the individual units received marching orders for their pre-attack assembly points. The attack, originally planned for 6 March, was postponed by 24 hours, however.

Meanwhile the SS Panzer Corps was already advancing vigorously in the general direction of Valki and east. The left wing, comprised of the SS Regiment *Thule*, made especially rapid progress, advancing along the Skorochodovo–Shelestevo rail line.

The enemy fell back. The Infantry Division GD had meanwhile moved into assembly areas in the Sidorenkovo–Chutovo area and was supposed to take the city of Valki as its initial objective. The division formed three attack groups, each of which had its own objective:

"Battle Group Strachwitz" (Commander Panzer Regiment GD) with reinforced Grenadier Regiment, in following march order:

> Panzer Regiment GD less I Battalion
>
> 2 batteries of III Battalion, Artillery Regt. GD close-defence squad
>
> III Battalion, Grenadier Regiment
>
> 3rd Company, Assault Pioneer Battalion GD
>
> 3rd Company, Anti-tank Battalion GD
>
> I Battalion, Grenadier Regiment
>
> II Battalion, Grenadier Regiment
>
> IV Battalion, Grenadier Regiment
>
> 6th Battery, Artillery Regiment GD
>
> remainder of III Battalion, Artillery Regiment GD

Assembly area Sidorenkovo–Chabanovka. Initial objective: Kontokusovo, then Perekop.

"Battle Group Beuermann" (Commander Fusilier Regiment GD) with reinforced Fusilier Regiment GD, as well as elements of the Panzer Regiment GD (I Battalion), the Artillery Regiment GD, the Assault Pioneer Battalion GD and the Anti-tank Battalion GD.

Assembly area southeast of Chutovo–northern edge of Chudovo. Initial objective: Rovni, then Kolomak.

"Battle Group Wätjen" (Commander Reconnaissance Battalion GD) with reinforced Reconnaissance Battalion, Assault Gun Battalion GD, and elements of the Artillery Regiment GD and the Army Flak Battalion GD.

Assembly area Artemovka–Skorochodovo. Initial objective: capture undamaged the bridges near Tarapunka and Kolomak.

The weather had become warmer; the snow was beginning to melt and the dark hue of the farm fields was already showing through in many places. Water from the melting snow ran with increasing speed along the ditches. Most of the roads, the designated march routes, were paved in this area and were thus able to support traffic, but the side roads turned into a bottomless something. It wasn't long before the men, still in their white-grey winter camouflage clothing and sitting on their faithful vehicles, were covered with a layer of brown earth. The wet conditions were almost more uncomfortable than the biting cold that had preceded them.

The beginning of March 1943 once again saw the German forces on the advance, something every participant in the war remembered so fondly from earlier days. Large numbers of vehicles of all types backed up at the departure points. Included were every type of tank; one could count more than a hundred, as well as the fast armoured personnel carriers and combat vehicles of the infantry. Eager officers and NCOs were on hand to give instructions, offer an encouraging word or pass round a bottle.

Morale was at its peak. Once again the German soldiers were buoyed by their own strength, the most obvious sign of which was the large number of tanks. The men sensed the coming success. Just as nature gets ready for a new beginning each spring, so the men of the Infantry Division *Großdeutschland* stood by their vehicles, ready for a fresh start.

Following a brief preparatory bombardment by the artillery, which really was not even required, the battle groups moved out of their assembly areas with the troops riding in their vehicles. It was early on 7 March 1943. The panzers rolled forward over the softened earth, dark monsters, followed by the long rows of combat vehicles carrying the men of the regiments.

Driving through Mosulevka, Alexandrovka and Molodetski, "Battle Group Strachwitz" arrived at the west end of the Kontakusovo collective farm without meeting any significant opposition. The first contact with the enemy took place there, but it was only the Soviet rear guard. There was a brief howling of engines, the hard crash of numerous tank cannon, then troops swarmed from the tanks and armoured personnel carriers. The advance soon resumed. The enemy were taken completely by surprise. The panorama of destruction, burning vehicles and houses, shot-up horse-drawn sleighs and guns, the twisted bodies of dead Soviets, was like a horrible dream.

At about 13.30 the battle group's armoured spearhead reached the south edge of Perekop without further resistance. Farther to the right the sound of fighting could often be heard. That was where the divisions of the Waffen-SS were attacking, their objective being the enemy forces sighted east of Valki. There too the enemy were soon overrun; the unrestrained flight of Soviet columns, guns and vehicles began.

Farther west the reinforced Fusilier Regiment GD, which made up the bulk of "Battle Group Beuermann," set off to the north from the Chutovo area. The route there was shorter, but more dangerous. The forest extending along the left flank threatened the battle group's advance, and from it the enemy fired shells and mortar rounds. Resistance stiffened at the multiple road junction in front of Rovni and especially at the effectively-destroyed river bridges, and was heavier than expected. Rovni offered the only possible avenue of retreat for the Soviet forces located farther to the west. If it fell, the bolsheviks near Shelestovo and Iskrovka would be cut off.

The German artillery went into position. Several salvoes and the action of the accompanying panzers enabled the fusiliers to rapidly approach the enemy positions. In order to avoid unnecessary German losses, the panzers went around the enemy, who were defending grimly in favourable positions, and attacked them from the rear. After an hour the enemy's resistance had been broken. In a wild flight the bolsheviks streamed out of Rovni to the north.

The path was clear, and the vehicles of the reinforced Fusilier Regiment GD rolled on toward Perekop to link up with "Battle Group Strachwitz."

At approximately 04.15 the reinforced Reconnaissance Battalion GD moved out on the left flank of the attacking Infantry Division GD. The weather was dreary and misty. The bulk of the battalion's squadrons advanced across open terrain due west of the rail line, and in spite of heavy flanking fire from Iskrovka, situated in the forest, it took possession of Shelestevo several hours later. The Assault Gun Battalion GD soon became embroiled in heavy fighting in and near Iskrovka while supporting the SS forces attacking there. After a hard struggle the attackers were able to enter the town and break the resistance of the stubbornly- defending bolsheviks.

Meanwhile the bridges near Tarapunka had fallen into German hands undamaged; the Russians had been prevented at the last minute from setting off 12 explosive charges. The 3rd Squadron, riding on assault guns, was moved forward to Kolomak, where it soon encountered elements of "Battle Group Beuermann," in particular III Battalion, Fusilier Regiment and I Battalion, Panzer Regiment GD. The fusiliers had orders to advance beyond Perekop to Kovyagi in spite of the onset of darkness, in order to win a favourable starting position for the continuation of the attack the next day. Everything now depended on preventing the fleeing enemy from stopping to catch his breath.

Division headquarters had meanwhile been moved forward to Chutovo. The general was at the front. Remaining in constant radio contact with his Ia, he urged the units to hurry. Together with his unit commanders, he was the driving force behind this race which absolutely had to be decided in favour of the attackers!

Losses were minimal: scarcely any killed, a few wounded. The first-aid facilities were moved up, always ready to accept incoming casualties. The 1st First-aid Company followed the rapid advance and set up its medical clearing station in Fedorovka, while another was established in Chutovo. In any case this was only temporary; for the next morning the advance would resume with all vigour.

The 8th of March brought extraordinarily difficult road conditions caused by blowing snow. The panzers of the Strachwitz Group, led by the Graf, or the 'count' as he was fondly called by his officers and men, initially drove from Kovyagi east to Shlyach, followed by the Grenadier Regiment GD. At Shlyach they veered north. The objective was to intercept the Soviet forces streaming back from the west. Contact with enemy forces on the left was possible at any time. The panzer attack, over hills and through valleys, encountered enemy forces, usually tanks, at various points in the terrain. These were immediately hit hard and destroyed; in all a total of 21 enemy tanks were knocked out. Stary Mertchik was soon reached, and a halt was called there in order to take on fuel and ammunition. The grenadier battalions joined the panzers after a difficult drive; they were riding in wheeled vehicles which had difficulty keeping up with the tanks.

The Fusilier Regiment GD initially screened these movements at the north end of Kovyagi along the rail line. Late in the afternoon it left the city and together with the tanks of I Battalion, Panzer Regiment GD under *Major* Pössel advanced due north. Its first objective was the Shuravli collective farm and later the Mok Merchik. Forward security positions were moved forward to the river.

For 8 March 1943 the Reconnaissance Battalion GD, reinforced by the Assault Gun Battalion GD, was under orders to block the Olchany–Bogodukhov road and halt Soviet road traffic rolling over it from west to east. Patrols were immediately dispatched to reconnoitre the roads leading to the target area. The battle group itself moved via Perekop to Kovyagi, in order to capture favourable jumping-off positions there. Unfortunately heavy drifting snow and blockages by vehicles of both regiments prevented the battle group from reaching its objective quickly. The last vehicle did not arrive in Kovyagi until about 16.00, as a result of which the battle group had to spend the night there. The patrols brought back interesting news: Lt. Gebhard reported that late in the morning his patrol and the Pössel panzer battalion had advanced to the Merchik via the Shuravli and Podgorny collective farms and Kovali. There the patrol sighted strongly-manned field positions and six tanks withdrawing before it. Local residents stated that there were four T-34s, 12 76.2mm guns, about 30 trucks and approximately 2,000 Soviet troops there.

The patrol led by Uffz. Karrsch reported that Novy Merchik was occupied by an enemy battalion. During the afternoon the reinforced Reconnaissance Battalion GD received a radio message from division with orders for the next day: the battalion was to block the road near Maximovka.

The Infantry Division GD's situation on the evening of 8 March was this: "Battle Group Strachwitz" had the leading elements of the Grenadier Regiment near Merchik Station, while its main force was still in Stary Merchik; leading elements of the Fusilier Regiment were holding security positions at the Merchik, while the main body of the regiment was still at the Shuravli collective farm; and in Kovyagi the reinforced Reconnaissance Battalion GD was making preparations for the next day to advance through the Fusilier Regiment GD's positions, cross the Merchik and occupy the high ground to the north.

During this advance it was imperative that the German forces once again set the rules of engagement and force the enemy to fight on their terms. Tactically, their primary objective was to destroy the Soviet forces farther to the west, but it was also important to establish contact with Army Group Centre to the north by the shortest possible route.

The mission of the armoured spearhead, "Battle Group Strachwitz" with the Grenadier Regiment GD, on 9 March 1943 was to block the Olchany–Bogodukhov road in order to prevent the enemy from breaking out to the east. Overcoming great difficulties associated with road conditions, the armoured group advanced to the specified road. Details of the operation are provided by the daily report of I Battalion, Grenadier Regiment, the unit immediately behind the spearhead:

"The Russians had infiltrated into the southern part of Stary Merchik during the early morning hours. When it became light 2nd Company put an end to this business. At 08.00 1st Company climbed aboard Tiger tanks of the Panzer Regiment GD, in order to secure the area between Kadnitsa and Repki Station to the west. 3rd Company, likewise riding on tanks, drove through Gosovo across the rail line toward Petropavlovka.

Both companies linked up near the 'work house.' Meanwhile all available soldiers and civilians shovelled snow off the road from Stary Merchik to Merchik Station, in order to create a passable link to the supply trains.

At about 12.00 I Battalion passed through and drove along the railway embankment as far as the 'work house.' From there the advance continued toward Klenovoye together with the panzers, which had occupied Maximovka after heavy fighting against enemy tanks; arrived there at about 17.00. Security forces deployed as follows for the night: 2nd Company near Tavrovka, facing west; likewise 1st Company in Popovka, together with the Tigers. They were therefore the elements of the Infantry Division GD deepest in enemy territory and the farthest north.

The 3rd Company occupied positions at the western outskirts of the village of Klenovoye, the 4th Company did the same at the eastern outskirts. Battalion command post I Battalion: Klenovoye."

The plan of the division command was obvious, namely to outflank the city of Bogodukhov to the northeast with its right wing and simultaneously prevent an outflow of enemy forces from the city. After initially following the advance by I Battalion, the Grenadier Regiment's III Battalion, with II Battalion behind it, drove through Petrovsky and Petropavlovka, meeting no significant opposition, and reached the "work house" north of Sukini, where III Battalion's command post occupied quarters for the night. The battalion's individual companies advanced another 500 metres to the north to a point outside Krysino, which was still occupied by the enemy, and secured there during the night.

The Reconnaissance Battalion GD, reinforced by the Assault Gun Battalion GD, with the 5th Battery of the Army Flak Battalion GD and two light field howitzer batteries of the Artillery Regiment GD, set out early that day for the intended advance across the Merchik. The combat report by the Reconnaissance Battalion Gd provides a factual, but exciting account of the day's action:

"At 05.15 on 9.3.43 the 3rd Squadron moved out of Shuravli toward Kirasirsky with a battery of assault guns, a 37mm flak platoon and two 20mm flak of the 1st Squadron. The village was taken after a brief firefight, and the battle group immediately continued on toward Sion. There the initially stronger resistance was broken by the assault guns. The battle group's next objective was Hill 188.7 north of the village.

At about the same time as the 3rd Squadron battle group moved out, 4th Squadron, together with the 1st Battery of the Assault Gun Battalion GD under Hptm. Magold, a 37mm flak platoon and the 2nd (APC) Squadron, set out to the east and advanced on the Voytenkov collective farm, which was reached an hour later. The two squadrons deployed immediately behind the village, where the two artillery batteries went into position to further support the attack, and advanced across the completely open plain toward the hills before Novy Mertchik. The village itself, which lay in the valley of the upper Mok Mertchik, could not be seen. The assault guns initially stayed back. The 2nd and 4th Squadron battle group advanced on the village on a broad front. There was still no defensive fire. The 2nd (APC) Squadron broke into Dolina, which lay farther to the west. Soon afterward the assault guns and 3rd Squadron entered the western part of Novy Mertchik, where the enemy stirred himself for the first time. The first mortar rounds fell some distance from the 37mm flak, which had driven into position quite close to one another in order to engage the enemy forces in the eastern part of the village. However the enemy soon spotted their targets and placed their mortar fire in their midst. The anti-aircraft guns and 4th squadron suffered casualties.

However the 2nd (APC) Squadron had meanwhile driven through the village and continued its advance on Hill 199.3. There it turned left and linked up with 3rd Squadron on Hill 188.7. Meanwhile the assault guns and 4th Squadron cleared the village of enemy forces. Crossing the Mok Mertchik was difficult, as the bridge had been completely destroyed and the ice, weakened by the warmer weather, was no longer strong enough. A way around was finally found, unfortunately not before one assault gun broke through the ice.

4th Squadron moved out again and attacked the village of Grigorovka across Hill 199.3. Fleeing enemy sleigh columns on the hills north of 188.7 were caught and quickly destroyed by the assault guns and 37mm flak. The advancing squadrons came under artillery fire from Alexandovka, which lay in the valley to the left of 188.7, as a result of which the mass of vehicles which had formed in the meantime scattered in all directions. The 2nd (APC) Squadron meanwhile advanced on Tarasovka in order to then turn toward Bayrak.

Meanwhile the 3rd Squadron charged recklessly down from the hill and attacked the village of Alexandovka in spite of heavy defensive fire. After the assault guns eliminated three 76.2mm anti-tank guns positioned at the edge of the village, the squadron entered Alexandrovka, where bitter house-to-house fighting once again broke out.

Meanwhile the battalion staff stood with the forward artillery observer on Hill 188.7 and watched as dense Russian columns fled the large, gently-sloping forest northeast of Alexandrovka. The mass of vehicles included guns, sleighs, trucks and even two tanks. The squadrons occupied defensive positions for the night, with the 2nd (APC) Squadron in the western part of Kirasirsky, the 3rd (VW) Squadron in Alexandrovka and the 4th (Machinegun) Squadron in Grigorovka.

It was the end of a very successful day, as the figures confirmed: 7 enemy tanks destroyed, including 3 T-34s, and 4 122mm guns, 21 76.2mm anti-tank guns, 16 47mm anti-tank guns captured, in addition to numerous sleighs, small arms, a backpack radio, anti-tank rifles and so on. About 300 enemy dead were counted.

At about 02.10 the staff of the reinforced Reconnaissance Battalion GD received a radio message from division, stating that it was to be relieved by the reinforced Fusilier Regiment GD and that the battalion should assemble in Kovyagi and await further orders."

The supporting units had played a major role in the success of this relatively small battle group, especially the 1st Battery of the Assault Gun Battalion GD under *Hauptmann* Magold, which accounted for the majority of the enemy tanks destroyed on that day in that sector. Hptm. Magold was recommended for the Knight's Cross on account of these outstanding accomplishments.

The following day, 10 March 1943, brought only limited gains in comparison to the preceding days. The roads and tracks were in desperate shape on account of the thaw, which affected the delivery of fuel supplies in particular. Many valuable hours were spent waiting for the tank truck to arrive with fuel. The Tigers alone consumed great quantities of fuel, especially in these difficult ground conditions, and it was they which most terrified the enemy, who lacked any effective countermeasures against the heavy tanks. The Tigers gave the German soldiers the superiority they needed for the coming days.

The only attempt by the enemy to break through occurred during the afternoon of 10 March, from west to east along the road. This was quickly smashed, however, primarily by the panzers. Several enemy tanks were destroyed. *Feldwebel* Rapp and his platoon of the 2nd Company/Panzer Regiment GD destroyed three T-34s, two of these by Rapp himself.

The enemy's bloody losses increased further as the panzers advanced to the outskirts of the Mussijki collective farm. The Soviets fled in panic toward Bogodukhov. Reconnaissance reported large columns withdrawing to the north. Meanwhile the division command had begun reorganizing its units and preparing for the attack on Bogodukhov. The Panzer Regiment GD, with its two battalions and the Tiger company, was instructed to position itself on the back slope of Hill 197.0 north of Krysino. The panzers were to swing northeast, cross the Merla east of the city of Bogodukhov and then enter the city from the north. The crossing over the Merla captured the day before by the Grenadier Regiment's I Battalion was to be used in this operation. Planning foresaw the Grenadier Regiment GD sending its II and III Battalions through Mussijki collective farm into the city from the south, while I Battalion screened to the north near Losovaya. The attack battalions would then drive through the city and continue to advance toward the north.

Meanwhile, in its positions on the hills north of Alexandrovka, the reinforced Fusilier Regiment GD prepared to seize the village of Krushchevaya Nikitovka, which lay on its left flank, with its III Battalion. At the same time the main body of the regiment, together with the assault gun battalion, was to drive past the village to the east, through Semenov Yar collective farm and enter the southwestern part of the city.

At about 11.00 on 11 March the units moved out for the concentric attack on Bogodukhov. Stukas had been bombing the city since early morning; the artillery continued the concert with its salvoes, softening up the city.

The grenadiers and fusiliers moved across the sun-drenched plains toward the objective as if on the training grounds. They advanced northward at a steady pace, widely spaced and weighed down by the heavy load of their weapons and ammunition boxes. Right behind the grenadiers and fusiliers, following from one hollow to the next, were the long columns of vehicles, in which sat the reserve units.

The anti-aircraft guns on self-propelled carriages likewise followed close behind the infantry, halting on areas of high ground and now and then firing a burst to chase an anti-tank or field gun from a stand of bushes or a group of houses. The outskirts of the city were soon reached. In the north the crash of tank cannon rang out. The panzers were already on the hills northeast of Bogodukhov, from where they engaged with outstanding success the Soviet sleigh columns fleeing toward the north.

The city drew all the men and vehicles like a magnet. The vehicles and infantry columns streamed into Bogodukhov through its many entrances and streets and filled it in no time. The first field kitchens were set up in the gardens scattered around the outskirts of this beautifully-situated town, and their stovepipes were soon emitting white smoke. At the same time the grenadiers of III Battalion drove through the city in their vehicles, and by evening they had entered Leskovka and Saryabinka, where they occupied defensive positions for the night. In the distance they could still see the last of the fleeing enemy sleigh columns.

As reserve battalion, I Battalion had meanwhile been moved forward, pushing its forward outposts as far as the northern outskirts of Senoye. The panzers remained on the hills about 4 kilometres north of the city to watch over these movements. Only the occasional shot was fired; the quiet of the evening moved in.

In the meantime the fusiliers had also occupied positions for the night in the western and northwestern outskirts of the city. The division command post prepared for the move to Bogodukhov. The Reconnaissance Battalion GD was likewise moved forward. Early the next morning it and the assault guns were to stay on the heels of the enemy, who were in full flight.

Meanwhile the Wehrmacht communique of 11 March 1943 spread the news that the Waffen-SS, which was attacking to the right of the division, was also making good forward progress. It stated that: "... In the Kharkov area our attack divisions drove the enemy back toward the city. There is fighting in the northern and western outskirts. Two Soviet regiments were outflanked and destroyed. Bomber and close-support Geschwader are smashing retreating enemy forces ..."

It was now vital that the enemy be kept on the run. All necessary preparations were made for the pursuit. Orders for the Infantry Division GD on the morning of 12 March: attack toward Bol. Pisarevka and break through in the direction of Grayvoron. Early that day the reinforced Reconnaissance Battalion GD was moved forward to spearhead the attack, together with the Assault Gun Battalion GD and the 5th Battery/Army Flak Battalion GD. These units set out toward the north. They were to be followed by elements of the Grenadier Regiment GD, then the Panzer Regiment GD and the fusiliers.

At 05.30, following a delay caused by clogged roads, the point unit assembled at the northern edge of Bogodukhov. The sequence:

> 8-wheeled patrol under Wachtmeister Roesch ahead of the point unit
> 3rd Squadron with 1st Battery/Assault Gun Battalion
> 4th Squadron with 2nd Battery/Assault Gun Battalion
> 2nd (APC) Squadron
> 5th Battery/Army Flak Battalion GD with 1st Squadron flak platoon
> 1st (Armoured Reconnaissance) Squadron
> HQ Squadron
> 5th (heavy) Squadron

The tracked vehicles worked their way forward over the road, which had frozen over during the night. The sun shone warmly, but a cold wind was still blowing.

At about 06.45 the attack spearhead encountered the enemy near Ivany-Berdyny and came under anti-tank fire. Subsequently the Assault Gun Battalion's 2nd Battery under Oblt. Schenk and the 4th Squadron attacked the village frontally. The latter lay extended along a slope leading down into a valley; after a curve in the road it continued up the opposite, completely treeless slope to the next hill. Positioned at the curve, concealed by a number of trees, was a 76.2mm anti-tank gun. Standing in his assault gun, Oblt. Schenk tried to pinpoint the gun's position. The first hit by the anti-tank gun brought the assault gun to a stop, the second ricocheted off the superstructure, killing the battery chief, who was left slumped over the hatch. The neighbouring assault gun, that of battalion commander Hptm. Frantz, was able to intervene, but too late. The battery chief was dead; two members of his crew died with him: Uffz. E. Kempter and *Gefreiter* G. Rausch.

The men of the accompanying 4th squadron leapt from their vehicles and advanced toward the houses on foot. The following 2nd (APC) Squadron veered off to the right and drove into the eastern part of the village with its armoured vehicles.

After a brief pause the fast Volkswagens of the VW Squadron drove up the opposite slope to secure the village which had just been taken. The units stopped to replenish their stocks of ammunition. The division commander's Fieseler *Storch* landed on an area of level ground. Armed with his knotty walking stick, he walked over to a group of commanders standing at the side of the road. He once again reminded them of the division's intentions: reconnaissance battalion scout ahead toward Bol. Pisarevka! According to statements by prisoners there was at least an artillery brigade with an anti-tank regiment there. In the event the enemy was too strong, the reconnaissance battalion was to hold back, wait for the panzer regiment's attack and then follow. Elements of the fusilier and grenadiers regiments mopped up the area surrounding the village.

The reinforced Reconnaissance Battalion GD set out from Ivany-Berdyny at about 09.00. The Army Flak Battalion GD's 5th Battery remained in the just-captured village and secured to the west for the time being.

The point unit encountered the enemy south of Bol. Pisarevka at about

10.00. The road was found to be mined. Eight guns were spotted firing from the eastern outskirts of Bol. Pisarevka alone: the artillery brigade! The commander of the reconnaissance battalion therefore decided to send 3rd Squadron and elements of the Assault Gun Battalion GD to the right through Maximovka toward Bol. Pisarevka in an outflanking manoeuvre, in order to intercept the enemy when they eventually fled the village following the attack by the tanks. The Panzer Regiment GD arrived before Bol. Pisarevka at about twelve noon and assembled for the attack. West of the road elements of the Fusilier Regiment GD; they were to accompany the tank assault. Waiting behind them in an endless vehicle column were the remaining fusilier battalions as well as the artillery and the grenadiers.

The panzer regiment moved out at 14.00 hours. The reconnaissance battalion followed right behind the attack, which rolled across the descending slope to the Vorskla Valley toward the village of Bol'shaya Pisarevka.

While the bulk of the Panzer Regiment GD, in particular II Battalion, and the fusiliers drove directly toward the village, the regiment's I Battalion, followed closely by the reconnaissance battalion, headed for the eastern edge of the village, in order to make a "right face" in the direction of Glotovo–Kosinka–Grayvoron.

Following an intense duel between the tanks and the enemy guns, the attackers broke into the village of Bol'shaya Pisarevka. Enemy guns, sleigh columns and groups of soldiers fled over the hills to the north. Others tried to flee east along the Vorskla Valley. German losses were minimal, with only wounded to report.

At about 16.30, as darkness was falling, the panzer regiment's I Battalion and the Tiger company attacked the small city of Grayvoron. It was a thrilling spectacle to witness this dashing tank attack. *Major* Pössel had developed the tactic of pinning down the crews of the enemy's heavy weapons with machine- gun fire from his tanks, then moving up slowly and destroying them. Flamethrower tanks followed in the second wave and burned out the enemy positions.

Right behind them drove the armoured personnel carriers of the reconnaissance battalion's 2nd (APC) Squadron, which was providing infantry support for the attack. They too had to face the enemy's anti-tank defences, but with much less armour protection than the tanks in front of them. The anti-tank guns, most of which were in open positions, were recognizable only by muzzle flashes at the edge of the village.

The nearby houses were soon ablaze and in the glow of the fires the attackers could see the gun crews at work. The flamethrower tanks pressed forward and from sixty metres sprayed a stream of cold oil that soon became a jet of flame. In an instant the target gun crew was shrouded in flames. One gun after another was silenced in this manner. The first tanks rolled past them into Grayvoron, followed by the nimble armoured personnel carriers and Volkswagens, which had meanwhile also found their way to the village. There were explosions everywhere and individual enemy tanks careened about, looking for a way out. As the armoured personnel carriers searched for the village's southern exit, where the reconnaissance battalion was supposed to assemble, a T-34 roared across the street in front of the command APC. The armoured personnel carriers moved ahead to the church and formed a hedgehog position there. Elements of the Grenadier Regiment GD (II Battalion) arrived and provided infantry protection.

At about 21.00 the situation began to gradually quiet down. Only at the eastern exit was the sound of enemy tanks and departing vehicles heard well into the night. Terrible road conditions continued to hinder the rapid delivery of vital fuel supplies, so necessary for the continuation of the attack. Refuelling was virtually out of the question before 13 March, as a result of which the division was forced to remain where it was. The time was used to improve the positions which had been captured and deploy appropriate security forces. The Fusilier Regiment GD was moved up to the north and northeast outskirts of Grayvoron to clear the terrain beyond the village of remaining Soviet soldiers. Patrols were also sent north across the Vorskla. New orders awaited the grenadier regiment's III Battalion. Their contents are best reflected in the order III Battalion issued to its companies:

On Reporting Form!

Sender: Date:

III/Gren.Rgt. GD   13. 3. 43 – 00.00 Hours

To 11th – 15th Companies

1. Gren.Rgt. is to reach Kosinka–Glotovo on 13 March, in order to begin probable attack to the southeast toward Udy early on 14 March.
2. March route: Leskovo–Ivany–Berdyny – –
3. March sequence: 1 platoon SFL. 18./ –
                                          III Btl./ –
                                          Rgt. HQ – HQ Comp.
                                          IV Btl./ –
                                          Anti-tank Btl., less 1st Comp./ –
                                          II Btl./ –
                                          1st Comp./Anti-tank Btl. GD
4. Starting time: 04.00 hours road fork 2,000 metres north of Leskovo.
5. III. Btl./ – in following sequence:
    11th Comp./ –, HQ III Btl./ –, 15th Comp./ –, 13th Comp./ –, 14th Comp./ –, 12th Comp./ – at 03.50 hours with leading vehicle 11th Comp./ – at road fork....
6. – – – –
7. – – – –
8. Anti-tank Btl. GD remains attached to the regiment for the duration of the march.

                                          A. B.
                                          Holzgrefe
                                          Lt. and Adj.

Finally, at about 14.00, the vehicles could move again, after all the tanks had been refuelled. The next objective was Borisovka, bypassing Golovchina. I Battalion, Grenadier Regiment was the closest infantry battalion behind the armoured spearhead and its report on the battle provides the most precise, detailed account available:

"At about 12.00 I Battalion moved out of Grayvoron behind the panzer regiment and ahead of II Battalion, Artillery Regiment GD. The armoured spearheads reached 2nd Company's security positions due west of Golovchin at about 13.00, drove up the road north of the lake, but south of the village itself, toward the brickworks, took fire from the north, made a left face and held there for the time being with its front facing north. Flamethrower tanks were deployed with 1st and 3rd Companies to clear the southern edge of the village of the enemy. In the process 1st Company blew up three enemy tanks.

2nd, 4th and 5th Companies initially remained behind as battalion reserve and moved up after the armoured spearhead at about 15.00. The latter had already made first contact with enemy T-34s at the entrance to the village. An intense tank duel resulted, with the enemy tanks positioned behind houses firing at the German attackers from good cover. Feldw. Diesel's tank was knocked out from 5-8 metres in this way. But soon one could see the first burning T-34s, while others sought to escape through the extended village to the east.

I Battalion had followed up in the meantime and likewise advanced as far as the entrance to the village without further contact with the enemy. There the troops left their vehicles and cleared the north end of Borisovka. Orders came to occupy defensive positions at the northern and eastern outskirts of the village, as enemy forces, at least a battalion, were reported approaching from the north. I Battalion's command post first at the western entrance to Borisovka, later in the northeast section in the vicinity of the fire defence tower."

I Battalion, Grenadier Regiment GD secured the area for the evening as follows:

1st Company and elements of 5th Company as battalion reserve. 3rd Company at the multiple intersection at the north end of Borisovka, next to 4th Company whose front likewise faced north. 2nd Company at the east end of the village.

The night passed relatively quietly, even if enemy tanks did make repeated forays into the village and near the eastern outskirts. One T-34 was destroyed from only 12 metres by a light field howitzer of 2nd Battery/Artillery Regiment GD in the immediate vicinity of the battalion command post.

Meanwhile the Panzer Regiment GD sat at the east end of the extended village, guarding to the east without the benefit of covering infantry. The Infantry Division GD's successful advance resulted in an extended northern flank. The hidden danger in this was that an enemy force penetrating from the north could not be countered immediately and in full strength. The positions still under construction; extending from Bol'shaya Pisarevka to the northeast edge of Borisovka, they consisted of a thin line of strongpoints.

Large stretches of the sometimes difficult terrain, especially north of the Vorskla and on the hills, offered an advancing enemy good approach possibilities. Orders were therefore issued for the terrain to be kept under observation to all sides and for the strongpoints to be set for all-round defense at all times. In that terrain the enemy could come from any direction under the sun, especially since it was a certainty that groups of enemy troops separated from their units and unaware of the situation were trying to reestablish contact with friendly forces.

On the other hand, aerial reconnaissance had determined that enemy columns, especially tank and artillery units, were approaching from the east through the Vorskla Valley. Undoubtedly these were units intended for the Battle of Kharkov, but which on account of the greater danger in the northwest had been redirected toward the Vorskla Valley.

Only by quickly concentrating all tanks, anti-tank weapons and the remaining available infantry reserves at the east end of Borisovka was it possible to counter this threat. The bulk of I Battalion/Grenadier Regiment GD was positioned at the northeast outskirts of Borisovka. The Reconnaissance Battalion GD and the Assault Gun Battalion GD were pulled out of their rest area, where they had spent 24 hours carrying out maintenance and repairs to their vehicles and immediately dispatched toward the southeast. Their mission was to disrupt prematurely the reported enemy tank assembly positions through a reconnaissance in force, so as to reduce the strength of the expected armoured assault before it got under way.

The following is the battle report by the reinforced Reconnaissance Battalion GD, which was the first to contact the approaching Soviet armoured forces and thus began the three-day tank battle near Borisovka:

"We set off at 09.00 on 14 March 1943. The reinforced battalion left the east exit from Borisovka, with 3rd and 4th Squadrons riding on assault guns forming the point. At about 09.30 hours the attack spearhead encountered two T-34s on Hill 221.2. The squadrons got down from the assault guns. The enemy tanks withdrew for the time being.

With its broad hills the landscape still presented a very peaceful sight. The 4th squadron with elements of the Assault Gun Battalion GD were sent wide through the hollow north of Stanovoye and reached the hill 2,000 metres north of Point 224.7. Movement by enemy tanks was spotted on the horizon in the area of Point 224.7.

In the meantime 3rd Squadron and 1st Battery/Assault Gun Battalion GD under Hptm. Magold had determined that there were strong enemy forces in Stanovoye. They subsequently attacked the village, whereby Hptm. Magold alone was able to knock out 14 enemy tanks in a daring attack in Stanovoye. By about 11.45 the village was in our hands.

Meanwhile an aircraft dropped a message which stated that about 120 enemy tanks and 80 trucks were approaching Stanovoye. On the basis of this pilot report and the already short ammunition supply, the commander of the Reconnaissance Battalion GD decided to initially withdraw behind the nearest hill at Point 221.2. Under the command of Hptm. Frantz, the assault gun battalion now took the initiative which was to be expected of it.

Battle was taken up with the leading enemy tanks–eighteen vehicles at first–which attacked Point 224.7. Under covering fire from the Magold battery the 3rd Squadron, which was still in Stanovoye, was able to leave the village at the last minute. Thanks to outstanding leadership losses were comparatively light: one killed and six wounded. While 2nd Battery was still covering the retreat, six more T-34s suddenly attacked from the flank. At this, suspecting that the reconnaissance battalion must have burst into the enemy tank assembly point by now, the commander gave orders for all elements to pull back toward Borisovka at once, but the Panzer Regiment GD was already there, ready and waiting for the attacking enemy tanks. The commander's attempt to personally establish contact with the panzer regiment in Borisovka failed, as eleven enemy tanks appeared in front of the village at about 12.30."

An impression of the battle from the point of view of the assault guns was provided by the commander of the battalion, Hptm. Frantz:

"As always, I was glad to receive orders from division to join the Reconnaissance Battalion GD battle group with my battalion. An outstanding teamwork had developed between these two units in the past months. Especially noteworthy was the ability to appreciate the peculiarities of our arm always shown by the commander of the reconnaissance battalion, Major Wätjen. In the morning the assault gun battalion set out from the east end of Borisovka with elements of the reconnaissance battalion riding on the vehicles. The 1st Battery under Hptm. Magold, who had joined the assault gun battalion during the defensive battles at Kharkov at his own request and who first learned to command assault guns during the retreat, took over the point position. The battery soon made contact with enemy forces, including tanks. Personal observation and reports radioed by this battery created the impression that the enemy was massing strong forces. While I was still considering how best to carry out an attack against the recognised enemy, one of our reconnaissance aircraft came toward us at low altitude. We immediately broke out the ground identification panels and fired smoke and illumination shells. The aircraft circled twice, in order to determine whether we were really German troops. Then he waggled his wings and dropped a message canister. We quickly emptied the canister and studied the map sketched by the pilot. According to this, six to eight kilometres distant there were about 100 to 120 enemy tanks and wheeled vehicles rolling toward us. This was it! The 1st Battery was pulled back from its present positions to the south somewhat, but not too far. The 2nd Battery was placed in a favourable defensive position in the area of Point 224.7. The 3rd Battery under Oblt. Wehmeyer was held back as battalion reserve and security forces were deployed to the southeast. There was a general ban on firing until approved by the battalion. Even while the assault guns were taking on as much anti-tank ammunition as they could hold (the normal quantity carried in an assault gun was 48 rounds, in such cases up to 100 rounds were packed in) the lightly-armoured vehicles of the reconnaissance battalion assembled in the direction of Borisovka as ordered. A proper tank battle was in the offing. Then the first T-34s came into view, ten to twelve vehicles. Deployed widely, they came straight toward our hill. The 1st Battery enquired whether it might fire at will. Permission was denied: 'Tell the crews again not to fire beyond 500 meters.' We wanted to give the enemy no opportunity to flee. Wave after wave of tanks came toward us. Some veered slightly north into a small valley and disappeared from our view, but part of our panzer regiment was supposed to be in position there or en route. We left the tanks to them. As soon as the specified firing range was reached the battle began. The first T-34s, five or six tanks, blew up. The next wave halted. They too were struck by the frontal fire. The 1st Battery enquired nervously whether it too might be allowed to join in. 'Not yet!' was the answer. Everyone wanted to knock out his share, but it was not yet clear whether all the reported T-34s were in the bag. Only then was the flanking attack supposed to be carried out with and from 1st Battery's position. More T-34s continued to move toward us. After it was clear that the enemy had not outflanked us to the south, the 3rd Battery was moved up in the direction of 1st Battery. The two assault gun batteries now began a flanking attack from the south against the enemy armoured forces which were attacking 2nd Battery frontally. We saw no T-34s retire. This was one of those rare cases after a successful tank battle when one could accurately count his own successes. Other weapons had not participated in the engagement at this location and we took possession of the entire field. Forty-three T-34s had been destroyed."

In recognition of the assault gun battalion's success in the past defensive battles and not least for this day's outstanding success, battalion commander Hptm. Frantz became the 228th German soldier to receive the Knight's Cross with Oak Leaves. Hptm. Magold, 1st Battery chief, and *Oberwachtmeister* Wegener, platoon leader in the 1st Battery, were both awarded the Knight's Cross. As well, numerous personnel received the German Cross in Gold or the Iron Cross. Here individual names may represent all the brave men of the battalion: Oblt. Wehmeyer, 3rd Battery chief; Obwm. "Mambo" Schmidt, 1st Battery; Lt. Reisenhofer, 3rd Battery; Oblt. Verch, battalion adjutant after the death of Oblt. Schenk and 2nd Battery chief; Wm. Kaspar; Obwm. Kliche, 3rd Battery (formerly senior NCO 1st Battery), who was seriously wounded in the earlier battles. Unfortunately there is not room here to mention all those who are deserving. All those who were there deserve recognition.

In the meantime I Battalion, Panzer Regiment GD had become involved in an intense tank engagement in which *Major* Pössel and his tanks decimated the enemy. Numerous enemy tanks fell victim to his guns, so that the total for the day (including the 21 destroyed earlier by the reconnaissance battalion battle group) was raised to 46. Truly a proud success!

The events of that evening (14 March 1943) and the following day are reflected in a personal account by a Panzer *Leutnant* (Lt. Pawel) of 7th Company, Panzer Regiment GD, who described this tough, but so successful tank battle as follows:

"Things got nasty as dusk fell on 14 March 1943. Machine-gun bullets whistled through the gardens on the outskirts of Borisovka and shells gurgled eerily overhead, recognizable by their bright red luminous trails. It was still quiet in our security sector, however we pressed the earpieces of our headsets tighter to our ears as if spellbound. Radio transmissions by our tanks said that there was feverish activity: enemy infantry was sneaking around our tanks, some were already in their rear; muzzle flashes from every direction, without doubt from enemy tanks.

For three hours there was the sound of heavy fighting; all around the dark night was lit by burning houses. Now and then there was an explosion, hundreds of tracers sprayed into the night sky, the ammunition from a stricken tank. Each man asked himself uneasily: ours or the enemy's? At about one in the morning on 15 March 1943 three attacks by enemy tanks against Borisovka's northern bridge were repulsed and eight T-34s destroyed. The enemy pulled back for the time being. They were undoubtedly gathering for a new operation however.

Then came the radioed order: '7th Company reinforce the defences at the north bridge!' We had been waiting a long time for this. Our four tanks felt their way along the road, the bright fireglow was our objective. We halted a short distance from the bridge and received a quick briefing and our assignments.

We crept across the bridge at safe intervals. Blinded by the glow of the fires, we were still able to see muzzle flashes farther down the street and then the first shells raced past us. We had to get out of there, the enemy had trained all his guns on the bridge. The driver of the first tank quickly realized what was happening; without waiting for orders to do so, he turned the tank off the road and disappeared into the safety of the darkness. The second tank followed close behind the first; the other two also managed to escape into the dark of night. We stayed close together and formed a circle for protection; for the air here, to the right side of the bridge, wasn't exactly pure.

Bursts of machine-gun fire whipped toward us from close range. 'Just keep shooting your machine-guns,' observed my gunner, 'that will make it easier for me to get you.' He was pleased that the Soviet infantry revealed its position in doing so. Several anti-tank shells were also meant for us, but they missed.

In the meantime we had taken up position in a hollow about 200 metres to the right of the road. It was a good firing position, but almost a mousetrap. What if the Soviets overran us and cut off the way back to the bridge? But why think about that; we had orders to hold. No one was about to surprise us, we were much too watchful for that and in the platoon everyone could depend on the others. The platoon leader scouted alternate positions and made contact with our tanks to the left of the road; they took over covering fire for our forward position. After a short briefing to the tank commanders on the distribution of fire, we were ordered to maintain radio silence. We were to open fire only on the radioed order of the platoon leader.

Critical minutes now followed. Suddenly the diesel engines of the enemy tanks roared to life scarcely 1,000 metres away. It wasn't two or even five T-34s, it had to be many more. We had to prepare ourselves for a tough fight!

The morning of 15 March 1943 dawned, the roar of engines slowly drew nearer. The tank leader spotted the outline of the first T-34 over on the road.

The gunners at their sights were already uneasy, but in the twilight they couldn't yet see their targets clearly. They held their breath and finally released their tension with a happy 'Aah' when the first T-34 finally came into the sight's field of view.

The loader meanwhile waited in feverish tension beside his gun, a shell in his hand and two more clamped between his legs; for every second was vital here. The radio operator wore a sceptical look as he once again checked his receiver; why hadn't the tank commander's order to fire come yet? They could already see five T-34s. With trembling fingers he felt along the connecting cables, they were in order. Unsuspecting, the T-34s ground their way through the snow and mud; seven were now in sight and their broadside was too tempting for the gunners.

What if they spotted us too soon? Then it would be better to open fire immediately and without orders. Surely the radio had failed just now! Or had the platoon leader even been put out of action? These and similar thoughts raced through the brain. Nevertheless firing discipline was maintained. Uncertain, the T-34s turned their guns half right and then half left; it was good that we were level with one another. Each gunner had known for some time which enemy tank he had to engage. The first two were the property of the man on the left wing, those following belonged to the comrades echeloned to the right.

Our nerves were stretched to the limit; the tank commanders glanced through their vision slits at the platoon leader's panzer. For a moment the calmness they had shown in many battles seemed shaken. Then, finally, the order we were waiting for: attention...safety off...fire!!! A mighty crash! Four–eight–twelve green, luminous trails of light in a matter of seconds. Between them brief radio transmissions; then only individual shots from our cannon.

Over there huge jets of flame and smoke. The last T-34 tried to turn around and became stuck. The crew jumped like cats from the turret, but were cut down by our machine-gun fire. Our tank drivers waved to each other happily. Now we had to reach the all-commanding hill in front of us, in order to steal a march on the enemy.

The counterattack was a success, but after our return to quarters the company painter had his hands full: for there were seventeen rings to be painted on our gun barrels as victory trophies."

So the second day of the tank battle near Borisovka had begun, 15 March 1943, which brought a defensive victory for the panzers in the early morning. The Anti-tank Battalion GD also played a role in the defence. Its 1st Company was able to knock out three enemy tanks in the sector of the Grenadier Regiment's I Battalion for the loss of one of its guns.

During the afternoon II and III Grenadier Battalions occupied the hilltops north of Borisovka bolstering the infantry complement of the town, which was in the very centre of the battle. The Fusilier Regiment also closed ranks and held the positions left (west) of the Grenadier Regiment GD, likewise facing north. In the afternoon the reinforced Reconnaissance Battalion GD, the bulk of which was defending the east end of Borisovka, received orders to drive via Grayvoron, Bayrak and Alexandrovka to the village of Udy on 16 March. From there it was to reconnoitre to the northeast and determine the whereabouts of the enemy's armoured formation.

Lt. Kollewe of the 13th Company described the impressions of III Battalion, Grenadier Regiment in its new defensive sector on the hills north of Borisovka:

"Off we went, the 13th Company in the point position. Once again there was debris everywhere, left behind by the enemy, in particular large numbers of anti-tank guns; there certainly was no shortage of them here. There was one such gun on every corner. Our panzers had been especially effective in Lokinsky. Masses of dead and weapons of every type lay everywhere. The enemy's losses just here must have been considerable.

Then the column halted on the road for some time. It was no wonder that we were now attacked by Russian aircraft; but their bombs and bullets were off the mark and in the end German heavy fighters prevented them from making further attacks on us. In addition to all this, some enemy tank was firing on the road and we were glad to finally get into Borisovka. We moved into our planned positions. I was given the northern sector: the road to Kryukovo. The steep road was impassable. As well we were told that the enemy was still sitting at the north end of the city. I therefore went back on foot until I reached the security positions of I Battalion. After being briefed I positioned my company in front of the 'collective swine farm' and on Hill 220. My only headache was the forest bordering on the west; but a solution was soon found for this:

II Battalion moved into my sector. I was thus able to send my 2nd Platoon and other elements to defend the wood. Uffz. Gebhard occupied the bridge from Krasny Kutok. In general the day was a quiet one, apart from a number of harmless enemy air attacks. On the other hand we watched with great joy as Stukas attacked Ktyukovo."

The 15th of March was another successful day of aggressive defence. The day's total of knocked-out enemy tanks reached 21. Thus more than 90 enemy armoured vehicles had been destroyed from 13 March up to and including 15 March. The Wehrmacht communique of 15 March publicly acknowledged this success:

"...west of Belgorod the Soviets tried to halt the progressing German attack with fresh forces. The enemy counterattack collapsed with heavy, bloody losses. The Infantry Division GROSSDEUTSCHLAND alone destroyed 44 of 60 attacking tanks in cooperation with the Luftwaffe..."

On 16 March 1943 the enemy again assembled strong armoured forces east of Borisovka, in preparation for an attack on the town the next morning. Twenty-eight T-34s carried out the attack, but after a brief firefight they withdrew to their starting positions. II Battalion of the Panzer Regiment GD under *Major* Thiede subsequently followed the retreating tanks to a point just outside Striguny, where it ran into a wasp's nest of new tank assembly areas. Heavy fighting broke out and II Battalion's situation was precarious for a time. It lost four of its panzers but was able to disengage from the enemy. In any case this action had proved that the Soviets were still not so weak as to allow the division's own attack along the Vorskla to be resumed.

Near Stanovoye the Panzer Regiment's I Battalion set out against a concentration of enemy tanks which had been discovered. The panzers charged into the assembly area, taking the Soviets by surprise. In a very successful engagement the battalion succeeded in disabling or destroying 30 enemy tanks within a few minutes. *Feldwebel* Rapp of 2nd Company, Panzer Regiment GD once again distinguished himself. He had stayed behind with his tank as a result of clutch trouble. While work was under way to correct the problem, Rapp's panzer was attacked by six enemy tanks which emerged from a hollow about 800 metres distant. He immediately opened fire and destroyed three of the T-34s in short order.

These bitter tank-versus-tank battles naturally overshadowed the accomplishments of the infantry. They were more spectators than active participants, and yet it was vital that they were there. For their work lay in the defence against and destruction of enemy infantry, who each time accompanied the attacking tanks in an effort to gain ground.

The infantry were skilled at setting up effective positions, especially those of their 'heavy artillery,' the 150mm infantry guns. This is reflected in a position sketch illustrating the field of fire of the Grenadier Regiment GD's 17th (heavy Infantry Gun) Company.

The 17th of March began quietly. There was no fighting during the morning, which led to the conclusion that the enemy had had enough of the previous day's losses. The fusiliers were moved closer to Borisovka and took over some of the positions formerly held by the grenadiers on the hills north of Borisovka. As well strong patrols were sent into the villages north of Borisovka. What the division was doing was pushing its forward positions as far north as possible while simultaneously freeing up other elements of its infantry for the continuation of the attack toward the east. However in the afternoon these movements and preparations were rudely interrupted. About 12 enemy tanks charged in from the northeast and broke into II Battalion/Grenadier Regiment GD's positions, causing an awful uproar. The defenders managed to destroy five enemy tanks in the first rush. However they could not prevent the remaining seven from entering Borisovka, where they hunkered down. The battle against these tanks went on well into the night.

In spite of the aggravating presence of a small, armoured battle group between its positions, the division command continued its own preparations unperturbed. The division must already have received orders to establish contact with the Waffen-SS units advancing on Belgorod and thus create a continuous line–including the 167th Infantry Division, which was supposedly near Udy.

Planning nevertheless continued, because it had to be expected that the enemy would concentrate his armoured forces, especially in the Vorskla Valley. The GD Division Ia, Obstlt. Natzmer, deployed forces to the southeast. At a suitable moment these were to veer straight toward Tomarovka in a flanking movement, attack the enemy forces near Striguny from the rear and establish a direct link between Borisovka and Tomarovka.

Appropriate preparations were made and the necessary orders issued. The late evening hours of that day, which had ended quietly apart from the uncomfortable but soon insignificant penetration by the enemy tanks, brought a special treat for the men of the Infantry Division *Großdeutschland*: the OKW had acknowledged their accomplishments of the past few days in its daily communique:

"In bitter defensive fighting between the 10th and 13th of March the Infantry Division GROSSDEUTSCHLAND, which is made up of volunteers from every German district, has smashed the bulk of three enemy rifle divisions and two anti-tank brigades and captured their entire complement of weapons. Twenty-nine tanks, 146 guns, and 107 mortars, machine-guns and anti-tank rifles were captured or destroyed in these battles, in which our grenadiers and panzers forced the Soviets to hastily evacuate further territory. More than 400 prisoners and many times that number of dead bolsheviks were counted."

On 18 March 1943 *Generalleutnant* Hoernlein received the Knight's Cross with Oak Leaves. Difficult terrain conditions on 18 March made it impossible to completely eliminate the enemy penetration in the northern part of Borisovka.

Nevertheless the division stuck to its plan and at approximately 10.30 set out toward Stanovoye, with the Panzer Regiment GD leading the way followed by I Battalion/Grenadier Regiment, in order to establish contact with the Waffen-SS to the southeast. The division expected to find the SS troops on the Kharkov–Belgorod road in the vicinity of Besonovka. Advancing enemy tank units were met near Chvostovka and heavy fighting broke out. After destroying 15 enemy tanks the advance was resumed over Point 240.5 toward Besonovka. Due east of the village the division's forces succeeded in establishing contact with elements of the Waffen-SS advancing toward Belgorod. Elements of I Battalion/Grenadier Regiment GD remained in Besonovka during the night to secure the town.

As was expected, there were still considerable enemy forces on the division's still unprotected northern flank, especially between Borisovka and Tomarovka and in particular in the latter village. The next objective was their destruction, and the division command had initiated measures to this end. Following in the path of the Panzer Regiment's southeastward advance were elements of the Fusilier Regiment GD from the northern front west of Borisovka. They were under orders to accompany the panzer regiment in its attack on Tomarovka on 19 March. These were followed, at about 18.30 on 18 March, by the Reconnaissance Battalion GD, once again reinforced by the Assault Gun Battalion GD. Its assignment was to secure to the north abeam Point 228.5, about two kilometres south of Kosytshev. This was to ensure that the panzer regiment was allowed to make its preparations at all costs. At about 22.00 Oblt. Spaeter and his 2nd Squadron reached Point 200.1. There the squadron's armoured personnel carriers and assault guns took up defensive positions in the deep snow, facing Kosytshev, which apparently was still occupied by the enemy. In any case, northbound column traffic from there was observed crossing Hill 222.5. The bulk of the reconnaissance battalion and the assault guns settled in for the night. Most of the fusiliers, who had become stuck in the still deep snow at the outset, spent the night on the badly drifted roads where they suffered terribly from the cold.

Patrols discovered that the terrain over which the attack planned for 19 March was to be made was impassable to wheeled vehicles. The division therefore issued orders for all available tracked vehicles to be prepared for the attack, which was to be carried out solely by the Panzer regiment GD, the Assault Gun Battalion GD and the elements of the Reconnaissance Battalion GD able to cope with the terrain. The infantry regiments, especially the fusiliers, were to follow if and when passable roads were found. The bulk of the Grenadier Regiment GD–less I Battalion–stayed in its positions at the north end of Borisovka and following the capture of Tomarovka set out from there to the east via Striguny.

The war diarist of the Reconnaissance Battalion GD described the course of this skilfully-planned and well-executed attack on Tomarovka on 19 March 1943 by the armoured elements of the Infantry Division GD:

"At about three o'clock in the morning Oblt. Spaeter reported that he and the 3rd Battery of the Assault Gun Battalion GD had repulsed an attack from Kosytshev by six enemy tanks, destroying one. Three further enemy tanks were destroyed toward morning. In the meantime contact was made with the approaching elements of the Fusilier Regiment GD on Hill 228.5, after they had spent the entire night 'milling' their way up the hill in the snow. At 09.30 the 2nd (APC) Squadron and the Assault Gun Battalion's 1st Battery set out to outflank from the right and attack Kosytshev, as the result of an independent decision by the commander of the reinforced Reconnaissance Battalion GD. A battery of I Battalion, Artillery regiment GD watched over the advance. Meanwhile Henschel 129 anti-tank aircraft appeared and, as so often happened in this area, dived on targets beyond Hill 222.5 which could not be seen from the ground. In the meantime several Ratas also appeared and the result was thrilling air combats. One Rata was shot down and spun into the snow about 100 meters in front of the commander's half-track.

Kosytshev was taken at 10.15. The 3rd (VW) Squadron combed the village and secured toward the west. Meanwhile the 2nd (APC) Squadron and the 3rd Battery of the Assault Gun Battalion GD occupied Hill 225.5 and there had a firefight with two enemy tanks which the 'butchers' (Hs 129s) had left alive. The Panzer Regiment GD had meanwhile been called back from its former position to the Kharkov–Belgorod highway to drive back the main body of the enemy located between Borisovka and Tomarovka."

In a fast attack from the east, at 11.50 the regiment rolled through Novaya-Derevnya, drove toward Tomarovka and there veered toward Borisovka in order to approach from the east in the enemy's rear and clear the advance road. The reinforced Reconnaissance Battalion GD joined the first part of the attack and followed to Tomarovka.

The leading elements of the Reconnaissance Battalion GD reached Novaya Derevnya at about 12.15. The road there was impassable for wheeled vehicles. Twenty-nine knocked-out enemy tanks were counted in the village itself–a success for the 'butchers' as well as the Panzer Regiment GD.

No one knew at first whether Tomarovka would be taken in the meantime, our own tanks were off and gone. Oberleutnant Spaeter felt his way ahead with his APCs and finally occupied Tomarovka, which had only been touched on the south side by the Panzer Regiment GD. Together with the Assault Gun Battalion GD's 3rd Battery, enemy troops which showed themselves in Tomarovka were engaged and defeated and two anti-tank guns were captured. The city itself was a field of craters after the earlier Stuka attacks. Scarcely a house was intact, the water tower was leaning steeply, the rail installations were as hard hit as the station itself.

The handful of men of the 2nd (APC) Squadron made their way on foot through the silent city over downed telephone wires, bomb craters and shattered trees. It was dead silent–not a sound far and wide. At the north end of Tomarovka an enemy column was spotted withdrawing to the north and was fired on. The panzer regiment had veered west at the city limits hours ago, and the APCs and assault guns couldn't enter the place because of the destruction. Oberleutnant Spaeter and his handful of crews were alone in this large city and they sought good firing positions for the expected enemy counterattacks.

The hoped-for reinforcements came at approximately 14.00 when the main body of the Reconnaissance Battalion GD at last arrived in Tomarovka. Suddenly a "lame crow," a slow Russian reconnaissance aircraft on skis, appeared, probably unaware of the presence of German troops in the city. Heavy infantry and anti-aircraft fire put a quick end to the bird.

The first grenadiers of I Battalion, Grenadier Regiment under Hauptmann Remer arrived at about 14.30. II Battalion, Artillery Regiment GD followed on foot. They had sought and finally found a way through Doltschik. Hauptmann Remer was temporarily placed under the command of the Reconnaissance Battalion GD and took over the defense of the town to the north and east.

In the evening our patrols encountered weak, retreating enemy forces, which were engaged in laying mines on the highway. On this day there was another stop in the division's offensive movements. The following infantry, which were supposed to occupy the recaptured territory, had not yet arrived. The first priority was to clear the area of isolated groups of enemy stragglers, occupy new positions and above all to conduct reconnaissance to determine the whereabouts of the enemy.

This job was given to the Reconnaissance Battalion GD; the Assault Gun Battalion GD under Hauptmann Frantz and 5th Battery, Army Flak Battalion GD were first released from its command on March 20, 1943.

In preparation for its new mission, the Reconnaissance Battalion GD moved to Pushkarnoye and Streletskoye, from where the individual patrols were sent on their way. The initial results of this wide-ranging reconnaissance showed the division command the latest state of the enemy movements: the Karrasch patrol dispatched toward Cherkasskoye-Olkhovka (and on the Kursk highway) encountered enemy tanks at the crossroads west of Vysokaya. The Meyer armoured patrol had a similar experience, meeting enemy forces in this area. The Rösch patrol, which was sent toward

Sadelnoye at approximately 17.00 that day, was unable to proceed any farther than Point 228.6 because of poor road conditions. The Kablitz patrol found that Dragunskoye was occupied by the enemy.

The outlying villages near Tomarovka were taken in isolated, small-scale operations, some against enemy resistance, which created more favourable defensive positions. In general, however, the units rested and used the opportunity to bring their weapons, vehicles and equipment back to order. On this day the sun broke through with spring-like rays and turned the ground into mud. This halted all movement by the wheeled vehicles. The snow disappeared and the first signs of green showed themselves on bushes, trees and shrubs.

The results of the reconnaissance had meanwhile been collected and revealed the following picture of the enemy to the division in Borisovka:

Enemy holding approximately the following line:

Schopino (about 10 km. north of Belgorod)–Beresoff–Sadelnoye–Dragunskoye–Butovo– Gerzovka, in which he apparently intends to establish a solid defense.

In general the days following March 20 passed quietly, while by night there were isolated enemy assaults on our security forces, some of which were far to the front. Night also brought the Soviet aircraft, especially to Tomarovka, which caused considerable unrest by dropping bombs for hours. On the very day the Reconnaissance Battalion GD was renamed the

Armoured Reconnaissance Battalion GD

March 22, 1943, the division was informed of its planned withdrawal from the front and transfer to a rest area in the rear. The regeneration of the division was to take place in the area north of Poltava. To this end contact was immediately established with the relieving infantry division as well as the 'L.A.H.', the neighbouring unit on the right.

The first units to be relieved were the elements of the Grenadier Regiment GD deployed in Pushkarnoye and the Armoured Reconnaissance Battalion GD in the same town. The corps ordered the Fusilier Regiment GD to undertake another attack in order to establish the main line of resistance to be held by the relieving infantry. This attack succeeded largely without serious fighting; only at Rackovo did heavy enemy resistance have to be broken.

Meanwhile the relief of the units proceeded as planned. I Battalion, Grenadier Regiment and the Armoured Reconnaissance Battalion GD were already on their way back to the new areas on March 24. The spectacle of the withdrawal was more than sad. The vehicles, especially those of the Armoured Reconnaissance Battalion GD, were in such need of repairs that each tractor or other tracked vehicle had to tow two, indeed often four, wheeled vehicles. The bottomless mud on the roads, which had been completely transformed into a thick, brown soup by the horse- drawn vehicles of the infantry, also added to the difficulty of this 'trip home on stilts,' as the soldiers were quick to call it.

It was mainly the 167th Infantry Division which took over the new positions here. On orders from the corps, a mobile reserve, consisting of the main body of the Fusilier Regiment GD, a GD panzer battalion, a GD artillery battalion, the Anti-tank Battalion GD and a pioneer company, remained until it was installed in the main line of resistance. The division began setting up its command post in Oposhnya on the Vorskla on March 26, 1943; it was to remain there until the end of June 1943. The individual units likewise moved into fixed quarters and after several days initiated their individual rest routines with training and regeneration."

"March 28, 1943 turned out to be a special day for many men and commanders, for the 20.00 news broadcast contained the following announcement: 'The Führer and Supreme Commander of the Wehrmacht awards the Knight's Cross with Oak Leaves and Swords as the 27th soldier of the German Armed Forces to Oberst Graf Strachwitz, commander of the Panzer Regiment Großdeutschland.' This was a fitting acknowledgement of the accomplishments of the young panzer arm of the Infantry Division Grossdeutschland. A further high point of the day was the simultaneous awarding of the Knight's Cross to Major Pössel, commander of I Battalion, Panzer Regiment GD."

"The days and weeks of rest and recovery on the Vorskla began. This period is very fondly remembered by all the participants. Wherever they were in the future, the days at Dikanka, Oposhnya, Velikye Budistsche, Poltava and the other quartering areas remained the best time of this war."

CHAPTER 3

REST TIME IN THE POLTAVA AREA

The division had in the meantime gone over to rest status between Kusemin and Poltava. Quarters were occupied in villages along the lovely Vorskla Valley on both sides of the road from Poltava to the north. The city itself, which began Russia's history as a European power with Peter the Great's victory over Karl XII of Sweden in 1709, was the major supply and transfer point for the entire supply of the German units stationed in the area; however, it was also the distribution point for all arriving personnel and supply goods. An endless flow of soldiers streamed into Poltava from home bases, replacement units, hospitals and recovery homes, the "new" to reinforce the units and the "old" to return to their companies, batteries and so on. The journey from home to the field units was described by a young officer candidate of the Anti-tank Battalion GD, who made his first trip to the east after basic training with the replacement-training battalion:

"Cottbus – early April 1943 – main train station – 5:45 P.M. They stood packed close together on the platform waiting for the local train, civilians and women from the Spreewald in their colourful local costumes. The field grey of the uniforms stood out among them. There were men on leave with children in their arms, wives and fiancees waiting with tears in their eyes; many silent thoughts wandered to heaven with the plea for a reunion soon at home.

In the midst of this swarm a group of young soldiers, their uniforms brand-new, the GD stitched on their shoulder flaps and their packs packed as per regulations on their still young and narrow shoulders. Then the voice of the station supervisor sounded over the platform: the train for Posen was leaving with the usual delay. It wasn't overfilled, nevertheless everyone pressed to get on board, and as they stood at the windows – young Hans Hömberg, Ulli Droste, Rold Burmeister, Papa Wahl, Count Steenborg, Siegmund Munke, and whatever their names might be – a high-spirited chorus of voices rang out over the platform: 'tough as canvas, solid as leather, and swift as chee-tahs!' The people looked in amazement at the car, and it was uncomfortable for the old front-line soldiers who once again had to leave home.

What did it matter to these youngsters, who had now got away from their training and no longer needed to suppress their feelings; for there they were standing down below on the platform, the ones 'who had always spoiled their happiness.' The strict training director was disgusted to hear his name in the repeating chorus. Beside him stood the course's 'mother,' Hauptfeldwebel Bordien, who always had to play the fierce senior NCO but who deep down inside was also only a man.

The final minutes passed, the time for departure arrived. Then the old mercenary song rang out over the platform: 'Vivat, now we go into the field...' The wheels rolled in the direction of Frankfurt/Oder. Small groups of soldiers sat together and exchanged the latest rumours over the situation in the Infantry Division Grossdeutschland's sector; others sang soldiers' songs and a harmonica hummed its soft melody. Across the Oder bridge, the river lying shimmering in the moonlight, the city itself dark – it was war after all. Shortly before midnight we had to change trains in Posen. Some freshened up in the waiting room or began writing the first postcards to home, while others ran to the telephone to say a few more tender words of farewell to a beloved maiden now far away.

Warsaw was reached in the morning hours and we assembled in the Wehrmacht home. Here sat the old soldiers from the front on their way home and the stay-at-home fighters from Warsaw, there members of the Todt Organization and the Reich Labour Service – all thrown together, tired and depressed. It was no wonder that a group of somewhat more than twenty men announcing their thirst for action a little too loudly stood out.

Once again the train rolled through the night, soldiers lay in luggage nets and bench seats, the signal lamps flew past, the wheels rattled on the tracks, and in the east the young day was obtruding itself. The train left Lvov. There were scarcely any civilians on board now and everyone stood tensely at the windows and gazed into the countryside. The plain stretched as far as the eye could see; the farm villages were shabby, the mud cottages run down and the straw roofs decayed. Now and then someone called the others to the window enthusiastically on spying a knocked-out tank or the remnants of a system of positions. The train stopped more often now; an ancient locomotive puffed and spewed dense clouds of smoke into the sky; at the stations the crew took on wood for the boiler and at these times women and children approached the cars. The dark sound of the foreign tongue reached our ears, they tried to make us understand and soon the bartering began. Bread was traded for eggs, butter wrapped in paper was exchanged for sundry items of equipment; one was no longer amazed to see men, women and children clothed entirely from Wehrmacht stocks. In the evening still the same monotone landscape as in the morning.

What was the name of the station, the end of the line towards which the train was striving? It was a sort of double name, which one could only pronounce if he coughed, sneezed or perhaps had a bit of a fever! There wasn't a lamp to light the way, just a pale gleam shimmering through the cracks somewhere in the distance, and we stumbled toward our long-awaited night quarters. It was a large dirty room with a few tables and benches, all of them already occupied; the air was thick enough to cut with all the pleasant odours of Arabia and in its midst the smoking wicks of the Hindenburg lamps. The youngsters stood there, not looking the least bit heroic. Their enthusiasm was gone too; now everything was tiredness and filth and – homesickness!

They unrolled their blankets, but dared not spread them out on the dirty floor. Their thoughts turned to bedbugs, lice and fleas and the entire atmosphere lay on their young souls like a great weight. They were disappointed and wanted to sleep but couldn't.

Finally morning came again and they confidently stormed the nicest and cleanest car at the front of the train behind the locomotive. There they stretched out and dozed on the benches, proud of their comfortable seats. – Until a veteran soldier informed them that the front car was vacant on account of the danger of mines and being blown up. However the courage of unreason and the fear of showing their own fear came over them and they felt almost like soldiers at the front in the middle of an action. They were after all already in the war zone. For when they looked out of the slow-moving train, they saw the wreckage of rail cars lying in the bushes and it became clear to them why they stopped at every station and why the train travelled only by day and so slowly.

Almighty God was watching over them, however, and they all arrived safely in Kiev. The train crossed the seemingly endless bridge and the young soldiers saw the green cupolas of the monastery high above on the steep bank. When they finally reached Poltava that evening, the distant front welcomed them with the first air raid alarm.

We gathered in a Russian barracks from the time before the First World War and waited for the vehicles from the units which were to be our future homes. Finally the trucks rolled into the square. There was a hasty farewell to former travelling companions and away we went – to the north.

The countryside on both sides of the road went on into infinity. The road ate its way through the countryside like a shiny snake, insatiable in its width, for countless wheel tracks ran beside it through the wheat fields and over still fallow fields. The boys were also amazed to find a road as smooth as

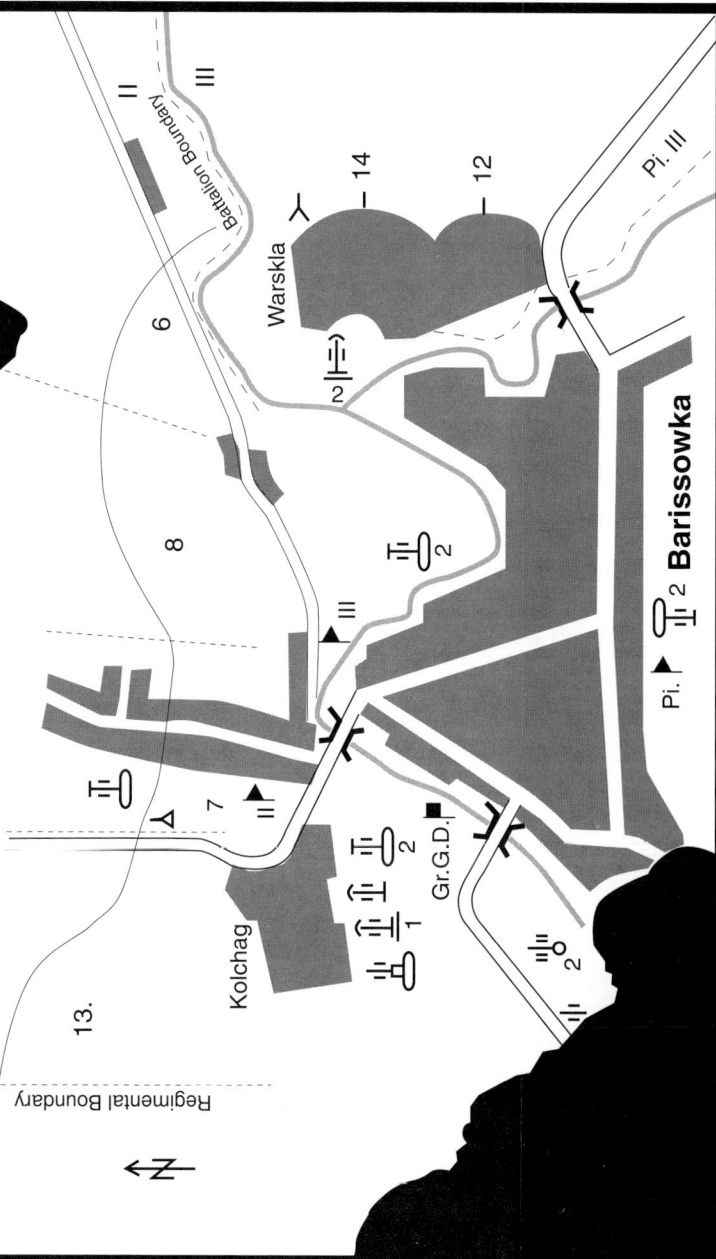

Sketch of Positions
of IV.Btl./Gren.-Regt. GD
on March 18, 1943
in front of Borrissowka

asphalt, but it was just hard-packed top soil, the famous black earth of the Ukraine they had heard about. Gazes wandered back along the road; one saw colourfully-dressed people walking, one here, the other there. A part of the family always seemed to be going somewhere in Russia. The women carried large bundles on their shoulders or backs; children barely half grown dragged unimaginable loads; goats and dogs scattered in all directions whenever a motor vehicle passed too close, and as cool as you please in the midst of this vortex the *pan*, the head of the family. Hours had meanwhile passed; we had passed through villages, signs everywhere warning 'typhus'; been amazed at the colourful diversity of the villages, and suddenly come to a halt in a small village. This was our destination, the quarters of the panzerjäger. Everyone got down from the vehicles. We formed up into ranks and waited for the battalion commander, Major Hacke. Heels clicked together, all eyes snapped front and suddenly we were ordered: 'Everyone around that tree – go – run, run!' Some caught on right away, others later, and so it was an 'open field' that raced across the grass. After they had returned to where the commanding officer was, lungs bursting, the first two were sent to the 1st Company, the rest were assigned as they returned. The six old friends were now separated for good. Gottfried Frenzel took Herbert Kessler under his wing, Siegmund Munke joined with Rolf Burmeister, the two slowest and also the tallest – Brösicke and Horst Walter – went to the 'Third.' Each man placed his pack on his back and they set off, between farms, over narrow footpaths along the hedges, which were showing the first buds, past a pond and through a water-eroded ravine. This was Saytshentsy, the village which was to impart to all of them their first deep impressions of Russia."

Yes this region of black earth, so rich in beauty and fruitfulness, provided the replacements their first and probably most pleasant experiences in the Ukraine. The older ones, those who had waged war in this land for months and years, no longer received this land with the same ardour. They simply took what they could use from it and supplemented their already ample diet with special trimmings.

All in all, the houses in which the soldiers were quartered made a hospitable and clean impression. The arrival of German soldiers brought no change to family life. Usually one room was left to the soldier, the Ukrainian family was partial to a second or side room. In general their lives followed two separate paths, except for the meals.

The Vorskla Valley, whose west bank offered an excellent view deep into the country to the east, was charming. The view of the river valley from the heights was especially unforgettable. The silver band of the Vorskla snaked past the chain of hills on the west bank. It was a shallow, fordable river that flowed through green fields and dark woods. The view to the north and east, over fields and more fields, was endless; to the south were lines of hills with dense, blue-green forests, individual white villages scattered among them.

The best part of the day was spent on training within the units, from squads to regiments, as well as maintenance on vehicles and equipment. At the repair echelons run by the shop foremen, numerous volkswagens, prime movers, trucks, tanks and guns, most of them disassembled into their component parts, stood and waited for repairs. One saw the drivers in their blue mechanic's overalls, oil-smeared and dirty, crawling about the innards of their vehicles; recognized the repair shop man, that specialist so indispensable to the troops, who always managed to put things right with the simplest means; watched the shop foreman or technical officer, who allocated new replacement parts or offered advice. These technicians were the most faithful, indispensable helpers the drivers of the combat vehicles had; it was thanks to their round the clock labour that most of the motor vehicles, tanks and prime movers were always ready for action. In the more dangerous situations – the recovery of a tank from the combat zone, for example – it was not unusual for the men of the repair echelons to have to carry arms while fulfilling their mission of retrieving a valuable piece of military equipment, then using their technical skill to restore it to an operational state.

This period of rest was in fact when the men of the workshops were at their busiest. Some transport sections of the individual battalions were en route to Germany to obtain special replacement parts for the units. The senior transport officer in the division headquarters had his hands full obtaining the parts as quickly as possible from the army vehicle parks. The quick and complete operational readiness of the combat vehicles depended to a large degree on their arrival.

As well as these technical personnel, the battalion IVa was also a busy man. The unit paymaster officials, responsible for feeding, clothing and paying the men, also did their best in this period to provide the units with much new clothing and keep the field kitchens well supplied with food from the country. In the eyes of the troops the best and most well liked paymaster official was the one who supplied the best clothing and food.

Yet another group of specialists stepped to the fore during the time of rest: the W.u.G. people, responsible for weapons and equipment. Each company had its weapons and equipment NCO, who watched over repairs to gun-type weapons and the upkeep of equipment such as gun carriages, gas masks, field glasses and so on, and even undertook minor repairs himself. He represented on a small scale what the repair echelons were to the vehicles on a large scale. His workshop resembled that of a watchmaker. Many modern small machines, special tools, often a magnifying glass as well, were the tools of the trade of these W.u.G. men.

Looming over everything else during a unit's period of rest was the question of supply. The work of the supply chain, taken for granted during periods of fighting, became obvious during these months, as the supply system played first fiddle for the outfitting and the regeneration of the units. On account of the excellent organization of the supply system, in the First and later the Second World Wars a motorized unit could operate eight to ten days without any supply whatsoever.

It was customary for the supply echelon of a battalion to include the following personnel:

> The Zahlmeister (paymaster official) or Intendant (a civilian
> official), responsible for foodstuffs, clothing and pay;
> The Waffenmeister (armourer-artificer official), responsible

for maintaining the weapons in working order;

The weapons and equipment officer, who administered the stocks of weapons, munitions, signals and entrenching equipment;

The engineering officer, in charge of the repair echelons. He was responsible for vehicle maintenance;

The technical inspector, who saw to it that the necessary fuel and tires were delivered;

The senior NCOs of the battalion staff and the companies, with the company clerks, the account and pay NCO, the staffs of the field kitchens, cobblers and so on.

As is generally known, the fighting units tended to look down their noses at the rear-echelon services. "Supply train slave" was one of the more gentle expressions used by the front-line troops to describe their fellows in the rear, "rear-echelon swine" probably one of the most stinging. However both elements were forced to rely on each other for better or worse. Woe to the rear-echelon services if the supply system failed to function! When the system operated smoothly not a word was said of it.

The rear-echelon services often had to battle marauding enemy groups in order to deliver supplies to the most forward elements. Immediately after occupying a new area the battle commander (in most cases this was the battalion paymaster official) had to set up an all-round defence. Many a member of the front-line troops sent to the rear-echelon for a time to rest soon returned to the front because life in the supply organization was too exciting. At the front he had a continuous front and fellow soldiers to the right and left. The "supply train slaves" on the other hand were usually on their own while delivering supplies and had to travel unfamiliar territory by night. Many acts of heroism went unnoticed. What the "supply train slaves" went through to supply their comrades at the front with what was necessary and often more!

The fighting and supply elements were always a whole, and one part could not survive without the other. It is for this reason that the accomplishments of the supply units are mentioned here. In the period 1 April 1942 – May 1943, which saw the operations from Kursk to Voronezh in summer 1942, from the Lower Don to the Manych, the heavy defensive fighting in the Rzhev area in the autumn of 1942, and the defensive battles in the southern sector of the Eastern Front in the winter of 1942/1943, the supply services delivered 30,561 tonnes of munitions, fuel and other important supply goods.

In delivering these supplies, the vehicles of the motor transport companies covered 2,165,144 kilometres, not counting the distances travelled while transferring units. This equates to 50 times around the circumference of the earth

The weeks and months spent at rest by the Infantry Division *Großdeutschland* were used to train the men (the veterans as well as the new ones) on weapons and equipment. This training was based on the wealth of experience gained in the past months of fighting and most of the exercises were based on actual combat situations. The Grenadier Regiment, which had its command post in Dikanka, established an instruction group for its battalions at Balyasnoye, where NCOs were trained on all the weapons used by the regiment. I Battalion provided a rifle company for the group, II Battalion a machine-gun company and III Battalion a heavy company. The focus of the group's efforts lay in terrain and field training.

The Armoured Reconnaissance Battalion set up a close-combat school under Oberleutnant Schubert, which conducted training in offensive patrol operations and the combating of tanks and bunkers from close range. There was a very real reason behind all of the exercises and the ongoing training; it was part of the intensive preparations for a new German offensive, whose objective was the elimination of the salient in the front on both sides of Kursk left over from the enemy's winter offensive. This attack was to lead off a new period of offensive action in 1943 which was to restore movement to the fronts.

The bolshevik enemy's interest in the organization, planning and the probable employment of the German units is apparent from their extremely active espionage network and not just in the area of the front. The well-known Soviet radio net – "Red Orchestra" – was very active in these weeks; it employed every German V-man working for the Soviets it could reach to learn the date of the attack and the armament and number of units involved as quickly as possible. The increased emphasis Moscow placed on ascertaining these details is evident from the radio messages sent by secret unit transmitters in these weeks, which were later made public.

13 May 43:

Dora to Director (Moscow):

(7.5.) – Assemblies of significant Russian forces visible to the Germans near Kursk, Vyazma, Velikye Luki. – OKW considers it possible that the Russian High Command is preparing simultaneous preventive strikes in several sectors, all these attacks based on the attack by Timoshenko in May of previous year aimed at interrupting the German build- up for the attack on Kharkov. –

30 May 43:

Director (Moscow) to Dora:

Urgent. Instruct Lucie to immediately ascertain:

1. Where on the southern sector of the Eastern Front is the German offensive to begin?

2. With what forces and in which direction is the blow to be carried out?

3. Apart from the southern sector, where and when is a German offensive planned on the Eastern Front?

We expect an immediate and detailed response from Lucie. Your sources are capable of answering these questions.

4 June 43:

Director (Moscow) to Dora:

During the next three months your attention and that of your people must be directed at obtaining precise and timely information concerning the plans and intentions of the OKW, the new formations of the German Army and troop transport, and the production and performance of the German aircraft and tank industries.

10 June 43:

Dora to Director (Moscow): – from Werther: –(4.6.) –

The following is all that is known at this time of the decisions taken since 27.5. changing earlier intentions: In the area of the 2nd Army and the 4th Panzer Army, movement of the motorized units assembled for the attack on Kursk were suddenly cancelled on Manstein's order on 28 May. This halted the massing of all mobile units of the 2nd Army and the left wing of the 4th Panzer Army.– Mobile units of the 2nd Army form the right wing of the 2nd Army behind defensive positions. – Left.(26 groups missing) initially postponed. Other changes in dispositions of the army not known. On the other hand.. (2 groups missing). fresh reinforcement of Luftwaffe combat forces on the Eastern Front.–

12 June 43:

Moscow to Dora:

Instruct Lucie to have operatives immediately acquire all information concerning heavy tank called Panther. – It is vital to determine:

1.   Design of this tank and technical characteristics;
2.   Design of its armour;
3.   Flamethrower and smoke discharger installation;
4.   Location of the facilities producing this tank and rate of monthly production.

The German soldier in the east suspected nothing of the treacherous goings on being conducted behind his back, but it did strike him as odd that rumours of a new offensive, which had been circulating for weeks, were continuing. Field training remained the first order of official business and a high level of emphasis continued to be placed upon it. Here, too, the objective was the complete integration of the replacements with the cadres of the individual companies, batteries and battalions

Frequent inspections by high and very high ranking commanders were an indication of the special nature of the training, which was to reach its conclusion in the not too distant future. The list of high-ranking officers who came to observe the exercises conducted by the division's units included General der Panzertruppe von Knobelsdorf, commanding general of XXXXVIII Panzer Corps; Generaloberst Hoth, Commander-in-Chief of the Fourth Panzer Army; and Generalleutnant Balck, acting division commander in the absence of Generalleutnant Hoernlein. All expressed their satisfaction with the high level of training and the good morale of the troops.

In their conversations with officers of the unit they also gave the first hints as to the planned operation, an attack with limited objectives code-named "Zitadelle." *Großdeutschland* was to play a role in the operation together with approximately fifteen panzer and panzer-grenadier divisions.

It was announced that the division was to receive a number of newly-formed units in time for the offensive, some of which would arrive in its present rest area. As was standard practice in the units of the Waffen-SS, a division escort company was added to the Infantry Division *Großdeutschland*. Its intended role was to guard the division command post, as well as serve as a mobile reserve for action at threatened areas of the front. Composition of the company was as follows:

> a rifle platoon
>
> a heavy machine-gun or mortar platoon
>
> an anti-tank platoon
>
> an anti-aircraft platoon
>
> a motorcycle platoon.

In general terms, therefore, the division escort company was a sort of small battle group suited to all operational situations. Eighty-three 3-tonne armoured personnel carriers arrived at Poltava at the beginning of June 1943, planned initial equipment for the APC battalion to be formed from the Grenadier Regiment's I Battalion. They were delivered to I Battalion's quartering area and the men became familiar with the new vehicles and their specific characteristics. It was felt that this new equipment would enable the battalion to improve on its performance in the previous battles. The battalion's outstanding commanding officer, Hauptmann Remer, received the Knight's Cross on 24 May 1943. The Artillery Battalion GD also underwent a reorganization during these weeks, with the addition of IV Battalion under Major Röckner. The regiment's organization was now as follows:

I and II Battalions each had two light field howitzer and one heavy field howitzer batteries, III Battalion two heavy field howitzer and one 100mm cannon batteries, while the new IV Battalion had one rocket and two light field howitzer batteries. As before, the Armoured Observation Battery remained under the direct command of the regiment.

Where the division's pioneers were concerned, their 1st Company was now completely equipped with armoured personnel carriers and a 4th Company, commanded by Oberleutnant Ebbrecht, a wearer of the German Cross in Gold, was formed. The resulting personnel changes are evident from the revised organization of the pioneer battalion:

Commander:	Hauptmann Chrapkowski
Adjutant:	Oberleutnant Bütenbender
Commander 1st Company:	Oberleutnant Wurm
Commander 2nd Company:	Oberleutnant Balletshofer (formerly Oberleutnant Höhne)
Commander 3rd Company:	Hauptmann Hückel
Commander 4th Company:	Oberleutnant Ebbrechht.

The Army Flak Battalion GD likewise changed its outer appearance in these weeks, completely reorganizing its batteries:

> 1st and 2nd Batteries with 37mm guns on self-propelled carriages.
>
> 3rd-5th (heavy) Batteries with 88mm guns.

6th Battery with quadruple guns.

In keeping with the division's expansion in personnel and materiel, there was a not inconsiderable strengthening in the unit's active anti-aircraft defence.

In the Armoured Reconnaissance Battalion GD, rumours intensified that the battalion was soon to become fully equipped with armoured personnel carriers and tracked vehicles. As a precautionary measure new drivers were trained on armoured personnel carriers and tracked vehicles in those weeks, retraining schools were set up and all the necessary measures were taken to take on strength new vehicles and new types of vehicle.

These supplements and new formations for the division undoubtedly marked the beginning of the reorganization of the former motorized infantry division into a panzer-grenadier division. Another move in this direction was the formation of a Third (Tiger) Battalion for the Panzer Regiment GD. The initial organization of the unit had been under way at Sennelager since mid-May 1943 under the command of Major Gomille. The battalion adjutant was Oberleutnant Dallmann, operations officer Leutnant Kerstens and signals officer Leutnant Welke.

Following the holding of Tiger courses at Paderborn, in mid-May the men for the new Tiger battalion began assembling at Sennelager. The quality of the crews was assured, as they were all experienced tank personnel. The men of the new 1st Company, Tiger Battalion were already members of the *Großdeutschland* Division. The new 2nd Company, Tiger Battalion was formed from soldiers of the 30th and 31st Panzer Regiments, while the personnel of 3rd Company, Tiger Battalion came from the 18th Panzer regiment.

Later, when III Battalion was incorporated into the Panzer Regiment GD at the front, the companies were renumbered:

> the former 1st Company became the 9th Company under Hauptmann Wallroth
>
> the former 2nd Company became the 10th Company under Hauptmann von Villebois and Oberleutnant Arnold
>
> the former 3rd Company became the 11th Company under Oberleutnant Bayer

The Tiger battalion was organized as follows:

> Headquarters with H.Q. Company, consisting of:
>> signals platoon with 3 tanks
>> scout platoon with motorcycles
>> pioneer platoon with 2 APCs and 4 trucks
>> flak platoon with 4 quadruple guns
>> reconnaissance platoon with 7 APCs
>
> 9th Company
> 10th Company – each with 14 Tigers
> 11th Company
> a heavy workshop company

The rest period included more than work on the expansion of the division and the ongoing training courses and field exercises. Time was also set aside for sport, leisure, relaxation and amusement. KdF groups went from quarters to quarters, offering amateur plays and theatre pieces; in the evenings groups of soldiers travelled to Poltava to see the famous Bolshoi Theatre and its excellent Russian entertainers. "The Gypsy Baron" was performed in German more than a hundred times and it was always received with great enthusiasm by the soldier audience.

Company evenings and battalion parties were held frequently, and with plenty of alcohol consumed offered a change in routine. It may have been at one of these parties that a song which soon found a place in the hearts of many soldiers was born. Many weeks and months later men could be heard humming the melody of the song in their foxholes and bunkers. The words to the first verse were

We're always jolly fellows and best cavaliers too,
my friend Meier, my friend Lehmann, and me.
We frequent the best coffee houses,
my friend Meier, my friend Lehmann, and me.

Boozy parties were not the only order of the day, however; there were other notable highlights as well. A concert of military music was held by torch-light on the evening of 20 April 1943 and was very well received by every-one.

Among the officers present were two who had received the Knight's Cross of the Iron Cross in the past weeks: Rittmeister Wätjen, commander of the "Hussars Battalion," decorated on 18 April 1943, and Hauptmann Frantz, commander of the Assault Gun Battalion GD, who on 14 April became the 228th soldier of the Wehrmacht to be honoured with the Knight's Cross with Oak Leaves for outstanding leadership and willingness to act.

In the final days of April 1943 orders were issued for elements of the division to move nearer the front, into the wooded country around Akhtyrka. Under cloudy skies the battalions of the Grenadier regiment GD marched north through Oposhnya and Kotelva, parallel to the Vorskla, bound for new quarters near Akhtyrka. They were followed at the beginning of May by the Assault Pioneer Battalion. The engineers were there to level the advance roads and reinforce the bridges in the area of the front in preparation for new action as part of Operation "Zitadelle." Because of the weight of the new panzers all the bridges had to be capable of bearing 60 tonnes.

The Panzer Regiment GD's I Battalion and elements of the Division Signals Battalion GD also moved into the assembly area near Borisovka. Movement had returned for some elements of the division and a return to action seemed to be imminent.

However, on or about 9 May, orders suddenly arrived to cease all movements. The offensive had been postponed for some time.

The bulk of the division remained where it was, undisturbed by all the to and fro, while the elements which had been moved forward set about establishing themselves in their new quarters. Training was resumed and the uninterrupted service routine continued. Because of uncertainty as to the enemy situation a mobile reserve was formed, which consisted of the following units:

> Grenadier Regiment GD
> I Battalion, Panzer Regiment GD
> I Battalion, Artillery Regiment GD
> 3rd Company, Assault Pioneer Battalion GD

All further march movements were forbidden and all practice radio traffic was banned.

In the Field Replacement Training Battalion GD, whose ranks were filled by a steady stream of replacements from Germany, the drilling and preparations for action continued unabated. While the training for the coming battles was in full swing, an order from Führer Headquarters reached the division, to the effect that:

"As per an order of the OKH, effective 23 June 1943 the Infantry Division GD is to be designated

Panzer-Grenadier Division GROSSDEUTSCHLAND.

This change reflected the reality of the increased allotment of tanks to the division and its equipping with a large number of armoured vehicles and the further expansion of the unit toward a panzer division. From now on the regiments called themselves panzer-grenadier and panzer-fusilier regiments and the word "panzer" soon appeared in every unit designation. The men were proud of this renaming; it raised them from the mass of former infantry divisions and added them to the list of fully motorized and armoured divisions.

They also knew of course that the weeks of rest were in fact about to come to an end. All the signs pointed to a return to action soon as part of Operation "Zitadelle" and the owners of the homes where the soldiers were staying were already whispering the date, which had been set at 29 June 1943, in their ear. It was a phenomenon which the soldiers still greeted with a sceptical smile, for they could not imagine that there were so many gaps in the net of secrecy that the population had the date of the offensive before they did themselves, but unfortunately it was so, and this was to have unpleasant consequences in the following weeks.

CHAPTER 4

WACHBATAILLON GD

Throughout the months of 1942 the routine of the *Wach-Bataillon Berlin* remained basically unchanged. The various watches were still mounted, honour companies were detached for receptions in the Reich capital and the successors to the former *Wach-Regiment Berlin* carried out their duties guarding the capital.

On 1 October 1942 the battalion was renamed

Wachbataillon GROSSDEUTSCHLAND

and thus became a part of the larger unit. Commander of the battalion was Oberstleutnant Gehrke, who stayed in close communication with the replacement units in Cottbus, with which an active exchange of personnel was maintained as with the division at the front. The watch battalion was increasingly becoming a collecting point for wounded and injured GD soldiers.

In autumn 1943 the watch battalion was required to detach an Honour Company GD to Belgium in addition to all the other tasks that it had to carry out. The company, which was equipped with Volkswagens and motorcycles, formed the guard for the Belgian king in Laeken Castle; the bulk of the unit was quartered in a barracks located only about 400 metres from the castle. The company commander was Leutnant Görlitz, senior NCO was Hauptfeldwebel Schimmelpfennig. Each day a platoon from the honour company fell out for guard duty at the castle, while a squad was always stationed at a hunting lodge. The soldiers frequently came into contact with the daughter of the King as well as Countess Rèthy, and as time went on a comfortable, friendly relationship developed between the soldiers and the court. The German soldiers were aware of their mission and approached it conscientiously with discretion and without treating those they were guarding as vanquished opponents. The behaviour of the guards was appreciated by the royal couple, who were supposed to feel the pressure of confinement as little as possible.

The German commander of Belgium and northern France, General von Falkenhausen, likewise welcomed the presence of a GD unit and the maintenance of a guard at his headquarters by GD soldiers. A squad always stood guard over the commander. General von Falkenhausen once declared that this honour company was probably the most capable combat unit in his area – at least at that point in time.

In the Reich capital itself the manifestations of total war were becoming increasingly evident. The Allies, who now were waging war against Germany on numerous fronts, sought to crush the morale of the population and destroy production sites through concentrated air attacks. Berlin became a frequent target and the bombers opened their bomb bays over the sea of houses that was the Reich capital. In spite of Germany's reinforced air defences, more and more Berlin dwellings were reduced to rubble.

With the growing frequency of enemy air raids another significant role was added to the duties of the *Wachbataillon GD*. The battalion and its men were increasingly called upon to help in rescuing people buried beneath rubble, in clearing away debris and in the repairing of vital installations.

In past years the number of foreign worker camps in the suburbs and outskirts of Berlin had grown dramatically. Watching over these was becoming an increasingly serious mission, and the *Wachbataillon GD* became involved. The tens of thousands of foreign workers employed in the German war industry, most of whom were unwilling conscripts, posed a growing threat to the inhabitants of the Reich capital. The authorities feared insurrections and revolt, the first sign of which would be work stoppages.

The command centres for the units stationed in and around Berlin developed an emergency plan, according to which these units would go into action in the Reich capital on the release of the code word "Walküre" (Valkyrie). The plan, developed by General Haupt, was intended to regulate the intervention of the troops against internal unrest and enemy parachute attacks and assist in enemy air raids.

All affected units had a copy of the order contained in a sealed envelope. As a result of the plan closer ties were established between the *Wachbataillon GD* and the Replacement Brigade GD in Cottbus, which was to prove valuable in the course of later events.

Division combat operations resulted in an increase in the demand for personnel as did the formation of new units for the division and other formations like the *Führer-Begleit-Bataillon*. On the other hand more and more convalescents were streaming from the hospitals to Cottbus. All this forced the Replacement Brigade (motorized) GD to carry out expansions of its units as well. The city's barracks installations had been inadequate for some time; the convalescent units, whose number was growing all the time, were usually moved to villages in the immediate surrounding area, while the barracks were reserved exclusively for the training of recruits. The demand for officer and non-commissioned officer replacements led to the creation of corresponding institutions; the training of specialists such as radio operators, telephonists, artillerymen, pioneers, tank drivers, armoured scout car crews and many others forced the brigade to form new companies and training groups, all of which had to be accommodated somewhere.

In the course of renaming many of the motorized infantry divisions as panzer-grenadier divisions, the name of the GD replacement and training unit in Cottbus and Guben was also changed. In April 1943 the former Replacement and Training Brigade (motorized) GD became the Panzer-Grenadier Replacement and Training Brigade *Grossdeutschland*.

During these weeks the GD replacement unit carried out a minor reorganization which resulted in the following external picture:

Panzer-Grenadier Replacement and Training Brigade
GROSSDEUTSCHLAND

Panzer-Grenadier Replacement and Training Brigade GROSSDEUTSCHLAND

Brigade Headquarters: Cottbus, Schillerstraß

Brigade Commander: Oberst Bandelow

with: Panzer-Grenadier Replacement and Training Regiment GD

(new artillery barracks in Cottbus)

Regimental Commander:Oberstleutnant Stirius (Major Bethge, Oberstleutnant von Courbiere, Oberstleutnant Schwarzrock)

Regimental Adjutant: Oberleutnant der Reserve Maeck (Oberleutnant der Reserve Bensinger)

Unit Vk.:   Military Administrative Advisor von Diepow

I Panzer-Grenadier Replacement and Training Battalion GD

as before

II Panzer-Grenadier Replacement and Training Battalion GD

(Alvensleden Barracks)

reformed as of 1 April 1943

Battalion Commander: Hauptmann von Heinitz

6th (M.G.) Training Company

7th (M.G.) Training Company

8th (heavy infantry gun) Training Company: Oberleutnant Lange

The former III Replacement and Training Bri was divided into:

IV Panzer-Grenadier Replacement and Training Battalion1

(Guben)

Battalion Commander: Hauptmann Walle

one anti-tank training company

one anti-tank training company

9th (Panzer-Grenadier) Training Company

10th (Panzer-Grenadier) Training Company

from 1944/45 also

11th (Panzer-Grenadier) Training Company:

12th (Panzer-Grenadier) Training Company: Obert. Weißenborn

III Panzer-Grenadier Replacement and Training Battalion

(Sachsendorf Barracks)

Battalion Commander: Hauptmann Trinks

9th (Pioneer) Training Company: Oberleutnant E. Kruger

10th (Signals) Training Company

11th (Signals) Training Company

12th (Pioneer) Training Company

Panzer Artillery Replacement and Training Battalion

(Guben)

Battalion Commander: Major Theermann
as before

Panzer Troops Replacement and Training Battalion
(Hermann Löns Barracks)
Battalion Commander: Major Senfft zu Pilsach
as before

The latter replacement battalion bore the name Panzertruppen Replacement and Training Battalion and was organized as follows:

Headquarters
1st-3rd Panzer Replacement and Training Company
4th Armoured Reconnaissance Squadron
Convalescent Company

In late autumn 1943 Major Hudel was named to command the battalion. As the Armoured Reconnaissance Squadron, in particular, received a rapid flow of convalescents at the end of 1943, making it more difficult to house everyone in the Hermann-Löns Barracks, some members of the replacement squadron moved into alternate quarters in Kiekebusch. Some of the men who went there were already trained and were available to the field forces as fit for active service personnel.

All the wounded and sick from the field forces were incorporated into the convalescent company in Madlow near Cottbus. Tank men recovering from wounds or injuries were included in the same company. The men remained in the convalescent company until certified fit or unfit for active service. In the latter case they were released from active army service. Personnel fit for active service received expanded training in the replacement squadron until they returned to the field forces. In order to meet the demand for replacement junior commanders, in April 1943 the Junior Commanders Instruction Company GD was formed under Oberleutnant Herbig. The company was quartered with and administered by I Battalion. Two OB (officer candidate) platoons were formed from the former OB platoon. Also administered by I Battalion, these were led by Oberleutnant Tisowski and Leutnant Alberti.

At the same time the 5th Reserve Officer Candidate Company under the command of Hauptmann Zetsche (later Oberleutnant Lauck) was stationed in the Sachsendorf Barracks with three supervisions.

1st Supervision: Oberleutnant Lauck
2nd Supervision: Oberleutnant Doege
3rd Supervision: Leutnant Leonhardt

Of the 90 candidates for officer training about 45 wanted to pursue active service. Almost half of the candidates were students from the Adolf Hitler Schools or Romanian officers. Some of the latter were long-time officers, several had even been decorated with the Michael Order, the Romanian decoration for bravery. Nevertheless, they participated in the entire training program, including the subsequent proving period at the front with the field forces. Later the Rumanians were transferred to the Waffen-SS in spite of loud protests.

Finally in late autumn, October 1943, the various officer candidate units

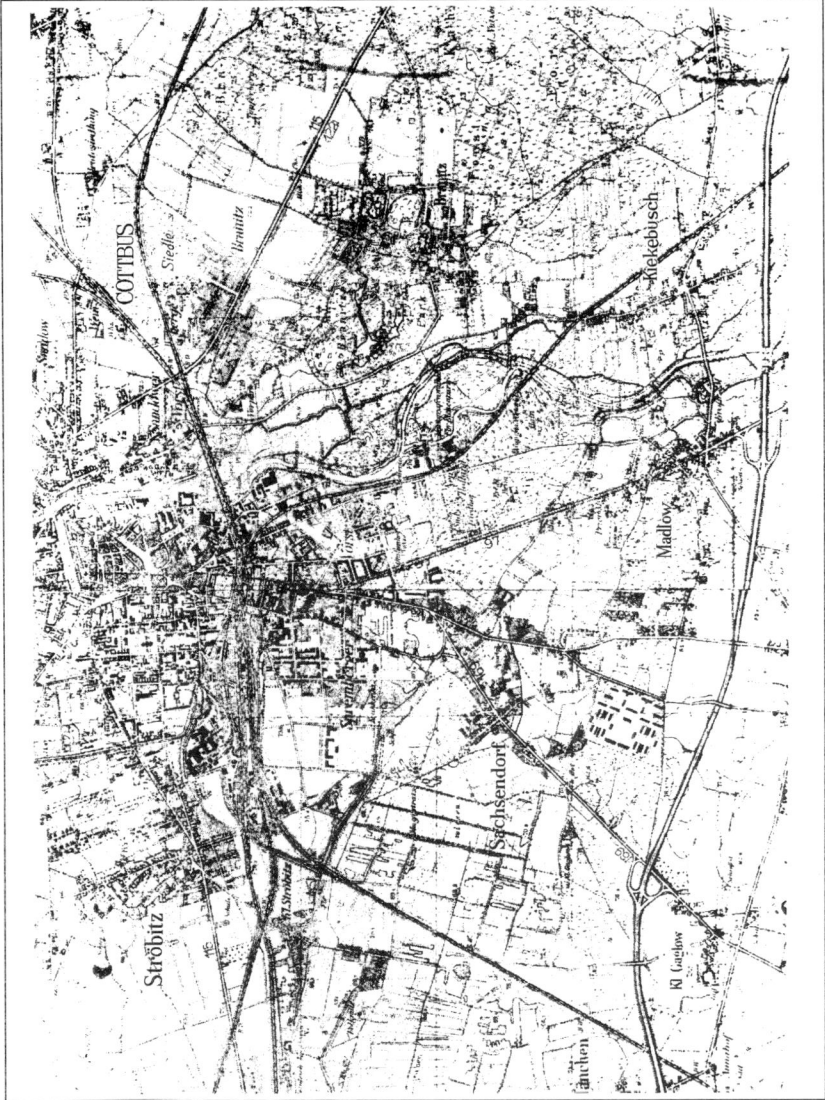

Cottbus

were combined in an Officer Candidate Company under Hauptmann Zetsche that formed the foundation for the officer candidate school which appeared later. All in all the service routine in Germany with the replacement units consisted of drills with live ammunition to prepare the men for action at the front. Understandably, those who came to the replacement units from hospitals as convalescents were not well disposed toward further training, having already trained before seeing their first action. They preferred to fill their time with leave and the comforts of life offered by their stay in Germany, whereby Cottbus and its inhabitants, who were very well disposed toward the soldiers, gladly helped out. A description of life in such a trained replacement or convalescent company prior to departure for the front is provided in an account by the former commander of a replacement company, Oberleutnant Dr. A. Metzner:

"The Sielowaners"

Leaf through all the lexicons, search all the atlases, scour all the books, records and archives, ask the world's geographers; you will not find the Sielowaner race. But they did exist: in Sielow, at the edge of the Spreewald, in Buckwar, their ancestral castle! Based there was a replacement and training company of the GD. And I had the honour to spend about six months among this constantly changing tribe.

The Replacement Training Brigade GD in Cottbus was a vital part of the GD unit. As well as drilling the replacements, the final polish was placed on convalescents there. However the personnel there also developed and tested new training methods and tried out new combat tactics, though only blanks were used. First-class leader and junior leader training was carried out there, and as well the recruitment of volunteers was conducted throughout the entire the Reich. At this time Oberst Bandelow, known as 'Prince Bandelow,' led the replacement and training brigade and filled the position very successfully. Not only he, but also Oberstleutnant Stirius, who elegantly directed the Infantry Replacement Regiment through almost the entire war, solidified our reputation at home, which was stamped by feats of arms at the front, psychologically, politically and propaganda-wise. We took full advantage of the character of the Replacement Training Brigade, its efforts to always come up with something new, the freedom we had in one of the somewhat isolated small villages that housed the company command post with our hostess 'Mother Buckwart,' and the gentle, trusting leadership of Hauptmann Beug, known to us all as 'Father Beug.'

We also worked hard at close-combat tactics and carried out tough endurance marches in order to accustom the soldiers to the rigours of the Russian Front. I explained to them the reason for such tough exercises, which could spare much blood and personally led field marches carrying rifle and assault pack. At the end we trained almost exclusively at night, even practised on the firing range at night for by now the war had also been largely moved to the night.

The usual orders arrived when a part of a company was ordered to the front: no outgoing letters or parcels, all leave cancelled and a strict ban on visitors. I felt it more reasonable to do the opposite. I granted special leave to the city for the mailing of parcels."

Preparations for a possible action in Berlin began to take up more time alongside the duties of training and educating the necessary replacements. The code-word "Valkyrie" also applied to the replacement training brigade. As one of the units based near the capital, it had to always maintain a unit at readiness in case a crisis might arise in Berlin. During the night of 31 July 1943 there was another of the familiar alarms, but this time it was for Berlin. The Combat Battalion GD was hastily assembled and placed under the command of Rittmeister Kuehn. The unit consisted of three heavy companies:

1st Company:	from the Junior Leaders Instruction Company under Oberleutnant Herbig, with two rifle platoons, 1 heavy machine-gun and mortar platoon and a pioneer platoon.
2nd Company:	with heavy weapons, such as heavy infantry guns, under Oberleutnant Lange.
3rd Company:	with armoured cars, motorcycles, anti-tank platoon and a tank platoon (Panzer II and IV) under Rittmeister Strauch.
4th Battery:	with one platoon each of light field howitzers and 20mm flak under Oberleutnant Kirsten.

The unit possessed a very mixed assortment of vehicles. It drove to the Blankenfeld area where quarters were occupied. The purpose of this action by the battalion was to be at the disposal of the military commander of Berlin and carry out a number of propaganda marches in strength in front of the various foreign worker camps, especially on Friday – payday. Nothing exciting took place during this time however; Berlin remained quiet. As a result the battalion returned to Cottbus on 21 August 1943.

Subsequent actions by specific units of the Panzer-Grenadier Replacement and Training Brigade GD, which mainly involved clearing, rescue and assistance actions in the Reich capital, took place under the special code-word "Ikarus." The first of these actions ran from 25 November to 10 December 1943. The unit's area of operations was Rüdersdorf and Köpenick, from where the units were moved into the city to provide assistance.

While the main body of the *Führer-Begleit Bataillon* was taking part in the winter fighting in the Kharkov area with the Infantry Division *Großdeutschland*, all that remained behind in the actual headquarters was a reinforced security company under Hauptmann Bölk, which continued the guarding of the city. In the absence of "Battle Group Pohlmann" the company received replacements from Cottbus, in order to enable the unit to meet its commitments but also to allow it to fill the gaps in personnel after the return of the battle group.

The exhausting duties in Führer Headquarters continued; numerous visits by foreign and allied heads of state required the soldiers of the army stationed there to provide frequent honour guards. They also had to be equal to any special missions assigned them and many difficult situations demanded skilled decisions. One such case occurred during the Christmas season. A representative of the Romanian government was visiting Hitler at the "Wolfsschanze" installation, while at the exact same time a representative of the French Vichy government was on his way to Führer Headquarters. Hitler wanted to avoid a meeting of the two delegations and left it to the commander of the headquarters to see to it that there was no meeting. Soon after the return of "Battle Group Pohlmann" in the early days of April 1943 there was a reorganization of the *Führer-Begleit Bataillon* at Mielau Troop Training Grounds and the escort battalion was simultaneously renamed the Führer Grenadier Battalion.

from:	became:
H.Q. FBB	H.Q. FGB
H.Q. Company, FHQu.	1st (Grenadier) Company
	2nd (Grenadier) Company
	3rd (Grenadier) Company
	4th (Heavy) Company
	5th (Panzer) Company
	added:
	4th (Heavy) Replacement Company
	5th (Replacement) Company
	Vehicle column

After a temporary return to the "Wolfsschanze" installation the battalion once again transferred to the Stablack and Zichenau Troop Training Grounds in East Prussia, where it was to complete its field training based on the battle group's experiences. On its return to Rastenburg, East Prussia in the second half of June 1943 the unit was again reorganized and its name was changed back to the *Führer Escort Bataillon*

from:	became:
one grenadier company	1st (Panzer-Grenadier) Co. (armoured)
3rd Grenadier Company	2nd (Panzer-Grenadier) Company
1st Grenadier Company	3rd (Panzer-Grenadier) Company
4th (Heavy) Company	4th (Heavy) Company
5th (Panzer) Company	5th (Panzer) Company
	6th (Flak) Company (new)
2nd Grenadier Company	7th (Fast) Company
	Vehicle column

This organization of the *Führer Escort Battalion* was intended to allow it to keep up with the ever-increasing scope of its watch duties, even though battle groups repeatedly had to be sent to the front, usually in winter.

The rigours of guard duty at Führer Headquarters and the strict rules for the soldiers involved in it, are revealed in the watch standing orders of the 2nd Grenadier Company commanded by Oberleutnant Janssen, which were written on 31 December 1942. The most important regulations are reproduced here:

Watch Standing Orders
for the Northwest and Southwest Field Watches of the
"Wolfsschanze" Installation

1. Duties of the Field Watches:

(a) The "Northwest" Field Watch guards the northwestern and northern outer perimeter of the "Wolfsschanze" Installation (right boundary: path 25 metres west of M 13 – M 12; left boundary: Görlitz Station – Schwarzsteinroad at Görlitz head forester's house); "Southwest" Field Watch the southwestern outer perimeter (right boundary: Görlitz Station – Schwarzstein road at Görlitz head forester's house, left boundary: airfield road at "South" Watch) against all attacks, monitors all pedestrian and vehicular traffic in and out of the installation and employs all means necessary to prevent unauthorized entry into the security zone.

(b) The "West" Watch is subordinate to the "Northwest"Field Watch, the "South" Watch to the "Southwest" Field Watch. The role of the "West" and "South" Watches is to monitor all pedestrian and vehicular traffic entering or leaving the installation. The papers of every person not known to the watch (including members of the Wehrmacht) are to be checked, entrance to the installation denied to the unauthorized and passes issued to persons with a valid reason for entering the installation. As well day passes issued by other watches are to be collected when the holders leave the installation.

2. Strengths of the Watches

1 officer or Feldwebel

1 enlisted man

(a) **Field Watch Northwest**
2 non-commissioned officers
27 enlisted men

(b) **Field Watch Southwest**
1 non-commissioned officer
18 enlisted men

4. Watch Superiors:

(a) the Führer

(b) the Chief of the OKW

(c) the Commanders-in-Chief of the three branches of the Wehrmacht

(d) the commander of Führer Headquarters or his deputy

(e) the commander of the Führer Escort Battalion

(f) the local commander

(g) the company commander of the 2nd Grenadier Company

(h) the local duty officer

(i)   the officer of the watch and his deputy

5.   **Salutes and Reports:**

(a)

(b)

(c)   Salutes and reports by individual sentries and patrols: Sentries and patrols on duty or on the way to or from the watch building will only salute the Führer and Supreme Commander of the Wehrmacht, as well as officers and offi cials of the Wehrmacht of officer rank, the SS and members of party organizations from Standartenführer up, if they approach to within saluting distance (about 30 meters).

10.   **Relief of Watch:**

Relief of the watch takes place daily at 12.00. The watch period lasts 24 hours. Relieving personnel shall assemble in the watch barracks at the disposal of the officer of the watch. The night patrols are to make their way to the watch bar racks at 17.30 and not return to their quarters until their last relief. Sentries and patrols are relieved on the officer of the watch's order after the guard mount is sounded. Relief of the patrols is to take place in roughly the centre of the guard area on the highest point in the terrain. The officer of the watch is responsible for ensuring that the relieving of the guard is carried out punctually and as per regulations. When the sentries and patrols go off duty he is to ensure that each man is equipped as required by regulations and is wearing a clean watch uniform.

11.   **Role of the Field Watch in Detail:**

Unless expressly advised otherwise, the sentry is forbidden to put down his weapon, to sit down, to lie down or lean, to eat, to drink, to smoke, to sleep, to talk unless he has official information or instruc tions to pass on, to accept gifts, go beyond his sentry area or to leave it before he is relieved.

Special Instructions to Sentries

6.   Sentries and patrols are responsible for security in their sen try and patrol areas and for security in the terrain immedi ately bordering them. They are to monitor and check all per sons and vehicles, watch for changes in the barbed wire bar rier and maintain a constant watch on the terrain in their area. Every sentry and patrol shall check the mail boxes, machine-gun posts, bunkers and towers, the air-raid trenches and telephones in their security area at least once during each relief. Contact is to be established with the neighbour ing sentry or patrol. The patrol area is to be patrolled in such a way so that no part of the terrain remains unobserved, while the sentry or patrol remains out of sight. By night the guard patrol route must be changed to enable the aims of the watch to be met in the prevailing visibility.

OPERATION "CITADEL"
Army Group Center and Army Group South
July 5, 1943

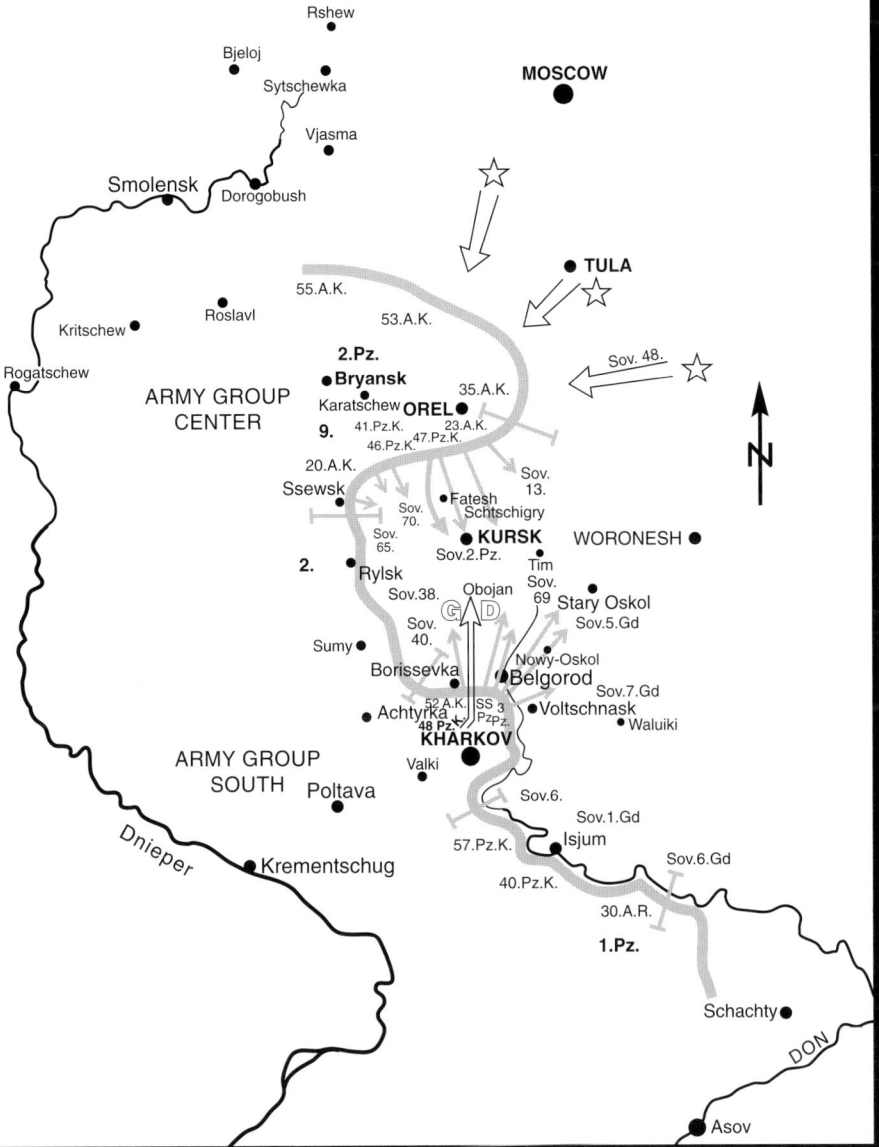

Rshew

Bjeloj

Sytschewka

MOSCOW

Vjasma

Smolensk

Dorogobush

TULA

55.A.K.

53.A.K.

Sov. 48.

Kritschew

Roslavl

Rogatschew

2.Pz.

ARMY GROUP CENTER

Bryansk

Karatschew

OREL

9. 41.Pz.K. 23.A.K.

46.Pz.K. 47.Pz.K. 35.A.K.

20.A.K.

Ssewsk

Sov. 13.

Sov. 70.

Fatesh

Schtschigry

Sov. 65.

KURSK

Sov.2.Pz.

WORONESH

2. Rylsk

Sov.38.

Obojan

Tim Sov. 69

Stary Oskol

G D

Sumy

Sov. 40.

Sov.5.Gd

Borissevka

Nowy-Oskol

Belgorod

Sov.7.Gd

Achtyrka

52.A.K. SS 3 PzPz.

48.Pz.

KHARKOV

Voltschnask

Waluiki

Valki

Sov.6.

ARMY GROUP SOUTH

Poltava

Sov.1.Gd

Isjum

Dnieper

57.Pz.K.

Sov.6.Gd

Krementschug

40.Pz.K.

30.A.R.

1.Pz.

Schachty

DON

Asov

103

Part II

ZITADELLE—AND THE AFTERMATH

CHAPTER 1

THE ATTACK

4. 7. 43 – 12. 7. 43   Attack in the Kursk area.

13. 7. 43 – 17. 7. 43   Defence of Kharkov

18. 7. 43 – 5. 8. 43   Defensive battle in the Orel-Briansk area

6. 8. 43 – 14. 9. 43   Defensive battle in the area west of Kharkov

15. 9. 43 – 27. 9. 43   Defensive battle in southern Russia and the fighting withdrawal to the Dniepr

28. 9. 43 – 31. 12. 43   Defensive battle at the Dniepr.

When the muddy period brought operations to a halt at the end of March 1943, both opponents on the Eastern Front had been battling each other in bitter fighting for nine months. In spite of the employment of all their forces, the Russians had been unable to prevent the Germans from reestablishing a firm front in the south and they were even forced to endure painful defeats. Furthermore, by voluntarily abandoning the salients in the front in the central and northern sectors, the German command had forestalled Russian intentions of excising these. The Russian armies badly needed to rest, regroup and replace their losses. They still carried the main burden of the battle. The German armies had undoubtedly suffered considerably, but as the counteroffensive south of Kharkov showed, they were still capable of quick and effective counterblows. The Russian command therefore felt it advisable to thoroughly overhaul its fighting instrument and not seize the strategic initiative for the time being.

On the German side a decisive operation like those of the previous two summers was now out of the question. This was due both to the heavy losses of the past year and the constantly growing strength of the Red Army, which was receiving a steady flow of supplies from its own armaments industry, which had grown tremendously, in addition to materiel from America. Furthermore the past year had provided clear evidence of the increasing flexibility of the Russian command in mastering operational situations, as well as of the undiminished tactical superiority of the German troops on the battlefield.

If a decisive success in the east could no longer be expected from offensive operations, it was obvious that the war should go over to the defensive. The German front was deep in enemy territory, it had sufficient room behind it to allow flexible withdrawals in the face of threatened Russian breakthroughs and subsequent surprise counterattacks to wear out and grind down the attacking force of the Russians. The last thing the Germans could afford was to offer the enemy an opportunity to destroy entire armies through strategic pig-headedness, often politically induced, as they had in the year past. The German field forces were so experienced and in spite of all the losses so conscious of their superiority over the enemy, that they were fully capable of a strategy of an operational war of attrition. Muddy periods, shortenings of the front and the quiet times that followed were very beneficial to the German divisions. The shock of Stalingrad had passed. Numerous units, including all the panzer divisions and a not insignificant number of infantry divisions, were pulled out of the front and were trained in an almost peacetime fashion. By implementing large-scale relief measures, even the divisions still in action at the front were able to withdraw units of up to regiment strength, place them in rest status and conduct weapons training.

Hitler may have realized that an offensive along the entire width of the front was out of the question. He did not, however, adopt a policy of letting the enemy attack first, in order to then strike him with a counterattack and inflict telling blows from a defensive posture. Instead he tried once again to seize the initiative from the enemy. The Eastern Front ran in roughly a straight line from Leningrad to west of Rostov. The sector chosen for the attack was a Russian salient west of Kursk, almost 200 kilometres wide and approximately 120 kilometres deep.

Operation "Zitadelle" was laid on for March-April 1943, with the intention of striking the enemy while he was still weak.

According to the directives issued by the OKH, the salient around Kursk was to be pinched off through a pincer attack against its corner posts by Army Group Centre – from the north – and Army Group South – from the south – and the enemy forces inside destroyed. The attack obviously entailed considerable risk for both army groups: the attack by Army Group Centre, Generalfeldmarschall von Kluge commanding, had to be made from the southern front of the Orel salient. Just as the enemy-held front around Kursk projected west deep into German lines, to the north the Orel salient, held by Army Group Centre, jutted east deep into the enemy front. As a base for launching Operation "Zitadelle," it offered the enemy the possibility of an enveloping attack, which if successful would threaten the rear of Army Group Centre's forces engaged in "Zitadelle."

The danger in Army Group South's area lay in the fact that the Donets region had to be held at all costs. Its exposed position offered the enemy the possibility of carrying out an attack from two sides with superior forces.

Undoubtedly it was true that the longer the enemy was given to restore his battered forces, the greater the risk to the army groups must become. Surprise was out of the question. The planning and scheduling of Operation "Zitadelle" were in the hands of the Commander-in-Chief of Army Group South, Generalfeldmarschall von Manstein, who had also made initial preparations for the use of German attack troops. A military study of this operation written by him after the war (von Manstein: *Verlorene Siege*, Athenäum-Verlag, Bonn, 1955) described the deployment and strength of the German forces as follows:

Army Group Centre

Ninth Army (*Generaloberst* Model)

Assault Group

XXXXVI Panzer Army Corps

    102nd Infantry Division

    258th Infantry Division

    7th Infantry Division

    31st Infantry Division Gruppe Manteuffel

XXXXVII Panzer Army Corps

    6th Infantry Division

    20th Panzer Division

    2nd Panzer Division

    4th Panzer Division

    9th Panzer Division

XXXXI Panzer Army Corps

    18th Panzer Division

    292nd Infantry Division

    86th Infantry Division

    10th Panzer-Grenadier Division

Attacking from the southern front of the Orel salient, these three corps had to break through an enemy front about 50 kilometres wide, with the two flanking corps simultaneously providing an offensive screen for the flanks of the attack spearhead. However the two neighbouring infantry corps to the east and west (east XXIII Army Corps, west XX Army Corps) were to expand the breakthrough front if the situation permitted. To these two corps also fell the job of guarding the deep flanks of the breakthrough group. Air support for 9th Army's attack was to be provided by the 1st Fliegerdivision.

Little more could be expected of the Second Army, which was holding a front of about 200 kilometres west of the Kursk salient with only nine weak infantry divisions, than that it engage the enemy forces facing it in order to enable the attack groups to encircle them.

It was possible to give Army Group South a greater scope for the "Zitadelle" offensive, since it had assembled two armies with a total of five corps with 11 panzer and 7 infantry divisions for the attack.

ARMY GROUP SOUTH

Fourth Panzer Army (Generaloberst Hoth)

LII Army Corps

    57th Infantry Division

    235th Infantry Division

    332nd Infantry Division

XXXXVIII Panzer Army Corps

> 3rd Panzer Division
> Panzer Grenadier Division *Großdeutschland*
> 11th Panzer Division
> two-thirds of the 167th Infantry Division

II SS-Panzer Army Corps

> Leibstandarte SS Adolf Hitler
> SS-Division Das Reich
> SS-Division Totenkopf
> one-third of the 167th Infantry Division

Armeeabteilung Kempf (attack sector)

III Panzer Army Corps

> 168th Infantry Division
> 6th Panzer Division
> 19th Panzer Division
> 7th Panzer Division

XI Army Corps

> 106th Infantry Division
> 320th Infantry Division

XXIV Panzer Army Corps

> Army Group reserve
> 17th Panzer Division
> SS Division Wiking

In the opinion of the army group high command, it was important for the deployment of the armies that the enemy commit his powerful operational reserves, standing east and northeast of Kharkov, into the battle straight away. At least as important as the drive on Kursk to pinch off the enemy forces in the salient, was offensive action to screen the assault from enemy armoured and mechanized units rushing to the scene from the east. For their destruction was also to be a significant objective of Operation "Zitadelle."

Armee-Abteilung Kempf was to continue holding the defensive front on the Donets from southeast of Kharkov to abreast Volchansk with one infantry corps. Offensively, it was given the task of screening the breakthrough operation toward Kursk to the east and northeast with one infantry and one panzer corps (a total of 3 panzer and 3 infantry divisions). In carrying out this mission the Armee-Abteilung had to break out of the Volchansk-Belgorod front on the Donets. The infantry corps would capture a defensive front to the east along the Korotsha, while the panzer corps would have to advance northeast in the general direction of Skorodnoye. A second panzer corps built around the 2nd Panzer Division, which was at first held back as army group reserve, was supposed to be placed at the disposal of the Armee-Abteilung as soon as it had won enough ground and freedom of movement to the northeast. Together with the first-named panzer corps, it was then to join the battle in open country to smash the enemy armoured units hurrying to intervene in the battle.

To the Fourth Panzer Army under Generaloberst Hoth was to fall the actual breakthrough to Kursk – toward the Ninth Army – and then the destruction of the enemy forces cut off west of Kursk. For this task it had under its command two panzer corps (including an SS panzer corps) with a total of 6 panzer and 1 infantry divisions, while a further infantry corps (LII Army Corps) was to join the attack on the western wing of the armoured attack group. If the breakthrough to Kursk and the destruction of the cut-off enemy forces succeeded relatively quickly, then the armoured units of the Fourth Panzer Army would also be able to take part in smashing the enemy's approaching operational reserve.

Obviously the two armies were allocated all the army artillery sent to the army group by the OKH as well as everything that could be made available in their own areas. Nevertheless, the artillery available to the attackers was extremely weak for a breakthrough through a positions system.

A further weakness lay in the fact that the panzer divisions had to be placed in the front line for breaching the enemy positions, because the OKH could not provide further infantry divisions for this purpose.

The attack by the two armies was to be supported by Luftflotte 4, with which the army group had worked successfully for so long. Unfortunately the air fleet's former commander, Generaloberst von Richthofen, was called away to Italy just prior to the attack. The forces of the Luftflotte available to support the attack consisted of 3 Stuka, 2 close-support and 4 bomber Gruppen."

The attack, which had been planned for weeks, was repeatedly postponed by Hitler in spite of the opinion expressed by the military commanders that he should either launch the attack early or abandon it altogether. Hitler, influenced by statements made by Generaloberst Model, wanted large numbers of Panther tanks, which had recently gone into production and which Model promised would assure a particularly decisive success. While, at the beginning of May 1943, there were approximately 686 panzers and 160 assault guns available for Operation "Zitadelle," as of 3 July 1943 a total of 1,081 panzers (half of which were Panzer IIIs) and 376 assault guns were ready for action.

German preparations for the attack on the Kursk salient had not escaped the notice of the Russians. In addition to their practice of immediately and thoroughly expanding every position, they built an extremely deep system of positions with wire obstacles and tank traps which was strongest in the deep flank of the salient, where it was bolstered by numerous tank-killing weapons. Strong reserves stood ready behind the threatened sectors of the front.

On 29 June 1943 the Panzer-Grenadier Division *Großdeutschland* received the definitive departure order for the assembly areas on the Vorskla northwest of Tomarovka. All preparations were made, the men anticipated a return to action.

On 30 June 1943 the units moved over dusty roads and paths into their areas, not without the familiar delays and traffic jams on the approach roads. Nevertheless, everything pressed "forwards" into the assembly areas.

Also in the endless columns of units streaming forward were the Kfz. 15s of 3rd Company, Panzer-Fusilier Regiment GD, then under the command of Oberleutnant Graf von Schwerin. Its strength that day was 2 officers, 15 non-commissioned officers and 104 enlisted personnel. It was one of the many companies of the Panzer-Grenadier Division *Großdeutschland* that in a few days would form the backbone of the expected infantry battle. Here are the names of those men, who like every other company were ready to put their lives on the line in the coming battles:

Company Commander *Oberleutnant* Graf von Schwerin

Company H.Q. Squad

Company H.Q. Squad Leader	Feldwebel Fuhrmann
Runner	Gefreiter Gabriel
Runner	Gefreiter Schultz, H.
Runner	Gefreiter Haase
Medic	Gefreiter Heidel
Dispatch Rider (heavy)	Gefreiter Zudger
Dispatch Rider (medium)	Gefreiter Andreas
Car Driver (heavy)	Obergefreiter Bartsch
Dispatch Rider (medium)	Gefreiter Schröder

1st Platoon

Platoon Leader	Feldwebel Kauert, Leutnant von Bremen

Platoon H.Q. Squad

Runner	Gefreiter Pennecke
Runner	Gefreiter Liebehenschel
Medic	Fusilier Ortenstein
Car Driver (heavy)	Obergefreiter Hess

1st Weapons Squad	**2nd Assault Squad**
Unteroffizier Teuber	Unteroffizier Gräfe
Obergefreiter Brill	Gefeiter Shulz, M.
Gefreiter Blänkner	Füsilier Hecht
Gefreiter Kowalewicz	Gefreiter Bodenberger
Gefreiter Härdtle	Gefreiter Schönknecht
Obergefreiter Glaser	Gefreiter Hohenegger
Füsilier Schorch	Gefreiter Lerke
Unteroffizier Deichsel	Gefreiter Pöhl (heavy car driver)
Obergefreiter Bunge	
Gefreiter Sommerfeld	
Gefreiter Jaap	
Füsilier Höwer	

Gefreiter Cardinal (heavy car driver)

3rd Assault Squad
Obergefreiter Uhrig
Fusilier Kaisers
Oberfusilier Großer
Fusilier Geilen
Gefreiter Braun
Gefreiter Völzke
Gefreiter Fintz
Gefreiter Ziolek
Gefreiter Zoufall (heavy car driver)

2nd Platoon
Platoon Leader   Feldwebel Sadeck

Platoon H.Q. Squad
Runner   Fusilier Abend
Runner   Gefreiter Hartmann
Litter Bearer   Fusilier Cremers
Car Driver (heavy)   Gefreiter Zaretzki

4th Weapons Squad
Unteroffizier Rauch
Obergefreiter Hildebrandt
Oberfusilier Tenelsen
Gefreiter Gliese
Gefreiter Neumer
Gefreiter Zedow
Oberfusilier Becker
Unteroffizier Dübbelde
Gefreiter Hannemann
Gefreiter Müller, G.
Gefreiter Buchholz
Gefreiter Schulz, R. (heavy car driver)

5th Assault Squad
Ubterofizier Stief
Füsilier Rompf
Gefreiter Püchner
Füsilier Lisiecki
Gefreiter Kremp
Füsilier Holl
Füsilier Heuer
Gefreiter Deckwerth
Gefreiter Focke (heavy car driver)

6th Assault Squad
Unteroffizier Schmitt
Obergefreiter Saßmannshausen
Gefreiter Mayerhofer
Gefreiter Copek
Gefreiter Fuchs
Fusilier Krüger, F.
Gefreiter Beckmann
Gefreiter Brückner (heavy car driver)

3rd Platoon
Platoon Leader — Feldwebel Meischke

Platoon H.Q. Squad
Runner — Fusilier Traue
Litter Bearer — Fusilier Schurig
Range-Finder — Obergefreiter
Endler Car Driver (heavy) — Gefreiter Puhlmann
Squad Leader — Unteroffizier Kursch

1st Mortar
Gefreiter Ruppenthal
Gefreiter Daesler
Gefreiter Hanke
Gefreiter Richter
Gefreiter Ostendorf
Gefreiter Gorwa
Gefr. Weil (heavy car driver)

2nd Mortar
Füsilier Prange
Füsilier Schmolke
Füsilier Schapitz
Oberfüsilier Bock
Gefreiter Döring
Füsilier Kröger
Gefr. Schröder (heavy car driver)

Fuel Truck
Driver — Gefreiter Skiba
Co-drivers — Obergefreiter Selinger
Gefreiter Brohm
Gefreiter Schulz, E.
Feldwebel Pfänder

Combat Train
Motor Vehicle Repair Squad
Senior Technical Sergeant — Oberfeldwebel Hennig
Mechanics — Gefreiter Schulz, E.
Gefreiter Lehmann, R.
Gefreiter Bohm (car driver)
Senior Driver — Gefreiter Sparmann
Motorcycle-Sidecar — Gefreiter Bradler
Medium Motorcycle — Gefreiter Gilbrich

Combat Train
Senior NCO — Hauptfeldwebel Muche
Equipment Officer — Unteroffizier Spies
Field Cook — Gefreiter Pirzer
Driver Large Field Kitchen — Fusilier Lohse
Driver Small Field Kitchen — Gefreiter Mahler
Field Cook Large Kitchen — Gefreiter Niesche
Field Cook Small Kitchen — Gefreiter Schulz, W.
Refueller — Obergefreiter Selinger

Orderly Office Driver   Gefreiter Grossmann
Driver Weapons & Equipment Car   Gefreiter Graßmann
Heavy Car Driver   Gefreiter Palm

Baggage Train

Accountant and Pay NCO   Gefreiter Mathesius

It is 2 July 1943; the individual units move into their assembly areas. The panzer-grenadiers set up their command post due south of Mostshenoye, while the division moves its forward command post into the wooded area west of the village. Tension lies over the responsible men, according to whose plans – in conjunction with those of the neighbouring divisions and the command centres – the attack will take place in the following days.

The terrain itself is hilly, broken by wooded areas and stream beds, some deeply eroded. The bottom land in the latter appears to be swampy. In the background a railroad runs from southeast to northwest, behind it a long, sweeping line of hills which blocks the view into the enemy hinterland. What lies there? Aerial photos show a maze of trenches, gun positions and anti-tank ditches – often kilometres long, earth bunkers and dug-in tanks in large numbers, then more trenches, apparently well-manned. Two strong defensive lines are made out, one near Cherkasskoye and one behind it, about at Dubrova. These seem to be the main defensive lines, this is where the battle will break out in all its severity.

Up front at the main line of resistance all is quiet. The static divisions positioned there have no direct contact with the enemy. Only patrols from both sides tread the ground between the fronts. The German positions are in the ground, before them a meadow and a brook, behind an almost commanding hill which just blocks the view to the north.

The division faces a difficult mission. It is in the attack's point of main effort. The day before the actual assault it must launch a surprise attack and take the commanding hill in order to acquire observation positions for the artillery and deprive the enemy of a view of the German preparations. The attack sector for the focal point division is consciously kept narrow; it measures barely two kilometres. Farther to the right is the 11th Panzer Division, still farther to the right the panzer divisions of the SS-Panzer Corps, while to the left, roughly in the area of Sybino, the panzers and armoured personnel carriers of the 3rd Panzer Division wait to attack.

Both regiments of the Panzer-Grenadier Division *Großdeutschland* have moved up. On the right the Panzer-Grenadier Regiment GD has assembled in valleys and ravines on both sides of Mostshenoye. During the afternoon III Battalion under Hauptmann Senger relieves a part of the static division south of Vasokoye in order to get as close to the enemy as possible. In the valley south of Loknya the panzer-fusiliers wait in the bushes and wooded areas. Their III Battalion under Hauptmann Polk also moves up to the main line of resistance, for together with its sister battalion of the panzer-grenadier regiment it is scheduled to storm the hill lying before them in the afternoon hours of 4 July. The panzers move up through the unfamiliar terrain behind the assembly area of the panzer-fusiliers, mainly by night. They include an independent Panther brigade with nearly 200 of the new, 44-tonne vehicles, which following Hitler's will are supposed to be the decisive element in Operation "Zitadelle." The attackers have been waiting for them; they expect everything of them.

But the men are sceptical. During the march into the assembly areas observers frequently noticed bright jets of flame spurting from the exhaust pipes, saw how now and then a Panther caught fire, forcing the crew to scramble clear to save themselves. More than six burnt-out Panthers littered the advance road. What would happen when the real thing began?

As well the crews of the new tanks did not seem exactly familiar with the conditions of the east. They wore new uniforms, which in itself said nothing; but most of them had not yet fought in the east at all, did not know the battle tactics of the bolshevik tanks, knew scarcely anything about the toughness of the enemy and his craftiness.

In these days it was the pioneers who had the hardest work to do: clearing mines! On the night before the attack alone, the Assault Pioneer Battalion GD's 2nd Company under Oberleutnant Balletshofer cleared more than 2,700 mines with only somewhat more than 10 men, and did so without loss. Where a fortified position had to be breached, the success of the attack depended to a decisive degree on the artillery. The guns had to smash a gap in the system of positions with their concentrated fire, especially at the focal point of the attack, while at the same time screening the flanks. Under the covering blanket of the artillery fire the infantry was then to break through the enemy positions, throw back the enemy and gain ground.

The commander of the Panzer Artillery Regiment GD, Oberstleutnant Albrecht, described the enormous, unforseen difficulties which the artillery faced in this sector, based on his own experiences:

"At this moment the mission of the artillery was to clear a path for the division by placing sharply-concentrated fire on the point of the break-in. However it immediately became clear to me that all we could speak of in this case was pinning down the enemy at first. Although the artillery of the units to our right and left – the 11th and 3rd Panzer Divisions – as well as army artillery was supposed to be placed under our command for the initial barrage, the promised quantities of ammunition were sufficient for only a short time. A sustained barrage, such as one remembered from the First World War, was therefore out of the question. In any case I was proud to have at my disposal artillery in the strength of three regiments, even if the affair had one or perhaps two hitches:

1. The German static divisions, from whose area we were to begin the attack, had no direct contact with the enemy. Between the fronts lay hilly terrain, which although traversed by patrols from time to time prevented a precise view into the Soviet system of positions. No one, none of the responsible infantry or artillery leaders, had ever really seen the enemy positions! And now, on the afternoon of the day before the attack, this terrain was to be taken in a surprise attack and the main assault made from this area!

Naturally for us artillerymen this was especially uncomfortable. For only after the Soviet positions had been located through days, even weeks of careful observation, could the fire be placed where it belonged.

2. The artillery could only reach the forward edge of the Soviet positions from the existing positions of the static divisions' artillery (insufficient range!). It was therefore necessary to make a change of position at the moment when a carefully-measured system of positions was vital and an extensive net of communications had to be available. Also it could only occupy the new positions area with or just behind the infantry. This meant that in this case we gunners would not see the enemy positions until very late on the day before or even the day of the attack itself. Time was therefore very short!

A difficult mission; it could be accomplished, but only if everything went well and above all if signal communications could be established in time and maintained. For there wasn't much time to prepare the positions; but how were the firing areas to be assigned to the individual regiments and battalions? How were the observation posts and position areas to be assigned? On the afternoon of the day before or on the morning of the day of the attack itself seemed completely out of the question, because it was simply too late.

Then came the saving inspiration: we needed aerial photos! We got them and they were very pretty, but unfortunately taken from a considerable height. A maze of trenches. Which were manned and which were dummy positions? The photo assessment centre of the 'Flivo' (air liaison officer) expressed itself cautiously and said, 'probably dummy positions.'

Work-filled days began. Discussions were held with the artillery commander, the subordinate units, the division and especially with the infantry, in particular with the fusiliers, in whose area lay the point of the main attack. We had to correct their expectations, which were much too high: there would be no sustained bombardment, and the actual barrage would only last so many minutes! We repeatedly emphasized that it had to be exploited. Finally the firing plan was ready. The Ia, General Staff Oberstleutnant von Natzmer, had allowed us to work quite independently and approved all the measures we proposed. This trust had to be justified!

At about 15.00 on 4 July 1943 the infantry, with III Battalion, Panzer-Grenadier Regiment, led by 11th Company, on the right and III Battalion Panzer-Fusilier Regiment farther to the left, launched a surprise attack in driving rain. The attack had a limited objective, namely the line of hills. However, with its excellent observation sites on the hills, the Soviet artillery quickly saw through the plan and inflicted the first, painful losses. All of the artillery commands had moved their vehicles as close as possible and waited for the order to move forward. Scarcely had our infantry begun climbing the opposite slope when the armoured observation and signals vehicles roared off, driving in a zigzag pattern like warships, in order to avoid the well-aimed enemy artillery fire. Miraculously there were only minor losses in men and vehicles.

In the course of the briefings all the commanders had been warned of the possibility of mines. We were soon proved correct. The damned things were everywhere. Hauptmann Theermann, commander of I Battalion, Panzer

Artillery Regiment GD, had already had his second armoured observation vehicle blown up from under him, signals vehicles were put out of action. Hauptmann Kuhlmann, the battery commander, was severely wounded by an exploding mine. The bad news poured in. Everyone moved through the terrain only with extreme caution. What had happened to our planned tempo? I had serious doubts that we would be able to make it at all by dawn of the day of the attack! Would the complicated and out of necessity so sensitive artillery fire control mechanism be ready by early morning? Oberleutnant Gröss and Oberleutnant Burchardi, the adjutant and operations officer, worked feverishly.

Hauptmann Maiwald, regimental signals officer, raced about setting up the lines. Everything would be highly provisional; there wasn't time to lay double lines. The main thing was that we had the lines together by the time of the big barrage; after that the commanders could fire by tactical viewpoints."

The attack on the afternoon of 4 July 1943, which was led off by a Stuka attack at 14.50, proved to be a difficult affair, contrary to expectations. Resistance and other obstacles were stronger than expected. Immediately after the last bombs fell, 11th Company, with the main body of III Battalion, Panzer-Grenadier Division GD behind it and supported by the 1st Battery of the Assault Gun Battalion GD, the 1st Company, Anti-tank Battalion GD and the 4th Company of the Assault Pioneer Battalion GD, stormed forward toward the hills. Losses mounted, but by about 16.00 the right section of the line of hills due west of Butovo was taken. Heavy mortar and anti-tank rifle fire were indicative of the strength of the enemy. At almost the same time as the attack began, waves of enemy fighter aircraft appeared and intervened in the fighting on the ground. From the unit on the right – the 11th Panzer Division – which had also taken part in the attack, it was learned that it had veered toward Butovo at about the same time. At precisely 16.45 the new positions were firmly in German hands and the view to the north was clear. Farther left, with III Battalion, Panzer-Fusilier Regiment GD, things did not go quite so well. The battalion commander, Hauptmann Bolk, lost a leg to a mine and had to be evacuated to the rear. There too the troops moved toward the slope in driving rain, however it was hours before it was reached. Very well-aimed enemy artillery and mortar fire repeatedly forced the attackers to halt and start again. The hill due southeast of Gerzovka was finally taken after darkness fell and the position nearest the Russian forward outposts was occupied. The attack's objective was finally reached, but at the cost of very painful losses.

So, after an at times very difficult struggle, the starting point for the great attack on July 5 was reached and the conditions for the moving up of the tanks and artillery achieved. While the infantry dug in up front and exchanged fire with the enemy, among the artillery the tension and excitement mounted. The men in the command posts and the gun positions knew that everything depended on the initial effects of the barrage. If that went wrong, everything went wrong. Here is a continuation of the account by the commander of the Panzer Artillery Regiment GD, Oberstleutnant Albrecht:

"Look at the clock; one a.m. My God, it will be light soon, they still have to range in – if all goes well. Time is quickly running out. Several battalions have reported ready to fire. The ranging in begins. However there is still no contact with our neighbours and the army artillery under our command.

Then finally Major Süßmann, commander of II Battalion, comes and says, 'My operations officer has just been killed in the hole beside me. Head torn off, frightful! We are ready to fire, adjustment fire complete.'

A bright spot, in spite of the sad news; the closest battery has completed its adjustment fire, but contact with the infantry is still broken because the panzers are fumbling about the country. Even the Panzer-Fusilier Regiment GD has no better information concerning the battalions. They have their own worries.

A half hour to go. 'Contact, Maiwald?' — 'Not yet!' Another quarter hour passes, there's only ten minutes until the attack begins! It's enough to drive one to despair. The successful start to the summer offensive depends on my barrage.

'Contact established!' shouts Maiwald triumphantly; we are in touch with all the units!! All the command posts are called; they report ready to commence firing. Now just let the line hold until I call for the barrage. The adjutant repeatedly calls the command posts to see if they're all really still there. At last it's time. The barrage will begin in one minute!

I begin to count. Ten seconds to go. 1 2 3 4 5 6 7 8 9 – fire!

There is a single, rumbling crash; shells roar, howl and hiss over our heads toward the Soviet positions. The barrage! Thank God! Everything goes as planned. How grateful and glad I am! Now the infantry must move out, I think, especially the fusiliers, III Battalion."

Yes – the infantry left its positions and attacked, but there was something wrong with the fusiliers. The Panzer Regiment GD and the panther brigade were supposed to attack with them, however they had the misfortune to drive into a minefield which had escaped notice until then – and this even before reaching the bolshevik trenches! It was enough to make one sick. Soldiers and officers alike feared that the entire affair was going to pot. The tanks were stuck fast, some bogged down to the tops of their tracks, and to make matters worse the enemy was firing at them with anti-tank rifles, anti-tank guns and artillery. Tremendous confusion breaks out. The fusiliers advance without the tanks — what can they do? The tanks do not follow. Scarcely does the enemy notice the precarious situation of the fusiliers when he launches a counterattack supported by numerous close-support aircraft. The purely infantry companies of III Panzer-Fusilier Regiment GD, or the 11th, 12th and 13th Companies, walked straight into ruin. Even the heavy company suffered 50 killed and wounded in a few hours. Pioneers were moved up immediately and they began clearing a path through the mine-infested terrain. Ten more hours had to pass before the first tanks and self-propelled guns got through and reached the infantry.

Once again the account by the artillery commander reveals the precarious state of the situation during this exciting phase:

'The enemy fire is especially heavy before the attack lanes of the fusiliers, but the tanks? Where are our tanks? Aren't they supposed to move out with

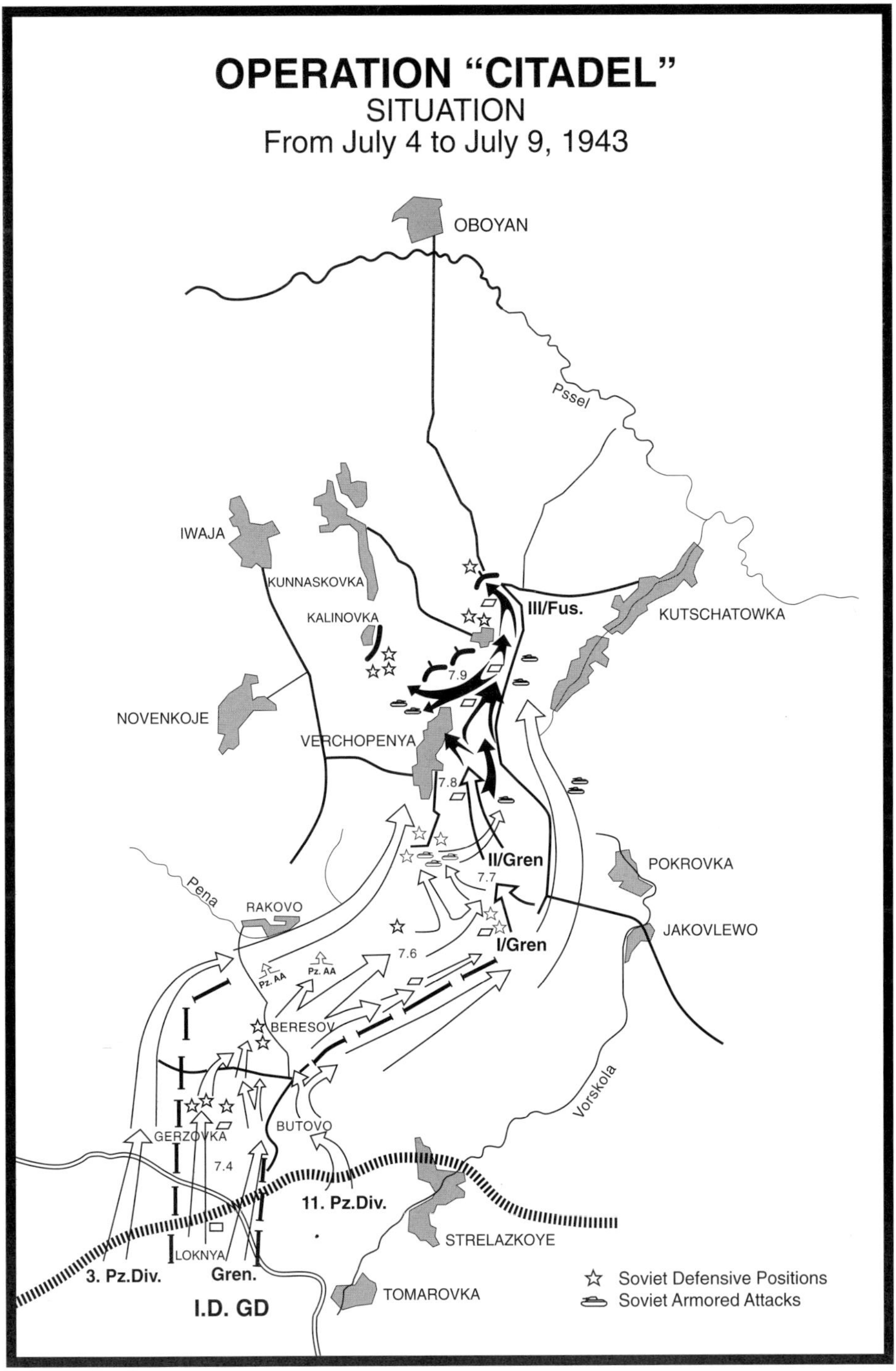
OPERATION "CITADEL"
SITUATION
From July 4 to July 9, 1943
OBOYAN
Pssel
IWAJA
KUNNASKOVKA
KALINOVKA
III/Fus.
KUTSCHATOWKA
7.9
NOVENKOJE
VERCHOPENYA
7.8
POKROVKA
II/Gren
7.7
Pena
RAKOVO
JAKOVLEWO
I/Gren
7.6
Pz. AA
Pz. AA
BERESOV
Vorskola
BUTOVO
GERZOVKA
7.4
11. Pz.Div.
STRELAZKOYE
LOKNYA
3. Pz.Div.
Gren.
I.D. GD
TOMAROVKA
Soviet Defensive Positions
Soviet Armored Attacks

the infantry? Then the bad news arrives; they're stuck in the mine field and cannot move. Any movement can bring further losses. First pioneers must come and clear the mines.

Meanwhile we observe the fire with our naked eyes. Everything is shrouded in dust and smoke. The enemy observation posts certainly can't see anything more. Our barrage is now over. The firing has become calmer and now is distributed over the specified areas as per the firing plan, at the same time it has wandered from the forward trenches farther to the rear. Are the infantry there? We can see some movement, but nothing specific.

Then General Hoernlein arrives at my forward command post. 'How is it going Albrecht?' — 'Everything as ordered, Herr General; the barrage went as planned, quite outstanding!'

'Any news from the infantry?' — 'Not yet!'

After a while Oberst Kassnitz, commander of the panzer-fusiliers, arrived. 'Good day, Kassnitz – how is it going?' The general's question.

'Shit, Herr General! My third battalion hasn't moved out yet,' said Oberst Kassnitz.

'Why?' replied the Division Commander.

'They waited for the tanks but they didn't arrive; and then they too didn't move.' A devilish situation. I remembered that the dashing young commander of III Battalion had been severely wounded yesterday; his successor probably wasn't as well oriented. A pity!

The entire barrage in the bin? The preparations, the worries; all for nothing!

'Yes, what will we do? Can't you fire the whole thing over again?' asked Oberst Kassnitz.

All I can say is, 'Out of the question, Herr Oberst. We don't have the ammunition.'

'Well Kassnitz,' observes the general, 'that won't work even with the best of intentions.'

General depression! My high spirits are gone. Then finally we get some good news: the grenadiers have taken advantage of the fire, have broken the bitter Soviet resistance in the trenches and are now advancing rapidly toward the hills. The general immediately moves the fusiliers to the right wing and sends them in behind the grenadiers. Everything is going to be all right after all.

Suddenly tanks appear behind us, more and more of them; they have a very long gun, a completely new type. Oh yes, the new Panther! Once again, however, our enthusiasm is dampened straight away; our tanks which have been able to free themselves from the minefield are now bogged down in a swamp which extends along a small stream. Patrols out at once! The available pioneer resources are totally inadequate for this job; it will take hours.

The breakthrough at the point of main effort is therefore out! My lovely barrage! In view of this situation the corps transfers the point of main effort to the right where the 11th Panzer Division has made better progress than we. Quite contrary to expectations! Not until the afternoon do we get moving again, after first overcoming the unfavourable terrain and the enemy resistance."

The grenadiers were more successful in exploiting the artillery barrage to break into the enemy positions, whereby they were further aided by the favourable terrain. The almost clockwork nature of the grenadiers' attack is evident in an account in the diary of the Panzer-Grenadier Regiment GD, which describes the first day of the attack:

Weather: Sunny, fair, scattered clouds, no wind.

03.00	Adjustment fire by our artillery.
04.30	Regimental commander forward in APC.
04.50	Artillery barrage.
05.00	Our artillery and tanks move out from the line Butovo – Gerzovka, with assault guns and 4./Pz.Stu.Pi.Btl. GD with the grenadier attack battalion, III Battalion under Hptm. Senger.
09.15	Point 237.8 west of Cherkasskoye reached! 12th Company veers west. Our tanks have difficulties in front of the anti-tank ditches in the Gerzovka bottom land. Right neighbour – 11th P.D. – at Hill 237.8. Left neighbour – panzer- fusiliers – abreast of us. Heavy enemy air activity.
09.00	Direct hit by bomb on regimental command post. Losses: regimental adjutant Hauptmann Beckendorff, Leutnant Hofstetter IV Battalion (adj.), Leutnant Stein Anti-tank Battalion GD, killed.
10.00	Order from Division Ia to Panther brigade: advance on Point 210.7. I and II Battalions range in. Execution delayed by halt in front of anti-tank ditch. II Battalion has difficulties moving up as panzer battalion has blocked the way.
11.00	Bridge is built over the Gerzovka bottom land – about in the middle of the division's lane of attack.
13.50	Soviet attack with seven tanks in direction of Korovino (against the fusiliers), our III Battalion also there.
13.53	All seven attacking Russian tanks destroyed by our tanks. Occasional outbursts of air activity by the enemy.
14.30	Leading elements of I Battalion and Panther brigade at the anti-tank ditch. Point II and IV Battalions south of Point 229.8 and in valley.
15.30	Panther breaks through temporary bridge over Beresovyi bottom land.
17.50	Regimental command post moved to west end of Yamnoye.
19.00	Bethke Battalion (II Btl.) instructed to attack Cherkasskoye from direction of Butovo via 237.8. 11th Panzer Division northeast of Cherkasskoye. Early afternoon attack by elements of I Battalion with tanks against north part of Cherkasskoye. I Battalion storms enemy battery and enters northwest part of Cherkasskoye.
19.35	II Battalion attacks southwest part of Cherkasskoye. Attack

by II Battalion soon called off on account of movement of our own troops in front of southwest part of Cherkasskoye. Flamethrower tanks of 11th Panzer Division already having an effect there. Heavy enemy air activity during night.

By late in the evening the attack's first objective had for all intents and purposes been reached. This was certainly the case on the right wing, where the capture of Cherkasskoye, one of the decisive corner posts of the first line of resistance, had been a complete success. Losses were relatively light, however the death of the adjutant of the Panzer-Grenadier Regiment, Hauptmann Gerhard Beckendorf, an uncompromising idealist, was especially painful. No less tragic was the hero's death of Obergefreiter Karl Treumann of the Assault Gun Battalion GD.

Forward elements of the left wing of the Panzer-Fusilier Regiment were due southeast of Beresovyi and had contact with its sister regiment on its right. The panzer-fusiliers had also largely reached their objectives, although at the cost of considerable losses. Seen as a whole, however, they were echeloned somewhat to the rear. The severe wounding of the regimental commander of the panzer-fusiliers, Oberst Kassnitz, in the front lines was a painful loss. He was quickly moved to the rear, but his injuries were so severe that he died in Germany on 29 July. Once again the Panzer-Fusilier Regiment GD had been hard hit by the loss of a regimental commander. Major Graf Saurma, commander of II Battalion, Panzer Regiment GD, was badly wounded in the stomach. His wounds were so serious that he too died on the way to the rear. Hauptmann von Gottberg took over command of II Battalion.

Night settled over the battlefield and covered it with silence, but everywhere helping hands were busy in support of the troops at the front who had been in heavy combat all day. Vehicles carrying food, motor ambulances, fuel trucks and munitions vehicles moved over the new advance road. Pioneers again went to work, building serviceable crossings over the swampy area.

Following a rain-soaked night, dawn began breaking on 6 July 1943 at about 02.30. II Battalion, Panzer-Grenadier Regiment GD set about clearing the southwest part of Cherkasskoye of groups of enemy troops still there. This put an end to the rifle fire which had been flaring up there since the previous evening. The enemy now showered the town with increasingly-heavy artillery and mortar fire, which unfortunately resulted in further losses among our ranks. The grenadiers therefore moved out early against the enemy's second line of resistance which lay near Dubrova.

In the meantime, in the river valley west of Yarkiy, the panzer-fusiliers prepared for a further advance. The objectives assigned them by the division were the villages of Kalashnoye and Lukanino, which lay northeast of their line of departure. Their comrades of the Panzer-Grenadier Regiment subsequently moved out at about 10.40 from due north of the road leading from Cherkasskoye to due south of Dubrova toward Point 237.7 and then Point 241.1. Leading the way was I Battalion under Major Remer, supported by the Strachwitz panzer group, consisting of I Battalion, Panzer Regiment GD and the Panther brigade.

The sequence of this attack group:

> I and II Battalions, Panzer-Grenadier Regiment
> elements of the Artillery Regiment GD
> command echelon Panzer-Grenadier Regiment
> Headquarters Company, Panzer-Grenadier Regiment
> IV Battalion, Panzer-Grenadier Regiment

During the night the boundary with the 11th Panzer Division, which was attacking on the right, had been established on the new line Butovo village–Dubrova road.

The *Großdeutschland* armoured assault pioneers also got no rest during the night. A multitude of mines had to be cleared from the extensive minefields laid by the bolsheviks in order to clear the way to the northeast. To this end two pioneer companies were placed under the command of the regiment spearheading the attack, the panzer-grenadiers. The pioneers also loaned valuable support in the storming of enemy positions. Sadly the pioneers had already lost the commander of the new 4th Company, Oberleutnant Ebbrecht, wearer of the German Cross in Gold, who was killed on the first day of the attack.

During the night the Armoured Reconnaissance Battalion GD was moved forward to Cherkasskoye. Its initial instructions were to reach the village of Yarkiy together with the attached Assault Gun Battalion GD. The first reconnaissance sorties were carried out to villages in the north, where heavy resistance was encountered, as expected. Finally, the battalion occupied defensive positions on a line from Point 210.7 to Point 210.3 north of Yarkiy, all the while under fire from enemy artillery, mortars and 76.2mm anti-tank guns. The 3rd Panzer Division, which was attacking on the left, advised that the division's tanks were due south of Savidovka attacking the village.

It therefore appeared that the attack was making slower progress in the left attack lane of the Panzer-Grenadier Division GD than in the one farther to the east. There, at about 14.45, I Battalion, Panzer-Grenadier Regiment GD and the panzers reported that the advance was proceeding smoothly and that the area south of Dubrova could be taken. However a heavy battle developed in the broad corn fields and flat hill terrain there against the bolsheviks grimly defending their second line of resistance. Earth bunkers, deep positions with built-in flamethrowers, and especially very well dug-in T-34s, excellently camouflaged, made the advance extremely difficult. German losses mounted, especially among the panzers. The infantry fought their way grimly through the in-depth defensive zone, trying to clear the way for the panzers. Finally that evening the brave panzer- grenadiers of I Battalion under Major Remer were able to advance by Dubrova and take Hill 247.2 where they dug in. There I Battalion, Panzer-Grenadier Regiment and the panzers of the Strachwitz group set up a hedgehog defensive position. All in all, however, it appeared that the breakthrough had not yet succeeded; instead the attackers were still sitting in the midst of the enemy's defensive zone.

The regimental headquarters of the Panzer-Grenadier Regiment followed up during the night and pushed its units, in particular II Battalion, as close to Dubrova as possible. The objective of this was to expand the penetration of the enemy positions into a breakthrough the next day and thus finally reach the open field of battle. Numerous Panthers had already been put out of action; the panzer regiment was forced to abandon many of its tanks on account of hits or track damage inflicted by mines and leave them for the following repair echelons for repairs.

The panzer-fusiliers concluded the day successfully, reaching their assigned objective in spite of considerable losses. The 7th Company lost many good comrades, among them the ever-smiling medic Joachim Baron, who succumbed to his wounds the following night. The 1st First-aid Company in Yarkiy was forced to deal with an increasing flow of wounded, especially mine-related casualties. A measure of satisfaction was warranted, however, in the fact that the evacuation of casualties to the rear proceeded smoothly.

Leutnant Holzgrefe was killed on 6 July by a direct hit on the command post of III Battalion, Panzer-Grenadier Regiment, along with battalion medical officer Dr. Sandmann and Unteroffiziere Seitz and Mischke. Numerous casualties also resulted from the unusually heavy attacks by Soviet close-support aircraft, which lasted all day. These attacks always took place at the moment when German fighters were absent.

The night was unsettled. The front, especially in the division's right attack lane, consisted merely of a line of strongpoints. Farthest advanced was I Battalion, Panzer-Grenadier Regiment, at Point 247.2 together with the bulk of the panzers. The village behind and to the left –Dubrova– was still heavily occupied by the enemy. II Battalion and other elements of the Panzer-Grenadier Regiment GD were farther southwest, approximately at Point 241.1. Contact with I Battalion was very loose and had been established by patrols from the 11th Panzer Division.

Relatively far to the rear was the Panzer-Fusilier Regiment at Lakanino, ready to attack northeast against the still heavily- defended Olkhovaya Gorge and hills west of Sirtsev. For it the actual battle still lay ahead. It was of vital importance to the tactical group that the penetration of the enemy system of positions be expanded into a breakthrough to the west during the coming day. All the necessary preparations were made.

At dawn on 7 July the panzers and elements of II Battalion, Panzer-Grenadier Regiment first took Dubrova, before veering northwest with I Battalion, Panzer-Grenadier Regiment GD. Unfortunately for the attackers, at this point the Panthers suffered enormous losses in tanks knocked out and the fully-deployed Strachwitz panzer group drove into a minefield which had not been identified, frustrating all further movement. An advance by I Battalion, Panzer-Grenadier Regiment GD was thus stopped for the time being. The panzers and panzer-grenadiers tried to maintain their positions under very heavy fire, and the lack of mobility of the tanks cost them further losses. The adjutant of the Panzer Regiment GD, Hauptmann von Seydlitz, suffered a serious stomach wound and was rescued only with great difficulty. Finally the remaining tanks of I Battalion, as well as the few remaining Panthers succeeded in crossing the minefield, in the course of which they became involved in a sharp tank-versus-tank engagement late in the morning. II Battalion, Panzer Regiment GD veered west and sought to escort I Battalion, Panzer-Grenadier Regiment to the scene of the fighting. The Remer Battalion finally arrived at about 11.30 and joined the battle. Meanwhile, farther to the north, II Battalion, Panzer-Grenadier Regiment GD launched an attack in the direction of Sirtsev but progress was slow. By radio the battalion commander reported considerable losses to enemy fire from anti-tank guns, mortars and 102mm cannon.

The panzer-fusilier regiment had meanwhile gained a foothold in the Olkhovaya Gorge with its III Battalion on the right, while on the left I Battalion took up the assault on Point 1.2 north of Sirtsev. Very heavy attacks by enemy close-support aircraft disrupted these movements considerably; in some places the fighting in the system of positions entailed heavy losses. The advance proved to be slow and laborious; heavy close-quarters fighting broke out over every single position.

Finally the enemy withdrew from Sirtsev under the pressure of this concentric attack by both GD regiments. Masses of Soviet troops streamed in a northwesterly direction toward Sirtsevo. By evening a small armoured group from the Armoured Reconnaissance Battalion GD and the Assault Gun Battalion GD, in cooperation with I Battalion, Panzer-Grenadier Regiment GD attacking from the east and aided by pressure exerted by the panzer-fusiliers from the south, succeeded in occupying the decisive Hill 230.1 against strong enemy armoured forces. The hill represented a favourable jumping-off point for further attacks to the north and against Sirtsevo. This was also the end of combat operations for that day; essentially it appeared that the Soviets' second system of positions had been successfully breached. Night fell and brought no rest. The sky was fire-red, heavy artillery shells shook the earth, rocket batteries fired at the last identified targets. Soon the Soviet "crows" were in the air, dropping large numbers of small bombs on the fires and other visible targets.

A sleepless night was followed by a sunny day. The first objective of 8 July was the capture of the well-defended village of Sirtsevo. Just as the attack was about to commence, however, the four panzers of II Battalion, Panzer Regiment's screening force under Leutnant Hausherr were knocked out of action. Leutnant Hausherr was killed along with his gunner and loader. It soon turned out that this tank-versus-tank duel was only the forerunner of a Soviet armoured advance by nearly forty tanks. The assault, launched from Sirtsevo, also hit the Strachwitz group at Point 230.1. Strachwitz's crews destroyed 10 enemy tanks in short order, but this advance by the enemy also showed how strong were their forces in Sirtsevo. Nevertheless at about 10.30 the panzer-fusiliers moved out of the ravines south of the village and headed north, while I Battalion, Panzer-Grenadier Regiment GD together with the tanks advanced on Sirtsevo from the east. The attackers broke into the village at about 13.50 in the face of heavy anti-tank fire from the west bank, after which they mopped up the remaining Soviet defenders in Sirtsevo. The 3rd Panzer Division's 6th Panzer Regiment assisted in this attack from the west.

In the meantime the Armoured Reconnaissance Battalion, reinforced by the Assault Gun Battalion GD, had received orders to attack Verkhnopenye from its previous positions. Since Sirtsevo was not yet in our hands at that point, the battalion commander decided to advance northeast through Gremuchiy. There the battalion met III Battalion, Panzer-Grenadier Regiment GD, which obviously thought it was in Verkhnopenye and had caused some confusion in the command staff by reporting same. An explanation of the true situation made it clear to the battalion command that they were in fact in Gremuchiy. The limited load-bearing ability of the only available bridge held up the Armoured Reconnaissance Battalion's advance for some time, and in the end the division decided to leave it where it was to guard the right flank. This measure quickly proved to be the right one. The first enemy tank attack from a northeasterly direction followed soon after the battalion had formed a semi-circle north of Gremuchiy. Scarcely an hour passed that waves of enemy tanks 20 to 40 strong did not attack. The Assault Gun Battalion GD under Major Frantz was able to destroy a total of 35 enemy tanks and 18 heavy anti-tank guns there in the course of a few hours. The positions, which extended in a semicircle from the road in the east across the M.T. station, were held. That evening the anti-tank battalion under Major Hacke, which had previously been successfully deployed with the panzer-grenadiers, was sent to bolster the Armoured Reconnaissance Battalion. Meanwhile II Battalion, Panzer- Grenadier Regiment GD, together with I Battalion, Panzer Regiment GD – including the regimental commander Oberst Strachwitz – and the few surviving Panthers advanced past Point 230.1 to the north. That evening this force became involved in heavy fighting with fresh Soviet tank reserves at the eastern end of Verkhnopenye. III Battalion, which had followed on the right, likewise became engaged in heavy fighting, but to the northeast of Verkhnopenye. That evening, after refuelling, the Gottberg Panzer Battalion (II Battalion) was pulled out of Sirtsevo and likewise sent in the direction of Verkhnopenye. Stuka attacks had done effective preparatory work and the main body of the Panzer-Grenadier Regiment GD clawed its way into the town of Verkhnopenye. Extending for a kilometre along the Penza in a north-south direction, it was a tough nut to crack. The effect of enemy fire from the west bank of the Penza on the mass of panzer-grenadiers attacking from the south and east was especially uncomfortable and disruptive.

The panzer-fusiliers were therefore withdrawn from the Sirtsevo area and sent north behind the backs of the panzer-grenadiers due west of Gremuchiy. In the next days they were to gain ground to the north between the Armoured Reconnaissance Battalion GD and the panzer-grenadiers. The account of the events of 8 July 1943 cannot be concluded without mentioning the courageous flak gunners of the Army Flak Battalion GD and their three heavy 88mm, two 37mm and one 20mm quadruple anti-aircraft guns. Apart from the eighty-eights, most of the guns were assigned to the individual infantry battalions by battery or platoon to augment the units own anti-aircraft defences against the often heavy attacks by enemy close-support aircraft. The following account by Leutnant G. Haarhaus, platoon leader in a 37mm flak battery, describes his experiences working with the panzer-grenadiers:

"My platoon of 37mm flak had been, so to speak, married to Remer's I Battalion, meaning we were under its command, for some time and were therefore well accustomed to it. Everything really ran like clockwork.

Once, with the Russians showing no intention of letting up, the infantry sat exhausted in their holes and waited for the tank support that had been promised. The panzers were late in arriving however. The Russian close-support aircraft were quicker to arrive on the scene. Every two hours they came sweeping in. Each aircraft dropped 50-60 small bombs, raked the infantry positions with their fixed weapons and then disappeared again.

For us of the flak there now began a worthwhile mission, especially since Major Remer had ordered: shoot them down! We did shoot down more than a few.

A typical attack went like this: 'Aircraft 6' shouted the lookout standing by the gun. Everyone ran to the weapons. The gun barrels raised and the K1 (gunner) peered through the reflector sight. Then the gun commander screamed: 'Aircraft in sight! Sustained fire!' The gun began to bark, but then the wings of the approaching, low-flying enemy aircraft lit up: machine-gun fire. This was the signal for the gun crew to make itself as small as possible behind the oh-so-thin armour shield and continue firing. 'Thirteen, twelve, eleven, ten, nine, eight, seven, six, five...' bellowed the range-finder. Then he took cover behind the gun tractor since from there range-finding was estimated. It howled, whistled and cracked all around. The enemy machines roared over the guns at a height of only a few metres, flew a wide circle and began another pass.

We brought down three of these fellows that afternoon, however half of one crew was knocked out of action by gunfire."

The morning of 9 July 1943 saw the Panzer-Fusilier Regiment GD advancing beneath a cloudy sky past Verkhnopenye to the east toward Novoselovka and Point 240.4. There, however, it was halted by a very strong defence of anti-tank guns and tanks. At about the same time – about 06.00 – the Armoured Reconnaissance Battalion, bolstered by the Assault Gun Battalion GD, was carrying out the division order for an advance toward Point 260.8 along the road to Oboyan. The attack was preceded by Stuka attacks on what appeared to be enemy armoured spearheads and troop concentrations farther to the north. Waves of dive-bombers dropped their loads with precision on the Russian tanks. A tall pillar of flame erupted each time a crew was sent to "commissar and Red Army heaven." Under cover of this really outstanding air support the battle group of the Armoured Reconnaissance Battalion GD approached Point 260.8. Observations revealed that to the east the 11th Panzer Division, which was still partially equipped with the Panzer III, was preparing to attack along the road to the north.

At about the same time, about 07.00, the panzer-grenadiers again set out against Verkhnopenye with II and III Battalions in an effort to finally take possession of the town in spite of heavy flanking fire from the west. "Battle Group von Strachwitz" supported the advance from the southern tip of

Verkhnopenye with about 19 Panzer IVs (long), 10 Tigers and about 10 of the surviving Panthers. At the same time, in a massed attack, Stuka wings dropped their bombs on recognized targets in the town and on the west bank of the Penza in order to soften up the objective. Finally, at about 08.35, the commander of II Battalion, Panzer-Grenadier Regiment GD reported that he was in the last houses in the northern part of Verkhnopenye, which meant as much as the capture of the hotly contested town. The strong flanking fire from the west continued, an indication that our left neighbour had been unable to keep up with our advance: he was still farther to the southwest and was heavily engaged with enemy tank concentrations.

With the good progress of the panzer-fusiliers in the direction of Novoselovka and the reinforced Armoured Reconnaissance Battalion toward Point 260.8, the Strachwitz panzer group was pulled out of the area south of Verkhnopenye as quickly as possible and sent to the northeast. It soon reached Point 240.8. The panzer group then drove through the Armoured Reconnaissance Battalion battle group in the direction of Point 240.4. Our tanks soon ran into the enemy tank concentrations, however, which were sighted from a distance of 2,500-3,000 metres. A major tank-versus-tank battle developed, with the Stukas providing continuous support. Hill 243 was reached after heavy fighting and the panzers halted there initially. On the horizon were burning and smoking enemy tanks. Unfortunately three of 6th Company's tanks had been knocked out as well. Oberleutnant G. Authenried was killed by a direct hit on his tank's turret. In the further course of the engagement Hauptmann von Wietersheim succeeded in carrying the attack as far as the anti-tank village of Novoselovka and reached the hill. This in turn enabled the panzer-fusiliers to continue to advance and they arrived at the road fork due south of Point 244.8 on the road to Oboyan. There they called an interim halt.

After reports of this success were received, the Panzer-Grenadier Regiment GD was withdrawn from the division's right attack lane at Verkhnopenye and elements sent to Novoselovka. However, the difficult situation of the 3rd Panzer Division on the left forced the division command to change its plans. The Panzer-Fusilier Regiment GD held farther north and northeast of Novoselovka and south of Point 244.8. I and III Battalions and the regimental command of the Panzer-Grenadier Regiment GD were now committed west and northwest of Novoselovka and screened the front to the north and northeast. Panzer Group Strachwitz had to turn almost ninety degrees in order to leave its former location on the road to Oboyan and head for Points 251.4 and 247.0. Its orders were to make a frontal attack on the enemy tanks in that area which were holding up 3rd Panzer Division's advance. The reinforced Armoured Reconnaissance Battalion followed this movement while screening the flanks to the southwest.

Our armoured spearheads encountered the first enemy tanks near Point 1.3, north of Verkhnopenye, at about 22.00, in complete darkness. The panzers halted to refuel and rearm and then wait until morning. In the meantime the Armoured Reconnaissance Battalion and the Assault Gun Battalion halted at a point south of 251.4.

These movements, the result of the difficult situation in which the 3rd Panzer Division found itself, brought the division units to Point 244.8 on the road to Oboyan, which was obviously the deepest penetration into the Kursk pocket by *Großdeutschland*. It was possible only at the cost of extremely heavy fighting and in some cases considerable losses. Names like Feldwebel Wolk and Stabsgefreiter Albrecht of 7th Company, II Battalion, Panzer-Grenadier Regiment GD and Unteroffiziere Guda and Plischke of 7th Company, II Battalion, Panzer-Fusilier Regiment GD stand for the hundreds of comrades who fell in these battles. They all lie in the Verkhnopenye – Oboyan area, fallen in the impetus of the last major German offensive on the Eastern Front!

The dark of night slowly passed over to the grey of the rising 10th of July. At about 03.30, the tanks of Panzer Group Strachwitz at Point 1.8 southwest of Novoselovka spotted the enemy tanks they had heard during the night in the water-filled valley before them. Soon afterward the first armour-piercing shells began falling; a battle between steel giants began this day of fighting on the southern front of the Kursk pocket. By 04.00 the first enemy tanks could be seen burning on the battlefield; but painful gaps had also been smashed in our own ranks. One of II Battalion's command tanks took a direct hit in the turret which killed gunner Unteroffizier König. The rest of the crew, some of them wounded, were able to escape from the tank. Oberst Graf von Strachwitz was also injured, by the recoil of the breech, while destroying an enemy tank and had to hand command of the Panzer Regiment GD over to Hauptmann von Wietersheim. The enemy armour was finally forced to withdraw at about 05.00, allowing our attack to the south toward Point 243.0 to slowly get under way.

Due south of Kalinovka the Armoured Reconnaissance Battalion GD, reinforced by the Assault Gun Battalion GD, carried out its assigned task of screening the right flank of the division's panzer attack to the north and northeast by advancing toward Point 247.0 south of Kruglik with its armoured 2nd (APC) Squadron. Patrols revealed Kalinovka and Kruglik to be rather heavily occupied, the enemy forces including a large number of tanks. When the point drove over the chain of hills from 1.8 to 251.4, about 15 enemy tanks were made out in a cornfield north of Kalinovka. Major Frantz moved out with two batteries of assault guns and elements of 2nd (APC) Squadron to chase the enemy armour away and try to reach the southern tip of Kalinovka.

Meanwhile the leading elements of the Panzer-Grenadier Regiment GD, namely I Battalion, appeared at Point 1.8 with orders to follow the attack. However these orders were changed at about 10.00; now the panzer-grenadiers were instructed to form a half-hedgehog east of Kalinovka, while establishing and maintaining contact with the panzer-fusiliers and the 11th Panzer Division on the right. The Strachwitz panzer group (von Wietersheim) had meanwhile reached the edge of Hill 243.0. However it was unable to advance any farther on account of heavy enemy flanking fire from the west. The group's objective was now a crossroads near Point 258.5, which like the forest to the west was heavily occupied by the enemy. III

Battalion, Panzer-Fusilier Regiment GD had also arrived and joined the battle behind the panzers, but all movement was paralysed by the heavy flanking fire from the west. The forward elements of the 3rd Panzer Division, which was attacking from the southwest with its rifle regiment, were also unable to approach.

Then in the early afternoon hours of 10 July the 2nd (APC) Squadron, reinforced by the assault gun battalion, entered the Kubasovskiy Valley. It passed through the valley and as darkness was falling reached the road from Kruglik to Point 258.5, about 1,000 metres south of Point 247.0. All enemy supply traffic on this road to the wooded area at 258.5 was thus severed, allowing the attack on this wood by our tanks to get moving again.

Eventually Point 247.0 south of Kruglik and Point 258.5 were taken before darkness fell. The arrival of darkness did prevent the enemy at Kruglik from being destroyed. Major Frantz, commander of the Assault Gun Battalion GD, described the dusk engagement at Kruglik:

"Together with elements of the reconnaissance battalion we had essentially achieved our objectives in the course of the day as per orders. A number of enemy tanks were destroyed in the process. Corn and sunflower fields were cleared of enemy infantry in cooperation with the armoured reconnaissance battalion. A constant irritation was the flanking fire from the village of Kruglik and the fact that the enemy road, part of which we could observe, was the scene of lively supply traffic. Unexpectedly the enemy failed to spot us, and in the course of the late afternoon we were able to advance through a ravine we had located in front of Kruglik. Hidden from sight in a valley, we worked our way toward the village as far as the hill. The 3rd Battery under Oberleutnant Wehmeyer and elements of the reconnaissance battalion initially remained there and successfully blocked the enemy traffic on the road. As dusk was now falling and I believed that the enemy in Kruglik might have become uncertain as a result of his road being cut, I tried to seize the village of Kruglik with the other two batteries of my battalion, the 1st and 2nd under Oberleutnant Brehmer. Widely separated, the assault guns of the two batteries drove at full speed toward the village. At first there was no defence at all. At 300 metres from the village – I already had the impression that the enemy had left the field – I suddenly saw fiery arrows coming toward us from the outskirts of Kruglik. Before I could figure out what they were, there were explosions directly in front of the mass of advancing assault guns. The vehicle next to me, I believe it was Wachtmeister Brauner of 1st Battery, began to stream smoke. Thank God it turned out to be one of the smoke candles that every assault gun carried. The vehicle had taken a direct hit on the bow plates but suffered no damage. The explosion and the effect of the projectile revealed that we were under direct fire from a Stalin Organ, the first time we experienced something like this in the campaign. Darkness slowly settled over the battlefield while the assault guns destroyed the Stalin Organ and the nests of resistance which repeatedly flared up at the outskirts of the village. The planned surprise attack misfired, nevertheless we – the armoured reconnaissance battalion and the assault gun battalion together – had once again achieved more than was expected of us."

A continuous defensive line was established during the night, as enemy counterattacks were expected with certainty in the next days. There was no movement by the division's units on 11 July; instead they and the 11th Panzer Division held the line they had reached, which ran roughly as follows: crossroads south of 244.8 (11th Panzer Division) – Point 233.8 (11th Panzer Division), the boundary between GD and the 11th Panzer Division – the hills east of Kalinovka (Pz.Gren.Rgt. GD) – Kubsovskiy Gorge to Point 247.0 (Armd.Recon.Btl.) – Point 258.5 (3rd Panzer Division). In general this day could be described as quiet apart from repeated advances by the enemy in company and battalion strength, some with tanks, against the positions of the Panzer-Grenadier Regiment GD.

According to statements by prisoners, the enemy appeared to already be committing strategic reserves, which had previously been resting in the distant rear. At least three tank and one mechanized corps under the command of the Soviet 69th Army and the 1st Tank Army were identified. The German command was thus able to assume that the enemy had sustained considerable losses in the battles so far. It appeared important not to let up, in spite of the severity of the fighting, and to pursue the attack.

The divisional orders issued during the night of 11/12 July 1943 were in keeping with this notion. Elements of the Panzer-Grenadier Division GD were relieved by units of the 3rd Panzer Division in their former positions and were transferred to the front of the attack lane in the area near Point 260.8 and to the north. The plan was for a continuation of the attack, primarily by the tanks and panzer-fusiliers, on 12 July in the direction of the Psel River, the last obstacle in front of Oboyan. It was learned from the division's neighbour on the right, II SS-Panzer Corps, that its spearheads had already crossed the river.

The artillery, anti-tank units and other heavy weapons were the first to be withdrawn from their positions in this reorganization and sent northeast. The Armoured Reconnaissance Battalion GD had no special role in the new plan. Like the Panzer-Grenadier Regiment GD it remained in the previous combat area at the disposal of the division. The panzer-grenadiers remained in their positions east and southeast of Kalinovka and waited for relief by the 3rd Panzer Division. The first of this division's units to arrive, at Point 247.0 south of Kruglik, was the reconnaissance battalion. It relieved the Armoured Reconnaissance Battalion GD early the next morning. The Assault Gun Battalion GD was placed under the command of the Panzer-Grenadier Regiment GD in its sector. Sadly, shortly before its departure for the new sector it lost the commander of 2nd Battery, Oberleutnant Bremer, who was killed by a sudden enemy artillery barrage.

Scarcely had the Armoured Reconnaissance Battalion GD been relieved at Point 247.0, when at 0620 the enemy attacked east with strong tank and infantry forces from the area west of the Kruglik – Point 254.5 and against Point 247.0. The latter position was soon lost and the Armoured Reconnaissance Battalion GD withdrew to the south. At the same time enemy armour and infantry attacked from Kalinovka against the positions of II and III Battalions, Panzer-Grenadier Regiment GD. The situation quickly became critical. II Battalion under Major Bethke, which was tied up by the enemy coming out of Kalinovka, found itself in a particularly precarious situation, which temporarily forced the battalion to withdraw from its positions. Unteroffiziere Merl and Neutsch and nine enlisted men of 7th Company, II Battalion, Panzer-Grenadier Regiment lost their lives in this fighting. Major Bethke was shot twice, in the neck and arm. Heavy close-quarters fighting broke out, in which the panzer-grenadiers in particular distinguished themselves. In spite of his wounds Major Bethke led a counterattack by II Battalion, which had moved up toward Kalinovka under the command of the regiment's operations officer, Leutnant Feldhaus. Feldhaus died a hero's death in this action. The battalion retook its former positions at about 18.00. Only then did the enemy attacks subside.

Oberleutnant Konopa took over command of II Battalion, Panzer-Grenadier Regiment GD. As a result of these heavy defensive battles the division's plans for a further advance to the north were initially overtaken. The units already on the move were recalled and placed in positions behind especially-threatened points. The panzers stood ready to counterattack, everything was organized for defence. The danger now lay on the left, west flank, especially since the 3rd Panzer Division was apparently too weak to win through there. The villages of Gerzovka and Beresovka were back in enemy hands and the danger that Soviet forces were advancing into the rear of the German attack divisions was increasing.

Then the division decided to attack south again over Point 243.0 with a battle group consisting of a panzer company, II Battalion, Panzer-Fusiliers, the reinforced Armoured Reconnaissance Battalion GD and the Assault Gun Battalion GD. The object of the attack was to move the 3rd Panzer Division back into its positions, but also to reduce the danger posed by Kalinovka. Appropriate preparations and reorganizations were carried out during the night of 13 July.

While further enemy advances against the positions of the panzer-grenadiers east and southeast of Kalinovka continued to be reported on 13 July, a cloudy, dreary day, elements of the battle group made preparations for the drive across Point 243.0. It was intended that it should advance past the Kubasovskiy Gorge on the north edge of the Distr. Tolstoye forest and "school" due north of it, while the von Wietersheim panzer group drove toward the same objective from the south. The object was to form a pocket around this wooded area. It was anticipated that the scheme would come to fruition on 14 July.

The reinforced Armoured Reconnaissance Battalion GD set off at about 06.00 on 14 July. Due north of Point 243.0 it linked up with the Assault Gun Battalion GD and II Battalion, Panzer-Fusilier Regiment which was waiting there as well as the panzer company. The commander of the Armoured Reconnaissance Battalion GD ordered the panzer company to begin feeling its way toward "school" at 08.15. The Assault Gun Battalion GD was to screen to the south and north, while the 2nd (APC) Squadron followed the panzer company with mounted troops. The panzer-fusiliers were to move up when the panzer company reached "school." Finally, at about 08.30, the

OPERATION "CITADEL"
SITUATION
From July 12 to July 17, 1943

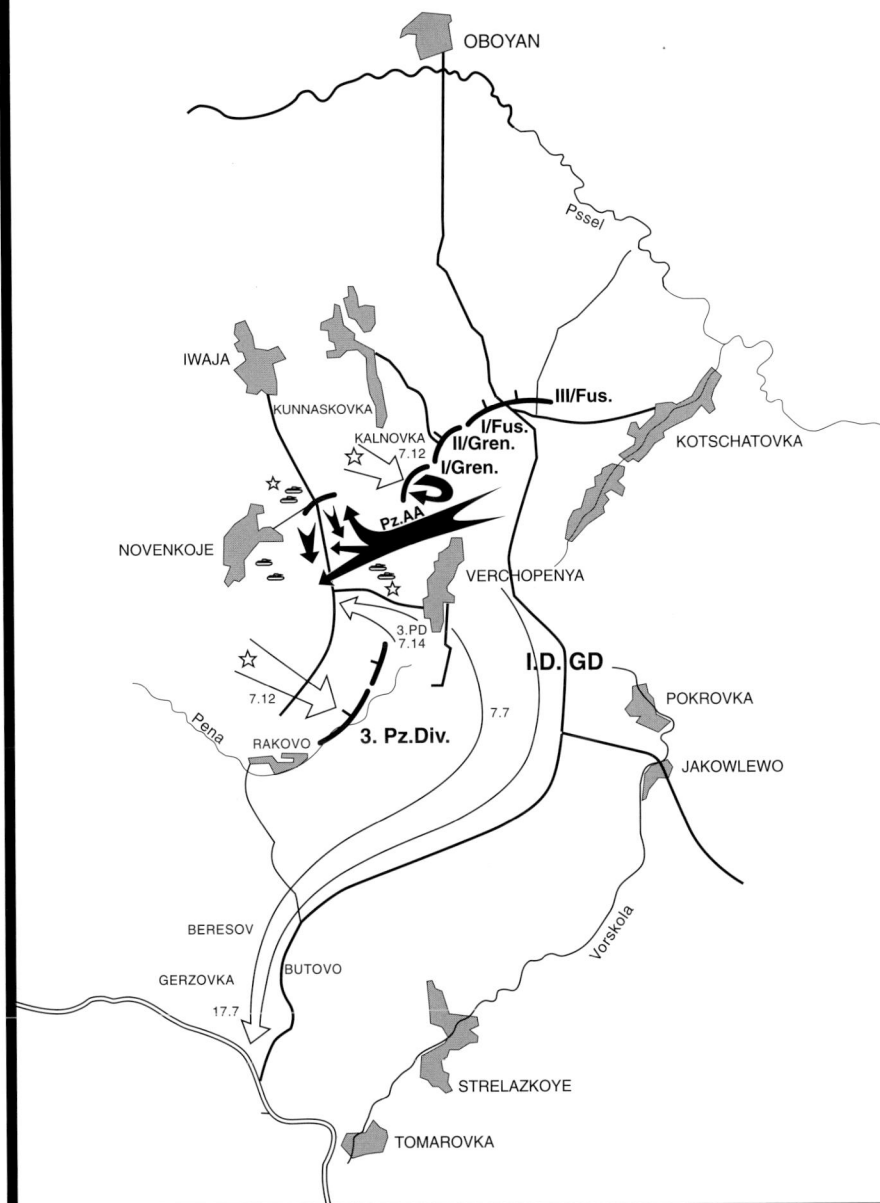

OBOYAN

Pssel

IWAJA

KUNNASKOVKA

III/Fus.

I/Fus.
II/Gren.

KOTSCHATOVKA

KALNOVKA
7.12

I/Gren.

Pz.AA

NOVENKOJE

VERCHOPENYA

3.PD
7.14

I.D. GD

7.12

POKROVKA

7.7

Pena

RAKOVO

3. Pz.Div.

JAKOWLEWO

BERESOV

GERZOVKA

BUTOVO

Vorskola

17.7

STRELAZKOYE

TOMAROVKA

panzer company set off toward the southwest via the Kubasovskiy Gorge.

As soon as the tanks moved out they came under heavy enemy tank fire from the area of Distr. Tolstoye and Point 258.5, as well as from north of the area of Point 247.0. After the loss of four tanks the panzer company withdrew to the back slope. At about 09.30 assault guns screening to the south reported an enemy tank attack from Distr. Tolstoye against 243.0, strength about fifteen T-34s. The assault guns knocked out three T-34s, after which the others turned around. This sudden advance by enemy armoured forces made it clear that the 3rd Panzer Division was not west of Point 258.5, as had been reported, rather about 2,000 metres farther east. The commander of the Armoured Reconnaissance Battalion GD therefore decided to extend his open left flank to the 3rd Panzer Division with the 2nd Battery of assault guns. With the serious anti-tank threat from Distr. Tolstoye a further attack on 'school' and 258.5 was impossible. The commander of the Armoured Reconnaissance Battalion instead requested that the 3rd Panzer Division attack 258.5 and Distr. Tolstoye in order to create the conditions necessary for the GD battle group to carry out its mission.

The 3rd Rifle Regiment in fact attacked 258.5 and Distr. Tolstoye at about 16.30. Afterward the commander of the Armoured Reconnaissance Battalion issued the following order: panzer company screen to the north, 2nd (APC) Squadron to attack north end of Distr. Tolstoye when the 3rd Infantry Regiment has reached Point 258.5. Panzer- fusiliers are to continue to secure Kubasovskiy Gorge to the north. The 3rd Rifle Regiment required more than two hours to reach its objective, Point 258.5. When this was finally reached at about 18.30, the 2nd (APC) Squadron advanced smartly across the road and gained the northern edge of Distr. Tolstoye. There it turned north and advanced toward "school" with the assault guns, which were once again with the battle group. This advance failed initially, however, as the enemy answered with heavy tank and anti-tank fire from Hill 240.2 and "school." It was learned that the panzer group had failed to reach Hill 240.2.

The assault guns and 2nd (APC) Squadron thereupon withdrew toward the Distr. Tolstoye forest's edge, while a battalion of the 3rd Rifle Regiment took over screening there. The falling darkness brought an end to the operation after it had enjoyed partial success. The detached units were released to their parent formations.

The units spent the next two days, 15 and 16 July, in the existing positions in constant defensive fighting against the Soviets, who attacked from the north and west, with tanks and with infantry, in up to battalion strength. All the positions were held. In the course of an offensive patrol near Novenskoye with his panzer company, Oberleutnant Lex succeeded in destroying 16 T-34s. It seemed as if the entire offensive had begun to stagnate, which was probably attributable to certain considerations in the senior command posts, but especially in Führer Headquarters.

Hitler had summoned the commanders of the army groups involved in the offensive, Generalfeldmarschall von Kluge of Army Group Centre and Generalfeldmarschall von Manstein of Army Group South, and briefed them on the latest state of the overall situation on all fronts (13 July 1943). The situation in Sicily, where the Western Powers had landed on 10 July 1943, had become serious. The Italians were no longer fighting at all. The loss of the island seemed probable. The enemy's next step might lead to a landing in the Balkans or in southern Italy. The building of new armies there and in the western Balkans was necessary. The Eastern Front had to give up forces and therefore "Zitadelle" could not be continued.

Feldmarschall von Kluge (Army Group Centre) declared that Model's army could not advance any farther and had already suffered 20,000 casualties. Furthermore the army group was forced to take away all of Ninth Army's mobile forces to counter the deep penetrations the enemy had already achieved against Second Army's front in three places. For this reason Ninth Army's attack could not be continued and also could not be resumed later. On the other hand, Feldmarschall von Manstein stated that, where Army Group South was concerned, the battle had reached its decisive point. Victory was within reach after the previous day's defensive successes against the enemy's strategic reserve, almost all of which had been committed to the battle. To break off the battle now would mean throwing away victory.

Since Feldmarschall von Kluge considered a resumption of the attack by Ninth Army out of the question and instead declared that he felt its withdrawal to its line of departure was necessary, Hitler, with the need to divert forces to the Mediterranean in mind, decided to call off "Zitadelle!"

On 17 July 1943 the OKH issued orders for all of II SS-Panzer Corps to be withdrawn from the front immediately and on the 18th for two further panzer divisions to be released to Army Group Centre.

One of the two panzer divisions was the Panzer-Grenadier Division *Großdeutschland*. The division was relieved by elements of the 3rd Panzer Division and moved back into the Vorskla Valley, into the area surrounding Tomarovka, during the night of 16 to 17 July and on the 18th.

Another painful segment of this unhappy war had come to an end. It was a brief but difficult period which had once again placed the initiative, the rules of engagement in the hands of the German forces. The German leadership had hoped for a straightening of the Eastern Front resulting in a shortening of the lines, as well as the destruction of considerable enemy forces and their strategic reserves. It was believed that after achieving this objective the war of movement of previous years could be resumed, and mobile warfare had always been the strong suit of the German units.

It was known that the enemy had suffered considerable losses in the fighting in the Kharkov and Belgorod areas, which had forced him to pause for a time to rest and regenerate his forces. It was further believed that the better morale of the Germans and their greater flexibility would once again give them the upper hand. All this lay within the realm of possibility and they remembered only too well the repeated urging by the Commanders-in-Chief of the two army groups which participated in "Zitadelle" for the rapid execution of their orders. They had total victory in mind, but this was not to be. The Allied landing in Sicily was the obvious reason for the cancellation of Operation "Zitadelle." Another, not inconsiderable reason may also be sought in the words "too late." For the delays in carrying out the attack and the repeated postponements made the forthcoming operation too apparent to the enemy. In this context the soldiers who were there recall that the owners of the houses where they were billeted knew the precise date of their departure days before they did.

For the men of the Panzer-Grenadier Division *Großdeutschland* this Operation "Zitadelle" saw them involved in an attack where the strength of their arms allowed them to enjoy the feeling of superiority. It is therefore understandable that optimism and a feeling of strength reigned when they left the rest area.

CHAPTER 2

IN THE FOREST OF KARACHEV

The transfer of the Panzer-Grenadier Division Großdeutschland into the Karachev area proceeded extraordinarily quickly under the pressure of events near Orel. The units had only just been able to assemble in the Vorskla Valley, when on 21 June the wheeled elements left the departure point of Grebenovka. While these drove to the new area of operations the tracked units and tanks were quickly loaded aboard trains and shipped to Briansk. At least 150 kilometres were covered each day and the first units, the wheeled elements of the Panzer-Grenadier Regiment GD, were able to occupy quarters near Karachev on 23 July. The drive, which at times was made in heavy rain, was no pleasure trip, because the drivers had to grind their way north over the rain-softened clay roads. The vehicles quickly passed through the villages of Sumy, Putivl, Yampol and Glukhov, while the tracked elements rolled over the Russian tracks on their open cars at high speed. Mines could be anywhere, laid by partisans in the woods. During pauses in the journey the "old timers" of the Infantry Regiment GD visited the graves of their comrades who had fallen in the Putivl and Glukhov areas during the advance of 1941. What had happened in these two years – yes had it really been only two years? To many it seemed like a lifetime!

During the days of the move the commanders learned about their missions for the coming battle in the forest of Karachev: northwest of Bolkhov the enemy had broken through the German lines on a width of almost 30 kilometres and was now advancing in a southwesterly direction through the almost impenetrable forests. The enemy had already penetrated more than forty kilometres into the German rear area and was threatening the city of Karachev as well as the road and railroad between Orel and Karachev. These two communications and supply lines, over which supplies for the German units in the Orel salient flowed day and night, were directly threatened. The mission of the Panzer-Grenadier Division Großdeutschland and the other arriving reserve units was to prevent these links from being severed and to destroy the advancing enemy forces.

It was also learned that the Supreme Commander had at first ordered that the city of Orel was to be held at all costs. Later, however, he left the decision up to the Commander-in-Chief of Army Group Centre, Generalfeldmarschall von Kluge. The latter reported to his superiors that he also wanted to hold at all costs, but that he intended to evacuate the rear-echelon units.

It is no wonder then that the first arriving GD units ran into the stream of infantry train units, which, in more or less good order, were trying to put distance between themselves and the enemy. Enemy bombing increased the nervousness of the withdrawal and its tempo. Endless columns of empty vehicles streamed in the direction of Orel; overfilled trucks from this area rolled west. According to certain rumours the enemy's armoured spearheads were already within six kilometres of the Orel-Karachev road and railroad. Exploding mines, set off by partisans, increased the fear of those striving to reach Orel.

Without waiting for the wheeled elements of the regiment, mostly the heavy infantry weapons, at about 04.00 on 24 July the Panzer-Grenadier Regiment GD moved out with three battalions to comb the wooded terrain northeast of Karachev, more to reconnoitre than to fight. The regiment's war diary provides details of the movements of those days:

Weather: cloudy with sunny breaks; periods of rain in the afternoon.

Attached units: I Battalion, Panzer Artillery Regiment GD (self-propelled), assigned to cooperate

1st Company, Anti-tank Battalion GD Division Escort Company GD

2nd Company, 104th Anti-tank Battalion

06.05	Preparations by I Battalion under Major Remer for advance on Shishkino. Preparations by III Battalion under Hauptmann Senger for advance through Karachev–Odrino toward (Bolshe) Narishkino. Arrival of II Battalion under Oberleutnant Konopa followed by tracked elements of III Battalion.
10.00	(Bolshe) Narishkino occupied by III Battalion, no enemy resistance.
10.30	Regimental command post in (Bolshe) Narishkino.
11.30	III Battalion takes Piryatinka, north of Narishkino, against light enemy resistance.
14.15	After brief reorganization II and III Battalions move out toward Alechino and southwest of it. Village is occupied. Enemy units identified from prisoners: 31st Guards Infantry Division, in this area since 23. 7. 1943. 551st Anti-tank Regiment of the 6th Anti-tank Division.
18.00	Attack by II Battalion under Oberleutnant Konopa on Mertvoye and Point 225.2 to the southeast.
21.00	Hill 225.2 in our hands. Regimental command post in wood south of Alechino.

This brief account describes the experiences of the division, most of which was still on the march, in the first days in this area. It was not exactly a hard battle, but it resulted in numerous individual actions. The enemy, who had penetrated the forest of Karachev with his points and small advance groups, was attempting to advance west through it parallel to the main road, appearing from time to time at the supply road and cutting it. He was in direct contact with the partisan units in the Briansk Forest. It seemed totally impossible to clear this forest region of the enemy or even gain control of most of it.

The mission given the fully-motorized units of the Panzer- Grenadier Division *Großdeutschland* was therefore extraordinarily difficult, indeed almost hopeless. Added to this was the fact that large areas of the forest consisted of swamps and moors, which for all intents and purposes limited travel to a few built-up routes.

The following description of a patrol near Karachev, provided by Obergefreiter Meissner of 1st (Armoured Reconnaissance) Squadron, Armoured Reconnaissance Battalion GD, reveals the difficulty of the task facing the companies:

"First we drove to Karachev. There was a halt just outside the city: our general was there. He gained our complete attention when he said that our mission was extremely dangerous and demanded the maximum attention and caution. In Karachev itself we were joined by Unteroffizier Karrasch and his patrol. For the first time four eight-wheeled armoured cars drove a patrol together; that had to be a good sign. Then we received our assignment from Leutnant Gebhard, the patrol leader:

In spite of heavy rainfall, the Soviets had succeeded in breaking through our front in the impassable forest terrain. They were currently threatening the main Karachev–Briansk road and had also cut a parallel road at one spot farther north. The previous evening a vehicle column had been ambushed near kilometre stone 23 and 28 of 30 men had been killed. We were now given the job of pushing through to the break-in point, supported by two Tigers and three flamethrower tanks, and keeping it open until a freshly-detrained battalion arrived. We moved away from the command post with the armoured cars in front, the tanks behind, but our joy in having such potent support did not last long. A Major took the tanks away from us in the last village before the break-in point. After brief consideration, Leutnant Gebhard decided to continue the mission with just his armoured cars.

As soon as we left the village heavy mortar fire began falling right between our vehicles. Now it began to get serious. Driving in the lead was Unteroffizier Karrasch, then followed our car with Leutnant Gebhard. In the third car was Unteroffizier Hartung, while Unteroffizier Schmidt covered the rear with his car.

The area was highly unsympathetic to us armoured car people: the road itself consisted largely of a raised, single-lane log road; right and left a swampy ditch and then impenetrable forest which we could not drive through. We could not approach our objective unseen, neither could we drive around it. The armoured cars worked their way forward like a caterpillar. The enemy might be anywhere. Our nerves were extremely tense. I had to light one cigarette after another for the crew. We drove a short distance, stopped and observed, then repeated the process. At each stop the radio operator informed the command post of our location.

Slowly we neared the suspected break-in point near kilometre stone 20; however nothing in the least happened. The first car drove forward, its engine making plenty of noise. We could definitely be heard deep into the forest. On we went. We passed kilometre stone 21, again nothing. Kilometre stone 22, nothing. Just beyond kilometre stone 23 an S-turn – halt! There were vehicles sitting on the road; the cars of the column. It was a sorry scene. The cars were riddled with bullet holes, windows shot out, items of equipment lay strewn about. Here a steel helmet, there a mess kit, a wallet still containing money.

We continued on, for the enemy had not yet been located. The lead car halted at the next bend in the road, at kilometre stone 24. Then a sharp crack ripped the stillness: anti-tank gun! The enemy had been found. The next order was not long in coming: 'Reverse, march!' We breathed a sigh of relief; we had completed our mission.

Suddenly there was a call from the last car: tanks from behind! Were they ours or Russian? Then we saw the crosses, they were German. It was our assault guns with mounted infantry. A general was personally leading the battle group. Leutnant Gebhard reported and described the exact position of the enemy anti-tank gun to the assault gun crews. The infantry now deployed to the left and right of the road; the assault guns were quickly able to destroy the anti-tank gun. We, however, drove back, and the order 'move out!' freed us of our mental strain. A drink of good liquor helped us dissipate the tension."

Under a rain-filled sky, which at times drenched the area in the afternoon, the panzer-grenadiers continued their vigorous attack. The villages of Krutoye, Umrichino and Shishkino, already more strongly occupied, were their objectives. By about 05.00 radio reports announced that all had been captured. At the same time I Battalion took Kusmenkovo. The line reached by the units now looked like this: north edge of Kusmenkovo (I), northeast edge of Progress (I), forest edge 1 kilometre in front of Alisovo (Bernhagen Company), Piryatinka (Division Escort Company and attached Regimental H.Q. Company). – II Battalion was still in the forest west of Alisovo and like I Battalion it prepared for a further attack on the apparently strongly-defended Alisovo. The subsequent objective of I Battalion under Major Remer was the village of Ismorosny on the Vitebyet River. The previously identified elements of the Soviet guards divisions, as well as an anti-tank and a mortar regiment, had already crossed the river to the west.

In the meantime the main body of the Panzer-Grenadier Division *Großdeutschland* had arrived. The panzer-fusiliers were on the approach and their leading elements arrived in the area east of Alechino. I Battalion, Panzer-Fusilier Regiment GD went into position there, its mission to advance on Shudre on the left of the Panzer-Grenadier Regiment GD. A first boundary line was drawn between the two regiments and ran approximately from Alechino to southeast of Shudre (both for the panzer- fusiliers).

Enemy resistance grew significantly and increasingly hindered a further advance. Nevertheless, the German forces had to try to capture the Vitebyet against the Soviet guards divisions, among which the "Red Banner" Division had been identified, in order to establish a new main line of resistance along the river. This was not accomplished until 26 July and the success was only partial. Early that morning II Battalion, Panzer-Grenadier Regiment GD set out against Alisovo frontally. The outskirts of the village were taken in the face of very heavy resistance and losses were not insignificant. The commander of the battalion's 7th Company was killed when the enemy threw back a live grenade. Feldwebel Werner, who had just been promoted for bravery in the face of the enemy, died a hero's death, while Feldwebels Braun and Barth of the same company were both seriously wounded. This left 7th Company without any non-commissioned officers. The oldest soldier in the company, Obergefreiter Harz, assumed command and was able to lead the unit to a successful completion of its mission. For these courageous actions Harz was promoted to Unteroffizier on the battlefield and was awarded the Iron Cross, First Class.

The only unit to reach the Vitebyet was I Battalion of the Panzer-Grenadier Regiment GD. Riding in their armoured personnel carriers and with the support of the Panzer Regiment GD, the troops of the battalion advanced vigorously and entered the village of Ismorosniy. This created a dangerous situation for the enemy, in that a German battle group had taken his jumping-off point. It appeared important to the overall situation that this position not just be held, but expanded and reinforced. It was also a certainty that the enemy would commit everything in order to recover Ismorosny. Heavy enemy counterattacks were reported there and at Alisovo at about 14.30. A critical situation arose at the boundary between III Battalion, Panzer-Grenadier Regiment GD and I Battalion, Panzer-Fusilier Regiment at Alechino as a result of a penetration by enemy tanks with infantry. Enemy forces with tanks broke into 11th Company, Panzer-Grenadier Regiment GD's positions, but the situation was cleared up by late in the evening after the destruction of five enemy tanks.

The division command now decided to hold the positions that had been reached and incorporate them into the new main line of resistance. The new line ran approximately as follows: village of Ismorosny – across the north edge of Kusmenkovo – Alisovo and further about 3,000 metres through the forest in a northwesterly direction to I Battalion, Panzer-Fusilier Regiment GD southeast of Alechino. The division's artillery was moved forward, strongpoints were set up, anti-tank and flak positions were scouted and occupied to defend against enemy tanks.

In the course of these movements Feldwebel Schlüter of 7th Company, Panzer-Fusilier Regiment GD was killed in the heavy forest fighting on both sides of Alechino. It was a heavy blow for the company, especially since Schlüter had only returned from leave on 24 July. The unit farthest to the east, the Panzer-Grenadier Regiment GD, was sent three battalions of the 45th Security Regiment to further reinforce its positions.

The 27th of July presented a contrary picture to the days before: the Soviets were constantly on the attack, especially against the sector held by III Battalion, Panzer-Grenadier Regiment. The enemy artillery fire, which was heavy at times, lasted until far into the night, however the defenders were able to successfully repulse all enemy attacks. The war waged by the infantry in this area of forest was probably among the most uncomfortable of any on the Eastern Front, for it demanded a lightning-quick reaction against an enemy who appeared suddenly. Often the small numbers of men were only metres apart. The enemy could strike suddenly from ambush. This was the fate of Wachtmeister Carls of 2nd (APC) Squadron, Armoured Reconnaissance Battalion GD, who led a patrol on foot into the forest north of Karachev but failed to return. During a later advance personal effects, weapons and a steel helmet were found and then several hundred metres further the cruelly-battered bodies. The patrol had walked to its doom in the forest.

The first combat orders for the Armoured Reconnaissance Battalion GD, which in the meantime had also assembled near Karachev, arrived during the evening of 27 July. Its mission was to reconnoitre the forest west of Varkiy and destroy the enemy south of the line Varkiy – Paseka. This order reveals that the enemy spearheads in the north were already much farther to the west, therefore trying to swing north and outflank the German units. Their objective lay near Briansk.

The 28th of July 1943 brought the first test of fire for the just-established main line of resistance on the division's northeastern front. The weather was dreary and rainy and threatened to soon turn the swampy subsoil into a watery moor. Again the Panzer-Grenadier Regiment GD's daily report provides closer details, which make obvious the changeable situation, but also reveal the defensive success achieved by the unit.

06.30	Heavy friendly air activity over enemy front line and rear artillery positions. The primary target of our air force is a raised road through a broad belt of swamp north of Shudre, over which all the enemy's supply traffic to the front appears to be flowing.
09.00	Enemy barrage on our front line with artillery, tanks and mortars as well as rocket launchers.
09.35	Enemy tanks with infantry in Alisovo.
09.38	Seven enemy tanks break through to the south near Kusmenkovo.
09.40	Two T-34s standing several hundred metres north of Kusmenkovo.
10.00	Penetration by enemy infantry against II Battalion, 45th Security Regiment is thrown back by our battle reserve (pioneer platoon).
10.20	II Battalion, 45th Security Regiment reports penetration against 8th Company with four enemy tanks. Counterattack by 7th Company, 45th Regiment. One 75mm Pak assigned to lend support.
10.25	Enemy infantry near Point 214.9.
10.40	One enemy T-34 knocked out near the regimental command post (north of Progress).

BATTLES FOR THE KARACHEV FOREST
July 24 to August 3, 1943

10.50	Situation at Kusmenkovo unclear.
10.55	Artillery reports: own infantry still in Kusmenkovo.
11.50	Direct hit on II Battalion command post: Leutnant Eckhardt Köpfe killed.
12.30	Slackening of enemy artillery activity. Main line of resistance back in our hands everywhere. 18 enemy tanks destroyed so far. I Battalion also reports fighting in Ismorosny.
13.20	Forward artillery observer reports: two enemy battalions and tanks assembling near 311.
14.50	Further preparations by an enemy battalion at the southwest corner of the forest north of Ismorosny. German Stuka attack by about 15 machines on Alisovo.

That afternoon the enemy assaults also abated against the shoulder position farther to the northwest, where elements of the Panzer-Fusilier Regiment GD had dug in. There, too, the defenders had held onto all parts of the main line of resistance. In carrying out its mission, the Armoured Reconnaissance Battalion GD had meanwhile fanned out to the north with numerous armoured patrols. Its main objective was to determine the exact location of the enemy. By noon the stream of radio communications from the patrols had allowed a relatively clear picture to be formed.

Panzer-Grenadier Regiment GD, which had come under at times intense pressure from enemy attacks that day, was holding a line Alisovo–Alechino along with the Panzer-Fusilier Regiment GD. To the left was "Gruppe Schmahl," whose positions extended roughly through Trubechina–Piryatina. The front then followed "Gruppe Major Klein" to the north with the 42nd Pioneers, who were still in Mal. Semenovka. A forward observation post south of Tvanovskoye Dvoriki reported major east-west movements by the enemy in Paseka, including eight guns and trucks carrying infantry in one case. This supported the suspicion that after the failure of his southward advances the enemy was attempting to swing out farther to the northwest. The fall of the villages of Krasaskiye and Novogorodskiye therefore had to be expected soon.

The first bad news reached the Armoured Reconnaissance Battalion GD in the afternoon: Major Klein's pioneers fell back from Semenovka, the villages of Krasaskiye and Novogorodskiye were also lost. In the early evening hours the first arriving units of the 293rd Infantry Division were sent against Novogorodskiye from Karachev.

The next 24 hours can be characterized as quiet, if one discounts repeated attempts by the enemy to mass forces and their destruction by our Stukas and flying tank-destroyers. In the north our situation appeared to improve again somewhat, after the first elements of the 129th Infantry Division arrived there and together with the 293rd Infantry Division recaptured the villages of Novogorodskiye and Mal. Semenovka. Meanwhile the Armoured Reconnaissance Battalion GD, which was operating in the same area, took a line from west of Varkiy to the village of Terebilovo, where it had little contact with the enemy. Our Henschel anti-tank aircraft made repeated attacks on enemy tank concentrations and it had to be assumed that there were stronger enemy forces to the north. During one such air attack the Soviets revealed a new type of anti-aircraft rocket in the form of a wire net with numerous explosive charges which was fired into the air. As a result subsequent attacks by German aircraft were somewhat more hesitant.

On 29 July the commander of the Panzer-Fusilier Regiment GD, Oberst Kassnitz, died in hospital in Breslau of wounds received on 5 July. He had been awarded the Knight's Cross eight days earlier.

Loud track noises from enemy tanks were again heard in front of the Panzer-Grenadier Regiment GD during the night of 30 June. This led the regiment to conclude that the enemy planned to attack this sector the next day. At about 09.00 about 30 enemy tanks were reported advancing west in front of the Panzer-Fusilier Regiment's lines on either side of Alechino. The objective of the enemy tanks appeared to lie in the south, roughly at Mertvoye. I Battalion of the Panzer Regiment GD immediately moved to counter this attack and was able to frustrate the enemy's attempt to break through while destroying a large number of Soviet tanks. Oberleutnant Risch and his Panzer IVs alone destroyed eighteen enemy tanks. Just arrived at Panzer Regiment GD was a Panther battalion, whose commander and adjutant reported to the command post for briefings.

There was also lively combat activity farther to the northwest with the Armoured Reconnaissance Battalion GD. Early in the morning of 30 July Rittmeister Spaeter reported hearing tanks and orders being given in the forest north of Point 211.7. Soon afterward 2nd (APC) Squadron was attacked in its positions there by two squadrons of Cossacks and about ten enemy tanks. The difficult terrain, which restricted visibility, made the squadron's defensive efforts more difficult. The half-tracked armoured personnel carriers simply couldn't drive off the firm roads without sinking immediately. On several occasions APCs suddenly found themselves facing thirty or more Soviets only metres away. Even the constant artillery support provided by II Battalion, Panzer-Artillery Regiment GD, directed by forward observer Oberleutnant Felsinger, brought little relief.

Finally four panzers, two Tigers and two flamethrower tanks, under Leutnant Fölke were sent to help. They were unable to reach the front line, however, on account of road difficulties and the weak condition of local bridges. The first significant relief was provided by two companies of the Armoured Assault Pioneer Battalion GD. This one day's fighting had cost 2nd (APC) Squadron the lives of two of its technical sergeants (Wachtmeister).

Higher levels of command by now realized that the salient near Orel could no longer be held in the present situation. A new shortened line east of Briansk – the so-called "Hagen Position" – was to be occupied instead. One precondition for the withdrawal was that all the units leave the "bulge" near Orel on a timely basis, while another was that the existing positions north of Karachev remain in place as flanking protection and the enemy not appear in the planned "Hagen Position" before the German troops. This new winter position was planned along the Desna River. All movements focused on this.

A fresh rumour circulated as far as the most forward foxholes; once again the Panzer-Grenadier Division *Großdeutschland* was supposedly to be transferred to the west or even south to the area of the Brenner Pass on the Italian border in the course of this withdrawal movement to the new defensive line due east of Briansk.

This was not yet the case, even though the first relief orders were being worked out. Everything was relatively quiet in the existing lines, but the position was not looked upon as favourable by the regiments. The panzer-fusiliers lay within shouting distance of the enemy in the tangled jungle of the forest, which prevented any kind of view of the enemy hinterland, especially for the artillery observers. The forest on either side and east of Alechino was impenetrable and no one knew what unpleasant surprise was being prepared in its depths from one moment to the next.

The panzer-grenadiers were in a similar situation; their positions lay in front of the enemy-occupied hills northeast of Alisovo. These allowed them to keep the enemy under observation as well as the crossings over the Vitebyet River – such as the raised road north of Shudre – which served as the Soviets' most important supply crossings. A certain improvement of the existing positions would have to take place to establish a future, definitive main line of resistance.

For this reason the division planned one more small advance to the northeast. Preparations for this were made immediately. The focal point of the attack was placed on the right. This area was held by the Panzer-Grenadier Regiment GD, whose positions appeared most favourable for launching the attack. The panzer- fusiliers on the left were to follow and as the attack progressed they were to move their positions forward through the forest farther to the east. Over the next few days the Luftwaffe carried out numerous attacks with what for this sector was a large number of aircraft against recognized enemy targets as well as the raised road north of Shudre. The objective was to soften up the enemy before the panzer-grenadiers attacked. The GD listening posts repeatedly intercepted uncoded enemy radio communications which revealed that they knew exactly who they were facing. A typical message intercepted in this sector was: "Großdeutschland is in front of us! We're not going to attack, we're digging in instead!"

The division reported nothing out of the ordinary on 2 August. The only significant event took place in the division's rear area, somewhere at the edge of the forest in the vicinity of Abrosimovo near Karachev. Rittmeister Spaeter of the 2nd (APC) Squadron of the Armoured Reconnaissance Battalion GD was presented with the Knight's Cross by the division commander. In a brief speech to the assembled battalion the commanding officer outlined the squadron commander's earlier accomplishments. The battalion itself was given a chance to rest, which it used to prepare for an early transfer into another area.

As the sun rose on a clear morning on 3 August 1943, the Panzer Regiment GD under the command of Major Pössel moved into the southern part of Ismorosny. Together with I (APC) Battalion of the Panzer-Grenadier Regiment GD it was to carry out the decisive assault to the northwest. For the operation the Assault Gun Battalion GD under Major Frantz was assigned to the right battalion of the Panzer-Fusilier Regiment GD, I Battalion under Major von Hanstein. The battalion was to assist the battalion as it advanced through the forest east of Alechino beside III Battalion, Panzer-Grenadier Regiment GD. The brief accounts in the war diary of the Panzer-Grenadier Regiment GD describe the course of the attack, in which all the artillery of the Panzer- Artillery Regiment GD as well as attached artillery battalions from other units, some with heavy guns, took part:

06.40	After heavy Stuka attacks I Battalion (Remer) begins attack from Ismorosny against wood to the north. This attack is
GD and	supported by I Battalion, Panzer-Artillery Regiment Panthers.
08.20	II Battalion and III Battalion (Senger) move out from forest positions northwest of Alisovo to the northeast. As well strong artillery and Stuka support. Attack accompanied by the von Wietersheim Panzer Battalion.
07.00	Thurau Company of I Battalion has broken into the forest.
09.05	I Battalion reports: strong flanking fire from the area 600 metres northeast of north exit forest road, north of Ismorosny.
09.20	Middle of forest reached, strong opposition.
09.30	According to report by artillery II Battalion (Konopka) about 1,000 metres northwest of northwest corner of Alisovo. Enemy position breached.
09.50	Preparations for greater concentration of all heavy weapons in front of each objective to be reached by the infantry, on order of the Commander-in-Chief, who is present.
09.50	Combing of the forest from the road to the southwest again making good progress in the face of limited enemy resistance.
09.55	Forest edge 500 metres both sides of road occupied. Contact with 45th Security Regiment on right. Two security companies moved up and inserted in forest with front facing north east.
10.15	Mission for III Battalion received via operations officer and radio: press ahead to eliminate flanking threat to II Battalion
10.18	Czaya Company has cleared forest, reached west end of forest (I Battalion).
10.25	Mission for III Battalion (Senger): If difficulty encountered in advancing, insert one company behind II Battalion (Konopka) and turn west.
10.15	All security companies have reached assigned area.
11.15	Orientation by Leutnant Wechmann of II Battalion: one company at nose of forest west of Number 6.0 with front facing north-northeast; a further company of II Battalion

	north-northwest of it farther to the front. Tanks (von Wietersheim) are to turn west. Gap still separates battalion from neighbouring battalion (III) on left.
11.30	Report from I Battalion: enemy infantry attack from north.
11.45	Enemy falling back northward from Alisovo toward "Yellow Hill" (6.0)! Engaged by artillery.
12.40	Orientation by Leutnant Wechmann of II Battalion: II Battalion in forest west of 6.0 ("Yellow Hill"). No contact to left (III Battalion). Three of our Tigers out of action, six T-34s destroyed.
12.30	6th Company of the 45th Security Regiment moved off.
13.30	Preparations by I Battalion to attack "Yellow Hill" (near Number 6.0) complete.
13.40	Order issued to III Battalion to establish contact with II Battalion.
14.02	Order to II Battalion: leave one company behind to guard to the west; prepare to attack "cornfield hill" with two companies.
14.22	I Battalion attacks, together with tanks.
14.55	Report II Battalion: have attacked! Artillery barrage from 60 barrels, Panzer-Artillery Regiment GD and attached artillery and heavy infantry guns of the Panzer-Grenadier Regiment GD. Contact established with III Battalion (Senger)!
15.13	Report II Battalion: attack making good progress.
15.15	Orders for I Battalion, 45th security Regiment: one company to II Battalion, two companies to III Battalion, in order to take over sectors of both battalions.
14.40	I Battalion on Hill 6.0!
16.00	II Battalion in defensive position due south of ridge, 1,500 metres south of Shudre. Right boundary is the road.
16.10	Bernhagen Company in front of Shudre is withdrawn.

This account, assembled from numerous reports, shows that I (APC) Battalion, together with the Panthers and other tanks of the Panzer Regiment GD, attacked at 06.40, initially toward the north then west toward Hill 6.0. Soon afterward II Battalion (Konopka) and to its left III Battalion, Panzer-Grenadier Regiment GD set out through the forest in a generally northeasterly direction and were able to capture the forest edge north of enemy-occupied Alisovo in the face of, at times, heavy opposition. The Panzer IVs of the von Wietersheim battalion provided support and destroyed most of the enemy tanks. I Battalion, Panzer-Fusilier Regiment GD under Major von Hanstein participated in the advance by the panzer-grenadiers by carrying out a forceful advance to their left. The panzer-fusiliers also gained a considerable amount of ground in the forest east of Alechino.

After the completion of the first phase of the attack there followed a brief period of preparation for the next assault. The new objective was the capture of Hill 6.0 and the advancement of the main line of resistance to the hills to the north, which offered a view of Shudre and the raised road to the north of it. With their capture the actual objective was reached. The companies of the 45th Security Regiment could occupy their new positions.

The day's losses had been considerable. It is known that radio operators Deutsch and Wolter (both of 14th Company), Obergefreiters Meier and Hechler and Gefreiters Ravenstein, Damaschke, Hölz and Steffens of 13th Company, III Battalion, Panzer-Grenadier Regiment GD left the battlefield, most with serious wounds. The other companies too had paid for the battle in the forest and cornfields with losses. The courageous commander of one of the companies of the Panzer Regiment GD, Oberleutnant Risch, who had enjoyed such success in the past days, died a hero's death in the battle for "Cornfield Hill."

However the success of this advance achieved what the operation's commanders had wanted: a usable main line of resistance with a good view of the enemy hinterland had been won. Scarcely had the night of 4 August changed over to another sunny day, when officers of the 8th Panzer Division appeared to assess the positions their division would be taking over. The 8th Panzer Division's 10th Panzer Regiment drove forward with its tanks as far as the forest near Ismorosny and there took over the GD positions; the panzer-grenadiers were relieved by the men of the 28th Panzer-Grenadier Regiment, also a unit of the 8th Panzer Division.

At this time several advance detachments were sent ahead to Briansk to make preparations for entraining. Morale rose again: out of the fire of this cursed position in the forest of Karachev; rest and food, preparations for new duties in a new area. They were a mobile fire-brigade again. It had been a costly struggle, but a successful one.

CHAPTER 3

WITH ARMY GROUP SOUTH AGAIN

The Armoured Reconnaissance Battalion GD was probably the first to reach the entraining station of Briansk after crossing the log roads through the dense forest. It was also the first after the division command to learn that the division's destination was not the sunny south or the Brenner, but Akhtyrka. The front was ablaze there; reports indicated that the enemy had broken through the well-known positions in the Tomarovka-Borisovka area. That was all that was known, except that haste was demanded. While the first panzer-grenadiers were entraining in Briansk on 5 August, that evening the armoured reconnaissance unit arrived at Boromlya, north of Trostyanets. The bulk of the squadrons detrained near Akhtyrka in the late evening hours. They were the first to arrive in the new battle zone.

However one other unit belonging to *Großdeutschland* detrained near

Sumy at about the same time and headed for the front via Lebedin: the future III (Tiger) Battalion, Panzer Regiment GD. After entraining at Neuhaus Station near Paderborn in July 1943, III (Tiger) Battalion was sent by blitz train to the Eastern Front. Each transport consisted of four Tiger tanks, two personnel cars and two munitions cars. The tanks themselves were loaded aboard special Reichsbahn "ssyms" cars capable of bearing 80 tonne loads. These were in themselves a problem, for each panzer had as standard equipment a set of loading tracks in addition to its normal driving tracks. The loading tracks were narrower in profile than the wider driving tracks. During loading of such a rail car the Tiger first took down the loading tracks from the car; then each of the 3-tonne driving tracks was removed and the loading tracks installed. On driving onto the "ssyms" car the Tiger carried the driving tracks with it between the installed loading tracks. Then the tank was braced. During unloading this process was repeated in reverse order.

Since the 9th (Tiger) Company (previously 13th Company) had already been with the division for some time, the new units formed at Sennelager for the new unit were the battalion headquarters with headquarters company, two battle companies and a heavy workshop company. Formerly designated 1st Company within the battalion, 9th Company, which was already with the panzer regiment, was under the command of Hauptmann Wallroth, Oberleutnant Stadler and Leutnant Folke. The majority of the company's personnel came from within the division.

The former 2nd Company, now 10th Company, was under the command of Hauptmann von Villebois with platoon leaders Oberleutnant Arnold and Leutnant Klose. Most of the company's personnel came from the 30th and 31st Panzer Regiments.

The former 3rd Company, now the 11th Company, was commanded by Oberleutnant Bayer. Platoon leaders were Oberleutnant Leussing, Leutnant Conrad and Leutnant von Waldow. The company's personnel were mostly from the 18th Panzer Regiment. Commander of the workshop company was Oberleutnant Stinshoff. The battle order of III (Tiger) Battalion was as follows:

Battalion headquarters with headquarters company, 3 fully-equipped Tigers (88mm KwK and light 2 machine-guns). Headquarters company included a signals platoon with three armoured vehicles, medium-wave radio squad, reconnaissance platoon with 3 medium and 4 light armoured personnel carriers, pioneer platoon with 2 armoured personnel carriers and 4 trucks. Flak platoon with three 20mm quadruple flak on self-propelled carriages.Scouting platoon with 4 VW Schwimmwagen, 4 motorcycle-sidecar combinations and 2 solo motorcycles. Three battle companies each with 14 Panzer VI, armed with 88mm KwK and 2 machine-guns. The 88mm KwK was a derivative of the 88mm anti-aircraft gun which had proved so effective in a ground role. There was only one major difference between the two versions: the anti-aircraft version was fired by means of striking pins, while the gun mounted in the Tiger, like all tank cannon, was fired electrically. This meant that by pressing the trigger the gunner completed a circuit which ran from the firing lever through the fixed striking pins to the shell, in whose base was located an electric opposite pole.

The machine-guns used in the Tiger were the MG 34 type. The MG 42, which was already in use by the infantry, was not used. Due to its high rate of fire and the resulting high consumption of ammunition, there was not enough room in the Tiger for the weapon. Of the two machine-guns one was in a fixed mount in the turret beside the main gun and thus its direction of fire could only be changed by moving the turret. On the other hand the second machine-gun, operated by the radio operator, was flexibly mounted in the bow of the tank in a so-called "ball mount."

The Panzer VI, or Tiger, had an overall length of about 7 metres, a height of about 3 metres and a width of 2.5 metres. The driving tracks were about 70 centimetres wide and together weighed about 6,000 kilograms. The Tiger was powered by a twelve- cylinder Maybach engine developing 700 H.P. Fuel capacity was 547 litres. Thus the Tiger was capable of driving only about forty kilometres in moderately difficult terrain before it had to refuel again. In the course of a single day's drive of forty kilometres a Tiger battalion with about 45 Panzer VIs expended approximately 24,500 litres of fuel, which the supply vehicles had to deliver each day. This total was further increased by the panzer companies' trucks, motorcycles, APCs and so on.

The engine cover plates of the Tiger were so heavy that it required three or four men to raise them. The Tiger carried ninety rounds of ammunition, armour-piercing and high-explosive, in internal racks. About 20 additional rounds could be stowed loosely in the turret. As well there were large quantities of machine-gun ammunition belts, egg-type hand grenades, smoke and tracing ammunition and the like.

The transmission of the Tiger was a miraculous piece of equipment. It was possible to shift gears without first engaging neutral just like in a modern car. It had eight forward and five reverse gears, as well as a so-called direction lever with three positions: forward, neutral and reverse. Unlike other tanks the Tiger was not steered by means of levers. Instead it used a steering wheel, similar to that of an aircraft. This steering wheel could easily be turned with a finger without great exertion.

Greater attention has been paid to the newest unit to join the GD for a reason. With its incorporation the division achieved a major strengthening of its panzer force. Now that its panzer regiment had three battalions, the GD Division was one of the most powerfully-armed units of the army, its equipment matched only by the divisions of the Waffen-SS. In the course of the past two years the earlier infantry division had become a pure panzer division.

When the first elements of the Panzer-Grenadier Division *Großdeutschland* began arriving in and north of Akhtyrka on 5 and 6 August, they were met by the spectacle of retreat, now a daily occurrence. The German troops streamed out of their former positions north of the Vorskla, near Borisovka-Tomarovka and further south near Kharkov in a westerly direction.

What had happened?

After the breaking-off of Operation "Zitadelle" the II SS-Panzer Corps and two panzer divisions (3rd Panzer and Panzer-Grenadier Division

Großdeutschland) had been withdrawn from the Kursk area. The Soviets were then able to reassemble and further strengthen their forces more quickly than expected. The salient now offered the enemy nearly ideal conditions for a breakthrough. The general weakening of forces on the German side was further exacerbated by the losses suffered by the German units, which could not be made good. This further increased the danger on Army Group South's northern front.

On August 3 the Soviet Voronezh Front launched the first major attack at the Kharkov-Belgorod area. The German front on either side of Belgorod was ripped open on a width of approximately 70 kilometres. The Soviet spearheads headed for Akhtyrka–Sumy–Poltava. From the immediate front-line area it was learned from the Fourth Panzer Army, which was in overall command there, that the enemy had already reached Borisovka in the Vorskla Valley, that III Army Corps with the 19th Panzer Division and the 255th and 332nd Infantry Divisions was supposedly encircled, that the situation north of the river sector was unclear, and SS units were still buzzing about somewhere farther to the south. For the time being that was all the information that was available.

For many of the German divisions deployed in this sector of the front the retreat was already in full progress. When the armoured reconnaissance vehicles of the GD arrived in Akhtyrka on 6 August the scene they found was one of disintegration: columns of infantry streaming rearwards, still-intact panzer units, even the newest Pak 43 anti-tank guns, all moving south over the dusty roads. The bridge over the Vorskla due west of the city formed a funnel for this stream.

Wild shouts greeted the GD men as they arrived: "War mongers!" "You swine who wish to keep fighting!" "Go home you blackguards!" These shouts were the mark of a beaten army, an unrestrained horde of men who no longer seemed to have any morale. For all this, the behaviour of the arriving units was even more determined. They set about moving all those whose morale had been shattered to the rear as quickly as possible and began restoring order, while they themselves prepared to offer resistance!

The arriving units of the Panzer-Grenadier Division GD, namely the Armoured Reconnaissance Battalion GD and then the pioneers, were at first placed under the direct command of Headquarters, Fourth Panzer Army and given their initial assignments. These took the following form: reconnaissance to the north, east and southeast, as well as occupying the initial resistance lines on a river line as far to the east as possible. If at all possible the potentially suitable Vorskla (in the north) and Pyadinka (in the east) Rivers were to be won and secured. In the south patrols were to drive as far as the Merla and establish contact with the Waffen-SS as soon as possible.

At about 11.00 the first armoured patrol commanded by Unteroffizier Rahlke, which was dispatched early on 6 August, reported Bogoduchov still free of the enemy, the village intact and most of the German supply dumps being plundered by the population. Nothing more was known of the enemy in this area. The Armoured Assault Pioneer Battalion GD under the command of Hauptmann Hückel detrained the same day north of Akhtyrka. It was immediately sent east, its destination the village of Novaya Ryabina-East at the confluence of the Vorskla and the Pyadinka. The next day, 7 August, brought more clarity over the enemy situation as well as the available German troop strengths.

The detraining stations of Boromlya, Smorodino and Trostyanets were all scenes of hectic activity. As the first elements of the panzer-grenadiers – H.Q., I (APC) Battalion and elements of IV Battalion – were detraining in Smorodino, further units like 1st First-aid Company and elements of I Battalion, Panzer-Artillery Regiment GD continued to arrive.

The bulk of the Armoured Reconnaissance Battalion GD, less 2nd (APC) Squadron, which was carrying out technical duties in Akhtyrka, pushed its patrols farther to the east and southeast and followed these by squadrons along the road to Bogoduchov. The city was reported free of the enemy early that day by a patrol led by Leutnant Gebhard. Meanwhile the 3rd (VW) Squadron took over the guarding of Kupyevacha, H.Q. Armoured Reconnaissance Battalion moved into Chodunayevka, while 4th (Machine-gun) Squadron moved to Zaphorozhets at first in reserve.

An armoured patrol under Unteroffizier Karrasch was sent northwest toward Swch. Marino east of the Pyadinka River. There it ran into five T-34s. The tanks and a large number of troop-carrying trucks immediately began pursuing the patrol. Then the enemy mobile force suddenly appeared at Kupyevacha Station, held by 3rd Squadron. It was forced to give up the village, which went up in flames. Only the southern part of the village could be held.

The Armoured Assault Pioneer Battalion GD had meanwhile arrived in Novaya Ryabina on the east bank of the Pyadinka. It immediately moved into strongpoint-type positions on both sides of the road to Bol. Pisarevka. This village, about 10 kilometres east-northeast of Novaya Ryabina, had already been taken by the Soviets; contact with the enemy had to be expected soon. It was also expected that the focal point of the enemy attack would lay there, as the road led directly to Akhtyrka. I (APC) Battalion was ordered to drive along this road and guard the bridge crossings over the Vorskla and the Pyadinka at Kirikovka as well as to the south at Yablotsnoye. The carrying out of these orders would result in at least a screen of German resistance nests in a semicircle around Akhtyrka.

The first serious engagements on 8 August occurred at different times, but at the same two significant points in the terrain: early in the morning two enemy tanks with mounted infantry attacked 3rd Squadron's positions near Kupyevacha, which had in the meantime been reinforced by the addition of three self-propelled anti-tank guns. The attack was repulsed by the squadron's 2nd Platoon. There were additional attacks during the day, but these too were rebuffed with the loss of several Soviet armoured cars. These attacks were seen merely as advances by point units, which in coming days would undoubtedly be followed by heavier attacks. This assumption was reinforced by reports from Leutnant Gebhardt's armoured patrol, which sighted considerable numbers of enemy infantry about 1,000 metres west of Bogoduchov.

Meanwhile Panzer-Grenadier Regiment GD, reinforced by I Battalion, Panzer-Artillery Regiment GD, two flak combat teams, 12th Company, Panzer-Artillery Regiment GD and the Armoured Assault Pioneer Battalion GD, occupied its positions. The pioneers remained in Novaya Ryabina, the Windeck Company (4th Grenadier) guarded the bridge at Klimentov, and the Czayka Company (3rd Grenadier) moved into the southern part of Yablotsnoye. Later arriving elements of III Battalion, Panzer-Grenadier Regiment GD, such as 13th Company, took over the defence of Yankovka, north of Kirikovka.

At about 13.35 Headquarters, Panzer-Grenadier Regiment GD reported that its command post was located 1,200 metres south of Swch. Vorovskogo, on the road to Akhtyrka. The Division Ia informed all the deployed GD units that III Army Corps, having broken out of Bol. Pisarevka through Ivaniy-Berdiny and Novo Sofiyevka, was now streaming from the southeast toward the Yablotsnoye river crossings and Novaya Ryabina with about 1,000 vehicles in order to reach the safety of the west bank. The enemy was pursuing this group of forces sharply as it fled west.

Passage of this battered German force was still in full progress when a force of seven T-34s with infantry attacked the east end of Novaya Ryabina. The enemy suffered a severe rebuff, however, losing several tanks to mines. The courageous pioneers under Hauptmann Hückel also managed to destroy three of the attacking T-34s from close-range. All of the strongpoints remained in our hands. This had undoubtedly only involved the spearhead of the Soviet attack. I (APC) Battalion positioned itself due south of Kirikovka, where it was thought the focal point would be the next day.

Further bad news arrived on the evening of that crisis-filled day: enemy armour had also reached the detraining stations of Boromlya and Trostyanets in the northwest; elements of the Panzer Regiment GD as well as II Battalion, Panzer-Grenadier Regiment GD were deployed at the latter site. In the city of Akhtyrka itself a mood of defeat reigned, caused by the passage of elements of the three formerly encircled divisions of III Army Corps, which alone had more than 1,000 wounded with them.

The local military hospital, which was relieved by the 1st First-aid Company GD, had its hands full caring for all the wounded. The work went on under a continuous rain of bombs from Soviet aircraft which also lasted through the night. The sun had not yet appeared on the eastern horizon, when in the early morning hours of 9 August Hauptmann Hückel's assault pioneers (two companies) moved silently into the houses and cottages of Staraya Ryabina which the Soviets had occupied during the night. Employing all the specialized pioneer close-range weapons at their disposal, the nests of enemy resistance were eliminated in a bloody close-quarters battle. The pioneers fired brief bursts from their submachine-guns and lobbed grenades through window openings. They blew up individual enemy tanks with mines. When dawn rose from the valley the last of the Soviets were gone, the burning cottages showed their way to the rear. The assault pioneers were the victors. Hauptmann Hückel's independent decision to eliminate this weak spot in the stabilizing front received the full recognition of the division command. It

DEFENSIVE BATTLES EAST OF ACHTYRKA
August 9 to August 12, 1943

DEFENSIVE PERIMETERS OF FORTRESS ACHTYRKA
August 12 to August 16, 1943

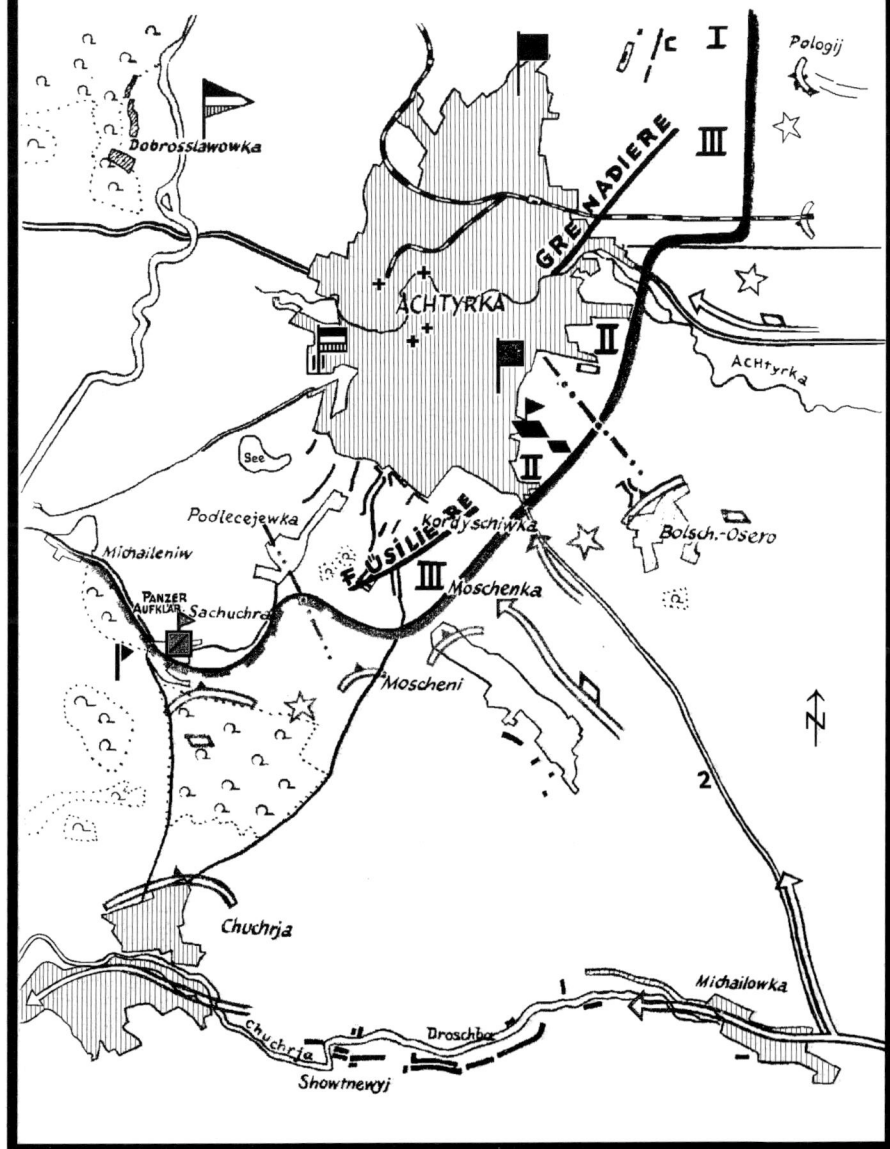

also later brought him the deserved recognition through the awarding of the Knight's Cross.

For the division in the forest west of Akhtyrka, however, there was still plenty to worry about. Even though its second regiment, the panzer-fusiliers, was in the process of detraining, incoming reports revealed a deteriorating situation in front of the screen of positions facing east. In many places the bulk of the enemy forces appeared to have arrived at the Pyadinka; north of the Vorskla at the Akhtyrka–Trostyanets–Boromlya rail line and in the southeast along the Bogoduchov road the squadrons, especially the 3rd and 5th near Kupyevacha and to the west, were coming under increasing pressure from the enemy.

In the sector held by the Panzer-Grenadier Regiment GD the enemy tried all day to gain a foothold on the west banks of the Pyadinka and Vorskla Rivers. With the limited forces available (considerable elements had not yet arrived) the regiment was unable to establish any continuous defence. The best it could do was fight a delaying action. There was no contact with friendly forces to the north. To the south there was loose contact with the armoured reconnaissance battalion, but its patrols could only observe, not stop a massed enemy assault. No reinforcements could be expected from the operational reserve for the time being, apart from the three divisions of III Army Corps assembling in the rear, whose fighting ability was doubtful after their breakout from the enemy encirclement.

Aware that it was on its own, the division command tried to make the best of the situation with the means on hand. It correctly recognized its first mission, to once again act as a mobile fire-brigade! It also realized that stopping the enemy in this sector was not possible; instead it would have to try and slow the advance of the vastly superior enemy, in order to give the senior levels of command a chance to establish a solid defensive line with new forces in a suitable area in the rear. In doing so full credit had to be given to the delaying action fought by the Panzer-Grenadier Division *Großdeutschland* between Vorskla-Pyadinka and Akhtyrka.

The division command had no influence on the battle zones farther north, where an outflanking appeared imminent, or farther south where two Waffen-SS divisions were obviously facing a similar task, namely that of holding up the enemy advance, more delaying than stopping it. If in these circumstances situations developed which forced a faster withdrawal of the divisions fighting the delaying action, this cannot be blamed on the units.

The events of 9 August illustrated the difficult nature of the task facing the panzer-grenadiers:

04.30	I Battalion reports: about 50 Russians have crossed the Vorskla west of Yankovka.
05.15	Enemy fire on southeast corner of Kirikovka.
05.45	Enemy battalion in march column sighted moving from Yankovka toward Kirikovka. One platoon of heavy infantry guns and one platoon of quadruple flak deployed against it.

	Road to Akhtyrka blocked by enemy. Heavy concentrations of enemy vehicles in area south of Kirikovka.
06.50	After attack by Bartsch Company (III Battalion) the road has been cleared again and is open.
07.20	Collective farm south of Kirikovka Station cleared of enemy.
07.52	Enemy attacks Czayka Company (3rd Grenadier) from both flanks at Yablotsnoye.
08.00	Five T-34s spotted south of Mayski Station.
08.25	Southeast section of Kirikovka cleared of enemy with assistance of flamethrower-armed APCs of the H.Q. Company.
08.30	Report from III Battalion: enemy pressing from south toward area 1,000 metres east of Garbusy.
08.40	Soviets move into Kirikovka in columns.
09.40	Enemy attack on Yablotsnoye.
10.00	Southeast tip of Yablotsnoye abandoned in face of strong pressure from enemy.
10.20	Oberst Terwitz, commander of 19th Panzer Division, establishes contact with Panzer-Grenadier Regiment GD.
10.50	Hauptmann Adler, commanding II Battalion following the wounding of Oberleutnant Konopka, arrived with two companies.
12.30	Enemy moves farther west north of Kirikovka. I (APC) Battalion - Major Remer - makes preparations to take Kirikovka southwest of the town.
13.45	I (APC) Battalion attacks Kirikovka! Leutnant Wolf Detlev Graf von Schwerin is killed.
14.15	Attack by I Battalion makes good progress.
16.45	13th Company, III Battalion attacked from behind in Yankovka-South by a force of approximately two enemy battalions.
17.45	Enemy attack preparations near Yekaterinovka, east of Yablotsnoye. The enemy moves farther to the south and southwest. Division Ia orders formation of new main line of resistance farther west to shorten our defensive lines.
23.30	Beginning of our withdrawal movements. New main line of resistance approximately so: Yankovka to hold, through Point 241.1, Veseloye–Zaphorozhets.

The southern tip of Kirikovka was also held until evening, after the Soviets reentered the town from the northeast. The situation south of the town was very unclear, especially since groups of enemy forces repeatedly appeared along the road, also from the southeast; even the command post of the Panzer-Grenadier Regiment GD had to defend itself on the road.

The withdrawal movements, which went on into the night, were aimed at a new line, but also at a reorganization of the battalions. The regimental command post was located at Barduny, III Battalion was still in Yankovka-South and Point 123.1, II Battalion echeloned to the rear toward the hills west of Veseloye-North, I Battalion still in the southern part of Kirikovka. At Point 1.5, due west of Nish. Veseloye, there was contact between II Battalion and the Armoured Reconnaissance Battalion, whose 3rd Squadron was holding the village of Vishnye- Veseloye, then 4th Squadron in Zaphorozhets, staggered to the rear 5th (Heavy) Squadron in Swch. Ilishevka and 2nd (APC) Squadron at Point 178.8 and Swch. Osetnyak.

At Point 161.2 on the road north of Zaphorozhets stood six Panthers of a recently-arrived panzer unit, apparently the 19th Panzer Division. A growing number of other battle groups reported in, such as 1st Battery, Nebelwerfer Instruction Regiment with the Armoured Reconnaissance Battalion GD.

Meanwhile, there was still no question of a consolidation of the front, for in any cases the forces available were not adequate to deal with the large number of hot spots at which quite strong enemy forces turned up. As well there was the fact that, although the Soviets respected the resistance at individual points, they soon discovered the gaps between them. They then simply advanced through these gaps. This forced our troops to improvise even further, meaning the rapid transfer of the defence to that point. There were simply shortages everywhere. There was one extended battle, this time on one side, the next time on the other. It was an exhausting mission for the units involved, which took a very high toll of the still available forces.

All in all 10 August demonstrated that the present, new positions were untenable, because the large number of armoured groups fielded by the enemy, up to thirty-six T-34s were counted in places, were repeatedly able to infiltrate through the gaps. The most dangerous situation in the division area was on the right wing, where the reinforced Armoured Reconnaissance Battalion GD and a few attached—some foreign—units had a not inconsiderable sector to hold. In the late morning hours of 10 August the enemy launched an attack toward Kupyevacha with a force of at least two regiments and accompanying tanks, approaching via Point 186.0-192.3. The weight of the attack was reduced by the quadruple battery of the "Jacob Battalion," but the defenders were unable to prevent an enemy battalion from driving through Prokopenk and entering Zaphorozhets, where it simply pushed out 4th (Heavy) Squadron, which was fighting a delaying action. The squadron subsequently dug in next to the Panthers at Point 2.0. It soon became obvious that the attackers were completely drunk and they completely ignored the German artillery, tank and anti-tank fire. Losses were correspondingly high, but with the masses of men available apparently not serious.

Leutnant Gebhard's armoured patrol reported from the battle group's right wing that Kosyevka, east of Kaplunovka, was occupied by the enemy and that enemy forces were moving from this village in a southwesterly direction. This underlined the enemy's intention of advancing as rapidly as possible to Akhtyrka on the open German flank. The danger was great that the enemy would arrive there before our units.

In any case the general arrived at the command post of the Armoured

Reconnaissance Battalion with news that the first panzer-fusiliers, apparently I Battalion, would arrive in the late afternoon. As well the panzers of I Battalion (Pössel) were going to undertake an advance through Kaplunovka in the direction of 192.3-178.4 toward 161.2 at about 16.00. The advance by the Pössel Panzer Battalion, which began at about 16.00, got no farther than Point 178.4, where it bogged down under heavy enemy fire, some from the flank. While this was going on about ten T-34s with mounted infantry rolled through unhindered along the road to Akhtyrka and forced the squadrons deployed there to withdraw their positions toward Veseliy Gay. Losses were heavy. At Veseliy Gay the squadrons were taken in and relieved by I Battalion, Panzer-Fusilier Regiment GD under Hauptmann Bergemann. This battalion immediately took over the positions at Veseliy Gay as far as the road (to the northeast), assisted by the 2nd (APC) Squadron under Rittmeister Spaeter with a panzer company.

Further elements of the division arrived in Akhtyrka, including the Assault Gun Battalion GD under Major Frantz as well as further elements of the Panzer-Artillery Regiment and the Panzer- Fusilier Regiment GD. During the night these units were sent toward the southeast.

The division command now found itself pressed to withdraw its left wing, the Panzer-Grenadier Regiment GD, to new positions farther to the west in order to achieve a shorter but also better-manned main line of resistance. Appropriate orders were issued to the commanding officer of the Panzer-Grenadier Regiment, Oberstleutnant Lorenz, to be carried out during the night.

All was ready on 11 August 1943. At 04.00 news reached the front from the supply trains that tanks were firing south of Akhtyrka. The 1st First-aid Company's main dressing station had already come under tank fire at about 03.30 and it had been forced to evacuate. In spite of the haste the move was an orderly one; the wounded were initially transferred to Yasenovoye. The enemy tanks had obviously come from a southerly direction, an area which appeared to be unoccupied. "Rumours" spoke of enemy tanks in Kotelva, farther south of Akhtyrka. The situation was uneasy; as dawn arrived the units at the front saw column after enemy column, all roaring toward Akhtyrka at high speed. There were huge dust clouds over the Bogoduchov–Akhtyrka road produced by endless march columns.

There was shooting in the city itself. Individual tank cannon were heard and occasional bursts of submachine-gun fire. Infantry had therefore already reached the gardens in the southeast part of Akhtyrka. There was minor confusion in our supply trains; arriving artillery, including the 105mm guns, went into position in the streets of the city, pioneers were taken from the panzer-grenadiers and drove at top speed into Akhtyrka. The division's forward command post in the city prepared for an all-round defence.

No one knew what was actually happening. Leutnant Dürig of the Armoured Reconnaissance Battalion GD, who drove into Akhtyrka on a motorcycle-sidecar, was fired on from a corn-filled garden and was fortunate to save himself, although he was badly wounded. The motorcycle was a write-off. Major Frantz's assault guns waited at the east end of the city in expectation of further enemy tanks from the east.

Before taking over their security positions at the east end of Akhtyrka the assault guns had had a special experience. Major Frantz described what happened:

"Arriving by rail, we were unloaded at the division's detraining stations north of Akhtyrka. At first I had only my 1st Battery and the combat trains of all three batteries with me. The remaining two batteries were still on trains somewhere. I received orders from division to take the elements on hand to a small village called Bolsh. Osero, east of Akhtyrka, about 3 to 4 kilometres away. No contact with the enemy was expected for the time being, however I was to deploy a security screen in any case. As I had been briefed on the overall situation by division and this, as the reader knows, was very unclear, I posted strong guards from the combat trains around our village at night. The guns of my 1st Battery remained on alert. Toward morning, it may have been 03.00, the sentries at the north end of the village reported loud tank noises. I drove there immediately on the motorcycle and determined that they must definitely be Russian T-34s. The security screen at the north edge was strengthened by two assault guns. Otherwise the trains, in particular, were made ready to march. The remaining assault guns remained at battle readiness. When dawn came it was possible to explore the situation further. Apparently an enemy battle group with 20 to 30 T-34s and mounted infantry had passed north of us in the direction of Akhtyrka and there run into our defences. In any case the Russian T-34s were widely deployed in wheat fields with a security screen to the west. Some of the crews had left their vehicles and were resting. As we were without infantry support, I decided to break through to Akhtyrka. Furthermore we had to reckon with the fact that this enemy battle group could summon infantry, which we could not cope with our assault guns alone. As the reconnaissance from the south part of the village in the direction of Akhtyrka had no contact with the enemy, I ordered my adjutant, Leutnant Bauer, to drive to Akhtyrka with the wheeled elements via the 'southern route' as quickly as possible, avoiding all combat. I still wanted to try and ease the situation in front of Akhtyrka by leading my assault guns to the city over the 'northern route.' So we drove out of the north part of our village at full speed, headed west in the direction of Akhtyrka.

As soon as we had approached to within 200-300 metres of the flank of the enemy tanks, the entire assault gun column, which so far had gone unnoticed by the enemy, turned right and opened fire. We succeeded in destroying a part of the completely surprised T-34s; I counted five burning. Then, however, the enemy settled down. The T-34s, especially those farther away, took up the battle. One of my assault guns was hit in the flank and knocked out. Wachtmeister Brauner and his crew, except radio operator Gefreiter Kilger, who was killed when the vehicle was hit, were able to bail out and run to other guns. We broke off the engagement and drove into Akhtyrka under very heavy fire. There we were taken in by our screen of anti-tank guns and tanks. In this way we had time to incorporate ourselves into the defences. My actions received the approval of the division command. With the exception of one assault gun, everything got through the enemy in one piece. The wheeled elements of the combat train suffered no losses at all."

Farther forward the panzer-fusiliers of Hauptmann Bergemann, the 2nd (APC) Squadron and several panzers held their positions near Point 2.2. There was scarcely any enemy pressure there, for the Soviets were moving without stopping in the direction of Akhtyrka on the far side of Vysokoye. It is astonishing that one can not speak of fear; more obvious was gallows humour and the awareness that they were actually quite strong with the concentration of forces in the city, even if there were enemy forces between them.

Only on the left wing, which was held by the panzer-grenadiers, did the situation look bad. Their positions were quite far forward and there was almost no contact with Akhtyrka. They had to withdraw, had to link up with the rest of their forces. The order to fall back to the main line of resistance was issued, but the Panzer-Grenadier Regiment's actions were also dictated by the enemy. The sequence of events just on the division's northeast front is best revealed by the reports it received:

04.30	Report from II Battalion from positions west of Nov. Veseloye, that enemy is attacking with strong tank forces. No contact to the right. II Battalion forms hedgehog around Point 146.6.
05.20	III Battalion reports enemy quiet.
06.35	Enemy observed in masses on the Bogoduchov–Akhtyrka road.
06.50	Order: all non-essential elements to fall back to Akhtyrka at once, in order to clear the city of enemy.
08.00	Enemy attack at Garbuny. III Battalion there. Further enemy preparations observed.

There was heavy fighting, some at very close quarters, at Point 146.6 where II Battalion had its hedgehog position. Leutnant Ahlfeldt, commander of 7th Company, was killed; Unteroffizier Rose of the same company also died a hero's death.

In the early afternoon the enemy pressure gradually slackened.

18.00	Following situation in the northeast sector (from left): Enemy has entered Bakirovka, from there advances in a southerly direction. Gruppe Lohmann holding north of Balyuki against increasing enemy pressure. Contact on left. Enemy incursion against III Battalion between railroad and road forces abandonment of Garbusy. Elements still holding at Barduny. Further enemy force from east with strong infantry and tanks. II Battalion at Point 146.6, no contact to the north. An enemy battalion with tanks sighted almost 7,000 metres behind the right wing in Verbovyi. For now it is not clear whether these are advancing north into the rear of the Panzer-Grenadier Regiment GD or continuing in the direction of Akhtyrka. At Point 2.2 stands I Battalion, Panzer-Fusilier Regiment GD with elements of the Armoured Reconnaissance Battalion GD. Bulk of the panzer-fusiliers plus the assault guns at the east end of

Akhtyrka awaiting the enemy. In the city itself, especially at the southeast corner, situation unclear. It is certain that there are at least minor enemy forces there with several tanks.

18.30	Report 17th Company: strong enemy movements from Petrovskiye to Bakirovka. Enemy attack on Kravchenki.
19.05	III Battalion reports heavy enemy attack from the direction of the sugar factory against its positions. Serious shortage of ammunition forces abandonment of positions.
19.07	Gruppe Lohmann abandons position near Balyuki and withdraws toward Akhtyrka.
20.00	Division order to move into positions at city limits of Akhtyrka. All heavy weapons to support defence there.

The movements toward the city of Akhtyrka, in some cases under enemy pressure, concluded in the early morning hours of 12 August. They led to the unification of the entire division in the positions at the outskirts of Akhtyrka, behind which all the divisional and some of the attached artillery sat in prepared positions. The guns were in a position to hammer the incoming enemy with heavy, aimed salvoes and considerably reduce the weight of his attacks.

As well, all the tanks and assault guns were assembled in the city, likewise ready to back up the infantry. The situation firmed up noticeably, even though the firefights in the gardens with the remaining enemy continued. Offensive patrols moved against the infiltrated enemy groups and destroyed them wherever they could catch them.

The 1st First-aid Company, which was based in Yasenovoye, reported handling more than 400 wounded in the previous forty- eight hours, which was indicative of the ferocity of the fighting during the withdrawal. The situation of the enemy around them caused more worry for the division command, which still had its command post in the forest due west of the city. All that was known of the enemy to the north was that he had long ago crossed the Akhtyrka–Boromlyz railroad to the west; what German units were there, it was supposed to be the 10th Panzer-Grenadier Division, was beyond its knowledge.

Even more dangerous for the division were the enemy movements south of its positions. Kotelva was definitely occupied by the enemy; the Soviets had penetrated to Belsk; enemy spearheads were said to be near Oposhnya in the south and in Budy to the north, indeed had even been sighted in the villages farther north. The division was threatened with encirclement on the west bank of the Vorskla. In spite of the situation in the position at the edge of Akhtyrka, which could be held with the support of the strong artillery forces available, the division issued orders for all armoured elements, which included I (SP) Battalion, Panzer-Artillery Regiment GD and I (APC) Battalion, Panzer-Grenadier Regiment GD, to withdraw during the night of 14-15 August and assemble west of the city. They were joined by III (Tiger) Battalion, Panzer-Artillery Regiment GD under Major Gomille, which had just detrained, and the bulk of the Armoured Reconnaissance Battalion GD. The division's plan: assemble during the night on both sides of Yasenovoye; departure of the armoured group at dawn under the command of General

Staff Oberst von Natzmer for a vigorous thrust to the south. Capture of the enemy-occupied villages of Grun, Kusemin and Belsk, destruction or chasing away of enemy forces on west bank of Vorskla.

While the squadrons of the Armoured Reconnaissance Battalion GD guarded the villages of Gnilnza and Pershe Travnya at Point 201.6, and the batteries of the 616th Flak Battalion trained their guns on enemy-held Dsyubi, "Battle Group Natzmer" rolled south at first light on 15 August. With I Battalion under Major Pössel leading the way, followed by III (Tiger) Battalion and the half-tracked armoured personnel carriers of I (APC) Battalion, the battle group advanced toward Grun. Meanwhile 2nd (APC) Squadron, Armoured Reconnaissance Battalion GD and the panzer company commanded by Oberleutnant Lex took the area immediately east of the road (between the Vorskla and the road) toward Budy, where the main body of the battle group was supposed to rendezvous. In spite of mines and considerable anti-tank fire the main force was able to enter Grun at about 13.00. Several super-heavy 122mm assault guns were destroyed there. This provided a demonstration of the clear superiority of the Tiger, which saw its first tank-versus-tank action there.

The advance continued without delay, and at about 15.00 the reinforced 2nd (APC) Squadron, which had been held up briefly at Rybalske, was able to report that it had linked up with the main force in Budy. An armoured patrol under Leutnant Gebhard which drove through Sinkiv and Dobshok toward Kusemin and Belsk reported that masses of enemy troops were fleeing south. The armoured battle group, 12 Tigers, 13 Panthers and two companies of Panzer IVs armed with the long 75mm gun, set off for Belsk at about 19.00. The objective was to take the small city and frustrate the enemy's aim of advancing farther to the north.

The reinforced Armoured Reconnaissance Battalion GD followed right behind the armoured group. A wild shoot-out developed against two enemy tanks and a few infantry at the gorge north of Belsk. One of 10th Company's Tigers, in fact the commander's vehicle, was knocked out by a determined enemy anti-tank gun. The tank's driver and gunner were killed, Hauptmann von Villebois and his loader were seriously wounded. Only the radio operator, an Oberfeldwebel, escaped with minor wounds. This incident, the first combat loss of a Tiger, showed that even a Tiger tank was not invulnerable if a disciplined anti-tank gun crew kept its nerve.

Finally the tanks advanced past burning trucks and houses into the village, where a security screen was immediately deployed. The whole night was spent flushing Soviets out of the cellars and ruins where they had taken refuge. This operation achieved a local success, for it put a considerable damper on the enemy. It was however unable to prevent the bridge over the Vorskla east of Belsk from remaining in enemy hands, which meant that the Soviets would probably turn up in Belsk again in a very short time. Patrols of the Armoured Reconnaissance Battalion GD determined that farther to the south other enemy groups and spearheads had already occupied Oposhnya and were feeling their way towards Budischtsche. This village lay only about 25 kilometres from Poltava! While the armoured elements of "Battle Group von Natzmer" were withdrawn to the area due west of or in the city of Akhtyrka, the reinforced Armoured Reconnaissance Battalion GD remained in Belsk until the evening of 16 August, where at about 18.00 it was relieved by Oberst Deutsch and about 150 pioneers. The battalion received orders to drive back to Akhtyrka and departed that same evening.

Meanwhile the senior commanders were formulating plans for a stronger attack by several German divisions from the Akhtyrka area to the south, in order to drive into the flank of the enemy forces at Kotelva and farther south and simultaneously establish contact with the Waffen-SS units believed to be in the area southwest of Bogoduchov.

On the other hand the enemy's situation was unclear; apparently he was assembling an entire tank corps near Kotelva and at the same time was bringing in fresh reserves against the SS units to the southwest. The proposed offensive action by the German side, with the Panzer-Grenadier Division *Großdeutschland* advancing in the centre, with the 10th Panzer-Grenadier Division behind and to the right and the 7th Panzer Division on the left, stood under a large question mark: they knew too little about the intentions of the enemy and in particular nothing about his reserves. It appeared, and this notion was felt particularly strongly by the division command, as if the enemy's strength southeast of Akhtyrka had been considerably underestimated. Statements by prisoners confirmed this fear, and so the division was quite aware of the difficulty of coming events.

The division carried out a brief reorganization, which resulted in the withdrawal of the Panzer-Grenadier Regiment GD and its transfer to the southern part of Akhtyrka and also included a twenty-four-hour period of technical service for the armoured elements the day before. At precisely 08.00 on 18 August a force led by the Panzer-Fusilier Regiment GD and the Assault Gun Battalion GD, followed by the entire Panzer Regiment GD with I (APC) Battalion of the Panzer-Grenadier Regiment GD set off down the road past Point 140.2 toward Kaplunovka. Following to the left was the rest of Panzer-Grenadier Regiment GD. The initial objective of the Panzer-Fusilier Regiment GD was the capture of Mosheni, while the other GD units were to reach the line Parkomovka–Kaplunovka.

The attack was led off by heavy Stuka attacks, in particular on the first villages to be taken, like Mosheni and Bolsh. Osero, while the batteries of the artillery regiments supported with heavy barrages.

The initial impetus of the attack resulted in the breaching of the enemy's main line of resistance; however the leading elements of the Panzer-Fusilier Regiment soon became bogged down in front of Mosheni. Unfortunately almost all the Tigers drove into a good-sized minefield south of Bolsh. Osero, so that almost the entire III Battalion with nearly 15 Tigers became bogged down and was unable to participate in the action until that evening. The track damage was so considerable that some of the Tigers had to go back into the workshops for repairs.

Major Frantz described the attack from the assault guns' perspective:

"Our mission was to support the attack by the Panzer-Fusilier Regiment. Incidentally, the target village of Bolsh. Osero was the same one we had left at the beginning of the battle for Akhtyrka after detraining. Oddly every soldier felt a certain curiosity when he was about to take a place where he had previously been and which had later been occupied by the enemy. It was as if one was about to visit a friend in peacetime. Of course the associated obstacles and surrounding circumstances were somewhat less pleasant in war. As per our briefing and orders, we took advantage of an artillery barrage on the edge of the village to drive quickly with mounted infantry to find gaps in the known minefield north of the village and then move up the bulk of the assault guns.

The plan worked surprisingly well, only two assault guns struck light mines and suffered track damage. The rest chanced upon a gap and were able to veer right north of the village and eliminate the anti-tank and machine-gun fire which flared up at the edge of the village. The rest of the assault guns were able to follow the tracks of those that had got through. With great satisfaction I realized that we had crossed the minefield in less than three-quarters of an hour. On learning by radio that our panzer regiment and the grenadier regiment, which were attacking west of the village, were stuck in a minefield, I immediately sent an assault gun to this battle group to lead the panzers through our gap. In the meantime we attacked southeast with mounted elements of the fusilier regiment. The enemy was apparently completely surprised by this surprising breaching of his mined main line of resistance. In any case we were able to seize the enemy artillery positions about four kilometres south of Bolsh. Osero after a brief firefight. The enemy gunners ran away from their guns in panic. Some were taken prisoner by our infantry. We halted on a commanding hill, posting security to all sides, and waited for the arrival of the remaining elements of the division. As planned, the panzers soon caught up with us as they continued their wide-ranging attack. By adapting to the development of the battle the division was in general able to reach its objective of the day."

The division subsequently issued orders for I Battalion, Panzer Regiment GD and I (APC) Battalion, Panzer-Grenadier Regiment GD to drive around the fateful minefield and then advance farther in a southeasterly direction. Remaining elements of the Panzer- Grenadier Regiment GD – II Battalion under Hauptmann Adler followed by III Battalion under Hauptmann Senger – moved on along the road and with the help of 4th Company, Armoured Assault Pioneer Battalion GD cleared the identified mine barrier. At 12.50 II Battalion reported that Hill 140.2 was in our hands and that they were continuing the advance toward Point 146.9. III Battalion secured the road south of Bolsh. Oserop south toward Mosheni, where the panzer-fusiliers initially got no farther. An enemy force of about fifteen T-34s, a number of anti-tank guns and strong infantry had dug in there. The Russian tank fire swept the road at 140.2 in an uncomfortable fashion.

About three hours after the start of the attack, Major Pössel's tanks and I (APC) Battalion reported that they had reached Point 144.7 and were advancing toward Point 181.4 north of Kaplunovka. The enemy was fleeing toward the north and northeast. Lively enemy activity in the air with bombing and strafing, especially of the road.

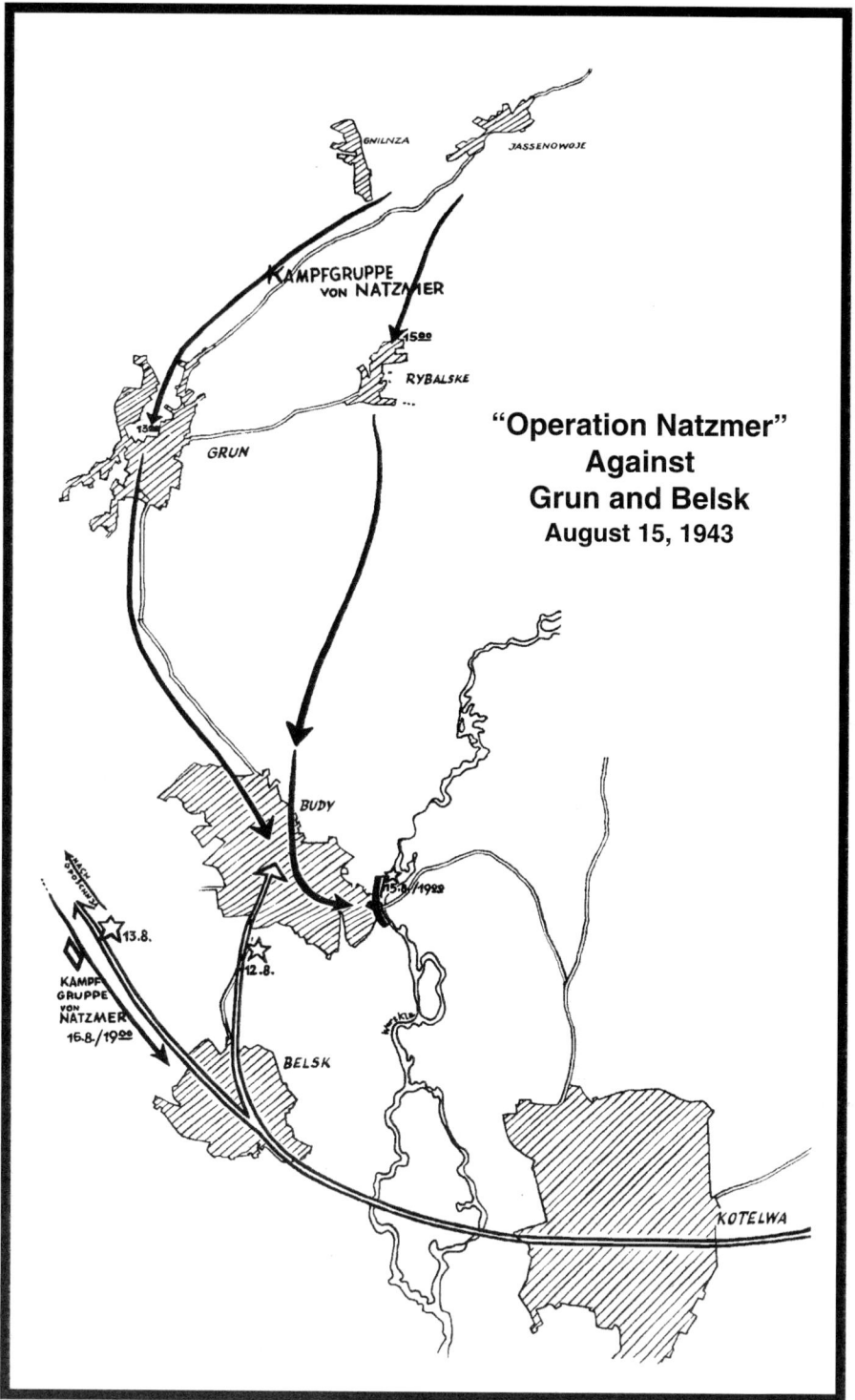

"Operation Natzmer"
Against
Grun and Belsk
August 15, 1943

New orders were issued at approximately 14.50. The Panzer- Grenadier Regiment GD was to veer west, with II Battalion from the area of 140.2 and III Battalion beside it, and attack Mosheni, which was still being stubbornly defended, from the east. The village had turned out to be a serious impediment to the advance by the Panzer-Fusilier Regiment GD as well as its neighbour on the right, the 10th Panzer-Grenadier Division, and everything had to be committed to break the resistance there.

Meanwhile the Armoured Reconnaissance Battalion GD had followed the panzer-grenadiers past Point 140.2 and was moving on Michailovka. On its own initiative the battalion attacked the village at about 19.00 and was able to capture the first houses in the northern part of the village. The enemy, who was initially taken by surprise by the attack from the southwest, reacted astonishingly quickly and fell back to the east from Kotelva with considerable elements. As a result of the delay at Mosheni he had enough time to withdraw the bulk of his units, so that the success on the German side was minimized. Still the leading German elements, the Pössel Panzer Battalion and Major Remer's APCs, were in Kaplunovka and on the road to the east of the town. The battle group was reorganized during the night; on the one hand because on the left the advancing elements of the 7th Panzer Division had not yet arrived, and on the other because significant counterattacks were expected from a northeasterly direction. The Armoured Reconnaissance Battalion GD initially moved its armoured elements only to the left flank of the division, facing northeast, and secured a line 178.8 – Swch. Osetnyak–Swch. Ilishevka – 167.1. The panzer-grenadiers moved their II Battalion forward to Kaplunovka, where it established its main position facing east-northeast. On the left to the northwest was III Battalion, approximately from Point 181.4 to Point 178.8. The terrain there consisted of low hills, so that one could easily see from one hill over the other. Most of these hills were covered with cornfields with pasture land in between. There were almost no trees, except on the isolated collective farms, most of which consisted of a few cottages and small, open gardens with a few trees. In many fields and meadows stood the familiar haystacks, which in the twilight were often taken for God knows what! Many of the low-lying areas and valleys were marshy and their suitability for vehicles always had to be checked.

With the enemy situation in the northeast unclear, during the night the panzer-fusiliers moved into Michailovka where they relieved the Armoured Reconnaissance Battalion and prepared for the attack south against Parkomovka. The panzers of I Battalion were supposed to advance simultaneously on the same objective from the southwest from Kaplunovka.

This attack by the two groups on 19 August was a complete success: Parkomovka was taken and a small bridgehead established across the Kotelva. Enemy resistance was comparatively light. The intention of having the Panzer-Grenadier Regiment GD follow this movement south had to be abandoned on account of the increasingly effective relief attacks from the northeast by Soviet reserve units.

A group of about ten enemy tanks was sighted near Osetnyak at roughly 05.15 and an infantry company near Ilishevka. The first enemy attack, in battalion strength with tank support, followed not five minutes later against the positions of III Battalion, Panzer-Grenadier Regiment GD. At the same time considerable enemy forces were discovered advancing on Point 178.8, and at approximately 07.10 II Battalion at Kaplunovka reported that further enemy forces were advancing southwest from Point 178.8.

There now began heavy defensive fighting in this sector on a line Kaplunovka (II./Pz.Gren.)–Point 179.9 (II./Pz.Gren.)–Point 181.4 (III./Pz.Gren.)–road to Swch. Osetnyak (Arm.Recon.Btl.)– Swch. Ilishevka–Point 167.1 (Arm.Recon.Btl.). The fighting continued with mixed success for the defenders until early on 24 August. It was a battle between guard units of both sides, which reached a level of severity, toughness and heaviness which was seldom equalled.

The enemy units were freshly-introduced guards airborne divisions, all young, very well trained and extraordinarily tough soldiers who would rather let themselves be killed in their positions than give up. They were in action day and night, backed up by a mighty force of tanks and anti-tank guns and supported by an active air force, consisting mainly of close-support aircraft. Their goal was not just to halt the German counterattack, but to destroy the German units.

On the German side the panzer-grenadiers and panzer-fusiliers of the Panzer-Grenadier Division *Großdeutschland*, with their heavy weapons, tanks and artillery, had seen days and weeks of hard fighting. In the end they were completely drained and exhausted, to an extent not seen before. The combat strengths of the companies had fallen considerably, strengths of 20-30 men in the rifle companies were the order of the day. The losses of the past weeks, especially among the leaders, had torn considerable gaps in the ranks, and some companies had to be led by men of Unteroffizier or Feldwebel rank.

Only in terms of weapons was the division at relatively full strength. The four battalions of artillery, including a self-propelled battalion equipped with Hummel and Wespe self-propelled guns, the first infantry regiment (grenadiers) with one APC battalion with about 80 armoured personnel carriers, the Panzer Regiment GD with a battalion each of Tigers, Panthers and Panzer IVs (long) and the assault guns of the Assault Gun Battalion GD, these bore the brunt of these battles, but also had to ensure that the backs of the fighting infantry were covered.

The Panzer-Grenadier Regiment GD undoubtedly saw the worst of the fighting from that day until 24 August. It shouldered most of the burden of meeting the Soviet assault with an unparalleled bravery. The attacks, advances, counterattacks and defensive measures were too numerous to describe in detail. The daily reports by one unit or another from this or that day may suffice. The following are by the Panzer-Grenadier Regiment GD from 20 August:

07.30	Infantry attack in battalion strength from 192.3.
09.45	II Battalion: enemy attack from 178.8 and 192.3 repulsed.
12.00	Osetnyak in our hands.

14.15	Two more attacks in battalion strength against II Battalion repulsed.
14.30	Enemy infantry 500 strong advancing south from area north of 178.8.
15.30	Orientation by Division Ia: at least three regiments identified on enemy side.
16.20	Enemy tanks with mounted infantry and following truck columns from the east toward Ileshevka.
16.40	Artillery reports: good effect on columns, munitions, trucks.
16.55	Twelve enemy tanks with mounted infantry broken through west of Osetnyak in direction of Bolsh. Osero, north of Udarnik. Regimental commander at III Battalion's forward command post since early morning.
17.15	II Battalion reports: 20 enemy tanks have veered east toward 181.4. Three T-34s in test station. Artillery reports that 7 enemy tanks have rolled through the firing positions of the 2nd and 3rd Batteries in valley east of Michailovka. Some guns out of action. Orientation by Division Ia: five enemy tanks with infantry at Point 171.1.
18.15	Regimental commander to Division Ia: 30-40 enemy tanks broken through near collective farms, about 10-15 of these knocked out.
19.50	Strong enemy attack directed against II Battalion at Kaplunovka. Battalion withdrawing to centre of town.
20.30	Enemy attack with tanks and mounted infantry against 12th Company, III Battalion south of Osetnyak. I Battalion, Panzer-Artillery Regiment GD reports 1st Battery put out of action by enemy tanks.
21.45	II Battalion reports: Forced out of Kaplunovka by enemy outflanking manoeuvre. Continuous main line of resistance exists from triangular wood to III Battalion.
22.30	Orders for new main line of resistance to II Battalion: due east of test station.
23.43	II Battalion reports: enemy moving past left wing with tanks and mounted infantry to south- southwest. In late afternoon an enemy assault gun was knocked out in the area of the regimental command post.

The situation seemed unclear, not just in the division's immediate combat zone but in the neighbouring areas as well. 1st First-aid Company reported that the enemy was outside Oleshnya and Lebedin and that its only road for evacuating the wounded was under enemy artillery fire. No evacuation of the wounded was possible at that time. During the night the first elements of the panzer-fusiliers located near Parkomovka, namely I Battalion under Hauptmann Bergemann, were pulled back and inserted on the division's left wing at Swch. Udarnik.

The following report was submitted on 21 August by the 3rd Company of the Anti-tank Battalion GD, deployed at Shemodanovka in the positions of II Battalion, Panzer-Grenadier Regiment GD:

"The night of 21 August was relatively quiet, but the first Soviet close-support aircraft came at dawn, heralding a hot day. Our gun was at Shemodanovka, in position in a harvested cornfield about 200 metres away from the road.

At about ten in the morning several Russian trucks with infantry drove past us on the road. Because of a shortage of ammunition for our anti-tank gun we weren't permitted to open fire on such a target. Then it was quiet again. In the afternoon our runner came with mail and some ammunition. Our gun tractor was about 400 metres behind us in a small valley. Then at about three in the afternoon it began.

German aircraft – He 111s – dropped countless high-explosive bombs right in front of our position, several dangerously close, but there was still nothing to be seen of the enemy. Because the terrain before us fell away somewhat and there was a ravine running across in front of us, we suspected that that's where the Soviets were making their preparations.

The Soviets attacked suddenly at 15.30; they tried to outflank us. This time the enemy attack was made without mortar support and also without artillery. Our gun tractor came over immediately in order to limber, so that we could withdraw if necessary. But things did not happen as we expected. Five minutes after the attack began our platoon runner, Gefreiter Steinke from Bessarabia, was killed by two bullets in the head. Gefreiter Drescher and I jumped for cover. In doing so Peter Drescher was shot in the heart and I in the shoulder, both with explosive bullets. We both passed out from loss of blood. I soon regained consciousness and tried to get out of the hole. With my Russian sniper's rifle in my hand, I realized that I was almost paralysed, then I passed out again.

When I woke up again the rifle fell in my lap. I saw that Gefreiter Dresche from Halle was wide awake even though he was bleeding heavily from his chest. Blood was running down from under my jacket. How I got out of the hole I do not know; I merely watched as Gefreiter Willi Müller from Sömmerda, Thuringia pulled me behind the gun tractor. Another two minutes and I would have ended up like Gefreiter Drescher, who was stabbed to death in his hole by the Russians with bayonets.

In spite of the heavy fire Gefreiter W. Müller dragged me to a grain shed, where the seriously wounded of 3rd Company lay. Oberleutnant Marx, the company commander, was also there, seriously wounded. Our artillery intervened at about 16.00 and gained some breathing room for us. Things were apparently not too good with the grenadiers either. When we drove away in the gun tractor I could see groups of grenadiers with raised hands being led away by the Soviets. Overturned and burning vehicles, empty gasoline cans, knocked-out tanks and dead, friend and foe, wounded heading for the rear, blown-up and abandoned guns, all this I saw on my way back to the main dressing station, where I was operated on immediately."

The division's accomplishments in a defensive role that day were acknowledged from above. That evening Generaloberst Hoth radioed: "Bravo GD!"

22 August 1943: Reports by the Panzer-Grenadier Regiment GD

02.00	Strong enemy attack on II Battalion with tanks.
03.20	Report from II Battalion: 8th Company still in its former position. 7th Company overrun. Russians outside II Battalion command post. Test station heavily occupied by enemy. Right wing of III Battalion overrun. II Battalion command post forced to fall back by advancing enemy. Order to I (APC) Squadron: blocking line west edge of Shemodanovka Valley. Artillery to place barrage fire in front of right wing III Battalion and on test station.
03.50	Beginning of morning twilight.
04.10	Fighting on 171.1.
04.30	Order on new line for II Battalion: road north of Shemodanovka, due east of mill to the stream.
04.50	Artillery report: friendly troops observed near test station. Our infantry on 171.1. Orders for Assault Gun Battalion GD: attack with an APC company of I Battalion north into flank of enemy force attacking III Battalion.
05.00	Blocking position one platoon of 3rd Company abeam windmill in bottom land. Formation of new main line of resistance there.
05.03	Artillery reports: Russians attacking 171.1 from the north. Two enemy tanks destroyed.
05.10	Right neighbour, II./20 and II./41, have contact with 7th Company in test station; this company is to be sent back to II Battalion by way of the right neighbour, as per order of the Division Ia.
10.00	Enemy attack on right neighbour, who falls back. 2 assault guns and 3rd Company sent there. Right neighbour then occupies new positions with contact with II Battalion on right wing.

Heavy close-quarters fighting raged in Parkomovka on 23 August, with the panzer-fusiliers defending themselves doggedly. A steady rain of mortar fire poured down on the defenders and this was largely responsible for their heavy casualties.

The destruction of 23 enemy tanks was reported from the northeast sector alone on the evening of the same day. Even if the enemy was able to gain ground, these gains were in no way commensurate with the enormous losses inflicted on him by the panzer-fusiliers and grenadiers. The positions held everywhere, even the communication between them remained iron fast.

The feats of the defenders in these days were superhuman. There was no rest at night due to continuous air attacks, enemy tanks driving around in their rear, and the reorganization of units and work on the positions. Then, during the day, they had to face enemy attacks, make changes of position and hold the positions. Hold, hold!!

Certainly everything that glitters is not gold; there too fear and the drive for self-preservation – and the spectre of the bolshevik massacre – caused the soldiers to fight to the last round. But from these motives, combined with the bravery of individuals and the example of their leaders, there developed a steadfastness that was admirable. Questions about the sense of this bloody conflict were scarcely ever raised on the battlefield, where it was a matter of to be or not to be.

During the night of 24-25 August the main line of resistance was moved back toward the south side of Chuchrja Brook as far as beyond the Krutenkaya Gorge, in order to shorten the front. This happened after the 7th Panzer Division was forced to give up the city of Akhtyrka on 24 August 1943. Contact to the south was established by the panzer-fusiliers (less III Battalion) via Point 165.7 to the west exit from Parkomovka. The movements to reach this new line generally took place with no pressure from the enemy, however they were revealed to him too soon by the premature and incautious burning of wheat ricks. It was scarcely surprising then, when defenders in Michailovka observed an enemy battalion streaming into the river valley at about 08.50 on 25 August. The Soviets also massed forces, including tanks, in the forest of the Krutenkaya Gorge, an indication that further attacks against the sector held by the panzer-grenadiers were imminent. Farther south enemy armoured forces assembled in considerable strength in the Chernyanski Gorge and in the village of Parkomovka, an indication that the enemy intended to advance west along this river valley toward Kotelva. From about midday on, the 25th of August saw continuous attacks on the entire main line of resistance. Limited penetrations were eliminated by counterattacks and by evening the units could report that the main line of resistance was firmly in their hands.

In the meantime the command posts had been informed that as part of a further shortening of the entire main line of resistance in the coming night the Panzer-Grenadier Division GD was going to be relieved and transferred, initially into the area near Oposhnya, for other employment. The division's positions were taken over by the linking together of the 7th Panzer Division in the north and the Waffen-SS units (Totenkopf) holding to the south. The only GD Division unit to stay behind was I (APC) Battalion of the Panzer-Grenadier Regiment GD, which occupied a prepared position southeast of Kotelva on the Kotelyevka Brook.

The division's movements during the night of 26 August 1943 took place without incident. There was relatively heavy bombing by the enemy but the pilots of the bombers were unable to locate their desired targets. The Panzer-Grenadier Division *Großdeutschland* was now placed under the command of General Lemelsen's XXXXVIII Panzer Corps, part of Armeeabteilung Kempf. The division thus left the combat zone where, in the past months, it had spent the long weeks of the attack, rest and refitting, and defence. The twenty-four hours until early 27 August the division spent in its old rest quarters at Dikanka-Oposhnya and Veliki Budischshe rekindled fond memories of the wonderful weeks in May and June 1943 when they had felt their full strength, probably for the last time.

What had happened in the meantime as far as the overall picture was concerned? Why were the former positions east of Kotelva abandoned and the division moved into the battle zone to the northwest? The major offensive by the Soviet Voronezh Front had smashed the first breach in the German defence lines. Farther south, this was followed by an attack by the Steppe Front which made unavoidable the abandonment of Kharkov by German troops on 22 August. The southern wing of the Fourth Panzer Army and the northern wing of the Eighth Army were both folded west, a consequence of the lack of adequate reserves.

The enemy poured into the rear area between Trostyanets and Poltava. Their strength came as a surprise to the Germans; the Soviets had recovered from the German counterblow of Operation "Zitadelle" more quickly than expected. As well they brought in considerable operational reserves which they had taken from other fronts. The Soviets intended to mass their forces for a breakthrough, and the area west of Belgorod and at Kharkov seemed most suitable for their tank units.

And yet, though the German units gave ground, through their bravery the enemy's intentions were upset enough to considerably slow their movements. The general line Poltava–Kotelva–Sinkiv essentially remained in our hands until 27 August and was, even if somewhat loosely, occupied by panzer and panzer-grenadier divisions.

On the other hand the situation in the Donets Region, in Army Group South's area, was even more ominous. The Sixth Army had initially succeeded in halting a dangerous Soviet breakthrough; however its forces were inadequate to restore the situation. Farther north, against the First Panzer Army, the enemy's attempt to break through had also failed to meet with the desired success; but there too German strength was exhausted. There were no longer sufficient operational reserves available.

These figures may illustrate the situation:

EIGHTH ARMY:

Front length:	Own units:	Soviet units:
210 km.	12 infantry divisions	44-55 rifle divisions
	5 panzer divisions	3 mechanized corps
		3 tank corps
		11 tank brigades
		16 tank regiments
		(in total about 360 tanks)

FOURTH PANZER ARMY:

270 km.	8 infantry divisions	20-22 rifle divisions
	5 panzer divisions	1 mechanized corps
	5 tank corps	1 tank brigade
		2 tank regiments
		(in total about 490 tanks)

At a conference of commanders-in-chief from the participating army groups at Vinnitsa on 27 August, Hitler acknowledged the dangerous situation facing Army Group South and declared himself ready to send further divisions from other army group areas.

Before it came to this, however, the Soviet breakthrough attempts in the south of the Eastern Front gained considerable ground and threatened to crush the positions of the Sixth Army. Army Group South therefore acted independently and ordered a withdrawal of the front to the so-called Tortoise Position, which for all intents and purposes initiated the evacuation of the Donets Region. Finally, on the evening of 31 August, Hitler gave Army Group South the freedom to withdraw the Sixth Army and the right wing of the First Panzer Army. All installations of military importance were ordered destroyed.

Finally, the difficult situation in the southern sector of the Eastern Front forced the defenders to adopt a mobile defensive strategy while maintaining the fighting power of their units to the maximum degree possible. The front had to be withdrawn to the Dniepr, a move which was supposed to result in a shortening of the front and provide reserve units. Corresponding orders were issued on the evening of 15 September. All the armies of Army Group South were to pull back to a line Melitopol–Dniepr River (to above Kiev)–Desna River. For the Panzer-Grenadier Division *Großdeutschland*, the carrying-out of these orders resulted in a multitude of actions in the period from 28 August to 15 September, which resulted in the entire division and individual units being shunted about the front constantly in the role of fire-brigade. The main objective was to deny the enemy a rapid advance at all those places where there were no German units, or to halt the Soviet thrust where the defenders were too weak. The term fire-brigade of the East gained its true meaning. There was scarcely a continuous main line of resistance in the Sinkiv battle zone during those three weeks. Wherever the enemy turned up the Panzer-Grenadier Division *Großdeutschland* was placed in their path; unfortunately this often happened too late, so that the danger could only be overcome at the cost of giving ground.

The division turned to this fighting style of plugging holes, of repairing the defensive lines and offering help in threatening situations, in its first action northwest of Sinkiv, to where it had been sent after its much-needed rest. The days from 28 to 30 August, while the division was occupied with these tasks, saw the enemy break through to the west, past the 34th Infantry Division and the 10th Panzer-Grenadier Division on the Vorskla. Danger loomed that the enemy might veer south and cut off the German units at the river; the north flank had to be shored up.

The battle zone was the area of Mytyashi, Osholay, Udovishenki and north of Udovishenki. Both regiments prepared for the drive to the north, with the 10th Panzer-Grenadier Division on the left and the 34th Infantry Division on the right. Tanks and assault guns supported the operation, whose goal was to advance the front toward the north. Several villages were taken, and then the attack bogged down under extremely heavy enemy fire.

Out of necessity it was decided to withdraw the entire main line of resistance to more easily-defended terrain due north of Levchenki. The troops, who found this attack and its subsequent abandonment incomprehensible, grumbled accordingly, most of all the armoured units, whose numbers of serviceable tanks had fallen drastically and who had just about reached the zero mark. Armoured patrols of the Armoured Reconnaissance Battalion GD discovered that the enemy spearheads, initially only reinforced patrols, had already appeared in the area east of Velbivka, and in consequence the measures north of Sinkiv appeared to be more or less pointless.

It is therefore scarcely surprising that the Panzer-Grenadier Division *Großdeutschland* was again withdrawn from its positions on 30 August and pulled back into the area due west of Sinkiv. The Ia's explanation of the situation revealed that the dangerous situation in the Kharkov combat zone made it necessary for the entire division to go there. The first orders were for the heavy weapons and tanks to entrain in Poltava; the tracked units departed.

But the move to Kharkov was cut short; at 16.00 on 31 August the Division Ia issued a new situation report. The enemy had broken through the 112th Infantry Division and the villages of Tepliy on the Sinkiv–Velbia railroad, Melnikov, Chervone, Sayarye and Yanovshichina had already been occupied by the enemy. The command post of the 10th Panzer-Grenadier Division was in Garazki. The city of Sinkiv was threatened with being outflanked by the enemy. The units of the Panzer-Grenadier Division GD still on hand were instructed to advance immediately, occupy a line Point 179.0–Dudenki–"Schp."– Melnikov, due south of Tepliy and prepare to counterattack to the northwest.

Orders superseded orders. The following is an order issued by III Battalion, Panzer-Grenadier Regiment GD to its companies:

III Battalion   **Date: 31.8.43**
Command Post

To: **13th Company**
II Battalion to attack Tepliy 13th and 14th Companies to give fire support. When II Battalion has taken Tepliy, move forward immediately; contact on right with 11th Company, left of fork-shaped ravine.

Second attack objective: Point 125.9. Move out on right of 'Fusilier' or left of 'Adler' (II Btl.), then accompany 13th and 11th Companies, reach and hold Point 125.9. Why are you not reporting by radio?

Senger

This attack was to be made without heavy weapons, which first had to be recalled at maximum speed. This confusing mix of orders was a cross for the division to bear, and it created the impression that certain commanders had it in mind to employ the Panzer-Grenadier Division GD in their combat zones as a mobile fire- brigade. Disagreement over this question seemed to result in the continual shunting-about of the division: first here, then there, and always there were attacks and advances in order to move other units into their positions.

A counterattack by the division near Tepliy on 1 September 1943 gained ground and was able to force the enemy back toward the north. The tanks, which covered 220 kilometres overland and then went straight into action after refuelling, supported the advance under the command of Major

Gomille. The assigned objective was reached on the evening of 2 September in the face of a strong enemy anti-tank defense. There was heavy enemy air activity all day, while the division's flak battalion was still stuck in the Poltava area.

During the evening of 2 September 1943 the forward elements of the Panzer-Grenadier Division GD were again pulled out of the front, being relieved in their positions by units of the 112th Infantry Division. The Panzer-Grenadier Regiment GD was the only unit to stay behind. It remained just behind the front from where it could intervene in an emergency.

This move saw the beginning of a process which could prove deadly to a division: it was pulled apart and its component units were deployed at various points along the front. The division's report from 3 September 1943, according to which the enemy had broken into the German positions due northeast of Oposhnya, already pointed in the direction the division was being drawn.

The combat strengths of the companies had reached a level which could scarcely be lowered: barely 20 men per company! 7th Company, II Battalion, Grenadier Regiment had seven men, led by Gefreiter Siche. Several companies were combined into one on account of a shortage of company commanders. The Panzer-Grenadier Regiment's III Battalion had only one company commander left, Leutnant Kollwege. At this time the entire Panzer Regiment GD had eight serviceable panzers. The rest were in the rear undergoing repairs. The Assault Gun Battalion GD reported an operational strength of 15 assault guns.

All the division's men were completely overtired, physically and mentally exhausted. Little attention was paid to food, all they wanted to do was sleep, sleep. It borders on a miracle that they could still fight at all.

On 4 September orders were issued for a 07.15 departure for the new Oposhnya operations area. It came as no surprise, however, that a counter-order was received while the men were still boarding the vehicles. The situation near Sinkiv, location of the 34th Infantry Division of XLVIII Panzer Army Corps, had so deteriorated that a GD battle group had to be committed once again.

Orders were issued for a battalion of panzer-grenadiers supported by the assault guns to advance from Daykalivka toward Sinkiv and then intervene in the area due east of the town with another battalion. II and III Battalions, Panzer-Grenadier Regiment GD set out for Sinkiv to the northeast; the situation was completely unclear. The attack's objective was Point 109.0, north of Sinkiv. By 19.00 the line: extension Velikaya road–Posharna–bridge in the centre of Sinkiv had been reached.

That same day, 4 September, the bulk of the division moved into the Oposhnya area, in order to carry out an attack from there north against the enemy advancing on Batki. As the Panzer-Fusilier Regiment GD moved along the dusty road, vehicle after vehicle, the regimental commander, Oberst Schulte-Heuthaus, stood at the side of the road, oblivious to the Soviet close-support aircraft which repeatedly attacked the columns. Suddenly there was a movement and the right arm of the commander, who was standing up in his car, flew away. It had been cleanly severed by a bullet. The commanding officer stood there like iron and watched his men while the doctor worked on his wound. Not until the last vehicle had passed did he turn to look at the serious injury. Schulte-Heuthaus very calmly organized his relief. Major Wätjen, commander of the Armoured Reconnaissance Battalion GD, took his place. Rittmeister Spaeter led the battalion in his absence.

The division commander's Storch, a small communications aircraft, took the commander of the Panzer-Fusilier Regiment to the aid station. The fusiliers were on the march to Oposhnya, however at Daykalivka elements, I Battalion, also veered off toward Sinkiv. The situation was still unclear. It was known that the panzer-grenadiers had taken possession of the city of Sinkiv on 5 September 1943, and that II Battalion, Panzer-Grenadier Regiment GD was going into position farther on the right, but the Soviets counterattacked immediately. They were initially halted at the outskirts of Sinkiv.

The much more dangerous point, however, lay at Batki and both sides of the village, where the enemy were able to make significant gains against the 11th Panzer Division. The Panzer Regiment GD and its command post were already in Sesekaly and to the north. The panzers suffered under heavy artillery fire, an indication that the front must be quite near. IV Battalion, Panzer-Artillery Regiment GD under Major Röckner was already in this area and it supported the defensive efforts of the 11th Panzer Division northeast of Oposhnya. According to information obtained by the Armoured Reconnaissance Battalion the focal point of the enemy penetrations apparently lay near Batki and in particular to the south. The first Soviet assault teams had been sighted in a shallow valley south of Besruki, on the Kotelva–Oposhnya road. From there it was only a few hundred metres to the first houses of Oposhnya's suburb, whose many gardens and trees made infiltration by the enemy a forgone conclusion.

Meanwhile in the area near Oposhnya and to the northwest, the Armoured Reconnaissance Battalion GD assembled near Saytshentsy, elements of the Panzer Regiment GD near Seni, and the Armoured Assault Pioneer Battalion GD and train at the northern outskirts of Oposhnya. A counterattack by pioneers and eleven tanks on 5 September aimed at capturing the line Hills 188.7 - 179.5 failed on account of the stubborn defense mounted by enemy troops in the gorge south of Besruki. The German forces were simply inadequate for the task at hand. The existing defence lines therefore stayed as they were.

The dangerous situation in the Batki–Oposhnya area, which posed a major threat to the supply base and the road to Poltava, forced the withdrawal of the elements of the Panzer-Grenadier Regiment GD still near Sinkiv. The grenadiers were relieved by elements of the 19th Panzer Division; "notwithstanding of the situation in this sector," as VII Army Corps ordered.

Once again the situation dictated a move to patch up the front. It is therefore important to examine these facts in more detail from the notes of the Panzer-Grenadier Regiment GD from 6 September 1943:

08.00	Last elements of the regiment disengage from the enemy and march through Daykalivka to the Panzer-Grenadier Division GD, the bulk of which is now deployed near Batki.

Fighting East of
ACHTYRKA

08.30	Corps order from VII Army Corps: Pz.Gren.Rgt. GD and two batteries of GD assault guns are again placed under the command of the 19th Panzer Division. Battalions on the march are to turn around and remain at the disposal of the 19th Panzer Division in the forest near 135.4, about 6 km. southwest of Sinkiv.
11.30	On an order from the 19th Panzer Division, III Battalion is placed under the command of the 73rd Panzer-Grenadier Regiment and deployed in the new main line of resistance on both sides of the road near Point 109.9, southwest of Sinkiv.
12.45	Corps order: a battalion is to be sent to the GD Division in Batki at once. II Battalion departs immediately; in Batki it is inserted into the division's main line of resistance at the northeast edge of the city.
14.00	III Battalion pulled out of the main line of resistance on order of the 73rd Panzer-Grenadier Regiment and deployed in new main line of resistance which runs from the windmill at the east end of Pryrulivka to the northeast edge of the kidney-shaped wood north of Pryrulivka. Right boundary: windmill – left boundary: southeast corner of the wood. An assault gun battery remains with III Battalion, the 2nd Battery is under the direct command of the 73rd Panzer-Grenadier Regiment. In the evening the enemy infiltrates the forest west of Shilivka from Shilivka.

In the meantime the situation has become more critical in the main line of resistance south of Besruki, outskirts of Seni, east end of Batki. The weak and battered German forces were simply no longer able to hold off the streams of enemy infantry and were driven out of their positions and forced to fall back to the west. Repeated counterattacks by lone tanks and armoured cars brought scarcely any relief. In spite of a vigorous defence, elements of the Armoured Reconnaissance Battalion GD were forced back to a new line from the north end of Oposhnya to Sauchomleni. This line held. At Seni-East it was even possible to move the machine-gun nests forward. The tense situation was eased somewhat at about 10.00 on 6 September; a radio message was received stating that the Panzer-Fusilier Regiment GD was approaching. At last reinforcements! The first elements of the regiment arrived in the afternoon and occupied a continuous line. The Armoured Reconnaissance Battalion GD itself was moved back to Saytshentsy as a mobile reserve.

Leutnant Welke, the signals officer of the Panzer Regiment GD, described the unclear situation dominated mainly by the superiority of the enemy:

"Our command post was situated at the south end of Oposhnya, where we made the acquaintance of the Stalin Organ. Appropriately, the command post was together with that of the pioneers in a large, isolated farm house. The main line of resistance ran along the edge of the village across from us. Some of our panzers were in the village, some farther forward in the security screen. Our farm sat picturesquely on a knoll with a good view to all sides.

We had laid down our lines. The radio operator sat in the SO 2 with his set on receive, in the house itself eggs sizzled in the frying pan, the sun felt warm on our skin.

Meanwhile, on the road the dispatch riders drove unconcerned to and from us. Major Röckner came too, as well as an assault gun unit leader. Finally, after much urging and plenty of jeering, the tanks and wheeled vehicles were finally camouflaged and a few foxholes dug.

While we were still at it we suddenly heard a distant howling. The sound, an infernal howling and screaming, quickly grew louder. We piled into the nearest hole four deep. Beneath me was an operator, then Major Gomille, then me and Major Röckner. Finally a couple of assault gun men who had been caught in the open jumped in too. The earth shook and my ears felt as if they would burst from the concussion; it went on for what seemed like forever. Wounded cried out, but no one dared leave his hole. Finally we made a beginning; with one ear in Ivan's direction to see if.... yes, he is, and again the rockets hissed toward us. Back into the hole again! There, a direct hit on the wounded in the house. It was terrible.

Together with Gomille and Röckner we collected the wounded and applied the first dressings. Then the radio operator informed us that there was increased fighting farther forward and especially to our left. An enemy infantry attack was in progress against our neighbour on the left.

When we returned that evening the command post had been abandoned; the houses were burning. All that was left was an ambulance taking on wounded. During the night we sought a new command post that seemed to us a little safer."

In the meantime the realization was made that the positions were not going to be held this way. Withdrawal movements were carried out, now here, now there. Losses to anti-tank guns and rifles hiding in the fields of sunflowers grew steadily.

The first alert units drawn from the supply trains were moved up to reinforce the combat companies. It could no longer be avoided. The first enemy groups had now entered Oposhnya; a heavy and bloody fight, the brunt of which was borne by the panzer-fusiliers, broke out in the town. Elements of the Armoured Reconnaissance Battalion GD went into position near Sesekali, northwest of Batki. Apparently the enemy had infiltrated there too.

In the course of the heavy fighting that day the commander of the Assault Gun Battalion GD's 1st Battery, Leutnant Grimm, was killed in close combat with enemy infantry in Sinkiv. The commander of the 3rd Battery, Oberleutnant Wehmeyer, was also killed together with two members of his crew, Unteroffizier Kallert and Obergefreiter Schreiber, in Oposhnya. Only Unteroffizier Druse was rescued; he had lost his eyesight.

The pioneers were also in Oposhnya; their pioneer equipment and flamethrowers as well as their training made them ideally suited to fighting in a built-up area.

There now follows an account by war correspondent Hans H. Henne, who was present in and near Oposhnya in those days:

Conversation in a Hole in the Ground

The hole in the ground was two metres deep. It was relatively dry. There was room in it for five men. When it became quieter we all climbed out except for a man who was wounded. He was waiting for the delivery of the food, when he would return to the rear. The commander was twenty metres farther to the right. The two runners remained near his command post so as to be on hand immediately if there was work for them. When we heard the mortars firing, we all found ourselves back together in our hole, with a crash so to speak. It happened quickly, as if we were swept from the field, and each of us had lovely blue marks, because in the darkness one jumped on top of the other.

One of the runners, a Gefreiter, was a quiet fellow. Sometimes, when we had to stay longer in the hole, he fell asleep and snored quite loudly. He must have had iron nerves. The other runner came from the pioneers, his mouth went like clockwork and he talked without letup, but it didn't bother any of us, for when he spoke we forgot to pay attention to the exploding shells and the shrill sound of the flying shards of steel that hacked into our cover.

Once a Feldwebel of the fusiliers jumped in with us. After he had caught his breath he lit a cigarette and listened quietly to what the fast-talking runner was saying.

The Feldwebel asked him what he had been in civilian life.

"I was training to be an actor," answered the runner. "I was at school in Vienna. I was just finished."

"Well, we have theatre enough here," laughed the Feldwebel. After a while the Feldwebel asked how long he had been a soldier.

Three months. I'm nineteen and I volunteered to serve in "*Großdeutschland*"."

It was quiet for a time. A star shell hissed into the sky and the runner who was a student actor in civilian life stood up, stared over the cover and called, "This is quite fantastic, I always find the light fantastic. It looks like a moonlit landscape outside." He had an enthusiastic face and looked like Will Quadflieg in the film "The Big Shadow."

The Unteroffizier, who lay at the entrance, climbed up and we heard him calmly walking to and fro. He seemed to have become bored.

"He has the Bronze Close Combat Clasp," said the Feldwebel.

The runner from the pioneers said proudly and almost pathetically, "We have one who was the first man of the division to be awarded the Silver Close Combat Clasp, at Oposhnya. He was my platoon leader."

The wounded man bent forward and said, "Yes, I know him. He's one of the quiet ones. One can't tell by looking at him that he's such a splendid fellow."

"Most of them are like that," said the Feldwebel. "The ones who make a lot of wind often turn out to be nothing."

"I was a runner with him in the platoon headquarters squad," said the former acting student. "I received my baptism of fire at Oposhnya. Whenever I

179

got a shock I looked to him. He was like a father to me."

We listened to the gunfire again and the Unteroffizier who had been walking to and fro outside leapt into the hole. He cursed, for he had struck his elbow on a supporting beam. We held our breath. Then there was a hissing above us. We squeezed ourselves close together, but the impacts were ten or fifteen metres away.

"Tell me how it was at Oposhnya," said the Feldwebel to the runner.

The runner coughed as before a scene and began. He talked very fast and his mouth worked like clockwork. He spoke High German, but a bit of his Vienna dialect always came through.

"We were twenty-two men and we had eight machine-guns. Our sector was one and a half kilometres wide, with a machine-gun about every two-hundred metres. Only in the forest were the holes closer together. The bolsheviks were between twenty-five and thirty metres away from us there. I was with the Unteroffizier. I had never seen a man as calm as he. In peacetime he was a master roofer, at the Kreuzberg. He certainly needed good nerves in his profession back then. He shared whatever he had, sandwiches, cigarettes or a drink of schnapps. He did it in such a way that no one noticed that it was from him."

"Wait," interrupted the Feldwebel, "I just heard something."

The runner fell silent, as if he had parked his mouth and we heard another dozen shells on the way. We felt the earth against our backs shake. The impacts were closer to the command post.

"Continue!" said the Feldwebel.

"Everyone was ready to walk through fire for him," said the wounded man, but as he was about to continue the runner took over. He spoke quite enthusiastically and it was fun for us to listen to him.

"Of course we always patrolled the positions at night. It was pitch black. The men lay two by two in the holes, which sometimes had water in them. The Unteroffizier spoke with them and one could see that it did everyone good. Otherwise he could barely put five sentences together. When someone asked him why that was so, he'd grin and say, "Well, that's quite enough!" Nothing more. You couldn't get anything out of him, but at night with the men he could speak volumes. He was no older than most, but he was like a father and one felt: he's right, he's old enough that he absolutely must know."

"One night we were in a hole. The 1st gunner was quite excited and said, 'Unteroffizier, the Russians are coming!' We listened and heard them crawling toward us. The 1st gunner wanted to fire, but the Unteroffizier restrained him and said softly, 'Man, stay cool, just stay cool!' We were all quite breathless – they were so close! Then a hand came from above over the cover and reached for the machine-gun. But the Unteroffizier had his machine pistol turned around in his hands and he struck. He was simply great. We tossed a few hand grenades under the noses of the others. They didn't come at night any more."

"Tell them about the right wing...!" said the wounded man. He seemed to know the whole story and his voice sounded as if what the runner was saying excited him greatly. Perhaps he would most liked to have told the whole thing himself.

"Yes, the right wing was open. I don't know on what day. We had been there fourteen days and were as wet as dogs. Suddenly there was nothing to the right of us and all at once enemy rifles began firing behind us. There was fire from every direction. I found the whole thing confusing but the Unteroffizier was calmness itself. 'What do we do now?' asked the squad leader. 'What should we do?' asked the Unteroffizier and grinned, 'We stay here and drink tea. But fun aside boys, we stay here, and none of the beasts is getting through here. That is clear. There's nothing more to say.' We were stuck, it was like we were on an island. It was a very desperate situation, but none got through us. In two days we fired 27,000 rounds of machine-gun ammunition. You can imagine that they didn't go into the air and that the bolsheviks bled constantly."

"Once, this was later on, a radio message came from battalion that the Unteroffizier was to report to the command post. That was the first time I saw him excited. 'Look out,' he said, 'I'm going to get chewed out.' His conscience was as clear as that of an angel. We always followed the wire to avoid getting lost. Then we arrived in the ravine where the chief was. Hansmann, that was the Unteroffizier's name, received the Silver Close Combat Clasp there for thirty assaults. He now already had thirty-eight. A few weeks later he received the gold clasp."

"And he wasn't wounded?" asked the Feldwebel.

"Yes, twice, but not badly. I wasn't there the first time but the second time it happened like this: It was Sunday morning at the road in front of Oposhnya. I was acting a little silly to make the others laugh. I said in Viennese, 'Boys, it's Sunday morning in Stephans Cathedral and there's a lovely organ concert.' Scarcely had I said it when I was lying on my nose. There was real organ music. The Unteroffizier got a fragment in his lower back. Afterward he said with a grin, 'There's organ concerts here on Sunday too, without your Vienna, only they affect your rear end instead of your ears.' He had a sense of humour and was an ice-cool fellow. "He was lucky," declared the Feldwebel.

"No," said the runner quickly, "He had a seventh sense."

Someone called from the command post. It was the voice of the adjutant. "I have to go!" said the runner who had been an acting student. His feet were as fast as his mouth. He was out of the hole in an instant. Just then a few shells fell nearby.

"Well," said the Feldwebel, who was peering over the cover, "The boy ran around that as if it were nothing."

"That's nothing to him," the wounded man was heard to say. "He makes so much wind with his mouth that he doesn't give credit to anything, but he is quite a lad."

We squatted in silence. I saw the figure of the Unteroffizier clearly before me. A man who had things in hand, one who feared nothing, one who gave nothing up for lost because he knew that all was not lost as long as one didn't give up on oneself. A master roofer from Berlin who lived at the Kreuzberg.

At noon on 7 September orders came for the Panzer-Grenadier Regiment GD, which alone was under the command of the 19th Panzer Division, to fall back to a new defensive line. Temporarily leaving III Battalion at Pryrulivka, the remaining elements of the regiment (less II Battalion, which was at Batki, and III Battalion) moved into the Pobeda–Romanki area, southwest of Daykalivka. On its arrival the regiment sent patrols to the north. At the same time the 19th Panzer Division occupied a new main line of resistance in the general line: Point 164.2, at the road, due south of Shilivka, which was held by the enemy,–south end of Kripky–Point 125.6, south exit from Daykalivka–Point 112.5, at the northeast exit from Birky, facing north. The occupation of the northeast exit from Birky was unsuccessful, as the enemy applied heavy pressure to the left wing of the main line of resistance in the afternoon.

The Panzer-Grenadier Regiment GD, which was without its II and III Battalions–the latter did not rejoin its parent unit until the night of 8 September–proceeded to assemble on the left wing of this formation. It established a temporary command post in Zvitoff and moved elements forward toward a line 116.9–139.7–107.0 (from left to right), which was occupied. This eventful day of combat came to an end as darkness fell. The night was relatively quiet apart from limited patrol activity by both sides. However, it seemed obvious that the enemy was in Daykalivka as well as on the road to Birky. The latter village appeared to be occupied, but more detailed information was lacking.

The maps of this combat zone again showed a somewhat continuous German defensive line, which ran roughly as follows: the 11th Panzer Division northeast and south of Oposhnya. German troops, mainly GD, still in Oposhnya and farther toward the northwest in the direction of Seny–Batki as far as Sesekaly. Through Pishnenky to Point 164.2, at the Sinkiv–Oposhnya road and from there in a generally westerly direction to the south end of Daykalivka, the 19th Panzer Division. From there elements of the Panzer-Grenadier Regiment GD through Points 109.0–116.9, due southeast of Birky. Even if there was no direct contact, the 112th Infantry Division was in position farther to the northwest.

The enemy appeared to have found the least resistance north of Sinkiv and consequently it was there that they gained the most ground to the west. There was a danger that the enemy might veer south at that point – north of Birky to Lyutenka. The corner post of Oposhnya, also the starting point of the railroad to Poltava, was already in danger.

The night of 8-9 September was also used to stabilize the existing strong-point-style positions by shortening the lines and moving the units closer together. This resulted in the following new main line of resistance for the Panzer-Grenadier Division GD, still without the Panzer-Grenadier Regiment GD, which was under the command of the 19th Panzer Division and on that unit's left wing:Oposhnya-North–Saytshentsy–Point 189.4 (north of

Babansk Gorge) Ivashenki, there contact with the right wing of the folded-back 19th Panzer Division. The panzer-fusiliers and armoured assault pioneers were still at Oposhnya and Saytshentsy, next to them at Point 189.4 the Armoured Reconnaissance Battalion GD. The Panzer-Grenadier Regiment GD, in the meantime strengthened by the addition of III Battalion, held a line of: 107.0, south of Daykalivka–Point 139.7–Point 116.9. The move to the new line took place in the course of general withdrawal movements, under the codeword "Bathtub." A new line designated 202 CC was also occupied from Point 141.9–Point 152.3–group of trees on the Birky–Dubini road.

The terrain on this wing of the defensive front was less than favourable and offered the advancing enemy outstanding approach possibilities. Vast fields of sunflowers, as tall as a man, offered scarcely any field of fire; the thinly-manned defensive lines, a consequence of the universally low combat strengths of the defenders, the enemy was always able to infiltrate at unobserved points and turn up in the German rear. The inevitable consequence of the lack of reserves was repeated withdrawals from the main line of resistance, because although it could probably be held at the front it was threatened from the rear.

The fighting strengths of the Soviets were astonishing; waves of 20 tanks with accompanying infantry turned up everywhere. Massed artillery blanketed the German positions with a hurricane of fire. Even though the enemy suffered frightful losses in many places, there were simply too many. They were overpowering. The night of 11 September once again brought orders to fall back and also saw the division reunited with the return of the panzergrenadiers. Apart from the 19th panzer Division, the neighbouring unit on the left was now the 11th Panzer Division under Generalmajor von Wietersheim, whose right wing maintained contact with the Panzer-Grenadier Regiment GD in the area of Vassile- Ustimovka.

The events of 11 September 1943 are described in detail in the daily report of the Panzer-Grenadier Regiment GD, which also gives a picture of the course of the day in the entire division area:

Assigned to support other units were: I Battalion, Panzer-Artillery Regiment GD and 12th Battery (rocket).

Under the command of other units were: the Armoured Reconnaissance Battalion GD, Army Flak Battalion GD and a battery of assault guns.

09.00 retake	III Battalion arrives in Makuchi and receives orders to Galijka, where the enemy has entered the northern part of the town, with assault guns. Armoured Reconnaissance Battalion GD moved through Koretski-South toward Point 1.2, northwest of Galijka, where it occupies a new position. Regimental commander now takes command of the entire committed regiment, including attached elements.
09.15	50 enemy troops move west on road to Galijka and set up mortars in town. Reconnaissance aircraft fires tank warning flare over Pokrovskoye.
09.55	Regimental order for III Battalion to occupy main line of

resistance from Shovno-Fedorovka to hillock 500 metres southwest of Galijka. To the left the Armoured Reconnais-- sance Battalion GD as far as the Vassile-Ustimovka road.

10.10	Stuka attack on Pokrovskoye-South and Galijka-North.
10.20	Enemy moves left past I Battalion. Strong enemy move- ments in Kolchecki, assault guns notified. Artillery destroys two enemy tanks with its fire. Air reconnaissance reports about 18-20 enemy tanks there.
11.30	Assault guns advance toward mill east of Makuchi. Regiment's forward command post in Masyuki-South.
12.00	Armoured Reconnaissance Battalion GD reports: line from road 1,000 metres east of 172.6 and road 1,000 metres west of 172.6 occupied. Pioneers of the 11th Panzer Division fleeing south past Point 169.3. Russians pursuing with strong infantry forces.
12.05	Enemy abreast Seeler Company (left wing I Btl.). A battery of assault guns sent to the Armoured Reconnaissance Battalion GD.
12.10	Enemy radio message intercepted: attack toward Makuchi, Romyany and Okari under all costs. Several of our Tigers subsequently sent there. Artillery has little ammunition.
12.40	Koretski occupied by enemy. 11th Panzer Division disap- peared into northern part of Vassile-Ustimovka.
13.40	Elements of Armoured Reconnaissance Battalion GD with thin screen on Hill 169.3. Contact established.
14.30	Approximately 150 enemy troops advancing west from Galijka.
14.46	Five enemy tanks destroyed. 250 trucks north of Galijka.
15.15	Assault guns report 11 enemy tanks knocked out.
15.30	55th Rocket Regiment arrives with "Stukas on Foot" (multiple rocket launchers).
15.52	Own right wing withdrawn toward northeast end of Makuchi. Enemy attack with two companies on left wing 2nd Company, I Battalion. Still no contact with III Battalion. III Battalion is supposed to establish contact immediately. H.Q. Company is inserted into the gap between the two battalions. Saytshentsy, defended by Panzer-Fusilier Regiment GD, has just fallen into enemy hands, Oposhnya threatened. Release of Armoured Reconnaissance Battalion GD by 's,' own front bent back from Chovno-Fedorovka to 172.7. III Battalion must take over the sector held by Armoured Reconnaissance Battalion. Assault guns drive to 2nd Company, I Battalion.
16.30	III Battalion has collected H.Q. Company.
16.38	Enemy attack halted in front of 2nd Company.

16.46	Three enemy tanks with mounted infantry advancing toward Seeler Company.
17.15	Beginning of relief from right starts. Enemy attacks near Galijka and Kolchecki halted. Counterattack by H.Q. Company leads to clearing up of situation – own losses heavy. II Battalion extends its left wing and at the same time takes over the position held by Armoured Reconnaissance Battalion GD, which is relieved to Deryagi.
19.00	Enemy attack on I Battalion repulsed. Withdrawal continues to proceed as planned. I Battalion takes over as rear guard.
22.15	I Battalion has occupied new positions. Regimental command post: Kirillo-Anovka.

The panzer-fusiliers were no longer able to hold Oposhnya after the enemy entered the city's extensive fruit and flower gardens. The main line of resistance now ran along the western edge of Oposhnya, supported by the Tigers of III Battalion, Panzer Regiment GD. The heavy tanks even made repeated forays as far as the northern edge of the city on 12 September. That same day 13th Company, III Battalion, Panzer-Grenadier Regiment GD, with a strength of 1 officer, 3 NCOs and 13 enlisted men, held the hill at Point 172.6, west of Makuchi, against every enemy assault with the courage of desperation.Assault guns provided as much support as possible in the dense fields of corn and sunflowers. The company commander, Leutnant Kollewe, described the fighting there:

"The remaining attacks were beaten off in front of the main line of resistance with the help of forward observer Oberleutnant Grundmann. My men were involved heart and soul again. It was a proper rabbit-shoot. All the while the Soviets pounded our positions with anti-tank guns. Once I was hit by five splinters, but they barely pierced my coat.

In the meantime the forward observer had also contacted the rocket launcher and with their help I successfully repulsed the last enemy assault of this day. Finally it became dark. A patrol returned; the Russians were behind us again in the cornfield. This meant we had to be careful, and I set up an all-round position as a precaution.

Subsequently our Kübel finally came with the food and rations. Wolter was standing right beside me and we talked about the general situation. Then, suddenly, a shower of Soviet mortar shells landed directly behind the Kübel. Those who had been hit cried out. There was no medic there, but Sturm immediately set about tending to the wounded. I was completely shattered. They all lay there – dead, wounded – all my good men! Everyone had to pitch in and help. I counted six dead and five wounded. I ran from man to man like a hunted wild animal. The Kübel was finished, completely wrecked, and there were no vehicles to be had.

Finally, finally, I obtained an armoured personnel carrier from Stöwer. Four of the wounded had already walked to the rear. We loaded Röhr, Rumey and Wurm into the APC. The latter cried out continually: 'Herr Leutnant! I'm dying, I'm dying!' Finally, after they were all gone, I was able to calm myself somewhat.

And these were my casualties:

Rühr | |
Rumey | | died of their wounds
Wurm | |
Uffz. Hauth | |
Uffz. Donauberger | |
Gefr. Gräfe | |
Stabsgefr. Goldewey | | all killed
Gefr. Graf | |
Gefr. Schulz | |

I ascertained that after this loss I was left with a total of eight men, including those from the elements placed under my command. My entire company headquarters squad was gone; they'd all been killed!"

The losses of the past days in the continuous defensive battles and fighting withdrawals are reflected in the combat strengths of the companies of two battalions of the Panzer-Grenadier Regiment GD on 13 September:

II Battalion	**III Battalion**
1:4	1:6
1:8	1:11
1:10	1:12

And still the main line of resistance remained as it had been set up: (from left) Point 169.3 (II Btl.)–Makuchi (III Btl.)–Point 173.4 (I Btl.)–Point 172.4 (near Skiby)–Koreshshina (fusiliers)–Ustimenko (fusiliers)–west edge of Oposhnya–city centre Oposhnya (fusiliers and pioneers).

Apart from minor penetrations, most of which were sealed off by brave assault teams formed by individual squads, the handful of men stood firm as iron with the help of the assault guns, tanks, anti-aircraft guns and anti-tank guns.

On the 15th of September the division finally received details of the large-scale withdrawal movement of the front, in total about 700 kilometres long, to the new Dniepr Line. The armies were to move toward just five Dniepr crossings, their mission to establish without delay a new front of about the same length beyond the river before the Soviets had reached or even crossed it. The Eighth Army's mission was made more difficult by the fact that, after crossing the Dniepr, it had to shift its front to the north to about 30 kilometres south of Kiev. It was to cross the river over the bridges at Cherkassy in the north and Kremenchug in the south.

In the initial stage of the Eighth Army's movements, strong panzer forces were to be left on the left wing in order to enable the army to disengage and fall back through Poltava toward Cherkassy and Kremenchug. The panzers were then to cover the army's withdrawal and follow as the rear guard.

The Panzer-Grenadier Division *Großdeutschland* was also assigned to these duties, the initial result of which was that it had to hold onto its existing positions for a few days longer. The extraordinarily difficult conditions

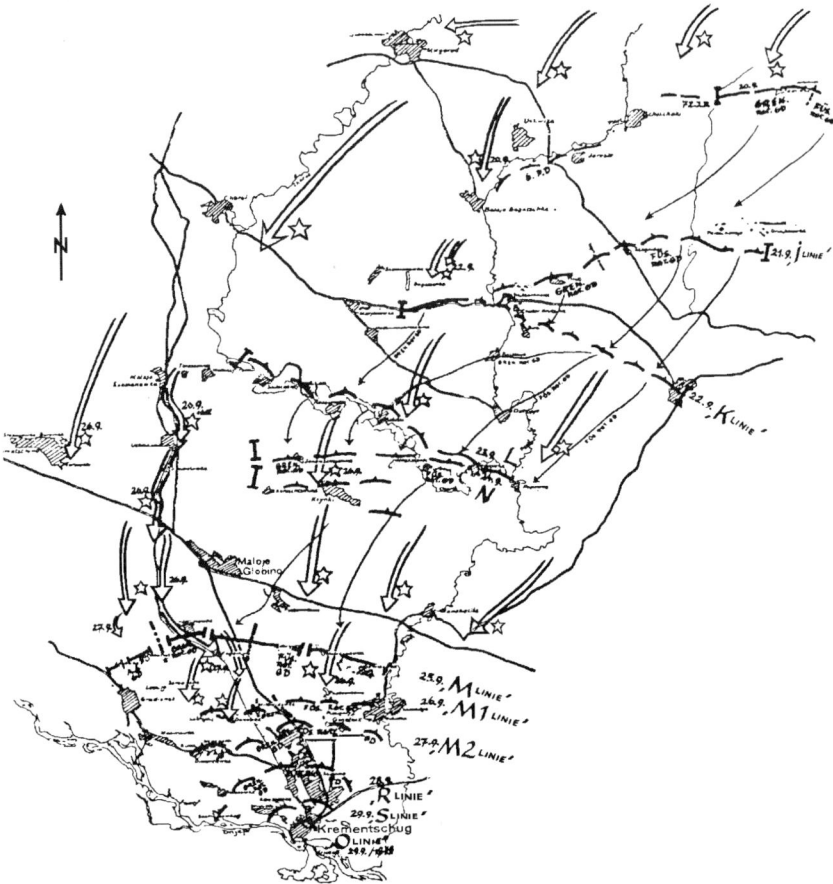

**RETREAT TO THE KREMENCHUG BRIDGEHEAD
ON THE DNIEPER**
September 20 to September 29, 1943

under which the withdrawal movements took place forced the army to adopt special measures to prevent the enemy from following up too sharply. Most of all the enemy could not be allowed to go over from the pursuit to a further offensive across the river as soon as he reached the Dniepr.

In an effort to delay the enemy advance, orders were issued for the units to carry out a policy of "scorched earth," a practice the Soviets had employed in past retreats. A partial withdrawal of the population could not be avoided, insofar as these wished to go voluntarily. Days of intensive work followed for the division headquarters and its command group as they prepared the withdrawal plan. Nothing could be overlooked. Lines of withdrawal were set down, which of course had to be coordinated with neighbouring units. The rail centres of Romodan and Poltava were prepared for demolition; however they continued in service in the evacuation of the wounded and difficult to move materials until the demolitions were carried out. Most of the workshops and baggage trains were loaded aboard trains and sent to the south bank of the Dniepr via Kremenchug. All damaged and "sick" tanks, weapons and vehicles were likewise sent to the loading stations for transport to the rear.

In the course of these measures, after handing over its remaining Panzer IVs the personnel of the former I Battalion, Panzer Regiment GD under Major Pössel entrained in Poltava and were transported through Germany to occupied France. In Bourges the men were to form a new Panther battalion for the *Großdeutschland* Division. It is therefore not surprising that the former supply roads to the west soon witnessed column traffic which far exceeded anything previously seen. In spite of the rain which prevailed in those days, vehicles of every type ground their way through the morass and softened earth toward the rear. The roads also bore a mixture of horse-drawn vehicles, civilian treks, herds of cattle, columns of prisoners and transport columns. Everything was moving toward the safety of the west bank of the Dniepr, where new rest areas and quarters waited.

The units were told that work had been under way on the west bank for months and that new positions and defensive lines had been created. They spoke of bunkers, gun positions, rested and new units, which were supposed to take in the badly-exhausted rear guards and give them a chance to rest and recover after crossing the Dniepr. Such rumours calmed the troops, corroborated as they were by figures given by the men engaged in building the positions – civilians under the command of German pioneers; yes they breathed easier and counted firmly on what they had been told.

The units of the Panzer-Grenadier Division *Großdeutschland* initiated the necessary measures for the withdrawal. The panzer-grenadiers combined their II and III Battalions into the "Adler Battalion." The former 7th Company was merged with the 8th and 9th Companies to form a new 7th under Oberleutnant Wiebe, the former 11th with the 12th and 13th resulting in the new 11th Company under Leutnant Berghoff. The heavy companies of both battalions, the 10th, 14th and 15th, were combined to form the new 14th (Heavy) Company under Oberleutnant Beck. The former commander of III Battalion, Hauptmann Senger, was named division train commander and took part of the battalion staff of III Battalion with him for this new mission.

On 18 September 1943 the newly-arrived Major Wack took over the Panzer-Fusilier Regiment in place of the wounded regimental commander, relieving Major Watjen, commander of the Armoured Reconnaissance Battalion GD, who had been filling the post in an acting capacity. Gradually, from about 18 September, information was released concerning the soon to begin withdrawal movement. As well there was increasing clarity where the overall situation was concerned:

> Mirgorod and Lubuy were in the process of being evacuated.
>
> A new line on both sides of Bodanovka would be occupied on 20 or 21 September in the first phase. In the course of this first withdrawal movement the 11th Panzer Division would be removed from the main line of resistance and the division's new neighbour on the left would be the 72nd Infantry Division.
>
> Enemy had broken through to the south west of the Psel. The 11th Panzer Division was to be committed against this enemy.

On 20 September the maps depicted the Panzer-Grenadier Division GD's main line of resistance – from which the withdrawal movements were to begin – as follows:

> (from right to left): west end of Momotvoka (fusiliers)–Point 161.5 –north edge of Jordanovka–stream course south of Yerokovka (exclusively fusiliers)–boundary of both regimental groups the stream.
>
> Stream–Point 2.0, south edge of Pavlovka (grenadiers)–Point 165.8 –Besrutshki-West (Division Escort Company and elements of the pioneers) contact point with the 72nd Inf.Div.: mill approximately 1,000 metres southeast of Samari.

In the course of occupying this line the 11th Panzer Division was relieved and moved west of the Psel. The enemy at first followed hesitantly and not until the afternoon did they become more aggressive, advancing in several places, sometimes with tank support.

In the meantime scouting for the next line of withdrawal "I" was in progress. This line was to supposed be reached during the coming night. Even before the details were worked out it was learned that advance enemy units had already reached Bogachka, due west of the Psel, and were threatening our supply lines, particularly the major Korol–Reshetilovka road. This enemy advance posed even more of a danger to the Psel crossing at Belozerkovka, the only bridge able to support the heaviest tanks. It had to be held at all costs, for on it depended in large part the successful retrieval of the heavy tank equipment. Taking these facts into consideration a new "I" line was laid down as follows: from right: Nadeshda (fusiliers)–Pestshanoye (fusiliers)–Sagaydak boundary fusiliers-grenadiers–rail line–Timki (grenadiers)–northwestern end of forest north of Krutcha collective farm (grenadiers)–to the Psel. Combat outposts to be left in an intermediate line until forced to fall back by enemy pressure. The von Wietersheim armoured group, with its eight remaining tanks, supported these movements and the withdrawal. The withdrawal of both regiments went according to plan.

In general the soldiers carried out the ordered destructive measures grudgingly; but they were also well aware that anything that stayed behind must become a disadvantage to the fighting troops.

First contact with the enemy occurred at about 10.00 on 21 September, when the Russians advanced tentatively on the left wing of the new defensive line near Bakeiskiy and Yerkovka. However the enemy pressure was not strong. In the meantime the Armoured Reconnaissance Battalion GD had been assigned to prepare the new "K" Line on its left wing to take in the arriving units and guard the left flank of the division to III Army Corps. For this purpose it was temporarily placed under the command of the Panzer-Grenadier Regiment GD and occupied the line Mostovovchina to Maryenovka along the road to Korol. The "K" Line was supposed to roughly follow the Reshetilovka–Korol road. To the right the Panzer-Fusilier Regiment GD still remained east of the Psel; the Panzer-Grenadier Regiment GD, with its right wing at the Psel near Birky, was to guard the road to the north.

Roads were assigned to both regimental groups, these running in a generally southwesterly direction toward Kremenchug. The regiments were also assigned crossing points over the various streams so that the withdrawal could proceed in an orderly fashion. The Panzer-Fusilier Regiment GD was assigned the Psel crossing at Ostupye and the Panzer-Grenadier Regiment GD the crossing at Balakliya. The next crossings were Fedorovka for the panzer-fusiliers and Subani for the panzer-grenadiers. Correspondingly all supply was halted.

The movement of the units to occupy the "K" Line began at about noon on 22 September. All units travelled by motor vehicle. There was contact with the enemy soon afterward on the left wing, when the enemy approached the main line of resistance between Bogachka and Semionovka with one hundred men. The bridge over the Psel River at Belozerkovka was already under enemy anti-tank and mortar fire, which made for an uncomfortable crossing.

The planned withdrawal of the larger units took place under the pressure imposed by time constraints, the movement area of the units and the freedom of action of the enemy. For the withdrawing troops it was important to maintain their mobility, have capable rear guards to conceal their intentions from the enemy and as well maintain iron discipline and nerves.

It was vital that the commanders of this type of withdrawal keep a rein on the following units, clear the rear area in preparation for the withdrawal movements in time and prepare new positions. Just the withdrawal demanded outstanding morale on the part of the troops.

On 23 September the movements of the Panzer-Grenadier Division GD east of the Dniepr continued toward the southwest. The "L" Line was occupied by evening of that day. Its general course was: the confluence of the Psel and the Korol near Popovka (fusiliers)–Fedrovka–Turbay (fusiliers)–border with Pz.Gren.Rgt. GD–Subani (grenadiers)–Radolovka (grenadiers)–Bilyaki (grenadiers)–Saytshentsy (grenadiers) contact with the Armoured Reconnaissance Battalion at Veselye Podol-Tarasovka (division boundary). Both regimental groups encountered problems crossing the Korol when the bridge at Fedrovka proved to be too weak for the heavy vehicles of the Panzer-Fusilier Regiment GD. The regiment was therefore also moved across the bridge at Subani in the Panzer-Grenadier Regiment GD's sector, which naturally led to traffic jams and lost time. nevertheless both units were across by the night of 24 September and the panzer-fusiliers and their supporting artillery were able to move into their assigned sector.

A look at the map revealed that the division's neighbour on the left, the 6th Panzer Division, as well as the remaining units of III Army Corps were withdrawing through Kremenchug and the ferry landing at Mazimovka, as a result of which the left flank of the Panzer-Grenadier Division GD was open. In order to shorten the lines in this sector a further withdrawal was undertaken on 24 September, to the "N" Line. This move brought no changes at the Korol.

The main body of the Panzer-Grenadier Division GD, however, turned back to the left and occupied the following intermediate line:

(from left): northern edge of Koreshchina – northern edge of Yanovshchina – Moskalenki and contact near Turbay with the Panzer- Fusilier Regiment GD. Here too rear guards were left at the Korol, whose job it was to delay the crossing of the river by the enemy for as long as possible.

The Armoured Reconnaissance Battalion GD, on the left wing of the Panzer-Grenadier Regiment GD, was under orders to patrol north in the area to the Dniepr. At about 15.00 on 24 September it reported that enemy spearheads had advanced to Malaya Senovka along the rail line to Kremenchug. The first enemy elements were already on the advance south toward Ustinovka.

The corps had ordered the bulk of the forces under its command to occupy the new line, but also that they leave strong rear guards in the old positions. The GD Division was too weak for this, however, and therefore decided to keep the bulk of its forces in the existing positions, as no major contact with the enemy had taken place. Only minor elements moved into the "M" Line which ran south of Maloye Globino. However, to meet the desires of the corps and further delay the enemy's advance, several intermediate lines were laid down between the former "N" Line and the new "M" Line, where new positions were once again occupied. The "M" Line ran roughly as follows: Demidovka (on the KR – Mansheliya road) Naydenovka (fusiliers) – Verguny (fusiliers) – Kagamlyk – northern edge (boundary with grenadiers there) – Ustimovka-South (grenadiers) – northern edge of Podolny (boundary with Arm.Recon.Btl.) – Anovka (Arm.Recon.Btl.). The "M" Line was meanwhile laid out as an intercept line and occupied by elements of I and IV Battalions, Panzer-Grenadier Regiment GD, elements of the Panzer-Fusilier Regiment GD and 1st and 2nd Batteries of the Army Flak Battalion GD.

The increasing contraction in the direction of the Kremenchug bridgehead, which was already marked by the course of the "M" Line, resulted in a corresponding strengthening of the German defence. The last elements of the 6th Panzer Division had left the combat zone east of Kremenchug for the bridgehead on 25 September. As well, the units moving through left strong elements, especially artillery, with the bridgehead garrison, which consisted of the 55th Rocket Regiment and Artillery regiment Büscher with three battalions.

The "M" Line was ultimately occupied on 25 September. Final orders for boundaries and sectors were issued and carried out. In Kremenchug itself, preparations to defend the city were under way and the evacuation continued. Both bridges, the road bridge and the railroad bridge farther to the north, were guarded by a heavy concentration of anti-aircraft guns. The Soviet Air Force attacked day and night in an effort to render the bridges unusable. The road bridge, whose surface was made of wood, was especially threatened. Its destruction would lead to considerable dangers for the garrison of the bridgehead, so the railroad bridge was modified to take road traffic as well.

The city of Kremenchug was a busy place. Vehicle columns, treks and herds of cattle still rolled west across the bridges. Pioneers and demolition squads scouted new positions and minefields. Batteries went into position in gardens. Foxholes were dug and observation posts erected. Side streets were sealed off with barbed wire obstacles and barricades.

Everything was set up for defence; the enemy was going to be forced to halt there and prevented from crossing the river. The Dniepr was of considerable width there and the current was strong. Lines of hills dominated the west bank, providing a good view to the east.

The last rear guards disengaged from the enemy at about 06.00 on 26 September. Soon their vehicles arrived in front of the left wing of the Panzer-Grenadier Regiment GD. In front of the sector held by the Panzer-Fusilier Regiment GD the enemy successfully pushed the security forces back as far as Naydenovka and advanced to Pustovitovo. There, however, they were halted. Statements from prisoners revealed that at least three Soviet divisions were facing the sector, including a guards airborne division which had seen action against GD at Akhtyrka. In the afternoon patrols sent out by the Armoured Reconnaissance Battalion GD discovered that an enemy force in company strength was advancing south near Matesha, west of Ustimovka. A further, much stronger column was on the march from Semenovka toward Ustimovka; the village of Terenyaki was found to be occupied by the enemy. German armoured groups made repeated forays and placed these columns under fire. These tactics resulted in heavy losses to the enemy; furthermore they were themselves compelled to deploy, bring their heavy weapons into position and prepare to attack. No sooner was this done than the German armoured groups disappeared and took up position on the next line of hills, in order to start the game all over again.

In this way the enemy's advance was repeatedly interrupted and time gained. This breathing space was used to scout new positions, make initial preparations and gradually occupy them.

On orders from the division, in the evening a further withdrawal was carried out to the "M-2" line. There was no significant pressure from the enemy. The new line ran approximately: western edge of Omelnik (fusiliers)— Pyatigory-North (fusiliers) – Milovidovka (grenadiers) – Donovka (II Btl. Gren.) – Zabrotski (grenadiers) – Mazimovka. Elements of the Armoured

Reconnaissance Battalion GD remained in Gradishsk for the night, while the remaining elements occupied new positions in the first position at the outskirts of Kremenchug as a precaution. It was learned from the division's former neighbour on the left, the 6th Panzer Division, that it had crossed the Dniepr with all elements and had occupied new positions on the west bank.

The tempo of the enemy's approach increased gradually, especially since considerable groups of Soviet forces were approaching the German Kremenchug bridgehead. Reports on enemy movements from 27 September revealed that they were expending considerable resources in an effort to break through the positions of the panzer-fusiliers at Pyatigory. At least one entire enemy regiment was identified in this one area. Repeated counterattacks with tanks, including Tigers, gained breathing room for the defenders and contributed to the holding of the positions. The German infantry was simply too weak to do the job alone. The artillery with its accurate barrages also added strength to the defence. The forward artillery observers who stuck it out at the front with the infantry were often the saviours of the situation and deserved to have their praises sung. The strength of the artillery and flak, the first batteries (heavy) of the former were already on the west bank, and an adequate supply ammunition permitted the bridgehead to mount an effective defence.

Considerable relief was provided by an advance by the Assault Gun Battalion GD, which drove to Loski collective farm and wiped out an entire enemy battle group west of Sredipolye.

At about 13.00 on 27 September 1943 the division issued orders for a withdrawal to the "M-2" Line, which in several places reached the outer limits of Kremenchug. The line ran as follows: Somilenki (fusiliers) – northern edge of Tereshkovtsy (grenadiers/fusiliers) – Nedogarki (grenadiers) – southern edge of Gulaki. beginning of the withdrawal was scheduled for 16.00; at the same time the first combat units would fall back from their previous positions and cross the bridge to the west.

One of these units was a battle group under the command of Major Gomille, commander of III (Tiger) Battalion, Panzer Regiment GD, with his tanks as well as 2nd Company, Panzer-Grenadier Regiment GD and I Battalion, Panzer-Artillery Regiment GD, which immediately transferred across the Dniepr for use elsewhere. The reason behind this was the need to counter Soviet paratroops which had allegedly landed west of the river.

On the 28th of September, the day before the ultimate abandonment of the Kremenchug bridgehead, the fighting units learned what was to take place in the next 48 hours. The Panzer-Grenadier Division GD was to be the last unit to leave the bridgehead. After blowing the bridge, the last elements of the division battle group were to cross the river in assault boats.

At 10.50 in the morning orders were issued for the withdrawal to the "R" Line for 18.30. The new line was to be occupied by infantry forces only. At the same time the bulk of the Armoured Reconnaissance Battalion GD and the artillery was to pull out. Only the Assault Gun Battalion GD was to remain initially to continue providing cover for the infantry in the bridgehead. The "R" Line was to be held by the Panzer-Grenadier Regiment GD on the left, the Panzer-Fusilier Regiment GD in the centre and on the right by a regiment of the 320th Infantry Division, which was expected to arrive from the northeast. All superfluous vehicles were to be moved to the west bank immediately. An "S" Line as well as an "O" Line, the last, were also planned, the latter to be held only by a battalion of panzer-grenadiers.

Occupation of the "S" Line—southern edge of Savino (fusiliers) – Kovalevka (grenadiers) – Krivusoki (grenadiers) – followed on the evening of 28 September, beginning at about 18.00. Elements of the Panzer-Fusilier Regiment GD were relieved and sent over the bridge to the west.

The armoured assault pioneers were now in their element. All of the streets of Kremenchug were mined except for three route through the city. Circular Teller mines and square S-mines were even laid in gardens; each pioneer was able to make use of his own imagination in selecting the most unlikely hiding places.

Given the dense net of mines and the uncertainty over the exact situation, it is understandable that many German vehicles also ran over these mines and sustained, in some cases, considerable damage. It was also predictable, however, that the expected Soviets were not exactly going to be happy about these surprises!

On the west bank of the Dniepr, meanwhile, the assault boats were prepared for the water action, well-camouflaged behind bushes and walls of houses. The successful retrieval of the last defenders on the east bank would depend on them and their crews.

The wooden road bridge was also under the protection of the pioneers. According to the fall-back plan they were to blow it up at 18.00 on 29 September. They must succeed, the destruction must be lasting. For this purpose they had brought in all available explosive materials, including aerial bombs of considerable size, which were to lend special force to the demolition and its effects. Then, with the rising of the blood-red sun, began the 29th of September, the day which was to see the end of a part of this retreat. In the Kremenchug bridgehead the last German units stood on the east bank of the Dniepr – ready to give it up.

The course of this day, so rich in events, tension and the giving of the utmost by each of the participants, will be taken from the dry daily report by the regiment which bore the main burden in those decisive hours, then Panzer-Grenadier Regiment GD under its commander Oberstleutnant Lorenz:

05.00 Not until 05.00 are the positions of the "S" Line occupied everywhere, contact with neighbouring units established. Timetable (for the withdrawal into the city) is: From 12.00 the remaining artillery, flak and heavy weapons as well as the remaining units of the 320th Inf.Div. From 17.00 withdrawal of the infantry toward the "O" Line, about 18.00 demolition of the bridges, 19.00 withdrawal of remaining infantry to bank of the Dniepr. Meanwhile I Battalion is to occupy the last bridgehead position north of the bridge.

08.00 Enemy attack in battalion strength at Mazimovka repulsed.

08.30 Enemy penetration south of Nedogarki in battalion strength. The right wing of I Battalion pulls back its security screen. Enemy veers to Pimentyevka. Of three enemy armoured cars which approached the anti-tank ditches near Nedogarki, two were knocked out, the third forced to turn away.

Own security positions still on Hill 85.4 and both sides of the road north of 85.4.

08.45 Seven assault guns arrive at regimental command post as last armour protection.

10.00 Commanders conference involving leaders of units participating in the withdrawal (or their adjutants) at the regimental command post. Planned course of the withdrawal of the units:

11.00 — part of artillery

13.00 — assault gun battalion less one battery

13.30 — anti-tank battalion

13.45 — rest of Panzer-Fusilier Regiment GD

14.45 — vehicles and elements of Panzer-Grenadier Regiment GD

15.30 — rest of artillery

11.30 Commander Panzer-Grenadier Regiment GD and division command post at Bridge Site North. At the same time Command Post South, manned by Major Pohlmann (panzer-fusiliers), set up on the west bank. Commander of I Battalion, Panzer-Grenadier Regiment GD, Major Remer, takes over command of the Panzer-Grenadier Regiment GD.

11.40 Enemy tank attack from Mazimovka with three tanks. Enemy attack in company strength repulsed by 4th Company. Aircraft reports 20 enemy tanks on Vlasovka–Krivushi road. 10 of these in Samusevka woods. 20 enemy motor vehicles in same area with infantry.

13.00 20 enemy tanks in area southwest of Mmhl., southwest of Kremenchug; 1 platoon of assault guns sent there for defence, initially on the raised road. After allowing themselves to be overrun our infantry is pinned down. I Battalion command post also overrun. Both medical officers missing. An enemy battalion attacks Krivuchi, another is advancing south from Point 75.1.

13.30 1st Company has disengaged from the enemy. Mines on raised road on river bank armed. Assault guns stand ready to defend northwest of Mmhl. Anti-tank troops of the SS and assault guns crossing the bridge are stopped and put to use. Regimental H.Q. Company takes over defense of bridge.

13.46 Two enemy tanks destroyed. Soviet artillery chief-of-staff of the 5th Guards Army captured with important material.

14.28 Panzer Group Vellen sent to II Battalion. An enemy battalion there. I Battalion's left wing withdrawn to "R" Line.

14.52 Assault guns which were stopped sent west across the bridge. Enemy tanks on bank of Dniepr turned back by artillery fire.

16.00 Withdrawal into "R" Position. Elements of III Battalion immediately cross bridge in vehicles.

16.42 Enemy bombing attack on road bridge. Wood hit and catches fire. Aerial bombs and explosives stored there explode.

16.45 I Battalion has occupied "R" Position; II Battalion still engaged in withdrawal. Enemy pursuing on left wing of II Battalion. Enemy firing heavy-calibre artillery into city, which is almost completely destroyed as a result of demolitions. Still in the bridgehead are: I and II Btl., 585th Inf.Rgt. (320th Inf.Div.), Rgt. H.Q. 585th Inf.Rgt., II and III Btl., Pz.Fus.Rgt. GD as well as I and II Btl., Pz.Gren.Rgt. GD. Enemy advanced to riverbank at quarry against 585th Inf. Rgt. with 30 men. II Battalion, Panzer-Fusilier Regiment sent to seal off the penetration.

17.55 Order to take over "R" Line. 4 more enemy tanks destroyed. Last assault guns roll over the railroad bridge.

18.45 Order to blow bridge. Riverbank cleared.

18.58 Bridge blown. 6 bridge piers were destroyed, 5 remain standing. I Battalion, Panzer-Grenadier Regiment GD immediately withdrawn further to the "O" Position.

19.30 II Battalion, Panzer-Grenadier Regiment GD crosses river. Two crossing points: western bridge with ferries and assault boats for panzer-grenadiers, east of the bridge with 25 assault boats for II Battalion, Panzer-Fusiliers and the rest of the 585th Infantry Regiment. I Battalion, 585th Infantry Regiment loses way to its crossing point, is even taken for the enemy. As a result crossing delayed until 22.25.

22.25 Commander Panzer-Grenadier Regiment GD leaves the east bank of the Dniepr in the last boats. All units released from subordinate commands. Enemy attempts to interfere with crossing with mortars. March into regiment's waiting area southwest part of Kryukov.

23.15 Report to Division Ia to receive new orders!

This dry, factual account of the events surrounding the crossing of the Dniepr River by the Panzer-Grenadier Division *Großdeutschland* is to be followed by the experiences of the men who played a significant role in the smooth execution of this difficult operation.

Those were hard days in the Kremenchug bridgehead which would not soon be forgotten. They were mastered by a group of men who, true to their voluntary oath, followed the orders of their officers, whom they trusted.

CHAPTER 4

THREE GREEN FLARES

The dry, official notes of the Panzer-Grenadier Regiment will be followed by war correspondent Henne's account of this day. Henne was present at the Lorenz command post during the evacuation. The events in the Kremenchug bridgehead left their impression, but in his lines there may be felt something of the tension that gripped all the participants in the bridgehead. Their job was to hold the bridgehead against the attack by the concentrically-merging units of the Soviet army until the evacuation could be completed as per the plan. Henne's account appeared soon after the events at Kremenchug.

"The car drove out of the marketplace very slowly, and it was unclear to me as to why it was moving at such a slow tempo. The houses to the right and left of us were burning, and the heat was so great that one had to hold his hands in front of one's face, and even then the biting smoke caused the tears to begin flowing. At the corner, where the street opened up directly into the bridgehead, it became apparent to me why everything was moving forward so slowly. I noticed several squads of pioneers laying mines. Seeing them working so close to the road, I began to realize how narrow the lane must be that already lay behind us.

I saw the big railroad bridge first. From this distance it gave the impression of strength and solidity. I knew that it was more than 900 metres long and that beside it there was also a wooden bridge spanning the Dniepr.

The nearer we came to the bridge the larger became the stream of traffic, for columns of vehicles of all types and sizes were pouring out of one of the other streets that must have ran along the railway embankment and from another whose end I could not see from my position. They turned into the open square and streamed into the mouths of both bridges, under the careful direction of officers and military police. It had been like this for days and the columns seemed endless. What struck me was the calmness with which everything took place. The traffic directors were scarcely ever required to shout or augment their voices with emphatic gestures, usually only when a careless driver strayed from his lane.

That was at about 12.00. I stayed with the bridge traffic-control officer for a while. I knew that he was the Ic of the division (Oberleutnant Ritter), but now that there was nothing left to add to the complete picture of the enemy's dispositions he had been assigned this traffic control job. He reported the beginning and end of the withdrawing units and carefully noted the numbers of vehicles. I was told that the vehicles currently crossing were those of an SS division and some of the division's. They were the last, however, all the others were already in safety on the other side.

In the city, or more accurately in what was left of the city, an important building was to be blown up at 14.00. I gathered from the conversations among the drivers, pioneers and runners, who were eating their meal in the shadow of a destroyed warehouse, that this event was being awaited with a certain amount of tension. As they talked about it I also overheard how many tons of explosives would probably be needed to blow up the two bridges. To my mind they were talking of fantastic figures, such as 70 tonnes for the railroad bridge.

At about 13.00 I saw the battle group commander drive forward. He was the commander of the Grenadier Regiment *Großdeutschland* and for the afternoon he had passed command of the regiment to one of his battalion commanders. I knew that this man wore the Knight's Cross and was known beyond the regiment for his courage and ability.

The battle group commander's command post was located in a house which stood just short of the bridge. Someone had written "Forward Message Centre" in chalk on the wall in large letters. Diagonally opposite this house, beyond a bunker and the square, stood another relatively intact house into which the general and the Ia – then General Staff Oberstleutnant Weiß in an acting capacity – had transferred their command post. From the moment the Oberstleutnant entered the house, at about 13.05, the outflow of vehicles appeared to enter a new phase, for everything went even faster, even smoother. The room, until days ago the tailor's workshop of some train unit and since then temporary quarters for many transiting units, was cleared in no time except for a small table and three stools. When the commander entered the telephone was already on the table, connected and ready to use.

On the table lay a map, on which were drawn three semi-circular rings with almost symmetrical radii from the centre point – from the bridges in fact. The first circle extended to the outer edge of the city, the second about to the centre, the third directly around our bridgehead. In the first line (or better said the first ring) at that moment were the grenadiers on the far left, then the fusiliers and finally the grenadiers of a regiment of the neighbouring division, whose main elements had already withdrawn across the bridge and were now likewise under the command of the battle commander.

First the commander and his extremely young operations officer stood in the room. I had the feeling that he was repeatedly going over the situation as he bent over the map. In curious contrast to the excited and hurried comings and goings outside, he exuded great calm and command. His battered and dusty officer's cap, a proper peacetime cap with its support wire still in place, sat stiffly on his head. His uniform scarcely differed from that of a common soldier. It was orderly, but was dust-covered and wrinkled and revealed that its wearer was as familiar with the mud at the front as he was with the map table.

The liaison officers of the regiments whose battalions were in the outer ring and whose vehicles had already pulled back across the bridges or were to leave in the next few hours reported in first. The next to report was the chief of the headquarters company, Oberleutnant Schoppe, a towering giant who had to bend low to get through the door. He cast a quick look at the map and received orders to take over the close-in protection of both bridges.

It was made clear to him that the main danger was to be expected from the west. 'How many men do you have?' asked the commander. He had eighteen men, came the answer. 'All armed to the teeth,' added the giant with a smile.

Just then the telephone rang. One of the officers passed the phone to the Oberstleutnant. As he identified himself the general walked into the room. As always he carried a walking stick. The officers stood and saluted, while the Oberstleutnant, who was listening into the receiver with great attentiveness, passed the general the other receiver so that he could listen in on the conversation. The voice at the other end of the line quickly and factually informed them that twenty enemy tanks had broken through. The general, who had the earpiece pressed to his ear, asked who was speaking. "Major

Remer," replied the Oberstleutnant softly, pointing to a point on the map with his pencil.

It was obvious to the commander from his conversation with the man he had appointed to lead his regiment that the enemy had a coup de main in mind. Advancing along the Dniepr with twenty tanks, their end objective was obviously to seize the bridges, prevent their destruction and simultaneously block them. Those of us who had a map looked for the point the commander had pointed out and estimated the distance at a glance. It wasn't quite four kilometres.

I suddenly noticed the commander sit upright as if the conversation had been cut off. He called repeatedly into the receiver: 'Yes, who's speaking? What's going on?' It was deathly silent in the room which was filled with officers, a Hauptmann from the pioneers had arrived as well as Rittmeister Heise, the general's adjutant, and his operations officer.

'What?' shouted the commander, 'enemy tanks?' He repeated: 'Yes, three enemy tanks, but no troop carriers .... You're sure you're not mistaken?'

It turned out that while the commander was speaking to Major Remer, the man at the grenadier regiment's switchboard saw three enemy vehicles approaching them from not too great a distance and in his initial shock mistook them for tanks. Finally, after repeated questioning and gaining confidence from the commander's voice, he admitted that what he saw were not tanks, but enemy infantry approaching in troop carriers.

I must repeat that during the time in which the report was received that twenty enemy tanks had broken through on the west bank, the general had instructed one of the operations officers, Leutnant von Prittwitz, to halt some assault guns which were just rolling past and summon the battery commander. When the commander had hung up the receiver, the pioneer Hauptmann saw that the time had come for him to report. He stated that the bridge was ready to be blown up.

'How many kilometres security zone?' the general asked back.

'About one kilometre, Herr General.'

"Good!' A new figure with a smoke-blackened face entered the room, the commander of the assault gun battery. I believe I recall that his name was Oberleutnant Sturm. The general took time to ask him whether he was related to a Herr Sturm he knew from Hamburg.

'No, Herr General,' replied the Oberleutnant.

'Where are you going?' asked the general.

'Across the bridge as ordered, Herr General.'

'You're turning around. Here' – the general pointed at the map – 'here twenty enemy tanks have broken through. Show them your teeth!' The battery commander was dismissed. The operations officer was instructed to stop any anti-tank weapons that were crossing or about to cross the bridge.

At that moment a heavy explosion shook the building, a cloud of dust sprang through the cracked panes and the door to the room flew open. The Rittmeister observed that that was probably the biggest explosion in the city.

'No,' replied the pioneer officer factually and without pausing to reflect, 'another twenty minutes.' I looked at the clock. There was in fact twenty minutes to go.

One order now literally followed hot on the heels of the other, precisely formulated and in German of great clarity. Three assault guns were assigned to secure three-hundred metres west of the bridge, four others three-hundred metres north. The chief of the headquarters company was summoned again and received orders to guard the assault guns. While he was squeezing his huge form through the door, an Obergefreiter came and laid several egg-shaped hand grenades, a hollow charge, an automatic rifle and machine pistols on the cold oven. They were to secure the command post. They had to be ready for any eventuality.

All the while vehicles roared past outside: tanks, guns, tracked vehicles, cars, motorcycles; order was exemplary and there were no delays whatsoever. Explosive charges continued to go off all over the city. Within the next few minutes the leaders of the assault boats and ferries which were to bring nine-hundred soldiers and any remaining vehicles across the Dniepr following the blowing of the bridge and the final evacuation of the bridgehead reported. 'Well, is it all going to work?'

'Of course, Herr General!'

'We have the ferries in an emergency,' observed the general to his battle group commander.

'How many men can one of these ferries take on; Lorenz, you should know that, you're an old pioneer aren't you?'

'About fifty, Herr General.' The leader of the pioneer battalion also reported in. I knew that he and his pioneers had distinguished themselves while fighting as infantry in the several-day defensive battle at Oposhnya. He was ordered to block all but three of the streets leading to the bridges with mines.

Finally a Leutnant reported. 'What do you want?' asked the general.

The serious-faced Leutnant declared that he had orders to blow up the house as well as all the other houses standing around the bridge.

'Immediately?'

'Yes, immediately, Herr General.'

'Well, then without me,' declared the general, smiling at such conscious-ness of duty. The other officers grinned. The Leutnant, still serious, turned and left. At that moment the earth shook, the house seemed alive. The shock wave came through the window and struck the wall, the door swung back and forth on its hinges as if moved by powerful hands.

That was the big explosion in the city. It was precisely 14.00. Everything worked right on time. While I climbed upstairs I heard someone ask if there were any reports from the second fusilier battalion. No, came the answer, nothing had been received yet and furthermore communications had been severed. Still the columns showed no sign of ending. The sun burned down and it was almost like a hot July day. A few sheep ran around somewhere and beside the wall of a house a calf stood and stared dumbly into the dust and the glare of the sun.

When I returned to the room someone had broken off the door to the adjoining room; those officers not needed at that moment were asked to wait there. The talk was that the enemy was now exerting greater pressure on the right wing; it was also said that there was no contact with several units at that time.

A runner had brought in the map case found on the bolshevik chief-of-staff of the 5th Guards Army captured in the grenadiers' sector. This so took my attention that for some time I only half listened to the continuing telephone conversations. The map case was well worn and in addition to several maps contained notebooks and photos. The latter showed a bald-headed man whose intelligent face bore hard features. While I thumbed through various identification cards, in walked the commander of the attached grenadier regiment of a neighbouring division, a small, agile, extremely good-natured looking Oberst with the Knight's Cross. He told the Oberstleutnant that he had contact with the fusiliers and that up above the enemy had been beaten back by the second battalion, I believe.

Just then a shout came from outside: 'Aircraft ... aircraft!' The Oberstleutnant ordered: 'Everyone into the bunker!' We pressed through the door into the dugout. It was pitch black and smelled awful. One couldn't help thinking that in quieter times soldiers had used it as a toilet; but no one cared right now. Safety was more important than smell. I believe someone even joked about it in the dark. The bombs fell to the left of the wooden bridge.

This interruption may have lasted three or four minutes. When we walked back into the command post it seemed as if nothing at all had happened. The Oberstleutnant was bent over his map again and spoke with the Ia of the division, who had come over from his command post. 'The twenty tanks,' the operations officer informed me, 'have beaten a hasty retreat, we got three of them.'

Much later – it was after the second Soviet air raid in which the explosive charge on the wooden bridge took a direct hit and then this little by little almost blew half of itself up, and after the division command post had been moved to the west bank – I noted a conversation between the Oberstleutnant and Major Remer. He said calmly and forcefully, 'Remer, everything must go exactly according to plan; but as well everything must be coordinated with the fusiliers. Then the 'Siegfried Line' must be held firmly, not fleetingly, so that we get all the vehicles out.' The operations officer was given the job of maintaining radio and radio telephone communication with the other bank.

At 16.30 it was learned by wire that the enemy had broken through at the quarry three kilometres east of the bridge site and was heading toward the bank of the Dniepr.

'That's all we need,' replied the commander calmly, 'I'll see what we have left.'

I had time and was compelled to watch him during this time. He was still calmness personified and showed not the least trace of tension. He smoked two of the cigarettes his orderly had laid out for him. He also found time to eat a few slices of bread and in his usual courteous style he didn't forget to invite the officers present to join in.

My note pad reveals that the enemy penetration at the quarry was halted by the artillery, which placed the enemy infantry under direct fire. It further states that at 17.00 the pioneer commander arrived and reported that the city and all important factories had been destroyed as ordered. The commander of the fusiliers, also a wearer of the Knight's Cross, turned up, but there was still no news of the second fusilier battalion. It began to get dark. The city was still burning. Outside it had grown quiet, now and then a vehicle rolled toward the bridge.

At 18.20 one of the bridge traffic-control officers reported. 'Is everything alright Ritter?' asked the commander. Reading from his note pad, the Oberleutnant listed what had crossed the bridge in the course of the afternoon. Only the assault guns were still missing.

At 17.40 a radio message was sent to the regiment: 'Assault guns pull back. Begin withdrawal at 18.00 and occupy 'R-1' position.' In the room it was almost dark. The commander asked the operations officer whether the green flares were there and how many and if they had weapons.

'Yes, all on hand, Herr Oberstleutnant.'

The commander paced back and forth, finally lit a cigarette. For a moment I tried to believe that the excitement of the moment had seized him after all. Once he declared while looking out the window, 'If only the assault guns would come...' At about 18.00 the Rittmeister and the general's adjutant came from the opposite bank by motorcycle. The Rittmeister wanted, as he put it, to gauge the situation.

'Inform the general,' said the commander, 'that everything is going according to plan. Put a guide over at the bridge so that my officer who is to bring the order to detonate to the detonation point will know immediately where he is and there's no delay due to a long search in the dark for the detonation point. Furthermore have them maintain a security zone of one kilometre over there. I think we'll be able to detonate at about 18.30.'

Finally the assault guns came. The commander of the battalion, Major Frantz, wearer of the Oak Leaves, reported personally. I was looking forward to meeting him, as I had heard plenty about him, but it was already dark. As he was leaving Frantz said to the Oberstleutnant, 'I wish you good luck!'

We were now alone. A few pioneers were standing around outside, others squatted in front of the house. They had poured fuel over the last part of the wooden bridge, whose explosive charges had not gone off, and it was now blazing fiercely. Now they were being employed as a sort of last line of security.

'I'm worried,' said one of the operations officers, 'that another vehicle is going to come.'

The major had heard the half-whispered comment and declared, 'There's no more coming, they're all across.' That was all he said. But there were no more doubts for us. In the penultimate ring there were now just grenadiers and fusiliers.

At 18.10 the operations officer jotted down a message: 'Bridge will be blown at 18.30. Am firing green signal flares.'

Immediately after the message was sent we moved out. We took the hand grenades and the weapons and walked across the square north toward the city. The street was littered with smouldering beams and pieces of metal and everywhere we picked our way around fallen wires and telephone lines. We had to hurry if we wanted to get out of the danger zone. I tried to imagine what was happening in the ring in front of us held by the grenadiers and fusiliers. There wasn't a shot fired and apart from the collapsing frames it was almost eerily quiet. There were twenty of us, officers, runners and radio operators. The pioneer companies and the headquarters company had disappeared into the dark somewhere to our left. No one walked too fast, as if to show that all this wasn't bothering us. In a few minutes the bridge behind us would go up. Then the river would be between us and those still over there. Now everything had to work as it had before. We stopped at a stone house and positioned ourselves at the wall which pointed toward the city.

The two radio operators climbed the steps of a cow-shed and set up their backpack radios there. The Oberstleutnant stood off to one side with the Oberst from the regiment of the neighbouring division and talked quietly with him. The operations officer, it was the small Leutnant Schneider, stepped forward and fired the signal flares. It was three green flares. They soared straight up into the dark sky, paused for a few fractions of a second like candles and then fell hissing toward the ground. I believe we were all thinking the same thing at that moment, but everyone acted as if it was nothing and went on talking about inconsequential things.

Now it must come. But all remained quiet. I heard the voice of the Oberstleutnant from the right.

'The radio operator – do you have contact...?'

There was no answer, but we heard the voice of a radio operator through the silence. He called loudly and accentuated: 'Schulte to Berta. – Schulte calling Berta. – Berta come in. – Berta come in...!'

Then it was quiet again.

'Do you have contact?' shouted the Oberstleutnant from the right.

'No, no contact!'

'Schneider, fire three green signal flares again,' ordered the Oberstleutnant. Certainly he was thinking something different than I, certainly he was convinced of what must and should happen, certainly he didn't doubt for a second the logical consistency of what was planned and what was now supposed to become fact. Perhaps a part of his brain was thinking: What if it doesn't go off – damn, why doesn't it go off – why is it taking so long – what's going on anyway – it's so blasted quiet here...'

The voice of the radio operator came again: 'Schulte calling Berta – Schulte calling Berta – Berta come in – Berta come in!'

A beam crashed to the ground somewhere and behind the cow-shed a flame leapt into the air. We lit a cigarette and I was just in the process of taking the first puff when the earth moved beneath my feet. That was it! I opened my mouth to head off the crash of the explosion but it was on us already. We waited another minute, listening to the buzzing of pieces of iron and steel, the dull pop of fragments falling into the carpet of ashes. We came out from cover behind the wall and walked back along the street. The wooden bridge was still burning and in its light we saw the silhouette of the blown railroad bridge.

Someone said, 'So now I can take my bathing suit off again, I was all ready to swim over there.' We walked slowly back to the command post. The calf lay to the left of the wall, it looked like it was sleeping. The house was still standing and appeared undamaged. I can't remember how long it was until Major Remer arrived and reported that he was holding the last ring, that everything was in good shape and there were no losses to report.

After the bridge was blown everything appeared to be in the best order. Three- or four-hundred metres in front of us the grenadiers and fusiliers lay behind the remains of walls and amid the rubble. The Sentz company command post, for example, was located not a hundred metres in front of the battle group commander's. A stream of orders followed. The pioneers moved from right to left down to the bank. Their shadowy outlines stood strangely still, illuminated in the darkness by the burning city.

'The comrades over there are slowly feeling their way forward, they're surely worried about mines,' said someone. I gave up trying to identify the speaker, for shielded from the light in front of us the darkness was like a wall around the command post. The dull buzzing of the assault boats came from the Dniepr. The first were now crossing. The enemy fired a few salvoes at the riverbank from the area of the quarry. The shells were wide and splashed into the water.

We stood around and I felt how great was the confidence and trust of everyone who was present in the Kremenchug bridgehead on this evening. Nothing more could happen now. What difference did it make if the enemy troops in the trenches fired across? It was a terrific evening, I would have given a lot if I had known anything that could match this atmosphere; this display of the colours, the fires, the shadows from the light, these scraps of conversation, this noise from the river. There came the men, one after another, still cautious in spite of the success of the operation, and the darkness of the riverbank swallowed them up.

We walked over the sand of the Dniepr. Someone I didn't know bent down, picked something up and said: 'So, I'm going to take this shell for my daughter.'

The wooden bridge was still burning. The commander stayed behind us, he and his young operations officer crossed in one of the last boats. Major Remer lay behind the embankment and waited until the last of his men had crossed. We walked across the sand. It was almost a pleasure stroll. It really couldn't have gone according to plan, I thought. One thinks a great deal while walking in the dark, that's an old fact. I could smell the water. My last vacation in Bansin came to mind, and I knew for certain that each of the 900 men had his own memories as he walked. One thought of his wife, one of his child who was surely walking by now. The Oberstleutnant was perhaps thinking something else, surely he was thinking something else. He had been the leader of a battle group. He had staked everything to disengage from the enemy without loss, as he had been ordered to do. He had seen to it that nothing was lost.

I don't know what was on Radio Moscow at night, but surely it was reporting the victory at Kremenchug and our complete destruction as we calmly and cooly stepped over the footbridge and climbed into our assault boats. We raced across the river and in a few minutes on the other side we were welcomed by the ancient security of the comradeship of those whose crossing we had covered."

Part III

CHAPTER 1

BATTLE ZONE KRIVOY ROG
(from 30 September 1943)

The Dniepr River, at least at this time of year, was undoubtedly seen as a formidable natural obstacle, but the field positions, obstacles and fortifications which had been talked about for weeks were not there. It was soon clear to the soldiers that the enemy would soon seek to force a decision here, where rain and mud scarcely hindered movement at this time of year.

It was not just that this side of the Dniepr, especially the Krivoy Rog area, offered many worthwhile economic targets, the area was also very appealing from the operational point of view for the Soviets, who were caught up in the impetus of their attack. It was to be expected that they would commit everything, to the limit of their supply possibilities, to force a crossing of the Dniepr. So on the 5th of October they threw five armies – 61 rifle divisions and 7 tank divisions with about 1,000 tanks – into the attack in the Kremenchug–Dniepropetrovsk area alone. Their clear and dangerous objective was to break through to the Black Sea via Krivoy Rog and Nikolayev, encircling and destroying the German units cut off by their breakthrough.

The German side on the other hand had to man and hold a front of nearly 700 kilometres with a total of only 37 infantry divisions. Given the low combat strengths of the units, which for divisions were often only about 1,000 men, perhaps 2,000 with replacements, the situation had to be viewed from the outset as hopeless. Of the seventeen panzer and panzer-grenadier divisions at the disposal of the army group in this sector, scarcely any still possessed any real attacking strength. The number of tanks had fallen on an equal scale to the strength of the regiments.

It is therefore not surprising that German command posts began receiving reports of enemy crossings of the Dniepr on 29 September 1943. Enemy paratroopers also appeared in the western hinterland, their mission to prepare bridgeheads on the west bank. According to reports from the units, at the outset there were four focal points for the crossing of the river in Army Group South's command area:

On the northern wing of the Fourth Panzer Army north of Kiev and in the area of the Eighth Army south of Kiev, roughly south of Pereyaslev. In the First Panzer Army's sector on both sides of Mishurin Rog south of Kremenchug; likewise in the area of First Panzer Army north of Dniepropetrovsk.

As appropriate reserves were not on hand, all units immediately available were moved in to seal off and if possible eliminate the bridgeheads. Among these units was the Panzer-Grenadier Division *Großdeutschland*, which had been the last to leave the Kremenchug bridgehead. Without even an hour's rest it was diverted south.

Yes, even while crossing the river, the unit leaders received the order to move to the area west of Mishurin Rog immediately after completing the crossing and reorganizing. There they were to launch a counterattack against the enemy forces which had crossed the river.

The senior command posts were well aware of the danger posed by these enemy bridgeheads. With the orders to defend, unavoidable given the situation, they planted the first seed for the overtaxing of men and materiel which would finally be deadly to the ability to resist and morale of the field units. But the German soldier fought to the death.

Reconnaissance revealed that the local situation on both sides of Mishurin Rog, the future scene of action for the Panzer-Grenadier Division Großdeutschland, was characterized by two focal points that the enemy appeared to be attempting to form on the west bank of the Dniepr: one was a still-weak enemy battle group which had crossed the river between Soloshino (east of the Dniepr) and Mishurin Rog (west of the Dniepr) and entered the hilly terrain northwest of Mishurin Rog. Its spearheads already commanded the Uspenskoye–Kommunar–Mishurin Rog–Likhovka road and were impeding German supply traffic. On 29 September 1943 I Battalion, Panzer-Fusilier Regiment GD under Hauptmann von Basse, reinforced by I Battalion, Panzer-Artillery Regiment GD, was sent against this enemy. The German force was able to occupy positions east of Kommunar, roughly at Point 70.4 and to the south. The planned action in this sector by the Panzer-Grenadier Division GD was rendered unnecessary by the intervention of the 23rd Panzer Division, whose mission was to drive the enemy near Kommunar back to the east. I Battalion, Panzer-Fusilier Regiment GD and I Battalion, Panzer-Artillery Regiment GD were temporarily placed under its command for this purpose.

Far more dangerous and significantly stronger were the recognized enemy movements southeast of Mishurin Rog, roughly east of Likhovka. The enemy was said to have appeared in this area with elements of five divisions and was threatening the hilly country east of Annovka. The pillars of this defensive area were still held by the 23rd Panzer Division at and north of Mishurin Rog, the SS-Cavalry Brigade (Fegelein) at Point 118.0 and the 1st Infantry Division at Point 163.8.

The GD's mission was to drive back the enemy and to reduce the bridge-heads to the maximum extent possible in cooperation with the units still standing. Here once again every available weapon had to be committed, everything had to be done to destroy the enemy.

However, not even the most urgent demands could conceal the true weakness of the German forces after the weeks of fighting and the retreat. The low combat strengths of the regiments made necessary further mergings of companies and battalions. Officer shortages were on such a scale that many companies were commanded by men with the rank of Gefreiter. Even the stream of replacements from the field replacement battalions could no longer make good the losses.

The backbone of the infantry, the panzer arm, had probably reached its lowest point in operational combat vehicles at this time. The Panzer Regiment GD reported that it had one (!) panzer ready for action, and that III (Tiger) Battalion had a total of ten Tigers on hand, all the others having been knocked out or undergoing repairs. At this point these remnants were combined under the command of Oberleutnant Bayer (C.O. 11th Company). The following members of the battalion were still in action: Oberleutnant Bayer, Feldwebel Drenkhahn, Heinz, Schuh, Bonitz, Gussone; Leutnant Folke (9th Company), Obergefreiter J. Jensen (H.Q. Company), Oberleutnant Arnold (10th Company), Unteroffizier Erbrich (9th Company), Oberfeldwebel Friedebach, Obergefreiter Wendels, Obergefreiter Pritz (H.Q. Company), Feldwebel W. Schmidt (9th Company), Unteroffizier Kania (9th Company), Feldwebel Stukenbröker (9th Company), Unteroffizier K. Schmidt (9th Company), Unteroffizier Bühler (10th Company). Available for minor repairs at that time was 11th Company's repair echelon under Feldwebel Priester. The former commander of the Panzer Regiment GD, Oberst Graf Strachwitz, was forced to leave on account of illness when the Dniepr was reached. He was temporarily replaced by Major Pfeffer, commander of the 26th Panther Battalion, which was under GD's command. The situation of the Assault Gun Battalion GD under Major Frantz was much more favourable. In spite of the recent heavy fighting the battalion was able to report 25 serviceable assault guns – 80% of its combat strength.

In spite of the pitifully few hours available during the night of 29-30 September to rest and reorganize the units, the first elements of the division left for the new area of operations at about 06.15 on 30 September. Panzer-Grenadier Regiment GD marched in the following sequence – command echelon, H.Q. Company, II Battalion, IV Battalion, I Battalion – through Kryukov, Morosovka, Mlinok, Taranivka and Tarasa Grigoryevka to Mikhailovka, where 1st Company, I Battalion formed a security screen at Point 120.5, due east of the road, facing east to guard the division's assembly area. II Battalion, Panzer-Artillery Regiment GD was temporarily attached to the regiment.

The Panzer-Fusilier Regiment GD – without I Battalion – was moved up immediately and transferred to the Krasny Kut area to accompany the planned attack on the right, or south. The mission given to the Panzer-Fusilier Regiment GD was to advance out of the river valley on both sides of Krasny Kut through Zapolitshki- South in the direction of Taranzov.

Reconnaissance revealed that the enemy had crossed the hills east of Anovka at about noon on 30 September. A force of about 800 men without heavy weapons was advancing south in the valley south of Zapolitshki. The hill at Point 117.0 was occupied by the enemy. In order to prevent the enemy from taking the hills east of Anovka, at about 19.00 I (APC) Battalion, Panzer-Grenadier Regiment GD moved out of the valley near Krasny Kut and II Battalion of the same regiment north of Anovka to attack eastward with the objective of Point 177.0 and Zapolitshki. The object was to create a pocket around the hill country east of Anovka. To this end I (APC) Battalion,

Panzer-Grenadier Regiment GD swung out over the hills east of Krasny Kut and Point 177.0 in order to then turn north toward Zapolitshki. II Battalion advanced north of the road and soon became involved in heavy fighting north of Ivashki. Contact between the two battalions was established near Ivashki at about 20.40; the enemy, who had moved in in disorganized masses, suffered heavy losses.

The overall situation first became clearer in the evening: panzer-fusilier command post at Krasny Kut with III Battalion on the hills southeast of Anovka, west of Zapolitshki. Panzer- grenadier command post in Kom. Volya, with II Battalion at exit from Zapolitshki, with I (APC) Battalion due west of the road bridge west of Ivashki. Still en route were I Battalion, 77th Artillery Regiment and II Battalion, 293rd Artillery Regiment as well as a battalion of the 54th Rocket Regiment, which together with the Panzer-Artillery Regiment GD was to provide artillery support for the subsequent advance. Division command post in Verkhne Kamenistaya.

A continuation of the attack to the east to stabilize the situation was planned for 1 October. Boundary line between the two regiments was set as Point 98.5 west of Kom. Volya to individual hills northeast of Tarantsov. The Armoured Reconnaissance Battalion GD was assigned to accompany the attack from the area of Tarantsov-South along the valley to the northeast and cover the right flank. For this reason the command post of the Panzer-Fusilier Regiment GD was moved to Zapolitshki- South and the Armoured Reconnaissance Battalion GD placed under its command. Planned for 09.30 on October 1, the attack by the two regiments had to be postponed until 12.00 as preparations were not completed in time. Once the attack began, III Battalion, Panzer-Fusilier Regiment GD under Hauptmann Pohlmann captured the hill terrain northeast of Tarantsov in spite of enemy resistance. Elements of the Armoured Reconnaissance Battalion GD, in particular the 4th Squadron, followed these attack movements and took new positions about 2,000 metres east of Tarantsov from where they at least had visual contact with the most forward positions of the 306th Infantry Division south of Sokolovo.

The advance by I (APC) Battalion, Panzer-Grenadier Regiment GD and the Assault Gun Battalion GD against Point 172.2 initially reached this hill, however the considerable resistance mounted by the enemy forced them to withdraw as the infantry could not follow. Among the fatal casualties suffered by the assault guns were Wachtmeister Wilhelm Bindseil and Unteroffizier Joseph Maier. The attack was resumed during the night, this time with greater success. The panzer-grenadiers again drove north through the gorge as far as Ivashki, advancing the entire line farther to the northeast.

The terrain in this area was characterized by numerous hills and valleys. The summits of the chains of hills featured mounds of earth, mostly old burial mounds, which projected like pyramids and which offered a wide view of the surrounding countryside. They soon had their own designation: "Three-Nipple Hill," "One-Nipple Hill," etc, soon became well-known features to every soldier and on the maps.

In contrast there were deep gorges to be found everywhere. These were

The map shows German and Soviet troop positions and movements at the Dniepr River, October 1943. Labels include:

Tschernobyl
Korosten
Radomysl
Schitomir
Berdischew
KIEW
Fastow
Jagotin
1.ukrain.Front
7. Armeen
Heeres-Res.
2.Pz. Arm.
N
H.Gr. Süd
Bug
8.
Tscherkassy
2.ukrain.Front
früher Steppenfront
H.Res.
3.Arm.
Tschigirino
G.D.
Kirowograd
Krementschug
17.10.
Dniepr
3.ukrain.Front
DNJEPROPETROWSK
2 Armeen
1.Pz.
Piatichatka
Kriwoi Rog
Saporoshje
H.Gr. A
6.
4.ukrain.Front
Melitopol
4 Arm.
ODESSA
CHERSON
Perekop
SCHWARZES
MEER
ASOWSCHES
MEER
Sowj. Tr.
Deutsche Tr.
0 50 100 150 200 250 300 km
KRIM
Kertsch
17.

THE BATTLES AT THE DNIEPR OCTOBER 1943

210

FIGHTING IN THE
MISCHURIN ROG-BORODAYEVKA
BRIDGEHEAD
Sept. 30 to Oct. 17, 1943

211

dominated by thick woods and in places impenetrable brush. These clefts offered the attacker and defender alike excellent concealment and camouflage possibilities.

For the attacker these gorges gave rise to constant worries about being outflanked. Because of the restricted visibility the fighting in these gorges was difficult and very costly. They were also a favourite target for enemy aircraft. The artillery preferred these clefts in the terrain for their firing positions, while motorized units favoured them for parking their vehicles.

The greatest success of these few days lay on the division's left wing. There the village of Ivashki and the hills to the north of it were finally taken; this created the possibility of an attack against the flank of the enemy forces advancing southeast from Borodayevka. The hills on both sides of Hill Line 170 also offered a view of the Dniepr and the enemy's river-crossing traffic. It thus appeared important to exploit this success and now drive along the Anovka-North–Ivashki–Pavlovka road toward Borodayevka.

The situation on the right wing – elements of the Panzer-Fusilier Regiment GD and the Armoured Reconnaissance Battalion GD – was less clear however. The enemy held out stubbornly on the hills near Point 172.2 and in the gorges to the east, and received a steady flow of reinforcements from Borodayevka. The advance by the 306th Infantry Division also brought no success. But ultimately the swing forward by this wing was a decisive factor in determining whether the bridgehead could be reduced. It was of little consequence that Borodayevka fell into German hands if the relief thrust from Hill Point 163.8, or along the Dniepr to the northwest, to seal off the pocket which was being formed was not carried out simultaneously. It is interesting in this context how well-informed the Soviet command was over the situation on the German side. The Soviet radio net "Red Orchestra," active in Germany and the rest of Europe for years, had placed its paid observers in important positions everywhere. These kept the Soviets informed of German intentions. Here are several intercepted radio messages:

Dora to Director (Moscow)　　Reply from Teddy (30. 9. 43)

(a)　　Fixed defensive line does not exist at the Dniepr. Resistance at the Dniepr will be limited locally to important river crossings.

(b)　　No continuous system of defensive positions exists west of the Dniepr. OKH will concentrate stronger forces in front of the Kiev–Belaya Tserkov–Smela–Krivoy Rog line with intention of conducting mobile warfare and then withdraw these into the Dniepr bend on the Cherkassy–Vosnessensk line under Russian pressure. West of this line there are only secondary positions whose construction is still in progress, but which cannot be ready for use in a defensive role before winter.

Dora to Director (Moscow)　　Reply to Teddy (30. 9. 43)

(a)　　OKH really hopes to hold until onset of winter – only line Zhitomir–Uman–Pervomaysk–mouth of Bug.

(b)　　Since mid-September General Staff German Army has considered not only the Dniepr line from Kiev to Dniepropetrovsk as untenable, but also the entire area east of lower Bug and Vosnessensk–

Nikolayev line. General Staff considers prospects of organizing resistance Kiev–Belaya Tserkov– Cherkassy–Vosnessensk– Nikolayev in the event of purposeful and timely planning by the OKH as much greater than any effort east of this line. Dora to:

Director (Moscow)   Reply to Teddy (30. 9. 43)

(a)   .....

(b)   .....

(c)   6th and 7th Panzer Divisions to a large extent battered on arrival at Kremenchug.

(d)   For political reasons OKH speaks of major defensive success on the bank of the Dniepr, although it knows that Russian army corps, Russian divisions driving from Kiev to Dniepropetrovsk leave the OKH no doubts as to the intentions of the Russian High Command. Continue advance in direction of Dnestr with full weight!

The German soldiers in the Krivoy Rog battle zone were unaware of the traitorous radio game being played out in the ether. The Tiger crews, who in those days carried out an advance against Borodayevla with their handful of panzers, also knew nothing of it. From this area on both sides of Ivashki, on 3 October II Battalion, Panzer-Grenadiers attacked left (north) of the road, I (APC) Battalion, Panzer-Grenadiers right (south) of the road, together with the assault guns and under the artillery fire from several battalions, while waves of Stukas pounded Pavlovka. They pushed through the village and were able to occupy the western part of Borodayevka as well as the commanding Hill 147.4 north of the village. This was the greatest success in this combat zone so far, which for the Germans was of decisive importance. Fighting raged in both villages until far into the night; meanwhile the panzer-grenadiers of II Battalion tried desperately to hold out on the slopes of Hill 147.4. It was clear that the enemy had recognized the danger at this point and was committing everything in an effort to regain it. He immediately initiated counterattacks, which ran aground on the bravery and spirit of the troops defending this sector with heavy losses to the attackers.

The defenders did not come out of these battles, which were often fought at hand-grenade range, unscathed, however. German losses forced them to improvise and reorganize. The enemy tried to slip through gaps in the panzer-grenadiers' defensive line. Runners or drivers present at that point counterattacked immediately and were able to drive the enemy back. The last of the men were used to form reserves, which were held back behind the threatened defensive line in order to stabilize it to the degree possible. The individual anti-aircraft guns of the Army Flak Battalion GD were extremely helpful; their self-propelled weapons repeatedly sent hails of fire into the attacking enemy.

After this success at Borodayevka on 3 October, the Germans were forced to shift the focal point to the right wing for their coming attack, in particular in front of and at Point 172.2. The efforts of the division and its neighbours on the right, especially the 306th Infantry Division and the 9th Panzer Division which appeared farther to the right in front of Point 163.8, were aimed at pushing this right wing forward along the Dniepr. At least the infantry of the 306th Division succeeded in establishing direct contact with the right wing of the Panzer- Grenadier Division GD, so that now there could be talk of a continuous line in this area.

This day was a particularly painful one for the division's Armoured Reconnaissance Battalion. The leader of 2nd Battery, Oberleutnant Hans-Wilhelm Verch, and Gefreiter Karl Kaufmann were both killed in a sudden mortar barrage which was not a part of any operation. Leutnants Reissenhofer and Bauer and Fahnenjunker- Unteroffizier Lämmert were badly wounded.

The next days were marked by the extraordinary severity of the fighting for possession of the chain of hills north of Borodayevka and Pavlovka, which continued day and night with changing success. Events such as strong groups of enemy infantry breaking into Borodayevka and the immediate counterattack with two Tigers to recapture the decisive hill were also the order of the day, as was the sudden appearance of enemy armoured battle groups at Zapolitshki, which caused some consternation among the train units. Nevertheless the defenders, at the cost of considerable exertions and sacrifices, were able to stabilize the situation and in general maintain a firm hand on their own positions.

Losses, especially among the units fighting on the chain of hills north of Borodayevka, which were more battle groups than complete companies, were such that the command could calculate when there would be no one left in the position. The following account by Hans Bittner, a Gefreiter in 3rd Company, Armoured Assault Pioneer Battalion GD, in which he describes how he was wounded, reveals the bitterness of the fighting, especially the close- quarters struggle for the line of hills north of Pavlovka:

"Dawn arrived on my last day in action in Russia. Beautiful, clear weather! We were left of the road. Another day on the attack and once again we advanced with almost no resistance. Oberleutnant Krüger, our chief, was at the road itself, and as usual our beloved quadruple flak supported our attack.

We neared the escarpment which extended far to the left at right angles to the road. Then, suddenly, fire from in front, mainly explosive and submachine-gun bullets. One could tell by the sound they made on impact and the rate of fire. Bolshevik close-support aircraft attacked repeatedly, but without success. The escarpment in front of us was worse.

One after another the men around me were put out of action; it was terrible to hear the dull detonations of the explosive bullets. Finally we were within about 100 metres of the escarpment. Up and then dive for cover, take cover and up again, like on the training grounds! The escarpment in front of us had been fortified; the Soviet infantry positions were visible in three levels, they even included bunkers.

Our attack continued to make rapid progress on the right and left; only we were unable to advance any farther against this damned escarpment. Then the man next to me was hit; belly wound! He cried out; it was frightful and heart-rending.

I wanted to go to him, to help him. Then something struck my ankle. I fell. I pulled off my boot as I lay on the ground. A bullet had pierced the ankle bone from front to back. The man beside me raised his upper body and screamed 'medic!! medic!!' A shot rang out, right through the head.

I rolled back onto my belly, picked up my rifle and practised sharp-shooting with the rest of my bullets. One after another I took aim and shot them. A sarcasm had seized me; they would see that I was still there.

Meanwhile my comrades had advanced so far that some of the Soviets fled, the rest surrendered. I dragged myself to the dressing station. At the road sat our quadruple flak; the gunner had been wounded. Though bleeding from the head he kept firing like wild. Then a Kübel drove up. An Oberst jumped out and went over to this brave gunner. He took the Iron Cross, First Class from his breast and pinned it on the gunner's tunic."

No less decisive was the action by I Battalion, Panzer-Fusilier Regiment GD at Mommunar, in the battle zone of the 23rd Panzer Division. It was at first believed that the situation there could be cleared up quickly, however heavy fighting broke out. The enemy had moved reinforcements and heavy weapons into the gorges and valleys west of Mishurin Rog. It became obvious that considerable attempts by the enemy to break through had to be expected there as well.

The fighting in this battle zone, which was under the command of the 23rd Panzer Division, was primarily an infantry affair with no let-up day or night. It was a battle of the hand grenade and of the individual riflemen at their posts, in their machine-gun positions and rifle pits, details of which are scarcely known.

The personal action of a platoon leader often shines as the decisive act in a small combat sector. In this case it was Unteroffizier Poschusta of 2nd Company, Panzer-Fusilier Regiment GD, who earned the Knight's Cross.

Poschusta's actions were acknowledged two days later by an order of the day issued by the commander of the 23rd Panzer Division:

23rd Panzer Division   **Division Command Post, 8. 10. 43**
Commanding Officer

> I express my special recognition to Unteroffizier Poschusta, a platoon leader in 2nd Company, Panzer-Fusilier Regiment GROSS-DEUTSCHLAND, for his independent decision to drive into a recognised enemy assembly area on 6. 10. 43 and for the conduct of this operation.
>
> Willingly accepting responsibility, the company commander, Oberfeldwebel Alfred Waldow, masterfully supported this daring advance.

At about the same time the 23rd Panzer Division submitted a recommendation for the Knight's Cross for Unteroffizier Poschusta. He did not live to receive the decoration, however, as he died a hero's death in action at Neuweg on 6 November, one day before he was awarded the Knight's Cross.

In the meantime the exertions on the right wing of the Panzer-Grenadier

215

Division GD – mainly by III Battalion, Panzer-Fusilier Regiment GD and the reinforced Armoured Reconnaissance Battalion GD – continued, in an effort to establish contact to the front and toward Borodayevka. On 6 October they succeeded, together with III Battalion, 580th Infantry Regiment, 306th Infantry Division on the right, in furthering the advance, capturing the "three- nipple hill" east of Point 172.2. Clearing several of the gorges in this area proved especially difficult, because the Soviets defended them tenaciously. These same enemy troops complicated the German advance with flanking fire and inflicted not inconsiderable losses.

An attack that day by the 9th Panzer Division to recapture the decisive Hill 163.8 north of Proletarka bogged down in the face of heavy enemy resistance from the cornfields on the hills.

This attack was supposed to relieve the pressure, which for the defenders north of Borodayevka and at Point 147.4 was becoming increasingly urgent. They were barely able to hang on there. The Soviets threw increasing masses of materiel,including for the first time tanks, in an effort to gain possession of this decisive line of hills for good.

And still the few defenders hunkered down, often only 200 men every 800-1,000 metres, to resist this continuing assault. The fighting went on all day. There was also no rest at night, for under cover of darkness the Soviets tried to surprise and capture the most important points. They knew that in the dark of night the Germans' heavy weapons, the anti-tank and anti-aircraft guns, were as good as useless.

Also dangerous was the situation on both sides of Hill Line 170, roughly north of Ivashki in the sector of SS Cavalry Brigade Fegelein, which on account of its limited fighting power and poor morale repeatedly left its positions. New GD units had to be sent to support the SS cavalry, mainly alert units formed in haste from the trains and supply services. It was a special tragedy for the entire unit that hand-picked, irreplaceable specialists who could not be replaced had to fight in these units. If they surrendered to the enemy pressure from this bridgehead the entire front would again be in motion in a very short time. If this happened it would be almost impossible to stop it. A participant described the action north of Zapolitshki on 8 October 1943 involving the alert company of the Panzer-Artillery Regiment GD, which was under the command of Oberleutnant Mittelstenschneid of the regiment's Armoured Observation Battery:

"In the early morning hours of 8 October we, the alert company of the Panzer-Artillery Regiment GD, moved into position north of Zapolitshki, sealing off the Zapolitshki Gorge to the north. We dug in and waited tensely to see how the situation would develop. There was nothing whatsoever to be seen of the enemy, so that we had no idea of the strength of the Soviet forces facing us.

A prisoner taken the previous night had stated that it was a mortar company. The Soviets waited and watched. Only now and then was a shot fired.

Not until after it was completely light, did we realize what a difficult position we had put the enemy in by surprising him the night before. Eventually an anti-tank gun and four heavy mortars were moved in. Several of us eagerly set about moving the anti- tank gun and two mortars into position. Their sighting devices were missing but we planned to fire by guesswork.

Eventually, however, we were told that an attack from the west by tanks was supposed to take the enemy in front of us in the flank or drive him back across the hills north of us. We were instructed to place some of our men at the disposal of the panzers as escorting infantry.

Finally, at about 09.00, we saw the first tanks approaching from the left, followed closely by the infantry. At first there was no movement by the enemy; the tanks rolled on slowly and scattered fire over the field.

Suddenly brown figures stood up everywhere, a few at first, then more and more. They tried to escape to the north in a wild flight. That was the moment when we opened fire with rifles, anti-tank guns, artillery and mortars.

The panzers veered left to cut off the fleeing enemy. When the Soviets saw that escape was impossible they settled into position again, this time in an extended line of bushes, about 500 metres in front of our current position, and in a field of sunflowers behind it.

It was now time for us to attack. The alert company sealing off the gorge attacked frontally, while their security screen was supposed to advance east from the hills with its right wing at the western edge of Ivashki and then veer left. Meanwhile the left platoon was to swing wide to the west. Everything went smoothly for the first 200 metres, then we came under infantry fire from the bushes. We worked our way forward in stages, with both machine-guns providing covering fire. The escorting armoured personnel carrier swept the bushes with its machine-gun. This soon ended, however, for the gun jammed and the machine-gunner received a serious head wound.

We made slow but steady progress and approached the row of bushes. We reached the trench in front of the road in one final dash and then crossed the road. Only a few Soviets were fished out of the bushes; numerous dead lay all around.

In the meantime the panzers had advanced to the northern hills. While several stopped to stand guard, three of the tanks cautiously came back through the sunflower field toward us, in order to drive the Soviets toward us from behind. Once the panzers were near enough to our line at the bushes, we got up again to destroy the remaining enemy in the sunflower field. Again isolated Russians appeared from the field and came toward us with hands raised. They threw their weapons away and seemed happy to have escaped this debacle. We now saw at last the numbers the Soviets had dug in here. A multitude of holes showed us a strength we had not expected.

Rifle shots were still being fired from the sunflower field and the bushes at the road while the prisoners were being assembled and the captured weapons collected. We set out once again to comb the entire field and fished out more Russians. We were able to collect at least 150 prisoners, while we definitely left behind just as many dead.

And so this day ended for the artillery, who had now passed their baptism of fire as infantry."

The group comprising the remnants of III (Tiger) Battalion, Panzer

Regiment GD, under the command of Oberleutnant Bayer, commander of 11th Company, suffered a severe loss on the 8th or 9th of October. A joint advance against the well-known "seven- nipple hill," east of Point 172.2, was planned for one of these days. The operation was to be undertaken by several Tigers together with the 2nd (APC) Company, Armoured Reconnaissance Battalion GD and the following infantry. Employing all means available, this attack was supposed to finally place this decisive group of hills in German hands. The attack began in the late morning. While the panzers with their wide tracks made comparatively rapid progress in the difficult terrain and were able to pass through the tall sunflower and wheat fields with relative ease, the small number of one-ton armoured personnel carriers were left behind at the edge of these fields with twisted tracks. As well the men in the open APCs had to defend themselves against the numerous Soviets who, hidden in their foxholes, tried to toss grenades into the vehicles. The advance was thus slowed to a crawl. Contact was lost with the fast-moving panzers. Apparently the enemy had also realized that the tanks had lost their infantry cover and permitted them to drive through unmolested. They then sealed off the area behind the panzers with anti-tank guns and hand-held weapons and encircled them. Neither were the tanks, which were now under fire from all sides by anti- tank guns, able to break through to the rear; nor could the armoured personnel carriers pierce the Soviet blocking ring and establish contact with them.

Stukas and reconnaissance aircraft later determined that all the surrounded tanks had been knocked out and their crews killed or captured. By evening the radio listening service had learned the names of the survivors who had been taken prisoner. They included Oberleutnant Arnold (10th Company), leader of the panzer operation, Leutnant Folke (9th Company), Oberfeldwebel Friedebach (H.Q. Company), Obergefreiter Jensen (H.Q. Company), Obergefreiter Fritz (H.Q. Company) and Unteroffizier Müller (H.Q. Company). Leutnant Folke returned in 1953 after ten years as a prisoner, nothing more was ever heard of the others.

With this loss the number of operational tanks had fallen to zero. The effects of this were to make themselves felt in the decisive fight for Borodayevka in the following days.

On 9 October the Armoured Reconnaissance Battalion GD was placed under the command of the Panzer-Grenadier Regiment GD and deployed due west of Hill 118.0 to reinforce the forces on both sides of Hill 147.4. Rittmeister Spaeter, then leader of the Armoured Reconnaissance Battalion, was slightly wounded that day while Unteroffizier Thurn of the battalion staff was killed by a direct hit on the command post. Unteroffizier von Kreyfeld of the signals platoon was badly wounded. Oberleutnant Gebhard and a squadron of about 25 men occupied the left wing, Leutnant Beckmann the right. Their positions were partly on the hill, partly on the back slope. The enemy attacks, which were made in varying strengths, increased, indeed they became almost continuous. It was almost impossible to reach these forward squadrons by day; anti-tank guns and mortars fired at anything that moved. The battalion command post was at an isolated house whose roof and outer walls were completely riddled. Foxholes in the shadow of the wrecked house still offered the safest refuge. Losses were more than a cause for concern. The battalion's daily report provides a dry and factual account of the events of 10 October 1943 in the positions held by the Armoured Reconnaissance Battalion GD on both sides of Point 118.0:

"At 04.00, just as we were about to transfer our battalion command post because it was the target of continuing anti-tank fire, the T-34s again opened fire. They were knocked out by three assault guns in a matter of minutes, after which some degree of quiet returned. By 07.00 the command post was in the gorge at the southern tip of Pavlovka; Rittmeister Heise took over command of the battalion. A short time later eight Panthers in the middle of our sector drove as far as the hill on which sat the knocked-out T-34s. Oberleutnant Gebhard was also supposed to advance with his left wing. However this was impossible as the Panthers drew very heavy mortar fire from the enemy. The squadron was finally able to move up after the Panthers withdrew and the mortar fire abated somewhat. A forward artillery observer also appeared to lend support.

At about 16.00 Stabsfeldwebel Hahn, commander of the 5th (Heavy) Squadron's pioneer platoon, arrived with 20 men and was deployed between Points 147.4 and 118.0. The pioneers suffered heavy losses while moving into position; eight men reported to the command post with wounds in a very short time. At about 18.00 a T-34 with mounted infantry drove through on the left wing of Oberleutnant Gebhard's squadron. The tank commander casually climbed out to take his bearings. He was shot immediately by a sniper, after which the T-34 sped back toward the rear.

Three enemy tanks sitting near Point 147.4 likewise returned the way they had come. As darkness was falling a pair of eight- wheeled armoured cars established contact with Point 147.4. During the night Oberleutnant Müller and 4./Kr.6 relieved the panzer-grenadiers there. Battle Group Abel, whose positions extended to about 1,000 metres north of the northeast part of Borodayevka, established contact on the right wing of Oberleutnant Müller's battle group. Available heavy weapons were two 88mm anti-tank guns (motorized) beneath Point 118.0 and two self-propelled 75mm anti-tank guns from an attached unit in the western part of Borodayevka."

The fighting in this area continued without letup in the following days. Nevertheless, one could say that there were no significant changes in the main line of resistance on the line of hills north of Borodayevka–Pavlovka, although this was at the cost of much sacrifice and death. The handful of defenders repeatedly rose from their holes and launched the counterattacks necessary to maintain contact to both sides. It was like the final rebellion against the unavoidable. The hope of escaping this inferno was limited.

The thoughts on the minds of the panzer-fusiliers of I Battalion in the positions near Kommunar, where the pressure exerted by the far-superior attackers increased steadily, must have been similar. Gradually one piece of ground or another had to be surrendered and the panzer-fusiliers repeatedly fell back to the nearest hedge, the next fold in the terrain, taking cover in holes and bushes. Always it was the last way out when the enemy was already at the doorstep of their positions.

The expected major Soviet attack from the bridgehead on both sides of Mishurin Rog followed on 15 October. With its weight the assault broke through the thin German lines in the first rush. Extremely heavy fighting involving I Battalion, Panzer-Fusilier Regiment GD and I Battalion, Panzer-Artillery Regiment GD broke out near Kommunar when the main thrust of the Soviet infantry attacking from Kommunar and Kutsevolovka became apparent.

This initial enemy assault was halted in front of the positions of the panzer-fusiliers by the fire of I Battalion, Panzer-Artillery Regiment GD and an attached SS artillery regiment, due in large part to Hauptmann Theermann, the commander of I./Pz.A.R. GD. The weak German battle group was deployed in the complex, ravine-rich terrain in strongpoint positions. Hauptmann Theermann remained at the front in his armoured troop carrier, always at the latest focal point, where he employed radio to make the most effective use of his forward observers and observation posts. Theermann personally directed the battalion's fire, so successfully that the attacking Soviets, who began their advance at dawn on 15 October following an intensive preparatory bombardment, were halted. The Soviets suffered heavy losses and at noon the main line of resistance was still firmly in our hands.

At about 13.00 that afternoon the enemy overran the positions of I Battalion, Panzer-Fusilier Regiment with about sixty tanks followed by infantry. Once again it was Hauptmann Theermann who saved the day. Through his fearless actions the breaches in the line were sealed off by artillery fire, the enemy infantry which had broken through were pinned down or destroyed and finally the conditions necessary for the recapture of the abandoned main line of resistance were created. In the two days that followed the constant enemy pressure forced a withdrawal of the main line of resistance. Theermann's superior command enabled the artillery to inflict heavy losses on the sharply-pursuing enemy and pin down his spearheads, effectively supporting the withdrawal. Not a single gun was lost in the course of these movements.

Finally, on 17 October, with Theermann's help a continuous German main line of resistance was established along a general line from Troitko to Petrovka (from a letter of appreciation from the 23rd Panzer Division). Hauptmann Theermann was subsequently awarded the German Cross in Gold for his actions. The enemy attacks which were begun north of Mishurin Rog also had a corresponding effect in the southern part of this now contiguous enemy bridgehead, namely east of Likovka.

Early on the morning of 15 October observation posts on Hill 147.4–118.0 – Contour Line 170 observed a considerable massing of enemy tanks, which led to the conclusion that an attack was imminent. The Soviet Air Force was extremely active early that morning, more so than usual, which also suggested that an enemy operation was about to begin. This finally started at about 11.30, near Contour Line 170 and Hill 118.0, where the Soviets attacked with tank support and intense fire from heavy weapons. An immediate counterattack with the few panzers available gained ground, but it could not stop

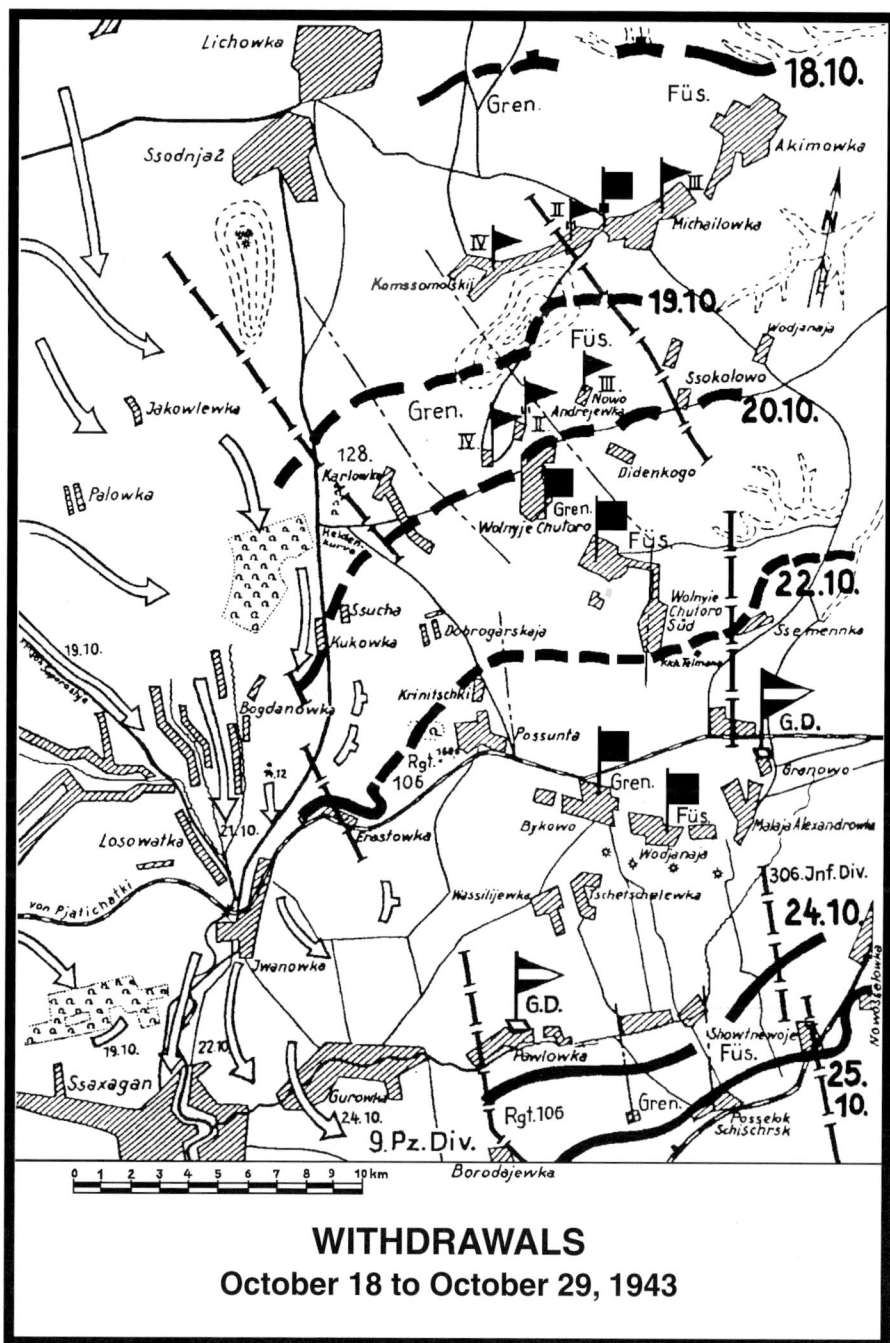

WITHDRAWALS
October 18 to October 29, 1943

Lichowka

Gren.

Füs.

18.10.

Ssodnja2

Akimowka

III

II

IV

Michailowka

Komssomolskij

19.10.

Wodjanaja

Füs.

Ssokolowo

20.10.

III

Nowo

Andrejewka

Jakowlewka

Gren.

128.

IV

II

Palowka

Karlowka

Didenkogo

Heiden-

kurve

Gren.

Wolnyje Chutoro

Füs.

Ssucha

Wolnyie

Chutoro

Süd

22.10.

Kukowka

Dobrogarskaja

kch.Telman

Ssemennka

19.10.

Bogdanowka

Krinitschki

G.D.

Possunta

Rgt.

106

Gren.

Granowo

Losowatka

Erastowka

Bykowo

Füs.

Malaja Alexandrowka

21.10.

von Pjatichatki

Wassilijewka

Tschetschelewka

Wodjanaja

306.Jnf.Div.

Jwanowka

24.10.

19.10.

22.10.

G.D.

Showtnewoje

Füs.

25.

10.

Ssaxagan

Gurowka

Pawlowka

24.10.

Rgt.106

Gren.

Possekok

Schischrsk

9.Pz.Div.

Borodajewka

0 1 2 3 4 5 6 7 8 9 10km

Ssakssagan
Gurowka
Posselok Schischorsk
Borodajewka
N
Ssawka
Tschumakowka
24.11.
Shelannyi
Schirokij Lan
Petrowskij
Shitlowo
zu Skilewataja
Kowalewka
Olgofeld
Kudaschewka
1.11.
29.10.
30.10.
Skilewataja
Nadija

9.Pz.Div.
Jekaterinowka
Pokrowka
Nikolajewka
Jagodnyj
Nikolajewka
2.11.
Miloradowka
181,0
Ssofijewka
4.11.
Krassnyj Orlik
Chalobudinskaja Grab
Nowo-Kijewka
G.D.
Jeristowka
30.10.
Utschastok Nr.-7
Businowataja Grab
Wessebja Dolina
170,9
Wes. Do.
4.11.
G.D.
Matutoi
306.Jnf.Div.
4.11.
Malaja Ssofijewka
4.11.
Perwomaiskoje
Leninka
Krassnoje Pole
Wassiljewka
161
Neu-Weg
16.11.
16.11.
Guljai Pole
9. Pz. Div.
G.D.
142,0
Ljubimowka
Dolgoje
Orlowo Grab
Gren. Füs.
22.11.
25.11.
26.11.
Schewtschenkowo
Alexandro-Belowo
C
18.11.
Sofijewka
D
22.11.
Schirokaja Grab
Menshinka
Jekaterinowka
Alexandrowka
Wehkaja Grab
E 28.11.
Tschernigowka
Tarassowka
E
16.Pz.Gren.Div.
G.D. Petrowa-Dolina
Siedlung
Lyssa-Gorka
Nasarowka
E₁
7.12.-2.1.
Perwomaiskij
Wyssokij
Michailowka
Ofrub
0 1 2 3 4 5 6 7 8 9 10 11 12 13 14 15km
Nowo Nikolajewka

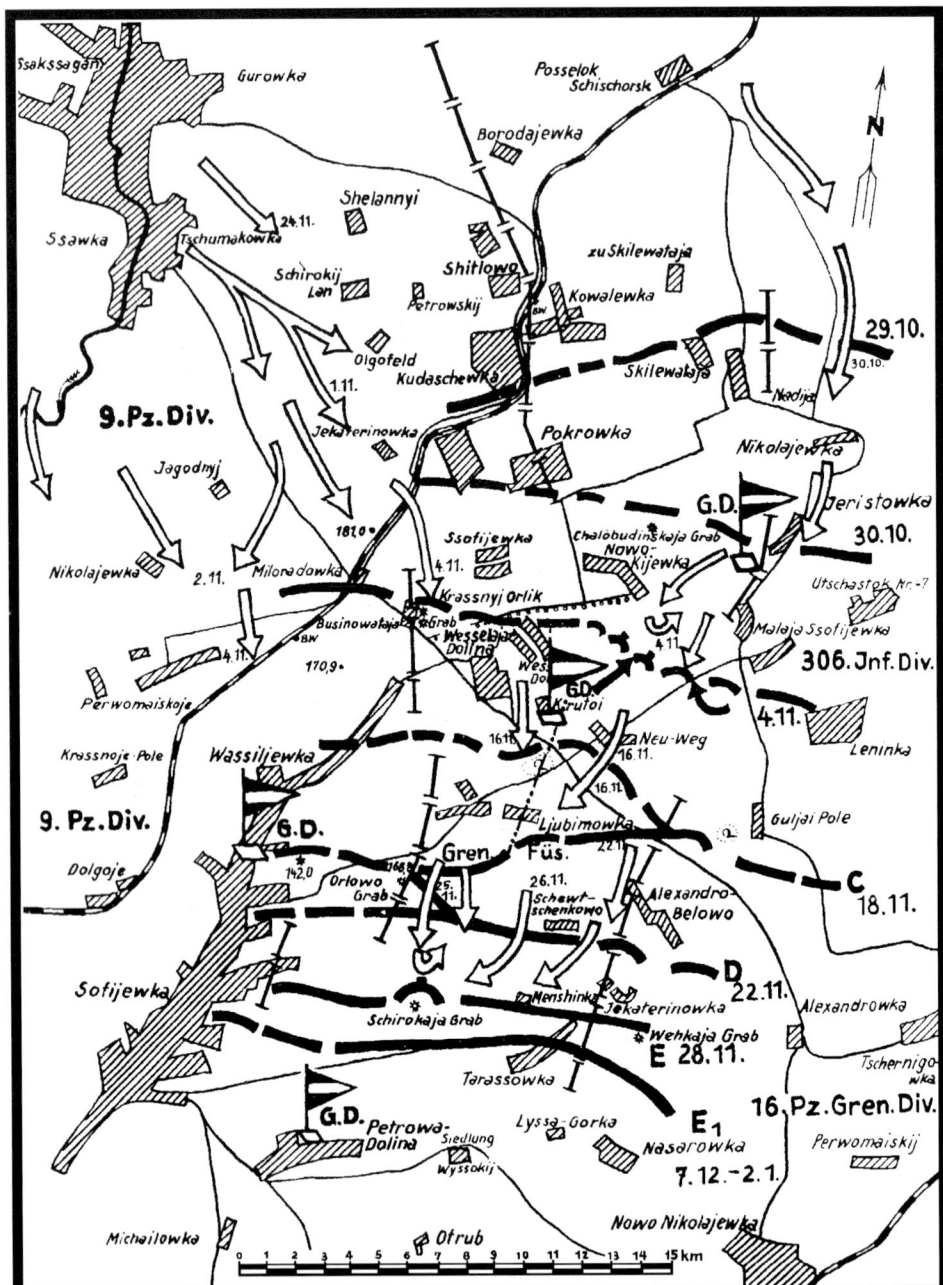

WITHDRAWALS
October 29 to November 26, 1943

the masses of attacking infantry. The enemy's losses were frightful, but he kept throwing ever more forces into the battle.

The battered and shrunken German battle groups (at noon that day the 2nd (APC) Squadron, Armoured Reconnaissance Battalion GD under Leutnant Beckmann was down to 1 officer, 2 NCOs and 6 enlisted men) joined ranks in the face of this superiority and sought to retain individual important points. In general the German positions moved to the back slope of the line of hills, where the defenders held out until evening with the support of the few tanks, assault guns, anti-aircraft guns and anti-tank guns.

However these positions were untenable in the long run, in the main because of the view possessed by the enemy up above. The division command therefore decided at about 18.00 on the evening of the 15th of October to withdraw the last battle groups to a shorter line, primarily to achieve an increase in fighting strengths. The line was fixed from Point 172.2—western edge of Pavlovka–tank hill–Contour Line 170 and farther to the west along the line of hills. These withdrawal movements were to be carried out during the night.

This order, which involved the abandoning of the decisive position near Hill 147.4 and the village of Borodayevka, ended the nearly fourteen-day-long attempt to eliminate the enemy bridgehead. This is scarcely surprising, since the Panzer-Grenadier Division GD had borne almost the entire burden of carrying it out. Completely worn out and without significant help from neighbouring units, it had tried to hold as long as there was a chance. Now it was over; the pocket, full of Soviets in the crowded bridgehead on both sides of Mishurin Rog, had burst apart. From it Soviet troops streamed into the open hinterland without meeting significant resistance.

On 17 October enemy spearheads were already nearing Tarantsov, where elements of 13th Company, Panzer-Grenadier Regiment GD tried to hold. Somewhere on one of the roads a lone panzer of 11th Company, III (Tiger) Battalion, Panzer Regiment GD, with a crew consisting of Unteroffizier Rampel, driver Unteroffizier Bahr, gunner Schreier, Krupka and Gussone, faced a large number of marauding enemy tanks and fought a bitter battle to save its own skin. Several enemy tanks, KV Is and T-34s, fell victim to the Tiger, the rest stopped in the face of such courageous stubbornness.

Repeatedly it was some sort of battle group from the two regiments and battalions which resisted at a ridge, a ravine or in a village to delay the advance by the enemy. Each of them knew that it was purposeless, that the superiority of the attackers was too great for them to stop it; but at least they could inflict losses on the Soviets, offer fresh resistance again and again to break the strength of their attack, reduce their fighting strength and destroy their hated tanks. Perhaps in this way they would be able to stop them somewhere.

On 17 October it again rained heavily, as it had in the previous two days. The ground was soaked, the unpaved roads had become bottomless and the vehicles pushed their way through the Ukrainian ground more than they drove. New defensive lines were occupied; the division's sector extended from right of the Sokolovo gorge left over the hills south of Point 172.2 to the hills north of Tarantsov, where contact existed with the 9th Panzer Division. In many places the Soviets attacked with waves of 20 and more tanks and endless masses of infantry, broke through the thin German system of positions, only to be halted again. The enemy tanks could not be prevented from driving through into the rear, for anti-tank weapons were no longer available in sufficient numbers, but time and again the defenders were able to separate the infantry from the tanks accompanying them. Not unexpectedly the marauding Soviet tanks caused great confusion among the train units, supply columns and even medical clearing stations in the division's rear area. Scenes of headlong flight, individual guns striving to get to the front and abandoned vehicles were signs of increasing confusion. Again and again, however, lone battle groups and trains stood up to the tanks, then tried to engage and destroy them.

This unrest in the hinterland was further heightened by the sudden appearance of enemy tanks and infantry columns in Popelnastoye and Pyatichatki, considerably farther south and deep in the rear of the units fighting near Likovka. Near Pyatichatki trains evacuating the wounded were shot up and set afire by enemy tanks. Some of the wounded were able to save themselves at the last minute and escape south on foot. The scene which greeted the counterattacking force at the station was a terrible one.

It was 18 October when this event was reported. Enemy forces had thus also crossed the Dniepr in the south, roughly in the area north of Verkhneprovsk and Kosinka, and were trying to reach the rear of the German units south of Kremenchug. There was a growing danger of encirclement. Would the defenders be forced to abandon their positions near Likovka in haste and without fighting? The situation was ominous, especially for the units of the First Panzer Army fighting in this area and farther north.

The commanding corps' order to offer the enemy stubborn resistance and to conduct a fighting withdrawal still stood. To stand and fight on in view of the increasing amount of fighting behind one's own front was simply a question of nerve. It became obvious to the division command that active reconnaissance in its rear was an absolute necessity, in order to keep tabs on enemy movements, move the trains and supply installations as close to its own positions as possible and in general protect its own.

For this reason the Armoured Reconnaissance Battalion GD was kept out of the general infantry battle and employed primarily to scout both wings and the hinterland. The orders given the patrols were standard reconnaissance duties: Where is the enemy? Where are our forces? Especially where is left neighbour? The shortages of weapons, the low combat strengths of the infantry units and the weeks of excessive demands had considerably reduced their worth as fighting units. Another factor was their limited mobility on account of their being equipped with horse-drawn columns.

Often enough the GD had to abandon positions because the enemy had broken through on the right or left with the resulting threat of being outflanked.

It became obvious on the evening of 18 October that new positions were necessary: Beskrovnoye–hills north of Kushtshino–crossroads about 1 km.

east of Point 164.5, also the division's left boundary with the 9th Panzer Division. Elements of this unit's 9th Armoured Reconnaissance Battalion were identified near Klin.

The armoured patrols of the Armoured Reconnaissance Battalion GD were out again on 19 October with orders to patrol along the left flank of the division and to the south. The Zwieg patrol was sent through Bykovo, Gurovka and Saxagan toward Pyatichatki and the Rösch patrol south on the highway past "heroes' curve," west of Karlovka. Their reports, the first of which was received by the radio station at 10.45, gave the following picture of the enemy: the enemy had occupied the road and wood about 5 km. northwest of Saxagan and was digging in there. The enemy had also entered Kukovka and was firing with anti-tank guns and anti-tank rifles on vehicles fleeing south. The GD's munitions dump with about 220 tons of munitions located in this area fell into enemy hands intact.

After these reports were received by the division the Armoured Reconnaissance Battalion GD was ordered to immediately advance into the Suka area to guard the division's deep flank between Kukovka and the 9th Panzer Division. Futher radio reports from the patrols revealed that on the one hand strong enemy columns were advancing through Yakovlevka–Pavlovka toward Dobrogarskaya and on the other through Zaporozhye–Sukanovka toward Losovatka. Furthermore, enemy tanks with accompanying infantry were also observed advancing from Rublevka through Vasilyevka toward Pyatichatki. As well enemy tanks had advanced through Sheltiye, which was occupied at 07.20, to the south and by noontime were firing on the Petrovo–Anovka road.

This information led to the conclusion that the enemy had broken through the 9th Panzer Division on the left and was trying to reach the deep flank of the Panzer-Grenadier Division GD. This fact forced the division command to the decision to dismantle its positions more quickly than anticipated and transfer them farther south while simultaneously reinforcing the left wing.

The division command post was moved to Granovo on the railroad west of Verchovtsevo–Saxagan. At the same time the units were pulled back to a general line: Sokolovo (fusiliers)–north of Didenkogo (fusiliers)–Volnye Chutora (grenadiers)–Krinitshki (grenadiers). On the division's left, where the front bent back toward the west, were the 106th and 128th Infantry Regiments.

On 20 October the situation in the Saxagan area began to stabilise when a counterattack by elements of the SS Cavalry Brigade Fegelein together with elements of the 114th Rifle Regiment advanced to the northwest edge of the city. There they were able to establish and hold a defense line. As well elements of the 16th Panzer-Grenadier Division were on their way from the south, their mission to retake the city of Pyatichatki the next day. However, the division's march was delayed considerably by enemy air attacks. In the meantime enemy attacks on the division's sector, carried out mainly by infantry, continued with undiminished intensity.

On 21 October patrols revealed the following about enemy movements, forcing the defenders to take further measures: enemy advancing with approximately eight tanks and infantry in trucks along the Bogdanovka—Losovatka road to the south, and according to latest reports leading elements are already near Drushe Nadeshdovka, due north of Erastovka. Massed enemy infantry likewise striving south past Point 141.2 (southeast of Losovatka- North) south of the road to Ivanovka. The focal point apparently lies in this direction. The enemy is endeavouring, in an overtaking pursuit, to outflank the left wing of the units farther to the east and attack these from behind.

In the area due east of the Bogdanovka–Ivanovka–Saxagan road the enemy initially guarded to the east with weak forces in order to screen his movements to the south. Nevertheless he advanced with tanks against Hill 160.6, due west of Posunta, which was seen as more than a reconnaissance in force. Assault guns of the Assault Gun Battalion GD knocked out the tanks, after which the enemy withdrew to the valleys west of Point 160.6.

On the basis of these movements the division once again ordered its positions moved, to be occupied as follows (evening of 21 October): western edge of Semerinka (fusiliers, also right division boundary)–Telmana collective farm (fusiliers)–Volnye Chutora-South (grenadiers)–north part of Krinitshki (grenadiers)–signal box near Point 160.6 (Arm.Recon.Btl. GD and assault guns).

The enemy bridgehead extended like a threatening finger far to the south, almost parallel to the Dniepr. The enemy spearhead pointed toward Krivoy Rog, which was burning in many places after frequent air attacks. Black clouds of smoke lay over the city, the central point of the industrial district, but it was still the scene of hectic activity, especially since the most important army dumps, supply bases, railroad terminuses and command centres were located there.

With signs of a further crossing of the Dniepr near Dniepropetrovsk a new Soviet point of main effort appeared to be in the making. Its objective was to be Krivoy Rog, where the two Soviet battle groups would meet and encircle the German units caught between them. The expected bad news came on 24 October when the Soviets succeeded in crossing the Dniepr on both sides of Dniepropetrovsk. At first, however, the initial enemy movements had no effect on the division. Instead the scheduled withdrawal movements continued in an orderly fashion. Even reports from the trains that enemy tanks had been sighted in the Kasanka area west of Krivoy Rog gave no cause for the introduction of further measures.

The 25th of October, the day the Soviets crossed the Dniepr on both sides of Dniepropetrovsk, saw the Panzer-Grenadier Division GD in positions which ran roughly as follows: Novoselovka (to the 306th Inf.Div.) –Shovtnevoye-South (fusiliers)–northern edge of Poselok Shorsk (grenadiers)–Borodayevka (Pz.Gren.Div. left boundary with 9th Pz.Div.). The division held these positions for several days, until 28 October; all enemy attacks, whose focal point lay near Poselok Shorsk, were repulsed. Not until the night of 29 October did considerable enemy penetrations against the division's right neighbour, the 306th Infantry Division, force it to withdraw its positions to a line from Potoki (division's right boundary with the 306th Inf.Div.) to the left to the northern edge of Skilevataya—southern edge of Kudashevka, where there was contact with the 9th Panzer Division.

The enemy had undoubtedly recognized the weakness of the unit on the GD's right, the 306th Infantry Division, and it now focused on the boundary between the two divisions, but especially on the left wing of the German infantry division. Supported by tanks, Soviet forces pressed along the Nikolayevka–Yeristovka road, advancing to a point just short of Yeristovka. Weak security forces from the 306th Division were observed at the southern end of the village on 30 October. When counterattacks by the division failed to achieve the desired success, the Panzer-Grenadier Division GD was pulled back to a line southwestern edge of Yeristovka–Chalabudinskaya–southern end of Pokrovka. The regiments made the move on 30 October with no pressure from the enemy, allowing them to occupy the new positions in peace.

At the same time, roughly on 31 October, armoured elements of the 16th Panzer-Grenadier Division were deployed to reinforce the 306th Infantry Division. Their primary mission was to secure Road 4 (DG.IV) from Nikolayevka south through Yeristovka and seal the area off against penetration by the enemy. This resulted in a pause in the fighting on the division's right wing, which for a time brought total quiet to the positions.

1 November also began as a quiet day, until at about 10.30, when the Ia passed a report to the Armoured Reconnaissance Battalion GD on the division's right wing that the enemy was attacking the 9th Panzer Division with a force of 50 tanks and infantry from Yekaterinovka southeast in the direction of Point 181.0. The battalion was instructed to begin reconnaissance immediately and initiate appropriate countermeasures. At about 12.05 the first enemy tank was observed at Point 181.0, which placed it left and behind the left wing of the panzer-grenadiers. Ten minutes later two enemy tanks with mounted infantry entered Miloradovka unhindered. The infantry of the 9th Panzer Division was on the retreat. The Assault Gun Battalion GD, which was under the command of the 9th Panzer Division in this sector, approached under the command of Major Frantz. In a short time it destroyed 21 enemy tanks in the valley near Krasny Orlik. This success temporarily dampened the enemy's enthusiasm for renewing the advance.

A counterattack by tanks of the 9th Panzer Division to recapture the old main line of resistance failed, however, and the entire main line of resistance had to be withdrawn to a new line. On 1-2 November this line ran as follows: Musitcha Trench, about 2 km. north of Malaya Sofiyevka (right boundary 306th Inf.Div.)–southern part of Novo Kievka–tree-lined road–Businov Vataya (left boundary 9th Pz.Div.). Once again the Armoured Reconnaissance Battalion GD was moved to the left side of the division as its watchful eye and ordered to observe the movements by the division's neighbour on the left, the 9th Panzer Division.

The strengths of the division's units: the Armoured Assault Pioneer Battalion GD consisted of two battle groups, one for use in the infantry role under Major Chrapkowski, the other for the pioneer role under Oberleutnant Krüger. I (APC) Battalion, Panzer-Grenadier Regiment GD had two companies, one commanded by Leutnant Ruder, the other by Oberleutnant Willert. The Panzer Regiment GD had so few tanks that there was only one panzer battle group in action at the front at any time. Most of the crews formed alert companies which were used in an infantry role. The soldiers bore the brunt of the battle. The defensive battle was fought by small groups of men, a handful of machine-guns, a few heavy machine-guns, and several flak crews. Whenever replacements did arrive, they were incorporated into these close-knit combat teams. The names of these men appear in no report, they are known only to each other and the memories of former company commanders. They lived for weeks in a hole in the ground that had become their second home, even though during the retreat the same hole had to be dug all over again in another place. They sat behind the wheel of a car, an armoured car or a truck. They steered the self-propelled guns through the terrain and in action, they drove into the waves of enemy tanks in panzers and assault guns or saw constant action behind guns, radios or at the operations table.

Their world was the sector in front of their foxhole, as far as their rifles would reach. Their lives were hard; their existence forced them to fight. In the trench they shared with a few comrades. There was room only for the essentials: a rifle, a machine-gun that worked well, sufficient ammunition, a piece of bread and a drink from the canteen to keep up their strength, a handful of tobacco for their pipes, now and then an hour's sleep to keep their nerve from failing.

They lay in the trenches and waited. Around them it was dark. Fifty metres to the right were two more guys and the same to the left; they knew that without seeing them. As per orders, they waited to defend the sector against any attack. They had to rely on everyone around them; whoever abandoned his hole placed his neighbours in deadly danger. Each man had to stay put no matter what, that was the iron rule of the front. The certainty of knowing that one's comrades were beside one, men who lived and fought in the same spirit of unspoken comradeship, was like a steel wall at their backs. Here no one was on his own, even when he squatted alone in his hole in the ground.

To have to lie and wait all day and night is a difficult art. The older, more experienced men maintained that assaulting, attacking, taking part in a daring advance was easier. There was more to victory here than the assault and the attack, however. This was the first thing the new ones had to learn. For one of them might lose his nerve on hearing a loud, bestial shriek of "hurray" from out of the stillness of the night, might want to jump out of his hole into the open. The older one would call a few calming words:

"Take it easy youngster, take it easy; they're just shouting!"

The old ones were those who had fought this battle for years, who knew all the enemy's tricks, who had tested their own tricks and knew how to employ them. They were the ones who had the nerve not to be afraid, who could wait until the right moment came. Their calm ruled their movements; they waited to fire, for they knew how precious ammunition was; they didn't raise their rifle or machine-gun until they were sure that their bullets would be on target. They tossed their hand grenades only when they would explode with deadly certainty in the onrushing enemy infantry, not a second sooner. When the Stalin Organs fired – and they could pick out that sound in the midst of battle with alert, practised ears – then they counted the seconds until the right time came to duck down into the foxhole. They had a certain feeling for what to do and what to leave.

They became accustomed to artillery shells and rockets like the sores on their feet. One was just as uncomfortable as the other; but since nothing could be done about either they accepted it and didn't waste any words on it.

But then the tanks came and with them the masses of enemy infantry. It was always the same and yet each time was different. Each time meant winning the inner battle, the conflict no one saw because it was fought out in lonely hearts. In the final decision each man had to come to terms with himself. Numerous objections, reservations and compromises emerged and swelled, threatened to burst the chest, provoked thoughts of a premature surrender, a quiet disappearance, the path of least resistance. But in the end stubbornness won out, the inexplicable drive to hold on, to stay put. When this point was reached the inner battle was won.

So they stayed in their tiny, often shallow holes and let the enemy tanks roll past, sometimes four and five times. But then they stood up, raised their machine-guns from cover, covered in mud and dust, and fired with a calmness and assuredness that always halted the enemy.

At some point, perhaps after weeks when the situation appeared to permit, the chief sent one man or another back to the train. They washed the filth from their bodies, slept dreamlessly for a day and a night, and for a few contemplative hours enjoyed being alive. Perhaps they wrote a letter home, listened to music on the radio, ate the best from the field kitchen. Then something called them back to the front to their comrades in the foxholes. Somehow it drew them back to where their world was. But never did they waste a word complaining that fate seemed to be dealing unfairly with them for having placed the heaviest burden on them.

Who but they knew of the manly joy that filled someone who had beaten off an attack and held his position or participated in a successful counterattack. Nothing in the world can equal such moments. They lived and fought in the highs and the lows of that war. There was the battle group commander, surrounded somewhere in the Krivoy Rog area, who radioed to division: "Don't worry, we'll fight our way out!" Their acts and deeds had nothing to do with time or place, neither with rank or age. Our thoughts turn again to those who stood out from the masses, made prominent by their actions, men found in any such fighting team: the Leutnant and his grenadiers who, already wounded, drove marauding enemy soldiers from their newly-won foxholes and emerged victorious. There is the First-aid Gefreiter who, although he knew that his company was surrounded on three sides, went forward six times to recover all the wounded; the Unteroffizier who, when his mortar position was overrun by enemy tanks and infantry, fearlessly walked over to the Soviet trenches and, in Russian, demanded his mortar back, and got it! There was the nineteen-year-old driver who was captured with his truck by the Soviets, but who managed to escape with the truck; or the Feldwebel whose Tiger was in the workshop for repairs when the enemy broke through. He engaged the enemy force of about 40 tanks without hesitation in his barely serviceable tank, coolly knocked out 17 Soviet tanks and escaped with his life.

The battle that began on the Pz.Gren.Div. GD's left wing at noon on 4 November was fought in this way. The by now almost expected attack by enemy tanks from the Krasniy Orlik gorge and the ruined houses of Businovataya struck the seam between the division and the 9th Panzer Division and very soon reached Point 170.9. Enemy infantry streamed south on a broad front without meeting any significant opposition. The infantry of the 9th Panzer Division had fallen back far to the rear and the only German forces still in that area were a number of detachments from the Armoured Reconnaissance Battalion GD. The danger that the enemy might break into the rear of the division's left wing, which was still holding out in its positions, led the division to order the left wing to fold itself back and make contact with the 9th Panzer Division at B.W. on the rail line. Armoured patrols from the Armoured Reconnaissance Battalion GD succeeded in carrying this out, once again placing a barrier in front of the enemy.

This day's fighting also brought an especially critical situation for Major Frantz, commander of the Assault Gun Battalion GD. Here is his report:

"Since in the previous battles the weakest part of our defence was always at the boundary with our neighbour on the left, the 9th Panzer Division, the assault gun battalion was given the job of guarding the left flank of the division, especially the artillery positions placed there for tactical reasons, against enemy surprise attacks from the 9th Panzer Division's sector. The boundary of the division lay on a rail line, which ran through the security sector on a high raised embankment. It suited us well for pure defence against tank and infantry attacks, because every tank coming over the rail line could be immediately engaged by the guns. However since our mission also included guarding the deep flank, it unsettled me that I had no view over the railroad embankment into the 9th Panzer Division's sector, where the sound of heavy fighting could be heard.

With my assault gun and its crew of Obergefreiter Scheffler and Gefreiter Witthöft, and with my escort, I believe it was once again Wachtmeister Brauner of 1st Battery, who was usually happy to fill this role, I therefore drove back along the rail line. The map indicated a railroad crossing several hundred metres in that direction. We found the crossing and drove across the rail line to investigate the situation in the 9th Panzer Division's sector. Our first look at the area, which was traversed by trenches and dotted with small trees, was enough to convince me that the enemy had apparently broken into the main line of resistance. I saw friendly anti-tank guns and artillery driving at full speed toward the rear and fleeing infantry, here and there a squad regrouping. I managed to stop a Feldwebel who in a brief report told me that the Russians had overrun our lines with numerous tanks and broken into the village behind a hill which lay in front of us. However since I could see no indication of direct enemy action on the hill, I decided to drive up to the hill with my escorting gun and see what was happening. I instructed my escort to follow 50 metres behind me and to the right to provide covering fire. In this way we reached the hill in a tall cornfield. Just as I was about to get my first look over the hill, I realized that there were fast-moving T-34s (in this situation it was impossible to say how many) coming through the corn at full speed only ten metres away. What was there to do? To take up the battle frontally made no sense, for the speed of the T-34s was too high and they were almost abreast my position. Signal to my escort: turn around and tag along with the Russian tanks as if nothing was happening. We drove down the hill with the very fast T-34s in sixth gear. Looking around from my hatch I saw the face of the Russian commander of a T-34 driving only 20 metres behind me. We looked into each others eyes and I now expected to see him close the turret hatch and train his gun on us. Nothing of the sort happened. (The assault gun had no turret and could not fire to the rear!) We rolled onward and I succeeded in reaching a valley to our right, which I had earlier chosen as my objective. It fell away somewhat more steeply and in this way offered a degree of cover to the left, in the direction of the attack. On reaching the valley I turned around and opened fire on the T-34s, which were abeam and somewhat ahead of me. My escorting gun now likewise opened fire from the same direction and position. In a very short space of time we succeeded in halting seven T-34s in flames. The completely disconcerted Russians milled about in all directions, because they didn't know where the fire was coming from. They ignored the area where we were, for they considered it their own territory. So we were able to knock out tank after tank. Only a few saved themselves behind the hill from which we had come. Among our still-fleeing infantry and the heavy weapons there was unbelievable jubilation. The will to resist was immediately reawakened after they saw that even these overpowering tanks could be stopped.

That we escaped from this situation remained an unexplained miracle to me and the two gun crews. That as well we were able to achieve a decisive defensive success filled us with pride. An appropriate radio report to the division with a precise situation report on the course of the main line of resistance in the neighbouring sector was met with the response: "Bravo, pick up a bottle of cognac this evening! Division commander'."

Scarcely had this gap been closed to a certain degree, when there was a dangerous penetration against the positions on the division's right wing. This incursion by the enemy could not be eliminated, at least not right away. The Panzer-Grenadier Regiment GD's request for permission to withdraw the right wing toward a planned line southwest of Neuweg, was turned down by the commanding corps with the argument that the area in question was absolutely vital as the starting point for a counterattack planned by the 14th Panzer Division the next day. Then the Armoured Reconnaissance Battalion GD was assigned to the panzer- grenadiers to eliminate the enemy incursion. The fighting in the area northeast of Krutoy raged far into the night, especially around the corner posts of the defense, which were still holding and which limited the extent of the enemy penetration. Bolshevik flamethrower tanks were at work there, escorted by T-34s and KV Is; by evening nineteen had been destroyed in heavy close-quarters fighting. II Battalion, Panzer-Grenadier Regiment GD was especially hard hit by this forcefully executed assault and losses were again heavy.

The 7th Company alone lost six killed; Unteroffizier Köhnen and his entire squad were listed as missing.

Again individual deeds by anonymous men who acted fearlessly stood out. When the enemy tanks and accompanying infantry broke into the positions, one of the APCs that moved off with the others as the counterattack got under way, broke down during the fighting. The starter ceased to work. At that moment the vehicle was rammed from behind by a T-34. Simultaneously the tank crew opened fire with submachine-guns and pistols on the grenadiers standing in the APC. The latter jumped out of the half-track. The tank then pushed the APC before it, all of this taking place in a matter of seconds, while the APC's driver was still at the wheel. Luckily the half-track was pushed up a slope and in this way reached the crest of a shallow rise. The quick-thinking driver now put the vehicle in gear, which caused the engine to start. In an instant the APC pulled away from the tank and raced back down the hill, oblivious of the shellfire, toward the German lines.

That evening a Leutnant of the Panzer Regiment GD drove forward in his tank, accompanied by an assault gun, in order to assume a more favourable position. The armoured vehicles halted and the Leutnant suddenly felt something cold brush the right side of his face. In the glare of an illumination flare he realized to his horror that what had just brushed his face was nothing other than the main gun of a T-34. At almost the same instant the turret hatch of the enemy tank flipped open and the enemy commander looked around. Before the Russian could even draw his pistol the Leutnant cut him down with his submachine-gun. Then the enemy tank began to move, intending to ram. Just as it was about to do so there was a loud crash. A German tank had fired a shell into the flank of the T-34, which caught fire and then blew up.

The well-prepared counterattack by the 14th Panzer Division on 6 November, with 200 new tanks and the support of nearly 100 Stukas, in the course of which the panzer-grenadiers hoped to advance their right wing back to the old main line of resistance, was a failure. The enemy tank, anti-tank, artillery and mortar fire, as well as the close-support aircraft which appeared again, halted our advance after it had gained 1,000 metres. The entire operation finally had to be called off by the corps. The only effective success lay in the successful drive into the former main line of resistance, which caught the enemy by surprise, and its subsequent capture by the panzer-grenadiers. Decisive assistance was provided by the armoured personnel carriers of I Battalion, which numbered twelve that day.

CHAPTER 2

War correspondent Henne submitted the following gripping account titled:

THE BIG NIGHT SINGSONG
I Battalion of the Panzer-Grenadier Regiment GD at Krutoy-Neuweg

As we turned into the village I tried to imagine how the newcomers, who had arrived yesterday, would cope with all of this. I therefore tried to look at everything through the eyes of someone who was seeing this landscape northeast of Krivoy Rog for the first time. It was clear to me that I had to start from the beginning again; they had an advantage over me in that they still recognized those things that were out of the ordinary, the strange, the achievement in its full degree. For them there was still no triviality here. They still saw difficulties where we had long since ceased to take them as anything out of the ordinary, and lastly they saw everything with the eyes of home. That was important to me.

The shabby village, which stretched out into the distance, appeared to be abandoned. However after we had passed the first cottages I noted that there were still a few women, bundled up against the icy wind, squatting in holes in the ground with their children. At the same moment a shell fell not far away from them, and I heard the excited lowing of a cow, which had probably been hit. A small, dirty youth stood beside another house and, by placing his hands around his mouth, imitated the sound of a shell.

Oberleutnant Konopka, who was in command of the battle group of the Panzer-Grenadier Division *Großdeutschland*, received me in one of the last houses before the row of poplars. It was said that he wore more decorations than anyone else in the division: the Knight's Cross, the German Cross in Gold, the Wound Badge in Gold, the Bronze Close Combat Clasp, the Silver Assault Badge and finally, crowning the right sleeve of his service tunic, four white stripes that said that he had personally destroyed four enemy tanks in close combat. I had imagined him as more rawboned, somehow as a warrior. But he turned out to be a quiet, extraordinarily courteous and obliging comrade, who from the moment of my entry into his command post did everything he could to make his guest as comfortable as possible.

The room was small. A straw mattress lay on the field cot. While the twilight filled the room I had enough to do to comprehend the atmosphere that prevailed there. Squatting in the kitchen of the room in which we sat were several runners and orderlies, who were in the process of removing their shirts in order to make several 'kills,' as they called them. In a short period one of them killed fifteen lice. The Oberleutnant, a leader in the labour service in peacetime, was full of stories, which he told in an extraordinarily lively fashion. He bristled with optimism, and I could imagine that that alone was often enough to encourage his men.

The Oberleutnant, this highly-decorated soldier, spoke of his plans for the future, of a farm that he so wanted to work after the war. If the house hadn't trembled from the impacts of shells now and then, one could have imagined that there was no war. The Oberleutnant said something to that effect and added: 'That's how we are, I mean we have inner peace, calm. The other,' he added with a gesture of his hand toward the outdoors, 'that can't really shake me any more.'

At about 17.00 a Feldwebel reported that replacements had arrived from home. They were fifty-three men. This time the Oberleutnant didn't put on his warlike fur hat, instead he reached for his officer's cap. He didn't put his coat on either, and I think that at that moment he was intent on providing an example to the men assembled outside with his own person that there was everything to be gained here at the front. We walked across the yard. The replacements stood on the village street as if they had been lined up with a ruler, cleanly shaven and their clothes neat and tidy. The Feldwebel reported. I think that all of us who had been here longer smiled a bit at the unusual scene a thousand metres behind the main line of resistance, but nevertheless I wished at that moment that the mothers and fathers of those boys and men could see how their sons were welcomed there. They were not pushed off to some battalion that needed replacements without further ado, instead they were welcomed like a wonderful gift from home and as its best donation.

An unusual joy lay in the faces, which raised themselves white from the twilight of evening. The Oberleutnant shook hands with each of them and had a good word for everyone. He knew a few men who had been with the battalion earlier. Numbers of companies and names of battles were spoken.

The Oberleutnant stepped back. His voice was firm, he spoke without hesitating in clear German. He told them that they had arrived at just the right time. The battalion was in a difficult situation, but it wasn't so difficult that they couldn't endure it. He hated stale aphorisms. He had just one thing to say, his motto: head up and then at the enemy. He had done it a hundred times, attacked properly, ran like a hare. After a week anyone who was of a different opinion was to report to him.

We drove in a troop transport to battalion in the darkness. The vehicle rocked through the darkness, and the Unteroffizier, whose face I couldn't recognize, stood upright beside the machine-gun and guided the driver with curt instructions like a pilot. For the first time I felt how very much this grenadier's vehicle resembled a boat. One didn't see the earth, but one felt the head wind. The vehicle moved as if on the sea. It was incomprehensible to me that the Unteroffizier didn't lose the direction. I could scarcely see my hand in front of my face.

There were six vehicles beyond an orchard – it was said that we were driving through an orchard. I first saw them when an illumination flare rose into the night sky. Beyond them was a ploughed field, and on it there rose two small hills, or as we are used to saying here, tits. A comrade once told me that they were nothing other than the graves of grand moguls. I don't know from what time they originate, but I can recall a story which, I believe, was titled 'Kurgane' and which told that these hillocks, which are to be seen everywhere here at the Dniepr, originated from the time of Genghis Khan.

I climbed out of the armoured personnel carrier and walked towards that of Oberleutnant Czayka, who was to carry out the nocturnal advance. It is difficult to say in a few words how it looks inside an armoured personnel carrier, but in any case it seemed to me as if I were sitting in narrow bunk in a U-boat. The light of two stumps of candles was not bright enough to see clearly the faces of those around me.

I had come just in time, said the Oberleutnant, offering me a drink from his bottle and a cigarette, for it started in a few minutes. Everything was prepared down to the smallest detail, as such an operation demanded. First a bombardment by rocket launchers and artillery – then off we go. Basically it was a nocturnal advance past our main line of resistance into the enemy. They intended to set off in six armoured personnel carriers, cause a great display of fireworks, drive the Soviets from their holes and show them that we're here.

Beyond that, he observed subsequently, we'll have no more spectacle during the night and will finally be able to sleep properly. The leader of the company headquarters squad, an Unteroffizier, was given the job of keeping an eye on the other vehicles to the right. The two radio operators, who were sitting in the rear, pulled back the tarpaulins until it was as if they were sitting in a gallery, completely separated from us. The driver said, 'Two minutes to six, Herr Oberleutnant.' Everything happened without orders and I noted that this small team lived by its own laws. The driver's first name was Franz and he was called 'fatty' by the Oberleutnant. One of the radio operators was called 'little father,' and I later heard that he wanted to become a teacher. Finally there was another, a first year medical student and a funny chap, who answered to the nickname 'pork borscht.'

I would have given a lot to make out the face of the Oberleutnant. I asked him his age. He was twenty-three, active and wounded seven times.

'This will be a spring without end,' he said laughing. He was calm personified. His sureness must have had a puzzling effect on those who knew this front and its frightfulness. The Unteroffizier, whose name was Walldorf, reported that all was in order. The Oberleutnant stood up: 'Forward!'

We drove slowly over the open plain. I could now see the tits more clearly against the lighter sky. 'Our main line of resistance runs left and right,' said the Oberleutnant, 'there are our foxholes. On the tits are the forward observers for the rocket launchers and the artillery.'

The headwind was icy. I imagined the soggy foxholes. 'The holes are about 100 metres apart,' said the Oberleutnant. The other vehicles drove in our keel line like ships. Someone called to us from the right, beside the hillocks. The driver braked.

'Herr Hauptmann,' called the Oberleutnant.

'Yes – is everything ready?'

'Everything's ready.'

'Then break a leg!'

'Thank you, Herr Hauptmann.'

'That was the artillery's forward observer,' said the Oberleutnant. The radio operator passed him the flare pistol.

'Starshell!' 'Starshell here, Herr Oberleutnant.'

The breech snapped shut. The Oberleutnant raised his arm and fired. The star shell hissed into the night sky and burst. Two white, two red and two green stars danced over us. That was the signal for the rocket launchers and artillery. The roaring of the guns started immediately. Everything was outstandingly well coordinated. It had an eerie sound, as if someone was blowing frightful notes through giant glass tubes. It howled overhead.

'It's spring for them now,' said the Oberleutnant. He turned around.

'Transmit: attack beginning!' One radio operator laid ten hand grenades on the seat beside me. The Oberleutnant shouted:

'Where is the man who is supposed to fire the red flare?'

'Here, Herr Oberleutnant!' came from the darkness.

'Watch out, my boy. If we fire a red flare, then you answer with red. Position yourself on the tit. Stay alert.'

The Oberleutnant turned to me: 'So we can find our way back,' he explained.

Through the darkness I could feel the looks of the grenadiers in their foxholes. Looks that were used to the darkness. A battalion, its numbers having dwindled, stared at the armoured personnel carriers. Pale, grey faces, bearded, dirty. Like clay figures, with wet boots, with sores on their feet, with hands that hadn't been washed in weeks. They stared over at us. Perhaps their hearts were racing. But no, they were used to it.

We moved off. Six armoured personnel carriers, each with three men. A driver, a commander behind the machine-gun or behind the cannon, another who passed the hand grenades.

The vehicles with the cannon drove on the right. To our left was the APC with the mortar.

'White,' ordered the Oberleutnant.

One of the radio operators passed him a signal flare. The shell rose high into the sky. An eerie scene. Moonscape or poor theatre background. A broad field, beyond it a field of sunflowers. The engines roared. The machine-gun on the right began to hammer away. Tracer ripped the darkness. Now the cannon fired. It sounded like an impacting mortar shell. The shell exploded a hundred metres in front of us. The APCs drove in a broad wedge.

To the right there was a shout of 'Hurray!' We moved off. 'Hurray – Hurray!'

Another flare! We saw the first foxholes. Hand grenades into them! Each vehicle was a raging, flashing column, throwing out streaks of fire. Every vehicle was a ship, ploughing through sudden darkness, and the headwind blew icy cold. On through the field of sunflowers, or was it corn...?

There, more holes! Into them with hand grenades.

'Hurray... Hurray!'

'Stay to the right, Walldorf,' shouted the Oberleutnant.

'Stay to the right!'

'White, pork borscht, hurry up!'

'White here!'

There was a flash of light, foxholes everywhere. The first hand grenade went wide. Another. Direct hit. All that I knew was that everything combined into a frightful chorus: the hissing, the shouts, the roar of the engines, the crash of the guns, it was ecstasy to us. We were caught up in it all, we had to shout. We stood up. The Oberleutnant manned the machine-gun. All the fighters who moved against the enemy by night looked like him, they changed, they were no longer themselves, they were sword and steel. It was hard to believe that he was only twenty-three years old, that he had been fighting in the east for three years, that he had been wounded seven times. Didn't he ever get tired? What powered him, what guided him, what kept him going...? The eyes of those in the foxholes behind him...?

Flashing light and endless hammering. There they are!

'They're running!' shouted the Oberleutnant.

Actually one could only see their legs, where the last glare of the light drove into the night. The rifles laid flaming ribbons.

'Hurray... Hurray!' The Oberleutnant sang loudly:

'This is a spring without end...' I knew that I would never forget this; I wished that I might be able to record all of this: this great night serenade by the men taking on an enemy superior in numbers.

A pair of boots stood in the middle of the field beside a foxhole. A soldier had taken them off; who could say where he was now, running in sock feet. A mortar position! Carry on!

To the right a ravine full of foxholes, then another field.

'Out!' shouted the Oberleutnant. It was still. Deathly still. No, the engines were humming!

'Walldorf!'

'Here, Herr Oberleutnant.'

'Turn around and move out!'

It was like a farewell song. The Oberleutnant hummed softly to himself. 'We must watch out. The comrades could have barred the way behind us,' he said. Walldorf fired a red flare. Another rose in the distance.

'That's the tits. You see, it was a good thing that we made this arrangement. It's easy to get lost.'

'How far did we advance?' asked the radio operator.

'Three kilometres. Signal to battalion and regiment: operation successful. No casualties.'

The rest was child's play. At 19.15 we stopped beyond the orchard, four-hundred metres behind the foxholes. The tarpaulins were unrolled.

'We have one wounded,' called the medical officer who had accompanied the attack. 'The mortar vehicle was hit up there.'

The Oberleutnant climbed out and walked over to him. 'Is it bad, my boy?'

'Bruises, Herr Oberleutnant.'

'Well, I'd say you were lucky, here are some cigarettes.'

When we were sitting together the radio operator called:

'But now it's time for Gustav!' He tuned in the Gustav soldiers' station. They were playing light dance music. We took a drink and smoked a cigarette.

'Now my men can spend the night in peace,' said the Oberleutnant. He lit a new candle. For the first time I saw his face, the face of a calm, young man.

Later we ate a sandwich. It was very cosy in spite of the close quarters. The commanding officer sent congratulations by radio, as did the Oberleutnant with the Knight's Cross in the field with the tanks. And the vehicles stood like eerie ships in the loneliness of the night. We laid down. The Oberleutnant up front beside the driver, his legs drawn in. It was getting cold. I heard the radio operator, the one called 'little father'; his teeth were chattering. The driver fired up the engine and it became a little warmer. I couldn't sleep and lit myself a cigarette. The Oberleutnant was sound asleep. I saw his face. It was bearded and dark. Only the radio operator was awake. It must have been even colder up front in the foxholes. But at least they could rest.

And the night passed. We got up at five o'clock. Morning was quiet. But at noon the Soviets attacked. The earth was a hell. The trial began anew. That is another story. But who would say that the front wasn't as hard as it was the day before...? Look at these men. I told the story of two hours, but it's always like that for them."

The enemy attacks subsided somewhat as a result of the effective defense. The defenders thus had an opportunity to shore up their positions, strong-points and machine-gun nests. How well it was that they did was shown early on the 8th of November, when continuous rain came to replace the sunny autumn days of late. Very soon all the roads became morasses. All foxholes that were not covered filled with water. Movement in open terrain was made extremely difficult.

The rain appeared to immobilize the enemy as well, for only his artillery and mortars remained active, firing every hour. The holding of the positions, which extended from Malaya Sofiyevka on the right, along the valley of the Busuluk, north of Veselaya-Dolina and along the row of trees to about 1,000 metres north of "nameless village" and from there to the south to the railroad, enabled the division command to pull various units out of the front line for a rest. In order to keep the lines manned, their places were taken by alert units from the trains, the artillery and the panzer regiment on a day by day basis. The Panzer Regiment GD formed two infantry companies which were named for their commanders.

These infantry companies were formed from members of the panzer head-quarters company, the trains and the tanks crews of III (Tiger) and IV (Panzer IV) Battalions. Led by Oberleutnant Stadler and Oberleutnant Velten, they were sent into the line after a week of infantry training. In those days they relieved I (APC) Battalion, Panzer-Grenadier Regiment GD and took over its positions. These extended along a ridge, bordered by a hillock on each end. There was no continuous trench system; the men squatted in foxholes which were inadequately covered against the cold, wet weather. Small groups of Soviets attacked daily, but these were always driven off by accurate machine-gun and anti-aircraft fire. The alert companies suffered casualties, primarily from the continuous enemy artillery, mortar and anti-tank fire, which was concentrated on the hillocks in particular. These losses could not be made good. Stabsfeldwebel Reichert, Gefreiter Kreideweis, Gefreiter Plottke, Franke, Mix and Dworczak died hero's deaths in those days. Others, like Gefreiter Meier and Unteroffizier Sommer, were wounded, but the positions were held and not an inch of ground was lost to the enemy.

The days until 15 November were cold and wet, with repeated attacks by the enemy. But the main line of resistance remained in our hands, even though repeated enemy incursions had to be ironed out with a minimum of forces.

The feats of the men were outstanding. Their number was small, their morale for that point in time was outstanding in spite of everything. On November 12 the commander of I (APC) Battalion, Panzer-Grenadier Regiment GD, Major Remer, became the 325th German soldier to receive the Knight's Cross with Oak Leaves, for his outstanding accomplishments as a commander during the summer months. This decoration was also an acknowledgement of the conduct of his men, who went through thick and thin for him.

The Panzer-Grenadier Division GD's front had to be pulled back as darkness fell (on 16 November); this came about as the result of a deep penetration, which could not be eliminated, against the 16th Panzer-Grenadier Division on the division's right. It occupied new positions in a line (from left to right): hills due south of 'nameless village," west of the Veselaya-Dolina crossroads, southwest of the Neuweg hills between Kisletshevatka Gorge and the road to the southeast. Initially the withdrawal proceeded according to plan.

The first rays of light pierced the dense fog, announcing the morning of 16 November. In the entire division sector all hell had broken loose. The Soviets had apparently noticed the withdrawal; they drove into it with considerable forces, including tanks, and caused tremendous confusion. The remaining tanks of the Panzer Regiment GD, mainly Tigers and Panzer IVs, moved off to engage the enemy; the assault guns, under the veteran command of Major Frantz, moved up to the ridges cautiously, in order to determine exactly where the enemy was. The counterattack squadrons of the Armoured Reconnaissance Battalion GD left their quartering area to drive to the threatened areas, and the batteries of the Panzer-Artillery Regiment GD prepared for all-round defense; each allocated one gun for anti-tank purposes. The heavy anti-aircraft guns, the proven 88mm weapons, pointed their barrels in the direction of the tank noises. All the division's forces and effort, especially that of the heavy weapons, were prepared for the defensive and for close combat.

The few panzer-fusiliers and panzer-grenadiers, as well as the alert companies, assembled again and were led by their officers and NCos into new holes and positions, where they dug in and prepared to meet the enemy attack.

Once again the Soviet tanks and mounted infantry felt their way forward through the dense fog. The defenders fell back before this superiority. Then they stopped and dug in again. And, thank God, our tanks and assault guns attacked; they fired on every enemy tank they could see. A Leutnant from Hamburg knocked out nine T-34s and a KV I; the Russians' tank losses must have been frightful, but their superiority was crushing; they continued to drive forward.

Not until they reached the outlying houses of Lyubimovka, were the infantry able to hold, master their positions. Many times Soviet infantry and tanks stormed down the hill toward the village, in an effort to capture the bridge at the outskirts; but each time they were stopped and forced to retreat by a light infantry gun, which cleverly placed its fire on that spot. This action by a single gun crew gave the defenders courage, they held.

Hauptmann Graf zu Rantzau, commander of a battalion of the Panzer-Artillery Regiment GD, related how a bolshevik flamethrower tank chased him over the open ground. He cast aside all his encumbering equipment and finally hid himself in a fox earth on a hill. Exhausted by overexertion, he fell asleep. When he finally awoke there were no Russians to be seen and he was able to rejoin his men unhindered.

The panzer-alert companies under Oberleutnants Stadler and Velten, unused to fighting as infantry, suffered grim losses that day. With only 18-19 men left from his infantry company, Oberleutnant Velten finally took up position on the back slope of a hill along a peach plantation and desperately fought off repeated enemy attacks. When the situation became hopeless, Oberleutnant Velten ordered those of his men not wounded to break through. He stayed in his command post with the wounded. The last to leave heard him say: "I'm staying with the wounded. If we can't hold any longer and the Russians do come, I'll shoot myself." He kept his word. The rest of the men were able to make their way to the rear.

When evening fell on 16 November an intermediate line was occupied, where the units could regroup and dig in. Altogether, 61 enemy tanks had been destroyed by the tanks of the Panzer Regiment GD and I Battalion, 26th Panzer regiment and by close-range weapons. This number alone is an indication of the severity of the fighting. With little loss of ground, the division was able to maintain control of its own field of combat, once again preventing the enemy from breaking through.

However 17 November brought no slackening in the enemy attacks. Beginning at dawn, the Soviets pounded the foxholes and makeshift bunkers of the forward German lines with artillery and mortars. It was the prelude to new attacks, which weren't long in coming.

Oberleutnant Konopka, commander of II Battalion, Panzer-Grenadier Regiment GD, was wounded. The former regimental adjutant, Hauptmann Kraussold, who by chance was on his way to the battalion command post, assumed command of the battalion. Enemy tanks turned up on both sides of Lyubimovka. Soviet infantry moved forward; it was a repeat of the previous day. The cry of "medic" rang out from every side. Wounded men dragged themselves toward the rear, others collapsed and fell. And then the Russians were in our positions; the hand-to-hand fighting began anew. The few defenders battled fiercely with the superior enemy. Hauptmann Kraussold was badly wounded; a shell fragment shattered his arm, another pierced a lung. But he stayed. Ignoring the pain, he had an emergency dressing applied to the wound, climbed into an armoured personnel carrier and led a counter-attack by his handful of men. This example in military heroism by the wounded Hauptmann inspired the grenadiers of II Battalion, and they stormed forward against the enemy. What had seemed unlikely a few hours before succeeded: the enemy were driven back again and the former main line of resistance was reoccupied.

The panzer-fusiliers of I Battalion likewise defended their positions stubbornly northeast of Lyubimovka; they refused to give up an inch of ground until it became obvious that they were alone on a broad stage. Finally the order reached them to join the general withdrawal toward the C Line, whose course was roughly as follows: crossroads 2,500 metres southwest of Gulyay-Pole – 500 metres south of cattle farm – hills south of Udova Gorge and Orlova Trench – Point 142.0. The withdrawal was made under very heavy enemy fire, with the tanks and assault guns providing a screen. Armoured Battle Group Gomille, which consisted of elements of the Tiger and Panzer IV battalions of the Panzer Regiment GD, once again stood out, destroying 29 enemy tanks. Oberleutnant Bayer alone knocked out ten enemy tanks, some from point-blank range. The assault guns also reaped a rich harvest from among the enemy armour, which attacked repeatedly: 18 KV Is and T-34s fell victim to their guns that day, and this without loss. Unteroffizier Bor of the assault gun battery had the highest total, sending eight enemy tanks "to heaven."

On the whole, it can be said that the assault guns were in competition with the panzers in the destruction of enemy tanks. By evening the anti-tank company of the Panzer-Fusilier Regiment GD was also able to report that Unteroffizier Lay and his gun crew had destroyed eight enemy tanks.

All these reports and accounts confirm once again the readiness for action of the heavy weapons, which as before gave the infantry their support in true comradeship in arms. Most are unknown, for they were usually assigned in small groups and platoons to the battalions and companies, especially in a defensive role, when they provided the infantry with needed support. This applied not just to the anti-tank units, but equally to the guns of the flak companies of the regiments, especially the Army Flak Regiment GD. These small 20mm anti-aircraft guns, like the 37mm weapons, which were called "barn doors," all too often formed the centre point of a counterattack, when they sent their shells like strings of pearls into recognized targets. The infantry advanced more readily under their screening fire, which extended in an arc into the enemy positions, for they knew that the effect of the flak shells made breaking into the enemy positions significantly easier.

The following account by war correspondent Henne, entitled *Three Green Signal Flares*, provides a graphic description of such an action:

CHAPTER 3

With the *Großdeutschland* Panzer-Fusiliers at Lyubimovka (17.11.43)

Although it was only coming up to 3 P.M. twilight was already beginning to fall, and I couldn't recognise all the people in the back room of the cottage. At the window sat the general. The collar of his long winter coat was still turned up; he must have come over from the grenadiers' regimental command post, which lay 400 metres beyond the ravine, a few minutes ago. Opposite him, bent over the wobbly table with the maps, was Oberstleutnant Niemak. He too had pulled on his coat.

'You've just set the next house ablaze with your fire!' I heard someone shout excitedly in the outer room. It didn't seem to bother anyone in here; it appeared that the close proximity of the impacts wasn't of any great concern to those sitting around the table.

The operations officer, Leutnant Boll, the director of a publishing house in Solingen in peacetime, was in constant contact with the battle group command posts, insofar as the wire communications weren't interrupted. Sometimes he passed the second receiver to the Oberstleutnant, who kept the general informed of the nature of the conversation.

Through an open door stepped an Oberleutnant. He was covered with dirt. His face, bearded and crusted with splashes of mud, turned to the Oberstleutnant, as he failed to notice the general. In a clear voice he reported that he had rounded up 25 stragglers and added them to his battle group. The enemy had now advanced to within 30 metres of the row of trees—he pointed this out on the map. He asked permission to enquire about the situation there, as contact with the right had been lost.

'They're coming through the gorge,' said one of the officers at the table.

The Oberstleutnant nodded and ordered the operations officer to contact the grenadiers' command post.

The general bent over the map; he talked with Major Wätjen, the commander of the reconnaissance battalion, tall, with a smooth fresh face, a wearer of the Knight's Cross. Then an Oberfeldwebel, walking with the aid of a cane, entered the room and reported. His face was swollen and he looked exhausted.

The general looked up briefly and said, 'Good day Dost!' Then, turning to the Oberstleutnant, he asked, 'What is Weber doing?' It seemed that he knew almost every man of the regiment.

Oberleutnant Weber, replied the Oberstleutnant, was still in the positions on the right with the few fusiliers he had left, just like Hauptmann von Basse.

Outside the impacting shells came nearer. They could hear the hiss of shrapnel. A small pig toddled squealing across the room. The CO of the Tiger battalion, Knight's Cross wearer Major Gomille, had prodded it awake with his foot as there was no room to get through the door.

'Leave our good luck pig in peace,' declared the general with a smile. Turning to the commander of the reconnaissance battalion, who wore a perplexed look, he explained: 'That is Susi.'

'She's been here as long as we've had our command post here, Herr General,' said the operations officer. He looked at Susi almost tenderly, but I don't think he was a great animal lover, rather he already saw Susi simmering away in the pan.

Oberfeldwebel Dost, a wearer of the German Cross in Gold and nine times wounded, leader of the fusiliers' operational reserve, had meanwhile laid down on the bed. From time to time he groaned.

'What's wrong with him?' someone asked.

'He doesn't want to go to the rear, even though his leg injury must be causing him terrible pain.'

The Oberstleutnant had meanwhile spoken with the grenadier command post.

'You must start at once!' ordered the general. 'The reconnaissance battalion with Tigers and assault guns will clear the gorge and place itself between Schewe and Weber. The gap must be closed immediately or there'll be hell to pay.'

'My Tigers have no fuel left,' declared the commander of the Tiger battalion. 'We are part way through the gorge, have knocked out two T-34s...'

The Oberstleutnant interrupted him: 'Have you sighted any infantry?'

'The infantry have bolted, two- to three-hundred men.'

'Try to get fuel from the assault guns,' ordered the general, 'but quickly, we must get going!'

A runner came over from the telephone exchange, which was in a neighbouring house. The Oberstleutnant took the message and quickly read it.

'Basse radios that he's under heavy pressure; he can't hold any longer.'

The general stood up. 'Let's get moving! I'm driving over to the artillery. I'll stop by here afterward.'

The shells fell nearer as the general climbed into his car. The enemy were firing armour-piercing shells. The general had scarcely reached the end of the village street, when the reconnaissance battalion's armoured cars emerged from a depression to his right. They drove into the gorge, widely spaced. The tanks, which had meanwhile obtained fuel from the assault guns, rolled forward between them.

I climbed onto the rear of one of the assault guns and we set off after them. Our progress was slow, as the steady rain had softened the ground. The roaring and droning of the engines drowned out everything. The gorge, as was typical for the landscape around Krivoy Rog, was completely barren. The slopes of the gorge were sparsely overgrown with short, yellow-green grass.

After about 400 metres the gorge made a turn. The two T-34s which the Tigers had destroyed were still burning there. Sometimes jets of flame, which must have ignited in the interiors of the tanks, spurted from their blackened turrets.

The reconnaissance battalion's armoured vehicles now drove out of the gorge very slowly. A gentle slope rose up before them. Here and there it was bedecked with shrubbery and sunflowers. The small APC of the reconnaissance battalion's CO, Major Wätjen, darted here and there like a startled bedbug.

We reached the top of the rise and at that moment we saw them, perhaps two-hundred metres away and moving toward us. All we could see in the misty air was grey shadows. It didn't look dangerous at all. Half concealed by the slope, they moved like a giant herd of sheep.

The vehicles spread out further and finally came to a halt. The tanks rolled ahead a bit farther. The reconnaissance battalion's cannon-armed vehicle, which was about three metres to the side of us, fired three shells into the rows of sunflowers. The first shell was long. It ricocheted off the ground a hundred metres in front of us and flew hissing and sparking into the air, but the others were on the mark. There was no more movement.

Suddenly the Tiger on the left began blazing away with its machine-gun. Thirty to forty dark forms stood up twenty metres in front of us. They ran right into the fire of the other machine-guns.

The commander of the assault gun stood upright in his hatch and shouted: 'The dogs stay down until the last minute. Watch out for the foxholes!' We saw them spring out of the ground in this way several more times, one, two or three metres in front of the other two tanks, which had moved forward some distance. They were shot down immediately.

The reconnaissance battalion commander's APC had driven away in the direction of the two T-34s in the gorge. The major established contact with Oberleutnant Weber and Hauptmann von Basse. It was still raining, and sometimes the wind blew clouds of fog over the rise. It became even more dusky. Occasionally a machine-gun fired a burst. An enemy anti-tank gun, which must have been somewhere on the other side of the rise, took potshots at the closest Tiger. Its shells fell three metres in front of the tank. Sometimes the tracer component of the shells flew high in the air after the impact and ignited in a flash of red.

The Tiger stubbornly remained where it was.

'Those boys have nerve!' said the Oberleutnant.

At that moment the tank fired its gun. We heard the shell cleaving the air. The sound was strangely high-pitched and sinister – the anti-tank gun stopped firing.

I drove back through the gorge with one of the assault guns, which had received new orders after the gap between the battle groups had been closed by the reconnaissance battalion. It was so dark that one could scarcely see four metres and we had to fire a white illumination flare every two or three minutes to avoid becoming lost. Their light was pale in the fog; the rays refracted, and I was reminded of the headlights of autos driving in thick fog. From time to time bursts of machine-gun fire came in from our left; the bands of tracer passed right in front of us through the fog. 'We've lost our way,' shouted the Oberleutnant.

'Or the Russkis have infiltrated back into the gorge,' remarked the radio operator, who had stuck his head out of the hatch.

We drove back. The Oberleutnant jumped out and, using a shielded flashlight, looked for old tracks. After about a quarter of an hour he climbed back in and shouted: 'I found the tracks of the APCs; we must stay to the right.'

'Right?...' asked the radio operator, astonished. 'I think left.'

'If we had kept going,' laughed the Oberleutnant, 'we'd have driven right into the Russkis. These gorges all look alike...'

'I'd just like to know if he's right this time,' I heard the radio operator say, 'you need to know your way around here.'

Nothing had changed at the fusiliers' command post. The commander stood at the table, bent over his maps. The operations officer spoke with the artillery, the rocket launchers and the grenadiers, and a runner arrived nearly every minute.

The Stuka control officer, a young pilot, was lying on the bed on the large oven, snoring loudly.

'What's up with the Stuka controller?' asked the Oberstleutnant. He appeared to have just noticed the sleeping man.

'He didn't sleep for three days and three nights,' said someone in the corner, where the icon hung. It had become quieter outside. Now and then there was a shot in the gorge behind the house. An orderly had draped the window with motorcycle coats and had placed several Hindenburg lamps on the table.

'If it wasn't for the damned fog,' declared the Oberstleutnant all at once.

'The boys can make their way through quite comfortably,' said the leutnant in the icon corner.

'Are there listening posts outside?' enquired the Oberstleutnant.

'Yes sir!'

The operations officer had summoned a stenographer and in a quiet voice he dictated a report for the regiment's war diary. Meanwhile the Oberstleutnant continued staring at the map; he seemed to be so engrossed in the terrain drawn on the map, that he heard nothing of what was going on around him. One of the runners laid a bundle of straw in the right corner and then brought a few sandwiches.

At about 20.00 the general's adjutant called and informed them that he had just learned that the Führer had awarded Unteroffizier Poschusta the Knight's Cross.

There was dead silence in the room for a few seconds when the operations officer repeated what the adjutant had said. The Oberstleutnant turned to me and said, 'Poschusta was killed twenty-four hours ago.' Turning to the operations officer, he said gruffly, 'Send this to Hauptmann von Basse at once. The fusilier regiment is proud of the decoration.'

When I stepped to the door I heard the sound of caterpillar tracks in the distance. The listening sentry was leaning against a tree, and if he hadn't made himself noticeable I surely wouldn't have known he was there. It was still raining. The wind was icy cold. Beyond the line of trees, where Oberleutnant Schewe and his battle group lay, signal flares rose into the sky. At 24.00 the commander lay down on the bed. The Stuka control officer sat on a stool by the window and murmured:

'I won't be needed here if this awful weather continues.'

On the table a candle was still burning. It was also quiet in the ante-room. All except two of the runners had laid down on the oven and were asleep.

At about 04.15 the listening sentry rushed in and shouted, 'tanks, tanks coming!' Everyone was immediately awake. The Oberstleutnant grabbed his submachine-gun and was the first outside. It was still pitch black. The sound of tanks was coming from the right. It was without a doubt enemy tanks. The operational reserve, which had been in the neighbouring house, raced up from behind and took up position against the wall.

'Keep quiet,' someone ordered.

Something was moving over at the tree line, but we couldn't see anything.

'That's a T-34,' said the Oberstleutnant.

Just then a voice called from the right: 'There comes another!' The Oberstleutnant instructed everyone to press themselves against the wall of the house facing the gorge.

A deep voice was heard to say: 'If there's no infantry with them, things are only half as bad.'

'But we've already seen them,' someone answered.

'They're following in large numbers.'

It had meanwhile become somewhat brighter, or perhaps our eyes were used to the darkness. The first tank drove back down the road and stopped at the tree line. At the same moment a second and then a third tank rolled around the corner of the house; the noise they made drowned out that of the first tank. The command post was surrounded on three sides by T-34s. Their engines made a frightful racket. The operations officer saw the gun of one of the tanks pointing at the door of the house. Something struck him: 'Damn, our maps!'

He dashed toward the door. The tank didn't appear to notice him. He passed through the ante-room and reached the wobbly table. The candle was out. He gathered up the maps, ran outside, and reached the rear wall of the house without incident. Farther down the street an enemy machine-gun roared.

'How many are we?' asked the Oberstleutnant.

'Ten,' came the reply.

'Who goes there...?'

No one answered. Someone came running up, gasping for breath, and called something in a hushed voice. He was carrying a box under his arm. The operations officer was the first to recognize him. He was the man from the exchange; he had gone back to rescue his portable switchboard.

Now they heard voices. The enemy infantry were working their way toward us. Submachine-guns roared, hand grenades exploded.

'The brothers are combing the houses,' whispered a runner.

The Oberstleutnant ordered: 'Go, into the foxholes!'

One after another they jumped into the foxholes the runners had dug to protect them from artillery and strafing fire. They were quite shallow. The tanks, which were sitting in front of the cottage door, withdrew to the tree line, and we could no longer see them. The first bursts now came in from the right, and shots were also fired from the gorge.

'The tanks have definitely made out our regimental command post,' said the Oberstleutnant.

'If we had a few more men we could take care of the brothers,' someone whispered.

'Back and through the gorge,' ordered the Oberstleutnant. They moved down the slope slowly and carefully, taking care not to silhouette themselves against the sky, which was becoming lighter. Increasingly heavy fire came from the right. They assembled near the grenadier command post. A few stragglers, perhaps fifteen men, stood there with no idea what they should do.

'So, boys,' directed the Oberstleutnant, 'get ready. Now we're going to go back and teach those fellows a lesson.' 'Have you any hand grenades?' asked an officer.

'There's a few left!'

Just then they heard the sound of engines to the right. 'It's the tank destroyer,' said one of the officers. 'It must be Unteroffizier Lay, he was further below.'

Somebody called: 'That's a gift from heaven!'

They waited. The white-washed walls of the houses around their command post were now clearly visible. The tanks loomed dark and massive against the sky. 'Stay out of sight,' ordered the Oberstleutnant. 'The comrades are in the foxholes over there and behind the houses. If they see us here, we've had it!'

I don't remember exactly who briefed the tank destroyer, but it suddenly appeared from the hollow. Everything happened quickly. The first shot was on target; and the second; and the third. The three T-34s were destroyed in three minutes. The Oberstleutnant led the charge; the men raced through the gorge. Cries rang out everywhere. They reached the house where the command post was and found the vehicles intact. The enemy withdrew, but during the morning they attacked six times out of the gorge and from the west in strong waves. The evening report submitted by the fusiliers put the number of enemy dead at 450. It was on the same day that 61 enemy tanks were destroyed in the sector of the Panzer-Grenadier Division *Großdeutschland*.

When they entered the room they found everything almost exactly as they had left it. Only the cigars, the commander's binoculars and the schnapps bottle were missing. The Oberstleutnant sat back down at his table and the operations officer spoke with a runner.

'How are things with Hauptmann von Basse?'

'The battalion is still in its old foxholes!'

'Good!'

After a while the Oberstleutnant looked up from his map. He showed not the slightest trace of fatigue.

'Where is Susi?' he asked, smiling.

'Herr Oberstleutnant, she was taken back to the train yesterday,' said the operations officer.

'Then it's all clear,' declared the Oberstleutnant. 'Susi is gone, our good luck pig – then of course such a mess was bound to happen...!'"

Not until the early morning of 18 November did the fighting die down, probably on account of the extremely heavy losses suffered by the enemy. The time gained was immediately put to use bolstering the positions, as well as reorganizing the units and incorporating the replacements that had arrived in the meantime. A sigh of relief went through the thin lines, even if evidence of fresh preparations by the enemy gave cause for further concern. The prowling about by T-34s on the enemy side of the lines and a resurgence of the enemy artillery and rocket fire made it appear that the period of quiet was to be of brief duration.

All remained quiet opposite the division's sector until about 09.00 on November 20. Then the enemy attacked at the boundary between the panzer-grenadiers and panzer-fusiliers. Counterattacks eliminated the enemy incursion there, but the same could not be said of the penetration, which was expanded almost to the point of becoming a breakthrough, against the division's neighbour on the right, the 16th Panzer-Grenadier Division, which was forced to abandon its positions. Even though this deep thrust by the Soviets was stopped by elements of the 13th Panzer Division, it forced the 16th Panzer-Grenadier Division and the right wing of the Panzer-Grenadier Division *Großdeutschland* to pull back their positions. On November 20 the Division's right wing was now lined up on the hills west-southwest of Vodyan Gorge to the hillock about 2,000 metres west of the cattle farm; from there the division's line followed its previous course to Point 168.8.

Major Wätjen, former commander of the Armoured Reconnaissance Battalion, left the unit to take up a new post in the OKH. Major von Schkopp took command on November 20.

Nothing special happened in the positions on November 21. There was a considerable increase in activity by Soviet close-support aircraft however. Several times through the day they dived through the low-lying cloud and blanketed villages and positions alike with bombs. The Soviet heavy artillery also came to life, firing at targets deep in the rear. The Army Flak Battalion GD suffered considerable losses, in men as well as equipment.

On November 21 the division ordered its units to fall back to the D Line, a move intended to shorten the front. The new line ran as follows: gorge about 2 kilometres southwest of Alexandro-Belovo straight west across the hills about 700 metres south of Shevchenkovo – along the Tupolova Gorge to Hill 168.8. The move to the new positions was to begin with the arrival of darkness. The division command was in Prtrova-Dolina at this time.

The rainy weather continued, turning the ground into a bottomless morass. Even the use of the armoured personnel carriers was placed in question, because they became stuck in the black earth. For the infantry in the foxholes the weather added considerably to their burden. The men suffered to an increasing degree from the wet and by night from the cold. The constant wearing of wet clothes and boots led to illnesses, which caused further losses among the fighting troops. Combat strengths dropped alarmingly.

It was therefore still impossible to withdraw the alert companies, which had been in action for weeks in relief of the regiments, and return the men to their actual duties. Most of these men were specialists, who could not be replaced on account of their long years of training on tanks, guns and the artillery.

An infantry company made up of tank personnel under the command of Oberleutnant Weikert, which had been deployed on the division's right wing, was completely wiped out during a counterattack. Weikert was killed. Scarcely any of the panzer men came back. The three panzer-infantry companies sent into action in the last three weeks had thus been almost completely lost; casualties numbered 60 men out of action and two officers killed. Talks with the Division Ia, General Staff Oberstleutnant von Natzmer, concerning this matter led to heated exchanges; but the division had to hold, there was no question of that. A sector 9,000 metres wide was being held by the two regiments with no more than 250 men in total; the single battle group of I Battalion, Panzer-Grenadier Regiment GD numbered 27 men; it held a two-kilometre-wide sector.

In the early morning hours of 26 November the enemy broke through at the boundary between the two regiments after a brief preparatory artillery barrage. Soviet tanks rolled south in the direction of the Shirokaya Trench unhindered. Accurate fire by Hauptmann Wülfert's Hummel and Wespe self-propelled guns (I Battalion, Panzer-Artillery Regiment GD) finally halted the enemy spearhead about 1,000 metres from the trench. The remnants of the infantry battalions hit by the Soviet attack (I Battalion, Panzer-Grenadier Regiment GD) was down to one Leutnant and 13 men, assembled on the Yekaterinovka-Sofiyevka road and regrouped there. In the meantime battle groups consisting of supply troops and artillerymen held the Shirokaya Trench and prevented a further breakthrough.

An account of what took place there was provided by Leutnant Welke, the signals officer with III (Tiger) Battalion, Panzer Regiment GD. He described the battle west of Menshinka as follows:

It was a misty, opaque late autumn morning. Enemy tanks had been reported for days. Major Gomille cast a glance outside the door of his cottage – he could smell tank weather. Even though there was no special order, he had the unit come to battle readiness immediately.

It slowly became lighter; the battalion was drawn up in a broad, open semicircle. Dense fog clung to the hills; all was quiet. But then powerful motors roared to life. I carried out a radio check: 'Sultan – understood, ready!' 11th Company was reporting many enemy tanks. Suddenly there was a wild outburst of firing; tracer ripped through the fog. Our infantry came running toward us, as if pursued by the Furies. They ran right past and took up position behind us. Then long streams of flame shot through the fog. The grenadiers shouted to us: 'flamethrower tanks!'

Then they appeared, large red stars on their turrets. They fired for all they were worth, sending jets of flame in the direction of our infantry. Major Gomille gave the order to open fire.

It was like being on the firing range. They came down a long slope on the side of the hill facing us. That day we had 18 Tigers in action – 18 heavily-armoured 88mm tank cannon, at that time still the best anti-tank weapon in existence.

I was in Major Gomille's tank. He guided me by nudging my right or left shoulder, until the pointed-post reticle of his periscope indicated that I had the correct target in the much smaller field of view of the gunsight. Then he tapped me lightly on the back. That meant: fire!

The tank's gunsight had a large spike in the centre and three small spikes on the left and right. These enabled the gunner to calculate the required lead for targets moving laterally and to compensate for the spin of the shell and the angle of parallax between the sight and the barrel. We had learned how much lead to use at home in the tank simulator or at the tank firing school at Putlos. I operated the elevating and traversing mechanisms until the first small spike to the left of the large spike was over the star on the turret of the T-34 – and fired! The smoke from the muzzle of the gun obscured my view for a fraction of a second. A glowing dot raced toward the Russian tank. There was a shower of sparks over there and in seconds the T-34 was shrouded in a huge cloud of smoke. A pleased Major Gomille clapped me on the shoulder: a hit!

Meanwhile other flamethrower tanks were burning. Another rolled through my field of view, and I had to turn the control wheels like mad to get the reticle on him. I fired, but I had allowed too much lead. Another of our Tigers got him before I could get off a second shot.

That was it. I couldn't see a thing for the dense clouds of smoke. The 76.2mm shells of the T-34s whizzed left and right past the turret; they were firing on the move, but it did them no good.

The slope was littered with burning wrecks; our Tigers concentrated their fire on the remaining Soviet tanks, which carried on at full speed. Moments later the whole thing was over.

Three or four T-34s broke through to the village behind us, where they caused terrified panic among the warriors in the command post. But in the end they, too, suffered the fate of their fellows, for below were self-propelled anti-tank guns, which took care of the rest. The Tigers that had been sent to the rear came back to join us.

We drove toward the burning wrecks in our SO 2. Every T-34 that hadn't burnt out and looked like it might be repairable, was fired on and set ablaze. The Russians suffered only total losses that day.

That day the daily report spoke of 29 enemy tanks that had fallen victim to our guns."

Finally, at about lunchtime, it was possible to see to what extent the enemy incursion into the regiments' positions had been crowned by success. Following the successful counterattack by the 13th Panzer Division (at about 13.00), it was the division's intention to launch a counterattack from Vasilyevka with the panzer-fusiliers and panzer-grenadiers and recapture the former main line of resistance.

This counterattack, in which elements of the Armoured Reconnaissance Battalion GD took part, was only partly successful. Still, all the panzer-fusiliers and the right wing of the panzer-grenadiers were able to reach their old positions. The left wing of the Panzer-Grenadier Regiment GD did not keep pace, and there was no news whatsoever of the 13th Panzer Division, which had moved east past Point 168.8. Darkness fell while all this was happening and forced a halt. Patrols of the Armoured Reconnaissance Battalion GD secured the area west of the Shirokaya Gorge; meanwhile the situation north of this point remained unclear.

Mopping up of the recaptured territory was begun during the night of 27 November. The area appeared still to be full of Soviet soldiers cut off from their units. From prisoners' statements, the Division Ia learned that a new Soviet rifle brigade and a tank brigade equipped with T-34s armed with a gun and a flamethrower had been on the attack since the day before, 26 November. The large number of flamethrower tanks, which struck terror in the hearts of the infantry, was thus understandable.

An enemy supported by flamethrower tanks was probably one of the most difficult things for the infantry to deal with. It demanded extraordinarily strong nerves and stamina, for the flamethrower tank's greatest effect was on morale. On the other hand they were very vulnerable and easily fell victim to short-range weapons and our own tanks.

A withdrawal to the E Line was ordered for the evening of November 27. This affected the right wing of the division in particular. The line ran: Vehkaya Trench – northeast part of Yekaterinovka – 100 metres along the road to the west – then northwest through the gorge south of Menshinka over Point 143.7–Shorokaya Trench and on to the west.

As far as combat was concerned, the next few days were uneventful, if one discounts the minor attacks by the enemy at various places along the front. On the left side of the division's sector, the Shirokaya Trench changed hands several times, before being lost to the enemy for good.

It was a lovely day. The excellent, sunny weather and the clear skies brought enemy aircraft. These caused a great fuss by strafing the front lines and bombing targets in the rear. The quadruple flak of the Panzer-Grenadier Division *Großdeutschland* shot down two Il-2 close-support aircraft.

A steady flow of reports concerning enemy attacks, incursions and counter-attacks provided the division command with further proof of the weakness of the units at the front. Each company, battalion and regiment formed a small reserve for the purpose of counterattacks; their sole purpose was the restoration of the situation in their respective sectors. These men were distinguished by their special fighting spirit, toughness and bravery; they were fighting teams that stuck together through everything and became pure close-combat specialists. Their weapons were submachine-guns, knives, spades, hand grenades, and their spirit. Without these tactical reserves, the shock units and assault platoons, the sector could not have been held.

The *Großdeutschland* armoured assault pioneers, who in the past weeks had likewise been employed mainly in an infantry role, were occasionally withdrawn from the front lines to carry out the duties for which they had been trained: erecting barricades, laying mines, digging tunnels and building positions in the rear, with the help of the available civilian population. There were virtually no pioneer officers left, almost all had become casualties.

Oberleutnant Krüger was the only officer still in command of his company. The commander of 1st Company, Oberleutnant Wurm, had just returned to the battalion after recovering from wounds and still walked with a limp. While laying mines he was caught in a Soviet mortar barrage and was fatally wounded in the head by shell fragments. Sergeants now led companies; they did so as a matter of course and were no worse than their predecessors.

The 5th of December brought the first snow. The eastern winter began, a season of great harshness in Russia.

On the same day the bulk of the division, except for six Panthers under Oberleutnant Giessen, began moving east to the army's right wing, approximately in the area of the 13th Panzer Division, where large concentrations of enemy forces had been observed. An attempt to break through the German lines was expected there; the army command hoped to meet this with the last available tanks scraped together from neighbouring units.

Thirty tanks were assembled in the 13th Panzer Division's sector: six from the 18th Panzer Division, fifteen Panzer IVs from the 13th Panzer Division and nine from *Großdeutschland*. In command of the GD panzers deployed there was Major Gomille. These saw their first action on 6 December.

Meanwhile, in the sector held by the Panzer-Grenadier Division *Großdeutschland*, the only available armour was the assault guns and Oberleutnant Giessen's six Panthers. The 6th of December brought numerous enemy assaults. Reserve Leutnant H. Schröder of the Assault Gun Battalion GD and his entire crew – Unteroffizier Christian Fleuchaus, Unteroffizier Wojciechowski and Gefreiter Wolfgang Klingenberg – were killed in the course of a counterattack.

During the night of December 7-8 new positions were occupied in the E-1 Line as a result of repeated enemy incursions against the panzer-fusiliers. This line followed the following path: Lyssa–Gorka–(settlement)–Vysocky–north of Sheltaya Gorge, from there due west, past Petrova-Dolina to the north. Quiet prevailed in these positions, apart from the usual enemy artillery and mortar fire, which fell on the foxholes throughout the day. The positions were improved through the building of bunkers, so that the men were at least given the opportunity to occasionally rest in a warm place.

Little out of the ordinary went on, apart from weak enemy advances, which were repelled, nightly harassment by enemy patrols and the usual artillery fire.

On the other hand the larger picture, especially to the west of the division's positions, seemed to be much more serious. The Soviets had gained further ground there, reaching the area of Alexandrovka, Snamenka and the Smela–Cherkassy railroad. Reports indicated that the Kirovograd–Krivoy Rog highway had already been cut; Kasanka was threatened. So the thoughts of the men were on the situation to the west of them. On the other hand word that the division was supposed to be moved to the Lemberg (Lvov) area to rest and refit gradually made its way to the front lines. The rumours said that the Ib, General Staff Major Müller-Eversbusch, had made preparations for the division's imminent departure on the fourth day of Advent, the 19th of December. However the soldiers were more than a little sceptical on account of broken promises in the past; their motto: We won't believe it until we're on the march! Nevertheless, advance detachments from the various units did depart in the direction of the Lvov – Ternopol area.

Christmas Eve 1943 saw the division in its old positions. The men had built themselves bunkers, laid down an almost continuous line of trenches, and here and there even organized a stove. All they wanted for Christmas was at least a few hours of rest. Packages and letters that had arrived in the past days were readied for delivery in the rear. The field kitchens cooked the best of what the country had to offer. Everyone was busy with the preparations, which were primarily for the men up front in the bunkers and foxholes.

At no time of the day or night was there peace and quiet in the forward positions. There was always something going on: friendly and hostile patrols were constantly active, seeking to learn the intentions of the opposition. Minor attacks at dawn or at dusk forced the defenders to constantly be on guard. The heavy weapons kept forward observers in the front lines, to allow them to react quickly when attack was imminent or preparations for an attack were detected. A radio operator belonging to 2nd Battery, I Battalion, Panzer-Artillery Regiment GD provided the following account of their actions, the brave forward artillery observers:

Christmas 1943 with 2nd Battery, Panzer-Artillery Regiment GD

'It was the evening of 23 December. Pitch-black night enveloped the end-lessly vast winter landscape of Russia. The sky was filled with glittering stars. I was sitting in a sleigh pulled by two small, shaggy ponies. The end-less expanse of Russia seemed to swallow up our tracks. I was on my way to the front, for the first time. A feeling of uncertainty had taken up residence in my young, eighteen-year-old heart, for I had no concept of war. Now and then one heard the dull roar of guns in the distance, and as a young man I saw the entire thing from a somewhat romantic point of view.

I had been assigned to 2nd Battery, I Battalion. None of my friends from my time in barracks was still with me. I was therefore alone, not only out-wardly, but also inside, for the comradeship in those many weeks in the bar-racks had been wonderful and I was sad that it was gone.

After a two-hour sleigh ride we reached our destination. I greeted my future comrades and soon we were getting along famously. I was to be used as a radio operator for a forward observer, and I didn't have to wait long. First, however, I had a chance to lie down and get some much-needed sleep. When I awoke it was already noon.

It was Christmas Eve day. The leader of the signals squad informed me that Wachtmeister Z. and I were to relieve our battery's forward observer up front with the infantry at dusk. I got ready to go, pulled on my snow suit and felt-lined boots, and as dusk fell we moved out. Loaded down with Christmas gifts from the battery, we tramped through the knee-deep snow in the dark toward the main line of resistance. Our progress was slow, as we repeatedly had to wade through snowdrifts in the darkness, but in an hour we reached our destination. We bade farewell to our relieved comrades. The Wachtmeister described the layout of the main line of resistance, at least as far as this was possible in the darkness. Then we settled into a small, two-man bunker, making it as Christmas-like as possible. The bare earth walls were bedecked with fir boughs and we lit several candles. A small iron stove crackled in the corner, giving the bunker a cosy warmth. There wasn't much talking, each of us was lost in his own thoughts, and the Wachtmeister even seemed to me to be somewhat depressed. He was much older than I and had a wife at home. But by the time this night was over I knew that there was something other than homesickness in his heart.

Soon it was my turn to stand watch in the trench.

It was Christmas Eve – silent, holy night. These thoughts filled my mind as I walked along the trench. It was as if fate had also allowed a silent, holy night to fall over the long front in the east, for all really was quiet, there and on the Russian side of the lines. Now and then a lone rifle shot split the night, or a red, green or white flare rose into the night sky and quickly extinguished itself. Every so often one heard a dull thump in the distance. My eyes strained to see anything on the enemy side. The strain was unnecessary, for there was no movement, so I could let myself dream a little. My thoughts built a bridge to home, to my relatives, to my two small sisters and to my father, who was also doing his duty as a soldier somewhere there in the east. From one of the grenadiers' bunkers came the old, familiar *Silent Night*. A slight feeling of homesickness crept into my breast, and I couldn't prevent my eyes from becoming moist. Why should I be ashamed? Homesickness was nothing to be embarrassed about. Anyway I was very proud that I was allowed to be there to stand guard for my fatherland. Soon I was relieved and walked back to our small bunker, where I got a couple of hours sleep.

So far 'going to war' had only had a romantic side for me, apart from the exertions and the bitter cold, but soon I was to learn better. I would soon discover how cruelly and pitilessly a war was fought, and what war really was, namely mass murder! Wachtmeister Z. shook me awake: 'The Russians are attacking, we need radio contact immediately.' All around us was one great inferno; a hail of heavy and light shells rained down on us. It was the first time I had experienced a bombardment. The disaster began to take its course before I could establish radio contact. A direct hit on our trench knocked me away from my set and threw me back against the wall of the bunker. I felt my face; nothing had happened to me, but my radio had been riddled by shrapnel. I crawled back out into the trench and asked Wachtmeister Z. if anything has happened to him. He replied that he was alright. His answers to my questions were brief and confused. As it was pitch black I couldn't see what had happened to him and I therefore asked him to come back to the bunker. There I saw the horror of war for the first time. He had been hit; his face and uniform were covered in blood. He had been struck in the head by a shell fragment and his brains were sticking out of his forehead. I laid him down as best I could, applied a bandage to his head and gave him a drink of schnapps. Then I crawled into the trench and called for a medic. But what I was doing was madness, for no one could hear me amid the crashing and bursting of shells. As it was only a side-trench, we had no direct contact with the grenadiers, and climbing out of the trench would have been sheer suicide. At first the Wachtmeister answered my questions, but soon he was completely unconscious. I was now alone and somewhat at a loss. What should I do? Had the Russians perhaps broken through? I couldn't possibly leave my Wachtmeister there alone. I would probably have been horrified had I known that at the same time not far from us the Russians had broken into our positions and killed a forward observer and his radio operator in the most brutal fashion. I now turned my attention to my radio set once again and in fact managed to get it working. I called the battery and told them what had happened. I received instructions to stay where I was; three men were being sent to recover the Wachtmeister. But hour after hour went by and no one came. Instead I received word that the three men had been forced to turn back several hundred metres short of our position by heavy enemy fire. I was told that I would have to wait until nightfall.

In the meantime I was afraid that the Wachtmeister would die in front of my eyes. However that was not the case. Our comrades came after dark and took him back on a sleigh. He was immediately flown to hospital, where he died several weeks later.

This was my baptism of fire. When this night and the following day were over my soul was torn and had grown older. I wasn't the same person I was 48 hours earlier when I sat in the sleigh and drove to the front. Nevertheless I remained a good soldier and did my duty until the bitter end of this war; I didn't desert spiritually either, I had just become another man overnight."

All of the men in the holes at the front, as well as those in the staffs and the command posts farther to the rear, wanted only one thing – a respite from the fighting. Apart from minor harassing fire Christmas Eve 1943 passed without incident. The heavily-laden commanders, company chiefs, platoon and squad leaders, went up to the front to cheer and encourage their men, but also to bring them small gifts, mail and parcels from home. The mail from loved ones at home was passed out, along with a handshake from the commander for every single soldier in the foxholes at the front somewhere near Vysocky or on the hills south of Nasarovka.

The senior NCOs, the mothers of the companies, were all on hand with their food trucks and NCO cooks, bringing the men the food and cakes that they had prepared with such love and skill.

There was emotion in the dirty, unshaven and tired faces of the soldiers when they saw all the work that had been done to bring a little beauty into this damned world.

Our hours of contemplation were numbered, however. On the first day of Christmas, 25 December, the Soviets set their sights on the town of Vysocky. They attacked with tanks and mounted infantry and forced their way into the town. The defenders counterattacked at once, supported magnificently by the tanks of the Panzer Regiment GD. The town was recaptured, but the Soviets attacked again and again. Vysocky changed hand five times, but at the end of the day it was in our hands. I Battalion of the Panzer-Artillery Regiment GD, with only six guns still in action, played a considerable part in this success. The brave forward observers were always there to direct fire on to the onrushing enemy, even though the situation seemed impossible.

Obergefreiter 'Ghandi" Canje of 13th Company, III Battalion, Panzer-Fusilier Regiment GD described this lonely struggle:

'On clear days I could see the Ivans assembling considerable numbers of tanks. I had a dark foreboding, for every night one could hear the tracks and engines of the tanks. Then the drunken Russkis bawled the *Internationale*. After dark we sent out a patrol to take a few prisoners. We knew that the Ivans were up to something. Things could get exciting.

I had been a squad leader for several days and the boys had fun making jokes about it. I had stood forward sentry duty for five days for one of them, because the danger of him falling asleep was too great. Hauptmann Frankenberg came on Christmas Eve and went from foxhole to foxhole handing out gifts. He also had several decorations to present and I was promoted to Unteroffizier retroactive to 1 December.

I said to the Hauptmann in proper Cologne dialect, 'Are you sure you haven't made a mistake?' (I was referring to the promotion.) He laughed heartily and declared, 'Don't worry Gandhi, go ahead and put on the braids!'

Then he passed on a greeting from Hauptmann Hassler, my old CO, who had recently come from II Battalion to III Battalion to inquire about me. I was extremely pleased to hear that 'Bubi' Hassler was asking about 'Ghandi,' the unit mascot.

I told my Leutnant, who was leading the company with 15 -20 men as a battle group on the right, that Ivan was up to something.

The first day of Christmas, 25 December, dawned with an eerie quiet and a heavy snowstorm. Then, suddenly, at about 04.00, death began drumming. The entire front was placed in an uproar. For several hours shells roared over our positions. As well as artillery, the Ivans fired mortars, anti-tank guns and Stalin Organs. Nothing remained intact. In my desperation I ran from foxhole to foxhole, checking on my squad. Those that hadn't run away or been killed waited patiently for what was to come. Then a battalion of female soldiers launched a direct attack against our positions.

In my distress I fired a series of flares: green/white/red. This was the sign that we were in serious trouble and required barrage fire from the artillery. I was a small island in the great flood.

Then I felt a heavy blow. I tried to wipe my nose with my right hand, and as I did so I saw that my right arm had been torn off and that there only a few bits of tattered flesh hanging down. My entire lower jaw was also shattered, one whole corner was gone. I dragged myself on with the last of my strength, for I was bleeding heavily. But gradually my blood-soaked clothing froze to my wounds and the bleeding slowed until it was just oozing out.

In this condition I took up my old machine-gun and fired into the attackers with my left hand. In my estimation it was an entire battalion. Finally I had used up all my ammunition; all I had left was a few hand grenades.

Lying in an empty hole, I now lost consciousness. I no longer felt any pain.

Now and then the severe cold woke me up. How long I lay there like that I don't know. All I know is that I suddenly heard a shout of 'Ghandi' and slowly came to again. Five or seven men had counterattacked with one of our tanks in order to rescue me. I knew that they found me covered in blood— and then the next eight days were darkness. I was operated on at the GD medical clearing station. Obergefreiter Kandt gave me a blood transfusion while I was unconscious. Then I was flown by Fieseler Storch to Nikolayev and from there to a hospital in Breslau.

I never saw the company again. Hauptfeldwebel Josef Henseler, who was then company commander, recommended me for the German Cross in Gold, which I received in hospital in Hanau on 20 October 1944. My record: 8 times wounded. Iron Cross, Second Class on 9.8.1942, Iron Cross, First Class on 14.11.1943, German Cross in Gold on 20.10.1944, Wound Badge in Gold on 6.6.1944.

That was my last day with the Panzer Division *Großdeutschland.*"

For forty-eight hours the Soviets tried to remove the corner post of Vysocky from the GD Panzer-Grenadier Division's front. Their efforts were frustrated by the bravery of the panzer-grenadiers and panzer-fusiliers deployed there, with frightful losses. After this failure they abandoned their plan and apparently went over to the defensive.

Two days later the enemy resumed their attacks. Most of these were crushed before they could get going and consequently the situation largely remained quiet.

Both sides patrolled actively in order to establish the precise location of the opposition's positions as well as to ascertain the enemy's intentions by bringing in prisoners for interrogation. There was more to these nocturnal patrols than one would commonly like to believe. They demanded the full participation of every man, including thorough preparations. Unteroffizier Berckholtz of 4th Company, I Battalion, Panzer-Grenadier Regiment GD, who led such a patrol on the night of 27 December, described what happened:

"Positions near Vysocky. At 23.00 I report as ordered with six men of my squad to the I Battalion command post. As patrol leader my mission is to learn the situation and strength of the enemy opposite our sector and if possible also bring back prisoners.

My people and I report to the company command post and leave our pay books and other papers there for reasons of security in the event we are captured. Then we set off, armed with submachine-guns and as many hand grenades as we can carry.

The snow eased up. We crossed our main line of resistance, with no noise and no talking. I knew the location of the minefields and we passed through unscathed.

After covering a stretch of about 400 metres we reached a hollow. The enemy fired off several red-yellow flares. Quick as lightning we threw ourselves into the snow and froze, only about 80 metres from the enemy position. I listened and observed what was happening in front of us. There was a great deal of vehicular traffic in the enemy's rear; we could plainly hear the Russian drivers cursing and urging on their charges. The *panye* horses were apparently having a hard time in the snow.

We crawled forward again a short distance. Once again they fired a flare. In its light we saw an enemy patrol of about 15 men to the side; it was moving toward our positions. We let the enemy patrol pass unhindered. Then we crept onward. There was nothing stirring in front of us; apparently we had come upon the boundary between two units, whose pickets were apparently rather thin. This fact encouraged me to advance another 200 metres, quietly and carefully.

We were now quite close to the Russian vehicles, for the shouting and grumbling now sounded quite close. Now we would go no farther; we stayed where we were and observed. I was able to ascertain that the enemy were unloading considerable quantities of ammunition and mines. The positions themselves appeared to be manned only by storm troops; for the time being the reserve troops were somewhat farther back. This suspicion was later confirmed by the prisoners we brought in.

As we withdrew carefully we heard individual shouts from the enemy side. We skirted the known foxholes and in doing so walked directly into another. There were two Soviets inside, one sleeping and the other dozing apathetically.

We had to act quickly. We cleaned out the nest without wasting many words, our pistols at the ready. The two Russians came out without offering any resistance, hands raised and knees shaking. We drove them back to our lines without further incident.

As we neared our positions I fired the agreed-upon signal, a star shell, to identify ourselves as a returning patrol. All the sentries in our sector had of course been informed of our operation, and so, happily and without losses, we returned to our company.

The most important thing was what the prisoners confirmed in their statements: namely that a major attack was being prepared over there, one which was to begin soon. As a result of this information we immediately initiated appropriate countermeasures."

The morning of 30 December brought another attack by the enemy, by a force of about 100 men. The assault was repulsed, however, with the help of the heavy weapons. The answer to the puzzle came to us over the enemy's loudspeakers that evening: they had expected the division to be relieved during the night of 29-30 December. The attack on the morning of 30 December was merely intended to ascertain the quality of their new opponent, but they were soon convinced that *Großdeutschland* was still there. It was interesting that the enemy had already been informed that the division was to be relieved. This led to all manner of speculation, especially on the part of the command posts.

The loudspeaker messages from the other side were worded as follows:

"No relief for GD. None of you will get out of here. Hell will break loose here in 24 hours!"

And in fact at about 21.00 on the last day of 1943 the soldiers heard hooting, shouting and roaring from the other side. That was a bad sign; in the opinion of the men in the foxholes the Soviets were getting drunk. Everyone was wide awake and tense. It was almost 22.00 when the first mortar round fell, the prelude to a ten-minute bombardment of our positions by guns of every calibre. Everyone fired illumination flares in order to see better, but no Russians came. Finally it was quiet again and it remained so until exactly 24.00.

Then someone shrewd found the key to this strange behaviour on the part of the Soviets: the bolsheviks were just saluting the New Year. For Soviet time was two hours ahead of the German; the barrage had thus taken place at exactly 24.00 according to their watch.

Exactly two hours later, at 24.00 German time, there was another powerful barrage, but this time one of our own – the German New Year's salute.

The new year arrived without further incident. However at first light on 1 January 1944 hostilities began anew near Vysocky with an intensity reminiscent of the previous days. The following account was provided by Leutnant Ruder, commander of 1st Company, I Battalion, Panzer-Grenadier Regiment GD:

"Those who experienced and first of all survived the battles in front of Vysocky at the end of 1943 and the beginning of 1944 will never forget this name for as long as they live. After the tough fighting withdrawal from the Dniepr, the division had dug in again in this area and refused to budge or yield no matter how hard the Russians tried to dislodge it. The sector's pivotal point was the village of Vysocky, or more accurately the positions in front of the village of Vysocky. Had the Russians succeeded in breaching and holding this line, the division's entire sector would have laid open before them, for from that commanding position they could see everything. At first the fusiliers held this sector, but by shortly after Christmas 1943 they were so reduced in number that they could not go on. A replacement had to be found.

That was I Grenadier Battalion, commanded by Major Remer. It still had a strength of about 100 men, a considerable fighting force at that time. The battalion consisted of two companies each with about 40 men and a battalion reserve of about 20 men. The latter stood by its armoured personnel carriers, ready to help wherever there was an emergency. I was then in command of 1st Company, while 2nd Company was led by Oberleutnant Willert. Both of us also had light infantry guns, mortars and 20mm flak; these were under our direct control and were positioned close to the front. Thanks to the wonderful cooperation with the crews of these weapons and the help provided us many times by the division's tanks and assault guns, we were never winded. They decided to place 1st Company in front of Vysocky. Until then I had been positioned left of Vysocky and had only sustained minor losses in spite of numerous attacks. We moved one night before Christmas with mixed feelings. The move went off without a hitch, for we made a great effort not to make any noise which might annoy Ivan. The new sector was about 1,500 metres long and had some crawl trenches, but otherwise only two-man holes in which to take cover from tanks. The platoon command post consisted of three small sections of trench, each of which was manned by four men. It was impossible to dig in any better. The ground was frozen hard and was covered with snow. The company's six machine- guns were distributed equally over the sector. On our first morning in the new sector the Russians greeted us with accurate mortar and anti-tank fire. I don't know whether they knew that it was us that they were honouring. There were minor attacks every day between Christmas and New Year.

These attacks were uncomfortable only because they were always preceded by heavy, and most of all accurate, anti-tank and mortar fire and took place in the early morning from out of the fog. The onrushing Russians were thus able to approach to within 20-30 metres before we could see and greet them. As well the Russians always sent penal companies, which were said to be forced to send us to the devil. Their stubbornness in the attack was unsurpassed. As a result they frequently broke into our positions. These incursions were always cleared up immediately thanks to the courage of every man. I was also lucky once again. My company's casualties stayed low, but we were all aware that things would get worse. The Russians were busy bringing up men and materiel and made no great effort to conceal this from us. They were obviously very confident.

On New Year's Eve loudspeaker propaganda replaced the gunfire and attacks. The lengthy harangue by the comrade was followed by German martial music. Then there was dead silence. I used the night to inspect my entire sector to the right, something I did every night. Although it was bitterly cold, in the morning there was the hated fog, which obscured our view of the ground favoured by the Ivans for their attacks. Everyone was feverishly tense. Suddenly, at about 06.00, there was a short but frightful bombardment. There was a direct hit straight away which killed four men, a painful loss. It was fortunate that none of the six machine-guns had been knocked out, for now white forms emerged from the fog. We scarcely believed our eyes. They came running towards our positions, man beside man, some even with arms linked. Our weapons opened fire at once. The machine-guns reaped a rich harvest. Thanks to their faultless fire the first wave was reduced to dead and wounded; but a second wave had already appeared, followed by a third. There were not as many, but they were just as stubborn. We couldn't destroy them all.

They broke into our lines at one of the platoon command posts. As ill luck would have it, it was the best-fortified and most difficult to reach command post. To cover the last thirty metres to it one had to cross open ground. It was impossible to determine the strength of the enemy force that had broken in. Ivan kept sending new people into the fight. As the visibility had meanwhile improved, they no longer charged wildly. Instead they worked their way very close to our positions by taking cover behind the dead and wounded, which was no less dangerous to us. Meanwhile the Russian anti-tank guns and mortars kept our holes under constant fire, in spite of the fact that they were also hitting their own people. The enemy incursion would have to be eliminated quickly or my entire sector would be threatened, but I had no men to spare. I therefore ran to the company command post, which lay just behind the main line of resistance, and succeeded in contacting the battalion. I asked Major Remer to send help as quickly as possible. But too late. The front had already begun to totter somewhere else and the reserves had been sent there. He had none left. Furthermore he was convinced that I could handle things myself. Strong language passed back and forth through the wire. The only choice left me was to help myself as quickly as possible or abandon the position in a hurry. My last reserve was my runner. I was determined to start a counterattack with him. The two of us therefore worked our way to within about 30 metres of the point of penetration. From there we could see an alarming number of Russian heads in the lost command post. The Russians had already spotted us and they began working us over, especially the troops moving up to attack. By means of hand signals I gave my people to understand that they should keep the Russians in front of us off our back.

They immediately opened fire, forcing the Russians to press their faces into the snow. I instructed my runner to stay where he was and give me covering fire. He was to come to my aid only in an extreme emergency. I would have to deal with the invading Russians alone. I jumped up, my submachine-gun at my hip, and began to run. At the same instant one of the Russians lobbed a grenade at me. I immediately took cover. The Ivan had given me a good idea. I had hand grenades too. I armed one, stood up and tossed it. Luckily it landed right in the middle of a cluster of Russians, who were waiting for me in secure cover. I immediately ran after my hand grenade and reached the point of penetration just as it exploded. The Russians had naturally laid flat, but they were already on their feet again, except for two who had been hit. I had my submachine-gun ready to fire from the hip, and I called out in Russian: 'Hands up!' Most of the Russians seemed ready to give up, but the one standing closest to me raised his rifle. I tried to shoot but nothing happened. My submachine-gun had failed me. I was done for.

The Russian had noticed that my weapon had jammed, it appeared I was lost. With the courage of desperation I struck the nearest Russian in the face with my submachine-gun. I made a mighty leap into the trench with the Russians, landing on one with my boots. I must have shouted and struck out desperately in my fury and desperation; in any case all I saw around me were raised hands. I had completely unnerved the Russians. They dropped their weapons. My runner, who now came to my aid, immediately set about disarming the enemy, while I armed myself with a loaded Russian submachine-gun. Finally we gave the Russians back their guns and brought them to my command post, but not before we put some men back into the recaptured section of the line. I had taken 10 Russians prisoner. Two had probably been killed by my hand grenade. Three light machine-guns, 4 submachine-guns and 5 rifles were found at the point of penetration, all of which we took to safety.

The Russians, too, must have witnessed and followed the whole drama. They showered us with furious mortar fire as we led the prisoners away.

They were almost successful. A small fragment struck me in the temple. Luckily it didn't have enough force to knock me down. I was able to carry on and bring the day to a successful conclusion. The Russians attacked the whole day and also tried at night with assault squads, but we held fast. Careful estimates placed the enemy's dead at 240 in front of my sector alone on this day. Unfortunately my company also lost many valuable and good comrades. Nevertheless we held this position for another five days without giving up a single foot of ground. However two days later we were in heavy fighting again."

Leutnant Ruder of 1st Company, I (APC) Battalion, Panzer- Grenadier Regiment GD was recommended for the Iron Cross, First Class by his commanding officer, Major Remer. His submission was accompanied by the following justification:

"Leutnant Ruder distinguished himself through a display of extraordinary courage on 1 January 1944, when the enemy attacked his company's sector with superior forces and broke into its positions. With only two men he raced forward from foxhole to foxhole, smoked the enemy out their foxholes with hand grenades and took nine prisoners in hand-to-hand combat. Leutnant Ruder swiftly reoccupied the main line of resistance and repelled all subsequent enemy attacks.

The defensive success achieved in this sector, which inflicted more than 60 dead and wounded on the enemy, and in the course of which 3 heavy machine-guns, 8 light machine-guns, 2 anti-tank rifles, 14 submachine-guns and 30 rifles were captured and brought to safety, was to a considerable degree due to the exemplary conduct of Leutnant Ruder."

signed Hoernlein   signed Remer, Major"

Farther to the right, however, immediately next to the right wing of the Panzer-Grenadier Division *Großdeutschland*, the enemy attacked the 16th Panzer-Grenadier Division with masses of tanks and infantry supported by extremely heavy artillery fire of every calibre. They broke into this unit's positions in spite of fearful losses and gained a considerable amount of ground. The right wing of the Panzer-Grenadier Division *Großdeutschland* held, but only as the result of an extremely strenuous effort. The division's alert platoons which were positioned there, including one from the Armoured Reconnaissance Battalion GD under Leutnant Heilmann, took heavy losses but were able to hang on. An enemy incursion against the panzer-fusiliers at Point 133.7 and the hillock dubbed the "heavenly breast" was largely eliminated with the help of Major Gomille's panzers. Leutnant Müller of the Panzer Regiment GD died a hero's death in this operation.

On the other hand, news reaching the division from other combat zones indicated that Zhitomir was already threatened by the enemy and that a major offensive operation by several panzer and panzer-grenadier divisions was supposed to start in that combat zone. The first withdrawal orders reached the Ia of the *Großdeutschland* Division during the evening. The division's positions were to be taken over by an infantry division. Tracked elements, including the panzers, were to depart immediately for the rear and

THE SOUTHERN FRONT
January 1944

DEFENSIVE BATTLES AT KIROVOGRAD
from February 7 to March 9, 1944

subsequently entrain in Pavlozoliye.

The scheduled relief of the *Großdeutschland* Division began on 3 January, after the situation on the right settled down and the 16th Panzer-Grenadier Division had successfully regained its former positions.

The first elements of the division to depart for the new area were the vehicles of the Armoured Reconnaissance Battalion GD, which assembled in Mereshino for this purpose. The other units of the division did the same, but all faced the problem of making their men, equipment and weapons mobile. The three-month retreat and the bottomless mud of the past weeks had finished off almost all of the remaining vehicles. As well the units lacked drivers, workshops and maintenance teams – and new vehicles had not yet arrived.

So the still-serviceable panzers teamed up with the guns of the artillery, the heavy flak's heavy tractors pulled trucks behind them, and the light tractors towed several field kitchens at a time. I Battalion, Panzer-Artillery Regiment GD had only two howitzers which had their permanent tractors, no motorcycles and practically no cars. Then there were the men, battle-fatigued, hollow-cheeked, their uniforms ripped and torn. The ranks had grown thin, many comrades were no longer there!

A lovely fire-brigade! "Princes in rags and tatters!"

So they assembled in and near Dynamo on the DG IV and from there went "on the road." Every vehicle, most with several others in tow, was to travel independently, as well and as quickly as it could.

The march route led through Kamenka, Bobrinets and Rovnoye into the area southwest of Kirovograd. After stopping briefly to assemble, the division was to continue in the direction of Uman. From there a major counterattack by the division and several German panzer and panzer-grenadier divisions was planned against General Vatutin's 1st Ukrainian Front, whose spearheads were engaged in a successful advance across the Uman– Vinnitsa line in the direction of the Bug. Headquarters, Eighth Army, which was in command, urged haste, for it was there that the danger was greatest.

The vehicles of the Panzer-Grenadier Division *Großdeutschland* were still skidding more than they were rolling in a westerly direction, on their way to Kirovograd, when southwest of the city an order diverted them towards the northeast.

The enemy had broken through on both sides of Kirovograd to the west and south; the Panzer-Grenadier Division *Großdeutschland* had to go there!

Part IV

FROM THE KIROVOGRAD AREA TO JASSY

5. 1. 1944 –	18. 1. 1944	Defensive battle for Kirovograd.
19. 1. 1944 –	6. 3. 1944	Static fighting on the Lower Dniepr.
7. 3. 1944 –	15. 3. 1944	Defensive battle north of Nikolayev and fighting withdrawal toward the Bug.
16. 3. 1944 –	26. 3. 1944	Employment in the rear area of Army Group South during the fighting withdrawal across the Bug and the Dnestr.
27. 3. 1944 –	25. 4. 1944	Defensive battles in Northern Bessarabia and in the foothills of the Carpathians.
26. 4. 1944 – 12. 5. 1944		Defensive battle on the Upper Moldau.
13. 5. 1944 – 19. 6. 1944		Static fighting in the area of Army Group South Ukraine.
2. 6. 1944 –	6. 6. 1944	Offensive battles north of Jassy.

CHAPTER 1

THE OVERALL SITUATION

In order to understand the change in orders for the deployment of Panzer-Grenadier Division *Großdeutschland* in the first days of January 1944, it is necessary to take a brief look back at events in the southern sector of the Eastern Front.

The following situation developed on the southern wing of the front roughly at the end of November 1943:

The German Sixth Army was holding the river line on the lower course of the Dniepr to a point halfway to Nikopol and as well was defending a small bridgehead in front of Nikopol against nineteen divisions and strong tank forces of the Soviet 4th Ukrainian Front under Soviet General Tolbukhin.

In the Dniepr Bend the sector held by the German First Panzer Army bent away from the river to the west and, as it stood then, the front ran from south of Zaporozhye to northwest of Krivoy Rog. The Soviet 3rd Ukrainian Front under Soviet General Malinovsky had been unable to breach the German front there.

The weak state of the German Eighth Army, which bordered the First Panzer Army, placed it in a critical situation. The continuous expansion of the Kremenchug bridgehead gave the 2nd Ukrainian Front under General

Konev a base of operations from which it could mass his armies undisturbed on the west bank of the Dniepr. It had also achieved a further crossing on both sides of Cherkassy, which in the end forced the Eighth Army to give up an almost 100-kilometre section of the Dniepr River and occupy new positions westwards.

In the area of the German Fourth Panzer Army the northward-facing positions ran from the Dniepr about 40 kilometres to the south past Kiev to the area northeast of Zhitomir. Farther to the north LIX Army Corps, though isolated, held the city of Korosten. Successful counterattacks in this area had initially halted the 1st Ukrainian Front under General Vatutin.

Without a doubt the German defence faced a threat of the first order in the gap between the left wing of the Fourth Panzer Army (northwest of Zhitomir) and the nearest fortified place, namely Korosten. Fears that something was brewing in the Kiev–Zhitomir area all too soon became fact, but the defenders could do nothing for lack of forces.

Beginning on 24 December 1943, the Soviet 1st Ukrainian Front, consisting of the 38th, 1st Guards and 1st Tank Armies, went to the attack west of Kiev on a broad front in the direction of Zhitomir. To the south, this main attack was expanded by the 40th Army south of Fastov.

Regroupings were undertaken on the northern wing of Army Group South in order to free up forces to avert an enemy breakthrough in the direction of Berdichev–Vinnitsa, for there were no reserves available.

On 31 December the picture revealed by the situation maps was of a breached front: there was no German resistance between Korosten and Zhitomir, while the northern wing of the Fourth Panzer Army was essentially holding due east of the Berdichev–Zhitomir road and XIII Army Corps was maintaining its positions around Zhitomir facing east and north.

North of Shashkov, the southern Soviet spearhead was advancing steadily toward Uman, in order to reach the rear of the German First Panzer Army which was holding farther to the east.

III Panzer Corps, with the yet to arrive Panzer-Grenadier Division *Großdeutschland*, was supposed to counter these dangerous enemy movements from the Uman area.

In the early days of January 1944 there were clear signs that the enemy intended to attack the Eighth Army's eastern front. The 2nd Ukrainian Front under General Konev was massing its forces, with the obvious intention of breaking through to the west on both sides of Kirovograd and linking up in the Uman–Permovaysk area with the 1st Ukrainian Front, which was attacking from the north. If this plan succeeded, the Eighth Army would face a similar fate to that which befell the old Sixth Army at Stalingrad.

Ground, signals and air reconnaissance identified the Soviet 5th Guards Army and the 5th Guards Tank Army making preparations east of Kirovograd and the Soviet 53rd Army north of the city.

CHAPTER 2

THE DEFENSIVE BATTLE FOR KIROVOGRAD

The Panzer-Grenadier Division *Großdeutschland*, which had been on the march west in the direction of Uman since its relief northeast of Krivoy Rog on 4 January 1944, was stopped on 5 January because of the enemy attacks on both sides of Kirovograd. Its units were assembled for deployment south of the enemy's point of main effort, roughly in the Rovnoye–Bobrinets area.

The two focal points which General Konev was about to form were obvious at the very start of the Soviet offensive, which began with barrage fire on 5 January: the armies of the 2nd Ukrainian Front did not attack the city of Kirovograd itself, instead they strove to break through north and south of the city, with the intention of linking up later to form a pocket.

The Soviets set off on their expected encirclement of the city with their superior armoured forces on 6 January. The German side did succeed in tying up strong enemy elements on the screening front through offensive action; but the Soviet 7th Mechanized Corps could not be prevented from crossing the Ingul River near Severinka and cutting the major road from Kirovograd to the west. The same thing happened south of the city, where Soviet forces drove toward the Ingul river line and sought to cross. The situation there that day was still completely unclear. The Panzer-Grenadier Division GD, which was being brought up as army group reserve, was supposed to close the gaps and thus create a continuous defensive front. The defenders anxiously awaited its arrival.

The 6th of January 1944 saw the Armoured Reconnaissance Battalion GD, the first of the division's unit to be relieved near Krivoy Rog, striving to reach its quartering area of Semenastoye, about 15 km. northeast of Rovnoye, in minus 10 degree temperatures and over ice-covered roads. Three armoured patrols had been under way for hours; they were to reconnoitre the situation on both sides of Kirovograd. Their reports showed that the enemy was already in towns and villages that had been designated as jumping-off points for the Panzer-Grenadier Division GD. For example, Novo Petrovka, about 8 kilometres southwest of Kirovograd, was occupied by the enemy. Further enemy movements to the southwest were observed in the river valley between Novo Pavlovka and Chervonniy. There was no sign of German troops.

A further patrol, which was scouting to the north, was able to make contact with friendly troops. The third patrol, which had been sent toward the villages of Anninska-Fedorovka, Marovka and Susnova, reported these occupied or about to be occupied by the Soviets with no apparent resistance. The greatest danger therefore lay southeast of DG IV, and it was apparent that the main body of the division would see action in the Sugokleya Valley.

The leading battle group, consisting of elements of the panzer- fusiliers, armoured assault pioneers and elements of the Panzer-Artillery Regiment GD, was diverted toward the villages of Rasdolya and Kompaneyevka while on the move during the night of 6-7 January, in order to seize its quarters and future assembly areas. This came off relatively smoothly, for a surprised enemy was scarcely capable of standing up to a determined group of men.

Meanwhile further elements of the division, in particular I (APC) Battalion, Panzer-Grenadier Regiment GD, followed closely by I Battalion, Panzer-Artillery Regiment GD, moved past and sent a group of half-tracked APCs ahead to scout toward Losovatka, which was also being approached from the northeast by enemy spearheads. First contact with the enemy occurred at daybreak. There was thick fog. Major Remer, with only a handful of men of his battalion and one field howitzer, quickly regrouped and launched an attack. He and his men were soon in the midst of the enemy; there was shooting everywhere – visibility was limited.

Following the motto: We are weak, therefore we'll just have to make ourselves strong!, they soon formed a circle and then drove round and round, firing to all sides. By blazing away with all guns, this tactic soon gained them some breathing room.

Meanwhile the remaining guns of I Battalion, Panzer-Artillery Regiment GD arrived and went into firing position. II Battalion, Panzer-Grenadier Regiment GD also hobbled toward the scene in its vehicles. During the night of 7-8 January both battalions set out through Losovatka toward Anninska, which soon went up in flames. The enemy were so surprised that they hastily withdrew into the ravines near the village of Muchartovka. Before the night was over the remaining houses were cleared of the enemy and positions were occupied.

In the meantime elements of the Armoured Reconnaissance Battalion GD, together with the attached 286th Assault Gun Battalion and the 934th Artillery Battalion, occupied the villages of Fedoseyevka and Chervonovershka. Their orders were to hold there until the attack on Fedorovka via Fedoseyevka by the panzer- fusiliers (planned for 8 January) began to take effect.

By the evening of 7 January it was already evident that an initial, strong-point-style of defensive line had been created as the result of the occupation of a line from Kompaneyevka through Rasdolya and Chervonovershka to Losovatka and Anninska which, although weak in forces, became the first barrier standing in the way of the enemy forces coming from the northeast. The division did everything it could to bring up the heavy weapons, and especially the armoured elements, as quickly as possible. Only the enemy's spearheads had arrived so far; the main force was still to come.

The division's plan was to move its positions as far forward of the river line on the hills in the Fedorovka–Anninska area east of Karlovka as possible, in order to meet the expected enemy armour in flat, open terrain. For this reason, on 8 January the panzer-fusiliers attacked Fedorovka via Fedoseyevka. After being relieved by their comrades of II Battalion in and around Anninska, the panzer-grenadiers of I Battalion, riding in their half-tracked APCs and supported by assault guns, resumed their attack on Muchartovka.

This attack was supposed to close the gap between Fedorovka and Anninska.

But the division command was also especially interested in the situation west of highway DG IV, or roughly the Karlovka-Veseliy area, especially since at first it was not clear where the enemy was and where there were still friendly troops. Once again it was the Armoured Reconnaissance Battalion GD which sent patrols to scout the situation. They soon reported that the bulk of the enemy's armoured forces was approaching.

The information provided by patrols on that 8 January revealed the following picture: twenty-two enemy tanks were fast approaching Point 202.2, due southeast of Karlovka, on the road from the north. This group of tanks halted briefly two kilometres south of this point, left four tanks there and rolled into the Sugokleya Valley to Karlovka with the bulk of the tanks and mounted infantry. The remaining villages northeast of Karlovka were reported occupied by the enemy by the Grau armoured patrol.

A further twelve enemy tanks were sighted in various villages.

In spite of unfavourable weather conditions and an occupied village in its path, Grau's armoured patrol was able to move deep into the enemy's rear. Driving along the railroad tracks, about 3 kilometres west of Kirovograd the patrol made contact with the 14th Armoured Reconnaissance Battalion (of the 14th Panzer Division), which was surrounded near Lelekovka. The latter unit intended to break out along the rail line, supported by tanks from the west. Presently it was being supplied from the air.

Danger point number one was the village of Karlovka and the road from Kirovograd to the south toward Losovatka, on the left wing of II Battalion, Panzer-Grenadier Regiment GD.

With some of its men riding on assault guns, on the morning of 8 January, I (APC) Battalion, Panzer-Grenadier Regiment GD attacked east toward the enemy-occupied village of Muchartovka and was able to fight its way in. Soon afterward there came alarming calls for help from II Battalion, which was being hard pressed in front of Anninska. The assault guns subsequently departed Muchartovka. The Soviets noticed this and drove into the village again with tanks and infantry. The few panzer-grenadiers of I (APC) Battalion tried desperately to hold. Orders were issued for them to fall back to avoid being cut off, and the panzer- grenadiers had to fight their way back. Tanks and assault guns arrived and, after regrouping, the battalion once again set out to attack the village. This time they took Muchartovka and hung on, eliminating the flanking threat to II Battalion, Panzer-Grenadier Regiment GD near Anninska.

However, our forces were simply too weak to hold both places. The Soviets began infiltrating back into Muchartovka as darkness fell; the sound of tanks was heard.

II Battalion, Panzer-Grenadier Regiment GD's struggle to maintain its positions on both sides of Anninska, especially to the east of the village, was a difficult one. It received capable support from anti-aircraft troops of the Army Flak Battalion GD, which engaged the enemy tanks at long range.

At this time Hauptmann Ruppersberg, the commander of 4th Battery, Army

Flak Battalion GD, was ordered to take command of 2nd (Heavy) Battery. He was an officer who was keen for action; tough, but fair to his men, valued by his superiors, not one for spit and polish, but a very brave soldier. Ruppersberg died a hero's death on the afternoon of 8 January 1944 on the road near Losovatka, due south of Anninska. Leutnant Haarhaus of the Army Flak Battalion GD described what happened:

'On this 8th of January Wachtmeister Rath received orders from Hauptmann Ruppersberg to go into position on the road near Losovatka with a flak combat team consisting of the 88mm guns 'Anton' and 'Berta.' From there, at 09.00 the combat team was led by the battery commander into positions which he had scouted himself. Unteroffizier Gierok took over 'Anton' and positioned it left of the road about 2,500 metres northeast of Losovatka. By 09.30 both guns were ready to fire.

Scarcely had the combat team oriented itself as to the immediate situation, when a Focke-Wulf 189 dropped a smoke shell near gun 'Anton' with the following message:

'About 15 enemy tanks with mounted infantry approaching on same road.'

Unteroffizier Gierok took the message and gave it to Major Remer, who had just pulled up on the road alongside the guns. He wished Hauptmann Ruppersberg good hunting.

Several minutes later the first four T-34s with mounted infantry appeared to the right of the road. While our infantry withdrew in the face of the beginning tank fire and took cover behind our flak artillery, both anti-aircraft guns opened fire on the enemy T-34s. Range was about 2,000 metres. The T-34s returned fire and very soon obtained a hit on 'Berta,' which smashed the left side outrigger and wounded the gunner. Meanwhile 'Anton,' under the command of Unteroffizier Gierok, scored three hits on a T-34 sitting to the right of the road. Heavy smoke poured from the enemy tank, which was disabled, and the crew fled.

Shot after shot raced from the barrel in the direction of the enemy, who turned away and disappeared behind the hill at top speed.

A fresh supply of ammunition had just been delivered, when another group of enemy tanks, seven this time, appeared on the hill. They approached rapidly under constant fire from our 88mm guns. In spite of the enemy's great numerical superiority, the gun crews accepted the unequal battle, ignoring the crashing and bursting of enemy tank shells.

'Anton' took a direct hit on its armour shield. The gunner was slightly injured. The gun crew nevertheless continued working and destroyed another T-34 with the next shot; but 'Anton' was hit repeatedly, until it was unusable and had to cease firing. Half of the gun crew was seriously wounded.

Hauptmann Ruppenberg, who had so far been with the 'Anton' gun, now went to 'Berta,' which was still firing. The next shot was another direct hit on the turret of an enemy tank. Pouring smoke, it sought to escape.

A change of targets was ordered, and after two more shots another T-34 had been destroyed. 'Berta' then took three hits, but these were ineffective.

Yet another T-34 was destroyed with two shots. The muzzle flash of a further T-34 was spotted on the hill. 'Berta' took aim and fired; but at the same instant there was another flash on the hill and a shell from the T-34 struck the gun's pedestal. This gun, too, was now out of action; most of the crew were severely wounded.

Hauptmann Ruppersberg, who was just talking to I Battalion, Panzer-Grenadier Regiment GD by telephone, was also badly wounded and died in a few minutes. All those still living were evacuated immediately and taken to the rear.

These were the last hours of this outstanding officer, who was posthumously awarded the German Cross in Gold. He received special mention in an order of the day issued on 14 January 1944:

'Hauptmann Ruppenberg fell as the leader of this battle group, which destroyed five enemy tanks, a shining example of the flak artillery of the *Großdeutschland* Division, which is always ready for action. He will live on in the division as an example of a heroic fighter.'

In the meantime the remaining tanks of the Panzer Regiment GD had detrained and were on their way into the area south of Fedorovka. Apart from the armoured groups under Oberleutnant Bayer (Panzer VI) and Oberleutnant Fischer (Panzer IV), which were already in action, there were at that time six operational panzers. The weather was icy cold; minus fifteen degree temperatures made the journey more difficult for the motorized elements being moved up for the attack scheduled for 10 January. It was planned that the Panzer Regiment GD, together with I (APC) Battalion, Panzer-Grenadier Regiment GD and elements of the Armoured Reconnaissance Battalion GD, under the command of Oberst Büsing and supported by the artillery of the Panzer-Artillery Regiment GD, would advance from the southeast toward Hill 191.1 north of Karlovka and the hill country southeast of Stary Danzig and occupy these, thus blocking the Sugokleya Valley; but most important of all, the main road from Kirovograd south to Losovatka, over which the Soviets were moving up their reinforcements, was to be cut.

The situation on the division's left wing was becoming even more threatening. At about 10.00 on the morning of 9 January, armoured patrols reported that enemy tanks had entered Konstantinovka and Dymino, about 12 kilometres southwest of Karlovka. They were thus abreast the panzer-grenadiers' regimental command post located in Losovatka. The only thing that was unclear was the actual location of the front line of the 14th Panzer Division, which was presumed to be in that area. Several patrols from the division's armoured reconnaissance battalion were sent to determine this. Meanwhile the Volkswagen-equipped units of the Armoured Reconnaissance Battalion GD took up position on the hills near Point 227.2, northwest of Semenastoye, facing the two enemy-occupied villages.

During the evening of 9 January the Grau armoured patrol reported sighting the most forward pickets of the 376th Infantry Division near Blagodatnaya, west of Gruskoye. Contact was finally made with the 14th Panzer Division, eliminating the uncertainty as to the situation on the left. After the breakout by its remaining units, the 14th Panzer Division planned to occupy positions near Veselye and Antonovka in cooperation with the 376th Infantry Division. The *Großdeutschland* Division command felt it important to close off the Sugokleya Valley and place a roadblock in front of the steady flow of new enemy units. Then, in conjunction with the 14th Panzer Division, they would finally be able to establish a continuous position.

During the night of 9 January, 1944, at about 23.00, the tanks of "Battle Group Büsing" moved off against Point 191.1, but they were halted by heavy flanking fire from Karlovka about 800 metres southeast of the village. The tanks adopted a hedgehog position there for the night. Bright moonlight illuminated the battlefield and made the task of the Soviets defending Karlovka much easier. Nevertheless, this first advance forced the Soviets to withdraw their spearheads, which had already advanced as far as Ivanovka. However the objective of the German attack remained the high ground near Karlovka and the blocking of the Sugokleya Valley.

Early on 10 January, German Stuka units approached; their primary targets were the enemy concentrations in the valley and the village of Karlovka itself. "Battle Group Büsing," accompanied by several APCs and seventeen (!) pioneers, subsequently set out again at lunchtime, this time against the village itself. Under heavy enemy fire it managed to penetrate several hundred metres into the village. However, because of the size and shape of the village (two by two kilometres) the attackers achieved only a limited success. By evening they were forced to abandon their gains.

After a brief regrouping, at about 17.00 the panzers and the few pioneers set off again, and this time they managed to drive 300-400 metres into the village of Karlovka. Losses were heavy. The attack force set up a hedgehog position, where it assembled and regrouped. At about 22.00, summoning all its strength, the battle group struck out once again. Several enemy tanks were destroyed; the courageous battle group forged ahead in fierce hand-to-hand and house-to-house fighting. The southeast part of Karlovka remained in German hands; nevertheless the hills offered a good view and the German-held part of the town drew concentrated fire.

It wasn't until about noon on 12 January that an order from division released the remaining elements from their exposed position in Karlovka and directed them back to their departure point. New positions on Hill 215.1 were to be occupied and improved. Together with the remaining handful of pioneers, who rode in APCs, at 06.00 the tanks that were still serviceable withdrew toward Point 215.1 and to Nasaryevka, where they were relieved that night by elements of the Panzer-Grenadier Regiment GD. The commander of the 2nd (APC) Squadron, Leutnant "Poldi" Beckmann, lost his life during the mopping-up operations near Karlovka on 12 January. He and all the other men of every rank had accomplished what must be considered a miracle: they broke the attacking strength of the 2nd Ukrainian Front under General Konev in its initial phase with only a relatively minor loss of territory.

Thirty-one Soviet rifle divisions from three armies and tank forces of the 5th Guards Tank Army were halted by the fire of German units ready to make the ultimate sacrifice. The Soviets did not achieve the desired breakthrough and the subsequent encirclement of the German Eighth Army. The defensive success southwest of Kirovograd also inflicted such losses on the Soviets that they remained quiet for the next few weeks and were forced to grant the German defenders a pause to catch their breath. It was only due to this circumstance that it was possible to stabilize the front.

The 14th Panzer Division was supposed to insert itself on the left side of the Panzer-Grenadier Division GD's positions and establish a continuous link to the 376th Infantry Division near Blagodatnaya. The insertion south of Karlovka of a newly-formed battle group under the command of the CO of the Armoured Reconnaissance Battalion GD, together with elements of the Armoured Assault Pioneer Battalion GD, a battery of the Panzer-Artillery Regiment GD and the Division Escort Company under Oberleutnant von Kameke, further strengthened the defences at the most threatened point, the Sugokleya Valley. Contact was established with the battle group's neighbours on the left, elements of the 14th Panzer Division; but in general things remained quiet, except for enemy movements before the front, which oddly enough were headed east, where the enemy apparently intended to form a new point of main effort.

On 16 January I Battalion, 26th Panzer Battalion, a Panther unit under the command of Major Glaesgen, arrived in the division area and was assigned to the Panzer Regiment GD, providing welcome reinforcement.

There was now also time to improve the positions at the front as well as those farther to the rear, the latter were primarily the responsibility of the train units, with the pioneers lending their support and advice. The bulk of the work went into creating three defensive lines – designated A, B and C – and laying down positions on both sides of Permovaysk along the Bug River line. The object of these efforts was to shore up the defences in preparation for the expected offensive by the Soviets. For the overall situation was more threatening than ever, especially farther to the northwest.

On 12 January, 1944 the 1st Ukrainian Front under General Vatutin advanced as far as Sarny on the lower course of the Sluch River; some elements even crossed the river and advanced on Shepetovka. The whole force of the Soviet advance struck the northern wing of Army Group South, held by the Fourth Panzer Army. There were no noteworthy reserves; it therefore remained doubtful whether this Soviet breakthrough, which had split the German eastern front in two, could be headed off and stopped. Energetic counterattacks at first halted attempts by the Soviets to sever the army group's vital links to the west, which saw them extend their attacks to the south toward Progrebishche and Shashkov.

There was no stopping the enemy forces from continuing their advance on Lutsk and Rovno, however, which resulted in a constant lengthening of the German front to the northwest. In this way the German forces there were stretched to the limits of possibility.

It must be remembered that the German Sixth Army was still on the Lower Dniepr near Nikopol, the most easterly point on the Eastern Front. The reason for stubbornly hanging on to this sector was the manganese mines near Nikopol. It was a personal order from Hitler, although tactically the salient in the front was untenable.

The entire southern part of the Eastern Front formed a diagonal line running from the southeast to the northwest, and given the weakness of the forces manning it there was little chance of it withstanding another major assault by the enemy. Orders were therefore issued for the trains and other non-mobile elements of the division to transfer to a new area west of the Bug. Only the combat echelons and the most important support units remained with the fighting forces. It was still quiet on their front; they had the impression that the Soviets were harbouring no new offensive intentions there.

To allow for the formation of reserves and to provide the 14th Panzer Division with a brief rest, the left wing of the Panzer-Grenadier Regiment GD's sector was lengthened by several kilometres and taken over by the Panzer-Fusilier Regiment GD, which had been relieved by elements of Corps Group A farther to the right. There was now direct contact on the left with the 376th Infantry Division. The main line of resistance held by the Panzer-Grenadier Division *Großdeutschland* was now 16,000 metres long and encompassed the villages of Antonovka and Veselye.

The Panzer Regiment GD now had more than 90 serviceable tanks, including those of the newly-assigned I Battalion, 26th Panzer Regiment. This potent force placed the division in the position of being able to stop several enemy attacks. The batteries of the Panzer-Artillery Regiment GD had carried out adjustment fire in their new zones of fire and had established focal points for the concentration of fire on designated points. These zones of fire were indicated on the division's maps.

The 27th of January, 1944 was a special date for all the members of the Panzer-Grenadier Division *Großdeutschland*: it was on that day that Generalleutnant Hoernlein, the division's popular commanding officer, was relieved after leading the division for two-and-a-half years. He had probably served longer with the unit without a break than anyone else. He had helped form the division and make it what it was. The Panzer-Grenadier Division GD was spoken of with great respect on the Eastern Front; it was also spoken of only in connection with its long-time division commander, who had shared the unit's fate in all circumstances and placed his stamp upon the division. Hoernlein was an exemplary front-line soldier, whose energy, strength, circumspection and unwillingness to yield to the enemy and to superior offices – which placed excessive demands on his forces – made him not only a superior officer who enjoyed the unreserved admiration of his men, but a universally-liked friend and comrade as well.

Rumours surfaced to explain his departure. One claimed that the Generalleutnant had sent a telegram to Führer Headquarters from Krivoy Rog, which said: "Is GD the only unit left on the Eastern Front? — Hoernlein!" Others tried to connect his departure with a dispute with the commander of the Panzer Regiment GD, Oberst Graf von Strachwitz. Whether true or not, every member of the unit was sure that their "Papa" Hoernlein had been with the division longer than anyone else and had shared its most difficult hours with them.

The final order of the day issued by Generalleutnant Hoernlein reflected his total solidarity with his men:

Panzer-Grenadier Division   Division Command Post,
GROSSDEUTSCHLAND   26.1.1944

My comrades!

"The Führer had transferred me away from the division to other duties.

For two-and-a-half years I have had the honour of leading first the *Großdeutschland* Regiment then the *Großdeutschland* Division. In this time the name *Großdeutschland* has become such a part of me that my departure comes as a heavy blow. I have endeavoured to combine in the division old Prussian military tradition with the ideas of the Führer. I have strived to make the division a unit whose inner strength and performance should not be exceeded by any other!

You have all followed me in this effort in exemplary comradeship and have shown that you are conscious of the obligation that goes with wearing our cuff title.

May the division continue on this road, always improve further, become even stronger internally and outwardly be the model for the German front-line forces. We owe this to the homeland, to the Führer and to our dead comrades.

I respectfully honour the many comrades who took their difficult path with natural, death-defying courage and whose sacrifice obliges us to end this war victoriously.

> But we the living should always look forward! The future will and must belong to us!

signed Hoernlein"

Generalleutnant Hasso von Manteuffel, previously the commander of the 7th Panzer Division, succeeded Hoernlein. At Targul Frumos and at Jassy he would soon have an opportunity to prove himself as the division commander.

On 5 February 1944, Major Frantz, long-time commander of the Assault Gun Battalion GD, left his battalion to join the general staff. No successor had yet been chosen. Oberleutnant Steffani, commander of 1st Battery, initially took over the battalion from Major Frantz, who had begun as a platoon leader with the GD in France and became an especially capable leader. His well-considered battle plans enabled him to achieve the maximum success with minimal losses. His troops loved him for his concern and his admirable energy. Frantz had exuded an atmosphere of confidence in countless crises. His independent decisions, which often decided the outcome of a battle, and his great personal bravery brought him the Knight's Cross with Oak Leaves.

On 27 January the majority of the Panzer Regiment GD, as well as the attached I Battalion, 26th Panzer Regiment, was temporarily attached to the 11th Panzer Division in the Cherkassy combat zone. The unit suffered heavy losses in the heavy fighting there, which lasted until 8 February. On 28 January Major Glaesgen, commanding officer of I Battalion, 26th Panzer

Regiment, was fatally wounded near Yesufovka while standing in his turret. Hauptmann Lemmer, the Panzer Regiment GD's senior company commander, was killed in action the same day. The well-proven Hauptmann Wallroth also died a hero's death far from his own unit in those early days of February. Many division members were wounded seriously, including Unteroffiziere Beller and Schelper. In spite of the very heavy losses inflicted on the Soviets and the outstanding success of the GD panzers, the sacrifice of these men on a, for them, foreign battlefield remains an especially painful memory.

CHAPTER 3

ON THE LOWER DNIEPR

Even though the lines in the division's sector were very weakly manned there was no danger at first. The Soviets dug in even deeper, laid extensive minefields and in general remained decidedly quiet. The units of the Panzer-Grenadier Division deployed at the front were in turn relieved for a day and sent to the rear to rest. A steady flow of replacements allowed company strengths to be brought up to an average level. In some cases units that had been merged were reorganized. For example, the surviving elements of III Battalion, Panzer-Grenadier Regiment GD, the majority of which were assigned to II Battalion, were released and a new III Battalion was formed.

The potential battlefield lay beneath deep snow; day after day the men had to dig out their foxholes, the gunners had to shovel the snow away from their guns, the trucks had to make their way through the snow-covered countryside. No decrease in watchfulness was possible in the front lines; every hour of the day and night the eyes of the men in the listening posts and machine-gun crews stared into no-man's-land. The endless monotony in the tiny, cold holes exhausted the men and now and then caused them to become stupefied. Everyone thought only of taking a rest and getting a good night's sleep.

In the rear areas things returned to normal: field kitchens and train units occupied fixed quarters, munitions and equipment were stockpiled in dumps, the pace of things achieved its daily routine. This rear-area activity was guarded by the Eastern Front fighters in their foxholes, small bunkers and slit trenches. 7th Company, Panzer-Fusilier Regiment GD was manning the positions southwest of Kirovograd on the rail line from there to the southwest. A member of the company described the sameness of the next few weeks in the open country east of Nikolayevka:

10 February 1944

"We've been in this awful place for weeks now! Chains of hills, broad slopes, between them a rail line with a sunken rail bed in places and a raised embankment in others; just as you like, but not a tree, not a house, just a puny thicket here and there.

We live in holes in the ground, some straw in one corner, a few boards over it. This has been our quarters for weeks.

It was a good thing that we at least dug our holes in the ground before the frost came. Yesterday two of our men were snatched from the position right beside the railway embankment. A sentry who was standing on the embankment only ten metres away saw nothing. In any case high grass and tall nettles made it easy to approach that spot by night.

12 February 1944

The nocturnal theft of two of our people had its consequences: we got a new company commander. Finally he came up front, placed his things in a corner by the tiny window, sought a place for himself to sleep in the other corner, chatted for a while and then went out with the runner to go to the positions.

15 February 1944

Heavy snowstorm since early today, can barely see 20 metres. As the food is being passed out freezing figures come in, all of whom want to get warm. All our things are wet; and now blowing snow and frost as well. Unteroffizier Rybak is wounded; he stays with us to get warm until the vehicle arrives with the food.

From 01.00 to 04.50 we wander from hole to hole, offering a few words of encouragement to the poor chaps, that is to say the old man talks to them, I just listen. At his urging shields are put up everywhere at night and small fires made behind them. With the blowing snow the Ivans don't bother us, and we can at least warm our food and thaw out the bread.

We return at about 04.30. At 05.00 battalion advises that there are Russians roaming about in our rear. The Company H.Q. Squad is given permission to go after them; the old man goes with us to search the area in question. Rather hopeless in view of the blowing snow. Well at least we tried.

18 February 1944

Out with the old man again; this time there are four of us. 'Combat patrol,' said the old man, 'everyone else as they are.'

Strongpoints are set up outside – a group of eight to nine men, with machine-guns, at least an NCO, good shield, a fire behind it and everyone gathered around it – with the exception of a sentry.

Boy, that's what they call the front now! A little fire every 300-400 metres, around it a few bundled-up figures! We caught a sentry sleeping in spite of the snowstorm, while the others sat behind their wall by the fire, unsuspecting. Court martial? Dereliction of duty in the face of the enemy? No, the old man gave him a smack and woke him up. We found that to be in order. Our four-man patrol came close to seeing action: two men were missing from the last squad. All that we can find out is that they didn't come back this evening.

Finally the chief learned where they had their foxholes – on the far right wing. The old man led us there: there was a foxhole, one could just make it out in the snow; but otherwise not a trace, no signs that the two are alive.

'They're gone!' someone said. 'Nonsense,' shouted the old man. 'Someone go in and dig out the snow!'

What should I say, the two of them were lying there, almost one on top of the other, their heads exposed beneath a few boards. The rest of the hole was completely snowed over, they were asleep!

It could easily have been their last sleep...

19 February 1944

The storm had abated somewhat. The chief reported to the rear that in his opinion something was going on in a cornfield farther to the right, opposite the second company in that direction. There had been noticeable changes in the appearance of the terrain.

The battalion opened fire on the cornfield briefly with its heavy weapons; we received its thanks. In the evening we had to send a patrol to the front. Finally, we succeeded in finding five men who were at least half-alive, who were capable of carrying out the patrol.

The chief and I went with them some distance and then took cover, ready to intervene if necessary. I don't know how long we lay there. Then the chief became uneasy and we set out to look for our patrol. We stumbled about in the darkness and the snow for a while but found nothing; we lay down again and listened to the front.

Finally we headed back. We were approaching a hollow when the old man froze. He dropped to his knees and fingered his submachine-gun. Then he crawled forward and waved. 'This isn't a very good place for us,' he whispered.

We had in fact landed among the Ivans and had stumbled onto an anti-tank rifle, but our Russian brothers had abandoned it and taken off.

20 February 1944

Weather better again. The disappearance of H. has cleared itself up. The poor fellow found a bunker on his way to the rear, laid down and went to sleep there – and froze to death.

At night the usual rounds of the positions. In the evening the Hauptfeldwebel comes with the food and rations. We're to be moved to the rear for three day's rest – praise God.

22 February 1944

We have bathed and are feeling rather chipper. The previous night's march to the rear seems like a grey shadow. Thanks to the dugout we of the company headquarters squad survived the snowstorm relatively well, but our comrades in the foxholes up front! After a kilometre the chief turned to us and had us halt; the column had fallen apart behind the company headquarters squad.

We had to go to the end of the company, and after marching another few hundred metres we all had a chum under our arm, helping him along. After the sixth kilometre every third man had to be helped by two others, and more and more were falling behind. Our chief was like a sheepdog watching over his flock.

We stopped and rested while standing. Onward, then a standing rest and then onward again. After the eighth kilometre there were men who could only be driven on by brute force, and still there was nowhere to take shelter. We had to keep moving. Once the old man said, 'Anyone who lies down is finished.' We had to keep plodding forward, the quarters had to be there somewhere. Lying down meant freezing. The old man kept urging the men on, now at the front, then at the rear, shuffling through the ice-crusted muck like the rest of us. We were just as exhausted as the others.

It took us more than 12 hours to cover the twelve kilometres. In the last 2,000 metres the senior NCO and some men from the train came out and helped carry the last of the men. Finally the first of the village cottages appeared. The chief stood and watched as the senior NCO literally shoved the lads into their quarters. That was our march to rest quarters.

28 February 1944

We were back in our positions, only this time to the left of the railway embankment. Sunday had ended badly. Three members of the company headquarters squad had volunteered to join a patrol. The old man was unsatisfied with this and he organized the affair himself. We went into the gorge which ran diagonally across the front in the direction of the Ivans. I fell out after 500 metres to provide cover from the left with a machine-gun. The chief and Weiß fell out after another 500 metres.

The remaining five members of the patrol then covered the remaining 600-800 metres alone. While our men lay to the left and right of the path in the snow, a Russian sergeant making his rounds plodded right past them. They let him pass, for their objective was to clear the bunker itself.

But there was a sentry. He opened fire and ran away. S. chased the sentry, while St. entered the bunker. A submachine-gun roared and Loges was fatally wounded. After this incident the whole thing fell apart and only S. and Fritz came back. The old man was very depressed over the death of Loges, who had often accompanied him, but also on account of St., whom he thought very highly of. We were lying there, waiting for the patrol to return, when suddenly shots and hand grenades shattered the silence. Dawn was already in the sky when we finally ran back down the slope to our own lines, less three men!

Körner returned from battalion yesterday at his own request to take Loge's place. This evening he is already dead. During the nightly rounds he and Fiss were standing with the chief by one of the holes, talking to those inside. The night was pitch-dark – from somewhere a single shot – Körner dead, Fiss wounded in the arm by the same bullet. Even in a quiet position time never passed without some action and without sacrifices; but in other sectors the Soviets had already broken into the German positions. Throwing them out again meant a return to action and fresh sacrifices.

Leutnant Munske, III Battalion, Panzer-Fusilier Regiment GD

February 1944

'Somewhere between Krivoy Rog and Kirovograd the fusiliers squat in their foxholes. Somewhere there is also Leutnant Munske's company command post. The Leutnant has been leading the company for fourteen days. The young soldiers see the older, stronger man as an example and model.

Many know where he came from and what he was before the war. They cling to their company commander with special enthusiasm. He is one of those fortunate men who, through their mere presence, radiate calm and security, and whom others follow blindly.

Some time earlier a hill was lost in III Battalion, Panzer- Fusilier Regiment's sector. One day there was a direct hit by an anti-tank shell on the battalion command post, which wounded the battalion commander and caused other casualties. Afterward the regiment issued the following order: the hill lying in the Munske Company's sector is to be recaptured, depriving the enemy of his observation point.

Munske Company command post. Squatting around the company commander are a few of the company's remaining NCOs. Munske informs them of the order from regiment. As they begin to grumble, he says in his calm voice, 'Children, I know what you're saying. Ivan has been able to dig in undisturbed for days, has placed barbed wire, the regiment knows this too. But if they still give us the order to take the thing, then that's just what we'll do. Somehow we'll do it.' In spite of this the mood remains depressed; a few jokes by Munske have no effect. They know that prior to many attacks the veteran front-line soldier has a feeling that all will go well. Before others there is the feeling of imminent disaster. That's how it is this time. The men sitting around their officer are battle-tested NCOs; they know what's what, and the debate shifts from for or against to how they should proceed. The company is only 35 men strong, and not everyone can be pulled out of the line. The attack plan is laid down as follows: surprise attack after dusk falls, roll up the trenches right and left, breakthrough to the hill by the Leutnant and two squads.

The Leutnant's laugh accompanies the NCOs on their way to the foxholes, but he himself is not so confident. For an hour he sits and scans the terrain, committing the route to memory. His eyes repeatedly come back to that damned ridge. The Russian positions are visible against it as grey flecks. The officer's face becomes concerned, the facade of optimism it wears falls away. The whole thing looks bad!

16.30. In the grey light of dusk forms move here and there through the terrain, whose extensive openness is filled with more and more shadows. Slowly and carefully the twenty men chosen for the mission feel their way toward the most forward Russian position. 50 meters from the Russian wire the Leutnant whispers instructions and they all move slowly toward the wire. Suddenly flames shoot up somewhere among the men, cries ring out – the Russians stir. The soldiers lay flat. The word 'mines' is whispered through the ranks.

From atop the hill bursts of machine-gun fire sweep the terrain, somewhere a mortar coughs. More whispering: 'two men dead, three wounded.' Then the mortar rounds started dropping. They are aimed at random, but the Russians are awake, surprise is lost. 'Back,' orders the Leutnant. The men fall back with the dead and wounded, while Munske and two men cover their retreat.

An hour later the Leutnant is sitting at the telephone talking to regiment:

'Yes, the attack failed, Herr Oberst, two dead and three wounded, one man wounded on the way back. The area in front of the wire is mined, several machine-guns, probably an observation post for mortars – and at least one anti-tank gun somewhere else!' The voice at the other end of the line croaks for a while; the Leutnant says 'jawohl' hangs up the receiver in resignation. He briefs the company headquarters squad leader: 'The same again. A squad of pioneers to clear the mines, three assault guns for the attack. They will be sent during the night. Attack tomorrow morning.'

The new plan is revealed as the food is being issued. Troops are assigned to guard the pioneers as they work to clear the mines and a new plan is made. The Leutnant grabs a few hours sleep, while the leader of the H.Q Squad briefs the pioneers. He is rudely awakened by rattling tracks and roaring engines outside. The assault guns! The door opens. A man wearing an assault gun uniform pushes his way into the dimly-lit room, the officer's cord gleams on his cap. 'Leutnant Döhn, leader of the assault guns assigned to you,' he says into the darkness. 'Man – Sigi – it's you!' Munske jumps to his feet. Two old comrades clap each other on the shoulder and shake hands. In peacetime one had succeeded the other. 'Man, in peacetime, how long ago was that, and now you come blowing in here!' They laugh, sit down in the corner and talk of another time until duty calls. The assault guns' mission: drive over the Russian main line of resistance with infantry riding on their vehicles, drop off the infantry just short of the hill and provide the assault with supporting fire. Into the debate comes a question from Leutnant Döhn.

'What do they have for anti-tank weapons over there?' They tell him that there is at least one anti-tank gun, but that its exact position is not known. Based on the terrain and the position of the enemy, Döhn considers the attack hopeless; his battery leaves the decision to him—after all armoured vehicles are difficult to replace. The fusilier regiment insists on the attack. 'Very well then, we'll go too,' says Döhn.

05.00. The fusiliers climb onto the three assault guns, the motors roar and the guns move off. From the open hatches the faces of the driver and commander peer into the night, which is dimly lit by stars. As well a light mist is forming. Munske squats on Döhn's assault gun and shouts instructions into the ear of his friend, who passes them to the driver via the intercom. The assault guns roll through no-man's-land, the hatches are closed, there is the lane through the mines. Shadows spring up, give directions, climb onto the assault guns. There are the forward enemy trenches! The roaring engines propel the assault guns over them. The handful of pioneers fall out to the left and right to cover the advance.

The tracks of the armoured vehicles clatter on the rising slope, the roaring of the engines rises in intensity. The assault guns slowly push their way up the hill with the fusiliers lying flat on their steel backs. The first bursts of machine-gun fire strike the flanks of the assault guns, the first aimed fire. 'Get down,' shouts the Leutnant. Still 100 metres to the ridge, but now there is fire coming in from all sides! The eyes of the assault gun commanders peer into the half light; seeing anything through the vision slits and optical devices in this light is out of the question. 'Aim at the glow of the fire,' orders Döhn. The assault guns fire a few shots; it doesn't make much sense. At least the enemy has the noise of the tracks and engines to aim with, we have nothing. Anti-tank shells and mortar rounds fall all around the assault guns, and bursts of machine-gun fire continue to strike their sides. Outside the handful of fusiliers attack. They move up between the assault guns, working their way toward the positions, dropping, getting up and running, dropping and getting up again.

The assault guns try to escape the fire coming from the anti-tank guns by moving forward and backward. In the leading gun Döhn has his eye clamped to the optical sight. He desperately wants everything to go well, but he can't obtain a proper target. There is Munske, another dash, ten metres to the second trench. Then tracer from a burst of machine-gun fire dances into one of the Leutnant's dashes. The two men beside him fall, then he throws his arms into the air. The bursts of fire continue and there is no more movement. 'Horst!' screams Döhn, as if the lifeless form up ahead could hear him. There is a crash, all too familiar – steel against steel. Döhn opens the hatch cover part way; the gun on the left has begun to burn, direct hit by an anti-tank gun! The Leutnant shouts out above the raging defensive fire, 'Back!' Then he opens the hatch all the way, gets out and goes over to the other assault gun.

The wounded gun commander is rolling on the ground. Döhn drags him over to the assault gun, which is falling back slowly. Two or three fusiliers appear, likewise dragging someone between them. Up onto the assault gun! Another wounded man is picked up. The few surviving fusiliers assemble behind the two assault guns that are still firing. Damn, where is the lane? There, the gap, held open by the pioneers.

Up on the ridge the defensive fire still rages. Its a good thing visibility was so poor or none of the assault guns would have come back. There are at least two or three anti-tank guns firing as well as mortars and machine-guns, and now artillery shells are falling on the area in front of the slope.

Leutnant Döhn leans over the entry hatch and directs his driver through the gap and back. Only two assault guns are coming back. Somewhere out there the lifeless body of the Leutnant lies among his fusiliers, somewhere flames lick against metal that was once an assault gun. Somewhere lie comrades you won't see again. Horst, thinks the Leutnant, Horst. He clenches his teeth and somewhere inside it hurts. His eyes continue to stare into the twilight. Are they burning just from staring?"

CHAPTER 4

Führer-Begleit-Bataillon with Army Group North
("Battle Group Bohrend" – FBB)

The German eastern front had been set in motion. The Soviets, since the end of 1943 constantly on the attack at various places on the southern German front, saw their chance everywhere and attacked from other, previously quiet points elsewhere on the front in an attempt to break through to the west.

Far to the north, Army Group North had been in fixed positions for more than two years. These extended from the Leningrad area across the Volkhov and Lake Ilmen and through Staraya Russa and Kholm to Nevel. The German Eighteenth Army had been forced to give up the close encirclement of Leningrad's southern front in January 1943 when it lost Schlüsselburg; the Sixteenth Army had voluntarily evacuated the salient around Demyansk, which it had held for more than a year, in February 1943 and now occupied stronger positions in front of Staraya Russa.

The relative quiet on Army Group North's front and the contrasting months-long, heavy pressure on the other two army groups had in recent months led to the withdrawal of thirteen divisions from the quiet northern front. When, at the end of December 1943, the Soviet 1st Baltic Front launched its breakthrough attempt against the German Third Panzer Army near Vitebsk, the Sixteenth Army was forced to give up two further divisions to shore up the front, further weakening Army Group North.

In the meantime the Soviets had assembled new reinforcements in the Oranienbaum bridgehead, on the Gulf of Finland and near Leningrad. It subsequently went to the attack on 14 January 1944, initially to break the siege of Leningrad and establish contact with the Oranienbaum bridgehead. This succeeded on 19 January in spite of a stubborn German defence. One day later an avenue to Oranienbaum was established, which left sufficient room to undertake new attack preparations. The Soviets scarcely stood still; they continued their operations to the west in an attempt to capture the land bridge on both sides of Narva.

On 18 January, soon after the beginning of the Soviet offensive from Leningrad and Oranienbaum, the Soviets attacked northeast from their bridgehead near Novgorod, north of Lake Ilmen, with the objective of taking the German Eighteenth Army and elements of the Sixteenth Army in the flank. After offering stubborn resistance, the German static divisions were finally forced to give in to the Soviet pressure and withdraw.

By 30 January the Soviet spearheads had broken into Yamburg on the lower course of the Luga, and from there they set out to break through towards the land bridge on both sides of Narva which, although fortified, was now almost devoid of troops. They succeeded in driving a wedge across the Narva River south of the city in a single thrust, threatening the German supply route.

It was on or about 5 February when this dangerous situation in the north led Führer Headquarters to form a battle group from the fully-equipped Führer Escort Battalion and send it to Army Group North as reinforcements for the Narva Front. At this point in time some elements of the FBB were conducting battle exercises at the Arys troop training grounds, while other elements were carrying out their guard duties at the Wolfsschanze installation. Additional elements of the battalion, units not on guard duty and the heavy companies, were in the Hindenburg Barracks.

The town of Arys was a lively place on the evening of 5 February; the soldiers had been issued passes. The alert order caught them totally unprepared. The movie theatres were alerted by telephone; motorcycle patrols raced through the narrow streets and called the soldiers with the cuff title back to their quarters. The barracks were soon the scene of hectic activity. Vehicles were made ready beneath the retractable roofs, weapons were issued, ammunition belts were filled and placed in boxes. And in the tiny rooms soldiers stowed their meagre belongings in their kit bags. The last man finally arrived at about 23.35.

The same thing was happening in Rastenburg, where elements of the new battle group were making preparations. Slowly the battle group began to take shape; its initial composition was:

> 2 rifle companies
>
> 1 heavy company
>
> 1 panzer company

> elements of the Führer Flak Battalion with:
>> four 88mm guns
>>
>> four 37mm flak
>>
>> six to eight 20mm guns on self-propelled carriages
>
> as well there was a signals unit with 3 field telephone and
>> 2 radio troops.

All in all, the battle group was equivalent to a potent battalion, command of which was assumed by Hauptmann Böhrend.

Further officers included:

> Oberleutnant Maletzki, commander of an armoured rifle company.
> Leutnant Freiherr von Knipsen, commander of the panzer company, with three platoons of Panzer IVs and one platoon of assault guns.
> Hauptmann Druckenbrodt, commander of the mixed flak battery.

The first transport trains departed during the night of 6 February and rolled without stopping through Tilsit and through Lithuania, Latvia and Estonia in the direction of Narva. The city itself could no longer be reached by rail, and the cars were unloaded on an open stretch of track in Weiware. It was 9 February. The vehicles had scarcely driven off the rail cars when the armoured personnel carriers set out for the battle group's assembly area. Its orders were to relieve a battalion of the *Feldnerrnhalle* Division. The Soviets opened fire with mortars as the battle group was taking over the positions; Unteroffizier Lucht became the first member of "Battle Group Böhrend" to be wounded. A few days later the commander of a rifle company, Oberleutnant Maletzki, was killed, the first of the unit's soldiers to die in action. The mission given "Battle Group Böhrend" was to screen the Kotlajärvi–Narva–Hungerburg communications road to the south and to simultaneously prevent any attempt by the enemy to break through across the Narva toward the station at Auvere.

The situation was as follows: SS-Corps Steiner, which was holding positions near the city of Narva and near Hungerburg, was under heavy pressure from the east. At the same time, however, west of the Narva the Soviets were attacking from the south in an attempt to sever the east-west communications road from Kotlajärvi through Auvere to Narva. The main objective of these enemy attacks was the railroad station at Auvere. Positioned there, with its front facing south, from Narva to approximately in front of Auvere, was the *Feldherrnhalle* Division. Beside it to the west was the 61st Infantry Division. "Battle Group Böhrend" was deployed right between the two divisions to guard the "seam" between the two units.

Extremely heavy fighting developed in the difficult terrain, part of which was swampy ground covered with brush and small trees. The anti-aircraft weapons commanded by Hauptmann Druckenbrodt proved tremendously effective. One rifle company was surrounded for an entire day. It managed to fight its way back to the German lines, but lost almost all its equipment and numerous men who were listed as missing.

Following a brief rest period in Jervi (Jöhvi) the battle group, together with elements of the *Feldherrnhalle* Division and the 61st Infantry Division, were placed under the command of the newly-formed "Battle Group Graf Strachwitz." This formation was led by Oberst Graf von Strachwitz, who had achieved such outstanding success in 1943 as commander of the Panzer Regiment GD. In March 1944 the FBB battle group took part in the successful armoured attacks by the Strachwitz group to clean up the situation south of Auvere. Numerous enemy tanks were destroyed, and the situation at Narva was returned to normal for the time being. Strachwitz was awarded the Diamonds to the Knight's Cross for his outstanding leadership and the great success achieved by the forces under his command.

Leutnant Famula, commander of a platoon in the Führer Escort Battalion's panzer company, distinguished himself in these battles and received the Knight's Cross. He was killed in action there several days later.

With the onset of the muddy period in the latter half of April, "Battle Group Böhrend," now under the command of Hauptmann Francois following the severe wounding of Hauptmann Böhrend in the early days of the battle, moved to the coast of the Gulf of Finland to counter repeated landing attempts by the Soviets. In about mid-May the battle group was relieved and released to return to Führer Headquarters; the first elements arrived in Rastenburg on 18 May.

The experience gained from the deployment of "Battle Group Böhrend," which was created at short notice as a result of the emergency situation at Narva, and its later success as part of Graf Strachwitz's armoured battle group led to the formation of a combat regiment. As per an order from Hitler, this reinforced regiment was only to be used at focal points.

The necessary preparations for the reorganization of the Führer Escort Battalion, which was to form the basis of the new regiment, got under way. Plans for the organization of the regiment were drawn up, requests for personnel were sent to Cottbus, for materiel and weapons to the OKH's Chief of Army Equipment, all with the notation: "Führer Order."

However these preparations, which were being pushed ahead in July 1944, were soon to experience an unexpected interruption.

CHAPTER 5

Großdeutschland in the South of the Eastern Front

The deceptive quiet in the Panzer-Grenadier Division GD's main line of resistance southwest of Kirovograd lasted from February until the first days of March 1944. A premature muddy period was heralded by rising temperatures, the melting of snow and the thawing of the frozen ground. Foxholes and bunkers drowned in ground water, the felt-lined boots of the sentries were wet and became uncomfortable; the fires behind the screens were often visible; fog lay over the Ukrainian soil more than ever.

During these weeks a reorganization of both of the division's regiments took place, made necessary by the low combat strengths of the companies. The heavy companies and the machine-gun companies were also amalgamated into one company. Designations reappeared which the men remembered fondly from earlier times: the proud "Sixth" had its name back, the name that had brought it fame far beyond the division under its former commander, Hauptmann von Courbiere.

Beginning in the early days of March, on or about the 3rd, there were distressing signs opposite the GD's front. Increased firing activity by the enemy suggested that something was under way over there. Intelligence confirmed the arrival of at least five Soviet rifle divisions in front of the Panzer-Grenadier Division GD's front alone; as well there were the corresponding enemy armoured units.

It was the latter that the soldiers in the foxholes heard the most of: the increased rumbling and roaring of tanks. The nightly shouts of Soviet soldiers directing traffic and the commands barked by whip-wielding *panye* drivers confirmed that ammunition was being moved to the front. The Soviets were making preparations, massing forces for a new attack.

The state of nervousness reached its climax on the 7th of March. All indications were that a major attack was to be expected in the next 24 hours.

In the peasant shack occupied by the Division Ia, General Staff Oberstleutnant von Natzmer, and in that of the 1st Operations Officer, Oberleutnant Graf Carmer, the field telephones rang almost without interruption. The LdN, head of the intelligence service, came in repeatedly with teletype messages, radio messages and notes intercepted by the Armoured Signals Battalion's field telephone and radio stations. Then the Ic, Hauptmann Ritter, came in again, armed with a large map filled with red entries representing the enemy build-up. Here too, in the brain of the division command, everything was focused on expected coming events.

Oberst Büsing, commander of the Panzer Regiment GD, was aware of the weakness of their defensive lines, especially in the left sector manned by the panzer-grenadiers. The areas astride the road from Kirovograd to Rovnoye and in the Sugokleya Valley near Karlovka had to be seen as probable focal points of enemy attacks. Therefore, on the evening of 7 March the CO of the panzer regiment issued the following order: "Everyone get ready! Command panzer and the entire combat echelon stand by for action on both sides of the road in the grenadiers' sector." The time had come, it was beginning here too. The Soviets had already begun their offensive near Proskurov and Shepetovka and on both sides of Uman.

At about 04.30 on 8 March a barrage of seldom-seen intensity began falling on the division's entire sector, also ranging to a depth of almost 12 kilometres. Shells of every calibre fell from the most forward foxhole to the command posts and woke every last man from his sleep. Everyone was immediately in position; the GD artillery initially bombarded its zones of fire, until it began receiving more precise target information from its forward observers. The panzers started their engines and waited for orders. But where was the enemy's point of main effort? Where would he appear en masse? Where would he attempt to break through?

Major Büsing drove to the southeast exit from Losovatka with his radio and command tanks, where he established contact with Oberst Lorenz, commander of the Panzer-Grenadier Regiment GD. Bad news had begun coming in from his sector, especially from the battle zones of II and III Battalions. Oberst Büsing stood with his company commanders and gave them their first mission orders. The enemy had obviously spotted the panzers, and his mortar and artillery fire, which was falling uncomfortably close to the tanks, continued to grow in intensity.

The platoon and company commanders squatted behind one of the tanks, maps on their knees, and listened to the words of the regimental commander. The signals officer was writing down radio messages on a note pad when a heavy shower of mortar rounds fell nearby. Instinctively everyone took cover, mud flew high in the air. Leutnant Eppke collapsed in the turret of his tank – dead. Oberst Büsing lay on his back, blood pouring from his forehead. The firing went on. An emergency dressing was applied and then Büsing was placed on a tank, which slowly made its way between the cascading fountains of earth toward the rear. Hauptmann von Wietersheim was summoned by radio to take command of the panzers. Oberst Büsing died at the Rovnoye medical clearing station at about 11.00 on 8 March, without ever regaining consciousness. Meanwhile the panzers rolled into the panzer-grenadiers' sector and engaged the onrushing Soviets.

The mass of the Soviet infantry discharged like a torrent into the boundary between the two regiments, III Battalion, Panzer- Grenadier Regiment GD on the right and II Battalion, Panzer-Fusilier Regiment GD on the left. They soon broke into Antonovka and Veselye, their initial objectives. The German heavy machine-guns and mortars fired everything they had, sustained fire; hundreds of Soviet soldiers were cut down. But thousands more followed; they drove past their fallen comrades south into the ravines and gorges which were so difficult to watch over. Shells from the artillery, infantry guns and anti-aircraft weapons exploded amid the brown-clad masses.

But it wasn't enough. Enemy tanks appeared and slowly pushed their way forward over the torn and shattered earth. The discharges of the tank cannon and assault guns, of the anti-tank guns and 88mm flak, merged into the din of battle; the man in his hole held on and fought for himself. Some men now ran away from this inferno created by the heavy weapons.

In the artillery firing positions, some of which unfortunately lay in front of a stream, the gun crews prepared for close defence. The sound of battle could be heard now, and lone enemy tanks appeared damned close to them; the gunners stared at their range-finders, which indicated that the shortest firing range for the howitzers was 1,800 metres. At lesser ranges they would have to fire over open sights, but the ranges were still in excess of that, they could still employ aimed fire.

Farther to the left, a change of position proved the undoing of the Panzer-Artillery Regiment GD. The enemy tanks and the attacking Soviet infantry arrived too soon: the bulk of the guns fell into enemy hands in close combat or had to be blown up. I Battalion sustained especially heavy losses.

The individual groups of infantry fought bitterly to hold their strongpoints; others were forced to fall back and occupy new positions. The weight of Soviet infantry simply crushed them. In the midst of this chaos they sought to make contact with the rear, assembled into small groups and clung to some significant point, a railway embankment, the edge of a ravine, near an anti-aircraft gun or in the vicinity of the assault guns or tanks. Many men had given up, their leaders dead or missing. They were unable to find their own people – all was confusion. Leutnant Wunnecke, commander of the 6th Panzer-Grenadier Company, was killed by mortar fire; Oberfeldwebel Heppes assumed command of what remained of the company. Somewhere on the railway embankment east of Nikolayevka 6th Panzer-Fusilier Company was strewn to the winds by the Soviet onslaught. Not until dusk did a few men meet up again. The pioneers also suffered bloody losses in the same area, and only scattered groups were able to reassemble that evening.

Here once again it was the heavy weapons which joined forces with individual groups of infantry to offer resistance. The 37mm flak on self-propelled chassis repeatedly sallied forth and poured their shells into the masses of attacking bolsheviks. They held their positions stubbornly and tried to halt the enemy's advance for at least a few hours. Or a lone 75mm anti-tank gun, its trails spread, sat in the cover of a row of trees and fired shell after shell into the oncoming enemy infantry. A squad rallied round it, a small group of panzer-grenadiers or the remnants of a panzer-fusilier platoon.

Not until dusk, with the arrival of darkness, did the sound of battle slowly die down. The din subsided. Only now and then did the sound of combat flare up again, machine-guns and submachine-guns hammering away in the falling darkness. Here and there figures rose up and dragged other wounded to the rear between them, or bent over crumpled forms lying on the ground and felt for signs of life. Parachute flares hissed into the sky, to be followed by streams of tracer arcing to the east like strings of pearls. The sharp crack of a tank cannon echoed over a ravine and disappeared in the distance.

The first day of the defensive effort southwest of Kirovograd was over. The enemy had penetrated deep into our positions; the weight of his attacks had strewn entire companies to the four winds and inflicted severe wounds. Yet, he hadn't broken through, his attack was still under our control. Anovka, Veselye, Kurlyugino, Point 200.9, Point 200.1 and Point 200.2 had been lost and were in enemy hands. The deepest incursion was about 5,000 metres deep.

The 9th of March saw the Soviets resume their attack at first light. In the ravines tank after tank streamed toward the positions held by the panzer-grenadiers and panzer-fusiliers, whose ranks had become much thinner. Heavy-calibre weapons hammered the positions; their shells ploughed up the earth. Von Wietersheim's and Major Gomille's armoured groups and the assault guns drove here and there to counter the enemy's armoured spear-heads. The crash of tank cannon repeatedly rang out over the battlefield, and fires and explosions were evidence of successes on both sides.

The enemy managed to break into Dymino. The panzer-grenadiers farther to the northeast were forced to give up their positions, and the village of Chervonye ultimately had to be evacuated by II Panzer-Grenadier Battalion. By lunchtime heavy fighting was raging in Yelisavetivka (Konstantinovka) and Ivanovka; the advancing Soviets could be seen from the division command post. Farther northwest Nikolayevka was lost in spite of a stubborn defence by the panzer-fusiliers. There, too, the evacuation of positions which until now had been held so steadfastly began. Movement came to our lines, interrupted only by counterattacks and local advances which created breath-ing spaces here and there.

Looming over everything, however, was the overall situation, which out of necessity had a great influence on the orders and movements of the Panzer-Grenadier Division *Großdeutschland*. Uman had fallen victim to the enemy offensive; the Soviets were on the march to the southwest, threatening the supply lines of the German units much farther to the east and forcing the German command to make fresh decisions. Once again there was a threat of envelopment and encirclement from the northwest, making all plans for the defense of the Bug River line senseless, as it was likely that the Soviets would cross the river before German forces could move into position to defend it.

Under the impression of this dangerous situation in the southern sector, orders were issued to German units in the southwest and farther to the east to fall back to a shortened defensive line, which initially was to run in a north-south direction roughly along the Bug and Prut River lines.

In this desperate situation everything depended on getting the German units still on the lower Dniepr out before the Soviets broke through south of Uman. This could only succeed if a durable front was established quickly as far to the north as possible. As well, it was vital that the enemy's southward advance be halted for good far to the west, north of Kishinev or north of Jassy at the latest.

Other units, those still on hand or brought from the Reich in the meantime, would have to intercept and halt the enemy armies which were advancing westwards north of Uman.

The 10th of March again saw extremely heavy defensive fighting by the units of the GD; these actions were already of a mobile nature. More than 43 enemy tanks were put out of action or destroyed. By evening the continuous Soviet pressure north of Ivanovka and along D.G. IV resulted in a breakthrough into open country. Every hill was fought over. Heavy house and street fighting took place in the villages. From the hills and observation posts the defenders could see column after enemy column advancing southwest. Meanwhile in the division's rear areas preparations continued for the transfer of the non-mobile combat elements, the damaged vehicles and workshops. With increasing haste these elements were sent west or assembled at entraining stations south of Rovnoye. The order was given to relocate all mobile elements of the division west of the Bug to Rumania.

The division's combat elements themselves had orders to fall back to a new line: on the evening of 11 March to the A-Line and later to the designated B- and C-Lines. Ongoing counterattacks allowed the division to throw out groups of Soviets that had penetrated the lines and thus maintain cohesion in its own ranks.

Route and departure reconnaissance was the responsibility of the Ia-March, the division officer responsible for the march movements. The march route was to the southwest, probably via Rovnoye and Novo Ukrainka, then west. Signs were posted to mark two march roads, on which the bridges were checked for load-bearing capacity.

Headquarters, Armoured Reconnaissance Battalion GD received orders to depart with the remaining elements of the battalion and scout the division's future rest area. As well the task fell to the battalion commander, as battle commander of the Eighth Army, to watch over the Bug River crossing near Miglya, about 8 kilometres southwest of Permovaysk. A battle group under the command of Rittmeister Schroedter, about 200 men strong, remained as a mobile reserve with III Battalion, Panzer-Fusilier Regiment GD under Major von Basse.

The enemy pressure lessened over the next few days, probably on account of the bottomless mud, but also because of the terrible losses the Soviets had taken and the transfer of their main effort to other sectors, which was undoubtedly connected to their heavy losses. As a result the division's planned movements were carried out smoothly. The B-Line was occupied during the night of 12 March. Only in the right-hand sector was there renewed enemy activity on 13 March.

The picture in the division's rear areas was a disconsolate one in those days: train units of every kind streaming toward the rear; vehicles creeping along, badly in need of repairs, trucks carrying kübelwagens; gun tractors with other wheeled vehicles in tow; among them *panye* wagons and herds of cattle, with military police as herdsmen. There were military and state police in questionable uniforms, captured vehicles, some of American origin, like Fords and Studebakers and many other types, barely still roadworthy. It was a really disconsolate sight.

The railroad station at Pomoshnya was doomed to death but still functioning. There the crippled vehicles were loaded aboard trains. All the while pioneers could be seen placing explosives. The huge station building itself towered over everything. It too was to be blown up in the coming days.

Finally, on 14 March, orders were issued for the elements deployed at the front to leave their positions as quickly as possible and march to their new areas. At this time the front line was still near Pechenaya, southeast of Point 227.6 in Sakarevka and farther to the northwest near Grusha and Shevchenko.

The Panzer-Grenadier Division GD's accomplishments in this battle zone were lauded in the Wehrmacht communique of 14 March 1944:

"In the southern sector of the Eastern Front, where a bitter struggle is being played out amid bottomless roads and completely muddy terrain, with fresh units being thrown in by both sides, our troops have repeatedly distinguished themselves against superior enemy forces through their exemplary steadfastness and unshakeable offensive spirit. Especially prominent in recent days have been the Panzer-Grenadier Division GROSSDEUTSCHLAND under the command of Generalleutnant Manteuffel, and the troops of LIX Army Corps under the command of Generalleutnant Friedrich-Wilhelm Schulz."

As well, the Commander-in-Chief of the Eighth Army, General der Infanterie Wöhler, sent the following telex:

"The great, hard-fought defensive success by the Pz.Gren.Div. GD received well-deserved praise in the Wehrmacht communique of 14 March 1944.

I congratulate the division on this high honour and wish it continued great success in battle.

Heil Panzer-Grenadier Division *Großdeutschland!*"

Wöhler
General der Infanterie and Commander-in-Chief, Eighth Army

Coincident with this message the division was released from the units of the Eighth Army to take up new duties in another battle zone. Relief of the division by infantry units began on 14 March and ended the next day. Because of the need for haste some elements were loaded aboard trains. The bulk of the division made its way to the southwest – toward new assignments. Their initial destination was said to be Permovaysk, more than that they did not know.

CHAPTER 6

THE 1029TH REINFORCED
GRENADIER REGIMENT (MOTORIZED) GD

Among the units of the Panzer-Grenadier Replacement Training Brigade GD (Oberst Bandelow) in Cottbus and Guben, the routine was a normal one for replacement troops. Units engaged in marches and exercises populated the city and surrounding areas, individual soldiers walked the streets more or less leisurely, vehicles, some fully loaded and some identifiable as driving school trucks, returned from drives, and in the barracks there was hectic activity as soldiers exercised and practised on heavy weapons.

This picture remained essentially unchanged, even in the fifth year of the war, although the number of convalescents was significantly greater than before.

The staff buildings – those of the Panzer-Grenadier Replacement and Training Regiment and of the brigade in the city itself – were the scene of constant activity. It was there that all the reports from outside came together; from there they were relayed to individual units. From there the training, composition, organization and requirements of the field divisions at the front were directed and organized. There too was the secret order from the commander-in-chief of the Replacement Army concerning the situation within Germany itself. Strengths of the various age- classes and the expected intake of replacements, the increasingly difficult situation in the war industries, the growing deterioration of war materiel, economies in many areas of daily military life – these were daily concerns. But there were other sources of concern: the consequences of the growing allied bombing offensive, the decline in the morale of the civilian population and especially among the foreign workers, the potential for internal unrest and the possible involvement of elements of the brigade. Among the secret directives and orders, the envelope to be opened on release of the code-word "Valkyrie" held a special place in the brigade's armoured safe. When placed in effect by the issuing of the code-word by the deputy commander of Corps Headquarters III, Berlin, it assigned a combat role to the Döberitz Infantry School, the Jüterbog Artillery School, the Krampnitz Armoured Forces School and the Panzer-Grenadier Replacement and Training Brigade GD at Cottbus and Guben against enemy airborne landings or in the event of internal unrest.

As the war went on the significance of the code-word "Valkyrie" grew; the Eastern Front was drawing closer and Germany was fighting a multi-front war. The deteriorating situation called for some unusual measures: clearing detachments in large cities, guard detachments at foreign worker camps, and supplementary detachments of battle groups to protect important installations.

In February-March 1944 the Soviets launched their major offensive. The German front was forced back and the Soviet threat drew ever nearer to the German frontiers. The full effect of total war became evident, even to the replacement and training units in Germany. Field replacement battalions had to be despatched to divisions at the front more often; more and more convalescent soldiers arrived at Cottbus and Guben, were taken on strength, equipped, and then sent back to the front. As well new units were formed to relieve decimated units and thus maintain the strength of the division.

The alarm that was issued in Cottbus and Guben on 5 March 1944, and for completely different reasons, came as a surprise, but in this case, too, the code-word "Valkyrie" was the reason behind the formation of a new GD unit, which was to bear the name;

1029th Reinforced Grenadier Regiment (Motorized) GD

Just as the code-word included precise implementing regulations, now the details of the new unit's organization and composition were specifically laid down. The main reason behind the formation of the new unit was the situation on the Eastern Front. The threat of a political overthrow in Hungary and Rumania demanded that further combat-capable German units be despatched to and employed in these regions.

The issuing of the code-word produced a great increase in activity at Cottbus and Guben in the days after 5 March, and within 48 hours of beginning the project the new regiment was beginning to take shape. Ultimately the unit was organized as follows:

1029th Reinforced Grenadier Regiment (Motorized) GD

Regimental Commander	Major von Courbiere (at Cottbus)
	Oberst Bandelow
Regimental Adjutant	Oberleutnant Mirow-Gläser
Operations Officer	Leutnant von Ludwiger
Signals Officer	Leutnant Röhling, as of 14 March
	Stabsfeldwebel Preuß
Regimental Medical Officer	Stabsarzt Dr. Schnering
IVa	Oberzahlmeister Salomoh
VK Officer	Inspektor Michel
I Battalion	Hauptmann Petereit
Adjutant	Leutnant Stier
1st (Rifle) Company	Oberleutnant W. Müller
Senior NCO	Feldwebel Adam
2nd (Rifle) Company	Oberleutnant Nachtigall
Senior NCO	
3rd (Heavy) Company	Hauptmann Brinken
II Battalion	Hauptmann Graf von Nayhauss
Adjutant	Oberleutnant Bensinger
4th (Rifle) Company	Oberleutnant Bitter
5th (Rifle) Company	
6th (Heavy) Company	
Regimental Units	
Commander	Rittmeister Kuehn
Regimental Headquarters	Leutnant Ratke, then Oberleutnant
Company	Hodapp, with motorcycle platoon, signals platoon
7th (Infantry Gun) Company	Oberleutnant Lange
8th (Antitank) Company	Oberleutnant Velten
9th (Pioneer) Company	Oberleutnant Kruse, then Leutnant Ratke
Artillery Battalion	Hauptmann Reichert
Adjutant	Oberleutnant Pruss

H.Q. Battery	Oberleutnant Jürgensen, then Leutnant Lattmann
1st (light field howitzer) Battery	Oberleutnant Kirsten
2nd (heavy field howitzer) Battery	Leutnant Spehr, then Oberleutnant Jürgensen
3rd (anti-aircraft) Battery	Oberleutnant Schürmann
Light Truck Column	Oberleutnant Röttger

The rifle companies each consisted of three infantry platoons, a light machine-gun squad with two weapons as well as a heavy platoon with heavy machine-guns and mortars. Old French Renaults served as squad vehicles. In general, however, there was no standardization of vehicles, which made things difficult for the repair services. There are reports of 156 different types of vehicle serving with this regiment!

The heavy companies each had a heavy machine-gun and an anti-tank platoon. The flak batteries, which were outfitted with brand new gun tractors, were equipped as follows: 1st Platoon with two 20mm quadruple flak on self-propelled carriages, 2nd (motorized) Platoon with three 37mm guns.

As far as the personnel complements were concerned, the companies were in almost all cases well off, and in some cases very well off, especially the pioneer and anti-tank companies. The following is a detailed look at the composition of the regimental units:

Headquarters Company

1 motorcycle platoon with old motorcycle-sidecar combinations from the training schools, an old Steyr light utility vehicle, 1 anti-tank platoon with three 50mm anti-tank guns and tractors, a large signals platoon with several 'Dora' backpack radio squads in Kfz. 1 vehicles, one 30-watt radio station in the half- tracked APC and several field telephone squads. The entire equipment complement appeared in no table of organization, was extremely motley and was in no way equal to later demands, especially in the area of signals.

7th (Infantry Gun) Company

3 light platoons, 1 heavy platoon with tractors; standardization of vehicles, at least within platoons.

8th (Anti-tank) Company

3 platoons each with three 75mm anti-tank guns and tractors, vehicles standardized.

9th (Pioneer) Company

Three platoons, well-equipped with mines, explosives, flamethrowers and rolls of barbed wire. No standardization of vehicles, but passably organized.

A large percentage of the enlisted men in the companies were recruits.

Within forty-eight hours of the issuing of the alert order the advance detachment, commanded by Rittmeister Kuehn with Leutnant Kaschade and several men, departed for Krakow, where they were to find more detailed orders for the employment of the 1029th Reinforced Grenadier Regiment. The corps headquarters based there gave Rittmeister Kuehn maps for the Neumarkt (Dunajec)–Zakopane area and explained that the regiment was to be quartered there. Initially there was no information as to the regiment's actual combat role.

Using these references the advance detachment arranged quarters, primarily in hotels and lodging facilities near Zakopane.

The first of the regiment's transport trains departed Neuhausen Station near Cottbus on 9 March 1944. The route they followed took them past the cities of Sagan, Neiße and Auschwitz and ended at Skawina south of Krakow. From there the division travelled overland to Neumarkt and into the Zakopane area, where the troops occupied their prepared quarters.

The surrounding countryside was strikingly beautiful. Scattered about the foot of the High Tatra, with its snow-covered slopes, rocky crags and dark forests of pine and spruce, were the large sports hotels, which took in the arriving soldiers. Most of the local inhabitants were Gorals, widely known as wood carvers. In contrast to the Poles farther north, they were very loyal toward the troops quartered there. Nevertheless the mountains between Neumarkt and Zakopane were said to be teeming with partisans, who exploited every opportunity to ambush lone soldiers and carry out acts of sabotage. Only the strength of the German garrison kept them from attempting larger actions.

Soon after his arrival in the Zakopane area, the commander of the 1029th Regiment, Oberst Bandelow – the first regimental commander chosen received another assignment – , made contact with the next senior command post, in order to learn details of what was planned for the regiment.

He learned that a new special purpose corps, LXXVIII Panzer Corps, was being formed under the command of Generalmajor Grolig. The corps was to consist of the 1029th Reinforced Grenadier Regiment (Motorized), the *Feldherrnhalle* Regiment, a unit similar to the 1029th Regiment, and the *Brandenburg* Instruction Regiment, the latter under Major Martin. The period allocated to formation of the corps was limited to a few days, and this was to be used primarily for training within the units and developing teamwork among the troops. This was achieved through daily march exercises on icy roads, field exercises and live firing.

While the corps prepared for its coming baptism of fire, probably in Hungary, on 18 March the regimental staff received departure orders for the next day. The Wehrmacht communique issued that day declared:

"German troops have been marching into Hungary since 4 A.M. on 19 March 1944..."

The orders stated: lightning advance to the Theiß, take over the guarding of the river crossings on both sides of Tiszadowogma and eliminate any interference with the German supply lines to the southern Eastern Front.

The battalions of the 1029th Regiment moved out at once. A snowplough which had just arrived from the central sector of the Eastern Front led the way, clearing the snow-covered roads. The march took the regiment through a snowed-in mountain world. To the left and right towered tall mountains,

1029th REINFORCED GRENADIER REGIMENT
(Motorized) GD

REGIMENTS STAB   S T A B S K O M P A N I E

I.

1. KOMPANIE   2. KOMPANIE   3. (SCHWERE) KOMPANIE

II.

4. KOMPANIE   5. KOMPANIE   6. (SCHWERE) KOMPANIE

7. (JG) KOMPANIE   8. (Pz. JÄGER) KOMPANIE   9. (Pi.) KOMPANIE

1. BATTERIE (le. F.H.)   2. BATTERIE (s. F.H.)

3. (FLA) B A T T E R I E

LEICHTE KOLONNE

I. Zug

Russen

Kp. Gef. Stand 1./1029 G.D.

Bitterberg

Plesa

Russen Berg

581

N

Viewing Point

BITTERBERG

almost completely shrouded by patches of mist and clouds. The roads were icy, with heavy snowdrifts.

The vehicles crawled along serpentine roads, bordered by dizzying precipices and deep gorges. The intervals between vehicles became ever greater. Soon they reached the border river of Dunajec, and the column drove on through its valley. There the snow was melting. The river itself was a foaming torrent raging between the crags. In every village the column passed the inhabitants showed their sympathy by waving and now and then tossing small gifts to the soldiers.

The column of vehicles continued on its journey, back into the loneliness of the mountains. Once again it encountered snow and snow-covered forests. Not until midnight of 19 March did the column stop; the last vehicles had to drive through the night to catch up with the others.

Lubowna, Presow, Kaschau – already on Hungarian soil. The border was crossed without stopping, the customs official scarcely stirred in his shack. There were already German troops in Kaschau, elements of the *Feldherrnhalle* regiment.

The population was very courteous. There too, to our surprise, there was much sympathy, cigarettes and friendly waves everywhere.

At about 21.00 on 20 March the point units arrived in the purely Hungarian city of Miskolc, which had a large Jewish population. Their arrival caused quite a stir. The elegant world of this city, in whose hotels and bars the war did not exist, was unsettled, more than anything by the warlike appearance of the newcomers. Members of the Hungarian Fascist Party served as guides. Several hours were spent there refuelling the vehicles and resting, for the regiment would soon resume its journey toward its actual destination.

The vehicles pulled out on the morning of 21 March while it was still dark, and they soon arrived in the planned security area along the Theiß. The units were quartered in the villages of Mezö-Kövesd, Nement-Bigg, Mezökerestes and Tiszadowogma. The blocking sectors were manned immediately, combat outposts set up and the heavy weapons moved into position. The Theiß itself had overflowed its banks and large areas of fields and meadows were under water. Headquarters, 1029th Regiment, as well as elements of I Battalion and the regiment's artillery battalion, remained in Miskolc at first, as there was some uncertainty as to the attitude of the Hungarians. The Honved and its general command had orders to mobilize, however there was much uncertainty as to whether they would obey them. On the one hand there was generally a great deal of sympathy toward Germany, on the other the orders reaching them were ambiguous, which resulted in a considerable amount of confusion.

While II Battalion kept watch on the Theiß crossings in the midst of a sympathetic Hungarian population without incident, the German garrisons in Miskolc and other cities found themselves in a cat and mouse game with the Hungarian troops and authorities. Only the skill of the German negotiators and command posts and the quick occupation of all the important points in the city prevented a confrontation.

Other German units arrived in the area by 31 March and relieved the existing garrison, including the 1029th Regiment. The companies and batteries received orders to entrain, which took place in Miskolc. They had new orders, which said that the 1029th Regiment GD was to reach the Hungarian-Romanian border and block the mountain passes there. Soviet spearheads were already in the foothills of the Carpathians, which had to be held at all costs.

The transport trains rolled through Szerencs, Tokay, Nyiregyhaza and Debreczen back toward the Hungarian-Romanian border, which was crossed at about 01.00 on 4 April. The trains rolled through the Dorna-Vatra Pass to Kimpolung, where the main body of the regiment detrained. Retreating columns were to be observed on the road beside the railroad tracks, as well as the occasional groups of prisoners. Anti-tank obstacles and barbed-wire entanglements were visible in the narrow valleys.

The detraining went quickly. The 1029th Regiment's 1st Company initially occupied quarters in Kimpolung and the 4th (Heavy) Company in Gura Humorului, while elements of the regimental units went to Vatra Dornei. All of these places were the scene of great confusion; they were all swamped with soldiers of every kind, staffs, supply units, female auxiliaries and so on.

In Kimpolung itself the German commander of Northern Rumania, General der Infanterie Auleb, who had his headquarters there (formerly in Czernowitz), had formed a "Battle Group Auleb." Elements of this battle group were supposed to secure the eastern exit from the Carpathians. With General Auleb were Generals von Sehmsdorf and Maderholtz, as well as a German general commanding the Koschna Pass. In Jacobeni – situated between Vatra Dornei and Kimpolung – were the last manganese mines available to Germany. Everything was to be committed to prevent these from falling into the hands of the Soviets.

The rapid retreat of the German eastern front was common knowledge, which unsettled the population and caused it to flee. There was a growing impression that the military command in this area had lost its head. There was a growing danger of panic and headlong flight with the approach of enemy forces. Therefore the arrival of the 1029th (motorized) Reinforced Grenadier Regiment GD was greeted with a sigh of relief, especially since the regimental command intervened energetically and tried to bring order to the blooming rear-area life and organize a regulation defence.

However news that Soviet tanks had entered a village 40 kilometres east of the Moldau and were now on the march toward Gora Humorului caused a renewed outbreak of panic. There were clashes of authority between the 1029th Regiment command and General Auleb, which were soon resolved in Oberst Bandelow's favour. Initially the 1029th Regiment occupied positions at the east end of its quartering area.

According to reports arriving at the 1029th Regiment's command post in Vama – located at the confluence of the Moldavita and the Moldau – "Battle Group Hauptmann Brinken" (elements of I Battalion), together with several German Carpathians companies, a battalion of Romanian border guards and elements of the Artillery Battalion GD, had put to flight a large Soviet mixed unit which included mortars and light artillery. An artillery piece, two 40mm anti-tank guns and several prisoners were captured. The enemy formation would probably have been destroyed, had not the inexperienced Rumanians, who were supposed to let the Soviets pass their mountain positions in order to then close the trap, not opened fire too soon.

Nevertheless the success was a welcome one, and morale was lifted appreciably, not least among the personnel of "Battle Group Auleb."

Statements taken from prisoners revealed that none of the members of this infantry unit, not even the older ones, had been in the army longer than three weeks. The youngest of the six prisoners came from the Don Steppe. In 1942, at the age of 16, he had served as an auxiliary with the 2nd Panzer Division, and had been captured by the Soviets fourteen days earlier while retreating with the Germans. The older auxiliaries captured with him had been shot right away, as they had previously served in the Red Army as reservists and were seen as deserters. The remaining five Soviet soldiers captured all came from areas occupied or recaptured by the Red Army in the past three weeks. They were taken as they were from their places of work; they were still wearing their civilian clothes and their only item of military uniform was a cap with the Soviet star. They claimed that the bulk of their regiment was made up of such soldiers, except for the officers. The Germans had almost always beaten a hasty retreat at the outset of battle and had offered scarcely any resistance. The results of this were that the Soviet officers became very careless.

Therefore the first defensive lines were established in this area by the Germans, whose intention it was to halt the Soviet advance in the foothills of the Carpathian Mountains. The 1029th Grenadier Regiment GD played a decisive role in this and the first defensive success near Gura Humora. In the course of time further German units came, so that gradually a continuous defensive line began to take shape. The positions extended along the crest of a line of hills which stretched between Gura Humora (Gura Humorului) and Manestirea Humorului. A line of wooded hills separated the German units from the Soviet positions, which were situated on the other side of the hills. Lively patrol activity developed on both sides.

The same day – 9 April 1944 – the 1029th Regiment ordered Rittmeister Kuehn to form a Carpathian battalion. The battalion was to be made up of so-called "Carpathian companies," units formed from stragglers and men separated from their units. "Battle Group Auleb" had formed these companies in the previous days in order to incorporate them into the defences. Previously seventeen of these companies had been on hand, some of which had already gone to the Ernst and Neuhoff Carpathian Battalions. Their value as combat units was limited, especially since they were short of arms and equipment. Nevertheless they were German soldiers, who could be made combat ready again with a reasonable command and provision of supplies. The two named Carpathian battalions were placed under the command of the 1029th Regiment GD and were now joined by the Kuehn Carpathian Battalion, which initially consisted of:

Mackert Company

Schulz Panzer Company (infantry role due to lack of tanks)

Böhler Company

The battalion's strength was bolstered by the mortar platoon of 4th Company, 1029th Regiment.

The Kuehn Carpathian Battalion's orders were to take over the defence of the Moldavita Valley and with it the left flank of the 1029th Regiment. It is noteworthy how Rittmeister Kuehn found his companies and how he moulded them into a battalion formation. He wrote:

"In Frumosul I found the 17th Carpathian Company under the command of Böhler, a panzer Leutnant. He told me right off that he had no knowledge of infantry warfare, but that he was willing to learn and would soon catch on. The company had no vehicles or machine-guns. In Vatra Moldavita I found another company. It was made up mostly of personnel returning from leave and men from a field replacement company who had been formed into an alert unit in Czernowitz under the command of panzer-grenadier Oberleutnant Schulz. Among the men of the company were numerous sergeants with the Iron Cross, First Class and the Close Combat Clasp. They all made a good impression. Finally, in Moldavita I discovered another company under the command of Oberleutnant Mackert. It had crossed the tall, snow-covered mountains from Putna over a mountain trail to reach this place. These, therefore, were the three companies of the Kuehn Carpathian Battalion."

In the following days another Carpathian Company, the 12th, under the command of Oberleutnant (Eng.) Merten, joined the battalion. It consisted almost exclusively of tank soldiers and brought with it several *panye* wagons and field kitchens. This company, too, was incorporated into the Kuehn Carpathian Battalion, raising its strength to four companies.

Rittmeister Kuehn achieved a passable level of organization with his unit in two days and assigned the companies the following defensive sectors:

1st Company, Kuehn Carpathian Battalion (previously the 17th Carpathian Company) in Frumosul

2nd Company, Kuehn Carpathian Battalion in Vatra Moldavita

3rd Company, Kuehn Carpathian Battalion (formerly the 12th Carpathian Company) in Moldavita Rusa

4th Company, Kuehn Carpathian Battalion (Oberleutnant Mackert Company) in Argel Battalion command post in Vatra Moldavita, attached mortar platoon of the 1029th regiment also there initially.

1029th Regiment forward command post in Vama.

Headquarters, 1029th Grenadier Regiment GD in Campulung, about 50 kilometres away from Vatra Moldavita.

The companies of the Kuehn Carpathian Battalion prepared for all- round defence in their villages, sent squad and platoon strength combat forward outposts up to 10 kilometres into side valleys leading to the enemy. Signals communication from the battalion to the 1029th Regiment was via fixed telephone link.

The armament and equipment of the companies varied greatly. There were enough rifles, but machine-guns, submachine-guns, pistols and optical equipment were almost totally lacking. Ammunition was scarce. There were few steel helmets, only every second company had a field kitchen. There were also shortages of coats and blankets, and the available footwear was just adequate.

It was several weeks before weapons were supplied, some by regiment and some by departing units. There was time, however, as the enemy was not yet a factor, and this was used for repair and maintenance of weapons.

A number of *Großdeutschland* men from the 1029th Regiment also joined the Carpathian Battalion to fill the vacant positions for trained squad and platoon commanders and at the same time create a solid framework for the unit.

While in the positions along the Humora from Gura Humora to Plesa the enemy remained at a distance and were engaged mainly with heavy infantry weapons and artillery. On 17 April the Kuehn Carpathian Battalion made its first contact with the enemy in Ciumorna. The Mander Squad, which had been sent ahead, was ambushed there by a Soviet offensive patrol of about 40 men. The squad, which belonged to the Carpathian Battalion's 2nd Company, lost two men killed in this encounter, however it was able to chase the enemy back into the mountains.

Details of the incident showed that the Soviet patrol had apparently been led by Romanian Huzules, mountain people of the Carpathians. In contrast the purely Romanian population was generally quite well-disposed toward the Germans. The terrain there, which consisted of lines of heavily-wooded hills with deep valleys, presented much greater difficulties. The north slopes of most of these hills were still covered in deep snow, which on account of the inadequate equipment of the soldiers deployed there caused the patrols great hardships. However, apart from occasional encounters in no-man's-land, the days that followed produced no significant combat. Further reinforcements arrived on the German side. Artillery and heavy weapons went into position, so that gradually it was possible to speak of a solidifying of the situation.

As the days went by it became obvious that the area near Plesa, on the upper course of the Humora in the sector held by II Battalion, 1029th Grenadier Regiment GD, was a focal point of the first order. Aware of the regiment's open flank, the Soviets were exerting heavy pressure against the German positions.

About two weeks earlier units of the 1029th Regiment had seized the monastery at Humora, inflicting heavy losses on the Soviets. Soon afterward an important hill with its pass and the small village of Plesa was occupied, as well as the hill to the south called Russian Mountain and the mountain to the west called Bitter Mountain or Bellringer. At that time II Battalion, 1029th Grenadier Regiment GD under Hauptmann Graf von Nayhauss and the units under its command (the Spangenberg Carpathian Company, elements of a further Carpathian Company, the Ghergel Romanian border guard battalion, a heavy anti-tank platoon of the 1029th Regiment and the battery of artillery commanded by Oberleutnant Kirsten) defended the Humora monastery, with strong, forward elements in Plesa, on Russian Mountain and on Bitter Mountain.

The Soviets made repeated attempts to retake the village of Plesa as well as Bitter Mountain, but each time they had been repulsed. Nevertheless the situation in this area remained tense. For its part, II Battalion, 1029th Regiment asked several times to be allowed to give up Plesa and Bitter Mountain in order to move to more favourable positions farther west. As well, Bitter Mountain changed hands several times on account of its wooded terrain and on 26 March was again in Soviet possession.

At this point 1st Company, I Battalion, 1029th Grenadier Regiment under the command of Oberleutnant W. Müller was ordered to storm Bitter Mountain and return it to German hands once and for all.

Thorough preparations were made for the operation, including the addition of a pioneer platoon equipped with flamethrowers which was under the command of a Leutnant. During the night of 27-28 April 1st Company, which had previously scouted the best way up the mountain, began its arduous climb. At about the same time the company's 2nd Platoon set out from Manestirea toward Hill 807 with orders to divert the enemy's attention from there. Finally, after a six-hour climb, 1st Company's advance guard under Oberleutnant Müller reached the planned departure position, right below the crest of Bitter Mountain itself.

It was early on the morning of 28 April when 1st Company began its attack, having hastily made preparations while still on the move. Company commander Oberleutnant W. Müller described the course of Operation Bitter Mountain and the days that followed:

"After a brief fire-fight with the Soviets, they fled the mountain and fell back through the forest east of Plesa. As soon as the men and I reached the crest, we (less 2nd Platoon) set up everything for defence. However that was easier said than done. Any counterattack by the enemy would come from the same direction as 1st Company and they would thus also be able to use the good cover to approach our positions. Furthermore they could now reach our right flank from Plesa, which was in their hands again. As well they could go around the foot on Bitter Mountain without being seen by us. Our positions were therefore threatened from practically every side.

With Bitter Mountain back in our hands again, at least for the time being, the pioneers, with the exception of a construction squad, were recalled by the battalion. We endeavoured to expand and secure in every direction the positions we had captured. The morning of 28 April was quiet, but in the afternoon a Soviet patrol approached unseen and in spite of bitter opposition it occupied and held the centre peak. The enemy now had a commanding position between Leutnant von Alvensleben's 1st Platoon and the company command post. Worst of all, enemy snipers were able to fire on anything that moved from there and we immediately began taking casualties.

Toward evening on the 28th telephone contact was established. We were able to reach the firing position of a light field howitzer, which fired several rounds at the Soviet-occupied peak.

The situation at the company command post remained uncomfortable, as it was attacked from various sides during the night. The Soviets attacked from the south, then from the west, then from the east. The two platoons in position at the command post had to turn their weapons south, then west and then east in order to defend their skins. As morning came on the 29th the Soviets fell back, leaving 1st Company in complete control of the entire mountain.

However the ammunition was now almost all used up, and before supplies arrived the Russians attacked again and once again reached the peak. It was the same show all over again, with snipers keeping everyone in check with their well-aimed shots. 1st Platoon was finally forced to abandon its positions under the pressure of the attacking Soviets, as a result of which most of Bitter Mountain was in enemy hands.

At almost the same time the Soviets began firing on the peaks with mortars from Plesa, which led to serious casualties. Two men were blown apart by direct hits, another was killed by a sniper. The situation was untenable. Gefreiter Ohnesorge went missing in this action. The men were all in, they could barely go on holding. Then Hauptmann Graf von Nayhauss, commander of II. Btl./1029 GD, decided to pull the rest of 1st Company out of its positions below Bitter Mountain. It was made regimental reserve and relocated to Bucsoia, where it stood down."

This Operation Bitter Mountain, which proved to be an unfortunate undertaking, cost 4 dead and 23 wounded.

Following these events, the units in the Humora monastery sector were relieved by Hauptmann Graf von Nayhauss and reorganized as the "Humora Monastery Group" under the command of Rittmeister Kuehn. A rifle company consisting of GD men formed the core unit of this not very homogenous group, which also included the Romanian Ghergel border guard and elements of the Carpathian Companies.

The group was deployed as follows: the bulk of the rifle company of GD men plus a medium mortar squad and a 50mm anti-tank gun in a forward position south of Plesa. Southeast of it on Russian Mountain two Romanian rifle platoons. In the Humora monastery the 6th Romanian Rifle Company under Captain Mironowice with a medium mortar platoon and a heavy machine-gun platoon of the Romanian heavy company and another rifle company. In the Madernita Gorge further elements of the Romanian border guard battalion, together with heavy platoons of the 1029th Regiment GD.

The only direct contact with the enemy at that point was near Plesa, which greatly eased the situation.

The subordinate Romanian units represented a rather difficult chapter, as the Germans were unable to exert any influence over their peculiarities. The Romanian border guard battalion, part of which was made up of stationary units, might serve as an example. Inadequate rear-echelon assets and lack of communications equipment were the order of the day. In addition to the battalion commander, Major Ghergel, the battalion staff consisted of just the adjutant, the interpreter and an operations officer. The latter was a university professor from Czernowitz. There was also a doctor there as well as telephone operators and a number of orderlies.

The Romanian rifle companies each had four platoons, each of four ten-man squads. Each squad had a light machine-gun. The companies were led by older captains, the platoons by sergeants, the squads by corporals. Most had little combat experience, however they were skilled at digging and excelled in camouflage and making a stealthy approach. The Rumanians were incapable of carrying out battle assignments independently.

The German soldiers were very much astonished by the sight of the Romanian company commanders striking their people when something didn't work.

Artillery units arrived and their heavy batteries took away any lust to attack the Soviets might have had; as a result the days passed relatively quietly. The first rays of the May sun melted the snow, even at higher elevations.

Other German blocking units arrived on 6 May, including the leading elements of the 8th Light Infantry Division. Officers from the unit who were to serve as guides reported to the battalion command posts.

On 8 May I and II Battalions of the 38th Light Infantry Regiment began taking over the positions. The relief of the 1029th Grenadier Regiment GD took place without incident, while the Romanian units and the Carpathian Companies at first remained in their positions under the command of the 8th Light Infantry Division.

The 1029th Regiment was released from the units of XVII Army Corps on 10 May. In the days that followed it travelled by road through Kimpolung (Campulung) and Dorna Sara along the Bistritza Valley to Roman, where the Ib staff of the Panzer-Grenadier Division GD under General Staff Major Usener was located. Orders were waiting there for the disbandment of the 1029th Grenadier Regiment GD, elements of which were assigned to their new units as they arrived in their quartering area near Roman. All the regiment's units arrived there in the period 11-15 May 1944.

Thus ended the story of a unit which, created in response to an emergency, had done all it could to bring honour to the name of *Großdeutschland* in spite of all obstacles, the difficult nature of the situation and unfamiliarity with the combat zone.

Part V

CHAPTER 1

IN RUMANIA

Targul Frumos and Jassy

Soviet armoured spearheads in front of the eastern slopes of the Carpathians?! Enemy infantry at the banks of the Moldau in Bukovina, deep inside Rumania!!

German troops retreating, fleeing masses of train vehicles, trucks and infantry struggling to get through. The rushed gathering of stragglers, the moving-in of alert units, mobilization of the last available forces. Creation of new defensive lines, establishment of firing positions, organization of the defence somewhere on the mountain slopes: what had happened? Where had the enemy come from?

On 8 March 1944 the Soviets launched a further offensive southwest of Kirovograd which the weakened German units could not stand up to. At almost the same time the order arrived to evacuate the area farther east and to occupy new positions farther west. The River Bug, a broad natural obstacle, was to be the new main line of resistance; the enemy was to be stopped for good at the Bug.

The offensive by the 2nd Ukrainian Front from the Svenigorodka area in the direction of Gaysin and Uman, which had been under way since 6 March, had placed the German Eighth Army in a most difficult situation, had pierced its positions and at the same time forced it to fall back to the south. Uman was lost on 10 March. By the 13th Soviet armoured spearheads had reached the Bug on both sides of Grayvoron, where, in an area almost 100 kilometres wide, they established several bridgeheads up to 30 kilometres deep. On 16 March they also reached the rail line to Odessa at Vapnyarka.

At the same time, farther northwest the 1st Ukrainian Front under Marshall Zhukov was at the gates of Vinnitsa, threatening to bring about the complete collapse of the German front.

Between the German Eighth Army and the First Panzer Army to the north there was now a huge gap in which there was no organized resistance. The Soviets had a clear path to the west; they had the opportunity to turn the flanks of the German armies. Elements of five Soviet armies had been identified opposite the left wing of the German Eighth Army alone. The momentum of these armies, which included a tank army, carried them toward the southwest.

On 18 March Soviet armoured spearheads reached the town of Yampol on the Dnestr River. Their arrival prevented the Germans from establishing a new defence line at this river barrier. In the course of the advance, two further Soviet armies and a tank army simultaneously veered south against the northern flank of the German Eighth Army and tried to destroy it between the Bug and the Dnestr Rivers. The Soviet armoured spearheads pursued the Germans across the Dnestr on both sides of Rybniza and by the end of March were nearing the Prut.

The German Eighth Army repeatedly lengthened its left wing in an effort to throw up a barrier in front of the enemy's armoured spearheads, which caused the Soviets to swing out even farther to the west in order to envelop the defenders.

The units of the Panzer-Grenadier Division *Großdeutschland* headed west, parallel to these movements by the Soviets, with most of the combat elements and the tracked vehicles travelling by rail. The trains rolled through Pervomaysk and Vradiyevka to Rybniza on the Dnestr, which was reached on 21 March. Reports kept arriving from the rail stations saying that the Russians were almost there. On 17 March the Railroad Liaison and Transport Officer called from Pervomaysk stating that the enemy was only six kilometres north of the entire line! Further transport by rail was in doubt. As it was impossible to entrain at other stations, some vehicles had to be blown up. Others sought to escape on the highway. The urge to drive west was irresistible in spite of the knee-deep mud, then renewed snowstorms, as well as overcrowded roads. Gun tractors pulled long trains of wheeled vehicles behind them. Any semblance of order dissolved.

The entire length of this stretch of highway was littered with bogged-down vehicles. There were overturned trucks, cast-aside *panye* wagons with broken axles and many vehicles that had been blown up. In the midst of the chaos were mud-splattered soldiers and officers, shouting, cursing, struggling in vain to untangle this hopeless mess. But their efforts were in vain. The Soviet close-support aircraft were omnipresent, strafing the columns and adding to the general atmosphere of chaos. Here sat a munitions train, blown apart, there a lone, blazing truck: signposts along the path of the German retreat.

The railway embankment was the only salvation. On it the columns of vehicles slowly made their way along the track; by following it they were headed in the direction of the German forces somewhere ahead. The point at which the division was supposed to assemble was repeatedly changed. On 24 March it was Floresti, approximately 40 kilometres west of Rybniza. Others claimed to have heard that the first assembly area was the city of Kishinev. No one knew for sure; but everything depended on the continually- changing situation that was dictated by the Soviets.

Halfway to Floresti the columns veered south; it now appeared that Kishinev was the first point of assembly.

Columns of vehicles also approached the Dnestr from Dubosary, from the northeast. They were able to cross on 30 March 1944 in severe cold. Kilometre-long columns backed up in front of the crossing, which at this point led to Rumania. In the valley of the Dnestr, with its vineyards and apricot and tobacco plantations, as well as in the nation's largest city, one could see German troops looting dumps abandoned by the Rumanians. It was a picture of a demoralized army.

The division headquarters arrived in Kishinev; almost immediately it received orders to march on. Calarasi-Targ, almost halfway to Jassy on the Kishinev–Jassy rail line, was the new destination. The division's combat elements were to assemble there and stand ready to attack in a northwesterly direction.

The division command had to rouse *Großdeutschland's* optimism in order to begin all over again. But they had to begin again if they hoped to stop the enemy!

The train units of the combat echelon were supposed to reach Jassy but were unable to get through. A path had to be cleared for them. Enemy spearheads, including tanks, were already north of Cornesti Targ, which sat astride the road and rail line from Kishinev to Jassy. This news reached the division command post in Kishinev on 31 March. The battalions were despatched that same night. The first elements arrived in Cornesti Targ on 1 April and immediately took up position there. The weight of the Soviet units had forced the battle groups of the 79th Infantry Division out of the positions they had only just occupied. Now they were to be helped back into their positions by the launching of a counterattack. II Battalion, Panzer-Grenadier Regiment GD was the first to take the offensive in this area, attacking at about 14.00 on 1 April.

By evening it had recovered the former main line of resistance, destroying seven enemy tanks in the process. Major Bethke, the battalion commander and former division adjutant, was seriously wounded; his place was taken by Hauptmann Heynitz. The other battalions soon arrived: III Battalion, Panzer-Grenadier Regiment GD advanced through Parliti Sat to Ungheni Targ, where its handful of men were supposed to occupy the hills in front of the town. A snowstorm struck on the very first day of this action, which was conducted by the bulk of the panzer-grenadiers under the command of Oberst Lorenz, with supporting tanks and assault guns and a battalion of the Panzer- Artillery Regiment GD. The storm came close to exceeding in force and cold temperatures anything seen thus far.

The soldiers had scarcely settled into their positions when further T-34s showed up along with Soviet infantry. Their objective was obvious: it was the road to Jassy, which was carrying all the German through and supply traffic. But they hadn't counted on the toughness of the GD men. They fought and held their positions in the heaviest snowstorms. Dead-tired, they roused themselves again and again and let their weapons speak. Their most effective support came from the assault guns, which destroyed a large number of enemy tanks.

Again and again the individual fighting man distinguished himself in counterattacks and advances intended to advance the main line of resistance. At the capture of Elisabetha it was Gefreiter Schindler of 11th Company, III Battalion, Panzer-Grenadier Regiment GD who came to the fore. Leading a machine-gun team, on 3 April he was one of the first to reach the outskirts of the village, where he inflicted heavy losses on the enemy, who were already wavering. Then there was Obergefreiter Eisfeld of the same company: while serving as platoon runner he put an enemy patrol to flight and mastered a dangerous situation.

On 4 April the enemy broke through to the highway and the town of Parliti and occupied Hill 154. Following brief preparations, on 5 April the panzer-grenadiers counterattacked. A closer look at what happened is provided by the diary entries of II Battalion, Panzer-Grenadier Regiment GD from 5 April 1944:

08.30   Weather: overcast, with good visibility. Beginning of attack on Parliti Sat. The 2nd and 3rd Companies of I Battalion and six assault guns are under the command of Battle Group von Heynitz (CO II Btl.). Swinging north, the 2nd and 3rd (APC) Companies, with Leutnant Bader's company in the centre, attack the town from the northwest. Meanwhile two Tigers screen to the north and west toward Tochiresti.

At the same time the Wechmann Company climbs onto two more Tigers and with these prepares to attack Hill 170.2, about 2 km. southwest of Parliti Sat.

However in the midst of preparations one Tiger, with a squad and the company H.Q. squad, breaks down; the other two squads and the one remaining Tiger reach, occupy and hold the hill.

Battle Group von Heynitz (II Btl.) is initially pinned down in front of the town of Parliti Sat by heavy enemy fire.

Hauptmann von Heynitz is killed, battalion adjutant Leutnant Geist is wounded.

Fahnenjunker-Oberfeldwebel Kalinowski dies a hero's death leading 3rd (APC) Company; Unteroffizier Piepenburg (6th Company) and 4 men also killed. An assault gun – Reserve Leutnant Josef Hensinger – is hit by an anti-tank gun and blows apart.

09.30   The left company succeeds in breaking into Parliti Sat; the Russians retreat to the west. The town is cleared of the enemy; only in the southern part is a group of Soviet soldiers able to hold out.

12.00   Hauptmann Meyer takes command of II Battalion. The unit occupies positions from the northwest end of Parliti Sat to and including Point 170.2.

16.00   The remaining enemy group in the southern part of Parliti Sat is destroyed; about 200 Soviets flee along the highway to the south and are wiped out by the heavy weapons.

Battalion command post: hollow about 1,000 metres east of Point 170. The night passes quietly.

The extraordinary bravery exhibited by Fahnenjunker-Oberfeldwebel Kalinowski, who died in the attack on Parliti Sat, was acknowledged by the placing of his name on the Honour Roll. The entry in the Honour Roll stated:

"Fahnenjunker-Feldwebel Kalinowski led his company, which rode into action on assault guns, with great courage at the Kishinev – Jassy rail line. Forced to dismount by barrage fire, and in spite of a serious leg wound, he led his men across an open, unprotected field against enemy tanks. He was fatally hit only a few metres from the hiding place of a T-34."

Oberleutnant Sturm, commander of the Assault Gun Battalion GD's 3rd

Battery, also distinguished himself in this attack. His leadership resulted in the destruction of numerous enemy tanks and, what was more important, the entry into the heavily-occupied town of Parliti Sat. He was recommended for the Knight's Cross of the Iron Cross, which he received a short time later.

The successful attack on Parliti Sat forced the enemy to pause at this point on the front. In the days that followed the division was able to move its positions farther forward. Large-scale retrograde movements by the enemy from the village of Tochiresti were observed and these offered the heavy weapons outstanding targets. In the few days that remained until Easter (9 April) the newly-won positions were expanded and fortified. Hostilities had almost ceased in this sector. Indeed, it was even possible to withdraw single companies from the front line and transfer them to the rear. There they were brought up to strength with replacements that had just arrived and were given a brief rest. It was a rest that the men needed very badly indeed after the strain produced by weeks of fighting. On Easter Sunday ("GD travel day") I and III Battalions of the Panzer-Grenadier Regiment GD were relieved, handing their positions over to II Battalion. The two battalions had been earmarked for action west of Jassy.

Major Remer, CO of I (APC) Battalion, Panzer-Grenadier Regiment GD, was relieved by Major Krieg as he was bound for a new post in Germany. Having served with the battalion through the early days when it had proved itself and its great successes, Remer now left the Panzer-Grenadier Division GD for good. His new post was a highly honourable one, namely commander of the *Großdeutschland* Watch Battalion in the Reich capital. Remer replaced Oberstleutnant "Kiki" Gehrke, who had been transferred to other duties.

The action carried out between Cornesti Targul and Ungheni Targul, a small-scale but very tough operation, received glowing praise in an order of the day issued by the Commander-in-Chief of the Eighth Army, General der Infanterie Wöhler, on 15 April 1944:

"In heavy defensive fighting in the Cornesti Targul–Ungheni Targul area during the period 1-7 April 1944, the Manteuffel Group prevented a breakthrough to the southwest and inflicted very heavy losses on the enemy. Destroyed were: 89 tanks (18 by close attack), 6 of these by the Armoured Pioneer Battalion GD, and 10 anti-tank guns. As well, the enemy lost large numbers of infantry weapons and 174 prisoners.

I express my thanks and recognition to the command and the brave field forces (Panzer-Grenadier Division GD, 19th Infantry Division, 23rd Panzer Division), which achieved this success in spite of the great strain and ongoing supply difficulties."

Wöhler, General der Infanterie

CHAPTER 2

THE BATTLE OF JASSY

Jassy, a city with over 100,000 inhabitants situated in Moldavia in a side-valley of the Prut, was now the target of the Soviet attack. By mid-April it was directly threatened.

All was still normal in the city on the morning of 10 April. It was like peacetime. There was even a street car still running, the last survivor of more peaceful times. A mass of vehicles forced its way through the streets and clogged the narrow thoroughfares.

From the front (to the west) there was bad news. Enemy tanks had been sighted on the road to Targul Frumos; they were ravaging the villages, setting everything ablaze. The terrified residents had fled with what they could carry before the Soviet hordes.

For those Germans and Rumanians who had become soldiers in order to keep the communists away from their boundaries, the appearance of the enemy had a devastating effect. In many cases they, too, broke and fled toward the west. Here and there they were caught and killed by the Soviets. Still others defended themselves desperately in the ruins of small towns. Then, finally, rescue came.

Early on 10 April the *Großdeutschland* Panzer-Fusiliers set out from Jassy to attack the flank of the enemy force that had broken through to the south between Jassy and Targul Frumos. Their objective was to destroy the Soviets, even though they had a force the size of an army corps.

Though they were small in number, the momentum of the panzer-fusiliers' attack, which was supported by tanks and assault guns as well as by II Battalion of the Panzer-Artillery Regiment GD, enabled them to take the hills near Danuan in the face of only minor resistance. There they regrouped. III Battalion, Panzer-Grenadier Regiment GD assumed the lead for the subsequent advance along the railroad to the west. Riding on their vehicles, the attackers drove to Podul Iloaei, where they freed a surrounded group of Romanian troops. With the latter's help they rolled up the Soviets and brought in a large number of prisoners. The advance continued down the highway toward Sarca. Leutnant Kollewe and his 1st Company entered the town, but not a shot was fired. The bolsheviks had taken refuge in the houses and had to be dragged out. They were completely surprised, for they couldn't believe that there were still German troops with the will to attack. Without pausing I (APC) Battalion, Panzer-Grenadier Regiment GD under Major Krieg took the point and drove to Valea Otlor, where the first serious resistance was met. Tanks and anti-aircraft guns moved up and that evening the infantry broke into the town. Following a brief close-quarters battle the surviving Soviets fled to the north; the town was in German hands.

The advance toward Targul Frumos was begun during the night. It was vital that this important city be returned to our hands. In spite of the darkness the attack was a success. The attackers broke into the city following a heavy bombardment which destroyed many Soviet resistance nests. The city was combed for enemy troops, insofar as the darkness allowed. For the most part the attackers established hedgehog positions on the outskirts of the city. Things slowly quieted down when dawn came. Most of the enemy appeared to have retired to the north.

Meanwhile the remaining battalions and the bulk of the Panzer-Fusilier Regiment GD moved up to join the point to set up forward combat outposts, especially to the north. At approximately 06.00 II Battalion, Panzer-Grenadier Regiment GD attacked the enemy-held village of Balteti from Sarca. Shouting fiercely, the grenadiers stormed the village. Later the battalion joined the attack north through Valea Otlor toward Palieni by the armoured pioneers and Tigers. Enemy resistance there was weak. A new defence line was manned on the hills about 1,000 metres southeast of Palieni and work began immediately to fortify it.

Near Targul Frumos meanwhile, contact had been established with German and Romanian units attacking from the west. The road from Targul Frumos east to Jassy was open again. Traffic returned to normal; the supply vehicles rolled.

The advance continued without letup, however, from Targul Frumos to the north and northwest, toward the advancing enemy. III Battalion of the Panzer-Fusilier Regiment GD reached the ridge southwest of Rusa on the far side of the marshy bottom land. On its left was I Battalion, which occupied defensive positions on both sides of Polieni on 13 April, relieving II Battalion, Panzer-Grenadier Regiment GD, while II Battalion of the Panzer-Artillery Regiment GD was in firing positions on both sides of Facuti.

Meanwhile, northwest of Targul Frumos, the panzer-grenadiers pushed the main line of resistance forward. Their forceful assault drove the bolsheviks out of the towns of Costesti and Pietrisi and by the evening they had reached the line Point 296 (on the Giurgesu highway) Point 274–Secaresti. Masses of Soviets fled, suffering considerable losses to the fire of the heavy weapons in the process.

That same day, from their positions in front of Bals, soldiers of 11th Company, III Battalion, Panzer-Grenadier Regiment GD observed the landing of a Soviet aircraft that had apparently lost its way. There was a quick burst of machine-gun fire and a party of men moved toward the aircraft. While the pilot was being picked up, his passenger tried to flee through the fields. He threw away one piece of equipment after another to help him run faster; but in vain, he was soon caught. He was an interesting catch: secret papers were found on him. The man was a major, obviously a liaison officer from the Soviet army group to the corps deployed in this area. Examination of his papers revealed important information about the objectives of the Soviet attacks.

Meanwhile Soviet resistance stiffened. Patrols revealed the enemy's forward positions: at the highway near Vascani–the north end of Barbatesti–Hill 344–edge of the forest south of Baiceni–hills north of Bals–south end of Ulmi Liteni–south end of Valeni Rusi and along the stream bed. Repeated armoured thrusts, like those north of Bals on 15 April, put the Soviets to flight locally, but resulted in losses. The courageous platoon leader Feldwebel Lux of 11th Company, Panzer-Grenadier Regiment GD was killed that day and an assault gun was lost as the result of a direct hit. On the other side of the coin, an armed reconnaissance toward Vascani by tanks and the armoured personnel carriers of I (APC) Battalion, Panzer-Grenadier Regiment GD resulted in 16 enemy tanks destroyed.

As a result of these operations it was obvious that the Soviets had moved in considerable reinforcements and would resume their efforts to break through to the south in the near future.

The obvious point of main effort of the enemy build-up lay along the Vascani–Targul Frumos and Bals–Targul Frumos highways. All hell broke loose in Bals on 16 April when the bolsheviks succeeded in ejecting the forward outposts of 11th Company, Panzer-Grenadier Regiment GD under the command of Feldwebel Nieswand from the town. An immediate counterattack by assault guns and Tiger tanks, which arrived somewhat later, resulted in the retaking of Bals, but it also confirmed the offensive intentions of the Soviets. The defenders had to expect a Soviet attempt to break through there.

In contrast things were quiet in the enemy positions opposite the panzer-fusiliers, apart from limited patrol activity and occasional artillery bombardments. One such patrol, which was carried out by Feldwebel Röger of I Battalion, Panzer-Fusilier Regiment GD and one of his men, became famous far beyond the realm of the division. Röger and his man disguised themselves as shepherds: they put on civilian coats over their uniforms, took walking sticks to serve as shepherd staffs and walked over to a herd of sheep grazing nearby. To the astonishment of his men, Röger and his companion moved slowly with the sheep toward the Soviet lines, which were visible in the distance. They drove the herd toward the railroad which ran along the bottom land in the valley before them.

Soon they reached the first Soviet foxholes. Feldwebel Röger softly murmured "good day" in Russian. He casually continued on his way, herding several sheep here, goading on stragglers with his stick there. At most the Soviet soldiers looked up briefly or joked among themselves, but for the most part they allowed the herd of sheep to pass without paying it much notice.

All the while the shepherd cast quick glances to his left and right, instantly registering in his brain everything he saw. There were two well-camouflaged anti-tank guns by a bush; there a heavy machine-gun. That decaying haystack had to be a radio station, perhaps even a command post; there were too many earth-brown figures running here and there. Farther to the rear sat two T-34s with their hatches open, to the left several 76.2mm anti- tank guns. Röger noted all of this without deviating for a moment from his role as shepherd.

Röger and his animals finally disappeared back into the hollow. There he left them on their own. He crept over to a railroad bridge, placed an explosive charge and blew the bridge to bits. Now wide awake, the Soviets fired wildly. But the shepherd, Feldwebel Röger, was able to return unharmed to his own lines, where he received a warm reception from his comrades.

and assault guns, of the anti-tank guns and 88mm flak, merged into the din of battle; the man in his hole held on and fought for himself. Some men now ran away from this inferno created by the heavy weapons.

In the artillery firing positions, some of which unfortunately lay in front of a stream, the gun crews prepared for close defence. The sound of battle could be heard now, and lone enemy tanks appeared damned close to them; the gunners stared at their range-finders, which indicated that the shortest firing range for the howitzers was 1,800 metres. At lesser ranges they would have to fire over open sights, but the ranges were still in excess of that, they could still employ aimed fire.

Farther to the left, a change of position proved the undoing of the Panzer-Artillery Regiment GD. The enemy tanks and the attacking Soviet infantry arrived too soon: the bulk of the guns fell into enemy hands in close combat or had to be blown up. I Battalion sustained especially heavy losses.

The individual groups of infantry fought bitterly to hold their strongpoints; others were forced to fall back and occupy new positions. The weight of Soviet infantry simply crushed them. In the midst of this chaos they sought to make contact with the rear, assembled into small groups and clung to some significant point, a railway embankment, the edge of a ravine, near an anti-aircraft gun or in the vicinity of the assault guns or tanks. Many men had given up, their leaders dead or missing. They were unable to find their own people – all was confusion. Leutnant Wunnecke, commander of the 6th Panzer-Grenadier Company, was killed by mortar fire; Oberfeldwebel Heppes assumed command of what remained of the company. Somewhere on the railway embankment east of Nikolayevka 6th Panzer-Fusilier Company was strewn to the winds by the Soviet onslaught. Not until dusk did a few men meet up again. The pioneers also suffered bloody losses in the same area, and only scattered groups were able to reassemble that evening.

Here once again it was the heavy weapons which joined forces with individual groups of infantry to offer resistance. The 37mm flak on self-propelled chassis repeatedly sallied forth and poured their shells into the masses of attacking bolsheviks. They held their positions stubbornly and tried to halt the enemy's advance for at least a few hours. Or a lone 75mm anti-tank gun, its trails spread, sat in the cover of a row of trees and fired shell after shell into the oncoming enemy infantry. A squad rallied round it, a small group of panzer-grenadiers or the remnants of a panzer-fusilier platoon.

Not until dusk, with the arrival of darkness, did the sound of battle slowly die down. The din subsided. Only now and then did the sound of combat flare up again, machine-guns and submachine-guns hammering away in the falling darkness. Here and there figures rose up and dragged other wounded to the rear between them, or bent over crumpled forms lying on the ground and felt for signs of life. Parachute flares hissed into the sky, to be followed by streams of tracer arcing to the east like strings of pearls. The sharp crack of a tank cannon echoed over a ravine and disappeared in the distance.

The first day of the defensive effort southwest of Kirovograd was over. The enemy had penetrated deep into our positions; the weight of his attacks had strewn entire companies to the four winds and inflicted severe wounds. Yet, he hadn't broken through, his attack was still under our control. Anovka, Veselye, Kurlyugino, Point 200.9, Point 200.1 and Point 200.2 had been lost and were in enemy hands. The deepest incursion was about 5,000 metres deep.

The 9th of March saw the Soviets resume their attack at first light. In the ravines tank after tank streamed toward the positions held by the panzer-grenadiers and panzer-fusiliers, whose ranks had become much thinner. Heavy-calibre weapons hammered the positions; their shells ploughed up the earth. Von Wietersheim's and Major Gomille's armoured groups and the assault guns drove here and there to counter the enemy's armoured spear-heads. The crash of tank cannon repeatedly rang out over the battlefield, and fires and explosions were evidence of successes on both sides.

The enemy managed to break into Dymino. The panzer-grenadiers farther to the northeast were forced to give up their positions, and the village of Chervonye ultimately had to be evacuated by II Panzer-Grenadier Battalion. By lunchtime heavy fighting was raging in Yelisavetivka (Konstantinovka) and Ivanovka; the advancing Soviets could be seen from the division command post. Farther northwest Nikolayevka was lost in spite of a stubborn defence by the panzer-fusiliers. There, too, the evacuation of positions which until now had been held so steadfastly began. Movement came to our lines, interrupted only by counterattacks and local advances which created breathing spaces here and there.

Looming over everything, however, was the overall situation, which out of necessity had a great influence on the orders and movements of the Panzer-Grenadier Division *Großdeutschland*. Uman had fallen victim to the enemy offensive; the Soviets were on the march to the southwest, threatening the supply lines of the German units much farther to the east and forcing the German command to make fresh decisions. Once again there was a threat of envelopment and encirclement from the northwest, making all plans for the defense of the Bug River line senseless, as it was likely that the Soviets would cross the river before German forces could move into position to defend it.

Under the impression of this dangerous situation in the southern sector, orders were issued to German units in the southwest and farther to the east to fall back to a shortened defensive line, which initially was to run in a north-south direction roughly along the Bug and Prut River lines.

In this desperate situation everything depended on getting the German units still on the lower Dniepr out before the Soviets broke through south of Uman. This could only succeed if a durable front was established quickly as far to the north as possible. As well, it was vital that the enemy's southward advance be halted for good far to the west, north of Kishinev or north of Jassy at the latest.

Other units, those still on hand or brought from the Reich in the meantime, would have to intercept and halt the enemy armies which were advancing westwards north of Uman.

The 10th of March again saw extremely heavy defensive fighting by the units of the GD; these actions were already of a mobile nature. More than 43

This daring, some would say foolhardy, action by the Feldwebel, a Swabian from Geislingen/Steige, was soon on everyone's lips. His actions were later acknowledged by the awarding of the Knight's Cross. Never again was the enemy scouted in this way by a member of the *Großdeutschland* Division.

The next few days passed quietly; the positions were fortified further. The men worked hard to improve foxholes, bunkers, machine-gun nests and firing positions. Fall-back observation posts were scouted and zones of fire established. Farther back in the division's rear, battered units of the division were rested and brought up to strength again; III Battalion, Artillery Regiment GD, which had lost almost all of its guns in the retreat, was reinstated as an active unit.

At the front the pioneers ventured into no-man's-land each night, placing barbed-wire entanglements and laying mines, especially in places that were difficult to see from the positions or out of reach of the heavy weapons. All efforts were directed toward defence, a static war, toward staying put where they were.

Subsequently orders came from above for a major offensive action in the division's left sector, with the objective of driving into the woods between Barbatesti and Vascani, in order to smash enemy preparations which were suspected to be going on there. A further objective, especially for the tanks, was Hill 372 and the hills near Dumbravita.

By 25 April all was ready. II and III Battalions, Panzer- Grenadier Regiment GD were to carry the weight of the attack. At about 04.15, after a brief artillery bombardment, the panzer- grenadiers sprang from their foxholes. The Soviets were taken completely by surprise. Their line breached, they fled in panic. The assault guns performed magnificently against the enemy's anti-tank guns, especially in the right attack sector under the command of Oberleutnant Steffani. Oberleutnant Diddens, a specialist in the destruction of anti-tank guns, and his battery alone destroyed 31 heavy anti-tank guns and three enemy tanks. He was named in the Wehrmacht communique, which declared:

"...the Soviets attacked north of Jassy with powerful forces. They foundered on the determined resistance of the German and Romanian troops. Local penetrations were sealed off.

An assault gun unit of the GROSSDEUTSCHLAND Panzer-Grenadier Division under the command of Oberleutnant Diddens especially distinguished itself in these battles on 25 April 1944."

The following is a list of the men of 1st Battery, Assault Gun Battalion GD who were there:

Battery commander: Oberleutnant Diddo Diddens
                       Unteroffizier Heinz Wenning
                       Gefreiter Josef Hirsch
                       Obergefreiter Karl Wöhrer
                       Leutnant Siegfried Döhn
                       Unteroffizier Hanns Schuster
                       Gefreiter Johann Ströcker

Unteroffizier Karl Heinen
Wachtmeister Otto-Heinrich Braun
Unteroffizier Helmut Schlegel
Kanonier Josef Martini
Unteroffizier Gerhard Scheffler
Unteroffizier Otto Feustel
Unteroffizier Werner Greiner-Mai
Kanonier Ferdinand Brück
Unteroffizier Rudolf Doskocil
Unteroffizier Alfred Jung
Obergefreiter Josef Stehle
Kanonier Alfons Deimann
Obergefreiter Willi Schmitz
Unteroffizier Kurt Knoch
Unteroffizier Werner Willeitner
Obergefreiter Herbert Laurent
Unteroffizier Hans Tietjen
Unteroffizier Herbert Mitschke
Unteroffizier Sepp Pollinger
Obergefreiter Leo Pieringer
Obergefreiter Andreas Meier

Farther to the left the Tigers and Panthers of the Panzer Regiment GD attacked along the highway to Vascani and were able to reach their objective in spite of considerable resistance, especially from tanks and anti-tank guns. This successful operation revealed that they had in fact driven into enemy attack preparations. The bolsheviks had massed strong infantry and tank forces. In spite of the success of the operation and the resulting booty in weapons and equipment, for many of the men, especially those of the Assault Gun Brigade, the coming of night was accompanied by sadness. One of their best, a man known for his cool bravery, and also one of the senior members of the GD's *Sturmartillerie*, Oberleutnant of the Reserve Reisenhofer, had been killed in this battle along with a member of his crew, Obergefreiter Franz Viehweg. His motto had been: "The life of an assault artilleryman is short, but tremendous!"

After the events of the previous day's offensive operation it was perfectly clear to the men and the division command that an enemy offensive was imminent. There were two obvious focal points: along the Vascani–Targul Frumos highway, and near Bals and the area south of Ulmi Liteni. The terrain in these areas was the most favourable for an attack by tanks, and it had to be expected that the bulk of the enemy's armoured forces would strike there.

The tanks and assault guns were sent into action on the hills between Vascani and Dumbravita again on 27 April. Believing that in this case, too, a good offense was the best defence, the division command sent them back into the hornet's nest of the enemy assembly area.

The tank battle raged for hours. The attack was an outstanding success; the panzers opened fire from a distance of 800 metres. After a few hits the first tank bearing the red star on its turret went up in flames. The panzer companies (the Tiger battalion was under the command of Oberstleutnant Baumungk) reported destroying large numbers of enemy tanks with only minor losses. Once again, however, there was little territorial gain even though the Soviets withdrew.

There was a surprise waiting for the tank crews when they inspected the knocked-out Soviet tanks: they were armed with a new 122mm gun. The shells came in two parts, with a huge propellant charge. So it was true what the German intelligence service had announced some weeks earlier: the Soviets were now using a new, much more powerful type of tank, the Josef Stalin, or JS for short. These new tanks subsequently became more prevalent, forcing the development of more powerful defensive weapons, especially anti-tank guns.

The defensive measures by the Panzer-Grenadier Division GD were accelerated, but were also concentrated in the areas likely to be attacked. Reserves were moved up and alert units were formed and positioned behind the main line of resistance. Alternate firing positions for the artillery were scouted, fall-back observation posts were set up, the radio equipment was checked in the event of a loss of telephone communications; all in preparation for what was coming.

Under the direction of the pioneers, prepared secondary positions were built deep in the defensive zone. Anti-tank barricades were erected on the roads leading into the city of Targul Frumos. Anti-aircraft guns went into firing positions. A breakthrough by the enemy had to be prevented at all costs.

The offensive expected on 1 May 1944 failed to materialize. Air reconnaissance, which watched over the enemy's assembly area all day, reported considerable masses of tanks and a large number of new artillery positions in the anticipated areas of main effort. At the request of the division commander, Generalleutnant von Manteuffel, the famous tank-destroyer Major Rudel and his unit were moved into the area. The Stukas bombed the woods and hollows, bringing death and destruction to the enemy. But at the main line of resistance all remained quiet; almost too quiet for this stage of the game. It was the calm before the storm, a calm which frayed the nerves of the defenders.

CHAPTER 3

DEFENSIVE VICTORY AT TARGUL FRUMOS

At precisely 04.20 on the morning of 2 May, there began a firestorm the like of which had seldom been seen before. The hail of fire lasted more than 60 minutes. Then waves of tanks, including the latest types, moved toward the German lines through the morning mist and the clouds of smoke produced by the artillery fire, which moved slowly to the rear.

The former commanding officer of the Panzer-Grenadier Division GD, Generalleutnant Hasso von Manteuffel, described the battle, which raged for three days with undiminished intensity, but which ended in victory for the defenders, as follows:

"North of the east-west line Podul–Iloaei–Targul Frumos–Seret the terrain was passable everywhere and was suitable for armoured combat vehicles. It also offered a broad field of fire. But it was unfavourable in that everywhere north of this line the enemy sat on the commanding hills, although they were 8-10 kilometres away from our forward positions and could not, as I hoped, make out the details of our defensive system. We therefore advanced our foremost pickets to about 2,500 metres north of T.F. (Targul Frumos). South of the east-west line there was rising terrain which gave us excellent observation sites and positions for anti-aircraft guns and artillery. There was also a Romanian field position in front of a deep, wide wooded area to the south, in which the completely terrified Rumanians now and then did some entrenching. The ground cover in the division area provided camouflage for the infantry positions, their heavy weapons and the assault guns.

Winter gave way to warm, sunny spring weather. The nights were clear, the days saw blue skies with excellent visibility. The subsurface was sandy and generally dry.

Due south of Targul Frumos there was a mountain from which the entire division sector and the probable area of the enemy attack could be monitored in the most ideal way through sight and sound. I moved my command post there in the last days of April.

The Field Forces in Action

Both infantry regiments were in the front lines, positioned in depth with strong local reserves in the hands of the regimental commanders. The Assault Gun Battalion was distributed among the two regiments and placed under their command. The division reserve consisted of the Pioneer Battalion and the Armoured Reconnaissance Battalion as well as the Panzer Regiment.

The Panzer-Artillery Regiment, well supplied with ammunition, its three battalions distributed over the entire sector, remained in the hands of the regimental commander, but was instructed to work closely with the infantry regiments. Concentrations of fire were not only prepared, but were, quite innocuously of course, test- fired and repeatedly checked. The heavy infantry weapons, including the infantry guns, were incorporated into the defensive fire plan. The division's flak battalion (4 batteries, of which 3 were 88mm guns), had one battery dug in north of T.F. for anti- tank defence, while the rest were deployed for anti-aircraft defence.

The Panzer Regiment around T.F. was at the disposal of the division commander. The repair services were close by so as to be quickly available.

There were ample stocks of munitions of all types and of fuel; this of course contradicts the fairy tale that has been told over and over again since the war, that we were supposed to be suffering from a shortage of ammunition at that time. Anyone concerned about supplies got them!

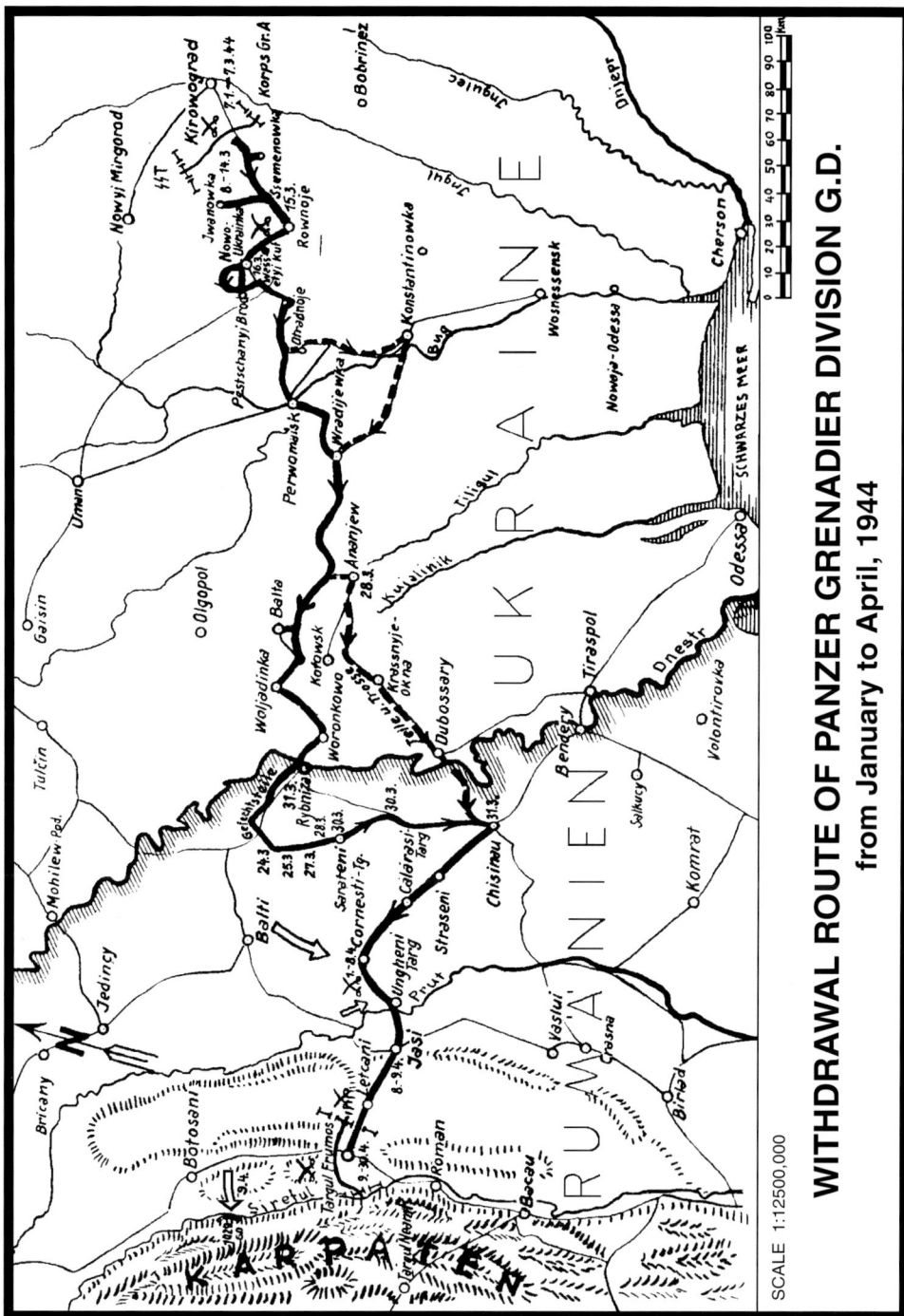

WITHDRAWAL ROUTE OF PANZER GRENADIER DIVISION G.D.
from January to April, 1944

SCALE 1:12500,000

319

BATTLE FOR TÂRGUL FRUMOS (Rumania)
from April 10 to May 5, 1944

The troops at the front had dug in deep, just as I had ordered, and were distributed in mixed battle groups in the defensive zone so that they could provide mutual fire support. The entire system of positions was scouted by the regimental commanders, submitted to me and then frozen in order to ensure uniform cooperation within the division.

Rations were good. The welfare of the troops in every respect was my first priority and the directive was carried out.

I announced the imminent offensive to the units and accordingly explained my thoughts and my battle plan to the commanders of the regiments and battalions and in part to company commanders on the spot in daily briefings. As a result of these pep talks the unit leaders, all of whom were close friends with each other, were briefed thoroughly. I make a point of emphasizing this because the interaction of all weapons and supporting units functioned in such an exemplary manner; the only other place one could find an example of such cooperation would be in textbooks.

My main concern was determining in advance how to employ the Panzer Regiment. Many possibilities were discussed with its outstanding officer corps, mostly together with the commanders of other arms, and the plan was frozen as soon as I had approved it. The planning was done in such detail that the individual companies could be told the route to and the area of their possible positions, allowing even the most junior commander to become familiar with the terrain, for a knowledge of the terrain formed the basis of their battle tactics—even more than tactical considerations! The latter should be left to the battalion commanders!

The Combat Potential of the Units

Deployed in the sector from Ruginoasa (in the left part of the division's area of positions) to the Seret River was a Romanian brigade, strong in numbers, well-equipped with automatic weapons, including German-made anti-tank weapons, and adequately provided with artillery. I had rejected an integration with my forces and accepted the risk (I regarded the use of the Rumanians in combat as such!) of leaving them on their own in a sector of positions. Any Russian attack that struck this sector would have to continue through Targul Frumos. I was confident that in such an event I could head it off there at the latest with elements of my division, which is exactly what happened.

The Panzer-Grenadier Division GROSSDEUTSCHLAND's combat potential was outstanding, its fighting spirit second to none. The troops felt themselves completely superior to the enemy and the battles in April had provided clear proof of this. Cooperation within the division was based on a high degree of trust and comradeship. All of the men were aware of the coming difficult mission and they had no doubts that they would master it in one way or another. All the troops therefore worked with commendable energy to prepare for the defensive battle which would demand their total commitment. The division strength (approximate values):

2 infantry regiments, each with 2 battalions of 4 companies each with 100 men as well as one battalion of heavy weapons.

1 assault gun battalion with about 40 guns.

1 pioneer battalion, at full strength.

1 reconnaissance battalion, at 2/3rds strength.

1 panzer regiment with: 1 battalion of Panzer IVs (approx. 40 tanks),

                               2 battalions of Panzer Vs (approx. 80 tanks),

                               1 battalion of Panzer VIs (approx. 40 tanks),.

1 armoured artillery regiment of 3 battalions, full complement of guns.

1 anti-aircraft artillery battalion with 3 batteries of 88mm guns.

Ample stocks of munitions and fuel.

The division was well-supplied with communications equipment (radio and field telephones). Painstaking effort went into creating an efficient signals net, although in principle I placed more value on radio communications than on telephone and telegraph lines. Almost all of the latter were destroyed by enemy fire on the first day of the attack.

The 46th Infantry Division had in the meantime been deployed on the division's right. It was a good division under a good commander (Generalleutnant Roepke). One could depend on it when the going got rough! This division had been instructed to bear the brunt of the defensive battle for 24th Panzer Division on its right. As it was not expected to be hit by the Russian attack, this division had released forces, some armoured, for the formation of a strong reserve. The 24th had limited experience as a panzer division, as it had only recently been reorganized as such.

The combat potential of the Rumanians was limited, indeed it was of no significance at all; in fact they were a burden upon us. Their officer corps was poor. This assessment applied to all the troops in the Romanian border positions (behind our positions, see above) and the cavalry division held behind the division's sector, which I had to look after. I placed little faith in any of these units, and this lack of faith was all too soon confirmed!

The Battle Plan

My battle plan was roughly as follows: As I could predict with a probability bordering on certainty that the enemy would attack with strong armoured forces in conjunction with strong artillery aided by good observation possibilities, I decided to repulse the attack through the use of the massed panzer regiment employing a mobile style of warfare. In my comments I left no doubt whatsoever that the division's regiments would have to defend themselves, for our panzers could not be everywhere. Various types of reconnaissance would be the basis for making the initial determination as to where the enemy would attack with strong armoured forces. These were to be attacked and destroyed by our panzers, which could then be used in other regimental sectors in the event that employment of the division was still necessary there. I therefore reserved to myself the right to commit the tanks and later took part in all phases of the regiment's attack. In fact until the morning of the day of the attack I had no idea where the focal point of the Russian attack was likely to be. I thought it most likely that they would strike the left sector; because the Russians surely hoped to put the Rumanians there to flight, and by exploiting this partial success be able to roll up my division. The success of my battle plan depended on: the accurate transmission of information obtained through reconnaissance and its dissemination to the entire division; the practical, painstaking expansion of the infantry's defensive positions; and well-thought-out firing plans for all weapons (the heavy infantry weapons, the anti-tank weapons including the elements of the assault gun battalion attached to the infantry regiments, the artillery and the anti-aircraft guns assigned an anti-tank role), which should be drawn up by taking into consideration the type of weapon, calibre and ammunition. Arrangements had to be made with neighbouring units to guard the boundaries between units, and heavy and very heavy concentrations of fire were prepared. Test-firing, carried out without attracting attention, formed the basis for the latter.

The division command post was just about ideal. As I mentioned earlier, it lay on a rise due south of Targul Frumos. Observation facilities installed there enabled the entire combat sector to be monitored by sight and sound.

In spite of the most careful preparations, the **decisive** factor in defence was the combat potential of the troops. It was this which allowed the defence to achieve the result it did: a huge fiasco for the Russians! There was no doubt that in any case the main burden of the struggle would be borne by the infantry.

We were in close contact with the air units of the Luftwaffe. Their support was promised; as always, this was largely dependent on the weather.

The Battle

The Russians took no action against the division at the beginning of April. There was little firing by their artillery as they were obviously conserving ammunition. Reconnaissance reported numerous new battery positions. As usual, the positional infantry stayed put until the beginning of the attack. The prisoners that were taken alleged that they knew nothing of preparations for an attack, but the enemy couldn't deceive me as to his imminent attack. All the signs pointed to 30 April or 1 May. The weather was fine, there were clear blue skies, the ground was dry. Conditions of visibility were very good.

Dawn came at about 04.00

On 1 May, the day before the attack, all was quiet at the front as before. At about noon air reconnaissance reported heavy massing of troops in the enemy rear. I therefore requested a bombing raid for the evening of 1 May, which was carried out. Numerous fires and explosions led us to conclude that the attack had been successful. Prisoners taken the following day confirmed this.

On 2 May 1944 the day began at about 04.00 with lively artillery fire, which was mainly concentrated on the forward positions and did not extend to the rear. Our camouflage must have been good, for losses in men and materiel were very low; it was thus essentially harassing fire, which, as was often the case with the Russians, they maintained stubbornly. Looking back, I believe that it was intended to soften up our infantry and heavy weapons positions before they committed their tanks.

The attack by the Russian armour began about an hour after the artillery opened fire, and about thirty minutes later tank fire began falling on Targul Frumos. I watched the tanks roll toward the city from my command post. Our infantry allowed itself to be partially overrun so as to leave the tanks to the 88mm flak battalion that was dug in at the northern entrance to T.F. The majority of the attacking tanks, about 25 in number, were hit and set afire, the rest, about 10, stumbled into our Panzer Regiment's assembly area and were destroyed there. I very soon had the impression that the main attack would come from the area northwest of T.F toward Targul Frumos and therefore ordered the Panzer Regiment to position itself behind a rise west of T.F. behind the sector held by the Panzer-Grenadier Regiment. Dug in on the rise, very well camouflaged, was a battery of assault guns. Approximately two companies of Russian tanks, about 30 vehicles, attacked the rise just as I was driving up to it.

The infantry deployed in front of the rise had allowed the tanks, which were moving at high speed, to roll past. The battery let the tanks approach to about 300 metres and then knocked out every one of them. Most of the enemy tanks exploded into tiny pieces. I later showed some of them to the experts to prove to them the outstanding effectiveness of our armour-piercing ammunition. We suffered no losses! Another Russian company drove indian file, that is to say one behind the other, past Ruginoasa, where the Rumanians had disintegrated as expected. It was spotted in time by a company of our tanks and completely destroyed. My initial impression was confirmed at about 08.00. There now came wave after wave of tanks, which we blasted and put to flight from well-sited, prepared firing positions. As I was speaking to the CO of the panzer regiment in his command vehicle (by radio), very large-calibre tank shells began whizzing past between our vehicles. They had been fired from great range. We soon ascertained that they were fired by heavy tanks from a distance of about 3,000 metres.

At first we both thought that it was a mistake on the part of a company of our Tiger tanks, for we had never met such heavy tanks from the Russians before. A company of Tiger tanks (Panzer VI) were ordered up, and they opened fire on these tanks. We could clearly see the shells striking the tanks but they bounced off their armoured fronts. The commander of the Tiger battalion, who was present, ordered the tanks to attack. They drove to within 2,000 to 1,800 metres of the enemy tanks and opened fire on them. Four of the enemy tanks were soon burning; three, as far as I could see, left the position at high speed. I ordered a nearby company of Panzer IVs to swing around Ruginoasa, give chase and destroy these tanks. These fast and manoeuvrable small tanks were fortunate to be able to approach to within 1,000 metres of the Russian giants and attack them from behind. The enemy tanks halted and we later learned that they had burnt out.

I have mentioned these Stalin tanks several times. Advantages: powerful gun, thick armour, low silhouette (about 51cm less than our Panzer V); disadvantages: slow, not manoeuvrable enough; as well, in my opinion their crews were not sufficiently familiar with the tank.

It would take up too much space to describe the battle in detail; therefore I will describe its course in broad outlines:

By about 11.00 the Panzer Regiment had destroyed about 250 tanks in the area of the Panzer-Grenadier Regiment's positions. I saw hesitation in the enemy attack. The Russians still had plenty of tanks, but they merely fired at us from extreme range without attacking. We at first had no interest in attacking so deep into the enemy positions with our tanks to finish them off – we hoped to take them on the next day or at another place. Meanwhile alarming reports had been coming from the Panzer-Fusilier Regiment (right division sector) since 09.00. Thirty-two Russian tanks had now entered the village in which the regiment's command post was located. Twenty-four were destroyed in a close-quarters battle in which even the regimental commander himself took part. The Panzer-Fusilier Regiment's lines were breached in several places, but it held fast. Like the Panzer-Grenadier Regiment, it had succeeded in separating the enemy infantry from their tanks and holding it up. The Soviet tanks now had to fight alone. I had promised my friend Oberst Niemack, the commander of the Panzer-Fusilier Regiment, that I would come to his aid with the Panzer Regiment at 12.00. The situation there had meanwhile become extremely critical. There was a renewed heavy attack by strong Russian armoured forces after 11.00. I therefore ordered the panzers to break off the battle in the sector west of Targul Frumos and assemble in the T.F. area.

The commander of the Panzer Regiment, who was in Targul Frumos, took the initiative and made all the necessary preparations to supply the regiment with fuel and ammunition as quickly as possible. A mixed battalion of Panzer Vs and VIs under the command of the commander of the Tigers was left behind in the Panzer-Grenadier Regiment's sector. I myself drove to the Panzer-Fusilier Regiment with a company of Panzer IVs. I assessed the situation and the terrain and sent the following panzer regiment to the attack while it was still on the move. It appeared on the battlefield at five minutes before twelve, exactly when I had promised the commander of the Panzer-Fusilier Regiment, which was holding out bravely. The panzer regiment's tanks immediately destroyed about 30 Russian tanks that were careening about in the regiment's rear area. By nightfall the intervention of the Panzer Regiment had completely restored the situation in this sector of the division.

During the latter part of the night, or before it became light, a half-battalion each of Panzer Vs and VIs was positioned in both sectors so that they could place fire in front of our infantry when it became light. On the night of 2 May the enemy's extraordinary losses in tanks, combined with the fact that nowhere had their infantry reached their initial objectives, led me to hope that the worst was over. I was to be proved right. The Russians attacked again on the 2nd and 3rd of May, but in spite of heavy tank support their attacks were shot to pieces in front of, and in places in, our positions.

Our bombers flew multiple missions on 2 May, including the Rudel Geschwader in the anti-tank role. They gave us effective support and even destroyed a number of tanks. They made highly effective attacks with bombs and guns on infantry and artillery positions as well as troop concentrations in the enemy's rear.

Our own tank losses had not yet reached ten vehicles, however a considerable number had sustained more or less minor damage. But thanks to the Panzer Regiment's outstanding supply organization and repair service there was virtually no drop in its strength, and it remained, as was so often the case, the courageous infantry's faithful helper.

The success was a great one: a breakthrough in the direction of Ploesti had been prevented, the enemy's losses in men and tanks were so great that they lost any desire to attack again as long as the Panzer-Grenadier Division GROSSDEUTSCHLAND was in position there. I estimate their losses at about 350 tanks destroyed and another 200 damaged.

It also found it important that we could now inspect the first Stalin tanks, which I had examined in detail and photographed. In my opinion our success was based on the following factors:

1. The accurate assessment of the situation in general.
2. The detailed defensive preparations, carried out diligently and reliably, which assured the closest cooperation of all arms within the division, and in which each weapon was able to exploit its technical and tactical characteristics to the full.
3. The marksmanship and skill of all the anti-tank weapons and the artillery.
4. The preparedness and steadfastness, as well as the bravery, of the artillery, the infantry, assault guns and the flak artillery as well as the aggressive spirit of the tank crews.
5. The exemplary fighting spirit of all officers, NCOs and men, who knew that each could depend on the other.
6. The accurate assessment of the situation in the various phases of the battle and of the terrain by the division command.

My battle plan was based on the following facts and the lessons of my past experience, which were confirmed:

The division had to defend, which meant hold, its positions, there was to be no fighting withdrawal; this had to be made clear to the common soldier, otherwise the infantry squad leader would believe that he was entitled to fight a delaying action and withdraw temporarily. The closest possible cooperation between the infantry and all the arms that supported it in battle – their own heavy infantry weapons, assault guns, artillery and pioneers- - formed the foundation of the defence; but the infantry also played first fiddle in the concert, and all the other weapons had to submit to their legitimate demands.

The armoured forces were to be held together and kept close to the front to counterattack and attack the enemy's armour.

The infantry headed the defence from resistance nests of varying strength and composition. Mutual support from position to position had to be assured.

Fire control of the artillery had to remain flexible and not adhere rigidly to the established firing plan. Maximum concentrations of fire had to be strived for in every case. It should in fact be destructive fire.

All other weapons had to subordinate themselves to the actions of the tanks wherever they were committed. In this way they provided the most effective help to the panzers and themselves. Obviously this included the exchanging of information. Frittering away of the armoured forces had to be avoided no matter what the circumstances so as not to weaken the defence's armoured core.

The panzers should not be satisfied with fending off attacking enemy tanks from good firing positions, rather they should destroy the enemy armour wherever it is seen or suspected. For this reason they must themselves frequently attack in order to destroy those enemy tanks supporting their attacking tanks from long range.

Movement and fire are to be coupled, in the battle of tank versus tank as well, to prevent oneself from being ambushed in a firing position by enemy reserves that have discovered the location of that firing position.

Commit only enough armoured forces to the defence as are needed to master the situation. The armour battle must be conducted in depth, that is to say that one must at all times have a reserve of tanks ready to go into action, especially of those with the large-calibre weapons (Panzer V or VI). One cannot be too strong in the attack, but at the same time one may give up the depth from which one alone can operate.

Since the tanks are dependent on their supply, recovery and repair services, their organization, workplace and working manner must assure that, following an engagement, the maximum number of tanks are available for use again in the shortest possible time. In my outfit they were under the command of a panzer company commander who was well aware of the needs of his comrades. In addition to good communications and the accurate shooting of the crews, the speed of the tanks on the battlefield, not on the road, proved to be a decisive requirement for a successful tank-versus-tank engagement in these battles; this was generally underestimated in peacetime. In these rapidly-played-out segments of the tank battle with their constantly changing combat situations, keeping tabs on the enemy by means of an uninterrupted and logically planned and executed reconnaissance effort, as well as the scouting of the terrain and finally the exchange of information between units, were further decisive foundations on which the battle was fought.

All panzer commanders right up to the division commander belong on the battlefield, specifically wherever they have the best view of the terrain and good communications with the armoured core. I was always where I could see and hear what was going on up front, that is to say on the enemy side and all around me. Nothing and no one can replace the personal impression!"

Reports by individual fighters, the battle groups and companies reflect the nature of the battle, their details supplementing the broad picture.

On the morning of 2 May 1944 the bulk of two Soviet armies and six rifle divisions began moving south to finally take the city of Targul Frumos, which was to become the basis and jumping-off point for future Soviet offensive intentions. Far to the left, right at the boundary with the SS-Division *Totenkopf*, the enemy's massed tank forces drove down and astride the highway and rolled over the forward positions of I (APC) Battalion, Panzer- Grenadier Regiment GD. Here and there individuals sought to save themselves by running away, while others dug in deeper and blazed away with everything they had. But against the tanks they were defenceless; all they could do was duck down, disappear into their foxhole and take cover.

However the panzer-grenadiers couldn't forget about the Russian infantry for a moment. They were there quickly, more quickly than expected. Fire ! Fire! Separate the figures from the tanks, drive them from the shelter of the steel giants or at least force them to take cover. 1st Company under the brave Leutnant Bernhagen was unable to disengage itself in time; suddenly the Soviets were upon it. Resistance was futile; the enemy's superiority was overwhelming. A few men raised their hands to surrender. But like the men of 1st Company who were even then just pulling themselves together again, they were simply shot down, killed, murdered.

Leutnant Hans-Karl Richter described his experiences:

"The 1st of May brought sunshine but the expected Russian offensive failed to materialize. No one had reckoned on that, including I Battalion. During the evening hours of 30 April we had walked all around the position again. We had placed trip- wires, laid rows of anti-tank mines and prepared fall-back positions for the four platoons at the edge of Dumbrovita. At about 22.00 I met Leutnant Dieter Bernhagen at a knocked-out T-34 that marked the company boundary. Our mood was not rosy. I expressed my doubts concerning 1st Company's unfavourable position when the expected Russian tank attack came. Dieter shared my concerns.

For half an hour we considered what to do if 1st Company and my 3rd Platoon, which was on the right wing, were overrun. Not much could happen to us in Dumbrovita itself and Leutnant Bernhagen hopefully expressed his doubts that 'Ivan' would ever get past the crest, alluding to our powerful Tiger tanks. We finally agreed that if the situation became hopeless he would try to reach Dumbrovita in order to set up a hedgehog position with 2nd Company. We decided on a rail line which veered to the west beyond Dumbrovita as the second blocking line. This promised better defensive possibilities against tanks. That same night I had a telephone line laid down to 1st Company's command post, so as to always have direct communication with Dieter Bernhagen. The line functioned well and Dieter gave me several important tips, because from his hill he see into the hollows and brush-covered areas in front of my company.

That night we waited in vain for the Russians. We heard singing and various commands, but otherwise nothing. The war seemed to have taken a break; but it just seemed that way. In the afternoon Major Schwarzrock came with several Rumanians. Once again we discussed the barrage fire zones and the behaviour of the Rumanians on my left wing. They sat side-by-side in their trenches like herrings and had probably made an agreement with the Russians not to move. They walked around on sunny days and no one shot at them. Instead Romanian officers at the west end of Dumbrovita shot at empty bottles. It really was a peaceful but deceptive picture. My only consolation was a rocket battery that had taken up position in the centre of town unnoticed by the enemy and three assault guns, whose crews were playing skat in the old rectory.

Soon it was night again. Not until dawn was the state of alert raised, and each of us hoped that the Russians had shifted their point of main effort. Had our Tigers robbed the Ivans of their guts? We ourselves didn't dare believe it. At about 22.00 we knew for sure. German aircraft dropped pyrotechnics far behind the Russian lines and then the heavy bombs followed. No one knew whether it had done much good. At about 01.00 we heard the sound of tanks. Battalion called and placed us on alert. I walked through the position. Not a man was asleep. At a quarter to two I again met with Leutnant Bernhagen at the T-34. There wasn't much left to say. Quite contrary to habit, the leader of my company headquarters squad, Feldwebel Boehne, passed us two glasses of schnapps. All he said was, 'We might need it soon.' Anyway there was not a trace left of the familiar 'spring without end' mood. We walked away. After taking a few steps Dieter turned around as if he wanted to say something else, but he just wished me good luck.

At 04.20 the world seemed to disintegrate. The front was ablaze. The flash of bursting shells was all that was visible as far as the eye could see. We cowered in our holes. Everyone knew that the big moment had come, the one we had already been waiting for for twenty-four hours. I kneeled by the field telephone; but what should I say? The command knew what was coming anyhow.

Feldwebel Boehne lay up above at the entrance to the cellar and watched. 'The swine,' was all that he said. Then we saw it ourselves. The enemy were now using phosphorous. The broad hollow between Dumbrovita and the hill on which 1st Company resembled a sea of fire. That had to be the focal point of the Russian attack. I cranked the field telephone in vain. The line had been severed. While I was doing this the ground began to tremble. A direct hit had almost levelled the house above our cellar. We looked at our watches and waited, but the firing continued unabated. When it finally appeared to leap over us an hour later, the air was filled with the roar of many hundreds of motors and the rattling of tracks.

Then machine-gun fire sprang up. We were outside in a flash. An unreal scene like we had never seen before met our eyes. In the broad valley about 80 to 100 tanks were racing toward the hollow, toward my 3rd Platoon. Star shells, mauve-coloured flares and thousands of tracers flitted in all directions. Why wasn't the artillery firing? The Rumanians were responsible for our sector. I sent a runner to the rear, but he returned with bad news. When the preparatory fire started, the Romanian artillery commander and the observation posts had left their positions, like their infantry, and had probably fallen back toward the much-talked-about bunker line. Now all we had left was the rocket launchers and the three assault guns.

But there was no time for reflection. The first tanks had already reached the outskirts of Dumbrovita. They didn't get far. The assault guns had been watching, and in a few seconds seven heavy tanks were in flames. Fahnenjunker-Feldwebel Gerber, who was in command of 1st Platoon on the left wing, suddenly came running across the open ground and he and his platoon occupied the west side of our planned hedgehog. Meanwhile, on the right wing our soldiers were fighting an almost hopeless battle.

The first wave of Russian tanks had already passed over them. Another hundred followed in the second wave, and they had infantry with them. Tremendous masses of infantry. It was time. When the first salvo of rockets landed in the midst of the Russians, I fired the signal flare. That meant pull back. Two squads of the 3rd Platoon were able to comply with the order and were taken in by us at the outskirts of the village. But the others stayed put; they probably saw no way out. They shot the infantry off the tanks, but then the T-34s were upon them. All at once the entire hill in 1st Company's sector seemed to be swarming with tanks. From a distance of 100 metres one could watch hand grenade duels, see soldiers jump to their feet and be cut down. Unable to help, we had to sit and watch.

We had posted four MG 42s on the rooftops and these fired without interruption. Then something happened that no one who was there will ever forget. A shout went through the ranks of the soldiers of 2nd Company. Ammunition gone, exhausted, some without weapons, our comrades stood up in their foxholes and raised their arms. Then we saw them fall. I don't know what happened, only that at that instant no one was thinking about cover. The men stood and fired rifles and machine-guns freehand. Our rocket launchers must have realized that something awful was happening over on the hill. Rockets howled over us without letup and tore huge gaps in the seemingly endless mass of brown figures. Still we stayed. Heavy rifle fire and a flurry of hand grenades were the first indication that the Russians had reached the first houses in Dumbrovita.

We fought our way back slowly, frequently fighting hand to hand. We stopped and set up a hedgehog position just in front of the rocket launchers. A Leutnant, probably the battery commander, had been very badly shaken up by the grisly murders on the hill. He lay on a roof with tears in his eyes, directing his battery's fire as it destroyed what looked like entire enemy units.

Suddenly there were Russian tanks thirty metres in front of the firing position; but the assault guns were standing guard. A few shots and three heavy tanks were burning. The crews didn't get far. Two tanks had broken through, however, and these split up the two platoons on the left wing. Two rifle squads and the company headquarters squad defended the battery's firing position until the last rocket had been fired. Then, at the last second, the brave Leutnant commanding the battery was hit. Badly wounded, we took him along in the prime mover. The assault guns had pulled back in the meantime. With a handful of men we slowly fought our way back to the rail line. The Russians had already crossed it. Finally, after a hand-to-hand struggle lasting 30 minutes, we were able to fight our way through at an underpass. Sadly our medic, Unteroffizier Hoffmann, was blown apart by a tank shell.

We reestablished contact with our people at about noon, the last squad of the battalion to do so. The day was not yet over, however. With four armoured personnel carriers I assumed responsibility for securing the left flank, which was open for many kilometres. I Battalion was scattered. There were small groups of men everywhere. With great difficulty Major Schwarzrock had managed to fight his way out of his command post, around which three T-34s were circling.

Tired and depressed, we sat in the armoured personnel carriers and waited for what was to come. The enemy hadn't penetrated far, but the soldiers could no longer stand the strain. The pickets on the hill must have fallen asleep, for suddenly there were four T-34s right in front of our half-tracks. However this time luck was on our side. As if summoned by a magic hand, the tanks and assault guns of the SS Division 'Totenkopf' suddenly appeared from the south; before any of the T-34s could take aim they had all been hit. Then there began a terrific tank battle, practically in no-man's-land. Oberst Rudel's Ju 87s swooped down repeatedly, showing the panzers the way. The four APCs of 2nd Company went with them, and they found plenty of work to do. The Russian infantry appeared to be following their tanks in thousands; now all the fury of soldiers who had seen their comrades fall to the murderer's hand was unleashed.

The attempt by the Russians to break through was frustrated. Until now little has been said concerning the details of the death of 1st Company and its brave Leutnant Bernhagen. I Battalion did its duty on 2 May 1944. In doing so it lost many of its best. Today the list of the missing includes the names of many comrades of 1st Company, proof that there, on the hills near Dumbrovita, Greater-German grenadiers gave their lives for Volk und Vaterland. Those who were allowed to survive these difficult hours should know the obligation they bear to them."

From their positions, the men of III Battalion, Panzer-Grenadier Regiment GD saw what happened to their comrades – and knew that for them there was only one choice. Somewhat farther back, at the edge of a hollow, there was a 75mm Pak. Crouched behind the anti- tank gun's armour shield, Unteroffizier Emde (4th Heavy Company, I Battalion) sat spellbound at the sight mount and stared through the telescopic sight at the approaching enemy tanks. Behind him, by one of the two trails, was his loader, the next armour-piercing round already in his hands. The gun tractor, which was off to one side, was hit by a shell and burst into flames. Then... a heavy blow, a flash of fire; the gun jumped back. In the area of the target a flash – smoke – fire. A tank blew apart. The loader rammed another shell into the breech; the anti-tank gun barked again, another enemy tank went up in flames. In less than twenty minutes Emde destroyed seven enemy tanks, just he and his loader. Then his gun was hit, and it was over. The firing stopped. The surviving enemy tanks noticed this and raced toward the lone anti-tank gun in order to run over it and grind it into the dirt beneath their tracks. Unteroffizier Emde and his loader were just able to reach safety. Later his commanding officer, Oberst Lorenz, awarded Emde the Iron Cross, First Class.

Due northwest raged the Battle of Giurgesti. II Battalion's 5th Company had been ejected from its positions, and its handful of men had fallen back to a section of trench several hundred metres in front of the village. Then a group of German soldiers emerged from the wood to the right: Leutnant Thurau of I Battalion had managed to fight his way through and went into position farther left near the highway. He had to hold, even though eight more enemy tanks had already arrived. Fire! Fire!! Armour-piercing shells brought them to a halt. On the road fork off to the left on the hill, near Point

298, they could see 26 enemy tanks and more than 300 men. Where was the regiment's pioneer platoon? Was it over there? Then Stukas came and dived on the mass of tanks. Smoke, dust, fire. For the moment there was quiet. To the right, the Russians had broken into II Battalion's trench. Oberleutnant Wechmann, together with several runners and a few stragglers he had picked up, stormed the trench and took it back, shooting wildly in all directions. The Soviets fled. The German right wing was again back in the main line of resistance.

Leutnant Morschek arrived back quite unexpectedly with his 24 men. They were held at the command post as battalion reserve.

Where was the neighbouring unit on the right? Where was the nearest machine-gun nest of III Battalion, Panzer-Grenadier Regiment GD? They should have contact on the left with Oberleutnant Wechmann of II Battalion, which was supposed to be in front of Secaresti. Where were they then? Hill 344 had been lost; it was in Russian hands. But the men of 11th Company were still holding out in the gardens at the north end of Cucuteni and were in contact with the Hauptmann commanding the company; there, at least, they were together.

Then, suddenly, two T-34s on the street. Hollow charges up! Frisch ran forward and set off after the tanks, but then two assault guns approached and opened fire. Frisch, now having reached the enemy tanks, armed the charge. Boom! Hurray, it's burning! There were loud shouts, arms were thrown in the air from joy. Then, from the side, machine-gun fire. Sustained fire. Time to keep their heads down.

What was happening near Bals, on the left? That's where III Panzer-Fusilier Battalion was supposed to be. Damned heavy firing there. Were they still there? It didn't look that way. The MG 42s were still firing, but the enemy tanks were already behind them. Now they were rolling toward Nicolne, where the artillery was. There was a flash, the guns of 1st Battery were firing over open sights. Boom! The first enemy tank blew up, then another and yet another. The battery had hit five enemy tanks, and while this was happening 2nd and 3rd Batteries were able to pull out and disappear toward the rear.

On the 'Kalmü,' Hill 256, there was still an observation post. Weren't they going to leave? Couldn't they tear themselves away from the panorama of battle, from their wide-ranging view to the north? Those were brave boys. Finally the enemy infantry were stopped. Oberleutnant Kendel of III Battalion, Panzer-Fusilier Regiment defended his road bitterly and single-mindedly, but he was unable to hold Nicolne. He and his men had to fall back to new positions farther south of the town.

And farther to the right, near Facuti, where the panzer-fusiliers had their command post, Oberst Niemack fought another battle. War correspondent Heiner Mayer wrote:

"Situated close to the wall of the house behind a cottage, the narrow opening led into the makeshift bunker. Below, the regiment's adjutant spoke without interruption to the battalion command posts. The Oberst sat in front of the entrance on a half-charred beam. If he bent down, the earpiece of the second receiver just reached his ear. Now and then he listened in. He said little. Beside him, on the bunker's earthen roof, lay a brown leather briefcase; inside were the most secret, important files and orders. Across the case lay a submachine-gun.

To the left a treeless path led down to a brook spanned by a narrow bridge. It was the only one across the very swampy stream bed. There behind the wall of a collapsed dam was an anti-tank gun, the sole available heavy weapon. Three-hundred metres farther down the brook sat a T-34, pouring smoke. It had been knocked out by the anti-tank gun several moments earlier. The village was burning from end to end.

The young operations officer came hurrying up and reported that 32 tanks had now been counted in the village. From the bunker the adjutant called, 'Herr Oberst, all communications have been lost, even to division!'

A formation of enemy bombers swept over the village. A growing hail of bombs fell among the foxholes on the slope. On the far side of the valley, behind the front, Soviet infantry went into position. Continuous bursts of machine-gun fire forced everyone to take cover. From the most forward holes someone shouted, 'Is the Oberst still there?'

The liaison officer from a nearby artillery battalion arrived with the news that there was one chance left to retreat, upstream. If the Herr Oberst wanted to attempt to establish a second line of defense there...

The Oberst cut him off and said forcefully, 'I hear retreat, there'll be none of that here! Are your guns still in their old positions?' The artilleryman replied that they were. 'Then fire as long as you have ammunition! ... By the way, ask my operations officer what I think of attempts to fall back!' The Oberst bent down in the bunker entrance: 'Just so that everyone is clear on this: there will be no such attempt here! Let each of my officers know again, by radio or runner: the village will be held no matter what!'

A Feldwebel came and reported that he had destroyed a T-34 with a panzerfaust a few houses away. His left hand was bleeding. The Oberst thanked him warmly and ordered him to have his wound bandaged and then come into his bunker.

Our infantry came back from up front. The rigours of five hours of close-quarters fighting could be seen in their faces. The Oberst knew them; he also knew what they'd been through that morning. Several of them were wounded. 'The tanks have broken in,' one of them reported, 'thirty-three tanks are tearing up our positions. Now they're entering the village. Herr Oberst it's simply impossible...'

The Oberst sprang to his feet. 'Impossible?... Do we know that? Oh, my fusiliers. Here we have hand grenades, mines, hollow charges, haven't we gone through situations like this before? Let them come. We are here and are tougher than thirty-three tanks.'

An Oberleutnant was brought in. Before they got him, he had knocked out the first of the thirty-three tanks among the houses. 'Bring me an Iron Cross, First Class!' called the Oberst. The adjutant took off his own and passed it up from the bunker. Above in the street a tank shell smashed the medical officer's house to rubble. Houses were burning all around. They could hear the rattle of tank tracks. Heavy artillery shells fell in the town. Rifle bullets hissed. Ricochets buzzed and howled before landing in the mud somewhere. 'Now let's get them!' shouted the Oberst, and he picked up his submachine-gun. The spell was broken...

Eight of the Soviet giants, some of the latest type, were destroyed in close combat, man against tank. The battle went on for hours. The rest of the tanks withdrew. The will of one man had overcome them; he was tougher than armour plate, tougher than columns of tanks."

And then, ringing out from the right, from the east, tank cannon; their hard crack was music to the ears of the men in Facuti. They had come at literally the last moment. The enemy tanks swung their guns around to the right to meet the new threat. Here and there one of them went up in flames, some withdrew to the north.

Tanks, armoured cars and APCs of the 24th Panzer Division appeared; they rolled past the village of Facuti and set out in pursuit of the surviving enemy tanks. The panzer-fusiliers followed slowly on foot. Soon II Battalion, Panzer-Fusilier Regiment was back in its old foxholes; on the left III Battalion stayed due south of Nicolne and dug in to stay. The town in front of them was full of the enemy.

And behind near Targul Frumos? Thirteen enemy tanks, including several Stalins, got through, while the others lay disabled in the field, were shot to pieces or blew apart. The Tigers, Panthers and Panzer IVs had finished them. The 88mm flak troops at the outskirts of the city enjoyed a big day. They kept up a hectic rate of fire. The main force of enemy tanks succumbed to hits from 88mm shells. Scarcely one of them returned to its departure position.

In the course of these bitter defensive battles, by the evening of 2 May 1944 the units of the Panzer-Grenadier Division GD alone destroyed 96 enemy tanks, some of them super-heavy types. The Panzer Regiment GD commanded by Oak Leaves wearer Oberst Langkeit was responsible for the greater part of this outstanding success. It destroyed a total of 56 enemy tanks. The 41st kill of the day brought the total number of enemy tanks destroyed by the regiment since it first saw action in March 1943 to one thousand.

Thus ended the first day of the great defensive battle in front of Targul Frumos. Even if ground had been lost, the positions as such were still firmly in our hands. Losses, especially men killed and the large number of missing, had been painful.

In spite of their bloody losses of the previous day the Soviets continued their attacks on 3 May 1944. Numerous tanks rolled into the positions of the grenadiers and fusiliers, some of them new; they formed points of main effort here and there but soon disappeared to the rear. But waiting for them there in ambush positions, deep in the division's combat zone, were the Tigers, Panthers and assault guns. The anti-aircraft guns concentrated on them, anti-tank gunners aimed at the steel giants' most vulnerable spots. It was tank slaughter again, an unparalleled massacre.

There was plenty of activity in the air the entire day by both sides. From the other side came close-support aircraft, the feared Il-2s, spewing death and destruction from their wing-mounted cannon and machine-guns. The Ratas spiralled above them and now and then dived down to attack some target they had spotted on the ground. The most commonly seen German aircraft were the Stukas, which dived howling on their targets and released their bombs just before pulling up. Their bombing accuracy was great. There were also the German tank-hunters, who took on individual enemy tanks with their cannon and destroyed them from the air.

On 4 May there existed the impression that the Soviet attack had lost some of its force. Concentrating their infantry and tank forces, the enemy now tried to break through only at selected points. They showered these objectives with artillery, mortar and rocket fire in an effort to totally destroy any and all resistance. And then they set off again, with masses of tanks and infantry, and sought to steamroller everything in their path.

Summoning the last of their strength, the infantry, who had been in heavy combat for two days, pulled themselves together to defend once again. One particular focal point for the defenders was the already famous "Kalmü"–Point 256. As the dominating hill position it exerted a special attraction on both opponents. It was now in no-man's-land; armoured assault pioneers of the GD stormed it several times, but each time they were thrown out of their positions. Each time, though, they regrouped and stormed this "Whore Hill," as it had become known, with flamethrowers and other assault weapons. On this day they finally succeeded in taking it for good.

Counterattacks by the battalions, some of which were down to 60 or 70 men, resulted in an improvement in their positions. The enemy were driven back. It was squad-size groups of men which repeatedly pulled themselves together and counterattacked. One such effort was organized by Hauptmann Mayer of II Panzer- Grenadier Battalion. He led his battalion headquarters staff and a squad from 8th Company in an assault which carried them back into Giurgesti. Mayer was wounded in the attack, while Oberfeldwebel Vies was fatally hit.

Otherwise 5 May was far quieter than the previous days; the Soviets were spent. Their strength was exhausted and all their bloody sacrifices had gained them nothing.

II Battalion, Panzer-Grenadier Regiment GD was tactically disbanded on account of its considerably weakened combat strength. Battalion headquarters and the Reinehr Company were assigned to I (APC) Battalion and the Morscheck Company to III Battalion. This measure was made necessary by the shortage of officers and especially NCOs.

Finally, on 7 May, the panzer-fusiliers counterattacked on the left wing of the division's sector with the assault guns and Panthers and supported by the armoured assault pioneers. Their objective was to take once and for all Hill 256, called "Kalmü" which was higher than any of the neighbouring hills. Possession of the hill meant a good view to the north into enemy territory and with it security, for from there any massing of tanks or enemy approach could be spotted in good time. Of course the Soviets were aware of this, and they transformed the hill into a fire-spewing fortress immediately after its capture.

The initial attempt failed, however a second attack made at first light with the support of 20mm flak on self-propelled carriages was more successful. The attackers entered Nicolne and tracer fire from the light flak drove the Russians from the town. Attacking from the left flank, panzer-fusiliers of the Regimental Headquarters Company under Oberleutnant Emminghaus, supported by pioneers, stormed the "Kalmü" Hill and took it in bitter hand-to-hand fighting. Artillery and rocket batteries pounded Point 256 to soften it up for attack. This proved successful and a short time later the positions were handed over to units of the 24th Panzer Division, which simultaneously took over this sector. The elements of the Armoured Reconnaissance Battalion GD deployed near Point 256 had to withstand significant Soviet counterattacks, which resulted in the hill changing hands several times. The fighting raged back and forth until 10 May. Statements by prisoners revealed that the regiments of the 3rd Guards Airborne Division had been completely wiped out in the fighting there. Leutnant Salzmann and Leutnant Heilmann of the Armoured Reconnaissance Battalion GD were killed in action on this hill which had cost so many lives.

From 11 May onwards all parts of the front became completely quiet. The enemy, who had hoped to force a breakthrough to the south with 300 tanks and numerous rifle divisions, had been frustrated by the iron will to resist of the men of the GROSSDEUTSCHLAND Division.

CHAPTER 4

THE FINAL BATTLES IN RUMANIA

The pause in the fighting in front of Targul Frumos in the sector of the Panzer-Grenadier Division *Großdeutschland* lasted until the end of May 1944. The peace was interrupted only by patrol activity, harassing fire and occasional skirmishes. Initially the enemy had no offensive intentions there, so impressed were they by the defensive readiness of the units facing them. Instead they turned their attention to improving their positions and laying minefields, which more or less indicated that they had gone over to the defensive, at least temporarily.

For the units of the Panzer-Grenadier Division *Großdeutschland* this time was highly valuable for reorganization, limited rest and refitting and taking in replacements. The 1029th Grenadier Regiment under Oberst Bandelow, which had been moved into the Roman area, was disbanded and the bulk of its personnel were absorbed by the division. The batteries of the 1029th Regiment, some of which were at full strength, allowed the division to reform the Panzer-Artillery Regiment's IV Battalion, which had suffered badly in the recent fighting. The former 1st and 2nd Batteries of the 1029th regiment became the 10th and 11th Batteries of the Panzer-Artillery Regiment GD, while IV Battalion's former 12th Battery returned to the battalion. The former 3rd (Flak) Battery, 1029th Grenadier Regiment joined the Army Flak Battalion GD, bringing the unit up to its authorized strength of six batteries.

The badly weakened II Battalion, Panzer-Fusilier Regiment GD was brought up to strength and placed under the command of Hauptmann Emminghaus. The former Regimental Headquarters Company of the Panzer-Fusilier Regiment was redesignated 5th Company, II Battalion, resulting in the following organization of the battalion:

II Battalion	Hauptmann Emminghaus
Adjutant	Leutnant Kaschele
Ops. Officer	Leutnant Behnsen
5th Company	Oberleutnant Möller
6th Company	Oberleutnant Kloft
7th Company	Oberleutnant Sadlowski
8th (Machine-gun) Company	Oberleutnant Pittelkow

In the meantime the personnel of I Battalion, Panzer-Fusilier Regiment GD under Hauptmann von Basse left for Germany, where the unit was to be reorganized as an armoured personnel carrier battalion at Fallingbostel Troop Training Grounds. There the battalion took charge of more than 50 half-tracked troop carriers armed with 20mm and 75mm cannon. At the same time the battalion's strength was augmented by personnel provided from the replacement training unit in Cottbus. The APC Battalion of the Panzer-Fusilier Regiment GD was expected to rejoin the division in June 1944.

Reorganization of the Armoured Reconnaissance Battalion GD as a fully-armoured reconnaissance unit was also begun at this time. Two squadrons, and later the remaining elements as well, were shipped to Cottbus to the Panzer-Grenadier Replacement Training Brigade GD. Hetzer armoured vehicles, based on the PzKfw 38(t) tank, were issued as reconnaissance vehicles, and the Volkswagen squadrons were equipped with half-tracked armoured personnel carriers. In the course of the reorganization, 2nd to 4th Squadrons were amalgamated into two squadrons. The battalion now consisted of the Headquarters Squadron and four other squadrons.

All in all, it was the beginning of a significant change for the Panzer-Grenadier Division *Großdeutschland*. The increasing difficulty of the struggle demanded more armour. Combat strengths of the regiments themselves dropped; regiments were reduced from the previous four battalions to three, each with just four companies. But at the same time the division became one of the most modern units in the German Army, distinguished first and foremost by an increased number of weapons and armoured vehicles. Increased mechanization demanded this measure, which admittedly on the German side could be applied only to a limited number of units at that time. As a result the GD came to be seen as a mobile fire-brigade, and more frequently than in the past it was deployed where it was expected that the enemy would break through.

By the end of May Rumania was ripe for further trouble. Aerial reconnaissance believed it had detected a shifting of enemy forces from the area northwest of Targul Frumos into the area northwest of Jassy, which suggested that they had new offensive intentions. The Soviets were searching for a German weak spot. This shifting of forces by the enemy resulted in the division command despatching armoured patrols provided by the Armoured Reconnaissance Battalion GD into the area northwest of Jassy to determine the enemy's intentions. The patrols discovered a massing of enemy forces in the area north of Letcani, very close to the Jassy–Targul Frumos highway. Something was brewing opposite the positions of the 46th Infantry Division. For a ridge was the only thing separating these positions from the highway, which was so vital to the German supply organization.

The direct threat posed to Jassy, the dangerous proximity of enemy positions to the highway and the apparent attack preparations in the gorges and ravines to the north forced the German command to take countermeasures. The Panzer-Grenadier Division GD received orders to immediately withdraw from its present combat zone and attack north from the area due south of Podul Iloaiei, Danian and Letcani.

On 31 May elements of the SS-Division *Totenkopf* began relieving the division's left wing, while elements of the 24th Panzer Division relieved the right wing.

The panzer-fusiliers were first to leave their positions. They had the shortest route into the assembly area and moved to the extreme eastern end of this in the area of north of Letcani. The batteries of the Panzer-Artillery Regiment GD went into position on both sides of the town and in the hollows behind the hills. They were strengthened by the addition of static artillery, including heavy rocket launchers, whose role was to support the attack.

The panzer-grenadiers took up position farther west, but north of the highway. With them was III (Tiger) Battalion, Panzer Regiment GD under Oberstleutnant Baumungk.

The initial objectives had been revealed: for the panzer- fusiliers, who would be attacking on the right, Hill 178.3, about 2,000 metres south of Isvoare Epurennu; for the panzer-grenadiers the hills on either side of Orsoaeia (Ursoaei). A common objective was the line of hills due south of the Prut Valley, as it was important to gain a vantage point overlooking the valley.

The infantry, tanks and assault guns attacked at first light on 2 June. The advance was supported by heavy fire from howitzers and rocket launchers and the first enemy-occupied villages were taken. Then resistance stiffened; they had reached the Soviet main line of resistance. The battle zone that the attackers had to traverse consisted of deeply-excavated positions, camouflaged minefields of unknown size and numerous anti-tank gun and mortar positions.

Farther right in the attack lane of the panzer-grenadiers, the Panthers of I Battalion, 26th Panzer Regiment under Hauptmann Graf Rothkirch were so held up by swampy ground that they had to go around, which cost time. Oberleutnant Hasler and his men stormed ahead, jumped into the trenches and rolled them up. Hand-to-hand fighting broke out. Heavy fire from Stalin Organs frequently forced the men to take cover, but each time the panzer-grenadiers advanced between salvoes.

The Tigers and Panthers exchanged fire with the enemy at extreme range, destroying anti-tank guns and setting enemy tanks on fire at ranges in excess of 2,000 metres.

However the enemy very quickly recognized the intentions of the Germans.

The Soviets committed whole swarms of close-support aircraft, which made things difficult for the attackers. The anti-aircraft gunners, as well as those of the Army Flak Battalion GD and the regiments' flak companies, did the best they could. With only three working guns, the flak company of the Panzer-Fusilier Regiment GD brought down a number of enemy aircraft in a few hours; the heavy batteries of the Army Flak Battalion GD alone claimed more than five enemy aircraft shot down that day.

These losses were not enough to deter the pilots of the enemy close-support aircraft, however. They repeatedly swept over the battlefield, dropped their fragmentation bombs and then returned to strafe the attackers. The latter were forced to take cover and the momentum began to go out of the German attack. Mine-clearing troops from the Armoured Assault Pioneer Battalion GD accompanied the advancing infantry spearheads. The mines, invisible to the eye and immune to almost all types of mine detector, were everywhere. Oberleutnant Krüger ran into an enemy counterattack but was able to fend it off and put the enemy to flight.

In spite of everything the advance continued. The bare, grass- covered hills were taken one after another. Far to the rear the anti-aircraft guns provided sustained covering fire, while the panzers shot up every anti-tank gun they could see as well as enemy tanks on the back side of the hills. This supporting fire played havoc with the enemy and reduced their firepower. This was the moment the panzer-fusiliers and panzer-grenadiers chose to force the next hill, to climb and occupy it. When they reached the top they placed sustained fire on the fleeing enemy.

During the fighting on June 2nd and 3rd, 1944, the 2nd Medical Company's medical clearing station was in a school in Jassy. Only the operating squad was there; 2nd Squad, like the other first-aid companies, was still on the march. The influx of wounded was large and increasing. The surgeons worked day and night, caring for the wounded and seeing to it that they were evacuated. But the flow of wounded continued, and soon there was no more room. The halls had to be used; soon another location was needed. And then there were the air raids on the city, which became heavier from day to day. The medical assistants and orderlies worked selflessly, day and night, without a break.

On 3 June the fighting raged on. The heavy weapons opened fire at first light, helping the attack groups as they strived to reach their objectives. The town of Orsoaei fell after heavy fighting. Unteroffizier Kühnanz of 6th Company, Panzer-Grenadier Regiment GD was killed and Major Süßmann, the commander of II (Self-propelled) Battalion, Panzer-Artillery Regiment GD, died a tragic death. Early that morning he set out with his adjutant, Leutnant Schürmann, his driver and the commander of the motorcycle squad, Unteroffizier M. Großpointner, in a VW Schwimmwagen to scout the area. They drove into a previously unknown minefield. A powerful explosion hurled the vehicle into the air and cast the occupants onto the ground in a wide circle. The major landed right on another anti-personnel mine, which blew him to pieces. The others were seriously injured; Unteroffizier Großpointner, the driver of the luckless vehicle, lost a leg below the knee and suffered other serious injuries.

By evening the infantry, especially the panzer-fusiliers, were able to capture the high ground on either side of Point 181 north of Zahorna. The attack objectives were taken in heavy close- quarters fighting at considerable cost, numerous enemy tanks were destroyed and a large number of prisoners brought in. There too the captured positions were immediately improved for defensive purposes.

The following two days, June 4 and 5, saw only local attacks by the Panzer-Grenadier Division GD aimed at improving its positions and expanding the area already captured.

After the shifting of elements of the Panzer-Grenadier Regiment GD to the right of the panzer-fusiliers, at approximately 14.00 on 4 June the men of the reinforced II Battalion, Panzer- Grenadier Regiment, together with the remaining handful of Tigers, attacked from the area north of Vanatori along the Jassy–Papricanii Coarb road toward the enemy-occupied town of Moimesti. By evening they had entered the village in the face of determined Soviet resistance. There were only four Tigers left, all commanded by officers, whose privilege it was to take command of the nearest serviceable tank when their own was put out of action. A nearby natural obstacle, the wood about 1,000 metres southwest of Papricanii Coarba, was defended by the Soviets particularly stubbornly and simply could not be taken.

As soon as the attacking groups reached their objectives, Romanian troops were moved up and these occupied the newly-won positions. However, the higher-ups were not very convinced of the Romanians' will to resist, and so German counterattack groups were held ready behind each of the Romanian positions and these were forced to intervene on more than one occasion.

That is exactly what happened west of Zahorna on 5 June, when the enemy, with considerable support from bombers and close-support aircraft, charged the Romanian positions on a 2-3 kilometre front and soon put the defenders to flight. Elements of the Armoured Reconnaissance Battalion GD were able to restore the situation by evening, returning the Romanians to their foxholes. Unfortunately this did not make for a rosy outlook for the future, especially for when the GD was no longer on the scene.

The losses of the past days once again forced the panzer-fusiliers to amalgamate units. The remnants of III Battalion were combined with those of II Battalion, while actual command of the regiment was temporarily in the hands of Major Krieg, filling in for Oberst Niemack who had been ordered to Führer Headquarters to receive the Swords. Niemack was the 69th recipient of this high decoration, which was awarded him for his courageous actions in front of Targul Frumos on 2 May 1944.

On 6 June the fighting finally died down somewhat; the men were able to better install themselves in the former Soviet trenches, which were now used in reverse to their intended direction. However the quiet was deceptive, for on 7 June the enemy counterattacked north of Zahorna with considerable air support. Hill 181 was lost and the Soviets managed to drive into Zahorna itself.

An immediate counterstroke, carried out by the Assault Gun Brigade GD under Oberleutnant Diddens and a battle group from the Armoured Reconnaissance Battalion GD led by Rittmeister Schroedter, returned Zahorna to German hands. However the attackers were pinned down by heavy defensive fire about 1,000 metres south of Point 181. Both battle group commanders, Oberleutnant Diddens and Rittmeister Schroedter, were put out of action with serious wounds. The German attack was called off and a new defensive line was occupied at the limit of the advance.

There now followed a pause in the fighting, apart from some local skirmishing, which allowed the German troops to more or less improve their positions. The accomplishments of the units of the Panzer-Grenadier Division *Großdeutschland* employed there are reflected in the following figures: in the period 2-7 June 1944 seventy enemy tanks were destroyed, 19 aircraft shot down and 45 artillery pieces and 36 anti-tank guns destroyed. The pioneers alone lifted more than 10,300 mines in this period, mostly under heavy enemy fire. The signals units constructed, operated and maintained a network of telephone lines 177 kilometres long, repaired 167 interruptions and received or transmitted a total of 1,763 radio messages.

With 17 enemy aircraft shot down, the Army Flak Battalion raised its total number of kills in a twelve-month period to 101.

The 2nd First-aid Company treated more than 2,000 wounded, at times under heavy bombing attack. The Assault Gun Battalion GD reported the destruction of 15 enemy tanks and took more than 90 prisoners.

In the meantime further Romanian units arrived in the division's area. These took over the recently-won positions, at the same time relieving the units of the GD. Eventually, by 13 June, the bulk of the division was in rest positions due south of the Jassy–Targul Frumos highway. Even there, however, the units were kept at a state of readiness for possible action in the former combat zone in the role of a fire-brigade. But at the same time it was announced that the division was going to be rested in an area where there was no immediate danger of further combat. The effect of this news was miraculous; to the few men still left it seemed unbelievable.

The necessary preparations for accommodating the units in their new rest area, located about 100 kilometres south of Jassy, began. The first units were moved south on 15-16 June. On 15 June Oberleutnant Diddens became the 501st soldier of the German Armed Forces to receive the Knight's Cross with Oak Leaves.

It was a fact; after months of heavy fighting and sacrifices, but also of honourable actions at the hot spots of the southern sector of the Eastern Front,

PANZER GRENADIER DIVISION "GROSSDEUTSCHLAND", July, 1944

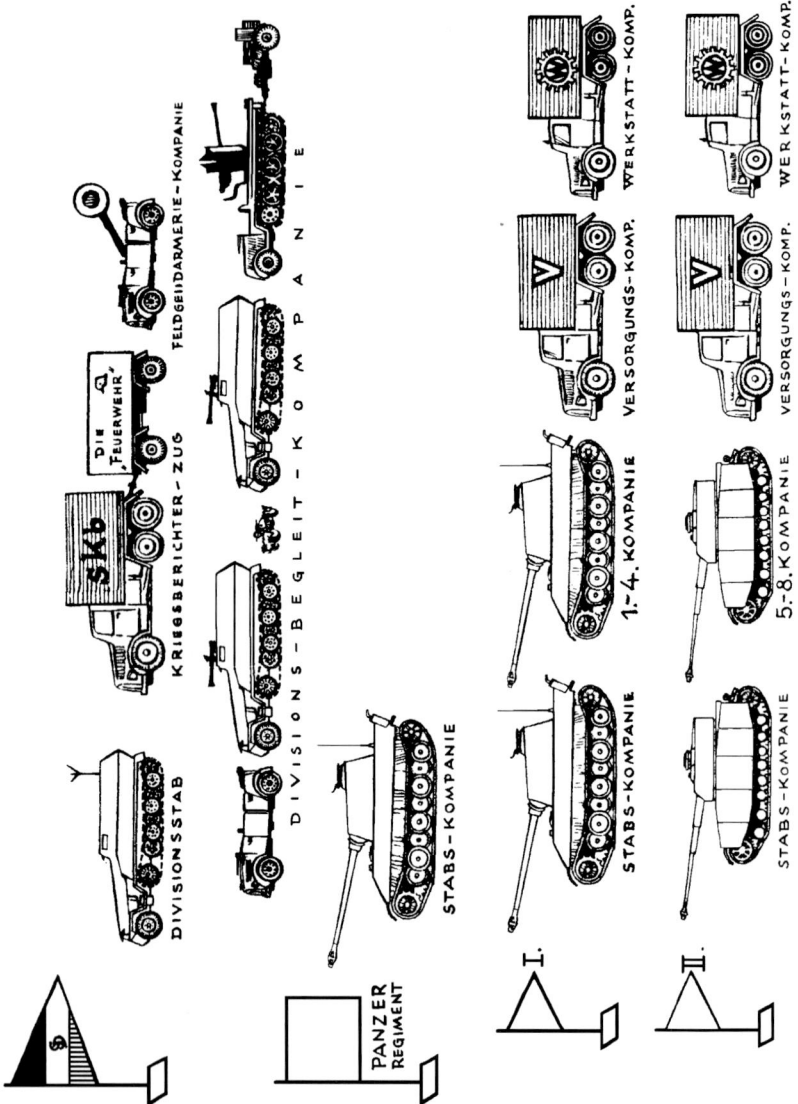

DIVISIONSSTAB

KRIEGSBERICHTER-ZUG

Die "FEUERWEHR"

SKb

FELDGENDARMERIE-KOMPANIE

DIVISIONS-BEGLEIT-KOMPANIE

STABS-KOMPANIE

PANZER REGIMENT

STABS-KOMPANIE

1.-4. KOMPANIE

VERSORGUNGS-KOMP.

WERKSTATT-KOMP.

STABS-KOMPANIE

5.-8. KOMPANIE

VERSORGUNGS-KOMP.

WERKSTATT-KOMP.

I.

II.

4.(m.)FLA-BATTERIE

6.(le.) BATTERIE

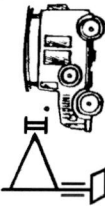

3.(SF.)BATTERIE [Hummel]

5. BATTERIE

1.-3. (SCHWERE) BATTERIE

5.(m.)FLA-BATTERIE

BEOBACHT. BTTR.

2.(SF.)BATTERIE [Wespe]

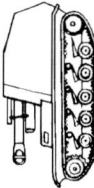

1.(SF.)BATTERIE [Wespe]

4. BATTERIE

6. BATTERIE

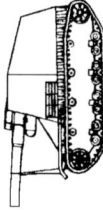

STABS-BATTERIE

STABS-BATTERIE

HEERES FLAK ABTEILUNG

STABS-BATTERIE

PANZER ARTILLERIE REGIMENT

I.

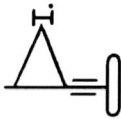

STABS-BATTERIE

II.

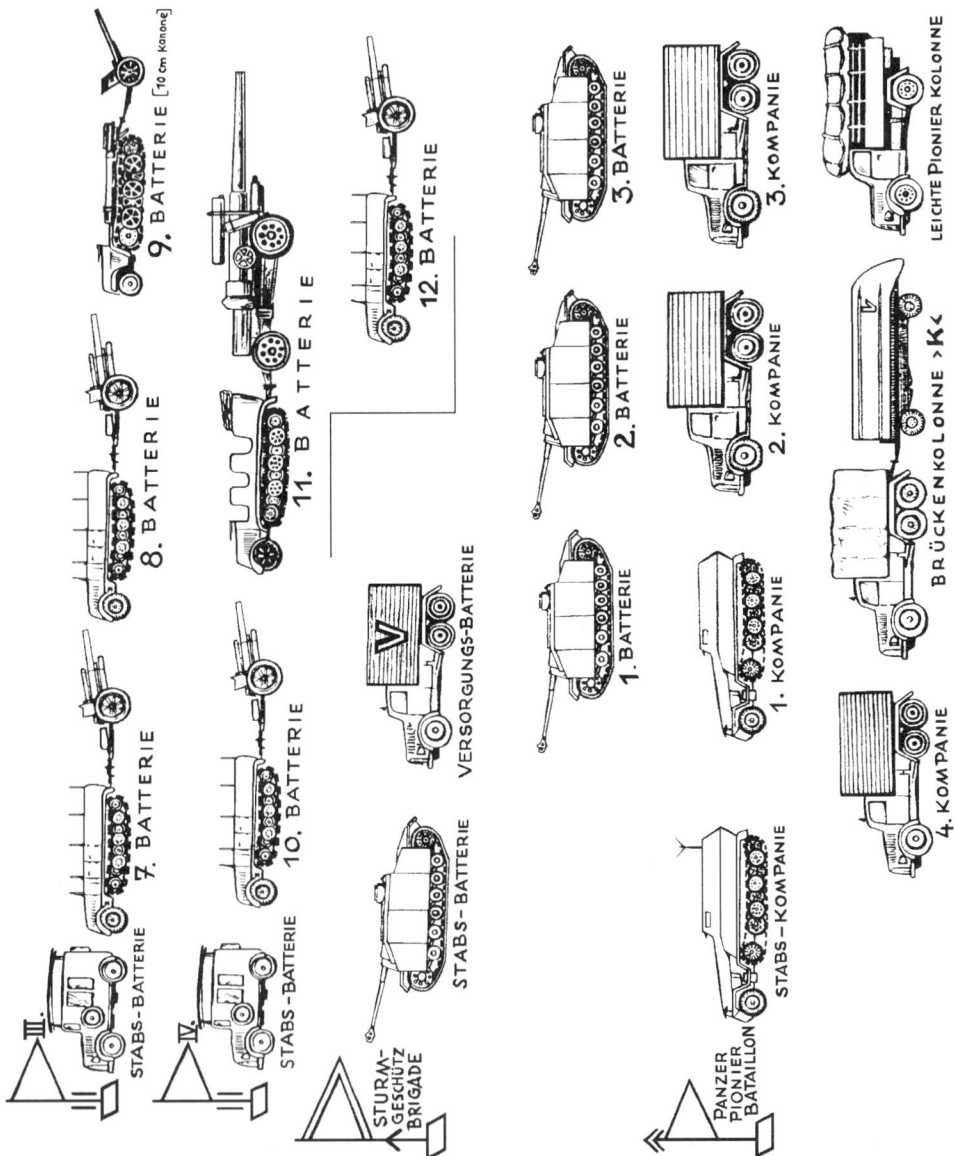

9. BATTERIE [10 cm Kanone]

8. BATTERIE

7. BATTERIE

III. STABS-BATTERIE

IV. STABS-BATTERIE

10. BATTERIE

11. BATTERIE

12. BATTERIE

V STURM-GESCHÜTZ BRIGADE

VERSORGUNGS-BATTERIE

STABS-BATTERIE

1. BATTERIE

2. BATTERIE

3. BATTERIE

3. KOMPANIE

2. KOMPANIE

1. KOMPANIE

STABS-KOMPANIE

PANZER PIONIER BATAILLON

LEICHTE PIONIER KOLONNE

BRÜCKENKOLONNE >K<

4. KOMPANIE

PANZER NACHRICHTEN ABTEILUNG — FERNSPRECH-KOMP.

FUNK-KOMPANIE

DIVISIONS NACHSCHUB TRUPPE

120 t 1.-6. KOLONNE

60 t LEICHTE KOLONNE

VERSORGUNGS-KOMP.

GERÄTE-KOLONNE

KRAFTFAHR PARK TRUPPE

1.-3. WERKSTATT-KOMP.

ERSATZTEIL-KOMP.

WAFFENMEISTEREI

VERWALTUNGS-TRUPPE

DVA AUSGABE DIVISIONS-VERPFLEG.-AMT

FLEISCHEREI-KP.

BÄCKEREI-KP.

FELD ERSATZ BATAILLON

1.-6. KOMPANIE

FELD-POST

SANITÄTS-TRUPPE

FELDLAZARETT

1.SAN.KP.   2.SAN.KP.

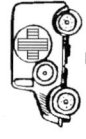
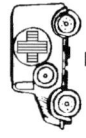
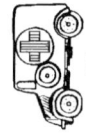

I.   II.   III. KRANKEN-KRAFTWAGEN-ZUG

the division was going to get a rest. The Wehrmacht communique of 9 June 1944 described exactly what had been achieved:

"...in the battles in the Jassy area German-Romanian troops under the command of Romanian Cavalry General Racovit, General der Panzertruppe von Knobelsdorf and General der Infanterie Mieth, with outstanding support from strong German-Romanian bomber and close-support squadrons, drove the bolsheviks from in-depth, fiercely-defended positions in heavy fighting and in doing so were able to significantly improve their own positions..."

CHAPTER 5

From Führer Escort Battalion (*Führer-Begleit Bataillon*) to Führer Grenadier Regiment and the Führer Escort Regiment (*Führer-Begleit Regiment*)

When the allies landed in Normandy on 6 June 1944 (the British on both sides of the mouth of the Vire and the Americans at the foot of the Cotentin Peninsula) heavy fighting was touched off in France which placed new burdens on the German Armed Forces. In Italy fighting raged south of Rome; in Finland the German-Finnish front on the Carelian Peninsula awaited a Soviet offensive. The German Eastern Front was fighting a desperate battle with barely cohesive fronts; the weight of the Soviet offensives and the increasing weakness of its own forces was steadily pushing it west, south and northwest toward the old borders of the Reich.

In Germany itself the allied air offensive was reaching its climax, paralysing to a growing degree the output of the war industries as well as the morale of the civilian population and its willingness to go on. With growing food shortages, an exodus from the crowded cities to the country, the knowledge of their own weakness and an awareness that there was no way out of the dilemma, most people gave in to their fate and kept fighting in deepest desperation for their very existence. The stubborn refusal of the western allies to come to any sort of an understanding, the growing fear of an invasion of Germany by the plundering and murdering Soviets, the behaviour of the German command (which bordered on absurdity) and the sense of powerlessness in the face of the enemy's superiority only stiffened German resolve to fight on.

At the bases of the German Armed Forces, especially those of the replacement training units, the older age classes, participants of the First World War, men bordering on old age, were under arms. They were the last levy, a desperate attempt to fill the gaps in the bloodied units and create the new units demanded by the many theatres of war. Boys of 15 and 16 years of age, most of them from the Hitler Youth, were given pre-military training designed to shorten their actual training time when they were called up. Replacements, replacements: it was the call of the fronts, the cry of the homeland.

Of the existing *Großdeutschland* units, the actual field division, the Panzer-Grenadier Division *Großdeutschland*, was fighting north of Jassy. Its strength rapidly deteriorating, it held its positions against the continuous

348

Soviet efforts to breach the front. At its bases in Cottbus and Guben, training of recruits by the Panzer-Grenadier Replacement Training Brigade GD had taken on an increased sense of urgency. The brigade provided the replacements needed to reform completely shattered units and reorganize others. It was also a collecting point for convalescents arriving from all over Germany; these men, having recovered from wounds suffered at the front, were used to form field replacement battalions. I Battalion, Panzer Regiment GD, which was in France waiting to be equipped with Panthers, was drawn into the battle on the invasion front and was placed under the command of unfamiliar units.

Following the return of "Battle Group Böhrend" under the command of Hauptmann Duckenbrod, the Führer Escort Battalion received sufficient replacements to bring it back up to its old strength and it went on carrying out its security duties at the Wolfsschanze installation near Rastenburg in East Prussia. Command of the battalion had passed to Hauptmann von Werther, who stressed the training of his companies in order to raise combat readiness. Parts of units were constantly detached to Arys Troop Training Grounds in East Prussia for live firing and battle exercises. In February 1944 other elements were transferred to Berchtesgaden to take over the guarding of those Reich Chancellory installations that had been moved there. Only ten days after the start of the allied invasion in the west, escort detachments of the Führer Escort Battalion were sent to guard the W2 installation at Margival near Soissons, in which the Supreme Commander spent barely twenty-four hours. With so many duties the division was rarely all together.

Following on the heels of the successful deployment of the armoured "Battle Group Böhrend," orders were issued for the expansion of the Führer-Begleit Battalion to the size of a regiment. The need to create new armoured battle groups was given further impetus by the success of the latest Soviet offensive. The surrounding of numerous "fortified places" had resulted in the complete destruction of more than thirty German divisions, and replacements for these had to be found quickly. As a stopgap measure the German command turned to so-called "small panzer brigades," which received priority in the delivery of tanks and other armoured vehicles. Initial plans called for the formation of a total of 34 small panzer brigades. It was intended that these would later (when time and materiel permitted) be expanded into so-called "big panzer brigades," even panzer divisions.

As originally conceived, the small panzer brigade was organized as follows:

> brigade headquarters and headquarters company
> one panzer battalion
> one armoured troop carrier battalion
> one panzer-grenadier battalion (if possible)
> one armoured reconnaissance company
> one armoured pioneer company
> one armoured anti-tank company
> one armoured signals company

one self-propelled flak company

one infantry gun company

one transport column

Development of this type of small panzer brigade was undoubtedly based on the regiment model, as its organization was basically the same as the latter.

At Führer Headquarters Generaloberst Jodl and General Schmundt were giving a great deal of thought to the guarding of the site. They feared that in the course of their advance to the west, the Soviets, who were well aware of the location and significance of the headquarters near Rastenburg, would bomb the installation or attack it with paratroops. This threat increased as Soviet troops neared East Prussia, and the installation was forced to adopt a defensive posture. This entailed strengthening the guard unit so that it would be capable of assuming the defence of the site.

In the past the headquarters had been divided, strictly locally, into three defensive zones:

1. The so-called outer ring: troops were stationed in the towns and villages around the headquarters, their mission being to guard the distant surroundings against attack.

2. The outer security zone: manned by elements of the existing Führer-Begleit Battalion, manning defensive installations with fixed heavy weapons.

3. The inner security zone: also manned by elements of the Führer-Begleit Battalion. The preparations for the reorganization of the Führer-Begleit Battalion, initiated in early 1944, went hand in hand with the intention to strengthen the unit. The striking power of the existing battalion was raised by training the men to the level of highly-qualified fighting men.

The beefing-up of the Führer-Begleit Battalion, which began in May 1944, and its reorganization as a regiment, took place under the command of Oberst Streve, commander of Führer Headquarters, Hauptmann Pieper, his Ia, and Oberleutnant Strauß. Selection of suitably qualified enlisted men and NCOs was undertaken by Hauptmann Kowalke at the Panzer-Grenadier Replacement Training Brigade GD in Cottbus.

Soon after the development of a new crisis situation in the north of the Eastern Front there was a call for a new battle group to be sent there immediately.

Hauptmann von Werthern was placed in command of the force, and in great haste he put together "Battle Group von Werthern," which consisted of two panzer-grenadier companies and a panzer company together with 88mm anti-aircraft guns, about 1,000 men all told.

The battle group was placed on alert on 6 June and departed shortly thereafter. Feverish preparations, formation and concentration of the individual units, issuing of brand-new weapons and equipment, personnel confined to base – all this marked the birth of the new battle group. Its destination was still unknown, though there was talk of a deployment to Lithuania.

The battle group entrained at the Arys Troop Training Grounds on 7 July and departed in great haste for the northeast. Trips to the front itself had become much shorter. After a train ride lasting several hours the units set out by road through Kauen to the east. The city resembled an overturned anthill. The endless stream of refugees mingling with herds of cattle; it was a scene of retreat, of chaos. The men of "Battle Group von Werthern" marched against the flow with determination and stubbornness, even though words like "war mongers" were thrown at them now and then. But eventually the road became emptier and more lonely. The slow, cautious advance into no-man's-land began. The battle group had already spread out; patrols were despatched, a screen was sent ahead on both sides. Action in this unfamiliar land was no longer far away. Then, at the point, machine-gun fire, Russian and German, back and forth, and the first radio messages flashed through the aether: "Battle Group von Werthern in contact with the enemy!"

The battle group saw continuous action near Anichkaya, somewhere in front of Vilnya, until August 1944. More than 3,000 men passed through the battle group as replacements for its losses in men and materiel. Hauptmann von Werthern was himself badly wounded on 24 July 1944 and had to relinquish command; only remnants returned to headquarters in August 1944.

The Strauß formation headquarters, which was to administer the initial organization of the new unit, was meanwhile transferred to Cottbus, where it was given a free hand by the replacement and training brigade. The result was a complete separation from the Führer-Begleit Battalion; the new unit was thus not created from or with the latter, but was a completely new unit formed from replacements and convalescents provided by the Panzer-Grenadier Replacement Training Brigade GD. However it was still intended that, following its formation, the new unit would be deployed to protect Führer Headquarters near Rastenburg.

The new unit, which was to become one of the first small panzer brigades, was christened in July 1944. Its name was:

Führer-Grenadier Brigade

By 19 July 1944 enemy spearheads were barely 100 kilometres from the headquarters. The town of Augustovo was threatened. Oberst Kahler, who had been named to command the Führer-Grenadier Brigade, was ordered to assemble the formation staff working at Cottbus and those units already put together in the Rastenburg area, where they were to assume responsibility for guarding the area surrounding the installation. Details of the unit's mission were contained in the first orders issued to it, by the Führer's Wehrmacht adjutant, General Schmundt, in Secret Command Matter No. 494/44. "Battle Group Kahler," as the elements of the new Führer-Grenadier Brigade (which was still in the process of being raised) that had arrived at Rastenburg were referred to, began its duties.

In June 1944 inquiries were made of all Wehrmacht offices as the result of deliberations under way by headquarters, the commandant of Führer Headquarters, the Wehrmacht operations staff and the Chief Adjutant. Their primary objective was to find a commanding officer for the existing Führer Escort Battalion, someone who, in addition to outstanding leadership and organizational skills, was capable of creating a special unit of highly-qualified fighting men. Finally they thought they had found the right man in Major Fabian, wearer of the Knight's Cross with Oak Leaves. He arrived in Rastenburg in mid-June 1944, was briefed on his responsibilities and with great elan and energy began sorting out the elements, companies and replacement units already in the area.

The Führer-Begleit Battalion was still a separate unit and went on carrying out its duties of internal security within the installation. It was intended that the fully-integrated battalion should be incorporated as a whole into an enlarged unit at a later date. Major Fabian's orders were to form additional units and later amalgamate them as a regiment.

Nevertheless, Major Fabian was the commanding officer of the Führer-Begleit Battalion as well as of the new regiment then being created.

New companies were formed in June-July 1944 to supplement the five existing companies of the Führer-Begleit Battalion, resulting in the following organization in July 1944:

Battalion Headquarters	Major Fabian
Adjutant	Oberleutnant Dyckerhoff
	Oberleutnant Arnold
	Leutnant Görlitz
1st (Grenadier) Company	Hauptmann Stoerk (in APCs)
	Leutnant Schuster
2nd (Grenadier) Company	Hauptmann Schlafen (in APCs)
3rd (Grenadier) Company	Oberleutnant Jungnitz
	(in Steyr four-wheel drive cars)
	Leutnant Gräter
4th (Heavy) Company	Hauptmann Schulte
	(mortars and anti-tank guns)
	Leutnant Mahring
5th (Panzer) Company	Oberleutnant Geisberg
	(tanks and assault guns)
6th (Flak) Company	Leutnant Reichmann
	Leutnant Strattmann
	Leutnant Schoone
	Leutnant von Malotki
7th (Fast) Company	Hauptmann Straube (in VWs)
	Leutnant Bahlser

References were already being made to a Führer Escort Regiment and Major Fabian was seen as its first commander. The reinforced battalion was stationed near the headquarters and in the city of Rastenburg for the immediate protection of the installation.

The demands for personnel made of the Panzer-Grenadier Replacement Training Brigade GD increased to a shocking degree as the war dragged on and tours of duty at the front became longer. Not only did the field division have a considerable requirement for trained men to fill the gaps torn in its ranks in battle; the increased demand for personnel for new units produced a situation which the brigade could not endure in the long run. The reorganization of various battalions of the field division as fully armoured units at various troop training grounds demanded replacement specialists. The mounting losses suffered by the Führer-Begleit Battalion's battle group in action at Narva was an additional drain on the replacement training brigade's strength.

And now, in July 1944, there was the formation of these new units, which also made considerable demands on personnel. The Strauß formation staff had priority in the selection of qualified men; Hauptmann Kowalke acted in similar fashion, backed up by Führer Orders and similar empowerments.

Then Rittmeister von Möllendorf, representing Major Fabian, also arrived in July with a considerable wish list for the expansion and bringing up to strength of the Führer-Begleit Battalion. He also sought to get what he wanted by means of a Führer Order.

Coming at about the same time, as they did, all these requests for personnel created many problems for the brigade's commander, Oberst Schulte-Heuthaus. He had to consider the urgency of the requests while preserving the core of his brigade.

At this point in the war the command seized upon a solution that had negative effects on the elite formations in particular; it decreed that several units should be created from divisions that had done especially well at the front. Individual units were taken from these divisions to serve as the foundations of new formations; as well, highly-qualified and long-serving members of units waiting to be sent back to these units at the front after recuperating from wounds were instead used in the formation of new units. This diversion of experienced fighting men, which soon became a regular occurrence, had a highly negative effect on the field division.

This practice did, of course, benefit the newly-raised units to a certain degree; however, even where they were concerned this was outweighed to a considerable degree by the use of inexperienced replacements. Although the ultimate result was two or more large formations, their performance was mediocre and none stood out above the others.

The Panzer-Grenadier Replacement and Training Brigade GD recognized the danger in this and used every opportunity to oppose it. In many cases the best fighting men were selected and grouped together to be trained as non-commissioned officers. Suitably-qualified men were training as radio operators, teletype operators, tank drivers, gunners, armoured car crewmen, APC drivers and so on, primarily to meet the increased demand for specialists. Brief courses were held for convalescents to acquaint them with the latest state of the infantry war on the Eastern Front and to familiarize others with the rigours of winter conditions in the east.

For these purposes and to provide more realistic training, the Panzer-Grenadier Replacement Training Brigade GD constructed a Russian village near Cottbus, which was faithful in every detail to the real thing in the east. Priority in use of the facility was given to the recruits, who were billeted there for the bulk of their training time, allowing them to familiarize themselves with situations they were likely to encounter in action.

After arriving at the Panzer-Grenadier Replacement Training Brigade GD, men who had recovered from wounds or illnesses were initially grouped into convalescent companies. There they were medically examined to determine their fitness for further duty. After their level of fitness had been determined, most were sent on a long home leave; on returning they either remained in Cottbus until they were fully recovered or, if found to be fit to a certain degree, were transferred to one of the cadre companies. The latter took in non-commissioned officers and enlisted men who were not yet ready for service at the front. In the course of time experience with these men, who had become unaccustomed to military service following a lengthy stay in hospital and indeed who were often disinterested in any further employment, made it necessary to split the cadre companies into three parts.

One group consisted of physically-fit NCOs and enlisted men with combat experience who were eligible for junior leader training. The eight-week courses, which incorporated the latest front-line experience, trained the men to be squad leaders or in some cases instructors for the training companies within the brigade.

The second group consisted mainly of enlisted men who required basic training again. Following this they either joined one of the junior leader courses or were assigned to one of the trained replacement companies.

Included in the third group were mostly NCOs and enlisted men who had been left disabled by wounds; they were retrained as clothing NCOs, equipment NCOs, orderly room NCOs, accountant and pay NCOs and so on for barracks duty. In the main they were made available to the brigade in order to release men capable of front-line use, though in some cases they were assigned to other army units for the same purpose.

The junior leader training given by the battalions proved to be an outstanding success, which resulted in candidates being assigned to a special company, the Junior Leader Instruction Company, under Oberleutnant Herbig. Its task was to train the replacements to be competent junior leaders and prepare them for service at the front. The company was organized as follows:

1st-3rd Rifle Platoons
4th Heavy Machine-gun Platoon
5th Light and Heavy Mortar Platoon

As may be deduced from the company's make-up, training was carried out primarily for the two panzer-grenadier regiments, the infantry units of the division.

During the twelve weeks of hard, intensive schooling, the company conducted realistic front-line training. The last fourteen days of each course were spent at the training grounds, with live firing and night and combat exercises. The course always concluded with an inspection, which was supposed to demonstrate the combat skills gained by the course, especially in the field. The growing shortage of specialists forced a further intensification of the training. In order to help ease the burden, in mid-June 1944 the 1st Conversion Company was formed. In the company qualified personnel were trained for special functions, received technical training and were taught to service highly-valuable weapons and equipment.

The primary function of the "Field Battle School GD" was the evaluation of experience gained at the front and its transmission in suitable form to the training companies. The school carried out specialized training in the standard close-combat techniques as well as the use of weapons in hand-to-hand combat. Suitable men were trained to become highly-qualified fighting men, tough on themselves and an example to the men. Major Gerbener, who had just recovered from a wound, passed on his wealth of combat experience to the men under his command.

CHAPTER 6

OFFICER CANDIDATE SCHOOL GROSSDEUTSCHLAND

Voluntary readiness – realistic training

The value of a unit is determined by the quality of its officers; their origin and character, as well as their abilities, training and skill determine the readiness and willingness to fight of the units subordinated to their supervision, care and orders.

Every unit moulds its officers and NCOs itself, offers them a military home and protects their rights, but in return demands their skill and their service. The unit is the personnel, who do their duty voluntarily or compulsorily. The officer and his junior leaders are responsible for them, even in situations of life and death. No higher authority can release them from this duty, a duty they must face up to.

The German people's will to self-determination, its will to fight to the end, grew as the military conflict dragged on and with the realization of our own weakness, our inferiority, of the shortages in weapons and materiel. The bearers of this will were often the young, the idealists, willing to dedicate their lives to a better future.

However the war had also produced an outstanding corps of leaders within the units. Junior leaders, squad leaders, platoon commanders and gun commanders had become masters of their craft after years of practice; they stood out above the mass of the soldiery and were recognized by them. Their opinion and their word often carried more weight than that of a young officer; the men followed them secretly or openly and trusted in their leadership. More than once they formed the backbone of an operation; their actions were an example to the others.

Such experiences and considerations caused the Panzer-Grenadier Division GD to take the selection and training of its officers and NCOs into its own hands. As early as 1 May 1942 these led to the segregation of officer candidates and their placement in an officer candidate platoon under the command of Oberleutnant Janke.

This measure was made necessary by the constantly growing demands by the field division for highly-qualified replacements. At the same time the division command had become convinced that a career as an officer should be open to every member of the field division. Proof that the chosen path of in-house replacement training was a correct one was provided by the expansion of the officer candidate unit to two platoons, command of which was placed in the hands of Oberleutnant Tisowski and Leutnant Alberti.

At this point changes were already taking place in the structure of the two platoons, which proved necessary in the interests of the field forces.

On one hand, consideration had to be given to the wishes of young volunteers who decided to apply to become GD Division officer candidates. These were mainly school graduates and other young men who had completed some sort of training. They signed up at the recruiting offices and after passing suitability tests were taken on strength as *Fahnenjunker* (officer candidates). They had to learn to be soldiers from the ground up.

On the other hand, there were those recruits who stood out above the rest during basic training in the replacement training units, and who appeared to be suitable for a career as an officer based on their character traits, quick perception and their outstanding military abilities. They were advised by their instructors and company commanders to apply to become career soldiers. The application then followed the normal chain of command.

The third category involved members of the field division, the front line forces, usually long-serving soldiers and NCOs whose personal conduct and behaviour in combat had qualified them for promotion. Most already decorated veterans, they were recommended for participation in a course by their company commanders and once accepted were sent to Germany.

The only differentiation made in all three groups was that of officer candidate and reserve officer candidate, O.B. and R.O.B. for short. Suitability had to be demonstrated during the basic training. If so appointed after basic training, the O.B.s and R.O.B.s were permitted to wear the silver-coloured double facing on their shoulder straps. Only then were they organized into courses in which they received specialized training toward their desired career as an officer. These courses lasted 4-6 months.

Among the conditions for the successful completion of the officer candidate course was the assignment of young officer candidates to the field forces for several months of proving at the front. Those candidates that had been selected from the front-line forces were assigned to officer candidate schools after completing the course. Those from the former group were not sent to the schools until they completed their proving period at the front. The officer candidate schools put the finishing touches on the candidates' training as officers, which was crowned by the awarding of commissions.

On 1 October 1943 the two officer candidate platoons were combined into an officer candidate company under the command of Hauptmann Zetsche.

1st-4th Supervisions:
1st Oberleutnant Lauck
2nd Oberleutnant Doege

3rd Leutnant Leonhardt

4th Leutnant Kolmitz

Over the course of the following months calls by the front-line forces for the officer candidate courses to include specialized training for the individual arms in addition to general officer training grew louder. Eventually, taking these requirements into consideration, the officer candidate company was expanded to such a degree that its initial organization was no longer adequate.

On 1 March 1944 the former company was organized into four, and soon afterward six, inspectorates (similar to that of the officer candidate schools) and placed under the command of Major Klüver, who soon afterward was granted the authority of a regimental commander. The new organization looked like this:

H.Q. Officer Candidate Unit, Pz.Gren.Repl.Brigade GD

H.Q. Company with Signals Platoon

1st - 4th Inspectorates for panzer-grenadiers

a 5th Inspectorate	with panzer, anti-tank and armoured reconnaissance sections
a 6th Inspectorate	with assault gun, armoured pioneer and artillery sections

In the headquarters company as well as the inspectorates (which were equivalent to companies) there was a cadre of personnel on hand who comprised the skeleton personnel, in a fashion similar to the officer candidate schools. The training staff, in an extended sense equivalent to a regimental headquarters staff, encompassed a large number of training officers and instructors as well as the inspectorate chiefs and their section officers. Working together, these created a training plan which served the demands of general and military training.

Naturally, military matters held pride of place, with tactics, weapons knowledge, equipment knowledge and command principles to company level and training duty forming the basis. In general terms courses were governed by two principles, training and instruction. Included in the first was weapons and equipment training, etc, while under the heading of instruction fell for example, gas warfare, patrol missions, the engaging of tanks from close range and so on. Following a brief theoretical discussion, each of these themes was tried out in practice, always taking into consideration the latest experience from the front.

Alongside the military training a considerable amount of time was set aside for promotion of general knowledge. The instructional staff included three instructors for general studies and a sports instructor for physical education, while a special section dealt with political instruction and provided suggestions in organizing free time. A good library was available to the students; personal leisure time was filled by group visits to the theatre and courses of lectures.

General discussions involving the course participants and training officers served to clarify questions that arose and helped students form their own judgements.

The instructional staff placed decisive importance on the forming of each individual personality. New methods, proposed by one or another of the training officers, were evaluated, in a fashion similar to that of Professor Hahn in his Salem Boarding School on the shores of Lake Constance.

Dominating the entire training program was the fact that everyone was a volunteer. This was the driving force behind independence of action, the inner incentive for increasing one's performance.

The quartering area for the officer and reserve officer candidates in Cottbus had no barracks fence. The decoration of personal areas, the individual quarters, was also left to the residents. It was supposed to be an expression of personal development. Not surprisingly, there were no padlocks on the officer candidates' cabinets and lockers.

After establishing an in-house officer candidate unit within the Panzer-Grenadier Replacement Training Brigade GD, the housing of which was greatly hindered by the crowded conditions in the barracks at Cottbus, the concept of an officer candidate village was proposed and very quickly put into practice.

With the assistance of several Reich ministries and various funds, however at first without informing senior command posts (in this case primarily the acting commander of Military Area Headquarters III, General von Kortzfleisch) about 50 wooden houses were erected on the Cottbus–Madlow road beneath spruce trees on the grounds of the Hitler Youth's regional leaders school in Neuholland. The so-called "private homes" each had two rooms. Contrary to any military plan, the houses were not constructed in rows but were strewn freely about the park-like setting. Supplementing the homes were a number of work barracks which served as classrooms, dining rooms, offices and equipment rooms. The Neuholland Guest House was converted into a mess and was also used as a lecture room for general discussions.

One question remained: how was this officer candidate village to be officially placed under the charge of the Wehrmacht. The entire facility had been created solely under the administration of the Panzer-Grenadier Replacement Training Brigade GD with no input from senior Wehrmacht offices, which would probably have held up the project. Rittmeister Bartram, one of the true GD veterans and restricted to home service as the result of wounds, was presently adjutant to the CO of the Replacement Training Army, Generaloberst Fromm. His relationship with the general was outstanding. The originator of the concept of an officer candidate home for the division suggested to Bartram that he invite his chief to take part in the opening ceremony. Using his charm, Bartram was able to guide his Commander-in-Chief to Cottbus, though before departing a rather sceptical Fromm said, "...exactly what am I supposed to do at this Feast of Tabernacles?"

The official opening took place on 17 May 1944 and was attended by a number of high-ranking officers, including the commander of the field division, Generalleutnant von Manteuffel; the commander of the Panzer-Grenadier Replacement and Training Brigade, Oberst Schulte-Heuthaus;

Reichsleiter Baldur von Schirach; General von Kortzfleisch, and others. The impression was outstanding, the program fitting and everyone was satisfied with the success of the undertaking.

The newly-created unit was also officially named, becoming the "Officer Candidate School *Großdeutschland*."

In the course of the next months work continued unabated under the command of Major Klüver. Organization of the school itself was completed in October 1944 and at the same time it was able to make available to the front the first officers trained there. Training under realistic front-line conditions occupied an increasingly large segment of the training timetable. The Hähnchen bunker camp near the autobahn was built specifically for this purpose. The individual inspectorates, some of which now consisted of four sections of about 40 men each along with their instructors, spent several weeks there, experiencing life at the front without leaving Germany. The earth bunkers were field-type affairs, which were built to front-line standards. The officer and reserve officer candidates lived in the bunkers as well as out of doors, and they very quickly became familiar with all the difficulties associated with such improvisations. From there they went to the field firing ranges where they frequently took part in live- firing exercises against movable targets. The targets were operated by the officer candidates themselves; squatting in a foxhole behind the human-shaped target, they experienced live firing under conditions very similar to those at the front.

All this served to train replacement officers for the GD field division as well as for other units. It was a confirmation of what was said in 1939 when the Guard Regiment was renamed the Infantry Regiment *Großdeutschland*, namely that this volunteer force also had to be the school of the German Armed Forces.

Part VI

CHAPTER 1

The Assassination Attempt in the Wolfsschanze
on 20 July 1944

Brooding heat had laid over the bunkers and wooden barracks of the Wolfsschanze installation in the forest east of Rastenburg since early morning. The usual hectic activity on the grass-bordered asphalt roads and concrete paths had given way to a sluggish listlessness. Only at the entrance to Security Zone I was the sentry ramrod straight at his post, for he knew that this watch was an especially important and responsible one.

Before him lay the handful of bunkers and bunker-like houses that stood within Security Zone I. Built rather close together, they included the "Chief Bunker" – House 11, in which lived the Supreme Commander of the German Armed Forces and Reich Chancellor Adolf Hitler. It was situated slightly off to one side near a pine nursery. In front of the house there was a well-kept lawn with small flower beds. Visible among the pines was a footpath; that was where Hitler's dog frolicked when it wasn't quenching its thirst at the brook that ran through the nursery. Not far away was the tea house; a simple, long wooden house that contained, among other things, the kitchen that prepared Hitler's meals.

Then there were the stenographers' quarters, the guest house and the bunker for the orderlies, servants and drivers, who were responsible for Hitler's well-being. Also there was the SD (Security Service) bunker, which housed SS-Gruppenführer Rattenhuber, who was responsible for Hitler's safety, together with several SD men, the bunkers of Göring, Bormann, Keitel and Dönitz, then the bunker complex of the chief of the OKW and the Wehrmacht Operations Staff, the signals bunker and the second kitchen. These were the quarters of the Supreme Command and as such were guarded closely by the Führer Escort Battalion. On that day, like every other, its most important task was the military protection of Hitler and his headquarters. On the other hand, from the very beginning Hitler's personal protection was the responsibility of the *Reichsicherheitsdienst* (Reich Security Service) or RSD; in the Wolfsschanze this function was carried out by Rattenhuber and a handful of men, about 11 in all.

Like the entrance to Security Zone I, that of Security Zone II, which encompassed the bunkers, houses and stone structures that housed the rest of the Wehrmacht Operations Staff, the messes and work barracks of the various departments and the headquarters commander, was guarded by sentries and guards. The entire installation was the responsibility of Watches North to South and East to West, which were mainly responsible for guarding the outer perimeter and whose equipment included heavy weapons. Theirs was a combat role; as mobile reserves they had at their disposal tanks, anti-aircraft guns and heavy weapons. The area surrounding the installation which was entrusted to them was also guarded by pressure-activated anti-personnel mines which, with their highly-sensitive detonators, were often set off when a rabbit or a deer strayed too close.

It was approaching noon on that 20 July 1944; the last relief was at 12.00; new guards arrived and assumed their posts. From their knowledge of the daily routine, the guards knew that the situation briefing always took place at noon in Security Zone I, inside the Führer Bunker. But the Führer Bunker was being worked on; men of the Todt Organization (OT) were strengthening the outer walls of the Führer Bunker, increasing their thickness from their previous one metre of concrete to four. The reason for this measure was fear of heavy bombing raids on the installation by the enemy. On this day the situation briefing had been moved to the guest house on account of the construction work. The guest house consisted of two of the latest type of Reich Labour Service barracks put together, with an entrance in the middle.

Like all such barracks it was made of wood, with only a layer of mortar plastered over the exterior for aesthetic reasons. The guards on duty that day had been alerted to expect the arrival of Mussolini, who was coming to meet with Hitler, at about 14.00. Everyone was therefore pressed for time. As usual, the briefing would begin punctually at 12.30 and would concern only the most important matters. Not many more than 20 people would take part; one was a representative of the BdE, the Commander of the Replacement Training Army, because the especially-important theme of the formation of new units was to be discussed. It was nearly 12.40; the situation briefing in the guest house had begun, preparations to receive Mussolini, who was expected to arrive by special train inside the installation itself, at the "Görlitz" stopping place, were under way. The schedule was set, everything else was put in preparation.

Then at exactly 12.42 German time, a powerful, but not overly loud, explosion shattered the stillness of the day; the men working in the vicinity of Security Zone I stopped what they were doing and listened.

What had happened? Had another one of those damned mines outside the facility exploded? Or was it something else?

Then two officers came hurrying down the concrete road toward Watch I; they showed their papers and rushed across the asphalt through-road to Field Watch South, which led to the airfield. The guard knew both men, General Staff Oberst Graf Schenk von Stauffenberg and his adjutant and escort officer Oberleutnant von Haeften. They had been there more than once and he also knew that they were from an office of the Replacement Training Army in Berlin.

The two men had scarcely disappeared into the forest when the field telephone in the guard house began ringing. "Alarm! Alarm! close all barriers immediately! Let no one in or out!" What was going on?

As it did every day, the Führer Headquarters courier aircraft had landed at the airfield near Rastenburg in the late morning hours of 20 July. As well as

"WOLFSSCHANZE" LAYOUT, in July, 1944

courier mail and several officers and civilians, the aircraft delivered General Staff Oberst Graf von Stauffenberg and his escort officer, Oberleutnant von Haeften, to Rastenburg. The car belonging to Hauptmann Pieper, the headquarters commander's Ia and temporary acting commander (Oberst Streve was away that day), was waiting to drive the two officers to the Wolfsschanze installation. All was normal; the officers were let out in front of the officers' mess in the spa, where Hauptmann Pieper was waiting. The men saluted each other and exchanged a few words; Pieper mentioned that he was a friend of Rittmeister Bartram, personal adjutant to Generaloberst Fromm, commander of the Replacement Training Army; Oberst von Stauffenberg had become Fromm's Chief-of-Staff only a few days earlier. An orderly in a white jacket with the silver and black *Großdeutschland* cuff band invited the men to sit down at a table beneath an oak tree in the mess garden in front of the spa. Roses decorated the table and bacon and eggs was served. Everything exuded peace and well-being, and soon the trio found themselves in a lively discussion of the situation. Rittmeister von Möllendorf, then the headquarters commander's adjutant, joined the group and sat down.

After a while Pieper got up and telephoned Feldmarschall Keitel, informing him of the Oberst's arrival from Berlin. They agreed that Keitel would call back when he was ready to receive Stauffenberg; until then Pieper could look after the guest. And so the group of officers remained seated and together discussed matters that affected them all. Stauffenberg seemed somewhat absent-minded, even nervous; he gave the impression of being rather scatter-brained, which was quite unlike him. Pieper thought: now they're burdening him with worries at the BdE.

Pieper always felt a touch of pity when he looked at this gigantic Oberst whom the war had scarred so terribly. He knew about the mine explosion in Africa that had cost him his right arm, an eye and two fingers of his left hand. The black eye patch that covered the eye socket made a sombre impression.

At about 11.00 an orderly approached the table and reported that Feldmarschall Keitel had called to say that Oberst Graf von Stauffenberg might come over. Hauptmann Pieper's car stood by to deliver the Oberst to Security Zone I, which also housed Keitel's quarters. Hauptmann Pieper walked the Oberst to the car, carrying his briefcase, which on this day was especially heavy and bulky. Curious, Pieper asked, "Why such a heavy briefcase, Herr Oberst?" The Oberst shrugged off the question, alluding to the mass of files inside. Pieper returned to his desk in the headquarters barracks; the orderlies cleared the table. Rittmeister von Möllendorf also returned to his duties.

As stated perviously, it was exactly 12:42 P.M. when the explosion shattered the quiet. A small cloud of smoke billowed from the guest house where, contrary to standard procedure, the conference was being held that day; window frames blew out and a man flew through the air and landed on the lawn outside the barracks. Figures crawled and jumped through the entrance; men staggered, collapsed or supported each other. Everyone in the vicinity rushed to the scene to render first aid. Ambulances were summoned; a growing number of men gathered around the barracks. Then Keitel helped Hitler outside. His clothing was blood-smeared, his pants hung down in tatters. Hitler was immediately treated by a doctor in the nearest bunker. It turned out that he had a large number of minor flesh wounds, a bruise on his right arm and minor shock. General Schmundt, on the other hand, was said to be seriously injured, as was General der Flieger Korten and one or two other persons. That was all that was known. The ambulances, some hastily summoned from Rastenburg, took away all the injured.

The security zones closed themselves automatically almost before the sound of the explosion had died away. The guards closed the gates, the field watches pushed obstacles called Spanish Horsemen into the entrances, preventing any movement in or out, as the watch standing orders prescribed in special cases. In addition, Hauptmann Pieper, acting on his own initiative, sounded the alarm by radio and telephone. All over the installation, however, officers and commanders of the guard had already acted on their own. No pass was accepted now; the guards let no one in or out.

Obergefreiter Jünnemann, a member of the Führer Escort Battalion's Panzer Company and a barrier guard at the South Watch exit, acted exactly as his comrades did. Spanish Horsemen had been placed across the exit. Feldwebel Kolbe, commander of the guard, saw two officers coming toward him from his right from the interior of the installation. One of them, an Oberst, imperiously and rather excitedly demanded that they be allowed to pass, but the Obergefreiter refused. The commander of the guard was similarly unimpressed; he explained to the Oberst that only the commander of Führer Headquarters could give such authorization.

Feldwebel Kolbe got on the telephone and called Hauptmann Pieper. Rittmeister von Möllendorf answered in his place, as Pieper had already rushed to the scene of the explosion. Over the phone Möllendorf gave permission for the men to pass, after all he knew the Oberst. After a few seconds Möllendorf's phone rang again; it was Kolbe, asking for confirmation that he had just spoken with Rittmeister von Möllendorf. When the latter confirmed that he had, a reassured Kolbe allowed the two officers to pass. This behaviour on the part of the commander of the guard was in keeping with watch standing orders, which required guards to immediately confirm all orders received by telephone.

The Oberst disappeared from commander of the guard Kolbe's view, climbed back into his car and drove away in the direction of the airfield. While passing through the deciduous forest the driver of the car saw the Oberst throw a large object into the bushes from the vehicle; however he was lost in his own thoughts and paid no more mind to this action on the part of his passenger.

Immediately after hearing the explosion, which he correctly guessed came from Security Zone I, Oberleutnant Dyckerhoff, one of the company officers and sometimes also an escort officer, immediately jumped into his Volkswagen and drove there past the guard. When he arrived several men were already investigating the circumstances and causes of the explosion.

364

The SS at once sealed off the actual scene of the explosion. Gruppenführer Rattenhuber directed the first inquiries himself. It was soon apparent that someone had attempted to assassinate Germany's military leadership, including Hitler, with an explosive device – but who were the culprits? Which of those that had taken part in the conference were no longer present? Dyckerhoff went through the list of names and very soon discovered, as did others, that Oberst Graf Schenk von Stauffenberg was missing. From an officer at the scene he learned that the latter was on his way to the airfield.

Dyckerhoff immediately rushed to the nearest telephone and had himself put through to the commander of the airfield. When asked about the Oberst, the latter said, "Oberst von Staufenberg and his adjutant are already here. They have just boarded the aircraft; the engines are already running!" Dyckerhoff: "Stop it! Stop it at once!" After a brief pause the airfield commander replied, "Not possible, the aircraft is already in the air." A strange story, thought Dyckerhoff, and he slowly returned to the scene of the assassination attempt.

The first thing an observer noticed on looking at the wrecked guest house was the flimsy nature of its construction. Was this why the bomb had failed to achieve the effect expected by the assassins? Only now was it apparent that only half the double barracks rested directly on the ground, while the other half sat over a hollow space. The reason for this was a depression in the earth, due to which part of the barracks was above the ground, supported only by several wooden posts; the blast wave from the explosion had thus been unrestrained and was able to spread unimpeded, especially in a downward direction. The windows and doors, which blew out, also helped allow the blast to dissipate to the outside.

The effect of this explosion within a room whose walls were made of concrete, such as perhaps the Führer Bunker, would have been unthinkable! No one would have survived.

Fantastic rumours were soon circulating, whispered from man to man: the Todt Organization had just tried to assassinate the Führer! An ambitious senior officer wanted to kill Hitler! Meanwhile the SS had hermetically sealed everything and the search had begun for the explosive device. Early suspicions concerned the soldiers of the Führer Escort Battalion who guarded this and all the other security zones.

The interrogations began. SS-Obergruppenführer Kaltenbrunner, head of the German intelligence service (Abwehr) after the removal of Admiral Canaris in February 1944, arrived, accompanied by about 20 SS men and detectives. Late in the afternoon Reichsführer-SS Himmler arrived at the South Watch, where he was promptly stopped. Oberleutnant Arnold, the commander of the watch sector, explained the reasons why he had been stopped. Himmler dismissed this with a smile and a wave of his hand: "Now then, commander of the guard, do you think that I tried to assassinate the Führer?" Finally he was allowed through and made his way to the scene of the crime. Increasingly the interrogations concentrated on the person of or the circle of persons around the actual culprit; and the name of Oberst Graf von Stauffenberg kept coming up. He especially came to the attention of the interrogators after they had interviewed Feldwebel Kolbe, who confirmed Stauffenberg's departure with his escort officer. The interrogations of Rittmeister von Möllendorf and Oberleutnant Geisberg, the only two officers of the Führer Escort Battalion temporarily forced to surrender their pistols, were conducted in a businesslike, even polite tone. These confirmed the suspicion that Oberst Graf von Stauffenberg must have had something to do with the affair. In the process it also turned out that Rittmeister von Möllendorf had lacked the authority to give Feldwebel Kolbe the order allowing the two officers to pass. But then there was his knowledge of Stauffenberg, perhaps also his nervousness or respect for the man's rank, but in any case it was soon clear that he and Oberleutnant Geisberg could not have been involved with the assassination attempt in any way. Incidentally, Rittmeister von Möllendorf was later killed near Houffalice during the Ardennes Offensive.

No members of the Führer Escort Battalion were arrested. Indeed the investigators repeatedly confirmed that they had behaved correctly during the past critical hours.

At any rate certain events shaded the mood of the grenadiers that evening and during the next 48 hours, namely the arrival in the installation during the night of 21 July of the first SS units and their move to hermetically seal off the entire installation, disregarding the existing guards.

One thing had almost been overlooked in all the excitement and confusion: the arrival of Mussolini. The special train was supposed to arrive at "Görlitz" at 14.00. It rolled into Rastenburg station as planned and Hauptmann Pieper, as acting headquarters commander, was notified of Mussolini's arrival. Pieper immediately relayed this information to Hitler, who initially decided to put off the visit until he gave further orders. What now? The train was already in Rastenburg, from there it was barely 20 minutes to the installation. He had to delay its arrival. Consequently, the train was first shunted about at the station for a time, and then headed out onto open track before slowly returning to Rastenburg via a roundabout route. The Duce remained oblivious to this delaying tactic. Finally, at about 3 P.M., the train was given permission to enter the installation and proceed to "Görlitz." The steps were pushed into place and the Duce left the car; waiting there for him as if nothing had happened was Hitler. The two men greeted each other briefly and warmly, and Hitler informed Mussolini of the assassination attempt which he had just survived. Hitler showed no signs of weakness during this first phase of their meeting; a black wrap covered his right arm, which was in a sling, and he extended his left arm to shake hands with his guest.

And what of the assassins? At this time all indications pointed to Berlin, more specifically to the Bendler Straße on the Tirpitz-Ufer, in the central office of the Commander of the Replacement Training Army.

CHAPTER 2

Berlin – Bendler Straße

Situated between the Landwehr Canal and the Berlin Tiergarten in the district of the same name is in itself an unremarkable street, which has nevertheless gone into history: it is Bendler Straße, at whose southern end, its front facing the Tirpitz- Ufer, stood the long grey building of the former Reichswehr Ministry, the later War Ministry. During the war its countless interconnected rooms housed numerous home offices of the Wehrmacht High Command, in particular of the OKH. In the sixth year of the war Bendler Straße was home to the Chief of Army Equipment and Commander of the Replacement Training Army, or Chef H Rüst und BdE in official German military parlance. Since 1939 this important post had been held by Generaloberst Fromm.

On 1 July 1944 the one-eyed, severely war-disabled General Staff Oberst Graf Schenk von Stauffenberg had become Fromm's Chief-of-Staff. Directly subordinate to Fromm was the Chief of the General Army Office, the AHA, General der Infanterie Olbricht, whose Chief-of-Staff was General Staff Oberst Merz von Quirnheim. Subordinate to the AHA were many additional departments, most occupied by older officers no longer suitable for combat duties. This office's senior-ranking officers resided on the second floor. On the side facing Bendler Straße was the office of the Generaloberst and his Chief-of-Staff as well as the waiting room and the room of his personal adjutant. In the summer of 1944 that was Rittmeister Bartram. As a senior member of the Infantry Regiment GD and then the Grenadier Regiment GD, he had been so badly wounded in the fighting in the Rzhev area at the beginning of 1942 that he was no longer fit for combat. In early 1944 Bartram therefore accepted a position as personal adjutant to Generaloberst Fromm in the Bendler Straße, which very soon afforded him an insight into the command centre of the Replacement Training Army. He saw the intricacies of organizational affairs, which included questions of personnel or materiel replacements, armaments, the testing of new weapons, financing etc.

The duties of the personal adjutant involved dealing with all the Generaloberst's personal correspondence, regulating all the formal and representative duties associated with the position, as well as the normal duties of an adjutant. The latter included control and administration of all secret command papers and command documents as well as announcing visitors who wished to see the Generaloberst for private or official reasons. On the other hand, all the house's internal traffic with the Generaloberst passed through the waiting room shared by him and his Chief-of-Staff, where two very skilled older ladies ruled and also kept up the all-important appointment book.

At the Bendler Straße 20 July 1944 began like any other day. The usual

**ARMY HIGH COMMAND
HEADQUARTERS**
Berlin – Bendlerstraße
on July 20th, 1944

activity was scarcely lessened by the oppressive heat. It was not until the afternoon that the "special events" began. It may have been 3 P.M. when General Olbricht received a telephone call in his office. It appeared that he had been waiting for it and that he breathed a sigh of relief when he recognized the voice on the other end of the line. The conversation was brief. The call came from Berlin's Rangsdorf airport, where the courier aircraft landed. Soon afterward Oberst Merz von Quirnheim was in General Olbricht's room, however he left quickly after the two exchanged a few words. The General dialled the number of the office of the military commander of Berlin and asked to speak to General von Hase. The latter also appeared to be expecting the call. Its sole topic was the codeword "Valkyrie."

"Valkyrie?" Had unrest broken out among the foreign workers? Had paratroops landed, was the capital of the Reich in danger? The troops in the capital and its environs had already been placed on alert and mobilized to action by the release of this codeword on a number of occasions. One recalls the formation of the 1029th Reinforced Motorized Grenadier Regiment on 5 March 1944 in Cottbus by the Panzer-Grenadier Replacement Training Brigade GD when the crisis in Hungary was nearing its peak. Then the order had come from the commander of Deputy Headquarters, III Army Corps. But this time it came direct from the chief of the AHA, General Olbricht, and the military commander of Berlin, was that not striking?

Since 1943 certain offices of the Replacement Training Army had kept sealed envelopes, which were marked "secret command matter" and which could only be opened by officers, in their safes in the event that the codeword "Valkyrie" was issued. At the same time stocks of weapons were stored in certain places in the quarters, with which to quickly arm a specific contingent of troops.

The last such call had reached the Panzer-Grenadier Replacement Training Brigade GD in Cottbus on 15 July 1944; it was taken by the then Oberleutnant Delius, acting for the brigade adjutant, Hauptmann von Kügelgen. An unidentified voice had asked, "How will the GD behave on the release of "Valkyrie'?" Shaking his head, Delius, after considering the question, replied, "As the order prescribes!" That ended the matter.

Early on the afternoon of 20 July the Panzer-Grenadier Replacement Training Brigade GD received another call containing the codeword "Valkyrie." The caller also advised that effective immediately the brigade was under the command of General Geyr von Schweppenburg's IN 4. As per orders the units were to depart for Berlin at once.

Oberstleutnant Stirius, commanding officer of the Panzer-Grenadier Replacement Training Regiment and currently acting brigade commander (as Oberst Schulte-Heuthaus was on his way to Guben), sounded the alarm and issued the necessary implementing orders. The same took place in Berlin-Moabit, home of the Watch Battalion Großdeutschland. The battalion staff had just gathered in the mess, though Major Remer, the commanding officer, was still on his way when the call came from Berlin military headquarters and the city's military commander issued the codeword "Valkyrie." As soon as he arrived and learned of the call, Major Remer jumped into his car and drove to Berlin military headquarters on the Unter den Linden. There he was given detailed instructions.

During the subsequent briefing he gave to his officers, Remer said, "Assassination attempt on the Führer! Outcome uncertain. The army is assuming governmental power. The Watch Battalion's mission: surround the government quarter within the precincts. No one is allowed to pass, and that means no minister and no general."

Similar messages and calls were also received by the commanders of other units and formations in and around Berlin: the commander of the Army Ordnance Technician School was given the special mission of sending assault teams to occupy the arsenal; the commander of the Army Armourer-Artificer School was given special instructions to surround the palace. Also called were the commanders of the 311th and 320th Regional Defence Battalions, the Armoured Forces School at Wünsdorf, the Cavalry School at Krampnitz and so on. All were to follow the special order "Valkyrie II," according to which the alerted units were to immediately depart for specified points within the Reich capital.

While the companies of Watch Battalion GD (incidentally the only active unit inside Berlin) were still making preparations to depart, General Olbricht's Chief-of-Staff, General Staff Oberst Merz von Quirnheim, delivered several prepared teletype messages to the Bendler Block's (OKH) message centre for transmission. Soon the teletype machine was clacking steadily as it transmitted the first order over the wire to the command authorities in the Reich and the occupied territories. All were worded the same as the following:

Teletype Message FRR HOKW 02150/20.7.44/16.45 Ia 126/44
Secret Command Matter

To the Military Area of Bohemia and Moravia!

I.   Internal Unrest

An unscrupulous clique of non-combatant party leaders has, by exploiting this situation, tried to stab the hard-fighting front in the back and seize power for its own selfish purposes.

II.   In this hour of greatest danger the Reich government has proclaimed martial law in order to maintain peace and order and has simultaneously entrusted me with exclusive power by placing me in supreme command of the armed forces.

III.   I therefore order that:

1. I entrust exclusive power (with the right of delegation) to the territorial commander of the Replacement Training Army, simultaneously appointing him commander-in-chief in the home theatre of operations; in the occupied western territories to the Commander-in-Chief West (Commander-in-Chief of Army Group B); in Italy to the Commander-in-Chief Southwest (Commander-in-Chief of Army Group C) and in the southeastern area to the Commander-in-Chief of Army Group F.

In the occupied eastern territories to the Commanders-in-Chief of Army Groups South Ukraine, North Ukraine, Centre and North and to the

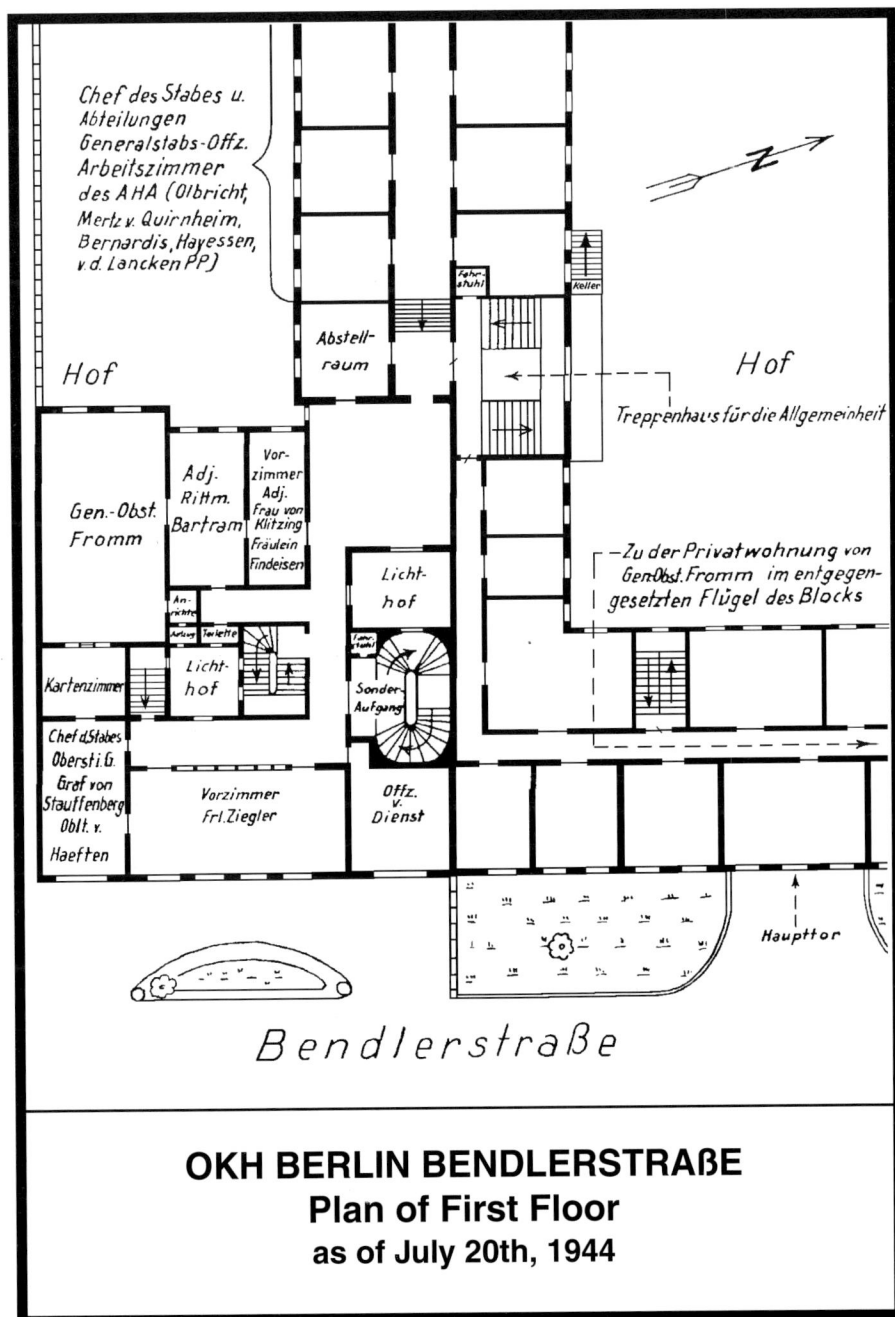

Chef des Stabes u. Abteilungen Generalstabs-Offz. Arbeitszimmer des AHA (Olbricht, Mertz v. Quirnheim, Bernardis, Hayessen, v.d. Lancken PP)

Hof

Hof

Abstell-raum

Fahr-stuhl

Keller

Treppenhaus für die Allgemeinheit

Gen.-Obst. Fromm

Adj. Rittm. Bartram

Vor-zimmer Adj. Frau von Klitzing Fräulein Findeisen

An-richte

Anrichte Toilette

Licht-hof

Zu der Privatwohnung von Gen.Obst. Fromm im entgegen-gesetzten Flügel des Blocks

Kartenzimmer

Licht-hof

Licht-hof

Fahr-stuhl

Sonder-Aufgang

Chef d. Stabes Oberst i. G. Graf von Stauffenberg Oblt. v. Haeften

Vorzimmer Frl. Ziegler

Offz. v. Dienst

Haupttor

Bendlerstraße

OKH BERLIN BENDLERSTRAßE
Plan of First Floor
as of July 20th, 1944

Wehrmacht Commander Ostland for their respective areas of command. In Denmark and Norway to the Wehrmacht commanders.

2. Subordinate to the holders of exclusive power are:
   (a) All offices and units of the Wehrmacht in their area of command, including the Waffen-SS, the RAD and the OT.
   (b) All public authorities (of the Reich, the provinces and the municipalities), especially all municipal, security and administrative police.
   (c) All office holders and organizations of the NSDAP and its associated units.
3. The entire Waffen-SS is incorporated into the army effective immediately.
4. The holders of exclusive authority are responsible for the maintenance of order and public safety. In particular they are to see to:
   (a) The security of communications installations.
   (b) The neutralization of the SD. All resistance to the military executive powers is to be broken ruthlessly.
5. At this hour of greatest danger for the Fatherland, unity of the Wehrmacht and the maintenance of full discipline are the foremost law.

I therefore obligate all commanders of the army, navy and air force to support with all available means the holders of exclusive authority as they carry out their difficult missions and to ensure that the directives issued by them are followed by subordinate offices. The German soldier is faced with an historic mission. His enterprise and conduct will determine whether Germany is saved. The same mission faces all territorial commanders, the high commands of the branches of the Wehrmacht and the command authorities under the direct command of the high commands of the army, navy and air force...

The Commander-in-Chief of the Wehrmacht
signed von Witzleben, Generalfeldmarschall
F. d. R. Graf Stauffenberg
AHA/Stab III/44 Secret Command Matter,
For Commanders Only, from 20 July 1944.

This message was signed von Witzleben. Others were signed Fromm, but in each case the name Graf Stauffenberg appeared below.

It was approximately 4 P.M. General Olbricht, chief of the AHA, had a conversation with Generaloberst Fromm. Generally such discussions lasted rather a long time, especially since the AHA was the most important office of the Replacement Training Army and the formation of new units was being debated at that time.

Rittmeister Bartram, personal adjutant to Generaloberst Fromm, described these moments:

"It was already 4:15 P.M. The Generaloberst intended to leave at 4:00, and I had already said goodbye to several acquaintances. Through the waiting room I heard the voices of the Generaloberst and General Olbricht. I was thinking to myself that I would have to stay longer, when suddenly the door of the chief's room opened and the Generaloberst excitedly called to me that I should stay in case he needed me! I gave no further thought as to why, but I did become curious when I heard loud voices coming from the room, which led me to suspect a heated argument with General Olbricht.

After a while things quieted down again and finally I stuck my head through the door to the Generaloberst's room to see whether he was still there. Fromm was on the telephone with Generalfeldmarschall Keitel at Führer Headquarters. I heard him ask excitedly if there were any orders for the Replacement Training Army and if anything else should be done. The answer was apparently no. Then the Generaloberst turned angrily to Olbricht and said to him, "You've just heard for yourself, the Führer is alive and there are no grounds for overhasty measures!"

At this point it should be mentioned that General Olbricht called on the Generaloberst at about 4:15 P.M. and as always was admitted straight away. Olbricht told Fromm that he had received news that an assassination attempt had just been carried out at Führer Headquarters and that the Führer had been fatally injured. He allowed himself the question as to whether they should take special measures, eventually including the release of the Valkyrie order. The Generaloberst was astonished that Olbricht had received this news and not he himself. It was subsequent to this that he spoke with Feldmarschall Keitel.

Once again from the experiences of Rittmeister Bartram:

"Olbricht now opened up and said to Fromm that responsible men had prepared for this eventuality and had formed a new government. Was he ready to stay at his post as BdE in this new government and lend a hand? The order for the release of Valkyrie had already been issued.

At this I saw Fromm jump to his feet excitedly and I heard him cry out: "That is a conspiracy! What's going on here? Who issued the Valkyrie order?' Olbricht merely replied that he and his chief-of-staff, Oberst Merz von Quirnheim, had issued it.

Fromm sent for the latter immediately. When General Staff Oberst Merz von Quirnheim then appeared, the Generaloberst, who was very agitated and red-faced, shouted: "How did you come to give the Valkyrie order? You know that it can only be issued by me. Are you hiding under a blanket with your chief (Olbricht)?' Then, turning to Olbricht, he said, "What is all this about a new government and the assassination attempt? I just spoke on the telephone with Keitel; there was an assassination attempt, but the Führer is alive! What you have done is high treason; I declare you both under arrest. No one leave the room..."

As he spoke these words General Staff Oberst Graf von Stauffenberg walked through the door and said to Fromm, "You are wrong, Herr Generaloberst, the Führer is dead! I myself set off the bomb; I have just come from Führer Headquarters and saw that no one was left alive in the barracks.'

Then Fromm exploded and screamed, "This is a revolution, that is high treason; you are also under arrest Stauffenberg! You know that the penalty for high and state treason is death! You will all be shot by a firing squad.' The door opened again and Oberleutnant Haeften stepped in with pistol in hand; the highly-agitated Fromm rushed at the officers standing before him. Stauffenberg now drew his pistol and both men aimed their weapons at Fromm. Stauffenberg said coldly, "Herr Generaloberst, it is not you who is arresting us, but we you, if you do not support us. Please go with your adjutant into his office and do not leave it! Armed officers will be guarding the door!'

What choice did we have after being disarmed. We had to bow to force. Oberleutnant von Haeften accompanied the Generaloberst and me into my office and cut the telephone cord with a knife. Soon we were alone; the Generaloberst walked back and forth in a cold fury, saying repeatedly, "Something like this has never happened; an officer laying a hand on his supreme commander; the German uniform is defiled forever; never again can one wear this coat with honour. My officers guilty of high treason!...'

He was unable to calm himself for a long time. But then we began thinking about how we could get out of this situation. For apart from us two and the two participants, no one in the entire office knew what was being played out. Fromm thought of the infantry school in Döberitz. But how to contact them, the telephone was out. As a GD man I thought of the Watch Battalion GD in Moabit and decided to try (my watch showed just past 5 P.M.) to reach Major Remer by telephone from my waiting room. But there, apart from my two rather excited secretaries, I saw two heavily-armed officers, who immediately pointed their submachine-guns at me. We therefore did not get out of the room.

From Fromm's room we heard a constant jumble of voices."

Bartram tried to reach the outside world via a second hall and the toilet. His main objective was the permanent guard on the ground floor belonging to the Watch Battalion GD, which must be manned by an officer of the watch battalion. Or had the latter been disarmed and replaced by other officer guards?

Time went by. Finally Bartram managed to reach General Kennes and told him of the Generaloberst's situation and the fact that he was being held prisoner. But the result was negative. General Kennes simply thought Bartram was mad; he didn't believe him. Why not? So far not the slightest indication of what was happening in the Generaloberst's offices had filtered through to the outside.

During one of his repeated forays Bartram ran into General von Kortzfleisch, commander of Deputy Headquarters, III Army Corps and was able to lead him to the Generaloberst's room. There Fromm described the situation in the Bendler Block and in Berlin. The Generaloberst instructed Kortzfleisch to immediately crush the conspiracy with force of arms and free him. Kortzfleisch returned the way he had come; however for some time nothing at all happened (von Kortzfleisch was also arrested by the conspirators soon after leaving Fromm and was consequently unable to initiate the requested counteraction).

And yet, elsewhere in Berlin the first countermeasures were taking shape. After executing the order given him by the city's military commander, Generalleutnant von Hase, Major Remer deployed his companies in the government quarter and took the required measures to seal off the area. Now, in the course of the late afternoon, he went to the Berlin military headquarters at Unter den Linden 1 for a second time to finally obtain more detailed information about the events surrounding Adolf Hitler. Remer became suspicious when he learned that Generaloberst Beck, retired since the beginning of the war, had been seen in the streets, in uniform and in a military vehicle; the appearance of unfamiliar officers in his barracks area was inexplicable, and the evasive way in which Generalleutnant von Hase answered his pointed questions made him wonder.

What to do? Then one of his escort officers, the severely disabled Leutnant of the Reserve Dr. Hagen, who had contacts in the Reich Propaganda Ministry, stepped forward and suggested to Remer that he contact the Reich Defence Commissar of Berlin, Reichsminister Dr. Goebbels, directly. With 20 men under the command of Leutnant Buck, Remer set out to see Goebbels and was admitted immediately. There he reported on the events in Berlin and the peculiarities that he and his men had encountered in the last hours. He also declared that he had orders from the city's military commander to arrest him, Goebbels.

It was approximately 6:30 P.M. when Goebbels put through a priority call to Führer Headquarters and asked to speak to Adolf Hitler. Goebbels spoke briefly with Hitler then passed the phone to Remer, who now heard for himself the voice of his supreme commander. The later instructed Remer to ruthlessly crush the revolt. He alone was responsible in Berlin, said Hitler, only he had all power in his hands. These conditions would remain valid until the arrival of Reichsführer-SS Himmler, whom he had named commander of the Replacement Training Army effective immediately.

Major Remer acted at once. Major Wackernagel, who had stayed behind in the message centre, telephoned from the Panzer-Grenadier Replacement Training Regiment GD and informed Remer that the bulk of the brigade, acting on orders contained in "Valkyrie II," was already on its way to Herzberg to occupy the Deutschland radio transmitter. Armoured patrols were also en route to Herzberg and the transmitter. Acting in place of Oberst Schulte-Heuthaus, who was alerted on his way to Guben, Oberstleutnant Stirius drove ahead to the Deputy Headquarters, III Army Corps, reporting to Berlin as per orders. On his arrival there all was dark; the doorman reported that General Kortzfleisch was out. General Freiherr von Thüngen was standing in for him; with him was Oberst von Herford. Stirius asked who was in command and what should be done. Oberst Schulte-Heuthaus also arrived with Oberleutnant Delius, but was unable to obtain a clear answer. They then checked with Cottbus again, where they had received their first accurate information from Major Wackernagel. The Oberst was to drive to see Goebbels immediately; there he would learn all he needed to know.

Despatch riders were immediately sent in all directions, primarily to annul the battalions' order to fire.

The Oberst and commanding officer of the Panzer-Grenadier Replacement Training Brigade GD drove to Hermann Göring Straße 20. There he and Oberleutnant Delius, his escort officer, entered the house of the Reich Minister.

Shortly before 7 P.M. the first report concerning the bomb attack on Hitler that afternoon at Führer Headquarters was broadcast by the Deutschland radio transmitter; it was also announced that the latter would himself speak at a later hour. Generaloberst Fromm and his adjutant Rittmeister Bartram heard the news on the radio that had been left in Fromm's room, where they were still being held. They left the radio playing softly so as not to miss Hitler's statement. They wanted to hear Hitler's voice so that they could be certain that he was alive. Meanwhile Bartram had also managed to bring Generals Specht and Kunze, both of the OKH, to Fromm's room and convince them that he was being held captive. From them they learned that Generaloberst Hoeppner was already residing in Fromm's office as the new BdE and that Generaloberst Beck was also present. Numerous teletype messages had been sent; there was feverish activity. All outgoing teletype messages were marked "Signed Fromm" F.d.R Stauffenberg.

The communications centre in the Bendler Block was not occupied by the conspirators, either out of carelessness or forgetfulness. The former LdN (director of the signals service), a Leutnant, carried out his duties as before. He had the first teletype message sent, however on closer inspection of its contents he became suspicious and then simply stopped sending any more. Thus some of the planned orders failed to reach their destinations. Two days later the Leutnant was promoted to Hauptmann for his actions.

It was nearing 9 P.M. Rittmeister Bartram went to Fromm's office on behalf of the Generaloberst and asked Generaloberst Hoeppner if he and Fromm might be allowed to go to Fromm's private apartment, which was located on the same floor but in another wing of the Bendler Block. Hoeppner allowed this and had both prisoners taken away through the corridors, escorted by two armed officers.

Rittmeister Bartram describes what happened next:

"The two armed officers took up their posts in front of the Generaloberst's private apartment. Inside the apartment was a telephone, which apparently still worked. Fromm was hesitant to use this line to make contact with the outside world. He decided not to, assuming that the centre was occupied by the conspirators; on the other hand he was hopeful of a counter-action and didn't want to interfere.

We debated how to get away from our watchers without making them suspicious. Finally I went to one of the guards and asked him to allow us to fetch the radio for the Generaloberst, as he wished to hear the 10 P.M. news. He had no objections and let me go back, probably assuming that a man who had had a leg amputated posed no danger.

Just before I reached the hall to our offices I heard shots fired there. I came around the corner and saw a large number of general staff officers of the

AHA, all of whom I knew, in front of our office. Weapons in hand, they hurried into Stauffenberg's and Fromm's room. This must be the counter-action, for they approached several other officers and disarmed them. There were questions and shouts: where was the Generaloberst?

I called to them, 'I'll fetch him!' and hurried to Fromm's private apartment. It was about 10 P.M. when we both returned to the offices. There we saw the armed officers holding several of the conspirators (Olbricht, Merz von Quirnheim, Stauffenberg, Beck, Hoeppner, von Haeften) in check in Fromm's room.

Fromm placed himself in the doorway between the map room and his office and said something to the effect of: 'Gentlemen, I am back! Now you are my prisoners. I have caught you in the very act of high treason and according to the existing laws you are to be shot on the spot by firing squad.' As he spoke he made a sweeping gesture toward the general staff officers, probably to designate them as them firing squad. 'Please surrender your weapons.' This they did. 'I am seeing you, Generaloberst Hoeppner, for the first time; I don't know what your role is in this, you will be taken to the Wehrmacht jail. Do you gentlemen have any requests?'"

General Olbricht asked to be allowed to write a letter to his wife, and his request was granted. The others gratefully declined.

Then Generaloberst Beck asked for a pistol so that he might shoot himself. Fromm gave him a pistol, whereupon Beck shot himself in the head; however he merely succeeded in wounding himself. With great difficulty he raised the barrel to his forehead again and fired a second time. Beck collapsed badly wounded into his easy chair, but he was still alive. Meanwhile Fromm turned to his personal adjutant and instructed him to bring one officer and ten men to serve as a firing squad.

On his way downstairs he ran into Oberleutnant Schlee, commander of 4th Company, Watch Battalion GD and a wearer of the Oak Leaves, and several men. Fromm's adjutant passed the order on to Schlee. A short time later Leutnant Schady (later killed at the Oder) appeared and identified himself as commander of the firing squad. Fromm ordered Oberst Claus Graf Schenk von Stauffenberg, Oberst Merz von Quirnheim, Oberleutnant of the Reserve von Haeften and General Olbricht taken away and brought to the courtyard of the Bendler Block. Preparations were to be made for the executions. A Feldwebel administered the coup-de-grace to Generaloberst Beck, who was still alive.

It was just past 10:30 P.M. when Major Remer arrived at Bendler Straße to determine the state of affairs. With him were his predecessor as commander of the Watch Battalion GD, Oberstleutnant Gehrke, and his adjutant, Hauptmann Bechtel. Remer had run into the pair by chance a short time earlier. Oberleutnant Schlee followed them at a short distance.

Generaloberst Fromm gave Major Remer a brief account of what had taken place in the Bendler Block in the past hours and then had him relate what had happened in the city. Remer suggested that Fromm go with him to see Goebbels, where he would learn all the details. Together they drove to the Propaganda Ministry, arriving shortly before 11 P.M. While Generaloberst

Fromm hurried upstairs, his adjutant, Rittmeister Bartram, at first remained below in the hall. Numerous party leaders and military officers were present, debating the day's events excitedly. It was almost midnight when the last radio bulletin said that Hitler was going to speak. A short time later his voice was heard; he spoke of an unscrupulous clique of officers which had treacherously tried to assassinate him. Only providence had saved him and from this he took strength. While his words were still fading away, Bartram became uneasy about his chief's lengthy absence. He went up the stairs to Goebbels' rooms and was informed in the hall that the Generaloberst was being held alone in a room. Bartram eventually found him, sitting on a stool, pale, dejected and depressed. When Bartram asked if he had any orders for him, Fromm just shook his head resignedly.

Then in the hall Bartram met Kaltenbrunner, who together with a member of the SD took the Generaloberst and drove away in a car.

In the morning, as the individual companies of the Watch Battalion GD were still returning to their quarters, SS- Obergruppenführer Jüttner, acting on behalf of Himmler, took over the affairs of the BdE in the Bendler Straße. Interrogations, the arrest of at least 8 members of the office and searches of the most secret safes followed. A sort of mobilization schedule for an intended uprising was found. The first connections were identified which had led to the plot against Hitler.

As related previously, the first units of the *Leibstandarte SS Adolf Hitler* arrived at the headquarters in the Wolfsschanze installation shortly after midnight on 21 July 1944 and occupied all important points within the site. An entire SS company sealed off Security Zone I; in Security Zone II and at the field watches the men of the Führer Escort Battalion were soon standing guard together with SS men. It was a grotesque affair, traceable to Himmler's wish to use this moment to outmanoeuvre the Wehrmacht and push the Waffen-SS into the foreground. It is also certain that General Burgdorff, as representative of the Führer's Wehrmacht adjutant, was in on this train of thought.

When the Waffen-SS subsequently moved an alert platoon under the command of an SS-Sturmführer into Security Zone I, there was friction between the Führer Escort Battalion's alert platoon under Leutnant Jaenicke which was already there and the SS men. Only the level-headed intervention by the commanders prevented the situation from deteriorating to the point where shots were fired.

An attempt by the Waffen-SS to take over the outer watches alone and drive the GD men from their posts likewise failed as a result of the quick intervention by Oberst Streve, headquarters commander, and the Waffen-SS commander, who in joint negotiations came up with a mode of joint action. The Waffen-SS commander, an astronomer in civilian life, was a reasonable, clear-sighted man, who in all these discussions emphasized that it was futile to get in each other's hair now, especially since it had been confirmed to him several times that the men of the Führer-Begleit Battalion had definitely done their duty. It was therefore agreed that initially they would stand guard together and then they would see.

It took perhaps two or three days for everyone in the headquarters to realize the impossibility of this situation as well as the unacceptability of the attitude being displayed toward the men of the Führer Escort Battalion.

When visited by his supreme commander in hospital in Karlshof, Generalleutnant Schmundt, severely injured and fighting for his life, made Hitler promise not to allow this injustice against his army guard, which had served so faithfully all those years, to go on. Finally the SS offered to withdraw all SS units deployed in the installation, provided an SS company (the 3rd SS Grenadier Company, LAH) was attached to the Führer Escort Battalion. This was agreed to in joint negotiations and subsequently implemented. The remaining Waffen-SS units moved to the outer edge of the security zone and remained there about 14 days before departing, carrying out no duties inside the installation during that period. As well Hitler requested that one man from each company of the Führer Escort Battalion be sent to see him. He received the men, whose honour had been badly injured, spoke to them in very heartfelt words and appreciatively reaffirmed his complete trust in them.

This behaviour on the part of Hitler was probably also due to the intervention of Generalleutnant Schmundt, the great patron of the GD units, who in his final hours took a pen and wrote a testament to Hitler: in it he implored Hitler to bring about a reconciliation between the Wehrmacht and the SS and not to allow the Wehrmacht to become the plaything of other forces.

Part VII

CHAPTER 1

FROM VILKAVISHKIS TO MEMEL

The Pz.Gren.Div. GD's "Horizon Crawl"

6. 8. – 4. 10. 1944   Offensive and defensive operations in East Prussia, Lithuania and Latvia; breakthrough to Army Group North.

5. 10. – 9. 10. 1944   Defense of Tryskiai and fighting withdrawal toward the city of Memel.

10. 10. – 28. 11. 1944 Static defensive operations in the Memel bridgehead.

The Panzer-Grenadier Division *Großdeutschland's* weeks-long period of rest and refitting in the area between Vasluiui and Bacau in Rumania ended on 24-25 July 1944. None of the men could have known that this was the last almost carefree period of rest the division would know. Once again they had enjoyed thoroughly one of the most beautiful areas in Europe, even if the days were filled to the limit with hard training. The incorporation of replacements and recruits, who had arrived from home to fill the gaps in the ranks; the evaluation of recent experience, especially in close combat and anti-tank operations; the reorganization of one or another unit into battle groups possessing a high level of weapons and firepower; the delivery of wheeled and tracked vehicles and their incorporation into the units; all these activities went on constantly. I (APC) Battalion, Panzer-Fusilier Regiment GD, which had been formed in Fallingbostel in the meantime was incorporated into the regiment; III Battalion was brought back up to strength and issued new weapons.

The former Armoured Assault Pioneer Battalion GD formed additional companies, establishing the framework for a future Armoured Assault Pioneer Regiment GD. The new units included a headquarters company, which received an anti-tank platoon from the Anti-tank Battalion GD which had just been disbanded. The company's commanding officer, Oberleutnant Bütenbender, had his hands full turning his new company into a capable instrument of war. Among the members of the anti-tank platoon of the Headquarters Company, Armoured Assault Pioneer Regiment GD were Obergefreiter Andreas Adelhardt as gun commander, Gefreiter Viets as gunner, Gefreiter Kurt Weller as loader, Gefreiter Helmut Besta, Gefreiter Leonhard Giesa and Gefreiter Walter Leschke. The "Steppe Nobleman," as the men called their company commander, Oberleutnant Bütenbender, was accompanied by his runner Gefreiter Pflanz. Based in Deleni, the artillery, too, trained hard; communications equipment was checked and the gun tractors were given a thorough overhaul. Hauptmann von Buddenbrock assumed command of the Assault Gun Brigade GD.

In spite of the many hours spent training, spurred by numerous inspections, the troops still found time to enjoy themselves. Sporting contests were held within the battalions and there was a regimental sports fest; evenings of entertainment put on by the companies were quite common. But it was the GD's front-line company of entertainers that provided the most fun and amusement with its carefully-selected program. The company started its program with a variety show. the competitors taking part in the show were Obergefreiter Majewski, Unteroffizier Zimmermann, Unteroffizier Wiese, Obergefreiter Zeh (tenor), Unteroffizier Nürnberger, Schirrmeister Boje (magician), Obergefreiter Breuer, Unteroffizier Ritter, Obergefreiter Neumann, and Obergefreiter Meier.

It was at this time that the song that was to stay with the Panzer-Grenadier Division *Großdeutschland* to the end of the war, indeed even into captivity, was created, the song:

Highway Nights

Melody: Majewski   Lyrics: Nürnberger

First it was the Dniepr, then it was the Bug,
later the Dnestr and then the Prut.
Retreat, what an exquisite word,
we're left with the highway – from town to town.

Refrain: Highway nights are stormy and cool,
highway nights – quite without feeling,
no stoves, no blankets,
nowhere to stretch our legs.
Highway nights – without coffee and bread.
Differential failure! – Batteries are dead.
I can do without this trip.
Highway nights are sh.. adieu.
Kfz. 17 built for radio operators,
on Russia's roads, bumpy and unpaved.
Stuck – and no one to pull us out,
what can we do – hollow charge up!
Highway nights.....

The following version was sung by Unteroffizier Willy Nürnberger and Unteroffizier Walter Wiese in Schleswig-Holstein:

Kahlholz days – Samland is lost
Neuhaus' torment – Pillau – Neutief.
It doesn't want to rain — Oh Pan Potchevu,

Blessings from the "Butcher" and the
"Stubborn One" as well.
Highway nights.
Then came the spit – one last try,
a mess – everything goes to pot.
We waded to Hela and to Bronholm,
that was no mistake – we pushed off!

And then the modified refrain:

Baltic nights are stormy and cold,
Baltic nights – quite without feeling.
No cabins, no blankets
and nowhere to stretch our legs.
Baltic nights – without coffee and bread,
the boat overloaded, but a sea voyage is necessary!
I can do without this trip
Baltic nights are sh.. adieu!

It was Unteroffizier W. Nürnberger who, one foot on a stool, plucked the strings of his guitar and let his melodious voice ring out. Many, many comrades heard him, picked up the melody and words of "Highway Nights" and took them along with them.

However this period of peace and quiet came to an end on 25 July 1944. Not all of the units had been brought up to their authorized strengths; there simply weren't enough men. For example the 9th Company of the Panzer-Grenadier Regiment GD had a total strength of 180 NCOs and men, the 11th Company about the same, while the 12th (Heavy) Company, with two heavy machine-gun platoons, mortar platoon and light infantry gun platoon was almost at full strength. As a result of experience gained in defensive operations, each battalion now had a so-called *Jagdkommando*, most of which consisted of three or four squads. This was the unit commander's counterattack reserve, or, simply put, his last reserve.

The Panzer-Grenadier Division *Großdeutschland* now left for good the command of the Eighth Army, after having fought as part of this formation in the past months. The Commander-in-Chief of the Eighth Army, General der Infanterie Wöhler, issued a special farewell order of the day, which said:

"I am losing a division whose name is intimately associated with the difficult and successful battles of the past year, of which I will name only the notable spring battle on the Upper Moldau. Always at the focal point of the action, an opponent feared by the enemy, and an inspiring example to our own divisions, the Pz.Gren.Div. GD never lost its bold offensive spirit, even when faced with the enemy's vastly superior numbers and in serious danger, and brought honour to the name it bears. Where the GD stood, the enemy's will was broken!

I am proud, GD Panzer-Grenadiers, that you stood in the ranks of my army, and I honour with a grateful heart the outstanding work done by your leaders, led by your division commander Gen.Lt. von Manteuffel, and your exemplary bravery and loyalty

New and difficult tasks lie ahead of you. You are setting out on the most decisive passage of arms of this war. I am certain that you will bring it to a victorious conclusion for

Führer and Reich."

Heil Hitler! – Pz.Gren.Div. GD
signed Wöhler, Gen .der Inf.

The vehicles, gun tractors and tanks rolled to the entraining stations. Most of the transport trains were despatched from Vasluiui Bacau, the panzers' point of departure, which was also the destination of some vehicle columns.

A number of units, such as I (APC) Battalion, Panzer-Grenadier Regiment GD, first drove through the Carpathians to Vatra Dornei on the Hungarian border and entrained there. For the men the drive through the mountain forests and over the barren passes was an impressive experience.

The transport trains pulled away from the loading platforms on the 26th and 27th of July, although some did leave later. They steamed north through the Carpathians and Hungary, passed through Budapest and Lavic-Sillien, crossed the Jablunka Pass and then travelled across Germany to Gumbinnen via Oppeln, Breslau, Lissa, Posen, Gnesen, Thorn, Allenstein and Insterburg to Gumbinnen.

They were in Germany. The enemy was at the frontiers. It was their job to defend them!

Following their breakthrough in the centre of the Eastern Front in June 1944, the Soviets held to their goal with undiminished energy. The retreating German armies were unable to stop them. Every attempt to establish a new, stable German front was wrecked at the outset; this was the sole purpose of the Soviet spearheads headed for Baranovichi, Vilna and the area south of Dünaburg. The weakened German armies fought a mobile battle with armoured battle groups in an effort to at least slow down the enemy spearheads and allow a continuous German front to be set up farther back in the rear areas.

In the central sector the German Second and Fourth Armies were able to maintain at least a semblance of cohesion, but the southern wing of the Third Panzer Army was completely up in the air and was being forced back ever farther toward the north. But there the Soviet 3rd White Russian Front was driving almost unopposed toward Vilna, whose German garrison was just able to fight its way out to the west. The city fell into enemy hands on 12 July 1944. Masses of enemy troops poured northwest into the area between Dünaburg and Vilna and Army Group North was placed in imminent danger of being cut off. Hitler rejected the idea of withdrawing Army Group North to a line farther to the west, although this was the only solution that might have allowed a consolidation of the front. Instead panzer units were withdrawn from unthreatened sectors to form a German armoured attack force which was to reestablish contact with Army Group North. This idea of Hitler's ignored the true situation however. First of all it had to be borne in mind that Army Group Centre, with only 16 German divisions, was facing at least 160 Soviet divisions, which meant that the enemy had achieved a ten to one superiority in numbers.

Although reinforcements for the Third and Fourth Panzer Armies were slow in arriving, the defenders initially succeeded in halting the Soviet advance, which had lost some of its momentum, on a line along the Neman from west of Grodno to approximately north of Kovno (Kauen). The German Fourth Panzer Army was even able to parry a dangerous Russian breakthrough toward Augustovo just short of its objective, and by committing several panzer divisions drove the enemy back toward the Neman.

But while the German central front temporarily stabilized itself in mid-July, fresh Soviet units attacked in the south and as well stormed Army Group North's front with increased strength.

By 21 July Soviet spearheads had reached Ponevich, about 150 kilometres west of Dünaburg, and only eight days later, on 29 July, the first Soviets reached the Gulf of Riga at Tukums! The tenuous link that had existed with Army Group North was now severed for good, the army group cut off. At about the same time, to the west Soviet spearheads drove into the Kursenai area, west of Schaulen.

But the Soviets were also on the move in the centre of the German Eastern Front, at the boundary between the German Fourth Army and the southern wing of the Third Panzer Army. On 2 August they occupied Vilkavishkis, the last Lithuanian city before the German border.

These offensive moves by the Soviets forced the Germans to make use of the reserves coming from Germany, the same reserves that were earmarked for the operation to restore contact with Army Group North. Now they were sent into action as soon as they arrived, initially to restore the situation on either side of Vilkavishkis (Wolfsburg). The enemy had to be forced back from the East Prussian border at any price and the front stabilized.

Transport of the units of the Panzer-Grenadier Division *Großdeutschland* received the highest priority and the trains were designated "blitz trains." After passing through Breslau, Allenstein and Insterburg the trains began meeting refugees everywhere; they greeted the men in the rail cars with sighs of relief. It was 3 August 1944 when the first of the GD units detrained in the dead of night – at Ebenrode, Eydtkau, Gumbinnen, Trakehnen and other stations. Pickets were sent out at the most easterly stations, however these reported no contact whatsoever with the enemy.

As the units arrived they moved into readiness positions from which they were soon to go on the offensive. The enemy situation in this combat zone was unclear; all that was known was that the Soviets had taken Vilkavishkis on 2 August and now occupied the city. The German positions, which were called the East Prussian Defence Position, ran in a north-south direction on both sides of the city and formed a dense ring around it. It was manned mainly by so-called "East Prussian Divisions," units consisting of young, inexperienced recruits, regional defence forces and alert units. Due to their lack of solidarity and the absence of fighting spirit they could scarcely be compared to battle-tested units. On the other hand their equipment was brand-new, with MG 42s, panzerfausts, bazookas, guns and vehicles all fresh from the factories – small matter that the troops had little idea of what to do with them. And yet they tried to halt the Soviets with the courage of desperation.

On 4 August, due north of the city of Vilkavishkis, the Soviet shock troops resumed their offensive toward the west. Their first assault broke through the thin defensive lines. Soviet spearheads were soon moving toward the area north of Wirballen, and forward elements were at the German border. However, at first it seemed as if the enemy penetration was limited. North of Wirballen several German assault guns under Oberleutnant Müller stood guard, their front facing north; northwest of Gumbinnen at the Kovno—Gumbinnen rail line, a flak battle group prevented the enemy from veering south. On the whole, however, the Gumbinnen–Ebenrode–Wirballen–Vilkavishkis road and rail line were in immediate danger of being severed.

The leading units of the Panzer-Grenadier Division GD, which detrained between Gumbinnen and Wirballen during the night of 3-4 August, immediately drove through Schloßbach into the division's assembly area, at and north of Wystiter Lake, south of Wirballen. As the local mobile reserve, they were kept at a constant state of readiness. The first to take up quarters there were the battalions of the Panzer-Grenadier Regiment GD under Oberst Lorenz. The main body of the division was still on its way there.

News of the enemy attack due north of Vilkavishkis reached the commander of the Panzer-Grenadier Regiment GD at his command post in Skardupiai, east of Vistytis, sometime on 4 August. At the same time orders arrived for the regiment to form a battle group to attack northeast from the area due north of Wirballen, drive back the enemy and restore contact with the German units holding out farther north.

Oberst Lorenz put together his battle group and handed command of the regiment over to Major Schimmel in order to have a free hand to direct the attack. During the evening of 4 August II and III Battalions moved out and headed north for the assembly area between the city of Wirballen and the Kovno–Gumbinnen rail line. Initial objectives were assigned. III Battalion, Panzer-Grenadier Regiment GD under Rittmeister Kuehn was to attack along the Wirballen–Skiaudiniskiat–Skardupiai road, remaining east; II Battalion under Oberleutnant Schmelter, whose objective was Hill 51 due east of the town of Obsrutelia, would advance west of the road; the general direction of the attack was northeast. As soon as I (APC) Battalion arrived, it would be deployed on the left next to II Battalion.

Fire support for the attack was to be provided by close-support aircraft as well as by elements of an artillery regiment of one of the East Prussian divisions; the latter had been instructed to cooperate with the attack force. Reinforcements arrived in the form of the regiment's heavy infantry weapons as well as the first Tigers, which had only just arrived by train.

At about 08.25 on 5 August, following brief preparations, both battalions of the Panzer-Grenadier Regiment GD attacked northeast from the front lines. Straightaway friendly close-support aircraft roared past overhead toward the enemy positions.

Resistance was initially weak. The escorting assault guns under Oberleutnant Müller spotted and knocked out a dug-in T-34. The leading elements of III Battalion soon reached the town of Skardupiai. Farther left II Battalion kept pace. Then resistance stiffened; heavy artillery pounded the objectives that had already been taken. The attack was temporarily halted until cooperation with the close-support aircraft, which had so far been inadequate, was straightened out. A resumption of the attack was planned in the afternoon.

The panzer-grenadiers resumed their attack that afternoon following a preparatory artillery bombardment. They gained ground in the face of stiffening Soviet resistance. On the left the armoured personnel carriers of I (APC) Battalion also advanced, but they were stopped before reaching the common objective, Hill 51.

On Oberst Lorenz's order the attack was cancelled for the day, in order to regroup and allow heavy weapons to be moved up during the night. Losses were not inconsiderable; almost every rifle company had twenty casualties. The wounded were tended to at the medical clearing station at Eydtkau. Further transports arrived in the rear, including those carrying the Panzer-Fusilier Regiment GD, which moved into the assembly area.

There was no resumption of the attack in III Battalion's attack lane to the right of the road from Wirballen to the northeast on 6 August. However the panzer-grenadiers of I and II Battalions attacked with support from several Tigers and after some heavy fighting took possession of Hill 51. Four of the Tigers, tanks C 11, C 12, C 13 and C 14, were knocked out. Among the crew members of the four tanks were Oberleutnant Leusing, Unteroffizier Tesmer, Obergefreiter Bormann, Feldwebel Förster, Obergefreiter Nadler, Obergefreiter Bräuer, Obergefreiter Galle, Unteroffizier Bahr, Gefreiter Figl and Unteroffizier Maierhoff. Most of these men returned wounded to the line of departure. The opposition that day was provided by 72-ton Stalin tanks, armed with a 122mm gun. With its superior firepower, the Josef Stalin had ended the Tiger's dominance on the Eastern Front.

The toughness of the fighting for Hill 51 was reflected in the loss lists. 6th Company, II Battalion, Panzer-Grenadier Regiment GD alone lost one NCO and five men killed as well as 20 wounded.

When the 7th of August passed quietly in the newly-won positions, toward evening the elements of the Panzer-Grenadier Regiment GD deployed there were relieved and moved to the rear. Something was brewing in the Vilkavishkis area.

Orders were issued for an attack by the entire division against Vilkavishkis, the key point on the Kovno–Gumbinnen road, situated in the middle of an open plain. On 8 August the unit commanders scouted assembly areas for the attack, which was to take place the next day.

The Soviets had meanwhile fortified the town's houses and gardens, installed heavy weapons, anti-tank guns and mortars in concealed positions and placed heavy tanks in the cover of barns and stalls. Their field of fire was excellent; they had a good view across the cornfields, meadows and ploughed fields. At the very edge of the city, in the south and east, there was a two- metre-deep anti-tank ditch, which was impassable even to the heaviest tanks. This was part of the East Prussian Defence Position and represented weeks of work by the German population.

Hidden minefields in terrain suitable for tanks were also supposed to make a potential attack more difficult. Between these there was marshy meadow country, almost impassable to tracked vehicles. The objective of the Pz.Gren.Div. GD's attack was to attack far away from the enemy's main line of resistance and out of the effective range of their artillery. The division would advance through the East Prussian Defence Position to the northeast, drive east of the city of Vilkavishkis deep into the enemy-held salient north of the city, and cut off the enemy forces farther to the west from their communications with the rear.

It was the morning of 9 August at about 04.15; mist rose from the marshy fields and meadows. Tanks, assault guns, half-tracked APCs, staff cars and tracked vehicles towing anti-tank and heavy infantry guns moved off on a broad front, as if on a roundabout, first east until they were south of the city, where they picked up the infantry, and then north. Leading the way were the armoured personnel carriers of I (APC) Battalion, Panzer-Fusilier Regiment GD, which together with the tanks were to strike the decisive blow to the east and north this day. They were followed closely by the infantry of II and III Battalions, which advanced on foot in squads right behind the armoured vehicles.

The mist still shrouded everything, preventing the Soviet defenders from seeing clearly the attack being directed against them.

Nevertheless, there was sporadic rifle fire and isolated bursts of machine-gun fire, and now and then a round from an anti-tank rifle struck the armour of the advancing vehicles.

Generalleutnant von Manteuffel had committed his division without firing a single shot. The surprise was complete. Not until the mist lifted, by which time the tanks and APCs were already east of the city, did the enemy, as expected, open fire with artillery, Stalin Organs and anti-tank guns. Heavy 150mm assault guns joined in the concert, however by now the attack by the panzer-grenadiers and panzer-fusiliers was in full swing. The panzers and assault guns, with the accompanying APCs, rolled toward their objective.

The moment had now come to send the fusiliers' sister regiment, the Panzer-Grenadier Regiment GD, from its assembly areas directly south of Vilkavishkis against the southern outskirts of the city. Its mission was to take the southern outskirts of Vilkavishkis and enter the city from there. The assault was led by III Battalion, Panzer-Grenadier Regiment GD.

The vehicles moved forward over the gravelly roads amid the milling crowd of advancing units as fast as the enemy fire permitted. Then it was time for the troops to leave their vehicles. Weapons in hand, they swarmed out and moved toward the enemy. There had never been so many enemy aircraft in the air before; they came in groups of 18, swooping down and releasing their customary fragmentation bombs. Their cannon fire repeatedly forced the panzer-grenadiers to take cover, as did the rocket salvoes from Stalin Organs and captured German rocket launchers being used by the

Soviets.

Then the first mines exploded; only a few hundred metres from the first houses on the outskirts of the city, elements of 9th Company, III Battalion, Panzer-Grenadier Regiment GD had walked into an uncharted minefield. There were casualties and cries of "Medic!"

A despatch rider sent by the regiment approached from the rear; it was Obergefreiter Bauer, bringing new orders to III Battalion. He roared up the road on his solo machine. Then...a cloud of smoke and pieces of the motorcycle flew into the air, the Obergefreiter was thrown from his seat: mines! Bauer was killed instantly. Farther right the armoured personnel carriers of I (APC) Battalion under Major Krieg were now making progress. Then, however, they became bogged down in a marshy meadow. Under heavy anti-tank and machine-gun fire from in front, they were forced to withdraw. The APCs made an about face and headed back the way they had come. It was now about 14.00. The three rifle companies had reached their objective, the old German trenches at the southern and southeastern outskirts of Vilkavishkis. Now it was time to move up the heavy weapons, to immediately prepare to defend the newly-won positions.

Farther to the right the Panthers and Tigers were exchanging fire with enemy forces dug in at the east end of the city. One of the Tigers was hit. It was the command tank. Major Baumungk and his driver, Unteroffizier Holzhauer, were badly wounded. Nevertheless, Hauptmann Bock continued to advance even though losses among the tanks were becoming more acute. Heavy tanks and well-camouflaged anti-tank guns made the going difficult. Leutnant Kurz, a platoon leader in 10th Company, was fatally hit. Oberfeldwebel Machleit, another member of 10th Company, was killed. Feldwebel Drenkhahn, Obergefreiter Schellhase and Gefreiter Jentsch, members of the crew of tank C 24 of 11th Company, died hero's deaths. Most of the tanks were damaged, some so severely that they had to be towed off the battlefield. However, after a brief halt Hauptmann von Basse, CO of I (APC) Battalion, Panzer-Fusilier Regiment GD, roared past to the east of the city with his armoured personnel carriers and assembled at Vilkavishkis' northern access road. New orders: drive on to the road-rail crossing, about 2,000 metres farther north. The advance was resumed at a high tempo. Now and then they passed a burning enemy tank; lone soldiers and whole groups of Soviets fled, the elite regiments of three divisions. The Soviets had positioned an entire guards corps there; now it had been chased from its positions and scattered to the four winds.

Hauptmann Basse's armoured personnel carriers were soon at the railway embankment. II Battalion, Panzer-Fusilier Regiment GD followed and took up position with its front facing north and northeast.

In the city of Vilkavishkis heavy street fighting had been raging since noon. Several Tigers helped the panzer-fusiliers and panzer-grenadiers fighting in the streets. A recently-introduced anti-tank infantry gun, equipped with a short barrel and capable of engaging tanks, proved to be an outstanding success. Here and there houses went up in flames. Panzerfaust projectiles crashed through windows, bursts of machine-gun fire chirped past street corners. Casualties were heavy on both sides. The houses had to be cleared one by one. It was a vicious struggle, made more difficult by the gardens and bushes. The fighting raged back and forth until darkness fell; Soviet relief attacks from the northwest and east were repulsed by hastily scraped-together reserves. The Panzer-Fusilier Regiment GD moved its command post to the north end of Vilkavishkis. Oberst Niemack knew no other way but to lead from the front; he had to be up front with his men.

Soviet close-support aircraft remained in the air until darkness fell, bombing and strafing. There wasn't a vehicle that hadn't been hit. Many had had their tires shot through, many others were just charred hulks. The dead and wounded were recovered: among them were many good comrades, many best friends; nevertheless the city of Vilkavishkis was back in German hands!

The fighting abated gradually during the night; there was one counterattack from the east, but it was stopped some distance from the city by the Panthers. The flak stood guard; the 20mm and 37mm weapons mounted on self-propelled carriages moved into favourable positions from which they could fire on the forest's edge east of the city.

The infantry, especially the Panzer-Grenadiers, occupied new defensive lines at the east end of the city in the old German positions, which there ran through cornfields. Contact was made to the north with III Battalion, Panzer-Fusilier Regiment GD under Hauptmann Kendel, which for its part was in contact with I (APC) and II Battalions. The defensive front faced mainly north and east.

East Prussian units arrived, reinforcing the captured positions and beefing up the defence.

The 10th of August dawned dull and grey. Everyone was on edge in anticipation of counterattacks by the Soviets. There had already been contact with the enemy at many places. Known enemy assembly areas were placed under concentrated fire in an effort to dampen the enemy's enthusiasm for a renewed assault before one began.

Apart from a few skirmishes in the north the day passed quietly for the panzer-fusiliers. The only notable incident occurred when about 100 Soviets broke out of the city by slipping through the lines of III Battalion, Panzer-Grenadier Regiment GD from behind. The enemy soldiers disappeared into the dense woods and thickets east of the city.

There was little significant change on 11 August 1944; the city of Vilkavishkis was in our hands, the highway west to Wirballen was usable again. Contact was made with other German units holding positions to the north and northwest, resulting in a cohesive defensive line. The Wehrmacht communique issued that day spoke of the successes won in this combat zone:

"...southwest of Kauen (Kovno), a counterattack has retaken the city of Vilkavishkis. In the last two days the enemy has lost 69 tanks and assault guns there, as well as 61 guns..."

Further East Prussian units arrived in the evening and began taking over the recently-won positions, relieving the GD units there. The same night the battalions moved into the area to the southwest and southeast of Vilkavishkis and rested. Departure was not expected before the evening of 12 August. The division was, however, still earmarked for the operation to restore contact with Army Group North as part of an armoured battle group; but first it had to reach the area west of Schaulen, where preparations would be made for the drive north.

Schaulen, which was occupied by the Soviets on 29 July, was located in the northern part of Lithuania. Heavy fighting was reported in the area to the west of the city near Kursenai. The danger of a breakthrough by the enemy to the west, to the Baltic Sea, was huge; the last overland link to the elements of Army Group North in the Courland was in danger of being severed.

The Panzer-Grenadier Division *Großdeutschland* received orders to move out immediately with all elements. Together with other armoured units it was to halt the enemy advance and restore contact with the elements of Army Group North holding out at Tukums.

II Battalion, Panzer-Grenadier Regiment GD under Hauptmann Schmelter moved off on the evening of 18 August; behind it on one march road were the other battalions, the artillery, the flak, the Armoured Reconnaissance Battalion GD – the entire division.

The march route was as follows: Schloßberg–Haselberg–Trappen (cross the Memel) –Willkischken– (14/15. 8. 1944) –Tauroggen – on the Tilsit-Schaulen road – then to Pakrazantis, turn north, Krazia – Kolainai; reach the Telsche-Schaulen road near Luoke, farther north to the Schaulen–Liebau rail line and turn east.

While still on the move the leading elements (men of II Battalion, Panzer-Grenadier Regiment GD) went to the attack from the area west of Kursenai. Their objective was the Venta and the town of Kursenai on its east bank. The attempted surprise crossing of the river failed; the enemy had incorporated this natural barrier into their defences very well. Heavy weapons of every calibre fired from every nook and cranny. This resistance forced the division command to assemble its own heavy weapons and commit the entire division. As the other panzer divisions had not yet arrived, the division had to risk an attack without protection for its flanks in the north and south.

Movement into the assembly area was made difficult by very heavy Soviet air activity, which also prevented II Panzer-Grenadier Battalion from continuing its advance to the river line itself. Losses were heavy in this open country: the 6th Panzer-Grenadier Company lost Unteroffiziere Müller and Lange, Obergefreiter Weynand and Gefreiter Walter killed, and 2 NCOs and 7 enlisted men wounded. Flanking threats from the north and south became serious; III Battalion, Panzer-Grenadier Regiment GD, which arrived on 16 August, had to be sent north toward Silenai immediately with only limited preparation. There was no time to carry out battlefield reconnaissance. Leutnant Winkler, commander of 11th Company, was wounded. To III Battalion's right the armoured personnel carriers of I Panzer-Grenadier Battalion were striving more to the northeast toward the Venta. Even farther right II Battalion, Panzer-Grenadier Regiment GD had become bogged down in completely open terrain.

Nevertheless, by evening the Sileani Estate had been taken and the Venta reached. The attackers advanced with relatively effective cover provided by thickets, brush and features of the terrain. As darkness was falling some brave grenadiers swam the river to fetch a boat that had been spotted on the other side. They all returned, though every one of them had been wounded. Like one of the assault guns, they had fallen prey to a mill dam that had been heavily mined.

Oberleutnant Schmidt, the commander of I (APC) Battalion, Panzer-Grenadier Regiment GD, nevertheless managed to cross the dam with a group of men from his battalion after dark. They advanced to the centre of Kursenai without meeting any resistance and took up positions around the market place.

Farther south the armoured personnel carriers of I (APC) Battalion, Panzer-Fusilier Regiment GD approached between the road and the railroad tracks, led by 1st Company. They veered south into the open terrain looking for a place to ford the Venta.

In the platoon leader's APC of 1st Company's point platoon sat Oberfeldwebel Seeger, his H.Q. squad leader Unteroffizier Röger, an Oberleutnant from II Battalion, Panzer-Artillery Regiment GD serving as a forward observer and his radio team, and the remaining members of the platoon headquarters squad. They were driving at considerable speed up the road toward Kursenai; trees and bushes prevented them from being seen from the town. As the half-track rolled around a bend in the road, its occupants found themselves staring at a Soviet 150mm howitzer, only a few metres away, its barrel pointing straight at them. There was nothing to do but get out and storm the gun. This they did, shouting loudly as they charged. The APC itself pulled back around the bend. Oberfeldwebel Seeger cried out and collapsed, badly wounded. He had been shot from the nearby wood which was apparently still occupied by the enemy. The Oberleutnant was seriously wounded in the same manner, but Unteroffizier Röger was already on the running board of the gun tractor and fired his submachine-gun into the driver's cab.

The other Ivans on the gun tractor, probably the gun crew, jumped down from the vehicle and began blazing away at Röger, who quickly disappeared beneath the tractor. Miraculously, he emerged unscathed when his men of the platoon headquarters squad arrived. The gun was in their hands. Although the Soviets in the forest maintained heavy small-arms fire, the armoured personnel carriers of I (APC) Battalion, Panzer-Fusilier Regiment GD rolled on and reached the Venta from the right. Once again it was Unteroffizier Röger who led the way, finding a ford across the small stream. He received the Knight's Cross at the end of August for this and other actions.

The crossing of the river took place under fire from the Soviet weapons, and the chase continued on the east bank—now toward the town of Kursenai from the south. The break-in succeeded; the town was finally taken after heavy house-to-house fighting with support from tanks and assault guns. The Soviets fled to the north and east. The artillery moved up immediately, and forward observers occupied suitable observation posts in order to place directed fire on targets to the east.

Pioneers (mainly the 1st and 2nd Companies) also moved forward to repair the bridge and make it passable for heavy vehicles. Heavy air attacks on the bridge site inflicted considerable casualties; fresh waves of aircraft arrived every few minutes, and they finally succeeded in partially destroying the bridge. Within a few hours the courageous pioneers had repaired it again, but the cost was again high.

On 17 August elements of the Panzer-Grenadier Regiment GD were also moved forward to expand the bridgehead to the north. Panthers of I Battalion, 26th Panzer Regiment under the command of Hauptmann Graf Rothkirch made an advance to the north, and with only six operational tanks they destroyed nine enemy tanks and numerous anti-tank guns. Hauptmann Rothkirch was awarded the Knight's Cross for this action. Acting on his own initiative, he drove northeast and opened the way for the panzer-grenadiers to continue the attack. This independent decision by the commander of I Battalion, 26th Panzer Regiment, based on his correct assessment of the situation, opened the door for an advance east in the direction of Schaulen.

Positions were occupied to the northeast in order to prevent possible flanking attacks by the enemy and to screen preparations by our own units, in particular the Panzer Regiment GD and elements of the Panzer-Fusilier Regiment GD, for a further attack to the east. The unit defending to the northeast (III Battalion, Panzer-Grenadier Regiment GD) was attacked several times in the course of 17 August (Thursday), finally by a battalion-size force of Russian infantry. Intervention by assault guns under Hauptmann Adam and the battalion's reserve platoon under Feldwebel Käs restored the situation after some heavy close-quarters fighting, but at the cost of losses in killed and wounded. It was only the bravery of this intervention group that allowed the positions in the north of the front to be held.

During the afternoon the artillery moved its observation posts into the town of Kursenai and the church tower in spite of continuous, heavy enemy fire. The batteries made a change of position and the armoured personnel carriers of I (APC) Battalion, Panzer-Fusilier Regiment made ready. The attack was then resumed on both sides of the road in the direction of Schaulen. The initial objective was the small town of Kuziai, or more precisely the crossroads south of the town.

A series of hill lines running crosswise to the direction of the attack, most covered with forest, had to be crossed. This was an ideal situation for the defenders, but a terrible one for the attackers. The enemy put up stubborn resistance with anti-tank guns, mortars and tanks concealed in the forest and behind the hills. There was heavy fighting for every hill, and flanking fire from the forest had to be eliminated. An increasing number of our tanks and APCs were damaged or destroyed, reducing the number of armoured vehicles available to support the advancing infantry.

The division's flanks grew longer, and forces had to be detailed to guard these as the other units assigned to the attack were not in position.

The remaining elements of the Armoured Reconnaissance Battalion GD. (no more than a battle group as the bulk of the unit was in Germany under-

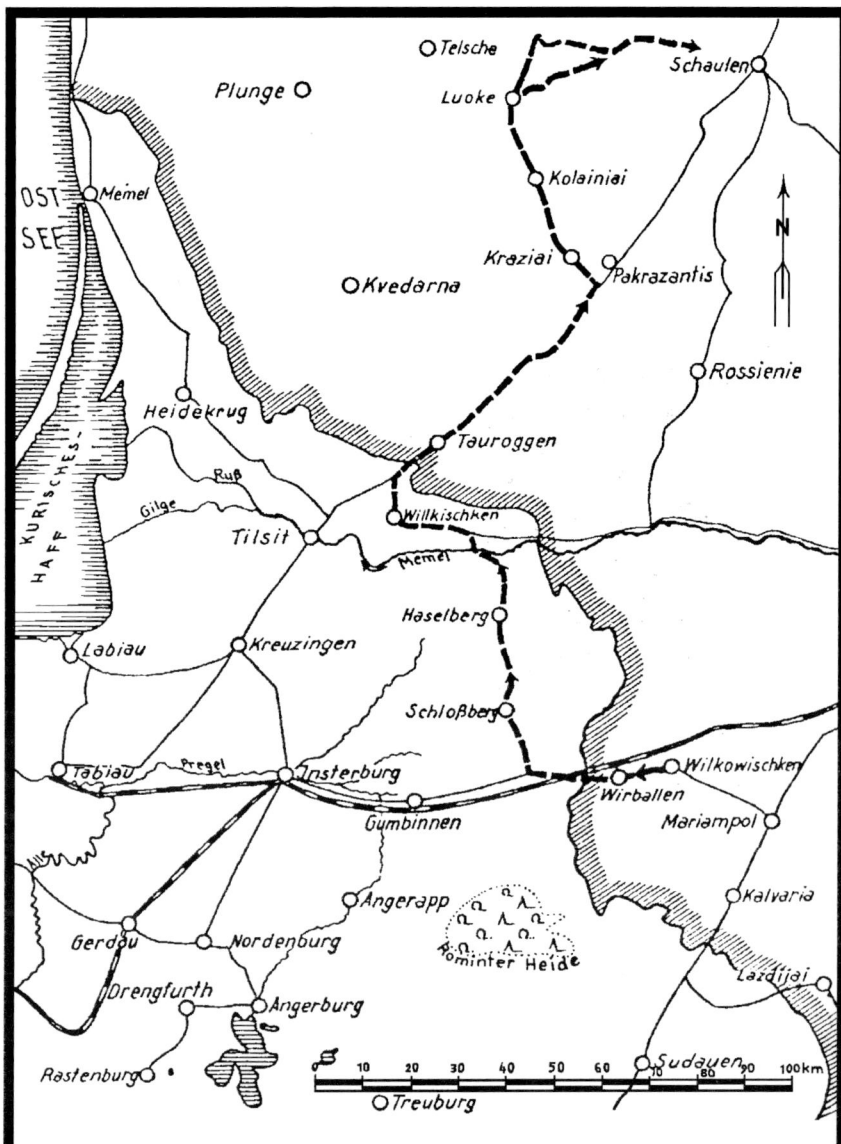

MARCH FROM WIRBALLEN TO SCHAULEN
from August 12th to 20th, 1944

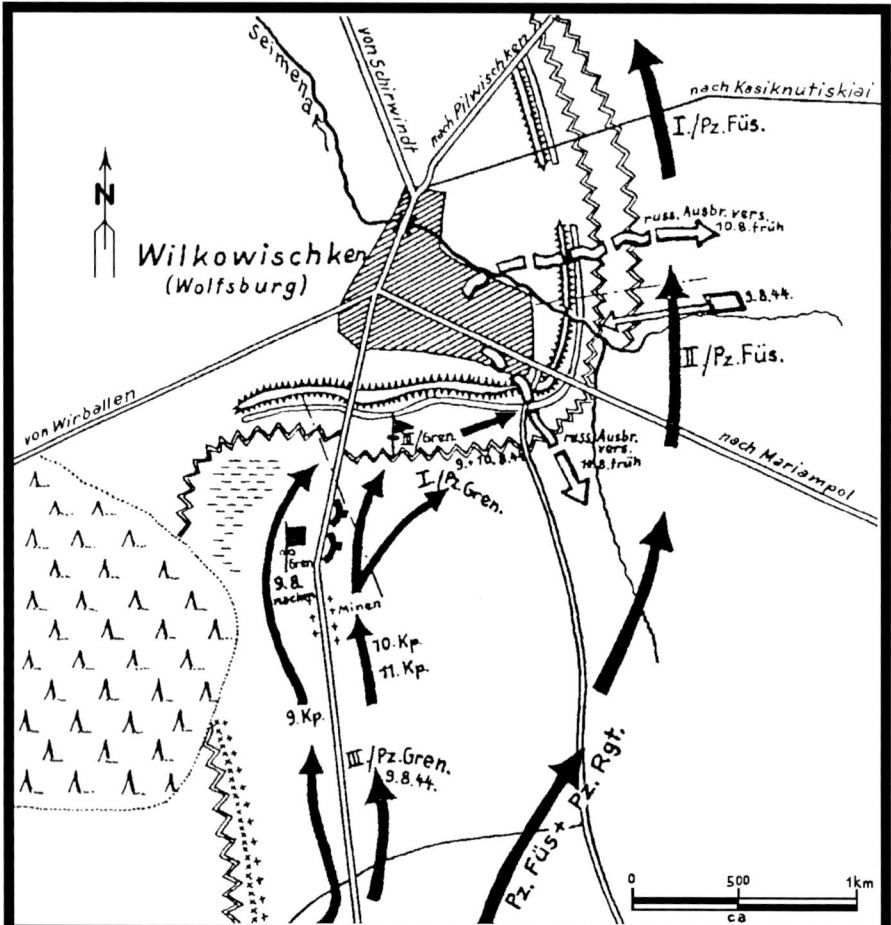

Map labels:
- Seimena
- von Schirwindt
- nach Pilwischken
- nach Kasiknutiskiai
- I./Pz.Füs.
- N (compass)
- Wilkowischken (Wolfsburg)
- russ.Ausbr.vers. 10.8.früh
- 3.8.44.
- II./Pz.Füs.
- von Wirballen
- II./Gren.
- I./Pz.Gren.
- 9.+10.8.44
- russ.Ausbr. vers. 10.8.früh
- nach Mariampol
- no. Gren. 9.8. nachm.
- +Minen
- 10.Kp.
- 11.Kp.
- 9.Kp.
- III./Pz.Gren. 9.8.44.
- Pz.Füs.+ Pz.Rgt.
- 0 ... 500 ... 1km ca.

ATTACK ON WILKOWISCHKEN,
August 9th to 10th, 1944

going reorganization) were relieved by units of III Battalion, Panzer-Grenadier Regiment GD and then deployed to secure the area north and northeast of Kursenai. The available Tigers of III Battalion, Panzer Regiment GD travelled overland to the Guragiau area, south of Kursenai, to guard against attack from the south. Only the few Panthers of I Battalion, 26th Panzer Regiment and the vehicles of the Assault Gun Brigade GD were carrying on the attack to the east. The 18th of August saw the panzer-grenadiers advance toward the Kuziai crossroads and the panzer-fusiliers drive toward Amaliait. All that was known of the enemy was they they were in prepared positions in Kuziai and at and south of the station. The panzer-fusiliers were supposed to attack this bulwark from the south and then resume their advance to the east. But it was the evening of the 18th before the points reached the bottom land in front of the objective, finally halting there. Quite surprisingly, 10th Company of III Battalion, Panzer-Grenadier Regiment GD, which did not receive the order to dig in in time, reported that it had advanced right up to Kuziai station without meeting any resistance whatsoever and was waiting there. The enemy had apparently not yet noticed its presence. Inexplicably the company received orders to advance no farther, and was instead told to wait for the artillery barrage the next morning.

The barrage began at about 03.30 on 19 August, but it was not on the station to the south, rather on the town of Kuziai itself, which gave the attackers no relief. The 9th and 11th Companies of III Battalion, Panzer-Grenadier Regiment GD attacked on their own and were able to link up with 10th Company at the railroad station. There, however, they were pinned down by heavy artillery, mortar and rocket fire which began with the arrival of daylight. The companies suffered heavy losses in killed and wounded; the attack had to be suspended for the time being.

The sound of heavy fighting was heard from the southwest on the afternoon of 19 August. The attack there by the panzer-fusiliers of I (APC) Battalion was beginning to make itself felt. The resolve of the Soviets at Kuziai Station now weakened and they fled their positions. III Battalion, Panzer-Grenadier Regiment GD moved into the positions, veered north and occupied the town of Kuziai.

Contact with the panzer-fusiliers under Hauptmann von Basse was established at the crossroads south of the town; orders were given to regroup in preparation for a continuation of the attack. II Battalion, Panzer-Grenadier Regiment GD had meanwhile moved up to join the attacking forces; Generalleutnant von Manteuffel talked to the attack battalions and explained his plan for the subsequent attack on Schaulen.

The situation remained as before: armoured personnel carriers and panzer-fusiliers together with tanks south of the road and rail line, panzer-grenadiers with assault guns north of the road and rail line. Next objective: Purviniai and the area to the south. Resistance had weakened; the panzer-grenadiers and panzer-fusiliers set off at 18.00 and rapidly occupied enemy trench positions about 1,000 metres east of the crossroads. The occupants of the trenches either fled toward the woods behind them or were cut down in the positions. The town of Purviniai was occupied with no fighting. By approximately 20.45 leading elements were close to the crossroads near Kuzaviniai, which lay in a shallow valley. The troops could barely distinguish it in the darkness. Orders were therefore issued for everyone to dig in, front facing east. A number of assault guns were positioned in the infantry positions, however the bulk of the brigade was in a wood somewhat farther to the rear.

During the night of 19-20 August orders arrived to halt the advance on Schaulen. The reason for this was obvious: the Pz.Gren.Div. GD had forced its way like a wedge through the difficult terrain to a point due west of Schaulen, with no protection for its flanks. These open flanks on both sides had gradually consumed all available forces. The attack group itself had lost too much of its striking power to continue attacking east. The division command also saw a continuation of the attack as too risky under the circumstances, especially as reports that the enemy had recovered from their initial shock and were preparing to counterattack west were increasing.

Leaving behind strong combat outposts to guard the crossroads just in front of Kuzaviniai (in this case the 11th Panzer-Grenadier company under Leutnant Ortner) early on the morning of 20 August III Battalion, Panzer-Grenadier Regiment GD and the assault guns withdrew to new positions on either side of Purviniai, making as little noise as possible. III Battalion's positions, which linked up on the left with those of II Battalion, extended from the town of Purviniai to the south. There was no direct contact with the panzer-fusiliers holding farther to the southeast, however. The gap between them, about 2,000 metres wide, had to be watched over by alternating patrols.

In the course of the day the enemy moved forward cautiously, but without attacking at first. However in the afternoon the Soviets carried out heavy artillery bombardments. The enemy also became more active in the air. Close-support aircraft concentrated their attacks on wooded areas in the rear, which the enemy suspected were sheltering troop concentrations and firing positions. Seen as a whole, however, the day passed with no serious fighting.

On that day, 20 August, Oberst Niemack, commander of the Panzer-Grenadier Regiment GD, issued an order of the day praising the eagerness and the success of I (APC) Battalion under Hauptmann von Basse. The words, "They're killer lions," repeatedly spoken in the heat of battle by Niemack in reference to the battalion, led to it being dubbed the "Lion Battalion." As well the battalion was given permission to apply the lion to their vehicles as a special recognition marking.

Panzer-Fusilier Regiment   Rgt. Command Post, 20 August 1944
    GROSSDEUTSCHLAND
    Commanding Officer

I Battalion has fought extremely well in the battles of the past days.

In recognition of its proud success, with the authorization of the division commander I decree that the battalion may apply the lion to its APCs as a special recognition marking Niemack.

Another minor withdrawal of the front took place while it was still dark on the morning of 21 August. Marshy meadows in front of the new positions made them more difficult to get at. It was from these positions that they would meet the expected enemy attacks. The new positions also made possible direct contact with III Battalion, Panzer-Fusilier Regiment GD south of the rail line. Arrangements were made with Rittmeister Radloff, commander of the panzer-fusilier battalion, for a joint defence. The heavy weapons of both regiments ranged in on prominent terrain features and suspicious wooded areas and made preparations for concentrated fire on known and suspected assembly points. The battalions' efforts were all of a defensive nature.

During the evening hours of 22 August reconnaissance personnel of a panzer division arrived at the regiments and battalions; they were officers of the 14th Armoured Reconnaissance Battalion, with orders to prepare for the relief of the GD. The units of the division were relieved during the night; they moved into the area due west of Kursenai for a brief rest. I (APC) Battalion, Panzer-Grenadier Regiment GD immediately set off in the direction of Tryskiai and continued north through Laizevai and Autz into the area west-southwest of Doblen. The other battalions followed by the same route as they were relieved.

In this area southwest of Doblen German armoured units had succeeded in driving to within 20 kilometres of the elements of Army Group North near Tukums. Approaching from the area west of Schaulen, the Pz.Gren.Div. GD's mission was to drive northeast from Autz together with the German panzer units that had advanced that far and establish a link with Army Group North. On 20 August 1944 Oberst Graf Strachwitz and his panzer group had mounted a unique armoured charge, breaking through to Tukums then veering east along the Gulf of Riga to the outskirts of Riga. Following this example, on 24 August the German units near Autz were to emulate Strachwitz and expand and enlarge the narrow corridor his advance had created. The initial objectives were Doblen and then Mietau, from where contact was to be established with the elements of Army Group North still holding out in Riga.

The Soviets initially assumed a defensive posture in this region, as their intentions seemed to lie in another direction. They apparently lacked the necessary forces to react immediately to the attack in the area west of Doblen. The outlook for the German panzer units was thus favourable, and hopes for the ultimate relief of Army Group North were justified.

The division units were supposed to pause briefly on either side of Lake Lilauce, north of Autz on Latvian soil, in preparation for the attack, after which they would advance in the direction of Doblen the same day. The arrival of individual units was delayed, however, and the planned attack was not carried out. Not until the morning of the following day did elements of the Panzer-Fusilier Regiment GD and I (APC) Battalion, Panzer- Grenadier Regiment GD move out of the area east of Lake Lilauce. Under increasingly heavy artillery and rocket fire, they advanced on Sanitorium Hill. Their objective was to take the commanding hill and create the conditions necessary for a joint attack on Doblen. Meanwhile elements of the Armoured Reconnaissance Battalion GD and the Panzer-Grenadier Regiment GD screened to the north, far to the north of the lake. There was no contact with the enemy. However, the enemy air force was extremely active. Close-support aircraft strafed known and suspected targets in the difficult terrain covered with brush, woods and thickets. The hated Stalin Organs also seemed to have become the Soviets' standard defensive weapon; they fired their salvoes into assembly areas and blanketed large areas with their rockets. Enemy minefields, most not immediately recognizable, claimed victims from the attackers and accompanying personnel. Oberst Niemack's *Schwimmwagen* drove into one such minefield and he was seriously wounded when the vehicle was hit by fire from a concealed anti-tank gun. A grave loss!

Finally, the attack of 24 August created the desired conditions. The battalions launched the decisive attack on Schaulen at lunchtime on 25 August. The men of the Panzer-Grenadier Regiment GD advanced along both sides of the Autz – Doblen highway, with II Battalion north and III Battalion south, supported by the assault guns of the Assault Gun Brigade GD. Farther south came the Panzer-Fusilier Regiment GD, accompanied by the Tigers and Panthers of the Panzer Regiment GD. The regiment's right wing forced its way northeast, due north of the Autz – Mietau highway.

Contact between units was difficult to maintain in the complex terrain. The enemy had all the advantages of the defender on their side; they had dug in at forests edges, at swamps and behind thickets and brush.

The attack began well, but it gradually lost momentum and finally ground to a halt at a heavily fortified and defended crossroads about 8 kilometres short of the objective. It was the crossroads at Lemkini-Skola, in front of Doblen. That evening the battalions finally dug in where they stood and went over to the defensive. Because of the limited available manpower the line consisted merely of a series of strongpoints.

In some cases combat strengths had fallen so low that battalions had no officers apart from the battalion commander, and companies were led by sergeants. In the infantry units companies were down to about 40 men.

Isolated operations by the battalions aimed at improving their positions could not hide the fact that they were incapable of continuing the offensive. The battalions fortified the positions where they stood, scouted firing positions for the heavy weapons and generally organized a defence in every detail.

The enemy remained quiet; they showed no inclination towards large-scale counterattacks. Both sides made repeated forays into enemy territory, hoping to bring back prisoners from whom they could obtain information as to the other side's intentions. Pioneers began laying minefields in front of the main line of resistance. The order to go over to the defensive finally legalized what the battalions had already done in the positions that marked the limit of the advance.

The Panzer-Grenadier Division *Großdeutschland* remained in these positions for several weeks; the units settled in, organized supply and became part of a new defensive line that extended from the area west of Schaulen near Kursenai in a generally northern direction west past Doblen and then to the northwest. The plan to link up with Army Group North was abandoned. Later renamed Army Group Courland, it remained surrounded and held its positions north of Tukums.

On 1 September 1944 Generalleutnant von Manteuffel handed over command of the division to the former commanding officer of the Panzer-Grenadier Regiment GD, Oberst Lorenz, who would lead the division until the end of the war. Before leaving, von Manteuffel visited each unit to say goodbye. One minor incident deserves to be mentioned: while talking with his men somewhere in the positions in front of Doblen, the subject of the size of the men of the GD, who were sometimes referred to as "tall ones," came up. There was a discussion as to who was the smallest among them. Von Manteuffel declared that it was probably he himself, for nowhere had he ever seen a smaller man in the GD. A bet was made that there was indeed a smaller man than von Manteuffel, with several bottles of liquor at stake. And sure enough such a man was found: Unteroffizier Orlovius of 7th Company (formerly 8th Company), Panzer-Grenadier Regiment GD was even smaller than his commanding officer. The bet was lost. Generalleutnant von Manteuffel lived up to his part and delivered the promised bottles to the winner.

Generalleutnant von Manteuffel was loved by the units under his command even though he was tough and uncompromising when it came to making demands of his subordinates; but he never demanded more of them than he asked of himself. His name is associated with the successful battles at Targul Frumos, Jassy and Vilkavishkis, where he demonstrated his command skills as an outstanding leader of armoured forces.

The front before Doblen remained quiet apart from limited activity by the enemy. The division's rear area, however, was the scene of hectic activity as new positions were constructed. At the front individual fighting men continued to lead the way. One such man was Gefreiter Czorny of 2nd Company, I (APC) Battalion, Panzer-Grenadier Regiment GD. In the course of a local offensive by the battalion to improve the main line of resistance, Czorny chased away the crew of a Soviet anti-tank gun with his machine- gun and captured the weapon intact. When the enemy gun crew, spurred on by their commissar, tried to retake their weapon, Czorny got up out of his hole and once again put the Soviet gun crew to flight. Taking advantage of the situation, he raced far ahead of his squad into the enemy positions and captured these too. In doing so he took out one of the positions from which the enemy had been pouring heavy flanking fire onto the battalion and brought about the desired improvement of our line. For this action, which had such a decisive effect on the local situation, Gefreiter Czorny was later awarded the Knight's Cross.

Obergefreiter Hans Sachs of 5th Company, Panzer-Fusilier Regiment GD describes the action which resulted in him receiving the Knight's Cross:

"While our I Battalion advanced far to the east, we had orders to destroy the Soviets still holding out in the forests. As soon as I went into position with my squad I discovered that enemy infantry and tanks were preparing to attack. I didn't waste much time thinking it over. There was nothing else to do but attack and we charged into the Ivans cheering loudly. The result was wild confusion, but we kept our heads.

One of my men destroyed a tank up close; but how many Soviets we killed was impossible to tell in our haste. The situation is favourable, I thought, and so we charged on (without worrying about the Ivans) and came upon a supply column, all lovely Studebakers!

We finished off another 15 Soviets hand-to-hand and captured a rich booty in munitions and food. From prisoners we learned that we weren't far from their rear-echelon units. I had my men go into position at a fork in the road, while I myself worked my way forward to see what was going on.

I hadn't gone far when, suddenly, a full Soviet company rushed our positions. Let them come, I thought to myself, then let them have it!

Everything happened so quickly that there was no time to think about what we were doing.

When we had fired the last shot and were finally able to have a look around, we found at least 25 dead, 18 wounded, two mortars, a heavy machine-gun, three light machine-guns and many rifles and pistols.

I never thought that I should receive the Knight's Cross for this."

The division remained in the Doblen battle zone. September 1944 was coming to an end with no great change in the main defence line, when on the 29th something happened in the sector held by the panzer-fusiliers that deserves to be recorded. This time the action was carried out by the men of the heavy company of II Battalion, Panzer-Fusilier Regiment GD, commanded by Oberleutnant Hoffmann:

"Low combat strengths as a result of the losses of the previous months meant that some of our positions were very thinly manned. Among the infantry companies deployed there contact with the enemy existed only at certain prominent points. The bulk of the Ivans kept their distance. II Battalion, Panzer-Fusilier Regiment had a relatively large sector to hold, as a result of which the rifle companies were somewhat overtaxed. At critical points, therefore, the positions were reinforced with several heavy weapons from the heavy company, especially where enemy tanks made their presence felt, even if only rarely.

In front of the main line of resistance of the company on the right wing there was a strip of land overgrown with low bushes, reeds and isolated trees. As it was also rather swampy, it was considered to be tank-proof. This area of terrain was thus only thinly manned, especially since there was no direct contact with the enemy there. By night only, Russian patrols occupied the edge of a wood lying about 800-1,000 metres away which was somewhat higher in elevation. The regiment usually ordered nightly patrols. This mission was rather hard on the rifle companies, because the men were simply exhausted from the daily and nightly tension. It is therefore not surprising that the heavy company, which had it somewhat easier manning its guns, was called upon to undertake these nocturnal missions.

Armoured Artillery Regiment GD with I and II Battalions, the Army Flak Battalion GD and the Assault Gun Brigade were to be sent to Headquarters, Third Panzer Army in Tryskiai. Departure was to take place on 5 October. The remaining elements of the division involved in the existing operation were placed under the command of the 4th Panzer Division. The Division Ia arrived in Tryskiai on the evening of 4 October and reported to Headquarters, XXVIII Army Corps. There he was informed that the division was to assemble in the area east of Tryskiai as army reserve. At the same time reference was made to the possibility of an enemy offensive in the next few days. The defenders knew that a Soviet offensive was imminent from air reconnaissance, radio intercepts and statements by deserters. Its most probable objective was the Baltic Sea and the final severing of the tenuous land link to Army Group Courland that had existed since August 1944. Although still small, the bridgehead northwest of Kursenai that had been won on 3 October was an indication of the likely starting point of the coming Soviet offensive.

It was known that an enemy force consisting of 19 rifle divisions, 3 tank corps and 1 artillery corps was facing the Autz sector (approx. 50 km. wide) alone. However by all indications there was not sufficient time to complete the partial withdrawal of the Panzer-Grenadier Division *Großdeutschland*, which was still looked upon as a potent force, and position it opposite the expected focal point of the enemy offensive east of Tryskiai.

During the night of 5 October 1944 the enemy successfully merged and expanded their bridgeheads across the Venta into a single bridgehead about two kilometres deep. Heavy air attacks early that morning on retreating train units of the Volksgrenadier division deployed east of Tryskiai were an indication of the attacks already under way against the main line of resistance. Due east of Tryskiai civilian construction teams under the supervision of the German civil administration had built a trench position. Nearly finished, it included dense barbed-wire entanglements and communications trenches to a second trench line. The enemy close-support aircraft fired on these entrenching detachments, resulting in tremendous confusion and a cessation of work.

It was between 08.00 and 09.00 when the sound of heavy fighting and the loud rumble of barrage fire was heard from the east. The Soviets, whose aim was to break through to the west, had begun their offensive. The German defences stood firm against the first two onslaughts; but when the third came the 551st Volksgrenadier Division was so decimated that it simply did not have enough men to defend the entire line. The Soviets were able to walk through the undefended sections of the line and push into the German rear. Deep penetrations were reported against the 551st Volksgrenadier Division and its neighbour on the left (north). Except for isolated sections that were still holding out, the front had been breached and there was no longer a unified command.

The Armoured Reconnaissance Battalion GD under Rittmeister Schroedter was immediately sent north through Svendriai to Pazizme with orders to guard the small German bridgehead over the Zizme near Tulkinciai and the forest narrows behind it. To the north the enemy had already entered the forest west of Pakepsteniat. Led by Rittmeister Schroedter, the squadrons drove into the attacking enemy force (roughly the size of a regiment) and quickly defeated it. Eighty enemy dead and 120 prisoners were counted. Without stopping to rest, the battalion, which had no heavy weapons, continued its drive into the enemy, who now moved up tanks and anti-tank guns. Not only did the battalion's forceful advance restore the former main line of resistance at this point, it also freed a trapped battle group of the 551st Volksgrenadier Division under Hauptmann Licht. The battalion held the line until approximately 03.00, even though the Soviets had outflanked it on the left and right by more than 15 kilometres and the unit was free to withdraw. Rittmeister Schroedter was later awarded the Knight's Cross for this action by the battalion.

In spite of this success by the Armoured Reconnaissance Battalion GD, the enemy could not be prevented from pouring like a rushing stream into the woods and open country east and north of Tryskiai. In the now-familiar fashion, waves of infantry-carrying T-34s, KV Is and Stalins streamed toward their next objective, using the elements of surprise and confusion to make a coordinated German defence impossible. The effect of this style of fighting on men exhausted by months of fighting (members of hastily-formed, scarcely homogenous units like the Volksgrenadier Division) was devastating. The result was chaos and headlong flight to the west.

Added to the other problems facing the defences was the depressing fuel situation: shortages were beginning to be felt, especially by the armoured units and panzer divisions. The Division Ib and the Quartermaster desperately sought the urgently-needed liquid. The commands of individual units also had to take the fuel shortage into account, employing their armour only where it was most needed. This limited the number of defensive points of main effort that could be formed.

The first elements of the Pz.Gren.Div. GD to arrive in the area southwest of Tryskiai, units of the Panzer Regiment GD and the Division Escort Company, were used to form a screen to the east and southeast. Simultaneously the Armoured Reconnaissance Battalion GD was recalled and sent north to establish contact with the elements of the 7th Panzer Division holding there.

The division commander arrived at the XXVIII Corps command post at roughly 13.00. There he received orders from the Commander-in- Chief of the Third Panzer Army to employ the elements of the Panzer-Grenadier Regiment GD expected to arrive in the late afternoon to seal off the Soviet breakthrough as far east of Raudenai (west of Kursenai) as possible.

The Panzer-Grenadier Regiment GD did not have an opportunity to see this action through, however, as the point elements of the regiment made contact with the enemy at about 14.00 approximately 8 kilometres north of Tryskiai; the road was blocked by enemy artillery and tank fire. I (APC) Battalion, Panzer-Grenadier Regiment GD immediately attacked southeast; but lacking any anti- tank weapons whatsoever, it was unable to fight its way through the enemy armour, which had already advanced beyond Virvycia, to reach the division. For this reason the Panzer-Grenadier Regiment GD was redirected from this area farther west through Tuciai, Pievenia and Juozapaiciai; the following units had already been rerouted through Vieksniai in the same direction.

At approximately 18.00 the division received orders to fight its way back toward the Windau Position and occupy the sector extending from Tryskai Station to the south end of the town of Tryskai.

The division command now tried to bring together its scattered units, some of which were deployed elsewhere. The reinforced Panzer-Fusilier Regiment was still to the north in the Doblen–Rusa area and had not yet been drawn into the events taking place farther south.

"Battle Group Langkeit" withdrew from its positions during the moonlit night of 6 October with no interference from the enemy. By 04.00 it was able to report that it had arrived in its assigned sector.

The morning of that day was relatively quiet, with the enemy only feeling their way forward cautiously; that afternoon, however, several attacks with tank support were repulsed. Finally the enemy was able to achieve a penetration against the sector held by the Division Escort Company, taking the wood which lay behind it. The Armoured Assault Pioneer Battalion GD, which had just arrived, had to be committed to seal off this incursion.

By the evening repeated Soviet attacks were exerting great pressure on the Armoured Reconnaissance Battalion GD's front, however an immediate counterattack prevented the enemy from breaking through. Here again it was the lone fighting man, often left on his own but with his fighting spirit intact, who saved the day.

While a part of "Battle Group Langkeit," Leutnant Roßmann of the Panzer Regiment GD had orders to cover the withdrawal movements in the Tryskiai area with the six Panthers of his tank company. Fighting as the rear guard, in a matter of minutes Roßmann destroyed three tanks from a group of enemy armour that was pressing hard. His Panther was hit and the radio was knocked out. All alone, he remained in contact with the enemy throughout the night.

The next morning Roßmann discovered that there were anti-tank guns and infantry in his rear and on his flanks and that enemy tanks were preparing to attack. Although completely surrounded, he decided to attack the enemy tanks in front of him. Roßmann's attack destroyed six of the tanks and eight anti-tank guns and put the rest of the enemy force to flight. Only then did he fight his way back to his own battle group, destroying an enemy supply unit consisting of truck transport columns and 13 anti-tank guns along the way. Following his successful armoured charge Roßmann rejoined his men safe and sound.

During the afternoon the Panzer-Fusilier Regiment GD was relieved in front of Doblen and Rusa and given its marching orders: it was to swing west through Moscheiken and Seda (Siady) in the direction of Telsche by the quickest means possible as part of the effort to regroup the division.

That afternoon strong Soviet armoured spearheads were reported advancing toward Luoke (Luknik). A rapid reinforcement of the defences there, which were weak, was necessary. "Battle Group Fabich," commanded by Major Fabich and consisting of II Battalion, Panzer-Grenadier Regiment GD, the 303rd Assault Gun Brigade and III Battalion, Panzer-Artillery Regiment GD, was assembled immediately and sent to the threatened area to restore the front and establish communication with the armoured elements of the 7th Panzer Division in the Kaunatava area.

However, the first radio communications from "Battle Group Fabich" confirmed that strong enemy forces were already advancing on Luoke from the east, southeast and northeast. A further radio message urgently requested food and munitions, as it was unlikely that supply would be possible in the days to come. Extremely powerful Soviet units appeared to be concentrating on Luoke, an important road junction, in an effort to completely destroy the battle group, which was squeezed into a confined area there. Scarcely had it reached the city and occupied its defensive lines after heavy fighting, when it was struck by attacks with numerous tanks from all sides. These lasted until late in the evening. The night itself was relatively quiet and was utilized by the battle group mainly to fortify its positions.

It was absolutely clear to every single fighting man there that when the sun came up on 7 October 1944 he would face another test of his steadfastness.

I (APC) Battalion, Panzer-Grenadier Regiment GD, commanded by Rittmeister Kuehn, and III Battalion, commanded by Hauptmann Brinken, under the regimental command of Major Schwarzrock, had meanwhile veered east at Nerimdaiciai, northwest of Tryskiai. There were brief preparations in the Laumiai area, then the battalions attacked the enemy forces that had already crossed the Virvycia. They subsequently occupied positions facing northeast beside the elements of the 7th Panzer Division still holding out in Tryskiai.

The field of view in the main line of resistance was limited on account of the dense forest and brush. Nevertheless there was contact with friendly forces, including the units of the 7th Panzer Division. I (APC) Battalion, Panzer-Grenadier Regiment GD, located between III Panzer-Grenadier Battalion (left) and elements of the 7th Panzer Division (right), still had about 22 operational armoured personnel carriers. Almost all were armed with the new 15mm machine-gun, originally a fixed weapon for use in aircraft, now installed in the APCs in a swivelling mount. This weapon had an extremely high rate of fire, 600 rounds per minute, and could fire tracing high-explosive and incendiary ammunition to 1,000 metres. The bulk of the APCs were concentrated in 3rd Company, while the remaining three companies had only a few vehicles. In these units the new weapons were mostly mounted on 3-tonne Opel Blitz trucks.

At the medical clearing stations the many wounded were in direct danger at this time, especially since most had been positioned to the side of the highway on account of the strafing of the latter by enemy aircraft. The medical facilities had to remain alert to where enemy and friendly forces were at all times. At this time most of the clearing stations were out of communication with the Division IV b.

The medical clearing stations had plenty of work to do; the wagons and motor vehicles of the ambulance platoons delivered a steady stream of fresh wounded from the battlefield, bleeding and fighting for their lives. The two focal points of the battle – Luoke in the south, Tryskiai in the north – produced considerable numbers of casualties. Evacuation of the wounded to the rear went on day and night. The journey was kilometres long and conditions in the rear areas were uncertain. As soon as the ambulances had unloaded their bloody cargo they headed back to the front against the stream of refugees and endless vehicle columns. The exploits of the ambulance drivers, subject to enemy air attack day and night, bordered on the unbelievable. To their credit, none of the wounded was left at the medical clearing stations.

At approximately 02.10 on 7 October (Saturday) the Ia of the Pz.Gren.Div. GD received a corps order instructing the division to hold the town of Luoke at all costs. It was to wage mobile warfare with armoured battle groups and prevent the enemy from breaking through to the west north of Luoke.

Beginning at 03.00, the division subsequently withdrew the elements in the sector south of Tryskiai to a line: stream line near Point 106.9 –Viesviniai–river loop west of Tauragenai–Ziljaliai. At the same time the left wing, the elements of the 7th Panzer Division still near Tryskiai and I (APC) and III Battalions of the Panzer-Grenadier Regiment GD, was withdrawn, making use of the river line to double back to the west. In spite of the poor driving conditions these movements were not hindered by the enemy. 3rd (APC) Company of I (APC) Panzer-Grenadier Battalion, which formed the rearguard, exchanged long-range fire with scattered groups of enemy troops. As a result of these movements a continuous front, though little more than a series of strongpoints, was again beginning to take shape.

The situation was especially difficult for "Battle Group Fabich" in and near Luoke. Fighting a desperate, costly battle against an enemy attacking from all sides, it was able to destroy numerous enemy tanks; but it could not prevent the enemy from driving past Luoke to the north, and in particular, to the south.

During the night I (APC) Battalion of the Panzer-Fusilier Regiment GD under Hauptmann von Basse once again had to despatch some of its armoured personnel carriers to the regiment's rearmost elements. Bringing up the rear, the trains had come under fire from pursuing enemy tanks and some had to be rescued before they could continue on their way. On the morning of 7 October I and II Battalions were abreast of Seda. After departing for the specified assembly areas, I (APC) Battalion, Panzer-Fusilier Regiment GD, which was driving point, ran into enemy spearheads southeast of Seda. The battalion deployed into attack formation and attacked the enemy, in order to drive them back and also screen the left flank at the edge of the forest northwest of Plinksiai Lake. Meanwhile II Panzer-Fusilier Battalion swung out to the west past I Battalion in the direction of Gadunavas, in order to position itself in front of the enemy on a broad front between Tavsola Lake and Plinskiai Lake.

As the bulk of the division's armoured forces were tied up in the middle of the sector, the Assault Gun Brigade GD was deployed toward Seda via

Telsche, Olsiady and Kalvarija to beef up the left wing. Its orders were to intercept the enemy forces reported there. At approximately 18.00 the brigade reported making contact with the enemy in the area of Berzenai. Following a brief exchange of fire the enemy withdrew toward Seda.

I (APC) Battalion, Panzer-Fusilier Regiment GD reported heavy enemy column traffic on the road north of Plinsksiai Lake heading for Seda.

Additional reports made it apparent that the enemy already had strong motorized and armoured forces deep in our flanks in the north and the south and was striving to achieve an encirclement. As there were no friendly forces worth mentioning either in the north or south, it became necessary to carry out a large-scale withdrawal to the "East Prussian Defence Position" abreast of Memel.

In the course of these withdrawal movements, on 7 October at about 16.00 the division received orders to withdraw the forces in the line Pieliai–Bedaukiai–Badmakiai to a line Visvieniai–Stulpinai–Tavsola Lake to prevent the enemy from breaking through to the west and southwest and to block the roads from Seda to Plunge and from Seda through Salanti to Krottingen. The next planned defensive line was the Tretovo–Plunge–Virkstos Lake line.

The units of the Panzer-Grenadier Regiment GD (less II Battalion) were the first to reach the specified line, at about midnight. Meanhile, at 21.45 a further order arrived from corps, calling for a rapid execution of the withdrawal into the area north and south of Plunge, located about 30 kilometres west of Telsche. The enemy had begun their encirclement attempt in the north and especially in the south. The danger existed that enemy spearheads might get to Plunge before the first elements of the GD arrived.

In all haste the units sent operations officers to the division command post, where they were briefed on their new mission by the Ia.

Command and control during the withdrawal was almost exclusively effected by radio, operations officers and runners. The division's radio stations sent and received about 300 transmissions each day. Brevity in orders, reports and inquiries was thus decisive in assuring the rapid transmission of information.

Further conditions necessary for a smooth withdrawal were precise scouting of roads and terrain, time staggering of all movements and strict march discipline on the part of all elements.

The troops moved into a new main line of resistance west of the city of Telsche at and north of the highway to Plunge. Acting as forward pickets, two lone APCs sat about 1,000 metres in front of the positions, watching and listening. Contact with friendly forces existed on both sides, which is reassuring to every unit leader concerned about his flanks.

At the highway, defended by I (APC) Battalion, Panzer-Grenadier Regiment GD, everyone was on the lookout. In front of them they heard the sound of tanks, and it was getting louder. Were the approaching tanks Soviet or German; friend or foe?

Then the first tanks appeared: they were Tigers of III Battalion, Panzer Regiment GD. They had been outflanked in their old positions by the Soviets in the afternoon, had waited for darkness and then rolled down the highway to the west at top speed. After several kilometres they roared into the midst of the Russian positions and simply drove through them. The breakthrough was completed without loss.

The soldiers of II Battalion, Panzer-Fusilier Regiment GD under Hauptmann Emminghaus stayed on both sides of Gadunavas, with their shoulders on the two lakes, until deep into the night. Supported by Hauptmann Graf Rothkirch's Panthers, they repulsed every enemy assault.

In the early morning hours of 8 October, II Panzer-Grenadier Battalion, which was still holding out near Luoke, broke out of its encirclement. The fighting was bitter. The battalion overran the enemy, drove through Telsche and Olsiady and at approximately 07.00 arrived in Plunge, where it was deployed in the Panzer- Grenadier Regiment GD's sector.

Employing mobile tactics, the Assault Gun Brigade GD and the 7th Panzer Division's armoured reconnaissance battalion withdrew to an area roughly abreast the north tip of Virkstos Lake–Mikyiai (to the northwest of the lake). Because of the way the situation on the south flank had developed the planned thrust toward Seda could not be carried out.

Enemy pressure on Plunge increased in the early afternoon. At the same time enemy tanks with mounted infantry were reported in the Anuziai and Budriai area – due east of the Minia River, east of Krottingen – thus already west of the "East Prussian Defence Position." The Division Escort Company was immediately sent to Kartena to block the bridges and a ford across the Minia there. On its approach the unit had to reopen the Plunge–Kartena road, which had been severed by the enemy west of Liepgiviai.

The Armoured Reconnaissance Battalion GD, which had been employed in the defensive front due to a shortage of available units, was originally supposed to reconnoitre on the south flank toward the Minis River line after reaching Plunge; but instead it was also sent toward Kartena before finally being rushed through Plunge, Plateliai and Salantai to Krottingen with the following orders:

(a)   Reach Jokubavas and secure the Memel bridgehead in the Genaiciai–Sasaiciai–Raguviskiai–Laumaliai sector until the arrival of the Panzer-Fusilier Regiment GD,

(b)   after handing over the defence to the Panzer-Fusilier Regiment GD move to Gargzdai and from there reconnoitre east of the Minia.

The battalion arrived in the Krottingen area at about midnight. II Battalion, Panzer-Fusilier Regiment GD, which had previously been held in the north and which was approaching via Mosedis (Masiady), was immediately redirected through Salantai into the area southeast of Krottingen.

In the meantime the division's supply units and trains had to be staggered far to the west. This created great difficulties in the delivery of supplies, especially of the necessary quantities of fuel. With the heavy east-west flow of traffic on the roads, the fuel columns and fuel trucks needed energetic and careful leaders to get through. Nevertheless they always delivered the fuel to the front on time, and consequently few of the division's vehicles had to be abandoned and destroyed for lack of fuel.

Unfortunately the latter included the greatest consumers of fuel: the Tigers.

A large number of them had to be sacrificed during the drive to the Memel on account of acute fuel shortage. One of the few Tigers still serviceable just outside Memel (Number C 24 with the crew of Oberfeldwebel Windheuser, Obergefreiter Nadler and Gefreiters Wolff, Schübler and Gussone, all of 11th Company) met its fate just beyond Krottingen. It was disabled by fire from a T-34 and its commander killed. According to radio messages from the units holding near Kartena, the Soviets were about to cross the Minia near Raguviskiai and were preparing to break through the Memel bridgehead positions as well. It was now of decisive importance to delay any further advance by the enemy at and north of Plunge; this would free up forces for use in the Memel bridgehead position on 9 October when the advancing enemy would be halted. Only in this way would it be possible for the remaining elements to stream through Krottingen into the Memel bridgehead position. To this end the division issued the following orders:

(a)   Beginning at 24.00 on the night of 9-10 October 1944, the division will withdraw "Battle Group Schwarzrock" (reinforced Panzer-Grenadier Regiment GD, II Battalion; Panzer-Artillery Regiment GD; III (Tiger) Battalion, Panzer Regiment GD) to the line Liepgiviai–south tip of Virksos Lake,

(b)   this move will free up "Battle Group von Breese" (Panzer-Fusilier Regiment GD; III Battalion, Panzer-Artillery Regiment GD; I Battalion, 26th Panzer Regiment), which shall then move into the Jokubavas area in the Memel bridgehead position via Plateliai, Salanti and Krottingen;

(c)   seal off Kolxzyk, north of Virskus Lake near Mikyiai, with a battle group consisting of the 7th Armoured Reconnaissance Battalion, the Assault Gun Brigade GD and I Battalion, Panzer-Artillery Regiment GD.

As darkness fell the division's units began the withdrawal, leaving behind a rear guard; the Panzer-Grenadier Regiment GD in a reduced position at Plunge, the Panzer-Fusilier Regiment GD in the old main line of resistance. It was the beginning of a foot- race between the retreating German units and battle groups and the Soviet armoured groups advancing on both flanks. The Germans were striving to reach Memel, which promised a friendly reception, safety and later (what a hope!) evacuation by sea. Alarming reports spurred the pace of the retreat. If they were to escape destruction it was going to require a total effort by the officers and NCOs and the trust of the men in their leaders.

And so "Battle Group Schwarzrock" (reinforced Panzer-Grenadier Regiment GD) occupied the assigned defensive line, while "Battle Group von Breese" (reinforced Panzer-Fusilier Regiment GD) sought to reach the Krottingen area by way of Plateliai and Salanti. The Armoured Reconnaissance Battalion GD was already battling strong enemy infantry and tank spearheads near Krottingen. After hasty preparations "Battle Group von Breese" attacked in the direction of Raguviskiai with I (APC) and III Battalions. It captured a line along the Minia and was able to hold this until evening.

During the attack Leutnant Neumeyer of I Battalion, 26th Panzer Regiment and his three Panthers gave support to I (APC) Battalion. After the artillery barrage (III Battalion) Neumeyer, acting on his own initiative, dashed ahead of the APCs and destroyed a total of six enemy tanks. This success inspired the following APC battalion, which made a rapid advance. As the advance continued the leading Panther, commanded by Leutnant Neumeyer, was hit in the running gear and disabled. Under continuous fire from four enemy anti-tank guns and several tanks, Neumeyer continued to engage the enemy and knocked out a further two enemy tanks, 2 anti-tank guns and 7 trucks. Meanwhile his stationary tank took hit after hit. Neumeyer did not abandon the Panther, however, instead he fought on. Finally the ninth hit penetrated the tank and wounded Neumeyer in both thighs. He immediately transferred to another tank and knocked out two more enemy tanks. When this Panther, too, was knocked out, he bailed out again and fought his way back to the panzer-fusiliers with his crew. Leutnant Neumeyer's actions, which had such an outstanding effect on the attack, were later acknowledged by the awarding of the Knight's Cross.

Meanwhile, following the arrival of the Panzer-Fusilier Regiment GD the Armoured Reconnaissance Battalion GD moved to the right into the Zvirbliai area, its front facing southeast.

The lengthy stand made by the Armoured Reconnaissance Battalion GD and the reinforced Panzer-Fusilier Regiment GD against a far superior enemy attacking with large numbers of tanks created the conditions necessary for the remaining units to flow behind this screening front into the Memel area and made possible the creation of the Memel Bridgehead.

Heavy Soviet artillery fire continued to fall on Krottingen. At 13.45 on 9 October the division received the following order:

> "The corps is fighting its way back toward the Gargzdai–
> Baugskorallen–Karckelbeck line manned by the 58th Infantry
> Division. The line is holding. It is imperative that the 7th Panzer
> Division and GROSSDEUTSCHLAND clear the area southeast of
> Krottingen and then place strong elements in mobile groups behind
> this line in the area east-northeast of Memel as quickly as possible.
> GD is to use the road through Polangen (Polange) to the maximum
> extent possible. GD shall initially leave a strong group to protect the
> important traffic centre of Darbenai and delay the enemy's advance."

At about noon the 7th Armoured Reconnaissance Battalion and the Assault Gun Brigade GD left the Notenai–Prialgava line and began fighting their way back toward Salantai. While elements remained at the north end of Salantai to hold the road and bridge open for the forces still east of the Salanta River to withdraw over, the main body of the battle group screened the Darbenai area to the north. In addition a well-armed patrol was placed on the road leading to Polangen neat Butinge.

At 12.00 "Battle Group Schwarzrock" abandoned the defensive line southwest of Virksos Lake; the last elements of the battle group crossed the bridge at Salantai at about 16.00 then drove through Darbenai and Polangen into the

Memel area. The march from Salantai through Darbenai and Polangen by the main body of the reinforced Panzer-Grenadier Regiment GD took place without interference from the enemy.

A dense stream of retreating units as well as every imaginable type of vehicle forced its way down the road. Discipline began to break down as they neared their destination. A heavy bombing raid was in progress as elements of I (APC) Battalion passed through the city of Polangen. The square was almost completely choked with wrecked and burning vehicles; dead and injured civilians lay everywhere. At the large airfield outside the city the runway was blown up.

Finally the old border of the Reich was crossed at Nimmerstadt. Along the former border ran the well-fortified "East Prussian Defence Position." The individual battalions of the Pz.Gren.Div. GD kept arriving until dark; as units arrived they moved into the positions north of Memel as indicated on the map. They were not, however, part of the Memel Bridgehead garrison as they had assumed; instead they were in a smaller bridgehead, whose outline was as follows:

> 1,000 metres south of the mouth of the King Wilhelm Canal–
> Leisten–Buddelkehmen–Zenkuhnen–Misseiken–Neufels outer
> works –Baugskorallen–Korallischken–Raddeilen–Paupeln– north
> end of Karkelbeck.

The mission given the defenders: Memel is to be defended against all attacks by the enemy. As the pillar between Army Group North and East Prussia, it is to be held to the extreme! The following are the sector assignments for the units manning the bridgehead:

Right: Pz.Gren.Div. GD with 220th Gren.Rgt. (58th Inf.Div.) and Pz.Fus.Rgt. GD

Centre: 7th Panzer Division

Left: 58th Inf.Div. with 209th Gren.Rgt. and Pz.Gren.Rgt. GD

Units flowed from the north into the Memel area throughout the evening and night and immediately occupied the sectors assigned to them. All available forces were committed so as to achieve the highest possible level of defensive readiness by next morning. Under heavy pressure from the enemy, "Battle Group von Breese" and the Armoured Reconnaissance Battalion GD fought their way back toward the new defensive line.

II Battalion, Panzer-Fusilier Regiment GD was still in a hedgehog position in a willow thicket east of Krottingen when it received a radio message from the regiment at about 20.00: "Battalions will fight their way through alone to Fortress Memel!" But this could only apply to II Battalion, since the other two battalions were defending positions southeast of Krottingen.

The following account describes II Battalion, Panzer-Fusilier Regiment GD's retreat:

"The company commanders squatted around Hauptmann Emminghaus. Council of war – maps spread out. 'Bloody hell – and on foot!' said Reismann casually. That afternoon the combat echelon had been scattered to the four winds by sixty T-34s. A patrol from the heavy company, led by its commander Oberleutnant Hoffmann, had found only a Kettenkrad at the vehicle park. There were still two 1-tonne prime movers, and these were now sent for. Fahnenjunker Henning's prime mover arrived with two anti-tank guns behind it instead of the usual one. The other prime mover had been knocked out.

While the council of war was in session the sentries reported the arrival of a Schwimmwagen; it was the chief driver of 8th (Heavy) Company.

The man was grilled ruthlessly about what had happened to the vehicles. According to him, those that hadn't been destroyed were safe. The mood picked up. After completing his report Obergefreiter Handtke received a satisfied slap on the shoulder from his company commander. Then the latter roared away: 'Vehicles fall in!' As darkness was falling the battalion pulled out and assembled on the road. The men mounted up and the vehicles rolled undisturbed to Krottingen.

The city presented an eerie picture, it was completely empty. The glow of fires over dark streets, now and then a soldier hurrying somewhere with his belongings slung over his back.

Hauptmann Emminghaus had been forced to abandon his Schwimmwagen after it broke an axle in a shell hole.

The commander of 8th (Heavy) Company led the way. On the road out of Krottingen was the bridge over the railroad; under it was a burning munitions train, above Ivan's night bombers.

The Oberleutnant got out and said to his driver, 'Go, full throttle—three kilometres, then stop and wait for the others to catch up.' He himself remained standing at the bridge, urging each vehicle to hurry. They flitted across like shadows while flames spurted from the burning rail cars.

Every now and then a bomb fell. One vehicle after another raced across the bridge, then all of a sudden it was over.

"Damn," grumbled the commander of the Eighth, 'where is my B-Krad?' It was no good, no more vehicles came. Their only choice was to run across the bridge in the dark, tongues hanging out. Then, one last vehicle approached—we got in.

When dawn came on 10 October we were in the middle of the stream of vehicles. An artillery unit had to choose a small nest like this to go into position or regroup, all the roads clogged, and up above Ivan with whole squadrons of bombers.

Cursing officers struggled to get through. At last we got moving again, and finally the church towers of Memel appeared on the horizon; grenadiers of our sister regiment had dug in to the right and left of the road. So on into Memel. It was a ghost town too. Then an air raid. Bombs fell somewhere. Go, move on!!

At a street corner was a limbered heavy mortar. The chief of the heavy company flirted with the idea of taking it along, but there wasn't time – onward! Open road, another air attack.

'Halt!' Several trucks roared past, they should have known better. 'Good God!!!' shouted the Oberleutnant, 'they're driving right into Ivan's arms.

Go, Handtke, step on it and go after them!' They caught up with the trucks just in time. 'Everyone out – end of the line!' We moved up slowly to relieve I (APC) Battalion and occupied a new defensive line at the outskirts of Memel."

By the morning of 10 October 1944 the defenders had achieved a level of readiness that allowed them to head off the enemy's drive to Memel and beat back their attack spearheads.

While in the morning the heaviest pressure was against 7th Panzer Division in the middle of the bridgehead, during the course of the afternoon the enemy carried out several attacks on the GD's sector in company to battalion strength. The Soviets penetrated about 700 metres along the Memel–Tilsit road but were driven back by an immediate counterattack.

The units of the Panzer-Grenadier Regiment GD, which was in the north of this combat zone, were arranged in the following sequence from the left on the Baltic Coast: I (APC) Battalion, III Battalion and II Battalion. All were on foot, manning hastily-dug holes on the watch for the Soviet attack which was sure to come. Rittmeister Kuehn, commander of I (APC) Battalion, Panzer- Grenadier Regiment GD, on the division's left wing in the Memel Bridgehead, describes the first few days in this positions:

Tuesday, 10 October 1944: Cloudy, windy.

After it became light I assigned temporary sectors, referring to the map, and as well despatched scouts to finally find this supposedly fabulously-built trench position. I myself drove to the church located in the north part of the town, in order to get a view of the area from the steeple. Even from there I could see no trenches and so I decided to have my battalion occupy a position at the north end of the town, extending in a great arc from there to Kunken Gorge. Since we were after all supposed to be defending a 'Fortress Memel,' it seemed to me important to hold as much terrain as possible.

Scouting farther north of the church I met a brave old rural police sergeant who was standing in front of his pretty white cottage in full war paint. He asked me rather timidly where our fighting troops were. When I told him that was us, he asked if he might now be allowed to withdraw to Memel, as he had received orders to fall back when the combat troops arrived. I felt sorry for the old man, and I couldn't help thinking about the fairy tale about the steadfast tin soldier. I asked him whether the entire civilian population had been evacuated. He answered, 'Yes, since yesterday.' There were still cows roaming the fields everywhere; obviously they had released the herds, because there wasn't time to get them away during the hasty evacuation of the town.

After I learned that there was an outpost of the Frontier Guard somewhat to the north, at his request I gave the old man express permission to withdraw.

Afterward I sought out the border guards and found them busy butchering geese. They gave my driver and me some lovely hot coffee, which did us good. The customs official in charge of the border post also reported that the civilians had been evacuated the day before. He subsequently turned pale when I informed him that he and his thirty men were now under the command of the battalion and were to begin guarding the coast immediately. He twisted and turned like an eel in his efforts to escape. Finally he asked for permission to drive to Memel to get new orders from his superiors. I told him he could go as soon as his men had occupied the sector assigned to them in the coastal dunes behind the main line of resistance.

The battalion's land sector was almost four kilometres wide; on the right (in and west of Kunken Gorge) was 2nd Company, in the middle was 3rd Company, and the area from left of the church to the beach was occupied by 1st Company. The APCs were positioned somewhat farther back in the village of Karkelbeck as a mobile reserve. Two APCs were sent ahead to Dargussen as forward pickets. They were under orders to repel enemy patrols that lacked tanks. Should enemy tanks or stronger infantry (a company or more) approach, they were to report this by radio if possible and fall back toward the main line of resistance. It had turned out that the radio sets in the new APCs were extremely unreliable. The experts in the signals platoon said that the tubes were too weak.

The 4th Company placed its mortars in position in the south part of Karkelbeck, the light infantry gun platoon in the north part of Rund Gorge. A forward observer from 4th Battery, which had been instructed to cooperate with the battalion, initially positioned himself in the church steeple. I strongly recommended to the artillerymen that they not show themselves at their turret hatches!

The battalion command post was set up in a house at the road fork at the south end of Karkelbeck.

I assigned Oberleutnant Derben to scout a passable road south through the forest for supplying the battalion, as we probably wouldn't be able to use the gravel road past the Kunken Gorge and Szodeiken Jonell by night as it was too close to the main line of resistance. I then drove to the regimental command post in Purmallen. On the way I found III Battalion's left flanking squad on the hill northwest of Szodeiken Jonell and explained to the squad leader where our right wing was (at his two o'clock position).

We subsequently found a long train with a mixture of freight and military cars near Kollaten, apparently abandoned by its crew. The highway from Nimmersatt to Memel and the road leading in from Krottingen were clogged with retreating and fleeing columns of every kind. Memel had been under continuous air attack since dawn. The city was obviously ablaze in many places. Another large formation of Russian heavy bombers approached just as we were nearing Kollaten. A battalion of Lithuanian auxiliary police in German police uniforms raced in panic across the fields toward the safety of the forest like a herd of frightened sheep. In doing so they offered the bombers a target too good to pass up. There were apparently numerous anti-aircraft guns in and around Memel, and these put up a murderous barrage. We saw several enemy aircraft shot down. It was only with great difficulty that we wound our way along the chaotically-clogged road to Purmallen. There I reported to Oberstleutnant Schwarzrock which positions I had occupied with my battalion and the reasons why. But I also pointed out that the position was only thinly manned, a two-man rifle pit or a light machine-gun nest every 150 metres! I also asked for anti-tank guns, as those assigned to us had been sent elsewhere in the past few days. These were promised, as well as support from the regiment's heavy mortar platoon. However the latter also had to help III Battalion beside us. Before I headed back, the battalion headquarters' senior NCO reported to me with a supply vehicle and another belonging to 2nd Company. When I queried him, he informed me that the field kitchens and the remaining elements of the battalion train had already withdrawn from Memel to the south! We were without our train. Subsequently a Gefreiter of 3rd Company reported back with two APCs; he had been detached to division on some sort of security assignment 24 hours earlier. Because of the heightened danger of air attack, I ordered the vehicles to maintain a greater than normal interval during the return trip. During a stop caused by approaching Russian bombers the grenadiers in the APC discovered that the train near Kollaten included, among other things, a car full of bread. As we hadn't seen bread for days, after returning to the command post I despatched a group of trucks under the command of the senior NCO to go back and fetch as much bread as possible. It turned out that the train was in fact abandoned and that one entire car was filled with cigarettes and chocolate, while the other cars contained other supply goods. The service cars turned out to be part of the Commander-in-Chief of Army Group North's command train. Our men retrieved a large quantity of writing paper from them, which was very important in view of the disappearance of our train. From then on the battalion's reports and orders were issued on paper bearing the letterhead 'The Commander-in-Chief of Army Group North!' Our salvage team reported that the train had already been plundered, and it was with a heavy heart that I sent a detachment there to guard it and at the same time informed regiment about the incident with the request that it have the train guarded, as we truly couldn't spare a single man.

In the meantime Oberleutnant Derben had returned from his scouting mission. What he had to report was shocking: in the forest south of Karkelbeck (barely 1,000 metres away from our command post) there was a large navy munitions dump, jam-packed with artillery ammunition for French 75mm guns. The dump personnel were stinking drunk and planned to blow up the entire place in about an hour! The resulting explosion would surely blow up the lovely forest, and our village as well. Furthermore Derber had found a passable road through the forest to the seaside resort at Försterei. He also found a navy flak battery at said resort with eight 128mm guns. The gun crews consisted of young men of the labour service under the command of navy gunners. The commander of the Försterei battery, a Kapitänleutnant, stated that the battery could also engage land targets and added that he would love to do so, all we had to do was specify the appropriate targets!

Unfortunately the battery had no one with training as a ground observer, and it also lacked the necessary field telephone cable to connect it with an observation post in our main line of resistance. However they did have outstanding 1:100,000 grid maps, which made it possible to quickly and accurately designate any desired target. The battery could then fire on specified targets by referring to the grid values we provided.

After a brief conference I sent Derben back to the drunks who were guarding the dump. He was to make it clear to the man in charge that in no event was he to blow the place up! Derben was to take whatever measures were necessary to enforce this order. Furthermore, he was to subsequently fetch a few of the navy maps from the Försterei battery and ask the battery commander to have field telephone cable laid at least as far as our command post. We intended to have our forward observers of 4th Battery and 4th Company direct the battery's fire against ground targets through our battalion switchboard.

Derben returned a few minutes later: the dump had not been blown up and the battery was going to lay down a line to the battalion command post. Incidentally: the battery was capable of engaging land targets at ranges of 21 kilometres! It could therefore reach Polangen airport. While on a brief scouting walk near the battalion command post we came upon about sixty Luftwaffe soldiers of regional defence force age under the command of an Oberleutnant. The men had set out from Polangen airport the previous afternoon and had come down along the beach. They were likewise press-ganged and placed on guard duty at the coast. The Oberleutnant asked for permission to bicycle into Memel to see the airport commandant, in order to request a truck to take away his men's excess baggage and to let him know where they were. I gave him permission to go.

Late in the morning the APCs in Dargussen reported enemy tanks approaching from the northeast. The observers in the church spire also saw about 15 tanks moving west from the direction of Grabben. At first everything remained quiet opposite the battalion's front. In the afternoon (the urgently-requested anti-tank guns had just arrived) enemy tanks attacked 1st Company's position at the church from the north. The spire was holed by shells and the artillery observers and the timberwork in which they had positioned themselves began to give way. The valiant commander of the 18-man-strong 1st Company, Feldwebel Zwillus, was almost killed by a falling rafter. He sprinted into the rectory and, standing at the window, described to me by telephone the course of the battle. He was interrupted when the tanks began firing into the house and he had to lie down on the floor. An anti-tank gun, which went into position at the last moment, knocked out the leading tank right in front of the church. The rest remained beyond the stream that ran north of the church. The only way across the stream for the tanks was a small bridge at the policeman's house, and consequently they had little opportunity to deploy. After the din subsided the battalion was sent a platoon of pioneers with mines and explosives. Oberleutnant Adam also arrived with three assault guns. Furthermore an Oberleutnant Straihamer (from another panzer division) was assigned to the battalion. He took over 1st Company; Feldwebel Zwillus, who was somewhat the worse for wear, was taken to the battalion aid station for a few hours to recover. The night passed quietly. Patrols reported enemy tanks in some of the dunes north of the lifeguard shack. Before it got dark, lookouts in the church observed a long column of infantry advancing through Grabben to the coast. Further, at least eight tanks were seen to drive into a wood about 1,000 metres north of the church following the failed attack.

While driving through the village on my way back from the church to the command post, I suddenly saw several dark forms on the main street. We stopped. It was three old women, who, in answer to my astonished questions, said that they had simply been left behind during the sudden flight on the 9th and now had no idea where to go. It seemed quite possible that other old people had been left behind in the village! For the time being the old women were placed in the care of Oberarzt Brodt.

In the evening there was another pleasant surprise: the NCO-led patrol we had left behind with heavy hearts on 9 October returned to the battalion safe and sound! The young patrol leader described their miniature odyssey: after completing ts mission at Ilgis Lake (observing Russian cavalry) the patrol returned to the main line of resistance just in time to see the last of the company's trucks disappearing in the distance. An old Lithuanian farmer told the men that their comrades had kept looking for them to the very last minute, but that in the end they could wait no longer and had driven away.

The patrol obtained a light cart and two ponies from the old Lithuanian and immediately set out on their journey west. As they rounded a corner leading to the bridge over the Salanta, the men saw Russian tanks ahead. They were able to turn the ponies around before the tank crews spotted them and fled south from the town. They crossed the stream at a shallow-looking spot several kilometres south of the town. The brave ponies were forced to swim, but they got the wagon to the other side. Once on the other side of the Salanta they fled southwest as fast as the exhausted ponies could go, constantly followed by the sound of pursuing enemy tanks from the north and east. Night had fallen when, in the midst of the forest, the exhausted ponies simply stopped and refused to go any farther. Unsure as to what they should do, the men climbed down from the cart. Suddenly they realized that they were right in front of a heavy tank. To their boundless relief it turned out to be a Tiger, our panzer regiment's rear guard! The tank commander told them that the tank was supposed to pull out not three minutes later. The faithful horses were set free and the men climbed onto the Tiger and returned to the battalion by the roundabout route of panzer regiment, division and grenadier regiment. Very, very happy to have the patrol back in one piece, I expressed my appreciation to the Unteroffizier and kept the men at the battalion command post for the night to ensure they got a proper rest. That same evening the prudent patrol leader was recommended for the Iron Cross, First Class."

The following account, by Oberleutnant Röhm, a battery commander in II Battalion, Panzer-Artillery Regiment GD, provides details of the Panzer-Grenadier Regiment GD's defensive sector and the first defensive success on the northern front of the Memel Bridgehead:

Memel, 10 October 1944

II Battalion of the Artillery Regiment arrived in Memel with the division rear guard under cover of night. The closer we came to the city the more clogged the roads became. Countless vehicles belonging to straggling units and trains; (the devil only knows where they all came from!) strove toward

418

the city. But we were old hands and night march tacticians and were able to struggle through; we reached the communications centre at the outskirts of the city shortly before midnight. However we knew that Ivan was right on our heels with strong forces and that the battalion would have to be ready to fire by dawn. Maps were used to assign the battery chiefs their firing position areas. They were reminded that the Memel Bridgehead had to be defensively ready by dawn, requiring them to get the most out of the overtired men. And it worked.

But even more happened in this half night; guns separated from their units, just sitting there limbered and doing nothing, were, with varying degrees of pressure, taken over. Precious ammunition for light and heavy field howitzers was taken from truck columns which had taken shelter en masse in the streets of Memel with absolutely no idea what was going on. A small group of determined men under Oberleutnant E. performed major miracles in this regard. Three batteries of naval artillery, equipped with anti-aircraft guns in thick concrete bunkers and capable of being used against ground targets, were placed under control of the battalion.

The battalion command post was located on the Purmallen Estate near the command post of the grenadier regiment, which was responsible for the northern flank of the bridgehead. When dawn came we were able to report to Oberstleutnant Schwarzrock that II Battalion was ready to fire in support of the panzer-grenadiers with 40 guns, 12 of its own and 28 requisitioned. Observation posts and forward observers were in contact with the infantry, the batteries had ranged in. The day could begin. And it did begin soon afterward. The Russians had been busy during the night. Full credit was due them for being able to prepare such an attack on our bridgehead while on the move in such a short time. Barrage fire from countless guns rained down on our positions, on the city, on the arterial roads, on the individual farms, literally taking our breath away.

It was going to be a hot day. What would things be like by evening? The telephone lines were gone in no time, but we had radio for just such an event. And that was vital. It was of decisive importance not to miss the moment when the enemy infantry made its charge.

Every firing position had good radio communications with the forward observers; each gun was trained on its barrage fire zone. The gunners were ready, the radio operators crouched beside their sets, and the observers squatted in their holes: scanning no-man's-land with intense concentration, cursing the dust kicked up by the impacting shells and the ground fog, which robbed them of their sight. At the command post the window panes in the good room and the roof were shattered. Imperturbable, Schwarzrock sat in an easy chair. His cigarette trembled a bit. Everywhere in the entire bridgehead there was smoke and flashes, howling and whistling; the city was ablaze, the impacting artillery shells were soon enough to burst the eardrums, the air was befouled, chunks of earth and shrapnel whizzed through the air. Shining down on everything was the sun, slowly rising over the horizon.

We listened to see if the whirlwind had begun to abate. No, it continued with undiminished ferocity. The division, the infantry, the pioneers, the assault guns and tanks, the artillery, everyone lay under cover, waiting, all senses tensed, ready to strike back.

For today was the day. We were surrounded, with only the sea at our backs. We would get out of this mousetrap only if we finished off the attackers.

Then our guns roared to life. They're coming! Attack on the entire front. The observers directed our fire as best they could. We had more ammunition than we had had for a long time. And so we fired salvoes and volleys at them, pounded them. They charged toward our positions in dense waves and they fell under our fire. A few got through; those that survived jumped into our positions with hands raised.

They were Lithuanians! The entire first wave of the attack was made up of Lithuanians, civilians which the Russians had picked up during their advance and which they now drove before them while attacking to act as a buffer and shield. But watch out, it was starting again.

Yes, massed artillery fire again, another attack. This time earth-brown forms approached our lines – and tanks. There was only a few tanks – but nonetheless! Our guns fired furiously. We were pleased that we had been able to make ourselves so strong in the few hours left to us during the night. The navy gunners performed magnificently. I had never seen these people before and my only contact with them was a single telephone line – the linemen did excellent work that day! The sailors (this was their very first battle of the war) had the range of every square kilometre around Memel; they also had sufficient ammunition and an astonishing rate of fire. In cooperation with the forward observers and infantry we were able to shoot up the enemy wherever they showed themselves. And our Tigers dealt with the few tanks. The Russians kept attacking, but the attacks became weaker and more sporadic.

It was high time for our batteries to move to their alternate positions. For if we knew the Russians, they had by now found our positions using sound locators and air reconnaissance. We moved into the new positions quickly and carefully. We were lucky. Scarcely had we left our old positions when shells started falling there. Scornful laughter on the part of the artillerymen and a slight shudder. If we had still been there! The only loss was suffered by the Fifth, a gun tractor. The sailors sat secure in their bunkers.

Things were now relatively quiet where we were, in the north of the bridgehead.

But what about the rest of the bridgehead? Bad, very bad! Ivan had broken through in other places. They already had tanks and infantry in the city and were ominously close to the harbour. II Battalion turned its guns to the east and south and blazed away at targets provided by unfamiliar observers. There were frequent changes of position to elude the enemy's damned sound locators. And there were the enemy close-support aircraft as well!

Yes, it was a hot day, just as we had suspected it would be that morning. However by evening it was clear: the division had beaten off the offensive against Memel, destroyed the enemy forces that had entered the city and had the bridgehead firmly in its hands.

The beautiful city of Memel had been shot to pieces, fires everywhere, the earth torn up and black, shot-up vehicles, shot-up equipment everywhere. But the front stood, ready to face new attacks."

On 11 October, after having moved up the bulk of their units and heavy weapons, the Soviets tried with every available means to force a break-through to Memel. At about 14.00, on the heels of a heavy preparatory bombardment, they attacked at various places on the defensive front with infantry in up to battalion strength supported by tanks and assault guns; however they failed to achieve the desired success. Once again an enemy penetration along the Podsseit–Stankus road was eliminated by a counterattack by the panzer-fusiliers. Five enemy tanks were destroyed.

The tanks of the Panzer Regiment GD also played their part in this success. The regiment had only just returned to action after making hasty repairs to its vehicles. In order to conserve fuel they were usually employed in a stationary role. They were positioned in ones and twos at intervals of 1,000-2,000 metres, in or just behind the front so as to be able to meet enemy armoured forces everywhere along the front. This method, which had a particularly reassuring effect on the infantry, proved increasingly effective and also had the effect of convincing the Soviets that they were facing a large number of German tanks in the bridgehead.

In spite of the fine defensive success, work continued at a fever pitch to beef up the main line of resistance and the positions in the rear. The main objective was to place all the men and weapons underground as quickly as possible.

To the joy of the defenders, two German warships appeared at sea on the misty horizon. On closer inspection they turned out to be the heavy cruisers *Lützow* (formerly the *Deutschland*) and *Prinz Eugen*. Their ship's guns provided effective fire support. Major Rudel, who had seen action in support of the GD many times, and his close-support fliers attacked enemy positions opposite the main line of resistance of the Memel Bridgehead.

The enemy's losses had been heavy. In tanks alone they had lost more than 150 in the past three days. When evening fell on 11 October and the day that had been filled with the sounds of battle gave way to darkness, in many places on the front the men heaved a sigh of relief.

The senior commands and the *Großdeutschland* division command shared the opinion, and justifiably so, that the first major attempt by the Soviets to seize Memel had failed.

CHAPTER 2

With I (Panther) Battalion, Panzer Regiment GD

On the same day, 5 October 1944, indeed at almost the same hour as the Soviets were launching their massive attacks east of Tryskiai in southern

Courland (Latvia) west in the direction of Memel on the Baltic coast, in the Narev Bend southwest of Rozan in Poland I Battalion of the Panzer Regiment GD, which had placed under the command of the 6th Panzer Division, made preparations to go into action.

By about mid-August, north of Warsaw the Soviet 1st White Russian Front, with 60 to 70 rifle divisions, 10 tank and mechanized corps and 3 cavalry corps, and supported by strong air forces, had forced the German Ninth Army back beyond the River Bug. On 22 August the Soviet 2nd White Russian Front also attacked between the Vistula and the Narev in an attempt to break through to the west. In a series of battles that lasted until 31 August 1944 the Soviets made numerous deep incursions into the front, especially against the German Second Army north of Warsaw, which forced the army to fall back in stages to the mid-point of the Narev.

After a brief interlude the Soviets resumed their effort to break through the German front on 3 September and ultimately drove the German armies back across the Narev. Although the German Ninth Army was able to hold Modlin, north of Warsaw, the Russians established a large bridgehead across the Narev near Pultusk at the boundary between the Ninth and Second Armies.

But on 5 October something was brewing in the Narev Bend between Ostenburg and Rozan, especially east-southeast of Mackheim.

During the period lasting from the 5th to the 15th of October, the Panzer Regiment GD's I (Panther) Battalion added fresh laurels to the name *Großdeutschland* while serving under the command of the 6th Panzer Division. Leutnant Vogelsang provides details of those days, which saw the battalion entirely on its own:

4 October 1944

On that day we were startled by a sound resembling distant barrage fire. Queries made of the 6th Panzer Division revealed that an attack by our forces to reduce the Soviet bridgehead was under way in the Ostenburg area. All was quiet in our combat zone, however.

5 October 1944

A day later the noise was closer; departure readiness was ordered, and toward evening the combat echelon moved out through Czerwonka in the direction of Perzanowo, where pickets were set up at the road as darkness was falling. The situation was as follows:

Major enemy penetration from the Soviet bridgehead to the Ostenburg–Rozan road;

I Battalion, Panzer Regiment GD's mission: counterattack with the objective of at least restoring the former main line of resistance.

6 October 1944

The battalion drove via Chrzanowo to Pruszki and formed up for the attack in a forest clearing there. Supplies were quickly distributed, after which mission orders were issued, according to which the battalion was to attack east with friendly infantry forces.

Soviet close-support aircraft soon discovered our attack preparations.

Several attempts to attack us with bombs and guns were soon abandoned after we put up concentrated fire with the machine-guns mounted on the turret cupola rings of our tanks, firing wildly into the air.

Finally, at about noon, we were ordered to battle readiness; the battalion rolled in the general direction of Mroczki–Rebiszewo and then veered south. On the right wing was 1st Company, left wing 4th Company.

7 October 1944

4th Company advanced with 3rd Platoon on the left wing, 2nd Platoon in the centre and 1st Platoon on the right, next to 3rd Company. The advance initially made good progress.

Just outside Napiorki lay a wood called the 'Towel Forest' which ran at right angles to the direction of attack. The 4th Company asked battalion whether the wood was free of the enemy and was told that it was. On the battalion's right wing the attack bogged down due to the slowness of our infantry and the onset of massive enemy countermeasures. Caution was obviously needed where the 'Towel Forest' was concerned.

1st Platoon, led by the platoon commander, drove toward the wood. Between us and the forest lay 600 metres of open ground; an ideal field of fire for enemy anti-tank guns if there were any present.

The platoon commander's tank came under fire about 300 metres from the wood. It stopped, then backed up. It was not seen to fire. While backing up the tank was hit a second and then a third time; luckily all bounced off. Finally after the last hit they spotted the enemy: a well-camouflaged T-34 in the forest. Two shots caused it to catch fire.

It was now apparent that the 'Towel Forest' was occupied by the enemy and wasn't about to be taken without artillery and infantry.

The company sat 600-800 metres in front of the wood and waited on the open plain for the radio message that would release it from its orders. Strong enemy defences had also halted our attack to the right of us. The company's losses – none.

Finally, in the evening, new orders: hold existing position! Infantry unavailable – therefore adopt an all-round defensive posture.

8-9 October 1944

At about one o'clock in the morning the fog became heavier, more dense. We could no longer see our own gun's muzzle brake. Leutnant Wächter ordered the tanks to move closer together.

The Soviets began firing with artillery and mortars. We had to withdraw out of range. There was mass confusion because no one could see a thing. Two Panthers were damaged and finally everyone regrouped.

The battalion had meanwhile been ordered to continue the attack. 4th Company swung out in a wide arc to outflank 'Towel Forest' from the left. After encountering mines we swung out even wider and were able to drive through to Napiorki.

The battalion destroyed 10 enemy tanks in the area of the 'Towel Forest' alone. Unteroffizier Larsen approached a KV assault gun that had withstood everything thrown at it and put it out of action from 100 metres. Then, security duty. The battalion was withdrawn during the night and moved back to a wood near Pruszkie. Our infantry took over the line reached by the battalion.

10 October 1944

A major Soviet attack was expected on 10 October at about 10.00. Barrage fire on our assembly area began punctually, right on the mark. The battalion moved out at once.Near Boruty we met friendly infantry, which were being hotly pursued by masses of Soviet infantry. The latter were halted by machine-gun fire and high-explosive shells.

The first enemy tanks likewise appeared from Boruty and we immediately opened fire on these. However the enemy quickly spotted us as well, and blanketed our position with artillery and Stalin Organ fire. We were unable to advance any farther. Leutnant Bernhardt, commander of 1st Company, was severely wounded by artillery fire while standing in his turret.

While the battalion was still stationary near Boruty, west of our position Soviet forces were driving north.

During the night the battalion moved to the rear again to take on supplies.

11 October 1944

Early on 11 October the battalion rolled north across the Ostenburg– Rozan road, drove back as far as the Zalusie–Rozan road and then turned inward, moving into position on the north slope of Hill 112, southwest of Rozan.

A fine drizzle made the entire situation even more unpleasant.

To our left, in the direction of Rozan, were elements of II Battalion, 11th Panzer Regiment.

As soon as the first of our infantry came back over the hill, we drove into hull-down positions.

It was the usual picture: in the distance masses of enemy infantry moving toward us. We opened fire at a distance of 500 metres, which resulted in an immediate halt by the enemy. Feldwebel Zeugner was at my two o'clock position, a little too far forward for the hull-down position. He was hit by an enemy anti-tank straightaway and the tank caught fire. Zeugner had apparently been hit in the stomach by a fragment; he had great difficulty getting out of the turret. Our medical Officer Dr. Franz reached him in minutes in a half-track ambulance, but it was too late. Feldwebel Zeugner was buried at the Heroes Cemetery in Mackeim a few days later.

To our left the Panzer IVs of II Battalion, 11th Panzer Regiment were involved in a fierce fire-fight with enemy anti-ank guns and ultimately had to withdraw. Our left flank was thus unprotected, and only by moving 3rd Platoon there was it finally (but with some difficulty) secured.

12-13 October 1944

Although the enemy ceased their attacks at this position, they increased the pressure elsewhere. An order radioed from battalion caused 4th Company to change positions with great haste.

Enemy forces were nearing 'Cross Road B' – the road from Zalusie to Chrzanow. 4th Company was moved to Zalusie and turned toward 'Cross Road B.'

Our infantry were in position in the ditches in expectation of the Russian

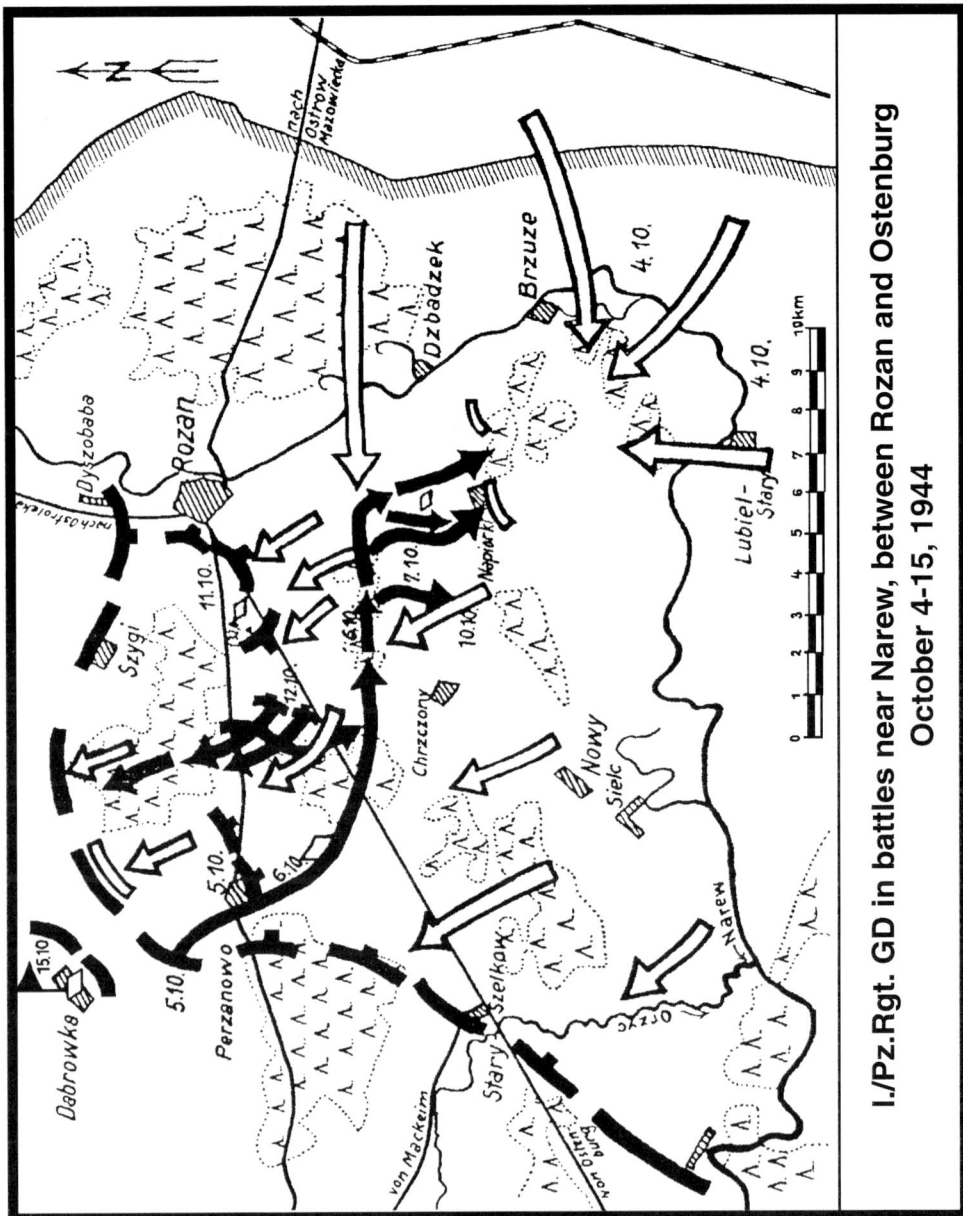

I./Pz.Rgt. GD in battles near Narew, between Rozan and Ostenburg, October 4-15, 1944

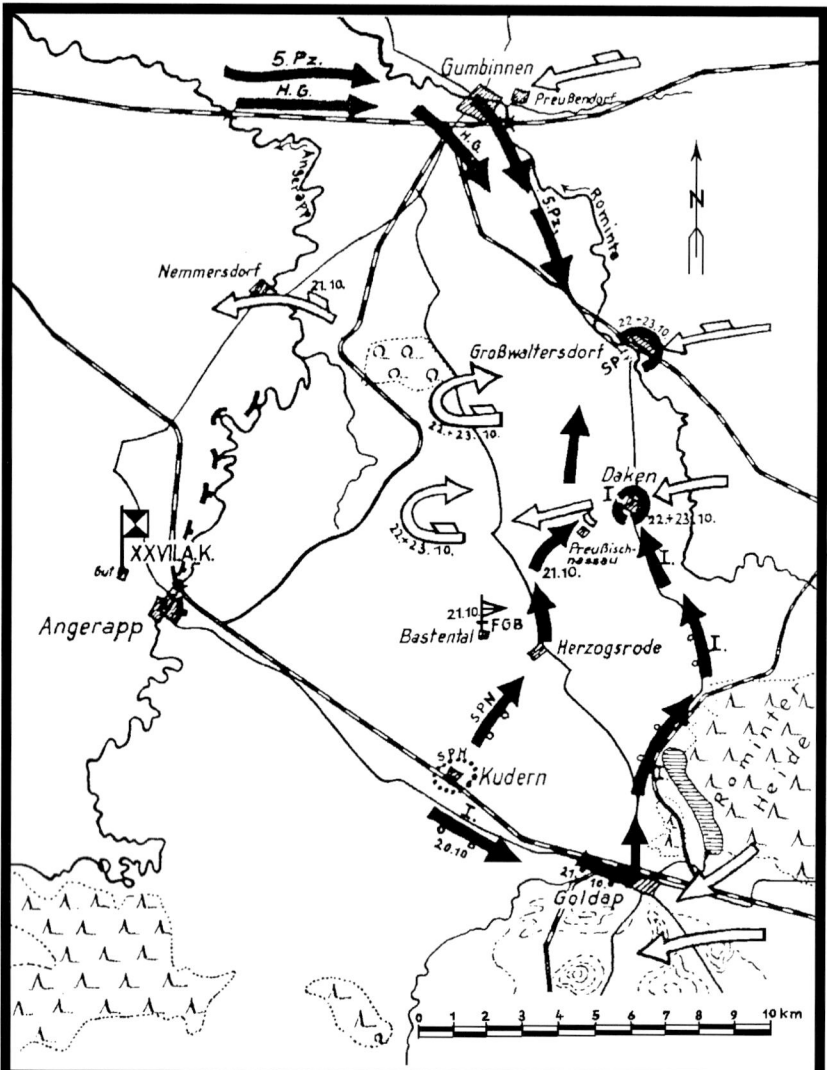

**Attack of the FGB near Daken and Großwaltersdorf
from October 21-23, 1944**

attack. We gave them machine-gun ammunition, as they had expended theirs. Shortly thereafter masses of enemy infantry appeared; initially the enemy took cover in the face of our concentrated fire.

When they rose up again, in particular on our right flank, our own infantry fell back in panic. Enemy tanks, including some Stalins, rushed past on our right without our being able to do anything to prevent them.

Immediately the order reached us to withdraw and assemble in the Lipniki–Czerwonka area; driving in reverse, we headed for the rear under cover. While doing so, Unteroffizier Larsen spotted a Stalin about 1,000 metres away at the edge of the wood and fired on it until the crew baled out.

On reaching the assigned area Leutnant Wächter established contact with the infantry commander, who instructed him to stand guard at the south end of the forest near Zalusie. 4th Company occupied this screening line; there was considerable battle noise and artillery fire from in front of us.

Once darkness fell we were brought to readiness each hour by radio. It was a difficult task keeping the exhausted crews awake, however the night passed quietly.

14-15 October 1944

Leutnant Wächter radioed at about 01.20 and instructed me to stand guard as far as Perzanowo, which meant extending the line by 2,000 metres.

Rising fog and darkness caused me to have serious doubts as to the effectiveness of so thin a line. At a walking pace it took about 90 minutes to brief each member of the platoon. Finally the tanks were in position at intervals of about 400 metres, as per orders. The fog prevented us from seeing or hearing anything. The sound of battle had died out hours ago.

Eventually, at about 03.00, 1st Platoon received orders to assemble in Lipniki and take on supplies. The 4th Company was already en route there. While replenishing was under way, Leutnant Wächter called the platoon leaders together and gave the following mission: after replenishing, the company would advance east on the forest road from Lipniki, turn toward Zalusie and stand guard at the forest's edge facing Zalusie. Efforts were to be made to enter the town itself.

By now the fog had lifted completely, and its place was now taken by a number of 'lame crows,' which circled above the village but dropped no bombs.

It was a magnificent dawn; the 4th Company departed in the assigned direction. Hand grenades and submachine-guns were set out for close combat as we entered the forest. The situation was completely unclear where the enemy were concerned, but the company arrived at the forest's edge due north of Zalusie with no hostile contact.

The panzers now got ready at the edge of the forest. Before the entire company had deployed fully, however, it came under heavy fire from the village. Anti-tank guns? They could see nothing; however around them large trees were collapsing like matchsticks. Very soon they spotted camouflaged KV assault guns which defied any frontal assault.

The company opened fire. Meanwhile enemy infantry cleverly tried to get to the forest from the village in order to outflank us, particularly on the right. Just as the tank battle reached its height, an entire battalion of Soviet infantry broke into the forest itself. The situation became very uncomfortable, especially since we couldn't do much to the KV even at 800 metres.

Orders came to withdraw. With the tanks providing mutual fire support, 4th Company threaded its way back along the forest road and reached the north edge of the forest.

New assignment: advance via Ponikiev to Soje. We scouted the forest north of Soje, however we met no enemy and therefore returned to the battalion in Dabrowka.

Leutnant Wächter and Leutnant Reißner were ordered to reconnoitre toward Soje with two tanks; the rest of 4th Company moved into a clearing near Dabrowka.

The two officers returned a short time later and reported that Soje was full of enemy infantry. Furthermore a strong assembly of enemy tanks was perceptible nearby."

So much for the diary of Leutnant Vogelsang, who described those days with 4th Company, I Battalion, Panzer Regiment GD. As for the fighting itself, that continued in the following days and saw the enemy gain a considerable amount of ground.

That was in fact the Soviet objective: to expand their bridgehead above the Lower Narev to the point where, after moving in and assembling their forces, they could initiate their last great offensive – against Berlin.

The map showed the extent of the bridgehead. It ran (from north to south) from the confluence of the Ozygi and the Narev due north of Rozan (the village of Soje–Czerwonka) south as far as Orzyc, on the Rozan–Ostenburg road. It formed a large salient extending into the German front near Ostenburg.

The Soviets achieved their objective of obtaining a sufficiently-large area in which to mass forces for subsequent operations within an enlarged bridgehead across the Narev.

Following a brief period of rest and refitting in Camp Mielau, the battalion again participated in a successful German counterattack, taking part in the liberation of Ostenburg. Unteroffizier Larsen was awarded the Knight's Cross for his bravery in these actions and for destroying 66 enemy tanks.

Finally, in mid-November 1944, the battalion was transferred into the Sensburg area of East Prussia, where it was reincorporated into the Panzer Regiment GD as I Battalion. I Battalion, 26th Panzer Regiment under Hauptmann Graf Rothkirch was simultaneously withdrawn and transferred to Hungary.

I Battalion, Panzer Regiment GD was absent from the division for more than a year. Nevertheless the battalion command performed well in seeing to the needs of the battalion while it was separated from its parent unit. Its naming in numerous reports is an indication of the willingness to fight always demonstrated by the men of this battalion.

CHAPTER 3

FÜHRER GRENADIER BRIGADE

First Action between Goldap and Gumbinnen

Following the assassination attempt of 20 July 1944, the battle group staff under Oberst Kahler, whose sole task was the rapid formation of the Führer Grenadier Brigade, was given another mission. Employing the personnel units arriving from Cottbus, it was to take over responsibility for the outer defence of the Wolfsschanze installation. On or about 25 July this second mission was handed over to General Denckert, so that Oberst Kahler could concentrate on his actual mission, the formation of the Führer Grenadier Brigade.

In its initial composition the battle group staff also formed the basis of the later brigade headquarters. In the second half of July it moved to Cottbus to activate on the spot further units formed from convalescents and replacements. The units previously formed in Cottbus by Hauptmann Kowalke, which arrived in the Rastenburg area on 19 and 20 July under Major von Courbiere, initially stayed in East Prussia, where they formed the foundation of the Panzer-Grenadier Battalion (motorized) FGB which was soon to be formed.

Personnel for elements of the later independent companies were also assembled around Rastenburg to await the activation of their units.

Among these units was 11th Assault Pioneer Company (Armoured) FGB; its first commander was Oberleutnant Max Horn, company officer Leutnant Hessmann, and senior NCO Hauptfeldwebel G. Strebel. The company's Table of Organization provided for three platoons and a 4th Flamethrower Platoon; Table of Basic Allowances 00712 provided the company with the following personnel: 6 officers, 31 NCOs and 217 enlisted men = 254. In the course of its formation the company was issued the following vehicles:

1 radio APC
4 platoon leader APCs
18 pioneer APCs
4 flamethrower APCs
1 Kettenkrad
7 motorcycle-sidecar combinations
1 Kübelwagen (for the company commander)
4 VW Schwimmwagen (for the platoon leaders)
1 car (for the maintenance sergeant)

9 trucks, with:
1 for fuel
1 for ammunition and pioneer equipment
1 for the armourer-artificer
1 for flamethrower oil
1 for rations
1 for field kitchens
1 for the orderly office
1 for the maintenance squad
1 - 12-tonne prime mover

At the end of July 1944 the Panzer-Grenadier Battalion (mot.) FGB under Major von Courbiere was in the area east of Rastenburg with its command post in Pohiebils, on the Rastenburg–Lötzen road. Elements of the battalion were still employed in the headquarters' outer security zone.

The battalion's initial personnel organization at that time was as follows:

Commanding Officer	Major von Courbiere
Adjutant	Oberleutnant Barkow, then
	Leutnant Rau,
	Leutnant von Maltzahn
Operations Officers	Leutnant Reichard,
	Leutnant von Maltzahn,
	Leutnant Bieselt
Battalion Medical Officer	Oberarzt Dr. Kornfeld
Paymaster	Oberzahlmeister Weidig
Commander H.Q. Company	Leutnant Grotewohl
Commander Survey Company (Observation Post)	Hauptmann von Kameke (from Oct. 1944)
Commander 1st Company	Oberleutnant Sachse
Commander 2nd Company	Oberleutnant Schorn
Commander 3rd Company	Oberleutnant Barkow
Commander 4th Company	Leutnant Härter
Commander 5th (heavy) Company	

Meanwhile at Cottbus personnel units for the future Panzer- Fusilier Battalion (Armoured), Führer Grenadier Brigade were put together and briefed on their future duties. Major Lehnhoff was placed in command of these, and during the period without vehicles he carried out several forced marches to train his men.

The battalion was later outfitted at Fallingbostel and its initial organization was as follows:

Battalion H.Q. Commanding Officer	Major Lehnhoff
Adjutant	Oberleutnant Krohn
Operations Officers	Leutnant von Alvensleben,
	Leutnant Mutius
1st-3rd Rifle Companies each with:	1 medium APC

	(company commander's vehicle)
	5 medium APCs with 20mm flak
	22 medium APCs with MGs
4th (Heavy) Company with:	28 medium APCs with racks for
	launching rocket projectiles
Company commanders at that time:	Hauptmann Walter Ludwig
	Oberleutnant Luchesi
	Hauptmann Lindemann
	Oberleutnant Schubert

The differing designations of the two battalions is allegedly due to the fact that Major Lehnhoff came from the Panzer-Fusilier Regiment GD while Major von Courbiere originally came from the Panzer-Grenadier Regiment GD, however this has not been confirmed. In any case the majority of the men, apart from the recruits and the men from other units, were former GD

men who continued to wear their cuff band. And so it was not by chance that most of the newly-formed units for the Führer Grenadier Brigade also wore the GD insignia on their shoulder straps as well as the cuff band. However it is also a fact that it was not a GD unit in the actual sense and the designation GROSSDEUTSCHLAND never appeared in its papers.

On 27-28 August 1944 the personnel units of the Panzer-Fusilier Battalion (armoured) of the Führer Grenadier Brigade moved from Wandern to

Fallingbostel, where they were issued vehicles. All the units of the Führer Grenadier Brigade were assembled at this training facility and in the surrounding area in order to receive vehicles and equipment and to carry out combined exercises aimed at turning it into a homogenous unit.

The Panzer-Grenadier Battalion (motorized), Führer Grenadier Brigade under Major von Courbiere, together with the independent companies, was transferred to Fallingbostel from the Rastenburg area on 7 and 8 September. There Hauptmann Kowalke took over the administrative control of the independent companies, prominent among which were the Infantry Gun Company, the Signals Company and the 11th (Assault Pioneer) Company. These were later joined by the 10th (Flak) Company and the Armoured Reconnaissance Company.

The organization of the brigade headquarters was also a temporary one at Fallingbostel; General Staff Major Webner was replaced as Ia by General Staff Major Weitbrecht. Webner became the brigade's 1st General Staff Officer. Oberleutnant Seldte became brigade adjutant, Rittmeister Strauß the IIa and Hauptmann Berg the Ib.

The first steps were also taken toward the formation of the Panzer Battalion FGB under the command of Major von Uslar-Gleichen. The panzer battalion was organized as follows:

Battalion Headquarters	(although there was no HQ Company, the headquarters included:) reconnaissance squad signals platoon pioneer squad maintenance platoon
1st-3rd Companies	each with 11 Panzer V Panthers
4th Company	with Panzerjäger IV medium tank-destroyers
5th Company	with assault guns
Supply Company	

The company combat strengths were about 80 men, while the supply company had a strength of nearly 150 men. Once again it was a picture typical of 1944: forming a unit with the maximum weapons and materiel strength using the minimum number of personnel, with the deletion of all supplementary elements, such as a headquarters company.

Little time was allowed for the welding-together of the Führer Grenadier Brigade in Fallingbostel; at the end of September, on or about the 26th or 27th, the brigade was loaded aboard trains and transported to the Arys Troop Training Grounds in East Prussia. Unfortunately this first common train transport was overshadowed by an accident. Two trains collided en route; the sad consequences were several dead and considerable damage to the vehicles.

After detraining in East Prussia, the elements of the Führer Grenadier

Brigade took up quarters in the area between Rastenburg and Arys as OKH reserve and continued their training. Since the first days of October Luftwaffe reconnaissance aircraft had been observing growing Soviet troop concentrations in the area south and southwest of Kauen (Kovno).

New artillery positions, statements by deserters and much increased enemy radio traffic were unmistakeable signs that the Soviets were planning a new attack. Five Soviet armies, with a total of more than 40 rifle divisions and numerous armoured formations, were massing. Their objective was to breach the German positions on the East Prussian-Lithuanian border and drive through to East Prussia and Königsberg.

On the defenders' side the positions of the Fourth Army commanded by General Hossbach extended in a gentle, eastward-facing arc from Augustovo through Vilkavishkis to Schirwindt on the Memel. The Fourth Army's mission was to defend the East Prussian frontier against the expected Soviet offensive. In the previous weeks the army had employed every possible measure that might increase its defensive potential. The construction of fortifications, especially on the south wing and in the centre to about the Vilkavishkis–Gumbinnen road, was in an advanced stage; the units were well-supplied with ammunition and ready for what was coming.

And yet the positions as such were only very weakly manned, as the Fourth Army had only seven experienced infantry divisions to defend its sector of more than 350 kilometres of front.

As well as a total of five corps headquarters, the army included six untested, newly-formed Volksgrenadier divisions, two security divisions, two cavalry brigades and a police unit which was most unsuited to front-line action. In comparison to the army's very large front-line sector and the size of the expected Soviet offensive, the available forces were totally inadequate, even in a time of positional warfare. At this time the army headquarters had no mobile, and more importantly no armoured, reserve at its disposal.

The very obvious concentration of enemy forces on both sides of Vilkavishkis led the German command to conclude that the Soviet army command was going to strive for a frontal breakthrough along the Vilkavishkis–Gumbinnen–Insterburg road. Consequently the Fourth Army prepared to meet the enemy thrust between the Rominten Heath and the Memel, ruthlessly stripping other areas, especially the south wing, of combat-experienced units, which were placed in the centre of its sector.

Finally, on 16 October, the units of the 3rd White Russian Front, which included powerful armoured formations, set out in a narrow wedge, strongly supported by close-support aircraft, along the Vilkavishkis–Ebenrode road. The initial assault resulted in significant penetrations. At first the Soviet point of main effort was north of the road, however on 19 October this was shifted into the area south of the road, striking the units of XXVII Army Corps. Nevertheless the defensive battle was conducted in such a way (by giving ground in stages) that it was possible to maintain the continuity between the corps.

On 20 October fresh tank forces of the Soviet 11th Guards Army broke through the German lines on both sides of Groß-Waltersdorf and by the 21st their spearheads had reached the Angerapp River at Nemmersdorf. Further waves of enemy tanks had also been spotted farther south in the area of the railroad station, and even farther south the fall of the city of Goldap to the enemy was imminent. In the north Gumbinnen was threatened by an enveloping attack from the northeast, the east and now from the southeast as well.

The battle had reached its climax; quick decisions were required on the part of the OKH, which was still based at Lötzen. Two armoured units (the 5th Panzer Division and the Parachute Panzer-Grenadier Division *Hermann Göring*) were hurriedly taken from the Third Panzer Army situated farther to the northwest and the Führer Grenadier Brigade was sent from the OKH reserve.

The brigade, which was housed in the Rastenburg–Lötzen–Arys area under Oberst Kahler, was alerted on the evening of 19 October by the release of the code-word "Rumpelstiltskin." The brigade's destination was the area due west and northwest of Goldap; wheeled elements were to reach the area by road, the tracked elements by rail.

As of 20 October the Führer Grenadier Brigade was placed under the command of the Fourth Army, at about the same time as the two armoured divisions, which were directed into the area west of Gumbinnen.

The army high command's plan was soon made known: the three units were to carry out a joint counterattack whose objective would be to cut off the advancing enemy spearheads from the south (FGB) and from the north (5th Pz.Div. and HG) in a pincer movement along the Rominte River, destroy them and establish a new German main line of resistance along the Rominte.

The first elements of the Panzer-Grenadier Battalion (mot.) FGB passed north through Goldap at approximately 06.00 on 21 October. The unit's mission was to advance as far north as possible along the Goldap–Gumbinnen road. 1st Company under Leutnant Sachse formed the point; it moved out, expecting contact with the enemy at any time. However the point was not fired on until it was about 800 metres north of Daken, at the brickworks. The town of Daken and the road that passed through it lay on a line of hills which reached its zenith at the brickworks. Leaping from their APCs, the grenadiers deployed to advance on the brickworks just as the main body of the battalion drove into Daken. The sound of heavy fighting was audible from the east, from the Rominten Heath, as the troops were leaving the vehicles. Soviet infantry crossed the stream and attacked the town of Daken from there.

Major von Courbiere quickly deployed his men and counterattacked in order to force back the enemy infantry. The effort was partially successful, and until the evening of this first day of fighting the Panzer-Grenadier Battalion FGB remained in this formation, with 1st Company ahead at the brickworks and the main body of the battalion holding position to the east.

Meanwhile the brigade headquarters set up its command post in the forest near Herzogsrode and took command of its units. The first to arrive was the Panzer-Fusilier Battalion (Armoured) FGB under Major Lehnhoff, which detrained about 8 kilometres west of Goldap and immediately began its advance. Mission: northward advance due west of the Goldap–Gumbinnen road; capture and barricade the Rominte crossings at Groß-Waltersdorf. The battalion advanced through Herzogsrode, but it ran into enemy armoured forces near Prussian Passau. There were wild exchanges of fire with enemy tanks and weak infantry, which lasted until evening. The Panzer-Fusilier Battalion (Armoured) FGB set up an all-round defensive position for the night in a hollow about 3 kilometres long. It was waiting for additional forces to arrive, in particular the Panther battalion under Major von Uslar-Gleichen, in order to resume the attack the next day. A security screen was thrown up on all sides and the cannon-armed APCs were positioned at the ends of the hollow. The few tanks, which were from another unit, were deployed as anti-tank guns. While it remained largely quiet during the day, at night the Soviets tried to enter the hollow; however in each case the panzer-fusiliers were able to keep the attackers at bay.

Meanwhile the Panthers of the FGB Panzer Battalion had arrived due west of Goldap, where they detrained immediately. The tanks came to battle readiness during the night and the crews were issued their mission orders.

When the first light dawned in the east on 22 October, reinforced Soviet forces again attacked the positions of the Panzer-Fusilier Battalion FGB near Daken and at the Rominte River, however every attempt to break through into Daken was repulsed. During the late morning increased battle noises were heard from the area west of Daken, with sounds of tanks moving and firing predominating. What they were hearing was an engagement between the Panzer Battalion FGB, which was attacking north, and enemy tanks, which had resumed their advance to the east.

Leutnant Taaks of 3rd Company was in command of the point platoon, and he set off with the Panthers of his platoon early on the 22nd of October. The gunner in Taaks' Panther, Gefreiter Rudi Becker, described what happened:

"On the morning of that 22 October the Panthers of 3rd Company moved out in the direction of the ball-shaped tree – a prominent reference point which probably lay behind the Russian main line of resistance. By the time we reached the rise in the road our tank had already taken its first hit from a Soviet anti-tank gun. The shell bounced off the commander's cupola, ripping out a hole as big as a man's fist. At first the commander, Leutnant Taaks, sat down on his little seat out of fright, but then he stood up again right away. But at the same instant, thinking that the shell had got him, I called out the target and gave the order to fire. I assumed that the Leutnant had seen an enemy tank and loaded an armour-piercing round. In the meantime the Leutnant had regained his senses and gave me the target – the anti-tank gun. I therefore pulled out the armour-piercing round and inserted a high-explosive shell. As bad luck would have it, the hit had knocked out the electrical firing mechanism. The emergency firing system, which was activated by a dynamo under the gunner's seat, had to be switched on in order to fire the tank's main gun. However everything worked smoothly, just as it had done so often in practice.

The first shell hit the enemy anti-tank gun and put it out of action. Just to

435

be sure, however, we put another shell into it.

Beside us on the right one of our Panthers was burning. We had driven past several enemy anti-tank guns and had only noticed one of them, because the others were so well camouflaged.

Then we ran into numerous enemy tanks, it might have been thirty or more. Later they even put the number at over 100."

The Panzer Battalion was now unable to reach the almost-encircled Panzer-Fusilier Battalion (Armoured) FGB; instead it became bogged down in the waves of enemy tanks flooding east and spent the entire day in heavy fire-fights west of Daken. An increasing number of enemy tanks were destroyed, but the battalion's own losses were also heavy. It was a difficult battle for the crews. The Panthers could only destroy the now familiar Josef Stalin tanks, with their 122mm guns, from a favourable position.

Finally elements of the Panzer-Fusilier Battalion (Armoured) FGB under Major Lehnhoff managed to advance to Groß-Tellerode, due south of Groß-Waltersdorf, from where they were able to fire on the bridge over the Rominte and in this way block it. The Soviet tanks and infantry streaming from the west tried to force a crossing of the river in order to escape the German encirclement. The result was bitter close-quarters fighting between the defenders and the retreating Russians. All in all more than 30 enemy tanks were destroyed in this combat zone, more important, the Rominte crossing remained in the hands of the panzer-fusiliers.

To the north the sound of battle intensified; the 5th Panzer Division and the Parachute Panzer-Grenadier Division *Hermann Göring* were driving south toward Groß-Waltersdorf. However at about noon on 22 October the situation of the Panzer-Grenadier Battalion (Motorized) FGB, which was defending Daken and initially facing east, became critical. The first enemy tanks appeared west of the battalion's positions at about 14.00 and began firing into the town. Then the Soviets also increased the pressure from the east; heavy artillery and mortar fire began falling on Daken and those of the battalion's positions identified by the enemy. Statements by prisoners revealed that most of the Soviet soldiers fighting at the Rominte belonged to the 12th Guards Rifle Corps "Red Banner" – they were thus outstanding and experienced fighters and members of an elite unit. Their mission was obviously to keep the Rominte crossing open for the tank and infantry units coming back from the west.

The "butchers," the Il-2s, bombed and strafed Daken without let-up. The battalion's anti-aircraft guns were able to shoot down several of these aircraft but could provide little relief from the air attacks. Eventually a well-aimed salvo of bombs put the last still-functioning anti-aircraft gun out of action, killing part of the crew. Leutnant Rau, the battalion adjutant, was fatally wounded at this time, along with many other panzer-grenadiers.

The situation in Daken became increasingly critical. 1st Company had long since abandoned its forward position and the bulk of the battalion had pulled back toward the town itself. The battalion was surrounded and radio and telephone communications with brigade were being jammed.

But still the enemy tanks, especially the T-34s west of the town, kept a

FÜHRER-GRENADIER-BRIGADE (FGB)

Organization, December 1944

FGB

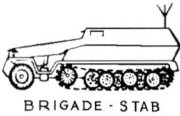

BRIGADE - STAB

STABS – KOMPANIE

Pz. AUFKLÄRUNGS - KP.

NACHRICHTEN - KP.

F L A – Kp.

STU. PI. KOMP

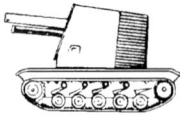

J G - Kp.

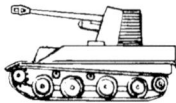

Pz. JÄGER Kp.

KRIEGSBERICHTER ZUG

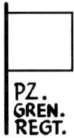

PZ. GREN. REGT.

STABS - KOMP.

Pz. FÜS. BATL. (gep.)

STAB

1. - 3. (SCHTZ.) Kp.

4. (SCHWERE) Kp.

VERSORG. - KOMP.

Pz GREN. BATL. (mot.)

STAB

1. - 3. (SCHTZ.)Kp. (Radf.)

4. (M.G.) Kp.

5. (SCHWERE) Kp.

VERSORG. Kp.

JNF.BATL
z bV
829

STAB

1. - 3. (SCHTZ.) Kp.

4. (SCHWERE) Kp.

VERSORG - Kp.

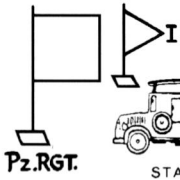

Pz.RGT.

STAB

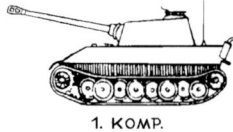

1. KOMP.

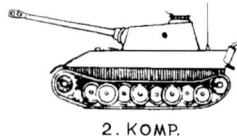

2. KOMP.

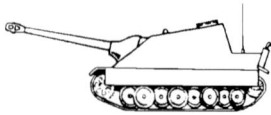

3. KOMP.

4. (Pz. JÄGER) Kp.

5. KOMP.

VERSORG.-KOMP.

WERKSTATT-ZUG

... IN ZUFÜHRUNG

STURM-
GESCH.
BRIGADE

STAB-und STABS-BATT.

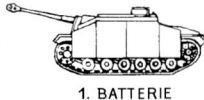

1. BATTERIE

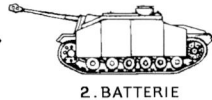

2. BATTERIE

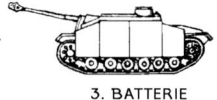

3. BATTERIE

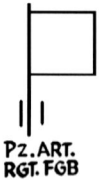

**Pz. ART.
RGT. FGB**

STAB

STAB-u. ST. BATT.

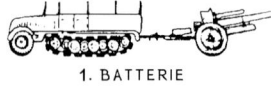

1. BATTERIE

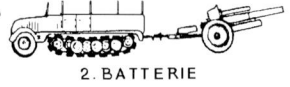

2. BATTERIE

3. BATTERIE

...IN ZUFÜHRUNG

VERSORG.-BATTERIE

FLAK
ABT.

1. BATTERIE

2. BATTERIE

3. BATTERIE

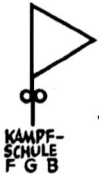

KAMPF-
SCHULE
F G B

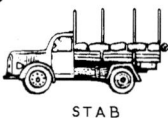

STAB

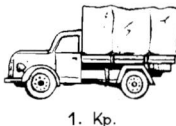

1. Kp.

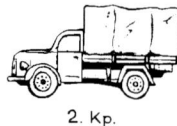

2. Kp.

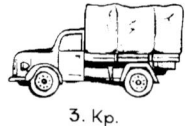

3. Kp.

**SAN.-DIENSTE
F G B**

SAN. Kp.

1. KRANK. KRAFTWAG.
ZUG

2. KR. KRAFTWAG. ZUG

**NACHSCHUB
TRUPPEN
F G B**

O. T.-KOLONNE

HEERES-KOLONNE

WERKSTATT-Kp.

respectful distance; attacks by enemy infantry, which lasted until dark, were repulsed. Yet the panzer-grenadiers felt more or less powerless against this assault from all sides, for they lacked heavy weapons and anti-tank weapons.

Then, as if by a miracle, a Panther appeared. The tank's commander, Unteroffizier Amann, had driven to Daken in error. Perhaps having lost track of the battalion, he had now landed in Daken, where he was greeted by a joyful howl from the panzer-grenadiers. The tank provided them with a decisive moral support, even if it wasn't 100% operational: the shell casing ejector was damaged. However it could still fire, and it had ammunition, and for the moment that was the most important thing.

And as the devil would have it, a shout rang out: tanks advancing on the village! As if out of nowhere, the first T-34 appeared at a street corner in Daken. It rolled slowly into a depression where all the vehicles of the battalion headquarters were parked. They had apparently caught the attention of the T-34, in any case it was moving toward the vehicles in a threatening way.

Then there was a crash; a direct hit on the T-34! Unteroffizier Amann's Panther had put the enemy tank out of action with its first shot. The Panther was quickly made ready to fire again, awaiting the next enemy tank. And they had to believe it wouldn't be long in coming. However, the presence of the Panther kept the others at a respectful distance. A handshake from the commander for the crew of the Panther, shouts of joy from the panzer-grenadiers, that was the thank you for the brave panzer men.

The 23rd of October saw no let-up in the fighting, although the overall situation had stabilized somewhat. The 5th Panzer Division had reached Groß-Waltersdorf in heavy fighting and it was on the verge of establishing contact with the hard-fighting panzer-fusiliers at Groß-Tellerode. It was about high time that relief arrived there; the enemy pressure from all sides, the fierceness of the fighting and the absence of supply, especially of ammunition, gave cause for considerable concern. The number of casualties was shocking, and had it not been for the courage of the individual fighting men and their leaders the positions could not have been held at all. By about noon on 23 October the remaining serviceable Panthers of the Panzer Battalion FGB were once again involved in heavy fighting with enemy tanks trying to smash their way through to the east.

The battalion itself was badly battered, and the battle was now fought by individual tanks. The tank of Major von Uslar-Gleichen, the beloved commander of the battalion who had already destroyed eight enemy tanks that day, was forced away by several enemy tanks and was finally badly damaged. The battalion commander's crew attempted to bail out. By chance the driver of the battalion's utility vehicle (an Opel Blitz all-wheel-drive truck) witnessed the disabling of the commander's tank and, disregarding the heavy tank fire, raced across the open country toward the scene. However, before he arrived an enemy tank scored a direct hit on the engine of the Opel Blitz. The courageous Unteroffizier was killed on the spot.

It proved impossible to get to the stricken command panzer. No one knew what had become of the commander and his crew. That evening, after a fruitless search, they were listed as missing in action. A deep sadness fell over the men who, in spite of the briefness of their service together, had learned to think very highly of their commanding officer.

Two days later, when the area was cleared of the enemy, the scout platoon went looking for the missing men. They found the battalion commander's badly-mutilated body, throat microphone still around his neck; he had been killed by a bullet through the back of the neck. The head of his gunner, a Leutnant, had been so severely battered that the bolsheviks had placed a towel over his face before they left the scene. The Unteroffizier driver had also been shot through the neck; it was nothing short of murder, for all had survived the disabling of their tank.

The weary panzer-grenadiers continued to hold out in Daken, fighting desperately for their lives. Finally, during the night of 23-24 October, radio contact was reestablished with brigade and they were able to describe the battalion's desperate situation. Orders came to withdraw from Daken that same night. All the vehicles (none were undamaged, many had been destroyed) were hurriedly pushed onto the Daken–Goldap road, where they were made ready to go. But then just as the last vehicle was out of Daken, a counter-order came from brigade stating that Daken was to be held. Major von Courbiere, who still had about 30 men with him, stayed behind while the main body of the battalion left the town and fought its way through to the west.

These elements later assembled in Herzogswalde at the brigade command post. The handful of men held their positions in and near Daken until the evening of 24 October. The situation had quietened down considerably that day, after the bulk of the cut-off Soviets had broken through to the east. During the night of the 24th the battalion command post was moved to Prussian Nassau, where the elements of the Panzer-Grenadier Battalion (Motorized) FGB were gradually reunited.

Seen on the whole, the German counterattack to destroy the enemy forces that had advanced to Angerapp had succeeded. Contact had been established at Groß-Tellerode between the 5th Panzer Division attacking from the north and the stubbornly-defending panzer-fusiliers, resulting in a somewhat tenuous link to Daken and to elements of the German units holding out west of Goldap. On 27 October elements of the *Hermann Göring* Division, also moving in from the north, took over the positions on the Rominte held by the FGB panzer-grenadiers; they were the last elements of the Führer Grenadier Brigade to be relieved. With this the fighting between Gumbinnen and the area north of Goldap ended temporarily, mainly due to the considerable losses in tanks and infantry suffered by the Soviets.

On 25 October 1944 Oberst Kahler, the commander of the Führer Grenadier Brigade, issued an order of the day concerning his men's first action. Its main topic was the bravery shown by the men:

Führer Grenadier Brigade   25 October 1944
Commanding Officer

Order of the Day

"Führer Grenadiers!

With our relief from the Rominte Position tonight, we stand at the conclusion of a three-day battle which will remain an unforgettable experience for all who lived through it. The days from the 20th to the 24th of October, which saw the Führer Grenadier Brigade in action in defence of the East Prussian soil of our homeland against the bolshevik hordes, became a crucial test for the young Führer Grenadier Brigade. At the same time it was also a crucial test for many from our ranks. It is up to each individual to decide to what degree each of us passed this test; to what degree the Führer Grenadier Brigade as a unit, one which has the high honour of bearing the name of our Führer, passed its baptism of fire, will be left to the judgement of those whose profession it is to do so. But you, my Führer-Grenadiers, may remember with pride that you had to withstand three days of heavy fighting at a focal point in the defence of East Prussia, and that you succeeded in preventing the enemy from achieving the breakthrough they were striving for.

I also express my thanks to all of you Führer-Grenadiers for what was accomplished by you in terms of preparedness, bravery and dutifulness. On this day I join with you, in proud sadness and filled with deep gratitude, in remembering all our comrades who sacrificed their lives for our Fatherland in the past days of fighting. As well as being with the many very young soldiers of our brigade who died heroically (officers, NCOs and men) none of whom will ever be forgotten in our fighting band, my thoughts today are with you, my comrades, but especially with my panzer men, on the occasion of the heroic death of their commanding officer, Knight's Cross wearer Major Horst Freiherr von Uslar-Gleichen.

Major von Uslar-Gleichen died a hero's death on the afternoon of 23 October 1944 after he and the crew of his command tank had destroyed eight enemy tanks in heavy tank-versus-tank fighting, providing a shining example to his men. At this time I would like to thank our outstanding panzer leader, our concerned commander and good comrade, Major von Uslar, who was taken from our midst by such a cruel soldier's death, for all that he was to his battalion and beyond that to the Führer Grenadier Brigade. Because of his life and his effect on others, his bravery in combat and his heroic death, he will go down in the history of the Führer Grenadier Brigade as one of the best.

And now, my comrades, we are constantly conscious of our lofty duty, fulfilment of which so often demands of us the deaths of Germany's best men: the duty to always and at any time give everything to cause the enemy's furious assault to break on our iron toughness. It is now up to us to defend the borders of our homeland!

And we, as the Führer's grenadiers, are called upon like no others to provide an example in fighting wherever a decision must be reached. The beginning has been made, I am counting on you, my Führer-Grenadiers.

Long live Germany! Long live the Führer!

Kahler

Postscript:

Insofar as the situation permits, this order of the day is to be shown to all members of the brigade by the unit leaders."

The deep Soviet penetrations on both sides of Goldap remained a serious threat, however; and it was only with great difficulty that these were sealed off for the time being by very weak German forces in a large salient around the city. The city itself had been occupied by the Soviets in the midday hours of 21 October.

A shortened main line of resistance encompassing more favourable terrain was necessary on account of the ratio of forces, but this could only be achieved through offensive action. For this purpose the 50th Infantry Division and the 5th Panzer Division were moved from the front near Groß-Waltersdorf into the area on both sides of Goldap and placed under the command of Headquarters, XXXIX Panzer Corps, commanded by Generalleutnant Decker.

While these units were making preparations on November 1st and 2nd, the German main line of resistance ran approximately from south of Goldap to a point on the western edge of the city, then north to the Goldap–Gumbinnen road along the Rominte. Weak German units tried to prevent the Soviets from expanding further; in particular there was a constant exchange of fire between the enemy and the 1091st Alert Unit at the northwest city limits. That unit sought to prevent the Soviets from advancing any farther by launching repeated counterattacks.

The most hotly contested points were the schoolhouse and the cemetery, and the pioneer platoon from the FGB's headquarters company also saw action there. Unteroffizier Nette and a runner were killed in one such offensive action in a hurricane of enemy artillery, mortar and anti-tank fire. Numerous Soviet snipers made any advance more difficult; it was a desperate struggle against an enemy superior in men and materiel.

The initial objectives of the attack were announced while the bulk of the Panzer Grenadier Brigade was assembling on both sides of the Goldap–Insterburg road: the 5th Panzer Division was to attack from northwest to southeast and take possession of the city. On the 5th Panzer Division's left wing, the Panzer-Grenadier Battalion (Motorized) FGB was supposed to reach the northern tip of Goldap Lake and occupy positions to the south on the western shore of the lake, facing east. The Panzer-Fusilier Battalion (Armoured) FGB, on the other hand, was supposed to swing south around Goldap and attack the high ground due south of the city, the most prominent feature of which was Hill 304, simultaneously supporting the advance by the 50th Infantry Division.

It was known that the enemy had positioned an enormous quantity of light and heavy artillery, mortars, anti-tank guns and Stalin Organs east of the city. The Soviets had set up powerful anti-tank barriers, especially on the high ground south of Goldap, the latter to defend the commanding plateau.

The attack units moved into departure positions during the evening of 2 November: the Panzer-Grenadier Battalion (Motorized) FGB along the Goldap—Gumbinnen road, command post on the Preßburg Estate; the

442

Panzer-Fusilier Battalion (Armoured) FGB south of the Goldap–Insterburg road east of the Goldap in some of the hollows and brush-covered areas that crisscrossed the area.

The initial elements of the 5th Panzer Division moved out against Goldap during the night of 2-3 November with the Panzer-Grenadier Battalion (Motorized) FGB on its left wing. There was no supporting artillery fire in order to maximize the elements of darkness and surprise. The objective, the north end of Goldap Lake, was reached at about 02.00. Positions were immediately occupied along the west side of the lake, as well as a blocking position to the north.

Early on 3 November the attack groups of the 5th Panzer Division attacked south, with the point of main effort between Goldap Lake and the city, guarded by the security forces to the north at Goldap Lake. The division's right wing pushed into the city.

At the same time, the grenadiers of the 50th Infantry Division set off from the southwest while the armoured personnel carriers of the Panzer-Fusilier Battalion (Armoured) FGB drove from the west toward the high ground around Hill 304. The swarm of half- tracks was met by extremely heavy anti-tank fire from numerous camouflaged and difficult-to-spot positions. While the infantry maintained a certain distance from the high ground and strove toward the city itself, the panzer-fusiliers sought to crack this anti-tank barrier at some point and get into the enemy positions.

They were unsuccessful. The casualties were frightful: Hauptmann Lindemann was killed; battalion adjutant Krohn was fatally hit as the command vehicle drove over an enemy trench. Oberleutnant Luchesi was seriously wounded, Leutnant von Mutius was killed, Hauptmann Ludwig and Leutnant von Alvensleben were wounded. These losses in officers and platoon leaders were an indication of the stubborn attempts to get the APCs moving again, to force open a way into the positions. But the attempt failed; the enemy anti- tank barrier simply could not be taken. The bitter struggle against the stubbornly-defending Soviets in Goldap went on for two days, until the situation was cleared up and the city was returned to German hands. On the evening of 4 November it was reported that the German city had finally been recaptured and that new positions had been established at the south end of Goldap Lake which were in contact with units of the 50th Infantry Division to the south.

Following these events the bulk of the Führer Grenadier Brigade was again withdrawn; it was initially transferred to the Kleinau–Herzogsrode–Rabeneck area as a mobile corps reserve. There it was granted a brief period of rest and refitting. Only the Panzer-Grenadier Battalion (Motorized) FGB remained in its positions on the north and west shores of Goldap Lake. Even though there was no more large-scale fighting in the next few days, the constant tank and artillery fire on the battalion's positions continued to tear gaps in the ranks of the defenders. Not a day went by that wounded didn't leave the battlefield and dead weren't taken to Goldap and buried in the military cemetery there.

Finally, during the night of 16-17 November, Silesian units relieved the

Panzer-Grenadier Battalion (Motorized) FGB, after which it, too, was moved to the rear.

On 30 November the brigade was pulled back into the Cottbus area, making the journey by road. There it was to continue the formation process, which had been interrupted, and fill the gaps that existed in men and materiel.

That day also saw the Führer Grenadier Brigade released from the command of the Fourth Army, which released the following order of the day:

The Commander-in-Chief　　　　　Army H.Q., 1 December 1944
of the Fourth Army

"On 30 November 1944 the Führer Grenadier Brigade left the Fourth Army.

The brigade was placed under the army's command on 30 November 1944 in crisis-filled hours, when the enemy succeeded in penetrating deep into the army's front north of the Rominten Heath. It was the mission of the Führer Grenadier Brigade, together with the 5th Panzer Division attacking from the north, to sever the lines of communication to the rear of the enemy tank forces that had broken through our front by driving into their deep flank from the south. The brigade successfully carried out this mission in the course of difficult fighting which was conducted with exemplary drive and determination. On 21 October 1944 it advanced through Daken as far as Hill 99 and on 22 October 1944 was able to occupy the bridge at Groß-Tellerode.

On that and the following day the brigade had to fight off heavy attacks against both flanks. In a determined defence the Führer Grenadier Brigade held the ground it had won. Elements of the cut-off enemy were beaten back to the east, but only at the cost of heavy losses. As a result of their defeat the enemy were unable to continue the attack. A breakthrough into the heart of East Prussia was prevented. The Führer Grenadier Brigade played a major role in this, and it can look back at this great success with pride.

The Führer Grenadier Brigade also proved itself in attack and defence in the subsequent fighting in the Goldap area which led to the recapture of the city on 5 November.

In farewell I wish to express my thanks and recognition to the proven Führer Grenadier Brigade and its commander. I wish that it might also be granted rich success in the future."

signed Hossbach
General der Infanterie

With the arrival of all the elements of the Führer Grenadier Brigade in the Cottbus area, the brief amount of time available was put to use for the refitting of the unit and its expansion into a "Reinforced Panzer Brigade." This involved an enlargement of the brigade headquarters and in particular the reinforcement of the brigade through the addition of new units.

The Panzer-Grenadier Regiment FGB was formed under the command of Oberstleutnant von Courbiere. The regiment's I Battalion was the former

Oberstleutnant von Courbiere. The regiment's I Battalion was the former Panzer-Fusilier Battalion (Armoured) FGB, its II Battalion the former Panzer-Grenadier Battalion (Motorized) FGB. The 829th Special Purpose Infantry Battalion, a unit of the regional defence force, which had previously been used to guard various headquarters buildings, was en route to become III Battalion.

Major Lehnhoff, since decorated with the Knight's Cross, was transferred to Berlin to take over command of the Guard Regiment GD. As well a regimental headquarters arrived for the future Panzer Regiment FGB, which had not yet been activated. There was a new assault gun brigade, initially with three batteries, plus an artillery battalion that was added.

Placed under the brigade's command were elements of a mixed flak battalion, three batteries initially.

The Führer Grenadier Brigade was allowed exactly eight days to reorganize itself. True, the individual units existed when the departure order reached Cottbus on 10 December, but they had not yet become a unit, a fighting team, which was ready for action. But the situation at the front left no more time. The units boarded the transport trains on 11 December and they left the loading stations headed west – to see action on Germany's western frontier.

CHAPTER 4

THE FÜHRER ESCORT BRIGADE (FBB)

Unconcerned by events at the fronts, and in particular in the east, the expansion of the Führer Escort Battalion went ahead in the Rastenburg area of East Prussia. Major Fabian had not permitted the months of July and August 1944 to be wasted. Instead, with the help of his officers and those of Führer Headquarters, he had used them to activate, organize and train additional units. The existing seven companies were expanded to eleven, initially without creating further battalions.

Cover designations were used for the new formations or fantasy titles were dreamed up. For example, the pay books of the men of the new 8th (Panzer-Grenadier) Company contained the following entry:

8.(Pz.Gren.)/V./Pz.Gren.Rgt. GD

The company's commanding officer was Oberleutnant Contag, its senior platoon leader was Leutnant von Malotki. The company was equipped with armoured personnel carriers and the training was hard and strict. In those weeks training was interrupted only by frequent foot patrols through the woods extending to the east, guard duty at the headquarters, or searches to confirm or deny reports of agents or enemy paratroops landing by parachute.

In addition to the formation of a further heavy company and the incorporation of two SS companies of the LAH, a special close combat company (the later 11th Assault Pioneer Company) was formed. Its order of battle, as well as its personnel, appeared in no table of organization. It was created as the result of experience gained in the war on the Eastern Front. In the first days of August 1944 a group of men assembled in the barracks who looked as it they had been hardened by sports and knew how to act quickly. The selection standards by which this group of men was chosen were extremely strict. A special obstacle course, which included a pit, a rabbit hole and a 15-metre-high diving tower, was set up to test the toughness and daring of this elite group. An indication of their willingness was the number of decorations for bravery they wore; there were six men with the Knight's Cross, even more with the German Cross in Gold.

The objective of this formation was to provide a fast close- combat company for the personal protection of the Supreme Commander.

Oberleutnant Schommer was chosen to command the company; by August he had activated four platoons. As 3rd Platoon was soon transferred into the installation itself as an alert platoon, it was necessary to create a 5th Platoon. All members of the company were issued the same equipment: panzer-grenadier uniform, but with white piping and the death's head insignia; a jump (parachute) jacket, called the "bastard's dress coat," and a paratrooper-style steel helmet. Armament consisted of an assault rifle, assault dagger and P 38 pistol.

The increasingly-strenuous training (which included hand-to-hand combat, judo and boxing) went on without interruption. The well-known boxer Kölbin was transferred to the company to help with the last-mentioned area of training.

In the final days of August 1944 Major Remer, on his way to the Panzer-Grenadier Division *Großdeutschland* to take over the Panzer-Fusilier Regiment GD, arrived at Führer Headquarters to report to Adolf Hitler. After unexpectedly promoting him to Oberst, in the first days of September the Supreme Commander ordered Remer to immediately form a battle group using units already activated for the Führer Escort Regiment, with the objective of taking over the defence of the headquarters which was now only about 100 kilometres from the front. At this time it was suspected that the allies were planning an airborne assault on the headquarters with two to three airborne divisions. Furthermore (like the Führer Grenadier Brigade then being formed) the battle group was also to be employed outside the headquarters as a mobile reserve within the so-called "Fortress Lötzen."

In carrying out this order Oberst Remer, taking into consideration the units already available, expanded the organization as follows:

Brigade Headquarters
Führer Signals Battalion
Führer Luftwaffe Signals Battalion (Air Warning Service)
Führer Flak Regiment "Hermann Göring" – with 14 batteries
Führer-Begleit Regiment with 11 companies
an APC battalion
a (fast) Battalion with VW Schwimmwagen and Kübelwagen
a heavy battalion with: a panzer company
an assault gun company
a flak company
an assault pioneer company
an armoured reconnaissance company
with the addition of a regional defense battalion, the 828th Special Purpose Infantry Battalion, originally intended to guard unoccupied installations; a medical company.

This unusual organization was mainly due to the special missions this unit was to take on. It is also partly due to the fact that it had to make use of existing units and formations. The individual units were equipped with the most modern equipment and the troops were all experienced front-line soldiers.

At the same time there also took place a division of the former command responsibilities in the Führer Headquarters itself:

Oberst Remer   became the installation's battle commander
Oberst Streve   remained commander of the headquarters.

This meant that the reinforced Führer-Begleit Battalion under Major Fabian was now placed under the command of Oberst Remer, the headquarters battle commander, as a headquarters defence unit; the headquarters commander was now responsible only for the internal workings of the headquarters.

In the meantime, however, the Soviets had advanced so far, with spearheads at the Rominte and in front of Goldap and Gumbinnen, that it seemed advisable to move the Führer Headquarters out of the "Wolfsschanze," east of Rastenburg.

The move to Zossen, near Berlin, took place in the period 28-30 November. The newly-activated close-combat company, 1st (Assault Pioneer) Company, accompanied the transport, while the main body of the Führer-Begleit Battalion continued to perform its duties in the "Wolfsschanze" installation. As battle commander, Oberst Remer also remained in the Rastenburg area for some time, however with Hitler's departure his mission ended.

The available time was now used to reorganize the available units of the battle group into a panzer brigade. The core of the new brigade was formed by the reinforced Führer Escort Battalion, which gave up its name in the process.

At the end of November orders came from headquarters for Oberst Remer to immediately transfer the brigade from Rastenburg to the west by rail. The first train left on 27 November and travelled to the Fischbach–Wittich area via Chemnitz, Schweinfurt, Aschaffenburg and Frankfurt am Main. From there the brigade units drove to the Prüm area in the Eifel Mountains, where the Führer Escort Brigade was supposed to assemble.

While still en route the brigade was reorganized in preparation for combat duty, with the following result:

Brigade Headquarters
Führer-Begleit Regiment with 2 battalions
828th Special Purpose Infantry Battalion
Führer Flak Regiment with 7 batteries
Signals Company
newly added: Panzer Regiment Headquarters, not yet activated
Panzer Battalion FBB – sent by Pz.Gren.Div. GD,
formerly II Battalion,
Pz.Rgt. GD with Panzer IVs.
Assault Gun Battalion – formerly the 120th Assault Gun Battalion –
rested and refitted.
Artillery Battalion – one battalion of the
120th Artillery Regiment with
2 light, 1 heavy battery.
one Todt Organization column and 1 army transport column.
one horse-drawn bakery and butchery company
medical company.

While the existing units were very well off regards personnel and equipment, this was not the case with the newly-added units. There were shortages of signals equipment and vehicles in particular.

Another serious shortcoming suffered by the ad-hoc formation was the inability of the Führer Escort Brigade to obtain a regimental headquarters for the panzer-grenadiers. Consequently the three panzer-grenadier battalions were supposed to be commanded independently and individually. The lack of a pioneer company also proved to be an aggravating shortcoming. Such a unit had been included in the formation of the brigade, but it had remained in Zossen to guard the headquarters there. Urgent requests were made for its return, and these were eventually granted. The company arrived in the brigade's assembly area just prior to its departure for the front.

Another depressing fact was that the artillery, which itself was inadequate, was not equipped with sufficient numbers of all- terrain vehicles.

The few days the brigade spent in the Prüm and Daun area of the Eifel Mountains before going into action in the west were used intensively to form and reorganize the brigade into a capable fighting unit. As well the troops received daily instruction at the company level. Leaders of all ranks were prepared for the missions to come through terrain briefings and map exercises. The Replacement and Training Battalion was very well equipped and staffed, in order to assure that training was smooth and effective.

Special emphasis was placed on providing the core units with the best available personnel, weapons and equipment.

The former II Battalion, Panzer Regiment GD (now incorporated into the brigade as the Panzer Battalion FBB) was equipped with the "Guderian" assault tank by the "Hermann Göring Works" in Linz, Austria. The vehicle in question was based on the Panzer IV, but it was armed with the very long 75mm tank cannon in a fixed superstructure. (Panzer IV/70)

The companies consisted of three platoons each with 4 tanks. 14 tanks formed the foundation of the battalion, which was organized as follows:

> Battalion Headquarters with reconnaissance platoon
>
> 1st-4th Battle Companies
>
> 5th (Panzer) Company – formerly 5th Panzer Company, Führer--
> Begleit Battalion under Oberleutnant Geisberg
>
> Supply Company
>
> Maintenance Company

Hauptfeldwebel Hildebrandt directed the affairs of one of these panzer companies, which was transported by rail to Traben- Trarbach and then set out by road over the snow-covered Eifel Mountains in the direction of Daun.

I (APC) Battalion, of the Führer Escort Brigade's armoured fist, was commanded by Major Fabian. Before going into action in early December 1944 its organization was as follows:

Overall Organization:

> Battalion H.Q. and Supply Company
>
> 1st and 2nd Grenadier Companies
>
> 3rd SS-Grenadier Company
>
> 4th (Heavy) Company
>
> 5th (Flak) Company
>
> 6th (Armoured Pioneer) Company (temporary)

1st and 2nd (Grenadier) Companies – company commander with

two 3-ton APCs armed with 20mm flak,
one with 30-watt transmitter. each of 3 APC platoons –
platoon leader's APC with 10-watt transmitter,
4 APCs with radio and 2 light machine- guns.
4th Platoon: 3 APCs with 20mm Flak.
3rd SS-Grenadier Company – similar
two 50mm KwK short on APCs
two APCs with 120mm mortars, as well as racks for 320mm rockets
each grenadier company had a total of 23 3-ton APCs.
4th (Heavy) Company – company commander
two cannon platoons with 75mm KwK short, also 6 APCs
1 cannon platoon with 75mm KwK long, also 6 APCs
1 heavy mortar platoon with 120mm mortars.
4 mortars, 4 APCs.
5th (Flak) Company – company commander
3 platoons with 20mm twin-barrel each platoon:
platoon leader's APC with one 20mm gun.
4 APCs with 20mm triple-mounted guns.
1 platoon: 37mm flak (SP) – 4 guns
6th (Armoured Pioneer) Company – company commander
4 platoons with flamethrower APCs – 5 APCs per platoon.

As far as equipment and weapons were concerned, the battalion was very well off for the fifth year of the war. It was also expected that employment of the unit in the west would bring about a turn for the better—to help balance the opposing forces and enable the defence to hold onto German soil.

The battalion went into action on 16 December 1944...

CHAPTER 5

THE MEMEL BRIDGEHEAD

The middle of October 1944 found the Panzer-Grenadier Division *Großdeutschland,* together with elements of the 7th Panzer Division and the 58th Infantry Division, in the Memel Bridgehead with its back to the Baltic, fighting a defensive battle against a superior Soviet force. The initial assault by numerous Soviet divisions, whose exact number is unknown, under the command of the 5th Guards Tank Army and the 43rd Army, failed to take Memel. The fortified city on the Baltic was in the middle of an area already occupied by the Soviets. Their attempt to seize Fortress Memel, to overrun it, failed. The German units, thanks to their bravery and the flexibility of their commanders, had been able to prevent the defensive front from crumbling. From approximately 13 October 1944 the pressure eased, but only temporarily, for there was no doubt that the Soviets would refuse to give up that easily. During the quiet period that followed, the only enemy activity was isolated attacks at Klausmühlen and Zenkuhnen.

The bloody losses suffered by the enemy in recent days, especially in front of the bridgehead, but also their long supply lines and the time needed to move in heavy artillery, forced the Soviets to pause to catch their breath and to reorganize.

Soviet intentions were all too clear to the Germans; it was now a question of who would be ready first: the German defenders: shoring up their main lines of resistance and fall-back positions and organizing concentrations of fire on areas of terrain over which the enemy were likely to attack – or the Soviets: massing new attack forces, with heavy and super-heavy artillery with which to soften up the German main line of resistance.

There was hectic activity for several days as both sides prepared for what was to come. In the bridgehead the numerically-weak infantry established themselves in trenches and bunkers, scouted fall-back lines and began fortifying them. Reserves, even if only a few men, were drawn from the units so as to have a squad ready to counterattack just in case. This was a tactic that always worked against the Soviets. The infantry weapons ranged in on specific areas. Radio and telephone communications were set up so that one would always remain serviceable in spite of the heaviest enemy fire. Finally all the ammunition that could be found was readied. The artillery, which to a very large degree bore the lion's share of the responsibility for the defence in such a small area as this, prepared combined barrages involving all available weapons. This in addition to the howitzers, included heavy flak batteries, naval guns and the heavy guns of the fleet unit lying off the roadstead.

It is like an earthquake when such a hail of 400mm shells strikes the earth. The ground writhes under the tremendous shock and groans and trembles as if it is about to crack at the affected place. This heavy weapon provided the German infantry, who suffered most from the effects of enemy artillery, with a valuable moral support. And there was one other thing: the shortage of ammunition for all types of heavy weapons which so often affected the German forces in the final months of the war, making many planned counterattacks all but impossible, did not exist at Memel. There was plenty of ammunition. A battalion commander's desperate call for an effective barrage in front of his men's positions would not go unanswered. This had not been the case for a long time.

It calmed the nerves of the men in the positions to know that a whistle could immediately bring down a rain of shells on the dense wood in front of them, where it was suspected that the enemy were massing their forces. But in the division headquarters, located in a cellar of the Althof Estate at the outskirts of Memel, they were under no illusions: the enemy would soon renew his offensive, probably in the next few days. All indications pointed to this: increased radio traffic on the enemy side, greater activity in the air, especially attacks on the main line of resistance, obvious ranging fire by additional enemy batteries on specific points in and just behind the main line

FÜHRER-BEGLEIT-BRIGADE (FBB)

Organization, December 1944

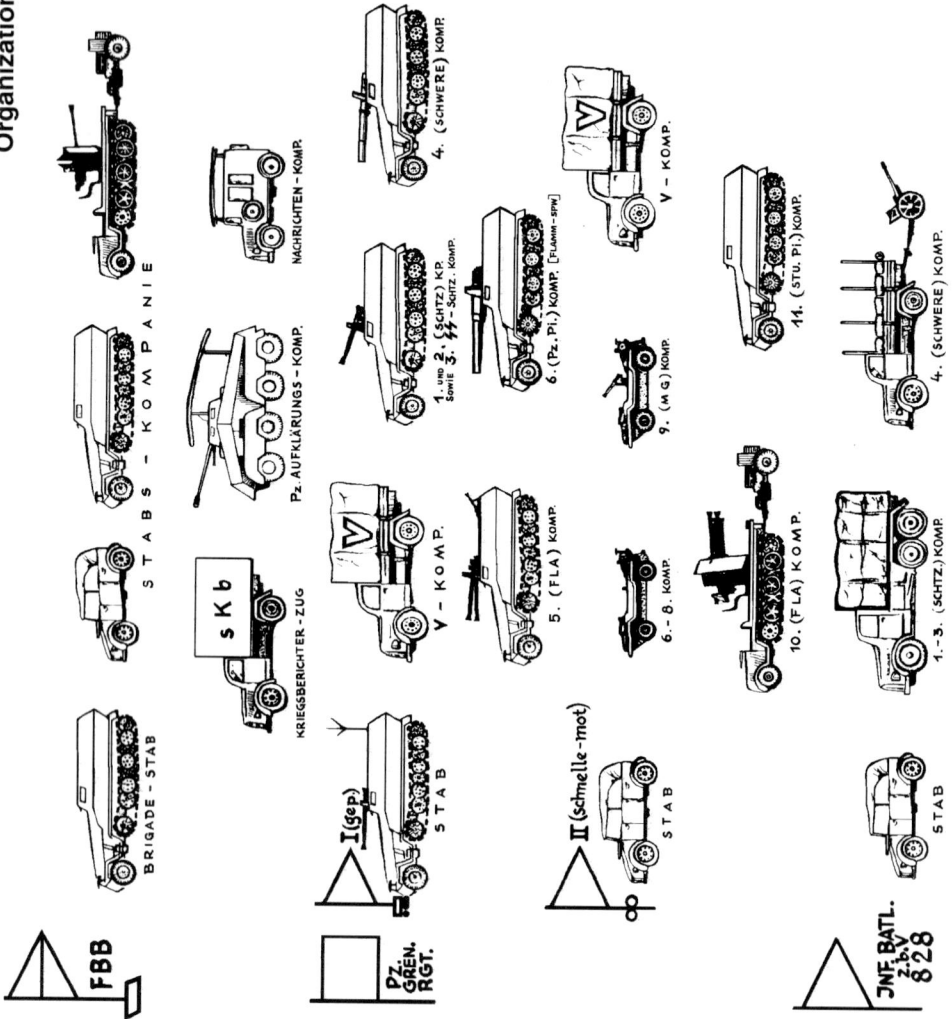

FBB

BRIGADE - STAB

STABS - KOMPANIE

sKb
KRIEGSBERICHTER-ZUG

PZ. AUFKLÄRUNGS - KOMP.

NACHRICHTEN - KOMP.

PZ.
GREN.
RGT.

I (sep)

STAB

V - KOMP.

1. und 2. (SCHTZ) KP.
Sowie 3. ƒƒ - SCHTZ. KOMP.

5. (FLA) KOMP.

4. (SCHWERE) KOMP.

V - KOMP.

6. (PZ. PI.) KOMP. [FLAMM - SPW]

9. (MG) KOMP.

6. - 8. KOMP.

II (schnelle-mot)

STAB

V - KOMP.

10. (FLA) KOMP.

11. (STU. PI.) KOMP.

4. (SCHWERE) KOMP.

INF. BATL.
z.b.V
828

STAB

1. - 3. (SCHTZ.) KOMP.

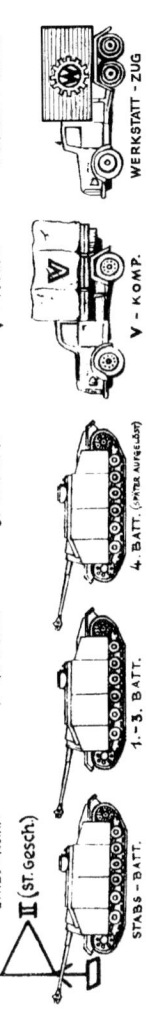
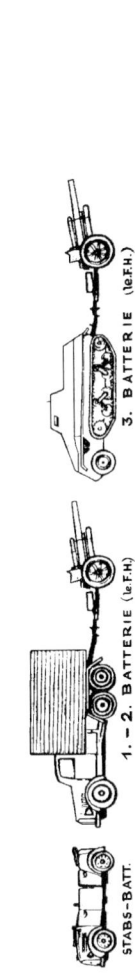
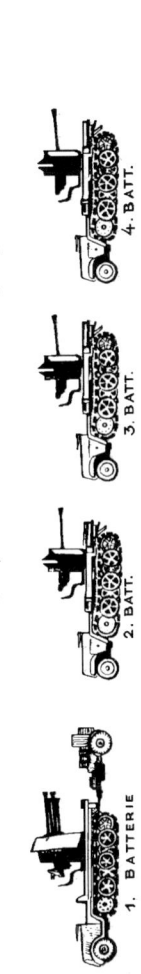
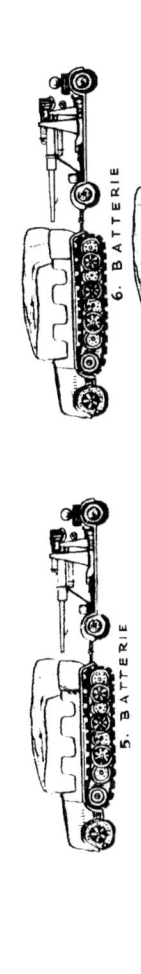

453

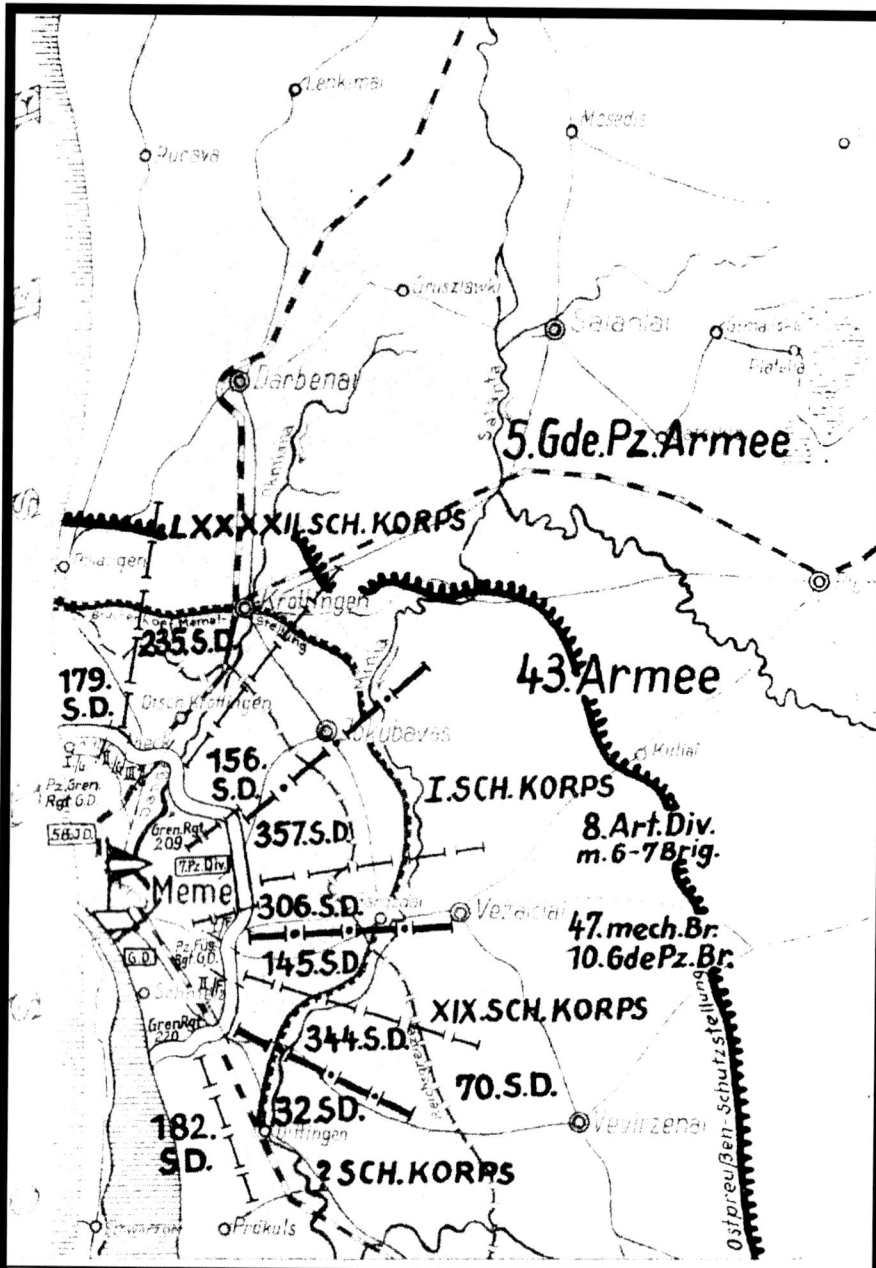

THE MEMEL POSITION
on October 10, 1944
9.00 Hours

of resistance, and increased probing of the German front lines by large numbers of enemy patrols seeking to snatch a prisoner from a foxhole. Something was definitely brewing.

Reports reaching General Staff Major Adler, Ia of the Pz.Gren.Div. GD, since the morning of 14 October revealed that the scale of the imminent enemy attack was far greater than initially thought. The nightly bombing raids by the enemy air force, the bombardment of the metropolitan area of Memel itself by heavy-calibre artillery and the subsequent drum fire by artillery and Stalin Organs on our main line of resistance, which lasted for over an hour, were early signs that the offensive expected on the 15th had begun early.

The Soviets attacked at 08.00. Their main effort, with numerous tanks, assault guns and close-support aircraft, was directed against the left side of the division's sector. While on the right the attack bogged down in front of the main line of resistance or was smashed by our artillery before it could get going, the enemy achieved deep penetrations near Hill 31 west of Kollaten in the sector held by the Panzer-Grenadier Regiment GD (III Battalion), along the Daupern–Klausmühlen road against II Battalion, Panzer-Fusilier Regiment and west of Missleiken in spite of fierce resistance. Klausmühlen and Jacken (to the south) were only retaken after the armoured reserve was committed, and farther south the former main line of resistance was recaptured.

As dawn broke the enemy also launched a tremendous effort to break through in the northeast of the main line of resistance against the panzer-grenadiers but gained little ground. Almost simultaneously they undertook a similar advance against II Battalion, Panzer-Fusilier Regiment at the railway line near Karlsberg

The commander of the battalion's heavy company, Oberleutnant E. Hoffmann, describes the enemy attack on the main line or resistance held by II Battalion, Panzer-Fusilier Regiment:

"Morning, 14 October; the geese cackled in the barnyard, the piglets squealed in the pen. We had prepared ourselves for a long siege. There was enough feed there for the animals.

The company headquarters squad of the 'Eighth' (8th Company, II Battalion, Panzer-Fusilier Regiment) was working on a bunker. Situated behind the house, it was almost finished. The sun illuminated a peaceful scene in the brilliance of autumn. Inside the house the mood was explosive. Major von Basse had objected to the positioning of Fahnenjunker Henning and his gun, and the C.O. of the heavy company to which the anti-tank gun belonged and Feldwebel Kuhn were discussing the matter further. Finally the discussion came to a close: 'No,' said the C.O., 'the cannon stays where it is – there's also a Tiger at the battalion command post, and together they can give a good concentration of fire in front of this hollow. And the Ivans definitely won't come over the hill with tanks, for they would be easy pickings there for the 105mm anti-aircraft guns of the naval battery. Therefore everything stays as it is!'

Suddenly the Ivans became active; artillery salvoes and zone fire in the entire central sector. The leader of the 8th (Heavy) Company's headquarters squad, Feldwebel Kuhnt, rushed to the telephone switchboard. The company commander went outside; he looked giddy. Time to get to our positions: steel helmet on, battle readiness, sentry at the corner of the barn; orders came for all weapons to come to readiness. Everyone asked the same question: what was going on?

Then the sentry came running: tanks, 200 metres!! The old man (the commander of 8th (Heavy) Company) shouted for panzerfausts. Then Feldwebel Kuhnt cried out, 'Herr Oberleutnant, the infantry gun platoon is running away!' The old man and Kuhnt dashed toward the infantry gun emplacement. Before they could get there they saw the limbered guns racing away over the ploughed fields in the direction of the Memel church tower. They stumbled into the emplacement and found Unteroffizier Walitsch standing there with his submachine-gun ready to defend his gun, which had been left behind.

'Oh, shit!,' said the old man. 'Man, now they must come through the hollow. Walitsch, leave the limber and man your gun. Barrage fire on the exit from the hollow. Runner! Runner! Go to the telephone exchange at once. Have them instruct all medium mortar squads and heavy mortars to place barrage fire on the hollow!'

While the lone small cannon blazed away, we worked our way through the wood; those two tanks had to be hiding somewhere. Ah, there they were! With their noses in the mud! They had bogged down within sight of the church towers of Memel!

A Wachtmeister from the 30mm Flak and a signals Feldwebel who had roared up on a motorcycle-sidecar combination let them have it with panzerfausts for good measure.

With the tanks out of the way the 6 or 7 of us toddled back to the command post. We still had no idea what was going on.

The sound of fighting had died down. At the linesman's shack the old man looked in the window; inside they were sitting down eating thick bacon sandwiches.

'Now then,' the old man said laconically, 'things are going well with you?' They jumped to their feet – there was an embarrassed silence.

'Well?'

Finally the gun commander stammered, 'Gun destroyed, one T-34 knocked out at close range!'

All the old man said was, 'Out!' They walked around the corner and there sat the anti-tank gun and on top of it an enemy tank!

'Napping,' murmured the old man to the Obergefreiter who was in command of the gun.

'It all happened so quickly,' said the Obergefreiter. 'When we came rushing out the tank was already on top of the gun and the tank commander was just driving down again. Then we tossed a hand grenade into the turret and that was that!'

'Well at least he's finished too – you Heinis!!' said the old man, already a little happier.

Two more T-34s approached the linesman's shack. There were shots from Karlsberg; aha – the Tigers were firing from up above.

Over at our barn several of I (APC) Battalion's half-tracks were burning.

'Hopefully the ammunition won't go up as well,' said the old man. The battalion command post was still undamaged. We saw soldiers so we carried on to the barracks complex. We made our way along the ditch beside the road, briefly exchanged fire with bailed-out Soviet tank crews and then saw what had taken place!

The leading enemy tank had run its nose into the trench. Behind it the rest had stopped and then fell victim to the waiting Tiger at the battalion command post. Simple target practice!

Then Fahnenjunker-Unteroffizier Henning, the positioning of whose anti-tank gun had caused such a controversy among the senior officers, came toward us.

'All clear,' he declared almost casually to his company commander, 'four enemy tanks destroyed!' All the chief said in reply was 'good,' but that word from the old man expressed more recognition than many decorations.

Dead soldiers littered the ground, items of kit—the enemy had caught an entrenching detail from the train." And now Fahnenjunker-Unteroffizier Henning's report:

"The enemy artillery fire was so thick that we had to jump into our fox-holes beside the farmhouse. I had just seen some of our infantry passing by, when suddenly the enemy tanks came out of the hollow and roared past us about 200 metres away.

I knocked out the last enemy tank, a Josef Stalin. Then, with the help of the infantry, we swung the anti-tank gun around. The gunner resumed firing while I ran over to the Tiger. The crew had shut the hatches and I was forced to pound away with a rock like a madman until finally the tank commander, a Feldwebel, looked out.

He then swung his turret around and fired into the enemy tanks from the side and ahead. In any case we were credited with four enemy tanks destroyed.

The commander of the 8th (Heavy) Company inspected the knocked-out tanks and declared with a grin:

'One of each type!' He pointed them out: 'There a Josef Stalin, there a Valentine, there a Sherman and finally a T-34, all finished!!'

The hits on the enemy tanks provided clear proof that our gun had been responsible for their destruction.

In the evening it was announced that about 26 enemy tanks had been destroyed in this sector alone—a considerable number."

The day passed much the same in the division's other sectors. A total of 66 enemy tanks were knocked out by guns or destroyed at close quarters, 36 by units of the division. The artillery recorded its highest expenditure of ammunition to date – 9,600 shells in one day.

Although the enemy had suffered heavy losses, our own casualties were also high; entire sections of Memel were in flames. However the Memel Bridgehead had passed a severe test on the first day of the enemy offensive.

By dawn on 15 October 1944 the main line of resistance was back in our hands everywhere; only in the north, near Karkelbeck, had our positions been moved back several hundred metres. It was only now that the details became known of the outstanding individual efforts involved in this defensive success.

Gefreiter Jensen of the Panzer-Fusilier Regiment GD, a member of an anti-tank gun crew, disabled two enemy tanks in a matter of minutes from a range of only 30 metres. As he was about to take aim at the third he saw that his gun was jammed. Acting quickly, he grabbed the nearest panzerfaust and stood up in the path of the onrushing enemy tank. He coolly waited until the tank was seven metres away, aimed the panzerfaust and fired. The projectile struck the tank's turret and put it out of action.

Four more enemy tanks were knocked out by individuals armed with panzerfausts.The initial Russian assault resulted in an incursion into the positions of II Battalion, Panzer-Grenadier Regiment GD at the Krottingen–Memel railway line. Without much further ado the men of the 5th and 6th Companies under the command of Leutnant Wenski counterattacked and drove the enemy back toward their jumping-off positions in heavy close-quarters fighting. Numerous Russian dead littered the ground; their automatic weapons fell into German hands.

Back in the southern sector, at the Dittauen–Memel railway line where the panzer-fusiliers of II Battalion had dug in, Leutnant Jetter, former platoon leader in the 8th (Heavy) Company and now battalion adjutant, led a counterattack by a handful of men to retake lost ground. The opposing forces were within hand-grenade range of each other. Light infantry guns and medium and heavy mortars were supposed to provide supporting fire, but the danger of shells falling short was great. Against his will, the commander of the "Eighth" finally gave permission to fire after repeated requests for supporting fire from the counterattack group. A total of eight barrels fired about 80 rounds, and apart from two of our men slightly wounded the barrage was a success. When he came back Leutnant Jetter, who was somewhat pale after having experienced friendly fire falling so close, merely reported that he had carried out his orders; 90% of the barrage had fallen on the Russians – the effort had been a success.

Replacements had arrived the night before the Soviet attack. An Oberleutnant and 30 men appeared at the command post of III Battalion, Panzer-Fusilier Regiment GD at the very moment the drum fire began. They immediately made ready, counterattacked and, supported by our tanks, drove back two enemy battalions and then reoccupied the old main line of resistance. The enemy left more than 200 dead behind.

Such examples illustrated the fighting spirit of the men in the defensive ring around Memel. It took great self-determination to plunge into the hurricane of fire that was the battlefield, and not everyone succeeded on the first try.

The following table shows the number of enemy tanks and assault guns

Date	Tanks	Assault Guns	A/T Guns	Marder II	Panzer büsche	A/T guns on APCs	Close Combat A/T weapons	
							Panzer-Faust	Hollow Charges
5. 10. =	13							
6. 10. =	8		9					
7. 10. =	17	1	1					
8. 10. =	5							
9. 10. =	23	7	6		2	3	4	
10.10. =	9	2	6	1				
11.10 =	6	4						
12.10. =	5							
13.10 =	1							
14.10 =	21		4			2	7	2
15.10. =	3							

total: 172 tanks and assault guns

On 16 October the Panzer-Grenadier Division *Großdeutschland* reported:
"In the period from 5-15 October 1944, true to their oath 8 officers, 42 non-commissioned officers and 202 enlisted men of the Panzer-Grenadier Division *Großdeutschland* died hero's deaths for Führer and Reich."

The situation in the Memel Bridgehead continued to firm up after the defensive success of 14-15 October 1944. Work on the positions continued. Each evening work parties from the rear- echelon units moved up to the front with spades, pickaxes and shovels. They laboured to shore up the bridgehead's defences on the north, east and southeast fronts.

The Ivans were doing similar work. They extended approach trenches toward the German positions, bringing their fighting positions to within about 200-300 metres of the German main line of resistance.

Now the daily and nightly routine of positional warfare set in as it had so often in this war: during the day occasional artillery duels; here and there a salvo on positions or assembly areas; now and then a burst from a concealed machine-gun at a visible target; from time to time a lone shot as a sniper picked off a careless victim – but otherwise all was quiet.

Almost every day there was some combat activity at one or another corner of the front, mostly as the result of an order from above, when an offensive patrol from one side tried to force its way into the positions of the other. Both hoped to learn the intentions of the other and for this reason they began capture operations aimed at snatching a lone sentry from his foxhole and bringing him back as a prisoner.

It is astonishing how quickly things returned to normal once the situation began to stabilize. Scarcely had the fighting died down when a zealous process of organization began, reestablishing the time of day as the determining factor in events: the food arrived daily at 12.00, the ammunition at 24.00, the early report to battalion was to sent by 05.00, because it had to be passed on to regiment at 06.00 and division at 07.00. The field post office was ready to hand out mail at 10.00; replacement parts were available and could be picked up at about 16.00. The appointments calendar triumphed, even in October of 1944!

In the Memel Bridgehead the officer in charge of constructing positions was the top dog, for the building of positions of every type, employing every refinement and trick of the trade, had top priority. Sector maps were produced, in several copies, colourful and dotted with positions—all for the satisfaction of the senior headquarters. The following is an account of those days in the positions and the battalion command post of I (APC) Battalion, Panzer-Grenadier Regiment GD:

"Gradually there now developed a certain daily routine of positional warfare. The continuous trench line was complete and had been blocked with wire obstacles; anti-tank mines were laid at the most important points as well as anti-personnel mines in certain places.

Night frost was a reminder that winter was coming. Pioneers built frames for bunkers in the forest in the rear; at night they were moved to the front and installed. Although our positions were at least three metres above sea level, it turned out that they filled quickly when it rained. Oberleutnant Straihammer was relieved on 27 October 1944. Taking his place as commander of 1st Company was Leutnant Albiez, a zealous young man. The reduction in size of the battalion's sector made it possible to rotate the two companies at the front so as to give the men a chance to spend 48 hours in the rest position in the rear, where they could sleep and clean themselves up.

On 28 October 1944 Hauptfeldwebel Biller of 1st Company returned from leave. He gave us a brief description of life at home. Then he at once set about working out the lists of missing, killed and wounded, as well as decorations and promotions which were due. The enemy stayed rather quiet following the intervention of the two heavy cruisers *Lützow* and *Prinz Eugen* in the most recent fighting. The two ships kept station off the coast, up and down (as the sailors say) and pounded the Russian positions in passing with their heavy guns, in the main opposite the regiment's right sector and that of its neighbour on the right. The Soviets fled their trenches in panic. An attempt by Soviet aircraft to bomb the ships was effectively frustrated by the ships' anti-aircraft guns.

Finally we were able to evacuate the remaining civilians. The large cattle were driven off, however most of the milk cows could not be saved. Strict orders were given to punish any slaughtering of stray cattle.

On 29 October 1944 all of the senior company NCOs met at the command post. There was a forceful discussion about the supplying of the troops at the front. I was able to use the opportunity to present the Iron Cross, First and Second Class to Obergefreiter Schäing of 2nd Company; he had distinguished himself in the fighting on 14 and 24 October as a sniper and outstanding lone fighter.

Leutnant Rejmont had meanwhile established a repair facility at our supply base. While searching for suitable materials he came upon a dump in Memel containing new APC roadwheels, something we had lacked for so long. One by one the armoured troop carriers were brought to the rear where they received new tracks. There was also an easing of the ammunition situation for the aircraft machine-guns and once again we had sufficient fuel.

Beginning of November – no large-scale operations by the enemy. In the nights both sides sent patrols creeping into no-man's- land. We determined that the enemy were also busy constructing positions for winter. The Soviets frequently sent over raiding parties whose main purpose was obviously to take a few prisoners and scout the positions of our heavy weapons. For the most part they avoided the Kunken Gorge, which must have been very uncomfortable for them. On several occasions the intercept team we had in the sector between the church and the coast listened in on suspicious telephone calls. In the morning patrols determined that the enemy trenches over there were full of soldiers. The artillery immediately pounded this concentration of Soviet forces and no attack ensued from there.

It now rained a great deal, and with very few exceptions all the positions were under water. We found two liquid manure pumps in Rund Gorge. They were put to use at night in a dammed-up section of trench; all night long they pumped water into a roadside ditch leading to the Russian position. However when day came the pumps had to be turned off, and in most cases the trenches filled with water again. Nevertheless, they brought us some relief."

The days continued to pass uneventfully in the Memel Bridgehead. Only 20 November 1944, a Monday, is worthy of special mention. On that day the supply ship *Fusilier*, about 6,000 tonnes or more, steamed too far north along the coast. It was about 2,000 metres abeam Quadrant 272 Q, level with the positions of I (APC) Battalion, Panzer-Grenadier Regiment GD, when, at approximately 08.30, it was discovered by the Soviet artillery. Thereupon it turned and sought to escape to the south in the direction of Memel. The Soviets attacked the ship, first with anti-tank guns then heavy artillery, and finally with Il-2 close-support aircraft. The vessel was hit several times; it lost speed and was finally left lying dead in the water just off the coast. By the time the naval coastal artillery finally, and with some difficulty, began firing at the identified Soviet batteries at approximately 10.00, the burning *Fusilier* was already drifted north stern-first and subsequently ran aground. In the evening twilight it was obvious that the ship was sinking.

On the morning of 21 November only the tip of the supply ship's forward mast was still sticking out of the water. All help came too late for the crew; they died hero's deaths in the waves off the coast north of Memel, among them the regimental pay official of the Panzer-Grenadier Regiment GD, Stabszahlmeister Seiler. A number of sacks of mail destined for the division were lost.

It was unrealistic to expect a highly-qualified combat division like *Großdeutschland* to be left unemployed in the Memel Bridgehead for further weeks, while elsewhere the German armed forces were locked in a life and death struggle on German soil. As well, high-level orders had been issued for reorganization and the creation of the Panzer Corps *Großdeutschland*, and on 1 November 1944 General der Panzertruppe von Saucken had been named the new corps' commanding general.

Thus the order for the withdrawal of the Panzer-Grenadier Division *Großdeutschland* from the Memel Bridgehead came as no surprise. The first detachments had already been sent to the Reich. The newly-appointed Chief-of-Staff, General Staff Oberst Bleicken, was in Führer Headquarters in Zossen to receive details as to how the order was to be carried out. The division was going to be transported by sea to the Sensburg area of East Prussia.

The first advance detachments from the 98th Infantry Division (from the Courland Pocket) reached the positions of the Panzer-Grenadier Regiment GD in the northeast sector on the evening of 21 November 1944. The units were relieved during the next few nights, routinely and with the imperturbability of experienced front-line soldiers who knew that extreme calm and silence were the best ways of guaranteeing a smooth departure.

The first companies departed for Memel on the nights of 22 and 23 November. There they were to embark on the ships that were to transport them out of the Memel Bridgehead. I (APC) Battalion, Panzer-Grenadier Regiment GD was the first to go aboard, embarking on the 6,000-tonne *Cometa* on 26 November.

Meanwhile, between Rastenburg and Sensburg preparations to receive the troops were in full swing. Major "Maxe" Fabich, the former director of the GD's forward message centre in Rastenburg, and the replacements that had meanwhile arrived from Cottbus scouted rest areas, arranged quarters and prepared to receive the troops. With the panzer-grenadiers of I (APC) Battalion on board, the *Cometa* put to sea early on 27 November, accompanied by two escorts and an armed freighter.

On 28 November elements of the Panzer-Artillery Regiment GD embarked on the 7,800-tonne *Wolta*.

On 30 November elements of the 1st Medical Company, together with other units, sailed from Memel aboard the steamer *Mimihorn*. The transports departed one after the other, all following the same route across the Baltic through the Pillau Lake Canal into the port of Königsberg, East Prussia, where they unloaded. Waiting there were railroad cars onto which the vehicles and men were loaded. Following a brief rail journey they detrained in the Sensburg-Rastenburg area, where they moved into the prepared rest quarters. I (APC) Panzer-Grenadier Battalion's assigned cantonment area was Warpuhnen–Sonntag–Sumrau–Dürwangen–Buschewen; 1st and 2nd Companies were quartered in Prusshöfen, the battalion command post in Warpuhnen.

Oberst Heesemann, the commanding officer of the Panzer-Grenadier Regiment GD, established his command post in Laxdoyen in the Rastenburg District. The regiment's III Battalion occupied its quarters in Sensburg. In Memel the embarkation of the Panzer-Fusilier Regiment GD under Oberst von Breese began very much later, on about 4 December. II Battalion boarded the *Wolta* and was transported safely and without incident across the Baltic to Pillau-Königsberg. II Battalion, Panzer-Fusilier Regiment GD moved into its assigned quarters in Prätlack, East Prussia. The regimental command post of the panzer-fusiliers was in Barten, East Prussia. Scarcely had the units moved into their quarters when the first orders for the reorganization and regeneration of the battalions, independent units and vehicle columns were issued. These reorganizations reflected the level of experience and prevailing conditions of the fifth year of the war. Many old faces reappeared. Men from Cottbus and from the schools, those recovered from illnesses and wounds, rejoined the ranks of the fighting division and gave it the stamp of a cohesive fighting unit one last time.

There were also many new faces, young war volunteers who had joined the armed forces at 16 and 17 to serve in this division. All of them (young and old) were assembled on East Prussian soil for a few weeks to develop into a new organization which was to carry on the traditions of the old *Großdeutschland* Division. They were all under the thumb of the war whose grim countenance now threatened the soil of their homeland.

They practised for what was to come on the soil of East Prussia, undisturbed and almost peacefully; they marched and toughened themselves, they developed new close-combat techniques, they hauled ammunition and dashed from cover to cover as if their lives were at stake. In the worsening cold, in the deep snow and in winter storms, they made the final preparations before going into action.

Part VIII

BATTLES IN THE WEST

CHAPTER 1

The Führer Escort Brigade and the Führer Grenadier Brigade During the Ardennes Offensive

When the Ardennes Offensive began in the early hours of 16 December 1944, taking the Americans completely by surprise, the German Armed Forces were following an order from Adolf Hitler that was based on problematical assumptions.

At that point in time, the foremost elements of the American and British invasion armies were still just west of the border of the old German Reich between Switzerland and Belgium. Only in the Baden area had the Allies set foot on German soil. The reconquest of France had unquestionably brought the Allies not only very long supply lines, but also losses in men and materiel. The now almost 800-kilometre-long front forced the enemy to commit all of the approximately 70 divisions they had on the mainland, so that the Allies could only create a point of main effort for the continuation of their attacks by denuding other parts of the front. As well the Allied units which had carried the attack so far were to some degree spent, and they needed to rest and refit before resuming the offensive.

The result was a situation which saw the Allies stayed put in the lines they had reached, apart from several planned local attacks, and in some places these lines were weakly manned in order to allow them to bolster their attack units.

Following its retreat to the *Westwall* (Siegfried Line to the Allies), the German front had firmed up to the point that it was quite capable of offering an organized defence. Indeed, with the availability of reserves which could be used according to a set plan, it was even possible to launch local counterattacks.

Besides, the outlook for Germany in its multi-front war was so dark that the Supreme Command was willing to consider desperate actions employing all and any means. Hitler's first consideration of exploiting such possibilities went back to August 1944. At that time he demanded a delaying action far in front of the *Westwall* to gain as much time as possible, not just to move up new forces, but also to create the necessary conditions for strategic counterattacks west of the borders of the Reich.

When, in the second half of September 1944, it became apparent that the allied pursuit was slowly running out of steam, Hitler began debating the idea of a counterstroke with increased emphasis. He could assume that seasonal bad weather would set in in late autumn, which would to a certain extent neutralize the enemy air forces. He therefore had it in mind to carry out his own counteroffensive before clear weather returned with the arrival of winter.

The area between Monschau and Echternach was first considered for the launching of the counteroffensive at the end of September 1944. The Germans had detected a weak spot in the enemy's front there, caused by the direction of the Allies' advance. Furthermore, it was almost the same area from which, in 1940, the German Army had come away with its greatest success of the war by exploiting the element of surprise.

An incorrect assessment of the relationship between Roosevelt and Churchill also played a role in Hitler's decision to take the offensive. He assumed that this was cloudy and that internal and external tensions would lead to discord. Hitler laid down the essential aspects of the offensive in October 1944, without letting the military leaders in the west in on the secret or even asking for their advice. He foresaw the employment of two panzer armies with a total of 28 to 30 divisions, 12 of them panzer or panzer-grenadier units. In spite of its weakened state, the Luftwaffe would be ready to intervene effectively with 800 aircraft.

In spite of all the counter-proposals by his army commanders (whose main concern was that the area to be traversed was too large) Hitler stubbornly pushed through his plan and ordered that the necessary preparations begin. The date selected for the start of the attack, 10 December 1944, was considered premature, but nevertheless that deadline was supposed to be advanced even more on account of a new offensive on the Roer by the Americans. However, technical problems and weather considerations forced three postponements of the attack date; 12 December and then 16 December 1944 was finally chosen as the first day of the offensive.

Two panzer armies were formed: in the north, the Sixth SS-Panzer Army under Oberstgruppenführer Sepp Dietrich, with four full-strength SS panzer and panzer-grenadier divisions, which was to break through the enemy positions between Monschau and the north end of the Schnee-Eifel. In the south was the Fifth Panzer Army under General der Panzertruppe von Manteuffel, who had commanded the Panzer-Grenadier Division *Großdeutschland* in 1943-44. The Fifth Panzer Army consisted of only three panzer divisions, four partly-incomplete infantry (Volksgrenadier) divisions and the Führer Escort Brigade, which had outstanding personnel and was very well equipped. Manteuffel's force was to break through with its left wing at the south end of the Schnee-Eifel and its right north of Vianden. Farther south, the right wing of the Seventh Army was to advance west with the attack forces, however its main role was to eliminate any flanking threat from the south.

The Schnee-Eifel, an impassable mountain chain where the American positions projected into the German front, was bypassed. The attack by the Sixth SS-Panzer Army did not achieve the desired decisive success. Its northern wing was able to gain little ground south of Monschau. After the 12th Volksgrenadier Division broke through the enemy positions northwest of Losheim after a two-day battle and the I SS-Panzer Corps had opened the way, the army centre and the southern wing reached a line extending southwest to the Trois Ponts area, south of Stavelot, after difficult and at times very costly fighting. On 18 December 1944 the Sixth SS-Panzer Army's attack bogged down there, far short of its initial objective of Liege. The close proximity of the very strong American Roer front, from which help was quickly summoned for the allied divisions whose front had initially been broken, must be seen as the reason for this, though the bravery of the attacking units there is beyond praise.

Far more successful was the methodical and well-thought-through attack by the Fifth Panzer Army farther to the south. With four infantry and two panzer divisions in the front line, it was able to punch through the enemy front. St. Vith, an important road junction, was bypassed as the enemy forces holding there defended the town with greater determination than expected, and Manteuffel's forces reached and even crossed the Our at several places. However it took the attacking divisions of the Fifth Panzer Army much longer to reach their initial objectives than called for in the timetable, especially since road conditions, obstacles such as blown bridges and parts of the *Westwall* and then the bitter resistance at St. Vith all resulted in considerable delays. The Führer Escort Brigade had to be committed to take the St. Vith area, through which ran the important advance road, also vital for the direct supply of the attacking German units. This mobile unit was thus initially lost for the actual drive to the Maas.

After detraining, the units of the Führer Escort Brigade under Oberst Remer moved out of the Wittich area through Prüm in the southern foothills of the Schnee-Eifel right up to the Belgian border. Their march objective was Schoenberg, on Belgian soil, on the right wing of LXVI Army Corps at the boundary with the Sixth SS-Panzer Army, which was advancing farther north. The latter's left-wing division, the 1st SS-Panzer Division LAH, also used the southern advance road due south of the Schnee-Eifel.

However, of all the elements of the Führer Escort Brigade moving up to the starting position, only I (APC) Battalion under Major Fabian had reached Belgian soil by the first day of the attack – 16 December 1944. The other elements were strewn over hundreds of kilometres on account of clogged roads, inadequate deliveries of fuel and terrible weather. By evening of that day the battalion's armoured troop carriers, which had been joined by the first four assault guns, had taken cover in the woods east of Lower Ameln where they waited for further orders. On the first day the battalion's route, which had taken it through Schoenberg in the direction of Wallerode–St. Vith, had to be moved north on account of the 18th Volksgrenadier Division's attack on the latter town and the uncertain situation there. Like the Assault Gun Battalion FBB under Hauptmann Franz, the vital Panzer Battalion FBB under Major Schnappauf was still far to the rear; the other elements of the Führer Escort Brigade could only guess where they were.

Not until 17 December was the bulk of the Führer Escort Brigade in place; the tank and assault gun units arrived at 15.00 after a forced march and assembled east of St. Vith. The commander of 1st Company, Panzer-Grenadier Regiment FBB, Oberleutnant Wolf, and his platoon leader Oberfeldwebel Lischak, set out on foot to scout ahead as far as Ameln. They were caught in a heavy shower of enemy artillery fire and Oberleutnant Wolf was fatally wounded. He was probably the first fatal casualty suffered by the brigade. Leutnant von Malotki assumed command of the Panzer-Grenadier Regiment's 1st Company.

Still on 17 December, I (APC) Battalion of the Führer Escort Brigade's Panzer-Grenadier Regiment participated in an armed reconnaissance toward Born as part of a battle group which included tanks and assault guns. The advance was halted by extremely heavy artillery fire before the objective was reached. In particular a barrier of American anti-tank guns prevented our tanks and assault guns from advancing any farther. The tactic of surprise had failed; the battle group was stopped short of Born.

Not until 18 December did Oberst Remer receive clear orders from LXVI Army Corps: the brigade was to advance past St. Vith with the corps in a generally westerly direction, without however attacking the town of St. Vith as such.

The Ia of the Führer Escort Brigade ordered the formation of an advance group, independent of the battle group still holding in front of Born with the bulk of I (APC) Panzer-Grenadier Battalion and elements of the FBB Panzer and Assault Gun Battalions. The make-up of the group was as follows:

Advance detachment:

> 1 armoured patrol – Armoured Reconnaissance Company FBB
>
> 1 rifle company in VWs – II (Fast) Battalion, Panzer-Grenadier Regiment.
>
> 1 assault gun company
>
> rest of II (Fast) Battalion, Panzer-Grenadier Regiment
>
> heavy infantry gun company
>
> flak company

Brigade H.Q. with rest of armoured reconnaissance company

Panzer Battalion FBB

rest of I (APC) Battalion, Panzer-Grenadier Regiment

Flak Regiment FBB

III Battalion, Panzer-Grenadier Regiment (828th Special Duties Infantry Battalion) (bicycle battalion)

Oberst Remer found the LXVI Corps command post in Weinsheim, about 5 kilometres north of Prüm; there he acquired further details concerning the current situation and received orders to set out with the bulk of the brigade through Roth, Auw and Schoenberg (Belgium) in the direction of St. Vith. No direct attack on St. Vith itself was ordered, instead the corps' intention to deploy the brigade west toward the Maas was confirmed. In no case was the brigade to allow itself to become involved in a struggle for St. Vith.

The situation in front of St. Vith on the morning of 18 December was characterized by the extremely determined opposition by the American defenders. Attempts to take the town by storm failed. The 18th Volksgrenadier Division, whose forward command post was in Wallerode-Mill, had initially been halted in front of St. Vith; there was no way of telling when the attack there would get rolling again.

The advance road through Schoenberg–Setz which had been assigned to the Führer Escort Brigade was completely clogged with the vehicles of the 18th Volksgrenadier Division and in a hopeless state. Even tracked vehicles could not drive along the side of the road.

Patrols were immediately despatched to scout a way around St. Vith to the north, but results were unsatisfactory. Consequently Oberst Remer decided to support a fresh attack by the 18th Volksgrenadier Division along the Setz (Atzerath)–Prümerberg–St. Vith road with his advance detachment which consisted of the bulk of II (Fast) Battalion FBB under Major Mickley.

The attack by the 18th Volksgrenadier Division, which was carried out with weak artillery support, failed to achieve success even though the FBB advance detachment was able to advance to the bend in the road at the Prümerberg. There, however, the 7th Company of the II (Fast) Battalion, Panzer-Grenadier Regiment FBB, which was advancing south of the road, suffered considerable losses to heavy anti-tank fire. Very heavy enemy artillery fire, especially on the wood surrounding the Prümerberg, increased casualties even further. Leutnant Esswein was killed along with many brave grenadiers. Senior Medical Officer Dr. Bartels, who had set up his aid station in a house to the right of the road, soon had his hands full. This failed attack on St. Vith showed that a further attack from the move, without assembling heavy weapons, was also doomed to fail. Added to this was the fact that the area north of the Setz–St. Vith road was the only one that appeared suitable for an attack by tanks from the east, and this involved an unfavourable assembly area "on the hill" west of the forest; the only access from the bottleneck of the road was in plain view of the enemy.

Oberst Remer decided to advance past St. Vith to the north on 19 December, using the Wallerode Mill–Meyerode road which earlier scouting had reported barely passable. The Meyerode–Medell area was reached late in the evening; contact was established with the battle group of I (APC) Battalion, Panzer-Grenadier Regiment to the northwest. The latter had succeeded in entering the town of Born in the course of the day, after the Americans fled in panic to the south and west as soon as the panzer-grenadiers attacked. The battle group under Major Fabian settled down in Born, having won a favourable starting position for subsequent movements by the Führer Escort Brigade.

The bulk of the battalions of the Panzer-Grenadier Regiment FBB assembled in and around Born with the intention of beginning an advance to the south at dawn on 20 December and conducting armed reconnaissance into the woods west of Born. Heavy enemy artillery fire fell on the town of Born almost without interruption and caused further, not insignificant casualties. Oberst Remer ordered the senior platoon leader of the 1st (Rifle) Company, I (APC) Battalion, Oberfeldwebel Lischak, to take his platoon into the wood west of Born and scout the enemy's strength there. Oberfeldwebel Lischak describes what happened:

"I didn't trust the forest and therefore asked Major Fabian to have two further platoons of my company follow on foot. We drove our APC about 500 metres into the wood along a forest lane and we could already see the opposite end of the wood. Then suddenly there were flashes and all hell broke loose! The other two platoons, which had followed on foot, suddenly found themselves in the midst of American infantry; as well we could make out at least 12 Sherman tanks, which wildly fired blind into the surrounding area.

We had to fall back. The leaders of the two infantry platoons, Oberfeldwebel Schneider and Stabsfeldwebel Bär, were both already wounded, as were a number of our men. Several had even gone missing in the confusion, and so we withdrew through the wood in the direction of Born.

Following our return I explained the situation to the Oberst. When Remer asked how many tanks I had seen, I replied, 'At least 12 to 15.' At this the Oberst declared that he had information that even twice that number was too low.

Unteroffizier Rothe, who went missing in this operation and was captured by the Americans, later reported that behind the American front he had observed about 80 tanks on their way forward."

The eager panzer-grenadiers of II (Fast) Battalion and their C.O., Oak Leaves wearer Major Mickley, put together a strong patrol for an attempt to raid the enemy artillery positions south of Born, approximately in the area between Hinderhausen and Roth, and in this way eliminate the vexing artillery fire that was falling on Born. Men of the specially-trained 11th Assault Pioneer Company under Oberleutnant Schommer were brought in to take part in the operation.

Obergefreiter Prowald, a participant, described the operation:

"We assault pioneers were near the viaduct in Born, which was also the site of brigade headquarters and its command post. During the evening hours of 19 December a patrol led by Major Mickley, with Leutnant von Rautenstrauch and Oberleutnant Schommer and his company, set out to scout a path through the American lines to the suspected enemy artillery positions and if possible ambush these positions during the night.

Following a forest lane the assault pioneers, walking single file, reached a road at the far side of the wood over which were rolling what appeared to be American supply vehicles. From their positions in the ditches at the side of the road they ambushed a number of Ami trucks headed toward the rear. The American soldiers were taken prisoner and the trucks were quickly rolled into the forest lane. This happened six or seven times without anyone on the enemy side taking notice.

Finally a lone jeep carrying two men approached. It too was stopped and the pair was taken prisoner. During the action, however, one of the two Americans suddenly fell to the ground; in an unguarded moment he suddenly jumped behind the wheel of the jeep, stepped on the gas and got away unscathed. The rifle shots fired after him had no effect.

That was bad: now those in the rear surely knew what and where we were. We waited half an hour but nothing special happened. We set out again indian file in the direction of the enemy artillery positions. Just as we were crossing a meadow a US reconnaissance aircraft appeared overhead, undoubtedly alerted by the escaped jeep driver. Scarcely had it disappeared (we were still crossing the meadow in developed formation) when several

American armoured cars appeared and sprayed us with fire. We had difficulty making out the enemy armoured cars clearly, as they were shrouded in smoke which only cleared from time to time.

Finally at about noon, after the armoured cars had disappeared, we reached the area in front of Hinderhausen where we thought the enemy artillery positions must be. We soon spotted them in a meadow; the barrels of the guns were facing in the opposite direction.

At the edge of the wood we made preparations for a surprise attack on the guns in the meadow before us. While we were making ready, an American truck came up from behind in the direction of the forest. We opened fire. Two American soldiers were killed instantly, but a third managed to flee in the confusion. Once again we feared that our plan would be betrayed.

The enemy artillery positions in front of Hinterhausen were guarded by one Sherman; it was positioned between the emplacements and the first house of the village.

Elements of II (Fast) Battalion as well as we of the 11th (Assault Pioneer) Company now attacked out of the forest across the open meadow and succeeded in capturing three houses which stood alone about halfway to the town. At first there was no resistance, no firing by the enemy. Apparently our advance had not been noticed. While the remaining platoons of 11th Assault Pioneer Company stayed at the houses to give covering fire, the company's 3rd Platoon moved along a sunken road toward the town. Our platoon leader, Feldwebel Kissmann, led the way. After crossing the road fork and reaching a bend in the road, we suddenly came under machine-gun fire from the emplacements. The sunken road protected us, if only to a degree, for anyone who looked over its edge was immediately hit in the head or neck by the enemy's well-aimed fire. We sat tight, unable to advance or retreat. Feldwebel Kissmann was also hit and was later taken prisoner by the Americans. While we were squatting there at a loss as to what to do, the covering Sherman suddenly came rolling around the bend in the road and opened fire with everything it had directly along the road into the group squatting in the sunken road. Panic! Everyone tried to escape this witch's cauldron, many wounded cried out, others groaned and fell to the ground dead. It was frightful. Where to go? Individuals repeatedly tried to put the damned Sherman tank out of action, but in vain. An Obergefreiter rushed the monster with an explosive charge; just as he was preparing to toss the charge he was killed by a burst of machine- gun fire.

Finally we succeeded in knocking out the Sherman tank and capturing its crew. Only a few of us were able to fight our way back to the edge of the forest; most of the wounded stayed behind or gathered in the three isolated houses. The enemy artillery, which by now had noticed the activity at the three houses, shelled the men hiding there mercilessly. Several of our wounded were killed as they lay in the houses on stretchers. Our comrade, the boxer Kölblin, surpassed himself there; under the heaviest fire he dragged two and three wounded at a time from the houses to the safety of the forest edge. When darkness fell we retraced our earlier path and made our way back to our departure positions."

After the failed operation against the enemy artillery emplacements near Hinderhausen, another chance presented itself in the forest south of Born. Major Mickley exploited this by moving his entire II (Fast) Battalion into the forest and taking up position at the Stavelot-Ligneuville–St. Vith road. By doing so he cut the supply route so vital to the American garrison of St. Vith. A battle group from II (Fast) Battalion was even able to move into Lower-Emmels and hold the town against all enemy attacks. Further attempts by II (Fast) Battalion to break through farther south toward Sart-Lex–St. Vith and block another communications road failed, however, in the face of well-aimed artillery fire from at least two or three American artillery battalions and anti-tank gun fire.

Oberst Remer therefore decided to initially cease attacking south and move up the main body of his brigade, especially his artillery and other units, through Born. In an unrelated move, in the early hours of the morning I (APC) Battalion's battle group under Major Fabian, supported by tanks and assault guns, set out from Born, bypassing the forest to the west, north toward Recht. The battle group arrived at dawn, catching the sleeping Americans by surprise. This success yielded a rich booty in tents, vehicles, weapons and prisoners. The battle group stayed in Recht, refuelled and waited for further orders. The Americans fled Recht in every direction and they were too deeply shocked to organize any countermeasures. The Führer Escort Brigade held the village of Recht with Major Fabian's battle group until evening fell. It had also taken Lower-Emmels and blocked the Ligneuville–St. Vith road with elements of II (Fast) Battalion under Major Mickley. Furthermore a strong patrol had been sent south in the direction of Sart-Lex–St. Vith with orders to sever this last road to the Americans in St. Vith. The bulk of the division meanwhile struggled to catch up with the point units, hindered by bottomless roads, marshy meadows and snow-covered terrain. Hour after hour passed before the men of III (Bicycle) Battalion under Hauptmann Gaum finally arrived. Leaving behind their only means of transport, their bicycles, they tramped ahead on foot in an effort to catch up. Shortcomings in the delivery of ammunition and precious fuel was cause for increased concern.

Farther to the north the Waffen-SS panzer-grenadiers of the Sixth SS-Panzer Army had become bogged down in front of Stavelot; they were unable to advance any farther in spite of all their bravery. In the Fifth Panzer Army's northern area the stubborn defence of St. Vith continued to hold up further movement in the direction of the Maas. The Führer Escort Brigade, which had been earmarked for the advance on the river, had to be diverted from this and committed to a flanking attack on St. Vith. Irreplaceable time for the subsequent conduct of the operation was lost; concealed in this delay was the seed which led to the failure of the Ardennes Offensive. At this point the most obvious success was in the central and southern area of the Fifth Panzer Army: the Panzer-Lehr Division under the command of Oberst Niemack, former commander of the Panzer-Fusilier Regiment GD, was nearing its first objective, Bastogne, and reckoned on its fall within the next 48 hours. Farther northwest German mobile units had reached Houffalize and were driving toward the Ourthe River line.

The enemy had not remained idle after their initial shock, however. As soon as Allied Commander-in-Chief General Eisenhower realized that the German action was more than just an attack with limited objectives, he scraped together all the available uncommitted reserves on the mainland. Eisenhower immediately diverted the 101st Airborne Division to beleaguered Bastogne and was able to bring relief to the American 10th Armored Division – which was sacrificing itself to hold the town – just in time. The Panzer-Lehr Division very soon found itself facing stiffening opposition which could not be broken in spite of the use of artillery and aircraft. Eisenhower's measures to localize the German attack went even farther, however: fresh reserves just arrived in England and France, an armoured and an airborne division, were sent to the Maas to head off frontally a breakthrough there by German units. Ongoing allied attacks were halted in sectors not attacked by the Germans. In this way several divisions were freed up and moved into the threatened area.

All in all, on 20 December the impression existed that the enemy had decided on their first countermeasures, and it was felt that those at Bastogne and in particular against the south flank of the Fifth Panzer Army posed the greatest threat to the German plans.

Due to delays in detraining in the Bonn area on 17-18 December after an almost seven-day rail journey from the east, the Führer Grenadier Brigade under Oberst Kahler did not arrive in time for the opening actions of the Ardennes Offensive. The brigade set out by road immediately, taking the shortest route to the front through the Ahr Valley via Adenau, Müllenbach and Bauler, Eifel. While on the move the brigade was joined by the 829th Special Purpose Infantry Battalion, consisting of battalion headquarters, 1st-4th Companies and a supply company. It was later incorporated into the Panzer-Grenadier Regiment FGB as III Battalion. The battalion was equipped with bicycles and a few trucks converted to run on wood gas. The first element of the Führer Grenadier Brigade, which was attached to the Fifth Panzer Army, to arrive was the APC Battalion under Hauptmann Hensel. It reached the Roth–Vianden area on the Germany–Luxembourg border on 19 December. The command post of the Panzer-Grenadier Regiment FGB under Oberstleutnant von Courbiere was moved forward as far as Heiderscheid; the regiment arrived there during the evening of 20 December. Its assembly area was Heiderscheid–Bourscheid–Vianden. However this was only the tip of the Führer Grenadier Brigade, the bulk of the formation was creeping west through the Eifel Mountains over icy roads. The brigade's tracked elements in particular suffered very badly from this overland march, which was so hard on their equipment.

The location of the Führer Grenadier Brigade's assembly area on the south wing of the Fifth Panzer Army was an indication of what its mission was to be: screening the army's left flank against an enemy advancing from the south. Part and parcel of this was bolstering the front of an exhausted Volksgrenadier corps in the Martelange–Boulaide–(Baschleiden) area and relieving elements of a parachute unit in the area of Tintange.

The mission was clear, only the units were still missing; the bulk of these did not find their way into the Heiderscheid area until 22 December. The tanks and tracked elements were still on the road, however. The APC Battalion under Hauptmann Hensel moved up as far as Neunhausen, west of Eschdorf, where it lay within range of the enemy artillery. During that same day the Panzer-Grenadier Regiment FGB moved its command post forward to Baschleiden and prepared to take over the first positions from the units waiting to be relieved there. Oberst Kahler undertook a limited counterattack with his APC battalion. Riding with him in his armoured troop carrier were his adjutant, Oberleutnant Seldte, and the leader of the FGB's H.Q. Company, Leutnant Koch. While the three were observing the attack from a hill, the APC was straddled by enemy artillery fire and sustained a direct hit. Kahler and his adjutant were badly wounded and Koch was killed. The brigade was thus robbed of its commander on its first day in action. After learning of this incident, Major von Courbiere rushed to the brigade command post in Eschdorf and temporarily assumed command of the brigade. Meanwhile the enemy artillery, anti-tank, tank and mortar fire on the Bourscheid–Heiderscheid road intensified, while simultaneously pressure against the German positions due south of eschdorf increased. The situation became increasingly unclear. The enemy were obviously making preparations to attack the shaky front held by the Volksgrenadier divisions, their obvious objective being to completely shatter the southern flank of the Fifth Panzer Army. Reports poured in of enemy attacks, even breakthroughs in the area between Bourscheid and Heiderscheid. The reports also spoke of the road between the two towns being severed from time to time. The Führer Grenadier Brigade was repeatedly forced to commit its units to counterattacks at various places, once south of Eschdorf, then in the area around Heiderscheid. The 829th Special Purpose Infantry Battalion (III Bicycle Battalion, Panzer-Grenadier Regiment FGB) under Rittmeister Rosenboom had to be temporarily attached to the 9th Volksgrenadier Division to act as a corsett-stay for that unit. It was the typical picture of a unit committed piecemeal under the pressure of events.

In an effort to exercise full control over at least the armoured elements of the brigade and to obtain some idea of the overall picture, on 23 December Major von Courbiere, himself slightly wounded, withdrew his command post to Bourscheid and ordered the Panzer Battalion FGB to carry out a reconnaissance in force against Heiderscheid, which was thought to be held by the enemy. Hauptmann von Schönfeld, commander of the battalion, deployed 2nd Company and elements of 3rd Company under the command of Oberleutnant von Wickern, with orders to carry out a feint attack to clarify the situation in the town.

The reconnaissance in force from Hoscheid through Goebelsmühle toward Heiderscheid was described by a participating member of 3rd Company, Panzer Battalion FGB:

"Our tank, commanded by Unteroffizier Müller, belonged to 3rd Company. We made our approach and at first found everything quiet at the outskirts of Heiderscheid. I envisaged once again how the Amis would likely react when we came. It was well known that when two German panzers turned up the Americans countered with at least seven; and when they didn't have them they stayed out of sight.

We were about to drive through a defile into the town, when we saw several Amis running and quickly fired two high-explosive shells after them. Before the third H.E. round left the barrel, however, we were ourselves hit, by a phosphorous shell. At the instant we were hit the turret was in the 11 o'clock position. As a result the radio operator couldn't get out as his hatch was blocked. We were unable to save him from the now burning tank and he burned to death. Our driver, Gefreiter Eder, got out safely, but he was mowed down by a machine-gun firing from the window of a house from a range of about 15 metres. Tank commander Unteroffizier Müller escaped from the turret with several burns; I myself was in the process of crawling out of the turret when I became caught. A mortal dread seized me that the lower part of my body would be slowly burned, but finally I managed to jump clear. Finally the gunner, covered with burns, also got out. Lying beside the tank, he screamed in pain. I tried to pull him into the cover of the tank, especially since the Amis were using us for target practice. As I was doing so gunner Schäfer was hit by an explosive bullet that almost severed his arm. Shortly thereafter he was hit in the stomach and was killed. I myself crept alone into the town to where the other panzers had stopped. In the course of the next few hours we all withdrew."

The armoured reconnaissance against Heiderscheid did clarify the situation – the enemy were in the town with numerous anti-tank guns and infantry.

The initial objective of the Americans was clear: to capture the crossings over the Sauer and send strong forces into the deep flank of the Fifth Panzer Army from their bridgehead north of the river. It therefore appeared important to establish a defensive line on the hills in front of the Sauer River (running roughly from south of Esch, both sides of Eschdorf, north of Heiderscheid to the area of Bourscheid) which was strong enough to halt the vigorous advance by the American units attacking from the south. It soon turned out, however, that the enemy forces, which included a concentration of artillery and tanks seldom seen before, were overpowering. The weather had meanwhile cleared and for the past twenty-four hours enemy fighter-bombers had been in the air constantly. An organized defence was soon completely out of the question. The brigade went over to fighting a delaying action in which it tried to turn up at numerous places, surprising the enemy and halting their points. It was impossible for the brigade to be everywhere at once, but it intended to hold the river crossings, especially the bridgehead near Eschdorf.

The brigade's command post moved to Esch on 24 December, behind the centre of its fictitious sector, as close as possible to its own defence line. There was desperate fighting for Eschdorf; very heavy artillery fire fell on the outskirts of the village and the bridge site. Hauptmann von Kameke and his men took up position in the town itself and tried to hold the rubble. Losses among the ranks of his brave II Battalion were fearful – but the sacrifice was in vain; the Americans entered Eschdorf. Finally, as darkness was

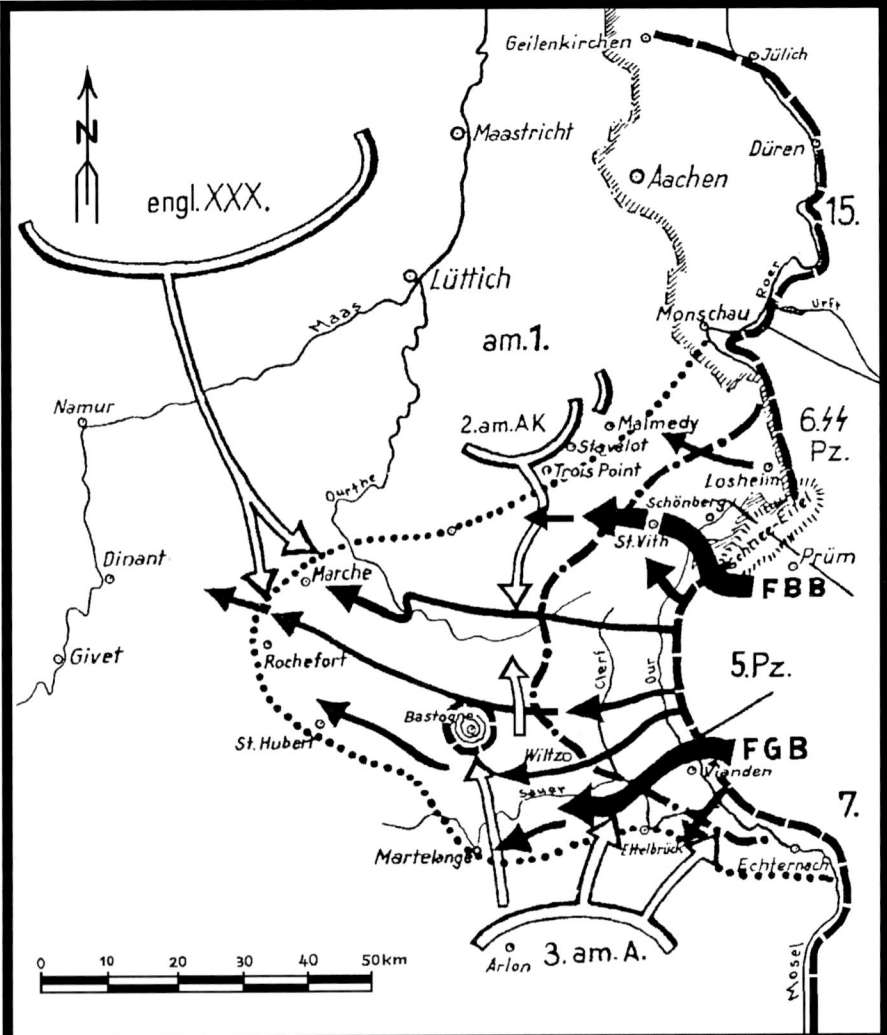

THE ARDENNES OFFENSIVE
Late 1944 - Early 1945

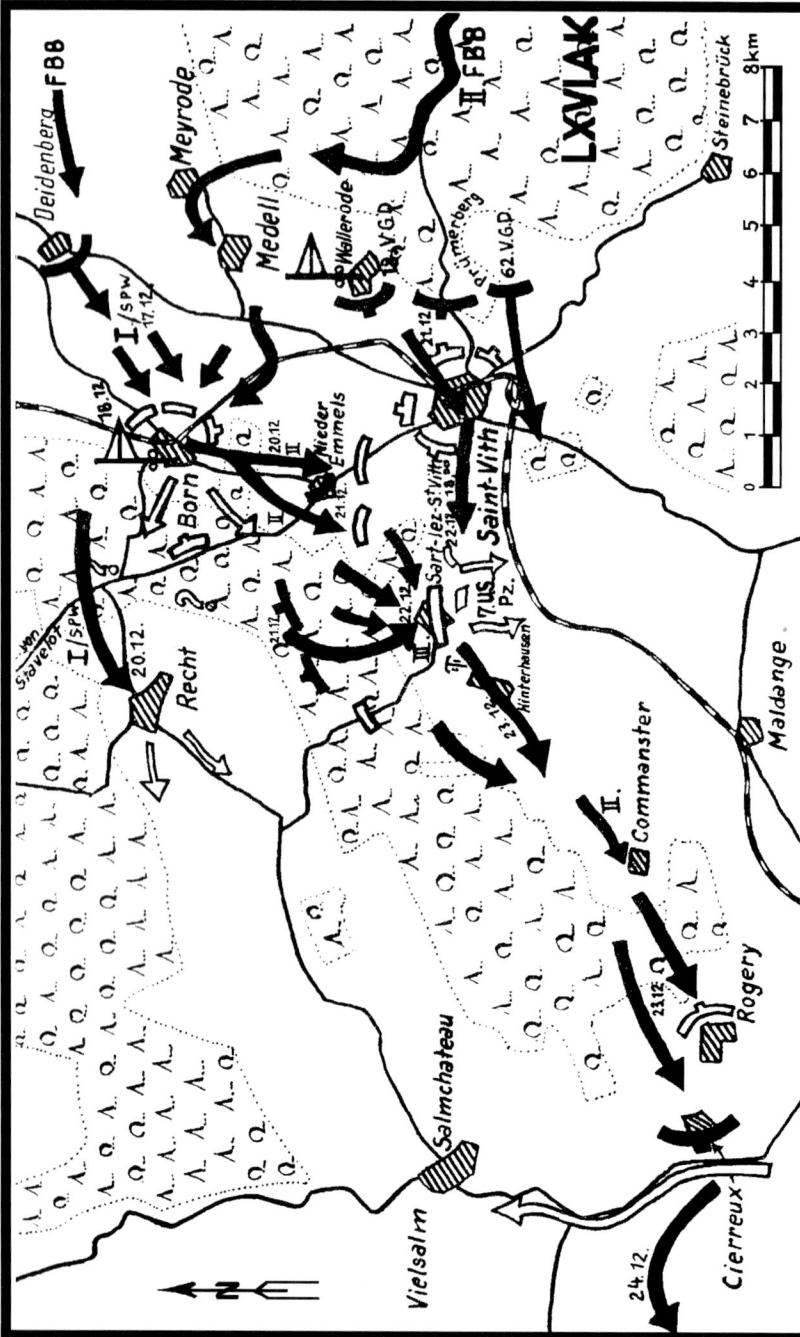

BREAKTHROUGH BY FBB at St. Vith-Hinterhausen
December 18 - 24, 1944

falling, the heap of rubble had to be abandoned. New positions were occupied on the wooded hills north of the village. Several battle groups of the Brigade Headquarters Company were surrounded in Eschdorf and remained behind in the village until 25 December. American tanks arrived and drove into the village; three were destroyed, but then it was over. Individuals and small groups of soldiers still managed to break through to the north to the positions of the brigade's II Battalion. Losses were heavy: Feldwebel Bullmann and Obergrenadier Anders killed; Obergefreiter Engert, Obergefreiter Maschky and Unteroffizier Eder wounded. Only 11 of the Headquarters Company's 25 men were still in action.

At this point the Americans had failed to cross the Sauer anywhere, including near Esch. Soon the defenders had the impression that the enemy were extending their efforts to the northwest in order to finally force a crossing of the river there. West of Eschdorf in the Liefringen area, however, the enemy appeared to be moving northwest without meeting any resistance. Were there no German troops there? Or was the massing of American forces there intended for a relief advance on Bastogne?

During the night of 24-25 December Major von Courbiere received orders to immediately move his I (APC) Battalion and the Panzer-Grenadier Battalion (however without the bicycle battalion) to Nothum, south of Winseler. Early on 25 December he was to advance from Nothum south through Dunkrodt-Mecher toward the Sauer near Liefringen and prevent a suspected enemy attempt to cross the river there.

At the same time elements of the FGB Headquarters Company were moved to Kaundorf, northwest of Esch, in order to occupy positions at the Sauer south of the town. These days were characterized by desperate attempts to establish a stable defence front along the Sauer and halt the enemy forces advancing from the south to the north and northwest. Their strength had been underestimated; General Patton's divisions, with very strong support from all arms, advanced steadily. Their first objective lay near Bastogne; the Americans wanted to establish firm contact with the US 101st Airborne Division under General Taylor which was stubbornly defending the city. On the German side it was a sacrificial battle against a superior force.

Notwithstanding the heavy battles beginning south of Bastogne for the flanks of the Fifth Panzer Army, the units in that army's northern sector, like the units beside them on the left wing of the Sixth SS-Panzer Army, continued their frantic efforts to finally take St. Vith. The American 7th Armored Division was still holding the city, and so far all attempts by the 18th Volksgrenadier Division and the 62nd Volksgrenadier Division, which had been moved in to bolster the attack, to take the city frontally from the east had failed. Farther north point units of the 116th Panzer Division had entered Houffalize, elements of the 2nd Panzer Division were advancing rapidly on Marche, and the armoured spearheads of the Waffen-SS units were striving west toward Trois Ponts and beyond. Only St. Vith held out like a pillar in the stream of the German attack. The leading elements of the Führer Escort Brigade were now in the wooded areas southwest of Lower and Upper Emmels, having been diverted from their actual march direction, namely west. They were now supposed to sever St. Vith's last supply road and initiate the fall of the stubbornly-defended city.

Oberst Remer marshalled his units in the wooded areas so that they could initially attack Sart-Lex–St. Vith, which would place them in position to attack the last supply road. II (Fast) Battalion FBB under Major Mickley assembled in a shallow valley due west of Lower Emmel; however its movements were spotted by the enemy, who pounded the assembly area with heavy artillery fire, seriously disrupting the battalion's preparations. The unit subsequently moved to the Bois d'Emmels wood and under cover of darkness effectively cut the Vielsalm–St. Vith road.

Meanwhile preparations were under way for the attack on Sart-Lex–St. Vith. When darkness fell the bulk of the brigade's armoured elements were moved forward into a wood due north of the objective. Before dark the brigade's artillery battalion moved into positions from which it could bombard the objective. Meanwhile III (Bicycle) Battalion under Hauptmann Gaum (on foot, having left its bicycles in Born) assembled in the Tomm-Berg area. Its assignment was to launch a surprise attack on the town from the northwest as soon as the panzers arrived.

The armoured group (2nd Company of the Panzer Battalion and the 2nd Battery of the FBB's Assault Gun Battalion) assembled in the area of Lower Emmel Heath at about midnight on 21-22 December. At approximately 01.00 III (Bicycle) Battalion reported that it had secured the assembly area in the Tomm-Berg area. The FBB Artillery Battalion placed observed fire on Sart-Lex–St. Vith and on identified enemy artillery positions west of the town. The armoured group moved off at dawn on 22 December 1944; however there was a delay when the leading tanks ran into mines at the south edge of the forest in front of Sart-Lex–St. Vith. These had to be cleared before the advance could be resumed.

Meanwhile III Battalion under Hauptmann Gaum launched a surprise attack on Sart-Lex–St. Vith from the northwest and fought its way through the town house by house. Contrary to expectations the town was stubbornly defended, with repeated counterattacks by American tanks. The delayed departure of the armoured group placed the men of III (Bicycle) Battalion in a sticky situation. The attackers had become the defenders, and they desperately crawled into the ruins of houses and cellars. Losses were frightful and the battalion's numbers dwindled. The Americans increasingly gained the upper hand and pressed the surviving groups of the splintered III Battalion. It was rifles and pistols against enemy tanks. Hauptmann Gaum held out in a cellar with the last panzerfausts and hand grenades. What was left of the battalion was finally overwhelmed and captured. Only a handful of men managed to escape in the morning twilight.

Then, finally, late that morning German tanks and assault guns rolled toward Sart-Lex-St. Vith from the north. They shot up the enemy tanks they could see and forced the rest out of the town in a heavy firefight. Hauptmann Gaum was freed. By about noon the town was again firmly in our hands. More than 20 American tanks were destroyed, several others captured intact and 50 prisoners were taken. The town remained in German hands even though the enemy artillery resumed firing soon afterward. Contact was established in the direction of St. Vith with the 18th and 62nd Volksgrenadier Divisions, which had finally succeeded in taking this troublesome obstacle. After a brief regrouping of the units and the summoning of the elements left behind, at about 08.00 on 23 December the Führer Escort Brigade, led by its armoured group, set out through Birkeler-Hinderhausen toward Kapelle. The brigade advanced on a broad front, with I (APC) Battalion on the right (north) and II (Fast) Battalion on the left on the advance road. The enemy's resistance appeared to have been broken; here and there abandoned tanks were captured intact and several other armoured vehicles were recovered from the marshy area east of Kapelle. For the most part there was no resistance.

To exploit this success, the mobile II (Fast) Battalion under Major Mickley was moved forward and, together with an assault gun which was assigned to it, took over the point. The battalion immediately set off through Commanster toward Rogery, while I (APC) Battalion and the artillery battalion joined the column. Beho was free of the enemy, but the Commanster–Rogery road was in terrible condition. Nevertheless the direct route was called for, as the bridge 1,000 metres northwest of Beho had been destroyed. Enemy forces were reported digging in east of Rogery. The artillery battalion went into position near Commanster to watch over the subsequent advance. Rogery was taken shortly before dark after a brief struggle and an hour later the advancing column entered Cierreux. Weak enemy artillery fire fell on both villages. Orders were received to resume the advance without delay, now to the side of the main road which crossed the direction of advance from south to north. The objective was the crossroads 3.5 kilometres west of Regné. There was no detailed information concerning the enemy situation or the location of friendly units. The point reported northbound enemy columns on the Bovigny–Salmchateau road; the brigade therefore immediately ordered the point to block the road south of Cierreux Mill and then trail the enemy columns, hoping in this way to gain as much ground as possible while it was dark without having to engage in any fighting.

The pursuit was soon detected, however, with the result that an enemy tank at the rear of one of the columns opened fire. This resulted in a heavy tank-versus-tank duel in which the two German assault guns driving point destroyed five enemy tanks and two limbered guns within five minutes. Wachtmeister Scheunemann alone knocked out five enemy tanks. In each case he approached to within 50 metres of the target and fired a flare; then, while the enemy were distracted, he fired at and hit an enemy tank. As the enemy column had apparently been halted by a blown bridge, it was unable to escape. Twelve more enemy tanks and twenty other vehicles were destroyed or disabled. Their crews fled into the countryside at the sides of the road. The Bihain–Regné–Ottre area was reached during the night and the vehicles stopped there to refuel.

The 24th of December dawned foggy as the last armoured vehicles approached the high ground around Regné over ice-covered roads. Contact was unexpectedly made with SS patrols which had reached the area. Undoubtedly they belonged to units of the left wing of the Sixth SS-Panzer Army. At this time it was also announced that the Führer Escort Brigade was being temporarily placed under the command of the Sixth SS-Panzer Army. A reconnaissance in force to the northwest, in the direction of Hampteau–Hotton, then later toward Durbuy, was planned by units of the army. But on this clear winter day all attempts to marshall motorized forces in preparation for the operation were frustrated by the enemy's air force, which was quite active. Consequently everything remained under cover and the units carried out maintenance and repairs on their vehicles and equipment.

Shortly before the beginning of the advance to the northwest, the army corps ordered the brigade to depart for Samrée–Dochamps–Amonines as darkness was falling on 24 December, to place itself at the disposal of LVIII Corps; but at the moment of departure the brigade's orders were changed; now it was to drive to Hampteau via La Roche. The brigade Ia, who had driven ahead to Warizy, was briefed by LVIII Army Corps. He was told that the Führer Escort Brigade was to take the village of Hotton and the bridge located there on 26 December and then continue to attack toward Noiseaux. To this end each unit received individual orders for their movement into the assembly areas. The following plan of attack was laid down for this operation:

"With the support of an assault gun company, II (Fast) Battalion is to advance to the right (east) of the Rendeux–Bas–Hampteau road and take the town. III (Bicycle) Battalion to advance to the left (west) of the same road through the Bois de Hampteau and take possession of the hills west of Hampteau.

Once the first phase of the attack has succeeded, the armoured group – including I (APC) Battalion – which is standing by in Rendeaux-Bas, shall drive through Hotton and, depending on the situation, either advance along the road or through Hampteau–Menil toward Hotton to take possession of the town and its bridge. The FBB Artillery Battalion is supposed to position itself so that it can support each phase of the battle with observed fire, while staying in close communication with each of the battle groups.

The bulk of the FBB Flak Regiment is assigned to air defence, because the shallow trajectory of the heavy batteries prevents them from performing effectively as artillery. However, as the attack progresses elements of the FBB Flak Regiment are supposed to eliminate flanking enemy fire from the north bank of the Ourthe. After the capture of Hotton the anti-aircraft guns are to be ready to take part in the blocking of the approach road."

In spite of moderate fighter-bomber attacks, the attack units were able to move into their assembly area during 25 December. The last units reached their departure positions at midnight. The attack began at about 09.30 on the following day, 26 December, and in spite of the extremely unfavourable terrain the units set off with great vigour. While the battalion on the right rather quickly took possession of Hampteau, III (Bicycle) Battalion fought its way through the Bois de Hampteau. I (APC) Battalion and the armoured group were ordered to move up. The leading troop carriers were approaching Rendeaux-Bas when an order from corps reached the brigade. It was to halt its attack and at once take all necessary measures for the immediate withdrawal of the brigade for other use. The brigade would be relieved in the positions it had reached by elements of the 116th Panzer Division.

I (APC) Battalion under Major Fabian, which had already arrived in the Rendeaux-Bas area, had the misfortune to come under artillery fire from positions on the north side of the Ourthe. The commander of 1st Company, Leutnant von Malotki, was killed. In escaping this mousetrap, from which normally there would have been no escape by day, many wounded men had to be left to their fate. It was simply impossible to recover them from the inferno without risking further losses.

As darkness was falling the brigade was finally able to disengage, at the cost of further casualties, and began its march south. The assigned march route was Halleux–Ronchamps– (southwest La Roche) road junction west of Champlon. The worst thing was that the fuel shortage was reaching its climax; almost half the vehicles had to be towed by others for the brigade to advance at all. The situation northwest of Bastogne made these measures necessary, however; near Bastogne the American relief units under General Patton driving from the south had established contact with the defenders of the city, the 101st Airborne Division. The Führer Escort Brigade's orders were now to attack south from the Morhet–Sibret area in the sector of the 26th Volksgrenadier Division, in order to close the west side of the encircling ring in cooperation with units of the Waffen-SS attacking from the south. It was 27 December 1944 when the first elements of the Führer Escort Brigade arrived in their new combat zone west of Bastogne.

At dawn on 25 December, the elements of the Führer Grenadier Brigade's panzer-grenadier regiment under Major von Courbiere that had assembled in the Nothum area on the night of 24-25 December set out on a reconnaissance in force south in the direction of Mecher-Dunckrodt and further toward the Sauer near Liefringen, in order to get there ahead of the suspected American spearheads. However the FGB's APC battalion came under heavy defensive fire as it neared the town of Mecher-Dunckrodt, managing to escape through a mixture of luck and skill. The Americans had obviously crossed the Sauer and therefore the brigade's mission was no longer valid. As well, it was realized that the enemy might now move northwest toward Bastogne without further resistance; but this would concede the relief of the 101st Airborne Division under General Taylor holding out in Bastogne and also threaten the Waffen-SS and parachute units still holding to the southwest.

Under ceaseless artillery fire of every calibre and uninterrupted fighter-bomber attack, the Panzer-Grenadier Regiment FGB held its ground in front of Nothum and made repeated futile attempts to attack south, but each attempt was frustrated before it could get going. Only with great difficulty and at the cost of considerable losses was it possible to maintain a tenable defence in the area between Nothum and Mecher-Dunckrodt. A number of assault guns, including those of 4th Battery, Assault Gun Battalion FGB under Oberleutnant Kümpel, were sent there on 27 December, but they were unable to achieve anything. Several of the vehicles were knocked out and the battery commander was killed.

On 27 December, meanwhile, the new brigade commander Oberst Maeder arrived from Courland and assumed command. He first had to search out all the elements of the brigade in order to ascertain the state of things. What he found was not encouraging: unit strengths, especially of the Panzer-Grenadier Regiment FGB, had reached a dangerously low level. By evening on 28 December the remaining elements of the Panzer-Grenadier Regiment FGB deployed south of Nothum had been withdrawn; they were temporarily shifted to Eschweiler for a brief period of rest and refitting.

By year's end, after the positions along the Wiltz had firmed up somewhat following the arrival of reinforcements, the command post of the Führer Grenadier Brigade was moved to Grümmelscheid, due north of Winseler. As well, after the successful breakthrough toward Bastogne by the Americans on 26-27 December the pressure on the south flank of the Fifth Panzer Army eased somewhat, as their main effort was now directed to the northwest. The fate of the remaining Waffen-SS and parachute units still south of Bastogne, which were supposed to close the ring around Bastogne in a joint effort with the Führer Escort Brigade attacking from the north toward Sibret, was now in doubt. The troops assigned to carry out this mission may not have known at that moment that the order was now impracticable in view of the completely misjudged situation at Bastogne. Oberst Remer readied his units in the area Flamierge–Chenogne–Pinsamont. All too soon he realized that the weak security screen set out by the weak 26th Volksgrenadier Division from Sibret to Morhet offered inadequate protection for his assembly area. As a precaution, therefore, on 27 December he positioned a battery of 105mm anti- aircraft guns and one of light field howitzers in Chenogne, from where they commanded the high ground west and south of the town. As well, the same day he moved the FBB's APC battalion and several assault guns into the Bois de Valet. The bulk of the FBB Flak Regiment was committed around Tronle and west of Flamierge in an air defence role, a move which immediately bore fruit, as the guns were able to shoot down 10 American gliders flying to the relief of Bastogne.

In the course of the afternoon the village of Sibret was lost to the enemy, something that was almost expected. Chenogne was also lost for a time, however it was recaptured by evening. Conditions for the planned attack south toward the Waffen-SS units deteriorated from half hour to half hour. And yet the order remained in force, and all the necessary preparations were made at the brigade command post in Tronle.

As per orders, during the night of 27-28 December the brigade assembled in the Chenogne area for the attack on Sibret. III (Bicycle) Battalion FBB under Rittmeister von Moellendorf (Hauptmann Gaum had been buried alive, gone missing, become lost!?) assumed responsibility for guarding the sector at the south end of the forest, north of Magerotte–Magery–Lavaselle, northwest of Morhet, as well as the sector south and southeast of Brul. The attack which began on the morning of that day did not get much farther than the wood south of Chenogne, for as the only attacking unit the brigade drew all the fire of the enemy artillery in and south of Sibret and all the other defensive weapons. The flanking fire from Villeroux was especially unpleasant. Soon the enemy forces in the area launched their own attack to the north and against Chenogne. There was heavy fighting at close quarters which lasted throughout the day, in the course of which the wood south of the contested town changed hands several times. The crew of a 105mm Flak distinguished itself in action that day. Positioned at the south edge of the wood south of Chenogne, it destroyed several enemy tanks in spite of heavy return fire, while the gun's crew fought off a number of attempts by the enemy to take out the anti-aircraft gun. Not until 30 December was the gun abandoned, after it had been rammed by an enemy tank. After a day of heavy fighting, in the evening the brigade reported that it was now too weak to carry out the required attack on Sibret. A cause of great concern to the brigade in its present position was the Bois des Haies de Magery, which was secured only by roadblocks and a few mines laid by an attached pioneer company of the 26th Volksgrenadier Division. By the evening weak elements of the 3rd Panzer-Grenadier Division had moved in on the left of the sector held by the Führer Escort Brigade. The grenadiers, cannoneers and tank crews dug in during the night in expectation of the coming attacks of the next day. It was always the night that brought some rest. The brigade command took advantage of the darkness to move up supplies, regroup forces, build new strongpoints and bring help to the front.

Things had reached the point where everyone knew what the senior command posts didn't want to admit: the offensive in the Ardennes had failed. Perhaps they could yet pull themselves together for a local operation, here and there undertake one last attempt to get the stalled front moving again. The enemy were far too strong, however; this was most obvious in the Sibret area, into which a steady stream of reinforcements was pouring. The situation in front of Chenogne became increasingly acute on 29 December, the second day of the Führer Escort Brigade's action in the 26th Volksgrenadier Division's sector. Throughout the day the enemy attacked the string of strongpoints at the edge of the forest and bushes south of Chenogne without let-up; the positions lay under a hail of fire from massed artillery positioned mainly southwest of Sibret and faced waves of tanks and ceaseless strafing and bombing by the omnipresent fighter-bombers. The defenders held their ground and recaptured lost positions, but the sacrifices were great. It was a desperate, seesaw struggle, and there was no hope of an improvement in the situation. The defenders were able to parry incursions by enemy infantry and tanks which penetrated as far as the outskirts of Chenogne (by now little more than a heap of stones) only by scraping up and committing the last reserve, a mere handful of men.

As if mocking the situation there, the corps ordered another attack on Sibret for the 30th of December, this time in conjunction with weak elements of the 3rd Panzer-Grenadier Division, even though considerably stronger enemy attacks had to be expected that very day.

Preparations went ahead nonetheless. They foresaw an attack toward Villeroux by the 3rd Panzer-Grenadier Division to take out the flanking weapons there, with a subsequent advance in the direction of Assenois where it was expected that the ring around Bastogne would be closed again with the help of the 1st SS-Panzer Division LAH attacking from the south.

The Führer Escort Brigade, which was subordinated to the 3rd Panzer-Grenadier Division for the attack, was ordered to advance on Sibret, take the town and then block the Neufchateau–Bastogne road to the south. The Führer Escort Brigade's plan of attack was as follows:

"After moving into its assembly area in the Chenogne area on the night of 29-30 December, II (Fast) Battalion under Major Mickley, together with an assault gun company, is to swing west and bypass the forest south of Chenogne on account of the enemy artillery fire, its right wing following the Brul River line, and attack and take Sibret from the north, opening the bridges at the north end of Sibret for the following armoured group.

The Panzer Battalion's armoured group with mounted APC Battalion will split up near Flohamont and if necessary support II (Fast) Battalion's attack on both sides of the Brul, but then drive toward Sibret in order to block the road leading southwest from Bastogne in the Belle-Eau area, as well as the road leading to Chlochimont.

The gap between Mande St. Marie and Sibret which will develop in the course of the attack is to be guarded by an assault gun battery and a light flak battery. The FBB Artillery Battalion previously deployed in the Flamierge area has taken up position in the shallow valley southeast of Rechrival. With forward observers accompanying both battle groups, its mission is to support the attack by placing observed fire on Sibret. There will be no preparatory artillery fire, instead fire on demand only after the start of the attack. The battalion is already ranged in on Sibret.

The Flak Regiment FBB's heavy flak battery shall likewise support the attack on Sibret with shells set for air burst and further engage targets which appear on the right flank. III (Bicycle) Battalion FBB will remain in its present sector at the edges of the forest with an attached light flak battery. The brigade will reserve an assault gun battery to be committed in the event of enemy tank attacks, especially against III (Bicycle) Battalion. As well the Heavy Infantry Gun Company shall establish an observation post in III (Bicycle) Battalion's positions."

The brigade moved into its assembly area; morning dawned on the 30th of December. The attack was scheduled for 07.30 in order to steal a march on the expected enemy attack. For experience showed that the enemy never attacked by day before 09.00. Shortly before the start of the attack II (Fast) Battalion FBB carried out a daring raid and snapped up the American infantry on picket duty halfway between Chenogne and Flohamont.

The brigade set up its forward command post at the south exit from Chenogne. II (Fast) Battalion moved off as it was getting light, while the armoured group, gaining ground to the south, deployed south of Chenonge. II (Fast) Battalion initially made good progress, but then bogged down in concentrated enemy fire in front of Sibret. The battalion commander, Major Mickley, a wearer of the Oak Leaves, the Wound Badge in Gold and the Silver Close-Combat Clasp, tried to get the attack moving again; however Mickley was hit and died on the battlefield from a severe stomach wound (shrapnel).

When the fog began to lift, the armoured group advancing toward Flohamont spotted two groups, each of about 30 enemy tanks, driving north: one toward the Morhet area and the other toward Jodenville. The panzers immediately opened fire and their first salvo left a number of enemy tanks in flames. However, as the Führer Escort Brigade's armoured group was itself on a gentle slope and soon lay under heavy tank and artillery fire, it initially pulled back with the grenadiers of II (Fast) Battalion FBB and continued the tank-versus-tank battle from the high ground between Mande St. Marie, including the wood which lay to the west. The grenadiers meanwhile pulled back to the southern outskirts of Chenogne. The unfolding tank battle cost the FBB's armoured group about four of its tanks over the next two to three hours.

The brigade's attack had obviously driven straight into an enemy attack. The collision was accordingly harsh and costly. Meanwhile reports arrived that a small number of enemy tanks were driving north through Lavaselle in the direction of Rechrival, causing tremendous confusion among train units in the Houmont area and even putting some to flight. The situation northwest of Houmont soon calmed down again, however, after one of the enemy tanks was destroyed with a panzerfaust and another was forced to turn away to the south. Furthermore the assault gun battery being held in reserve was sent to the threatened area to restore order. In spite of this the FBB's artillery battalion, whose emplacements were south of Rechrival, had to fight for its life. The guns destroyed three more enemy tanks with direct fire.

The continuous bombing raids and massed artillery fire had by now turned the town of Chenogne into a pile of rubble. Oberst Remer himself made his way back to Chenogne, the focal point of the enemy attack, and arrived just as an enemy tank attack through Mande St. Marie toward Chenogne was developing. He described the situation in detail:

"The situation in the town of Chenogne was extremely critical, as I found only a few damaged tanks and a handful of grenadiers there, holding out in cellars and the ruins of the town. I myself was paralysed as commander for a time, when an enemy tank appeared and stopped a few metres from the ruin in which I found myself. I still managed to send two radio messages to the armoured battle group from the radio-equipped troop carrier which was out of sight behind the house: "Town is being held to the last man'."

Not until evening were Oberst Remer and the handful of men with him freed from their unpleasant situation and Chenogne was held until darkness came. The commander of the Führer Escort Brigade went on to describe what happened:

"I was amazed that the enemy tanks and the American armoured troop carriers did not enter the town, even though they were taking no defensive fire worthy of mention from our side from the town of Chenogne. It later turned out that as a result of the continuous bombing raids on the town, our armoured battle group had positioned itself in a semi-circle around Chenogne, making clever use of the terrain, and had taken up the battle against the enemy tanks. Good results were achieved by the tanks at the north edge of the forest south of Chenogne and by the heavy flak battery at the south end of the Bois de Valet. This engagement was one of the toughest experienced by the brigade during the Ardennes offensive. In the course of the afternoon the attack was beaten off decisively; Chenogne remained in our hands. In my opinion the town could have been taken by an infantry company attacking on foot, as at times there were scarcely any of our troops occupying it.

Our own personnel losses that day were very heavy, but due to the fighting spirit and bravery of the German soldiers the day led to a complete success which cost the enemy 30 tanks. In my view the enemy attack concentrated too much on Chenogne. It would undoubtedly have achieved more success if the focal point of the attack had been placed with the battle group advancing toward Rechrival. For the spearhead of this group had practically pierced the brigade's defence while the bulk of the brigade was tied up in the battle for Chenogne.

A further failure on the part of the enemy was the fact that (as was so often the case) the brigade was left the night to quietly establish a new defensive front. The much-quoted axiom, "Sir, let the evening come, then the battle is won,' proved true even in this critical situation. The American forces could have spared much bloodshed if they had exploited the day's success during the night."

There was a regrouping of forces during the night on account of the changed situation, and the Führer Escort Brigade was once again placed under the command of LVIII Army Corps. Elements of the 3rd Panzer-Grenadier Division took over occupying the town of Chenogne. The boundary with the 3rd Panzer-Grenadier Division was: crossroads south of the Bois de Herbaimont–east end of Renuamont–west end of the Bois de Valet–Flohamont. On the left the boundary with the Panzer-Lehr Division was: west end of Lavacherie–road fork east of Pirompre–Remage.

Since all three battalions of the Führer Escort Brigade were equally exhausted and there was insufficient time to relieve the badly-battered III (Bicycle) Battalion, the units were ordered to hold the existing line Gerimont–Pinsamont–Rechrival–west tip of the Bois de Valet in their previous dispositions; this was done even though a resumption of the enemy attacks was expected on 31 December.

III (Bicycle) Battalion received about 100 replacements. Brigade was holding back two strong reserve forces whose mission was to counterattack immediately in the event of incursions by the enemy into the line. I (APC) Battalion and elements of the Flak Battalion were reserved for the key sector east of Rechreval, and for the west sector II (Fast) Battalion and the FBB Assault Gun Battalion. Furthermore a heavy flak battery was deployed in the woods north of Renuamont to deal with any breakthrough by enemy tanks north along the main road. The rest of the FBB Heavy Flak Battalion was deployed in the area north of Sprimont in such a way that it could engage any enemy tanks that broke through in addition to its air defence duties. Brigade headquarters was located in Lavacherie, forward brigade command post in Fosset with the armoured battle group.

The relief of the units in Chenogne itself by elements of the 3rd Panzer-Grenadier Division did not take place until daylight on 31 December. Enemy forces which broke into the town were ejected by the brigade's tanks, which were already in the process of leaving. During the day there were several enemy assaults against the sector held by the brave III (Bicycle) Battalion FBB. However these lacked the fury of the previous day and they were smashed by concentrated artillery fire. The defence line remained firmly in our hands.

The ebbing of hostilities on this last day of 1944 also made it possible to give the fallen commander of II (Fast) Battalion FBB, Major Mickley, a proper burial. The fallen officer was carried to his grave beneath a lone oak tree in front of a tall forest, in the presence of two companies of his old battalion and elements of the 11th (Assault Pioneer) Company. After the brigade commander had delivered his moving eulogy, the simple wooden coffin was lowered into the ground as a volley of rifle fire rang out.

The same day the brigade released an order of the day, in which it said:

"Effective immediately, II (Fast) Battalion, Panzer-Grenadier Regiment FBB will bear the name Mickley Battalion in honour of the personality and accomplishments of its fallen commanding officer."

II (Fast) Battalion took over the Gerimont—Pinsamont sector during the night of 31 December 1944-1 January 1945. The battalion reserve was in Tillet, to where a battery of the Assault Gun Battalion FBB was also moved from Amberloup. III (Bicycle) Battalion, situated in the sector south of Hubermont, was reinforced by the company in Pinsamont. The extremely tense fuel situation (some of the panzers only had enough fuel in their tanks for 10-15 kilometres) now made it necessary to keep the armoured vehicles close by. Often the tanks had to be left up front after a successful counterattack, in order to avoid wasting fuel. All non-combat vehicles were parked in the area north of the Ourthe.

Beginning at 09.00 the enemy attacked continuously, supported by tanks. Several enemy tanks which broke into Hubermont and Rechrival were put out of action by brave men of III (Bicycle) Battalion. A further eight enemy tanks were destroyed by the heavy flak battery positioned in the woods northeast of Renuamont. Prominent in this action was Unteroffizier Ahlemeyer and his crew, who alone knocked out six enemy tanks. The courageous commander of III (Bicycle) Battalion, Rittmeister von Moellendorf, died a hero's death in the close-quarters fighting in Hubermont. The stubborn, ruthless fight put up by this battalion, which had been in contact with the enemy without a break since 19 December, created favourable conditions for intervention by the armoured group, which was able to drive the enemy back to their starting position. Pinsamont was lost after heavy fighting. The company of II (Fast) Battalion FBB which had been ejected from there settled down on the ridge between Acul and Rechrival, with its front facing northeast. No counterattack followed, however, as Pinsamont lay in a salient projecting deep into the enemy's lines.

At approximately 14.00 enemy forces advanced on Gerimont. Several enemy tanks were destroyed and the situation was restored. The panzers of

Major Schnappauf's battalion repeatedly had to go to the front. The battalion commander, who came from the Frankenwald area, was always at the fore, there and at Hubermont and Rechrival, the brigade's other stubbornly-defended nests of resistance. Men like Unteroffizier Mucke, who drove without hesitation into the wave of Sherman tanks and gradually wore them down, formed the core of this armoured group, the backbone of the infantry. The ultimate abandonment of Chenogne by the 3rd Panzer-Grenadier Division made necessary a simultaneous withdrawal to the south exit from Millomont by the left wing of III (Bicycle) Battalion FBB.

Seen as a whole, however, enemy pressure initially abated in the following days; the reason was not obvious. It appeared that the enemy were moving in fresh forces in preparation for a new attack.

On the German side the defenders held the general line Tillet–Acul–Laval (chateau)–Hubermont–Millomont, and contact was established on both sides: with the 3rd Panzer-Grenadier Division on the left and the Panzer-Lehr Division on the right. The Führer Escort Brigade could still report 25 serviceable tanks and assault guns on 3-4 January as well as 15 under repair. A further 15 to 20 tanks, most of which had suffered mechanical breakdowns, still could not be towed to a repair facility on account of the lack of fuel.

The brigade's individual companies were in much worse shape; in general they were down to 25 to 30 men (each battalion thus had about 150 men on average). These were figures that were in no way comparable to the rations and offensive strength of the enemy.

The positions remained generally unchanged on both sides. The Americans now made repeated surprise attacks in an effort to break into the German positions. Counterattacks restored the situation. There was an inexplicable occurrence on the right wing of the Führer Escort Brigade, at the Bois la Chenaie forest, during the night of 5-6 January. Two companies, a total of about 60 men, simply disappeared. A brief outburst of machine-gun and pistol fire was heard from the area in the evening, then quiet. The positions were empty. Apparently the soldiers manning the positions had been attacked from behind. In this regard it must be said that the brigade's opponent there, the American 81st Infantry Division, fought with extraordinary skill. Patrols from this division were often discovered deep behind our lines in the Tillet area; they called out to German sentries in German, causing a great deal of confusion.

In the first days of January 1945 the picture on both sides of Bastogne was that of a pincers whose jaws were in the half-open position. West of Bastogne the Führer Escort Brigade, with the 3rd Panzer-Grenadier Division and the Panzer-Lehr Division, were holding a narrow wedge whose tip pointed south between Tillet and Flamierge and whose shank extended northward, forming a corridor in that direction. The maximum width of this corridor was 5 to 7 kilometres. The other jaw of the pincers was holding out in very heavy defensive fighting east-southeast of Bastogne, desperately maintaining the southwest flank along the hills in front of the Wiltz River line. There, between Donkholtz and Winseler, stood the men of the Führer

Grenadier Brigade, who in those days were struggling to hold open the Harlange—Donkholtz road for the elements of the 1st SS-Panzer Division LAH and the parachute units still holding out to the south and southwest. Almost cut off, these units had to restore contact with the northwest jaw of the pincers in the direction of Sibret, and their line of retreat through Donkholtz had to be kept open.

The retreat began; the attempt to take Bastogne and thus create the conditions necessary for a resumption of the advance toward the Maas had failed. Since 3 January 1945 the American counterattacks from the south in conjunction with British and American units advancing from the northwest, whose general objective was Houffalize, had become more noticeable. The German divisions which had advanced farthest west now had to retire east in time to avoid the threat of encirclement. But for them to be able do so both flanks had to hold, at Donkholtz and between Tillet and Flamierge.

Once the corps realized on 8-9 January that the Ourthe salient could no longer be held, foremost among the units faced with the growing danger of being cut off was the Führer Escort Brigade and the units on its flanks. Appropriate orders were issued; where the brigade was concerned, they called for it to cross the Ourthe exclusively at Wiompont at 05.00 on the morning of 11 January. The bridge was blown at 05.00 and the 9th Panzer Division took over the rear guard.

The worst thing for the motorized troops in this situation was the catastrophic fuel situation, which for weeks had paralysed almost all movement in and behind the front. It had now reached the point where at best each vehicle had twenty litres of fuel, where many vehicles had dry tanks after their last action and where deliveries were no longer reaching the front. Barely 24 hours were left before the brigade was to cross the bridge at Wiompont. Towing detachments were hurriedly formed and the available fuel was issued to prime movers, which then took four to six wheeled vehicles under tow. Darkness was falling as the train of tractors and towed vehicles ground its way through Flamierge and Salle toward the bridge. There were no American aircraft in the air, the front was quiet. Had the withdrawal escaped the notice of the Americans?

The armoured troop carriers of I (APC) Battalion FBB were the last to evacuate the positions at Hubermont and in front of Tillet, at about 20.00. They drove toward the rear, passing vehicles and tanks that had been blown up. No fuel – no help! One of the cannon-armed troop carriers of 1st Company, which was bringing up the rear, skidded into the ditch. It tipped over into a brook and ended up lying on its side. Unteroffizier Bürger, driver of the vehicle, said, "If you don't help me, I'll wait for the Amis. I'm not going to leave the vehicle." Two APCs were left behind to help. Meanwhile a despatch rider drove ahead to fetch a 12-tonne prime mover; the troop carrier had to be freed, cost what it may. The effort was in vain, however, the prime mover could not come. The commander of the stranded half-track, Unteroffizier Ringleb, broke down in tears. He didn't want to leave his vehicle. Then, to the relief of everyone, an Unteroffizier arrived with several canisters of fuel he had hidden somewhere. The APC was recovered, together with a prime mover, and both reached the north side of the river in time. As the vehicles fell back, here and there they passed intact guns that had been abandoned in their emplacements. There were no tractors, no fuel.

The last of the brigade's vehicles reached the crossing at Wiompont before the bridge was blown. They left a combat zone in which they had spent more than 13 days under the most arduous conditions.

Once again the brigade occupied the line east of La Vacherie–Avis Court–road fork south of the Bois de Herbaimont, in order to take in the last of the retreating units. Then, during the night of 11-12 January 1945, the Führer Escort Brigade was released from the command of LVIII Army Corps and became army reserve.

Twenty-four hours later the brigade marched through Ortho, Filly, Wibrin, Houffalize, Tavigny, La Villette and Troine into the Winerange—Donnange–Boevange–Deifelt area, where in the course of 13 January it was placed in rest status.

The brigade established its command post in Deifelt. The Führer Escort Brigade's entire quartering area lay under heavy attack by American fighter-bombers, while artillery fire fell on Dönningen–Deifelt. II (Fast) Battalion suffered the worst, with 60 casualties, at least 40 of whom died! It was frightful, and the troops were unable to defend themselves!

The Führer Grenadier Brigade was still in position on the lines of hills south of the Wiltz, roughly in a line Winseler–Rullingen–Nocher. But it couldn't be considered a real line: it was no more than a battalion here and there, armoured groups inserted among the Volksgrenadier Divisions to bolster their defensive strength. The poorly-equipped troops simply were not equal to the demands being placed on them by a battle of attrition of undetermined duration. As veteran soldiers therefore, the Führer Grenadiers had to do their utmost to intervene and restore the situation at least to a certain degree.

At dawn on 8 January elements of the Panzer-Grenadier Regiment FGB were assembled in the hollows south of Nocher in preparation for an attempt to retake the village of Dahl. The men set off early in the morning; it was extremely cold and the deep snow made it almost impossible for the panzers to advance. However at the very moment when the first houses were taken and the fighting in the village had reached its climax, the defending Americans mounted a powerful counterattack which simply swept the panzer-grenadiers out of the village again. Dahl was abandoned in disorder and only some of the units involved in the attack were able to retire to Nocher, perhaps 80 men in all.

After this failed attack the Panzer-Grenadier Regiment FGB moved into the Grümmelscheid area, where it occupied new positions at the mill on the north side of the Wiltz. It was a quiet position with no direct contact with the enemy. Meanwhile III (Bicycle) Battalion and the 9th Volksgrenadier Division were still waging a major defensive battle on the hills in front of Winseler. Deployed there from the very beginning in a supporting role, the heavy fighting had cost the battalion almost its entire personnel strength.

Now, after further serious fighting, it was waiting to be relieved, there was only a handful of men left, and these joined together to form a small group.

One battle group was the only element of the Führer Grenadier Brigade left in action. Consisting mainly of tracked elements and tanks, it sought to stabilize the situation in the Grümmelscheid–Donkholtz area. Meanwhile the infantry elements of the Panzer-Grenadier Regiment FGB assembled in a forest camp near Eschweiler, where they were to be reorganized.

The front had compressed itself; a few kilometres to the north the Führer Grenadier Brigade's sister unit, the Führer Escort Brigade, was about to see action again, as army reserve of XXXIX Army Corps. On the afternoon of 13 January a battle group made up of I (APC) Battalion and the Führer Escort Brigade's assault gun and artillery battalions was moved forward to Moinet, in order to take part in a counterattack from Michamps to the southwest by the badly-battered 167th Volksgrenadier Division commanded by General Tolksdorf.

The battle group's orders were: attack at dawn on 14 January from Michamps through Oubourcy, clear the wood southwest of Oubourcy and restore the main line of resistance previously held by the 167th Volksgrenadier Division. At the same time a battle group of the 9th Panzer Division was to attack from the Bourgcy area, north of the rail line toward Bastogne.

The battle group moved into readiness position during the evening. There was lively enemy artillery fire on the assembly area, however casualties were light. The attack began as planned at dawn on 14 January. The battle group reached the wood in the first rush; the troops left their APCs and advanced southwest through the wood on foot.

Now, however, it turned out that the 9th Panzer Division's battle group had not attacked on the right as promised; heavy flanking fire from the deep right flank, from the railway embankment, made any further progress by the Führer Escort Brigade impossible. The battle group itself suffered heavy casualties, in particular from shells bursting in the treetops, and in spite of its initial success it was forced to pull back into the wood again. A hedgehog position was established southwest of Oubourcy and there the battle group fought off enemy counterattacks all day.

While the fighting was still going on the brigade was placed under the command of LVIII Army Corps, which ordered another battle group from the Führer Escort Brigade, namely II (Fast) Battalion and two tank companies, to Derenbach as a mobile reserve. Furthermore the Panzer Battalion FBB was moved up to Hamiville at the disposal of the corps. These orders resulted in the total fragmentation of this homogenous unit and with it its fighting potential. Finally, after a direct appeal to Generalfeldmarschall Model, the brigade was returned to action as a unit. It received orders to occupy a defense sector extending from the crossroads 1 kilometre southwest of Moinet–hill east of Longvilly–west end of Oberwampach, and thus close the Bastogne–Clervaux road. On the right was the 167th Volksgrenadier Division and on the left the 5th Parachute Division. During the evening of that day, 15 January, heavy fighting broke out over Longvilly, which II (Fast) Battalion FBB was supposed to hold. Hauptmann Straube was seriously wounded, and medical officer Oberarzt Dr. Barthels assumed command of the remnants of the fast battalion which desperately held on to the rubble of the town, which was ablaze from end to end, until well into the night. Not until about midnight, when Longvilly was ordered abandoned and the battalion had withdrawn toward Chifontaine, did Hauptmann Behn take command of II (Fast) Battalion FBB. The next few days, from 16 to 18 January, were marked by persistent enemy attacks with heavy artillery and fighter-bomber support, especially on both sides of the Bastogne–St. Vith road, which seemed to be the focal point of the enemy's efforts. Once again all attacks were repulsed. The main burden of this defensive effort was borne by the infantry and the tanks, which often had to undertake several counterattacks a day. The fighting was especially hard on the grenadiers; squatting in their foxholes day and night with no relief, soaked to the skin by the frequent snow flurries, theirs was a superhuman effort. Cases of second- and third-degree frostbite became increasingly common. Relief at regular intervals, which patrols had revealed was the norm among the opposition, could not be carried out because of the lack of reserve personnel. The situation was further aggravated by the low combat strengths of the individual companies, which at this point had shrunk to 10 to 15 men.

The soldiers also had to cope with the downright bestial enemy artillery fire and the activities of their fighter-bombers. This constant bombardment not only resulted in material losses, but it had a demoralizing effect as well. There was scarcely a moment's peace and quiet. The phosphorus shells which caused even the snow to burn, explosive bullets that caused frightful wounds: all this wore down the defenders. And yet the individual fighting man had not given up. An enemy tank unit was spotted due north of Longvilly at dawn on 16 January. Two assault guns, which managed to approach undetected while the enemy refuelled, smashed the position and destroyed eleven of the tanks. Oberfeldwebel Hohn of the Assault Gun Battalion FBB exhibited a cool head, accounting for 7 of the enemy tanks himself. He was later decorated with the Knight's Cross for this feat. A further enemy attack, which temporarily reached the crossroads 1,000 metres southwest of Moinet, was halted by concentrated fire from the flak and artillery.

A special cause of concern for the Führer Escort Brigade was the state of the unit on its left, the 5th Parachute Division, which had taken over the positions of the 1st SS-Panzer Division LAH on 15 January and which was very much the worse for wear. Each time the enemy broke into Oberwampach elements of the FBB were sent via either Allerborn or Derenbach to restore the situation.

Those elements of the Flak Regiment FBB assigned to air defence duties reported downing two or three enemy aircraft almost every day, so that in the course of time the fighter-bomber attacks in the airspace above the brigade decreased significantly. Meanwhile new positions were scouted in the rear area; in the days that followed the brigade was supposed to fall back to these in order to shorten its defence lines and fortify resistance.

The first withdrawal of the lines, by about 2.5 kilometres, took place during the night of 19-20 January. The new position roughly followed the old prepared position in the rear: provincial boundary west of Troinle–west end of Baraques des Troinle–west end of wood east of Allerborn– along the road to Derenbach. As well, armoured elements of the Führer Grenadier Brigade, which was deployed to the left of the FBB, and about 10 Tigers of the 9th Panzer Division were temporarily placed under the command of the Führer Escort Brigade, as it still appeared very important to effectively block the road to St. Vith so as to ensure a smooth withdrawal by the elements of the army deployed farther north.

In the new line all members of the brigade's train units who could be spared, as well as every available gunner from the Flak Regiment FBB, were assembled into alert companies and employed as infantry. The by now completely exhausted remnants of I (APC) and II (Fast) Battalions moved into the Deifelt–Donnange–Lullange area for 24 hours to sleep and dry their clothing. The Artillery Battalion FBB went into position in the Donnange area, while the armoured group moved to Winerange. The elements of the Führer Grenadier Brigade and the 9th Panzer Division under the brigade's command were sent back to their parent units.

This action was the Führer Grenadier Brigade's last in this area, the bulk of the Panzer-Grenadier Regiment FGB having already transferred into the area around Marnach and the bordering forest on 16 January to rest and refit. There the regiment built bunkers in the deep forests, received replacement personnel and rested.

After standing by in the Marnach area as a mobile reserve until 25 January, in the course of the withdrawal of the German front the Führer Grenadier Brigade retired through Dasbourg, Daleiden, Juchen and Karlshausen into the wood near Neuerburg to continue the process of resting and refitting. This interval came to an end on 2 February, however, and the brigade marched east through Prüm, Daun, Ulmen, Kaiseresch and Mayen into the Polsch area, before continuing on toward Koblenz, Rhine–Niederlahnstein, where the brigade command post was also established.

Meanwhile the retreat of the German front continued. The Führer Escort Brigade was in action again. On 21 January a new position, following the line west end of wood east of Crendals–west end of Winerange–west end of Boevange–line of hills south of Boevange, was occupied as per orders. The brigade established its command post in Eselborn. The first elements of the Führer Grenadier Brigade were also pulled out of the line during these withdrawal movements and sent to the rear.

On 22 January they returned to the front, moving into the bridgehead positions around Eselborn and Weieherdange to cover the withdrawal beyond the Clerf (French: Clerve) River line by the divisions of LVIII Army Corps. The Artillery Battalion FBB was ordered into the area of Reuter, east of Clervaux, to watch over the withdrawal, while the Flak Regiment FBB was deployed in the Marnach area (heavy battalion) and at the bridges over the Clerf (light battalion) in an air defence role. The bulk of the Panzer Battalion

FBB also withdrew behind the river, while an assault gun battery was placed under the command of each of the two battalions still in front of the river.

The picture was always the same, day and night: retreating troops. Always above them were the enemy fighter-bombers, reaping a rich harvest with their bombs and guns. There was tremendous confusion, traffic jams everywhere, especially among the horse- drawn units. As well there was no fuel. Catastrophe loomed at the bridge over the Our at Dasbourg, farther in the rear. Numerous tanks had made it that far but now had no more fuel. Their hopes of finding some were dashed. They sat around the bridge site, offering the best possible targets to the enemy aircraft. In spite of the foggy weather enemy bombers repeatedly tried to knock out the military bridge over the Our. This they failed to do, but the stream of vehicles hurrying to reach the bridge scarcely abated at all. Burning vehicles cast their eerie light on the night scene and offered new targets, which the American night bombers homed in on and showered with bombs. Conditions were chaotic.

Then on 23 January an order from army group reached the brigade: it had been named army group reserve and was to extricate itself and move through Clervaux, Marboury, Dasbourg and Daleiden into the area south of Arzfeld.

There, on 24 January, Oberst Remer was informed by the Führer's army adjutant that the brigade was to be expanded into a panzer division. The additional units were standing by and the rest of the brigade was to transfer to the Mainz area in the next days prior to entraining for the east. It was 25 January 1945.

The Führer Order for the enlarging of the brigades to panzer divisions, dated 30 January 1945, was worded as follows:

To:

Führer Escort Brigade

Führer Grenadier Brigade

Both brigades are declared divisions on account of their actions and in recognition of same under the designations:

Führer Escort Division

Führer-Grenadier Division
